Hardly a Scholar

Hardly a Scholar

SECOND EDITION

Ken Shearwood, D.S.C.

Kennedy & Boyd

Kennedy & Boyd
an imprint of
Zeticula
57 St Vincent Crescent
Glasgow
G3 8NQ
Scotland

http://www.kennedyandboyd.co.uk
admin@kennedyandboyd.co.uk

First published by Tiger and Tyger in 1999, ISBN 1 90291 403 8

Second Edition first published by Kennedy & Boyd 2009

ISBN-13 978 1 904999 94 2
ISBN-10 1 904999 94 8

For
Biddie
Paul
and
Vanessa

On a rock

Acknowledgements

Quotations in the text have been taken from the following copyright works and acknowledgements are made to:

Soccer in the Fifties by Geoffrey Green; *The Edwardians* by J.B. Priestley; *English History, 1914-1945* by A.J.P. Taylor; *The English Tradition of Education* by Cyril Norwood; *Babbled of Green Fields* by Denzil Batchelor; *The Double and Before* by Danny Blanchflower; *Talking Football* by Alf Ramsey.

Extracts have been taken from: *The Times, The Guardian, The Daily Telegraph, The Daily Express, The Oxford Mail, The Oxford Times, The Evening Standard.*

If I have failed to ask permission of the holders of the copyright in any material I have used, it is an error of omission, and I ask pardon for it.

A warm hug for my dear daughter, Vanessa, who, as always, was such a help and encouragement, offering wise advice as she typed yet another manuscript for me.

My thanks are also due to Julian Smith, Paul Lawrence, Lew Hemming, Archie Smith, Jeremy McLachlan, Tom Griffiths, Chris Christian, Mark Buck, Richard Hudson, Stan Lenartowicz, Colin Maitland, my first editor, Ken Rhodes and — it goes without saying —Biddie.

Seascale in the 1930s.
Above: John Shaw, nephew of Bernard Shaw; Ken's father leading the line; KAS about to catch.
Below : John Shaw, Gertrude Shaw with 'fag'.

Foreword to the First Edition

Whatever Ken Shearwood is he is most certainly not a Mr Chips. He has given a great deal of his time to one institution, but not at the expense of an open mind and a vast range of interests. He is far too big a person to let that happen. Like many, I valued and needed his friendship at Lancing. Beyond that I have caught glimpses of the other Ken — in Mevagissey and Gorran Haven, through meeting people who served with him in landing-craft during the war and, of course, when talking to those who played football with him in the great days of Oxford and Pegasus. By a quirk of fortune I am reminded of him most days as I walk my black Labrador along the River Severn and into the garden of Ridgemount, Ken's house at Shrewsbury. And even after fifteen years I still miss those tall cups of coffee in Macari's Ice Cream Parlour as we scanned the newspaper and quickly sensed the narrowness and the absurdity of much of boarding-school life.

Personal memories and borrowed stories will not, however, do Ken justice. Of course, everyone has his favourite Shearwood tale and will not hesitate to tell it. I remember wallowing in the shallows of the Indian Ocean, stranded like a great red whale, as a rather loud Englishman (I never did know his name) regaled me with stories about Ken and Pegasus. But I am trying to think what makes Ken so special. *Whistle the Wind*, his first and best book, could well provide the key. A young naval officer, with five years of war under his belt, newly married, still restless and with a natural sense of adventure, tries his hand at professional fishing in Cornwall. His humour, generosity and adaptability shine through the pages, as does his genuine capacity for friendship.

Ken has what Neville Cardus called 'the common streak', common, that is, in the best and most valuable sense of the word, rejecting snobbery and exclusiveness, seeking and finding all men as they are. Cardus considered this quality to be the salt of art and life and Ken Shearwood possesses it in abundance. He is indeed a man for all people. Such a quality is part of his nature but I often wonder how and when it developed. I doubt that it was at public school. The less salubrious part of Derby where his father had a surgery may have played a part, as may his experiences on the lower deck during the early part of the war. Biddie's influence is inestimable. Whatever the source, this breadth of understanding when combined with wit, kindness and real interest in other people make him a remarkable friend. Through the passage of time and because he loves the place, Lancing has been the main beneficiary of his gifts and personality. Lucky Lancing.

Ted Maidment
August 1996

L'Envoi, Seascale, 31st August, 1931

Preface to the First Edition

It was during a school service in Lancing's great chapel that I began to think about writing a memoir.

Suitable titles, such as *The Blue Balloon* (see the Epilogue) and *The Merry-go-Round* were two I considered. But *Hardly a Scholar* won the day. Ten years later, after referring to the odd school diary and magazine, war scribbles, press cuttings and a host of memories, *Hardly a Scholar* evolved.

The story begins in Derby in the 1920s and describes preparatory and public school days, lower deck service in the North Sea, and landing-craft operations in Sicily and Italy. A postwar spell of inshore fishing in Cornwall preceded a four-year stint at Oxford and an eight-year association with Pegasus, the combined Oxford and Cambridge soccer side of the 1950s, that twice won the Amateur Cup at Wembley. For forty-five years I worked at Lancing as teacher, housemaster and registrar, with some football and cricket coaching thrown in.

Contents

Illustrations

24 Normanton Road, Derby

Chapter 1

Derby, Shardlow and Maidwell Hall

24 NORMANTON ROAD, from where I first glimpsed daylight in 1921, has long since been pulled down and in its place now stands the Derby Ministry of Labour Employment Exchange. It was a square, solid, ugly yet unpretentious, three-storey house, protected from the road by wrought-iron railings and a dingy hedge. Flanked by Christ Church on one side and a row of humble dwellings on the other, it was part of a busy thoroughfare down which carts rumbled and trams frequently swayed and clanged their way past our front door. Every so often a band of the Salvation Army would march down the road, while sandwich men wandered along the pavement competing with the huge Oxo and Bisto posters plastered upon the walls and wooden hoardings. Most intriguing of all was the dentist's surgery on the first floor directly opposite, where shadowy movements behind net curtains fed our imaginations to the full.

One of my earliest memories is of lying on a narrow sofa, the blind drawn, staring at the final flicker of firelight before falling asleep. From afar I'd detect the faint sound of a late tram, listen intently to its strident approach growing harsher every second, until finally, like some primeval beast bursting from out of the dark, it was there beneath my window, lights flashing, momentarily threatening, before grinding onwards to fade into the blackness of the night. At other times, particularly on Saturday evenings, the shrill voice of a woman singing across the road in the public bar of the Wilmott Arms, would penetrate the dark privacy of the room where I slept, which in the daytime I shared with my two sisters.

I vividly recall one wet winter's afternoon, sitting by an upstairs window watching a horse and cart approach. The small stooping figure of the man was dejectedly leading his huge beast along the tram-lines, his sole protection against the rain an old sack thrown across thin shoulders. He stopped. Taking a bucket from the cart, he methodically shovelled up a pile of horse dung. The job completed, he removed his cap and wiped his forehead. Taking the horse by the mouth, he continued his plodding way. Tiny sparks flew from the massive iron horseshoes as the stallion, slipping a little, took the strain. Several times a week the sharp cry of the rag-and-bone man rang out. Regular as clockwork, the organ-grinder arrived, parking himself beneath the dentist's surgery, where he would begin vigorously turning the handle of his hurdy-gurdy, filling the air with rumbustious music, evocative of the funfair. Further down the road a one-legged ex-soldier wearing his campaign medals, not yet a rare spectacle in Derby, sat most days on the pavement alongside his chalk drawings, before him an upturned cap. Every afternoon, promptly at five o'clock, the shout of, "Piper, evenin' news special!", the clang of our iron gate, and the rattle of the front door letter-box, heralded the arrival of the *Derby Evening Telegraph*.

At the back of our house was a fairly large garden with a tennis court, a sandpit, and a big greenhouse hung with heavy clusters of purple and green grapes, tomatoes and pot plants, a fragrant and fitting home for our chameleon. A curving herbaceous border discreetly hid the vegetable garden, while an eight-foot brick wall, its top embedded with evil shards of jagged glass, protected us from the world outside. When spring arrived the surrounding lime trees blossomed and hid its ugliness. Over one section of the wall the sunless and crowded playground of an elementary school confined the shouting children, ragged and poor, who played and fought, until their cries were silenced by the ringing of a handbell.

But on Sunday mornings the road was oddly quiet, except for the bells of Christ Church next door, tolling their message which we heeded not, for I never remember once attending a church service there.

Two trees stood between the back of the house and the tennis court. They were not tall trees, but old, well shaped and full of foliage. Many an hour I spent climbing them. Later, and in some haste, I was to seek their friendly branches as a refuge from our big bull mastiff who could, if overexcited, become suddenly rather frightening.

In summer my parents gave the occasional tennis party. Their guests in white flannels sat in deckchairs beneath the leafy shade of one of the trees, refreshed with cups of tea, fresh lemonade, thin tomato and cucumber sandwiches and home-made sponge cake. It was a strangely incongruous setting, surrounded as we were by unattractive buildings and small drab shops, slap on a busy thoroughfare with all its attendant smell, end-of-day rubbish and racket, bang in the centre of a big industrial town suffering from the depression of the Twenties.

My father was a doctor in general practice, who worked long hours and made little money, despite the fact that he was the senior partner of the largest practice in Derby. But that wasn't to say we did not live well. We had a nanny, loving and endlessly patient, bow-legged and tiny. She was a dear. We kept in touch through the years; I saw her the day before she died half a century later, frail as a fallen leaf, her memory crystal clear. We had a resident maid, sometimes two, and a woman who came in and did the family washing in a low ugly outhouse. Her tall son, Reg, used to clean out the medicine bottles with a crude brush on the end of a piece of wire, dipping them in a galvanised tub of water. It seemed to do the trick. He taught me to ride a bicycle. Eventually he took me onto the main road and showed me how to avoid getting my front wheel caught in the tram-lines.

My father's consulting room was on the left of our green front door, and sometimes we would hear the sound of crying as a child was vaccinated or underwent minor surgery. All the dispensing was done at home and the patients' waiting-room never seemed empty. "He's got another huge surgery," I can hear my mother saying with a sigh and look of resignation; his surgeries were always far bigger than those of the other two partners. Downstairs the pervasive smell of ether filled the narrow dark hall and the dispensary too contributed its own smell to the house. Above a hard wood working surface with a sink and the single blue flame of a Bunsen burner, ranged rows of coloured bottles, large and small. Here the dispenser, his face purple and veined, made up the bottles of medicine, neatly wrapping each one up and sealing it with bright red wax before sticking on the label of instruction. And all the time he was quietly robbing my father and the practice of a lot of money.

He was a tall, trusting man, my father, much liked, but most impractical. He smoked heavily, played picquet with my mother and played a good hand of bridge. Above all he had a splendid sense of humour. The phone would ring frequently and often he would be called out to a 'midder' case, sometimes twice a night. He suffered severe headaches from being hit in the head by a piece of shrapnel at Gallipoli and was granted a war disability pension of £42 a year. He served on the Western front, Gallipoli and Suvla Bay and was twice awarded the Military Cross and twice *Mentioned in Dispatches*. A Londoner, born at Norwood, he was a chorister at Westminster Abbey, educated at Whitgift, where he held the long jump record for some years, and always claimed that he had caught and bowled Jack Hobbs. But what I remember most about my father is the acrid smell of ether that clung to his clothes, and the eternal cigarette between his lips.

My mother was also a Londoner, one of a family of nine children. Her father was headmaster of a big London state school and a church organist. She was very pretty. Despite having plenty of domestic help, she still worked ceaselessly in the house. My father liked social life much more than she did, and I believe this had something to do with the break-up of the marriage many years later. I have a photograph of them taken together in 1916, just after they were married, my father dressed in a captain's uniform, his head heavily bandaged. Despite nearly seven decades, that faded and ochre-tinged photograph still holds them together forever in that fleeting moment of time.

Every summer we would take a house for a whole month somewhere on the coast. Early in the morning we'd set off, my mother having been up most of the night packing and preparing food for the picnic. Bowling merrily along in our maroon 1928 Ford, my father would quote from Belloc and Chesterton and sing the songs of the trenches. *Mademoiselle from Armentières* I remember was his favourite. When we were all getting bored with the long journey, there was one ditty in particular he would sing on such occasions, beginning with the line,'Down went McGinty to the bottom of the sea'. We would follow in turn, singing it as a round, taking an excessive and noisy intake of breath, before vociferously pronouncing the word 'Down', as each new round began. And always there would be sixpence for the first member of the family to spot the sea.

We had a governess until I was six, when I went to a small private school in Friargate run by Miss Maltby, who possessed a severe presence, offset by her partner, Miss Barbara, who was fat, jovial, breathless and friendly. I didn't do very well, but did win a prize, for the first and only time in my life; Kipling's *Just So Stories*, inscribed, 'For general improvement'.

Once, and once only, my mother decided she would drive me to school. A policeman was on duty in the town centre. He waved her on, she mistook the accelerator for the brake and had the constable not leapt for his life, she would have run him down. She never drove again.

Shortly before my ninth birthday it was decided I should go as a boarder to a preparatory school. One evening I was introduced to a guest of my parents who had come to dinner. He was smoking a Turkish cigarette, a habit he never gave up, not even in the classroom when teaching his favourite subject, history. I found myself looking up at a striking, florid face, with an aquiline nose and alert brown eyes full of merriment, beneath smooth black hair and a curling forelock. A Wykehamist of friendly mien, Oliver Wyatt had more than just the hint of a smile when I shook his surprisingly limp hand. He was headmaster-designate of Shardlow Hall, a preparatory school seven miles outside Derby. I was the first boy he had registered.

The reality of what was now about to happen hit me with sickening clarity. I was to leave the world I knew. To make matters worse, Nanny Houghton was departing for good. Like an enveloping mist, my cloak of security evaporated and I felt exposed and totally miserable.

The day of departure arrived; it was time to say goodbye. The slam of the front door had an awful finality. Of the short journey to Shardlow and what happened on arriving, I remember little. But I clearly recollect standing in a small boot-room, which contained a wooden frame for shoes, and weeping.

A few things stand out from the two years I spent at Shardlow. There was a large gravel area in front of the Hall beyond whose railings lay the playing-fields, trees and a deep pond. Here at break-time we all assembled and Oliver Wyatt, grasping a boy's hand in each of his, would chase after and touch another who would join the line. In the end a cordon of some fifty boys swept down on the last survivor. It was exciting stuff and I loved it.

There was a fat boy called Corby, prone to accident, `who won fame because he ate a worm, though I was not one of the privileged who saw him do it. The same boy nearly drowned when he fell through the ice one winter's afternoon. We built huts in the grounds, some of whose dark interiors we wired up and lit with torch batteries. Close by the Hall stood a magnificent cedar from whose branches the unfortunate Corby fell and broke his arm. But there was one in our midst who would scramble nimbly up into the great tree and with astonishing skill and balance run fearlessly out along the flat expansive foliage of its massive boughs. Miraculously he never fell. Once a fox ran through the changing-rooms — Oliver Wyatt was a great huntsman — and on another occasion when the hounds had killed, we were blooded on our cheeks.

Art was taught by a young Nordic master with smooth fair hair above cold blue eyes whose general manner frightened us. He moved silently about the classroom while we attempted to draw a flower in a pot. The room was very still and I became aware of his presence behind my chair. What I had drawn, with a hard unyielding pencil, must have maddened him, for suddenly he slapped my cheek with the back of his hand.

"Don't ever draw like that again," he warned softly. I was too frightened to move or speak, but I made up my mind there and then never again to attend another of his drawing lessons. Thus began my weekly headaches and bilious attacks which convinced our matron that the best place for me was the sickroom.

Above: My parent's wedding, 1916

Below: Father

Below right: Mother

Above: I don't seem to be helping, Lake District

Below: Family group, Lake District

For several weeks I managed to keep up the charade until, quite providentially, the art master disappeared and we had a new one, Gresley, son of the distinguished Derbyshire painter, himself now well known. He was kind and encouraging and I drew and painted a kingfisher. I still have it; pretty dreadful it is. More importantly, my bilious attacks and headaches promptly ceased, which was just as well since the matron was beginning to doubt their authenticity. But I did give her rather a surprise late one afternoon towards the end of a Michaelmas term.

I was hurriedly eating an orange and, being impatient to part two segments, popped them into my mouth, swallowed and immediately began to choke. Frightened out of my life I tore down the length of the hall, along a short passage and burst into the matron's room still choking. Alarmed, she started from her chair only to sink back as, with a dreadful hawking sound, I vomited the two segments of orange into her lap.

Returning in a bus from an away match, some of us began to throw things out of the window and enjoy ourselves. When we got back the headmaster was informed and we were all beaten there and then with a cane. That was a shock to me, it was also painful as well as humiliating, and I felt deeply ashamed that I had done something terribly wrong. There was quite a lot of beating, usually in class with a slipper. There was one senior boy called Rogers who was summoned from the dormitory and beaten on his bare behind. When he came back, shaken but undaunted, he showed us the weals. He left at the end of the year and went to the Royal Naval College, Dartmouth. We admired his courage.

Although small, I was good at games. The captain of our first XI football and cricket side was a tall mature boy called Fox, of Fox's Glacier Mints. His father had a chauffeur-driven pale blue Rolls-Royce which periodically swept majestically up the drive and parked opposite the wide flight of steps that led to the front door. Whilst batting one sunny afternoon in a practice game, I suddenly discovered what a half volley was and, with exhilaration, began to loft the ball all over the place. I had not done very well when batting in school matches and the cricket master, who was umpiring, angrily accused me of not having tried when playing for the school.

"If you can do it now, why couldn't you have done it in matches?" I was bewildered.

But by then the end of term was in sight and the exquisite excitement of those last few days and nights at school never ceased to thrill, just as the last few days of the holidays never ceased to cause the heart to sink, though, as the terms passed, this eased.

In 1932 the school moved from Shardlow to Maidwell, deep in the Northamptonshire countryside. In front of the Hall with its four domed lead turrets and separate chapel, stood the slender statue of Hermes, beyond which splendid trees and smooth lawns stretched towards a lake abundant with huge golden carp and fat brown trout, dark shadows that swam idly under and around the water lilies. From the banks we'd occasionally glimpse the sinister convolutions of a grass snake swimming on the surface, while bird-life darted and moorhens piped and splashed amongst the reeds where a pair of swans annually and diligently protected their nest and cygnets. Stepping-stones wandered across the water to Oliver Wyatt's other delight, the rock garden, where much of his spare time was spent in shabby old clothes tending rare plants and shrubs. He was later to become Treasurer of the Royal Horticultural Society and President of the Alpine Garden Society.

That I was lazy I would never contest. I had neither liking nor ability for Latin or French. Retaining the factual knowledge required for History and Geography I found difficult, chiefly because of my inability to concentrate for any length of time. Far too often my mind flitted hither and thither, studying a master's clothes and mannerisms, wondering what the boy in the front row was up to, speculating on when I would next be going out, above all conjuring up in my imagination the heroic deeds I would perform in the next school match. Maths, at which I was by no means good, I did, however, quite enjoy. For here there was anticipatory pleasure and some satisfaction in listening to the answers read out, and discovering that not all one's efforts had been in vain.

So I plodded on enjoying myself more and more on the games fields until, once again, I became afraid, this time of two masters. The first, Boojum we called him, was another Wykehamist who sported a large moustache, wore heavily framed spectacles with thick lenses. In rather a sinister fashion he padded softly around the school in rubber-soled shoes. He played the piano competently, walked with a curious spring in his step and liked to creep up and surprise us. He taught most subjects and, for a particularly bad piece of work, the culprit would be summoned to the front of the class, told to remove his slipper and bend over. The short sharp whacks that followed were invariably painful.

But the man we feared most was our Latin and games master. He was big by any standards, but to us he appeared enormous and threatening, with his powerful shoulders and deep-set, frequently bloodshot eyes, which peered fiercely out of his heavily jowled face. When there was work to correct he would call out our names, and those of us who were not exactly Latin scholars would approach his small table with trepidation. When my turn came I would stand at his side imbibing alcoholic fumes, and watch the prelude as he inhaled deeply from his cigarette, before carefully placing it in the ashtray alongside my exercise book. Taking up his pencil he would begin correcting my Latin composition, pressing fiercely with a spatulate nicotined forefinger, slashing through word after word until he reached the end, when it was time for another long drag at his cigarette. But far from having a calming effect, this served only to galvanise him into further frenzy. Seizing his pencil once more he'd strike one vicious diagonal stroke across my page of paltry effort, pressing so hard that often the lead would break. Finally, with a flick of his wrist, he'd send the exercise book flying across the room, at the same time attempting to clout me across the head, which I quickly learned to anticipate and avoid.

"Get away," he would say with quiet disdain, moving his left hand as though brushing crumbs from a table and I would retreat in disarray to retrieve my book, while the class, heads bent, tensely awaited the next summons.

On the rugger field he was equally formidable. As a stand-off I wore mittens on wet afternoons and before we began playing, he'd make us do some warm-up sprints. Then the game would start and he'd take part. "Tackle me low, tackle me low," he'd bellow, ruthlessly fending off boys right and left who failed to do so. The sight of those piston-like tapering legs and massive thighs bearing down on us was an awesome spectacle. Had our parents seen their gallant sons, some not so gallant, attempting to tackle low and bring the monster down they might well have been aghast. As for the forwards, they too had to be well and truly in the thick of things or there'd be trouble. One boy, his name was Andrea, insufficiently involved in a loose scrum, quickly found himself very much involved as he was picked up and tossed bodily into the midst of it. He emerged with a badly split lip which needed stitching. He later became head boy of Malvern.

But to give the master his due he praised us when we brought him down, or if there was a good three-quarter movement with the ball passed accurately and taken at speed.

He wasn't so keen on soccer though, the game I loved most. I have a very clear memory of scoring a goal in a practice match which he was refereeing. Unlike in his rugger he never joined in the play, I suspect because he hadn't much respect for the game and was no good at it. On this occasion I had dribbled neatly past three players, gone round the advancing keeper and scored a good goal, which gave me great pleasure, but only momentarily. An angry snort behind me and a sharp cuff across the back of the head put me firmly in my place.

"Why the hell didn't you pass the ball, you selfish little devil?"

I could think of no reply.

After a game he would watch with lascivious intent whilst we took our showers, seizing and tickling his squirming victims, running his hands over wet loins and squeezing their thighs tightly as he sat them on his lap.

He certainly put the fear of God into us and, if anything, his teaching periods grew worse. But, unlike the earlier drawing lessons, we had Latin every day, so bilious attacks were out of the question. The remedy was simple. When the occasion was ripe I would look at the work of one of the cleverer boys and make the necessary corrections, doing my best to ensure they were not too obvious. It proved successful. Indeed my deceit bore such fruit that it encouraged me to adopt a similar approach towards improving my other subjects.

There was, of course, the day of reckoning, looming ahead like some ugly cloud on the horizon — the end of term examinations. These I dreaded and, on the first day when the papers had been handed out and we'd been told, "You may now begin writing," I would pick up my pen and, with sinking heart, search for a question I could answer with some relevance. For the next hour I would sweat it out, glancing up as though seeking inspiration, listening to the smug scratch of pens on paper, as those about me, heads bent, scribbled away feverishly, until the invigilator's voice finally broke the silence and ended the ordeal. "Right, pens down, stop writing... I said, 'Stop writing,' that boy," and we'd hand in our papers.

Outside in the main hall, the animated chatter usually ended in general agreement that the paper had been an easy one, a verdict which sent cold shivers down my spine.

Eventually the marks would go up. Approaching the notice-board with a good deal of reluctance, I'd discover my name, if not at the bottom of every order, very nearly, which marred my end of term somewhat.

In the middle of one Easter term the school doctor, much to my dismay, stopped me from playing games because I had walked in my sleep, not without some personal danger, and he considered I was stressed and needed a rest. The dormitory window sills were both wide and low, easy to sit or stand on and I had walked in my sleep through an open window.

I had sleepwalked on several occasions before, but this night in particular, I dreamed that I was falling and, with a bump, hit the ground. Still asleep, I got up and began to walk deliberately round the school trying to get in by pressing the low windows with the palm of my hand to see if any were open. When I reached the changing-room area I found myself sliding down a coke chute into the boiler room. With difficulty I clambered out, still asleep, yet all the while curiously aware of what was happening. At last I came upon a door and on trying it found it open. At that precise moment I awoke fully. Alarmed, I ran down a long passage, past the masters' common room and up the broad stairway, pausing for a moment on the landing halfway up, where I listened to the silence of the house. Through the wide, low and lofty window I gazed at the dark woods that lay on the far side of a long grass terrace. A sliver of moon slipped from behind a cloud and from a distance I heard the church clock chime twice. I turned, quickly climbed the remaining stairs and tapped on the matron's door. She was not pleased and at first didn't believe my story. But when she saw the state of my pyjamas and feet, her manner changed. The following morning, the marks in the flowerbed indicated clearly where I had fallen some twenty feet and verified my story. Oddly, I had landed right beside the front door and yet had chosen to move off, still sleepwalking, all the way round the house.

My dream, I believe, was the consequence of an experience I'd had the previous summer in the Lake District, when I careered wildly down a long scree on Great Gable and completely lost control, somersaulted into the air, and crashed down on the loose stones of the scree, shaken, but undamaged.

As a precaution, bars were promptly put across the dormitory windows.

Perhaps from what I have written it would appear that I thoroughly disliked my preparatory school. Certainly, I still counted the days and final hours until, trunk and tuck-box securely lashed to our Ford's extended luggage grid, I would embark on another three months' exile.

When, however, I began my last year at Maidwell, it was with pleasant anticipation, for I was now a prefect, captain of games, no longer feared any master and life was good, except for one large blot on the landscape — the Common Entrance Examination.

Cheating, like a drug or an overdraft, once begun, is not easy to resist. Although I was aware that it was of no value to me morally or practically, I continued to seek help from the written work of others, and use aids to memory in form tests and examinations, never experiencing the satisfaction of success that is the reward of one's own labour. Consequently I drifted on just about satisfying the masters, labelled a bad examinee and warned in end of term reports that if I were to have any hope of attaining the standard required to pass the Common Entrance for Shrewsbury, there would need to be considerable improvement. In fact, when the time came, I did manage somehow to pass the wretched examination, but not without the aid of a few scraps of paper surreptitiously hidden about my person, and so scraped in, much to my relief and that of my parents.

The remaining three weeks of that last summer term at Maidwell were the most enjoyable of all, and I felt genuinely sad when the time came to say farewell. All leavers were presented by Oliver Wyatt with a small thin blue book with the unlikely title, *The Straight Left*, which did its best to prepare thirteen-year-olds for life at a public school, advising, amongst other things and, most forcefully, that 'New Men' should stick to their own year group and beware of friendship with senior boys.

As for our ferocious Latin and games master, he too presented me with a book on cricket, with a letter in which he wrote: "The enclosed is a small appreciation of all you have done as captain of rugger. The more I see you play the sorrier I am that you will from now on make soccer your first love as regards games, for quite apart from which is the best game, I feel quite sure that you could reach a higher standard in rugger. However, you will certainly do well at either."

Sixteen years later, towards the end of my fourth year at Oxford, I was about to have a quick lunch at the Kemp in the Broad, when suddenly I spotted the old tyrant sitting alone at a table. Astonished, I studied him for a few moments and experienced a degree of sadness. Was this really the same man who had so frightened us? He seemed to have shrunk and now looked frail, slightly shabby and much older. Perhaps he was aware of my gaze for he suddenly looked round and our eyes met. I got up, went over and we had lunch together. Our pleasure at seeing each other was mutual. He knew that I was captain of the Oxford soccer side and playing for Pegasus — it was the year we were to win the Amateur Cup at Wembley before a crowd of 100,000. But he had not forgotten his letter. 'I still think you would have done better at rugger," he said as we parted. I never saw him again.

Almost exactly half a century on, my wife and I visited Maidwell. It hadn't changed. The Hall itself, grounds and trees, were as beautiful as I remembered them. Approaching the main entrance I glanced up at the window from where I had fallen. The bars were still there. On entering we were greeted by a youngster who approached of his own accord.

"Can I help you, sir?"

"If you would, please. I was once a boy here." My remark did not impress him at all.

"We've got new kitchens," he continued, "Annie's still here. She's been with us for fifty-two years."

"Has she? And does the Pytchley still meet in the grounds?"

He nodded, and I conjured up a picture of Oliver Wyatt, high on horseback, resplendent in pink coat and cravat, beaming his pleasure, surrounded by peers equally colourful, yet strangely formidable, astride their huge champing mounts. The ladies, elegantly attired in black, seated side-saddle, veiled and superior, sipped their hot drinks while we boys made a fuss of the hounds. The whips cracked, the hunt moved off and we'd follow until the pack was out of the grounds and we were out of breath and allowed no further. Slowly and reluctantly we'd return to our lessons, only the distant baying of the hounds and intermittent sound of the horn breaking the cold crisp silence of a winter's morn.

"Would you like to see the kitchens?" I heard the boy ask.

"I think I'd better see your headmaster first," and, still chattering, he took us through to the handsome wing where Oliver Wyatt had once lived in considerable splendour, where some of us had received the cane. But the three magnificent hides of a Bengal tiger, snow-white leopard and black panther, that had so fascinated us half a century earlier, were no longer there.

Shopping with Mother, Derby

Chapter 2

Shrewsbury

I HAD NEVER VISITED Shrewsbury School prior to my going there, nor had my parents as far as I am aware. I'd been entered for three schools, Shrewsbury, Repton and Rugby, and Shrewsbury had won the day.

I first met the housemaster of Ridgemount with my parents in a pleasant drawing-room overlooking the river Severn at the start of the September term of 1935. I see him now looking down at me, the great square jaw, the mouth's firm line, the steady long gaze of those very blue eyes and the massive head crowned by flaxen hair. Smiling, he placed two huge hands upon my shoulders and, with slow deliberation announced, "He's very like his father." A heavily built man, ponderous in movement, A. E. Kitchen was an Oxford rowing Blue and a renowned coach. He was known as the Bull, but referred to by the house as Kitch; his pleasant wife was known as Ruthie.

To say that life at Shrewsbury was tough for a new man is an understatement and each of us experienced varying degrees of fear, though we'd never admit it or tell our parents.

For the first year we were known as 'scums' and were expected to go through the mill, as our predecessors had done for the past four hundred years and more. It was all part of the public school tradition and Shrewsbury was no exception, as we quickly discovered on the second night of the term, when Ridgemount, along with the other houses, held its Hall Elections. New men, the scums, and second year men were assembled in a small library on the right-hand side of the entrance to the house dining hall and told to wait and keep quiet. In due course the door opened and we were summoned. Entering the hall singly and with considerable unease, we were greeted with ribald comments, hissing and booing, which intensified as those who were disliked the most made their appearance.

In haste we took our seats on the long benches around the spare dining table, conscious of staring eyes and the sudden silence that had fallen. The scrape of a chair, as a monitor rose to his feet and strolled towards where we were sitting, broke the silence. Holding up a sheet of paper he proceeded to walk slowly round our table, stopping occasionally to lean over a boy's back and wave the paper before his eyes only to withdraw it, move on and do the same to another. Finally, amid cheers from the house, the paper was thrust in front of the unfortunate boy elected Hall Crier for the term. Every eye now watched as he clambered up onto the bench and stood nervously facing the house and monitors at head table.

"Oyez, oyez, oyez," he began.

"Louder, much louder," bayed the house.

"Oyez, oyez, oyez," he repeated to renewed shouts and, despite frequent interruptions and commands from the monitors to "Read that again properly," he did his best to struggle through several sides of ill-written script, its content intended

Above: Ridgemount

Below: Ridgemount House 1936

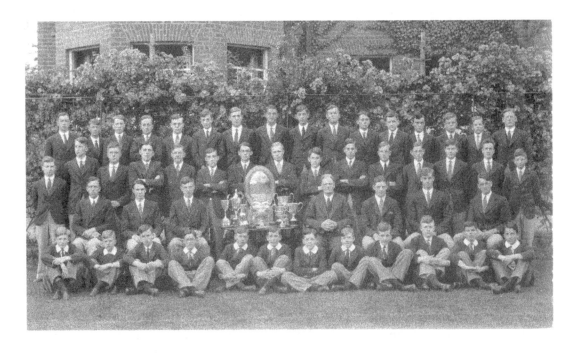

solely to humiliate and afford the house every opportunity to mock the solitary figure who would end with, "God save the King, and down with the Radicals."

As he read on, the names of boys who had been elected to postman, bell ringer and other jobs were cheered and booed according to the recipient's popularity. Hall elections did not enhance the beginning of each term for those first two years, but there was nothing we could do about it, since the green baize door that separated our side of things from Kitch's private side, always remained firmly closed on such occasions.

Each morning at seven o'clock the ringing of first bell summoned us from the warmth of our beds to stand in turn under a short pipe that projected from the wall and take the customary Shrewsbury swill, subjecting our bodies to gouts of cold water. The rumbling of pipes, the repeated flushing of the one and only lavatory, whose system could never accommodate the needs of forty-nine boys after a night's sleep, and the constant sound of gushing water filled the air.

Swilling was compulsory for all except monitors, who had the questionable privilege of plunging into a brimming bath of cold water. Those who sought to escape the ordeal of a swill on icy mornings were usually detected by a monitor running a hand down the culprit's skin, before sending him back for a proper swill.

Then it was off to first lesson, books beneath arms — the distant bell urging us on up the hill past Oldham's, the Common on our right, past the Moser building which housed the school's distinguished library, on past the less distinguished chapel and fourteen Eton fives courts — usually running the last stretch in order to reach the school buildings before the bell, high up on the end wall, ceased its ringing and our names were marked down as late for first lesson.

Forty-five minutes later we were on our way back for breakfast, followed by chapel and three fifty-minute periods. At half-past twelve we were free to do what we liked, kick a football, attend a cricket net, visit the school shop, work, or just do nothing.

After lunch some form of exercise had to be taken by all in their first two years, often it meant a 'tow' — a run. Shrewsbury was renowned for its cross-country running. The Royal Shrewsbury School Hunt had its own 'hunting' language, the School Colour holders given the title, Gentlemen of the Run. The R.S.S.H. took part in no less than twelve cross-country runs — the Bomere, the Bog, the Cruckton to name a few — the most important of all being the Tucks.

This was a compulsory event which took place in the early weeks of every Michaelmas term, when the whole school — the 'pack' — and a number of staff, which would include the headmaster and, in particular, A. H. Pearson, a Cambridge running Blue, assembled outside the Moss gates to run five miles. The huntsmen and whips, — significant in black capes, crossed whips on white vests — clasping hunting crops and horns, stood on the flanks of the five hundred runners. Then to the sound of the horns and with a great shout the pack would suddenly surge forward, the captain of running, the huntsman, leading the way and setting a gentle pace, his senior and junior whips marshalling the 'hounds' and rounding up the stragglers. There were four 'all-ups' which gave the runners brief breathers before the final run in from Tucks Bridge and the winner 'killed' by so many yards.

Apart from Wednesdays and Saturdays, which were half-holidays, there were two afternoon periods from a quarter to five, followed at 6.30 by a roll-call in the houses, tea which was the final meal of the day and Top Schools, another Salopianism for homework. At nine o'clock house 'dicks' — prayers — taken by Kitch or the head of house marked the end of the day.

During the week we all wore blue suits and stiff collars rounded at the ends, with the exception of new men below a certain height — and I was one — who for their first year wore Eton collars. On Sundays top hats and tails were the order of the day, short jackets — bum-freezers — for the Eton collar brigade. School praeposters carried walking sticks. Whenever any member of the school passed a 'brusher' — master — on the site, he would automatically raise a hand and touch his ear as a mark of respect. When going down town 'bashers' were worn, flat straw boaters encircled with a coloured ribbon denoting a boy's house, a black band if a member of the sixth form, a blue one if a member of the rowing eight.

For disciplinary problems in form there was extra lesson on Saturday afternoon, between two and four. A boy who collected three penal marks would have one hour's extra lesson, four penal marks would warrant two hours. It was a salutary, much disliked punishment and, for a games player, one to be avoided at all costs.

The school porter was Corporal Hartshorne, a small bald man with an explosive stammer and a spring in his step, reputedly an ex-flyweight champion of the British army, who had been through the First World War. Each day he would visit every classroom and with a sharp tap on the door, enter and present the form master with a book. In it, written in red ink were notices to be read out to the boys. In blue ink were the notices for masters. Not infrequently a master read out the wrong one.

At the end of the first three weeks, all new men faced a verbal test conducted by the house monitors. We had to know, with the help of the Brown Book, the Carmen Salopiense, the names and colours of the ten houses, eleven including Marycourt, the waiting house, the school's own language, and other pieces of obscure knowledge peculiar to Shrewsbury and its site. I don't think anything particularly unpleasant happened to those unable to answer the questions, other than to face a further test. But it was just another cloud that hung over us, causing apprehension and doing little to stabilise the shifting sands of insecurity we all trod in those early days at Shrewsbury.

For house punishments we were given penals which meant writing out lines of Pope or Milton, and sometimes a boy was summoned by the house monitors and beaten. Every so often during the course of the day the long cry of 'doul' — Greek for slave — rang through the house, followed by the noise of chairs being pushed back and the frantic rush as scums raced to the monitors' study because the last to arrive had to carry out the order. The forty-nine boys in Ridgemount were contained in four communal studies. The monitors' room of six had the advantage of a carpet, a few easy chairs and a coal fire in the winter.

A diminutive middle-aged matron called Trixie, more commonly known to us as Tee-Hee-Hee since she would preface any conversation with a chuckle and three such utterances, looked after our health with the aid of the medical officer, Dr Urwick, who drove a Rolls-Royce. A round-shouldered lugubrious house John, in a shiny navy suit, cleaned our quarters and served us in the dining hall. He wore a bow tie, possessed a pockmarked bulbous nose and neck and, wheezed heavily as he sailed sedately round the tables, leaning over our backs to plant before us plates of food. Much of his day he spent in the boiler-room, a narrow gloomy cavern of coke and tobacco fumes situated down a flight of steps underneath the house where, with sleeves rolled up and collar off, he washed and shaved in a chipped enamel bowl, rolled and smoked cigarettes and filled in his football coupons.

Sundays began with voluntary Holy Communion followed by breakfast, a forty-minute 'divvers' lesson, chapel and lunch. In the afternoon we'd go for a walk attired in top hats and tails, or blue jackets and bashers. The more privileged were allowed bicycles. After tea and Evensong came study lock ups, when we read the Bible in preparation for the predictable 'take a slip' and test during first lesson on Monday morning.

'Reading over' occurred at the beginning and end of every term, when the headmaster, H. H. Hardy, read out the names of the school from top to bottom. Approaching the nether regions, certain recognised characters who had not moved up the school list caused audible ripples of mirth. I learnt quickly that those who failed to progress faced the threat of superannuation, of having to find another school or, in Salopian jargon, being 'ruxed', sacked. It was hardly surprising that a good deal of 'cabbing', cheating, went on. Being an experienced hand, I quickly and with little hesitation joined the ranks, just about holding my own.

'Take a slip', ordered F. F. Monk, form master of Lower IV 2A in which I now found myself, and each of us would tear a 'penal' into three long slivers of paper in preparation for a test. It was a command I was to hear many times.

The headmaster, late scholar of New College, Oxford, gaunt and grim-faced, rode the site on a sedate and upright bicycle, mounting and dismounting in such a curious fashion that it was rumoured amongst the school that he had been wounded in the backside or, in our vernacular, shot up the arse.

There were forty-six assistant masters at Shrewsbury in 1935, seventeen from Cambridge, twenty-three from Oxford, thirty-two of whom were scholars or exhibitioners. Despite this, some of the teaching in the lower parts of the school was as dreadful as it was excellent in the top half. The Brown Book records that, in the Lent term of 1936, the classical Upper Sixth, taught by Street and Moore, the headmaster and Dawson, contained six pupils already awarded classical scholarships, three to Oxford, three to Cambridge, of whom one was to become headmaster of Eton, and another, though not yet a classical scholar, was to become Lord Chief Justice of England.

In contrast, K. B. Banks, a colossal man with thin but flaming red hair and a round flaming red face, taught us maths in the lower school. He would lumber into first lesson invariably very late, grunting and breathless, slump into his chair and with elbows on desk peer down at the form, red-rimmed and bleary-eyed, like some great stranded walrus. He would breathlessly gasp out a few alcoholic instructions to carry on doing the next exercise, then close his eyes and, breathing heavily, fall asleep. His subsequent career in the Royal Navy was not helped when he took some naval craft at speed down the Clyde.

Dickie Sale, form master of Lower IV form one, taught us history as well as other subjects. He possessed a fruity voice with an odd inflexion, had a curious gait, and an entrance which never ceased to amuse. Round the opening door a hand would first appear grasping a waving mortar-board, followed by a waggling head, accompanied by a prolonged noisy humming sound. With a flick of the wrist the mortar-board would sail through the air, more often than not landing accurately on its owner's desk or chair. "Um," he'd hum steadily, bending slightly forward, arms and gown waving, body swaying as he proceeded towards the front of the form: "Um, take a slip. Question one — um?" He was by now seated in his chair, and we were humming back at him. "Question one — um — what famous historical name — um — is at the top of page one hundred and eighty-two — um?" and moving his head from side to side, at the same time stroking his handsome moustache, he watched with a twinkle in his eye, whilst we scribbled our answers before looking up and signalling with a crescendo of humming that we were ready for his next question. This he acknowledged with raised arm, whereupon our humming ceased temporarily, though his did not. It was a performance he accepted, expected, orchestrated and thoroughly enjoyed and, though we did not learn much history, we remembered his lessons. Housemaster of Ingram's, he was a popular figure, an Oxford cricket Blue, a left-handed batsman who had played for Derbyshire. He coached us in the nets, bowling teasing off spinners, humming away the while, clad in a short-sleeved Free Foresters sweater, ever quick to smile and encourage. He was not allowed to drive a car, since he hummed and fiddled too much with the gears, all the result of a war disability — so we understood.

W. J. Pendlebury, Pendlehof we called him, was in charge of Middle IVB. He would sit motionless in his chair like some enormous eastern potentate, gazing down at the form through thick-lensed glasses, head immobile, only his eyes moving.

"Stand up, Ainsworth," he once commanded during a Latin test, and an open Kennedy's *Latin Primer*, resting on Michael's lap, fell conspicuously to the floor. He was 'swiped' by Dickie Sale, his housemaster, that evening. Had Pendlehof ordered the whole form to stand, the majority would have faced a similar fate!

"See if you can hit Charlie Larkin with a piece of chalk," challenged a member of Upper IV 2B, as we leant out of the only window, high up by the bell on the west wall of the School Buildings, and looked down to where a group of brushers stood chatting at the end of one summer morning's break. Grabbing a piece of chalk and without bothering to take aim, I threw it randomly in the general direction of Larkin, knowing the chance of scoring a hit to be negligible. Not so. With unerring accuracy the missile found its target, Larkin's head, which jerked like a puppet on a string. Glancing up at the open window of grinning faces high overhead, he set off at speed heading up the stairs for Upper IV 2B.

"Who threw that piece of chalk?" he asked breathless and angry, bursting into the form room where we were now all seated at our desks.

"I did, sir."

"Which house are you in?"

"Ridgemount, sir."

"I shall report you to your housemaster."

That evening, in the middle of Top Schools, I was summoned. Passing through the green baize door and along the passage, I knocked at Kitch's study and entered. He was seated at his desk.

"I understand that this morning you threw a piece of chalk at Mr Larkin and hit him on the head." He looked at me seriously with those very blue eyes. "Is that true?"

"Yes, sir."

"Then I'm going to beat you," and he got up slowly and produced a cane from the side of his desk. "Bend over."

I received three strokes, not very hard ones.

"Right, you may go," said Kitch.

"Thank you, sir," I replied.

"Ken," he said, as I reached the door. "It must have been a very good shot."

While playing inter-house soccer leagues in my second year I was seriously injured. I had gone for a ball which I had no chance of winning. The opposing back had attempted to volley a clearance, missed the thing completely, but kicked me with the hard toe of his boot — and they were hard in those days — over the right kidney. I finished the game in much pain and reported to our matron.

"Tee hee hee," said Trixie predictably, "I'll put a poultice of anti-phlogiston on," and, heating the glutinous substance over a saucepan of boiling water, placed the pad over the area. It was Saturday afternoon. "Come and see me before you go to bed."

I did so. I was about to enter her room when Kitch came through the green baize door. He looked at me steadily, then held my head between his huge hands.

"You are in pain." It was a statement.

I nodded.

"Have you rung the doctor?" he asked the matron. "I think you should."

"Has he a haemorrhage?" the doctor enquired of our timid, friendly little matron.

"Have you passed blood?" Trixie asked me with some embarrassment. I was by now in the house sickroom. I shook my head.

But early in the morning I passed blood all right and told the matron so.

"Tee hee hee," she began and told Kitch who rang the doctor. He came and saw me briefly later that Sunday morning.

A sharp constant ache gnawed deep within my back and I twisted and turned, unable to eat or sleep. On one side of the bed, adjacent to the wall, hung a bell push which I batted ceaselessly to and fro with the palm of my hand, vainly seeking distraction, for I now knew the meaning of pain.

On Monday the school doctor called again, but nothing seemed to happen and there was no respite from the penetrating ache and haemorrhage. On Tuesday morning, without warning, my father arrived with an eminent Derby surgeon. Dr Urwick was present and Kitch stood by the door as Mr Dyke examined me and quietly asked a few questions. I caught my father's kind, reassuring smile. Then they left, looking serious. Neither my father nor the surgeon had spoken to the school doctor. They kept that for when they were the other side of the sickroom door. Within half an hour I was moved by stretcher and ambulance to the school sanatorium, where I lay in bed for three weeks, my feet never touching the floor. I was visited by the school chaplain, Hum Beevor, who would first say a few prayers, which seemed to embarrass him almost as much as it did me. The headmaster's wife, Jocelyn, whose grandson I was to teach many years later, Kitch, Ruthie and the drawing master, Woodroffe, all popped in more than once. The last-named, who had brought me some drawing materials, possessed a somewhat frenetic appearance, with his unkempt hair, protruding lower lip, moist slightly ajar mouth and wild bulging eyes. His words came out in a torrent of spittle, but he was a kind man, in contrast to the sadistic creature I had come across at Shardlow Hall. I read *The Story of San Michele* and some novels of Buchan and Dornford Yates. My one great boon, for I was in a single room, was a wireless whose battery always needed recharging at the wrong time, and the frequent visits of a boy called Ellis whose friendly company was a great help.

Eventually Miss Goozie, the sanatorium matron, said that I could get up for a short time, but warned me that my legs might give way.

I promptly ignored her advice and attempted to go it alone. But for her timely intervention, I would have collapsed. I was allowed home for a week to recuperate.

There was now less to fear. As we moved up the house order our confidence grew, mine perhaps too fast. In 1938 the houses were connected by internal telephones so we could ring each other up, but only for serious purposes.

Bromley-Davenport, senior to me and an excellent mimic, who played the piano at house dicks and, when Kitch was not present, would jazz up the chosen hymn, suggested one evening Oldham and I ring up Barlow, a monitor in School House, a suggestion we promptly and somewhat unwisely followed. On hearing Barlow's voice we enquired whether he had some paper to hand.

"You have? Good. Then we suggest you take it in your right hand and screw it slowly up your arse," with which we hung up, secure in our anonymity, though not for very long.

R. R. Prentice, head of the school and head of School House, soon rang Woodrow, our head of house, and quickly discovered who had made the call. Bromley-Davenport was summoned by Prentice and returned unscathed. Oldham and I each received a summons to present ourselves at School House at 8.30p.m. the following Sunday.

Promptly, at the appointed time, we knocked, entered and stood before a row of comfortably seated praeposters and monitors who surveyed us with solemn curiosity. In front, a wooden chair was ominously conspicuous.

"What was the point of that call you both made to Barlow the other night?"

asked Prentice, surveying us during an initial and lengthy silence, which did nothing to put us at our ease. I had no ready answer other than to suggest it was done for a bit of fun. "And you?" asked Prentice, ignoring my comment. All eyes now focused on Oldham, who stood stolid and heavily built, his face flushed.

"Well," he blurted out forcefully, "It was really a question of one for all and all for one," a remark of such irrelevance that it completely baffled those we faced. It caused me to break into uncontrolled splutters of slightly hysterical laughter which, despite every effort, I could not stifle. It did not help our cause, mine in particular, and we were summarily dismissed to wait outside, along with a number of boys who had congregated in anticipation of what was about to happen. Oldham was summoned first and given six strokes, three from Prentice, three from Barlow. I received an extra three for frivolity. I know Kitch was aware of the incident, but he never mentioned the matter, for senior boys at Shrewsbury had great influence.

Prentice went on to have a distinguished career, both in the war and subsequently. Barlow became a squadron leader in Bomber Command and was awarded the D.F.C. and Bar. Oldham and Bromley-Davenport were both killed, the former in 1942 serving with the Rifle Brigade in North Africa, the latter on active service with the Cheshire Regiment in 1944.

I was now beginning my third year. Games continued to play an important part in my school career and I was representing the house at football, cricket and fives, but I was not good enough to play for the school. Earlier I had tried my hand at boxing, entering an event called 'Novices' Boxing'. In the first round I had been drawn to fight a day-boy, in those days known as 'skytes', derived from Scythian, or outcast, and regarded most unjustly as second-class citizens. To lose to a skyte — I cannot recall his name — was something one would not wish on one's worst enemy. My opponent was taller than me and he knew how to box. At 'Seconds out of the ring', I tore into him and promptly ran onto a good straight left. I tried again and again and, by the end of the three two-minute rounds, I had a bloody and painful nose, was thoroughly weak, dizzy, and well beaten. Later I was asked to be captain of house boxing and, recalling my previous painful experience, decided I'd better learn something about the noble art, if such it can be termed. I visited the gymnasium, where Sergeant-Major Joyce held sway in spotless white flannels and sweater, minus a few fingers lost in the First World War. There I was coached by the diminutive lightweight champion, Hartshorne, who gently tapped me about the head and body with dextrous speed, and then passed me on to David Bevan, a heavyweight Oxford Blue, a complete contrast, who would first remove his spectacles before putting on his gloves.

"Now, Shearwood," he would say slowly and deliberately, screwing up his eyes and peering myopically in my direction, "are you ready?"

"Yes, sir."

"Then we'll begin leading with our left," and he would deliver a stunning ramrod of a punch to the head which knocked me off my feet.

"Sorry, Shearwood," he would apologise, as I gingerly picked myself up off the floor, "you all right?"

"Yes, thank you, sir."

"Right oh, we'll box on then."

He certainly taught me to keep my guard up.

When the inter-house boxing competition took place, I fought at ten stone eight and under, beating John MacKinnon on the way to the final, knocking him down with a right cross which surprised me as much as it did him. John became Senior Clinical Lecturer and Consultant Cardiologist at Birmingham University. In the finals, keenly watched by the headmaster and many others, I had to box against Anthony Robotham, strongly built and a renowned slugger, who had all but knocked out two boys, both fights having been stopped. But I wasn't too worried, for I had now learnt how to protect myself and box a bit, and the one thing I was certainly not going to do was mix it with Robotham. Oddly enough, right from the start, my adversary approached me in a wary fashion, and the first round I know went comfortably in my favour. Jabbing away with my left, keeping up my guard and ducking to avoid the occasional wild swing from Robotham, I survived the next two rounds and, confident that I had won the fight, turned towards my corner when, to everyone's astonishment, the headmaster suddenly pronounced loudly and emphatically, "I have never seen such a disgraceful fight in all my life. You will box another two rounds and this time let's see some action."

So we fought another two rounds, which I fear disappointed the headmaster yet again. At the end of it all I was acknowledged the winner.

On the academic front I was getting by, or so I thought, until put to the test when taking the 'Ticket', the School Certificate Examination, in the summer term of 1938. We sat it in the Alington Hall and, despite my usual few aids to memory, I failed dismally. I took the examination again the following winter term, along with several others in the same boat. We were left much to our own devices, aware this time it was now up to us. I worked hard, rather enjoyed doing so, and achieved, without any aids to memory, the five credits necessary to gain Matriculation.

The Michaelmas term of 1938 began with Chamberlain's proud assertion, "I believe it is peace for our time," which, according to my mother, so incensed my father while watching the Pathe Gazette News in Derby's Gaumont Cinema, that he gave a loud angry snort when the prime minister appeared on the screen waving aloft his white piece of paper.

I wrote in my diary, Sunday, 25th of September: 'Long arguments and talks. The general opinion is there must be a war. Kitch, I hear, is very depressed and Taylor says it's a hundred to one there will be a war.' On the 27th: 'Gas-masks were tried on everyone.' On the 28th: 'Volunteers go down town to help with gas-masks. Hitler wishes to see Chamberlain, Deladier, Benito. Cheek!' On the 29th: 'News much better. In the afternoon played left-half for the second eleven against Shrewsbury Amateurs.' On the 2nd of October: 'This week has gone quickly. Everyone is very pleased about the news, but I do think the Czechs have got a bad deal out of it. Derby County won again. They are still top with Everton.'

But though we argued amongst ourselves the pros and cons of the Munich Agreement, I do not recall the political reality of appeasement, or the imminent threat of the Nazis being much discussed. The final paragraph in the October *Salopian* of 1938 had this to say:

'And what of the future? After Munich what? The dictators apparently go from strength to strength, from one blackmail to another... And yet we feel that something must crack in the totalitarian pyramid. The dictators have forgotten the truth of the maxim, *Quod te minorem dis geris, imperasl* War, war, on everyone's lips, in everyone's heart. If it had broken out, many of us here would have no thoughts of any future except that of conscription, death, annihilation... Aeschylus knew the frightfulness of war; he wrote, "Instead of the men who went out to fight, there returns back to their homes an urnful of ashes". But, mercifully reason and fear prevailed, and we can think of the future with more hope, if not with any certainty. As we see it, the only future for civilisation lies in the ideal of freedom of expression for the individual.'

In the final count, I suppose it can be said that a year of freedom had been gained, a year in which to rearm, though never sufficiently to equal the lost armaments and fortifications of Czechoslovakia, a nation which would have presented a formidable obstacle and been a welcome ally on Germany's southern frontier.

So life at Shrewsbury continued. Later that term, much to my delight, I found myself in the school soccer side coached by Alan Philips, a neat centre-forward, who would watch our matches seated on a shooting stick. He and Tommy Taylor, Corinthians and soccer Blues and both on the staff and eventual housemasters, would sometimes play against the XI, the latter on the right wing, neat and fleet of foot, crossing the ball accurately to his colleague, who invariably won the ball in the air despite a lack of height. We had a good side in 1938, good enough to defeat Charterhouse on 'Senior', our notoriously heavy ground, by ten goals to one, and this despite our opponents having placed a large teddy bear at the foot of their upright and, possessing a centre-forward of renown, J. D. P. Tanner, who later played for Huddersfield, Oxford and England. We too though had a useful centre-forward and captain, Michael Crawford, who was to play football for Cambridge and some games of cricket for Yorkshire. Those awarded their colours wore on certain occasions, round, dark blue velvet skull caps, silver-tassled and edged with silver braid, beautifully and expensively made by Affords of Shrewsbury.

Alan Philips was a good coach and respected, but it would have helped to have had more contact with the professional world. After all it was customary to employ a professional cricket coach, but then there were gents and players in the summer game, and the gents ruled the roost.

Much of my football I learnt from watching Derby County — the Rams — during the latter half of the 30s. It was at the Baseball ground that I first saw the great professional sides of Division One, first heard the excited roar of the crowd as the teams ran out from the tunnel, the home side immaculate in their shining black shorts and white shirts. This neatness of attire and ease with which they controlled, and unerringly struck the ball one to another prior to the kick-off, made a lasting impression on me. I was to see many of the great pre-war players and, of all their skills, it was perhaps their heading I admired the most.

My remaining six terms at Shrewsbury became increasingly enjoyable. There was no pressure of work. I never attained the sixth form. I began doing quite a lot of extra drawing with Woodroffe, and started to consider architecture as a career.

More than once, early on a summer's morning, when the curve of the river below shone in the sunlight, and no First Lesson beckoned, I would slip down town for a short wander around before breakfast. Only the house John was aware of my excursions, but he said nothing. A lugubrious old bird, he nevertheless allowed me to fill in my football coupons down in his stuffy, coke-ridden boiler room — that is until Kitch found out. I was summoned once more through the green baize door and along the passage down which one went for the occasional breakfast, dinner or swiping.

We were a lively lot in Ridgemount, perhaps too lively for some. As we hastened up the hill to our lessons, once in a while we ran into Doc Barnaby, innocently bicycling to school.

"Get him," the shout would go up, "get the old Doc," and despite his frantic efforts to peddle away, we'd catch up with the master, and push him off his bike. "Got to walk now, Doc."

"Rotters," he'd mutter, as we dashed on ahead chortling to ourselves, leaving him to remount and follow in our wake. He took it all in such good part that we got the impression he rather enjoyed running the gauntlet.

On Sunday afternoons in winter, there was always a welcoming fire in the hall, where those of us in our fourth year listened to the records of Hutch and Bing, toasted bread and ate crumpets, lavished in butter. We were invariably hungry and at the beginning of each term I brought back in my tuck box a Fuller's chocolate and walnut cake, plus a pot of Gentleman's Relish, both replaced at half-term. I must have eaten the best part of sixty Fuller's cakes during those five years at Shrewsbury.

Ascension Day was a whole holiday. I have a photograph taken outside The Corbet Arms, of Gibson, Lock, Crawford, Singleton and Stockton, all of us grasping pint mugs of beer, smoking pipes, the latter three wearing cloth caps. We enjoyed ourselves hugely, drank more than was good for us, lit a fire by the river's edge, laughed and never gave the future a thought.

Mondays were Corps days and, of course, there were Field Days when all four hundred of the OTC set off, breaking step over the Kingsland Bridge, marching down through the town, the band strident, the big drum banging away while the townsfolk paused and stared curiously from the pavement as we passed on our way to the station.

Those in command of the Corps were beginning to take things more seriously, as was apparent one Inspection Day when an old biplane dived on us when in column of threes. In pretence we aimed at it, shooting over the shoulders of the next in line; as the plane roared over our heads we wheeled about and shot at its tail. In reality I think most of our heads would have been blown off. Night operations were exciting, particularly against another school when it was unwise to be captured.

But if those in authority were adopting a more serious approach to military matters, Ridgemount certainly was not, as our musketry instructor and Bisley coach, Sergeant-Major Blud M.M. would readily have testified. Bow-legged, veined and purple-faced, he was, amongst other things, in charge of the indoor shooting range where, during one Corps parade, Malcolm Lock, Tim Singleton, Peter Stockton and I were detailed off for target practice. Spread-eagled on the cocoanut matting in the firing position, we prepared to shoot. Between the targets and ourselves — the middle distance I think is the correct term — was a miniature hill, bridge, a church and a house.

"I'll take the church," whispered Peter.

"I'll take the bridge," said Tim.

"I'll take the hill on the right," murmured Malcolm.

"I'll take the house," I said, as the targets came up.

"Fire," ordered Sergeant-Major Blud and up went the bridge, church, hill and house.

"Cease fire, bloody 'ooligans, the lot of you. Get out."

Every summer there was an Inspection, when we fixed bayonets and stood to attention in long lines for what seemed ages — not infrequently someone keeled over and fainted — presented arms, marched past, gave the Eyes Right and listened to Major James West's fruity and prolonged bellow, "Battalion".

We wore peaked caps, puttees which would come loose if not properly put on, baggy knee-length khaki breeches and high-necked prickly jackets with brass buttons, as worn in 1914. We had belts and webbing, waterbottles and long scabbards for our bayonets. The webbing we cleaned with blanco, the brass buttons with Brasso. The douls were responsible for cleaning their monitors' equipment. It would be hard to design a more uncomfortable uniform. Since I suffered badly from hay fever, Field Days in the summer were hell, and I would return from a day in the Shropshire countryside worn out, my eyes itching and red, my nose raw from incessant sneezing.

Ascension Day over, the long summer term got under way with cricket and rowing, 'tubbing' as it was called, the two main activities. Before going to bed, those seriously involved on the river would anoint their backsides with methylated spirits to prevent the Shrewsbury 'tubbing arse'.

Wandering over the site on a summer's afternoon, white figures scattered across the Common engaged in house cricket leagues, a visitor would hear the familiar sound of bat on ball, and faintly catch on the wind the distant splash of oars and the shouts of coxes urging on their crews as down on the river, fours raced, scullers practised, and the school eight prepared for the Henley Ladies' Plate.

In late June parents arrived for Speech Day, which began on Friday and continued till Sunday evening. Outside the main entrance to the ivy-covered red brick walls of the School Buildings, a senior brusher in gown and mortar-board

Above: With mother on Speech Day

Below: Call over

Above: Head of School Leslie Minford with Stanley Baldwin on Speech Day

Below: Shrewsbury 10, Charterhouse 1

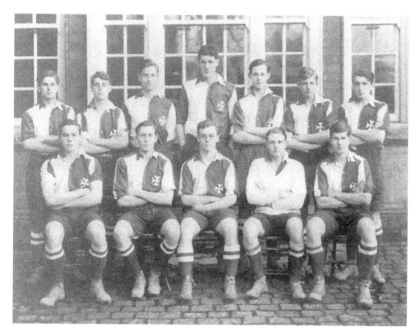

took 'call over', at his side the head of school reading out the names, ticking them off on a list. Slightly apart stood H. H. Hardy, hair cropped, his short military moustache bristling as he observed proceedings with a stern and sharp eye. A large assembly of parents watched from Central, as each member of the school touched his ear in the traditional manner and filed past, dressed in Sunday rig, tails but not top hats, though praepostors wore them and carried walking sticks. We all wore carnations.

Out on the cricket square the eleven were involved in a two-day contest with the Old Boys, the Shrewsbury Saracens, played, so Neville Cardus wrote in his *Autobiography*, perhaps a little euphemistically 'On the most beautiful playing-fields in the world'. In front of the pavilion, a grass bank of trees, known as the Tier, now no longer, stretched its friendly arm onto the Common. Here Stanley Baldwin in bowler hat sat on Speech Day in 1939, leaning forward, both hands resting on his stick, chatting with one of the cricketers, Leslie Minford, Classical Exhibitioner and Guinness Classical Scholar of Balliol, gifted all-round games player and head of school. At the far end of the Pier, flags flying tall in the breeze, four splendid marquees provided strawberry teas, while outside, seated in a semicircle, the school band in white flannels and straw hats played with gusto, until the cricketers came down the steps of the pavilion and play once more resumed.

There was a parade of Eights down on the river, a P.T. display on the lawn west of Central and exhibitions of various kinds. There were top hats galore scattered like black beetles in the fives courts awaiting collection when chapel was over. There were speeches and a school play to attend; my mother was fascinated when I pointed out the huge figure of Banks lurching unsteadily amid the parents, strolling outside the Alington Hall during the interval. Dinner in the evening at the Raven and a drive into the Welsh hills on Sunday for lunch, brought it to an end, and we settled down for the second half of the term. It was the last proper Speech Day for five years, the end of an era.

Most of August 1939 I spent with my family on holiday in the Isle of Wight. The weather was hot and I could see my father was restless as he stared out across the calm water at the gathering grey ships, his mind elsewhere, no doubt on what was to come. He was also, though unbeknown to us at the time, attracted to another woman with whom he would eventually live and marry.

Towards the end of the month I travelled to North Devon to stay with a friend and his family in an old farmhouse. I was dotty about one of his sisters aged fifteen, and had been so for some time. Bathing together in the heavy surf of Saunton sands one fine but very windy morning, when the tide was well out and we should have known better, a sudden unexpectedly heavy undertow swept her off her feet. Just in time I managed to grab her, clasping my arms about her slim form, holding her body close against mine, something I had longed to do all week, but lacked sufficient courage. It was a brief, exhilarating, at the same time alarming experience and, for a moment it was all I could do to hang on and resist our both being dragged out to sea.

On the morning of September 3, we gathered round the farmer's ancient wireless and beneath low, dark beams, listened intently to the weary voice of Chamberlain announce that we were at war with Germany, denying his prediction: 'Peace with honour. I believe it is peace for our time'. Sixty years earlier Disraeli had used identical words addressing the House of Commons, following his diplomatic triumph at the Congress of Berlin. But unlike Chamberlain's Munich, Disraeli's Berlin had proved a genuine contribution to European peace. Later that fateful day, the S.S. *Athenia*, carrying over a thousand passengers, mostly European refugees bound for America, was torpedoed by U-boat 30 some 250 miles off the Irish coast. War had begun.

We returned to Shrewsbury on Thursday, September 26 to learn that Cheltenham College had been evacuated on us. They were to stay for two terms. The Common that autumn witnessed the unique occasion of a soccer match in the morning, when Shrewsbury defeated Bradfield, cheered on by our visitors, and a rugby match in the afternoon, when Cheltenham defeated Rugby, cheered on by us. As well as could be expected the two schools got on with each other, though it was not wise they should meet on the stairs of the School Buildings, as one went down and the other went up at the change-over of lessons.

The Easter term of 1940 began with one of the hardest winters in years. The dormitories were freezing and the water pipes had iced up, which at least meant there were no compulsory swills or cold baths. Below, the river froze; up on the site there was skating on the Common.

So far the war had not intruded too much on our lives, apart from rationing and the blackout. But suddenly the 'phoney war' ceased dramatically; the Germans invaded the Low Countries, the French were defeated, and the bulk of the British Army, driven back onto the beaches of Dunkirk, was only snatched from disaster at the last moment.

The situation was tense, the threat of invasion a reality. Immediately a twenty-four hour guard was mounted on the Armoury, which housed a few Lewis guns and 400 Lee Enfield rifles. In no time a member of the Corps had inadvertently left 'one up the spout'; on emptying his rifle a bullet sped in the direction of Oldham's, which did not please the housemaster, Sopwith. We played our part in the defence of the town, alongside the Local Defence Volunteers, jokingly referred to as the Look, Duck and Vanish Brigade. The idea that we could have coped with a landing of German parachutists was too absurd to contemplate. Plans to stop tanks with Molotov Cocktails had already proved ineffective, since the petrol scattered too far when the bottle broke. To remedy this our science masters, Phillips, Matthews, Larkin and Taylor put their heads together and, by experimenting, established that an effective combustion could be achieved if the bottle had a covering of cloth. A demonstration was laid on, attended by a number of brass hats from the Barracks and Area Command. Hugh Brooke and Alec Peterson generously agreed to sacrifice their ancient Austin 12 to serve as the tank, which obligingly burst into flames when hit by the freshly improvised Molotov Cocktails.

On June 17, the day France surrendered, senior boys were ordered to keep their rifles and ten rounds of ammunition in their houses, under the care of housemasters.

The headmaster, who had experienced the First World War and was a stickler for detail, began using his Civil Service background, organising his staff to such an extent that David Bevan advised his colleagues: "If invasion comes, lock Hardy in the chapel."

But no one was more belligerent and patriotic than Corporal Hartshorne, who went on his rounds with an even brisker step, quoting repeatedly and explosively to all and sundry a saying Ernest Bevin had made when the nation stood alone after the fall of France: "We're in the Final now, sir".

There were more Field Days, Corps parades, night ops, guard and A.R.P. duties, and once a recruiting march through the town. As for Ridgemount, we played our part, co-operating cheerfully, though with customary frivolity, which caused Tom Taylor, who had now taken over the OTC from James West, to remark that either he or the Ridgemount contingent would have to go, and it certainly wasn't going to be him.

I recall many a happy memory of that last summer term at Shrewsbury. One is of an early start one June morning in 1940 to play a two-day match against Rossall. It was a glorious hot day and we drove the whole way with the hood of the bus down. We swam at the end of the first day's play in their outdoor pool, and then beetled off into Blackpool for a night out. Towards midnight and considerably the worse for wear, the bulk of the side somehow managed to clamber aboard the last tram back along the sea front, to be confronted by a far from pleased master in charge of cricket, Hugh Brooke.

"It's not even as though we're in a strong position. You're an absolute shambles," he snorted, a phrase he used constantly. Popular, upright, well over six feet and good looking into the bargain, his slightly amused expression, as though life was indeed all a bit of a shambles and not to be taken too seriously, belied the truth, evident when he later became ordained. An Oxford cricket Blue, he invariably wore a Harlequin cap and would enjoy demonstrating the late cut at which he was adept. We made amends the following day and won the match.

I recall a visit to Blenheim Palace where Malvern had been evacuated. *The Sketch* magazine photographed the match and published a page of pictures, one of me hitting a six on the way to 67. 'Brookie' had joined up. Harry Turner, the old Yorkshire pro had retired, and George Hart of Middlesex had taken over as professional. A young, soft-spoken, fair-haired Wykehamist, A. W. E. Winlaw, Cambridge scholar and cricket Blue, had joined the staff and helped with the coaching. Tim Singleton and Peter Stockton, both now at Oxford, came out to Woodstock and watched some of the match, Peter for a while seated astride one of the Duke's stone lions. He had not changed. The hot summer term of 1940 ended with a win at Repton by seven wickets, Mike Ainsworth hitting 154 on the first day — but then he was always better with bat than pen — followed by an innings defeat of Cheltenham, John Matthews, who was to play for Scotland and Cambridge scoring 112 and I scored 79.

We won the final of the cricket house matches and the silver bat, which pleased Kitch a great deal, particularly since in April he had resigned from his first love, coaching the school eight. *Picture Post* arrived and took photographs of the school, one of Kitch and me standing in front of Ridgemount on the private side, with the dark broad sweep of the river below. I thought it odd that he should choose me. I wasn't head of house and had never even been considered for it. I was too iconoclastic, too much one of the lads. But I think in a way he rather liked me.

It had now become apparent that our housemaster was slowing up. We didn't know there was anything seriously wrong, but there were signs that all was not well. At lunch he would carve the joint standing at the table in the bay window, Ruthie at his side, his house monitors around him. Slowly he would get to his feet, slowly take up the carving knife and fork with those huge hands and, very slowly and deliberately begin to carve. When he had finished, before sitting down, he would lift his great head and gaze for several long seconds at the body of his house as they chatted and ate their food, waited on by two maids and the unsmiling house John at the far end of the hall.

There remained only the end of term Bump Suppers, when each house held a dinner to celebrate the conclusion of Bumping Races, an annual event on the river in which twenty-six boats usually took part.

Ridgemount's Bump Supper of 1940 was, not surprisingly, frugal. In previous years we had sat down, some of us in dinner jackets, and opened our menu cards, neatly tied with the house colours, blue and gold ribbons, to reveal a substantial meal of: Salmon Mayonnaise — Roast Chicken, Ham and Tongue — Roast Lamb — Fruit Salad, Trifle, Raspberries and Cream — Ices — Dessert. Nonetheless we still enjoyed ourselves and after toasting the King — House — Crews — Head of House — Guests, and Kitch had said his few words, the leavers wandered up onto the site, once described by Thring as, 'the finest of any public school', to stroll on the Common and meet, mostly for the last time, our friends in other houses.

So my time at Shrewsbury came to an end and I bicycled away with Malcolm Lock to a forestry camp somewhere in the Welsh hills. There we shared a small tent and during the day wielded sharp axes and built great fires, which impregnated our clothes with the rich smoke of burning wood. To this day I find it the most evocative of all smells. In the evening we would wend our way down the hillside to meet Peter Stockton, who lived nearby with his parents in a peaceful old vicarage. We drank beer, smoked our pipes and chatted together till closing time, when we set off in the mist to climb, somewhat unsteadily, the winding path through the damp bracken till we reached the camp and our own small tent eight hundred feet up.

Ten days later, once more at the foot of the hill, we mounted our bikes and bade each other farewell. I watched Malcolm peddle off on his long journey home to Somerset before starting on mine.

We did not see each other again. He was killed in action serving with the Coldstream Guards at the end of the war.

I kept in contact with a few contemporaries in the years to come, mostly those involved in games. Kitch I never saw again, though I remember him well. Towards the end of his time in Ridgemount, he was being pushed up to school in a wheelchair

*Above: With Kitch looking down
river from Ridgemount
(Picture Post, 1939)*

*Right:: With Malcolm Lock,
summer 1940*

32

Above: A Six against Malvern at Blenheim Palace

Below: With Michael Ainsworth, who was to be my Best Man

by members of his house, until eventually in 1943 he .was forced to give up. At the ceremony in honour of his retirement he fell and broke his femur, but insisted on remaining throughout, despite intense pain. He showed great fortitude and died shortly afterwards of Parkinson's disease.

Today, looking at a house photograph, taken in 1936, which marked the end of my first year at Shrewsbury, evokes a host of memories. It is a summer's day. The ground and first-floor bay windows of Ridgemount are wide open. It is a low brick-built house, whose pleasant walls are partly covered with Virginia Creeper, though insufficiently to be obtrusive. Immediately behind the row of boys standing at the back on benches, is a tall hedge of rambler roses. In the foreground the faint sideline of a tennis court is etched on the dry grass.

It is a good clear photograph and, although fifty-eight years have elapsed, the faces are still as vivid to me now as they were then. In the front row, at the feet of the housemaster and his monitors, sit the new men, cross-legged, distinguished by starched Eton collars overlapping the tops of their blue jackets. All of us are looking intent and serious, apart from Kingston St B. Adams who is smiling gently, and the good-natured Thursfield, who left early and eventually became a vicar. Most of the new men have their hands clasped across their knees, though three have somehow contrived to hide their arms. Hall alone has his folded. I am second from the right, small and unsmiling, sitting on the grass next to Rutherford, whose ears protrude, a fact which did not deter him from becoming Head of House and Captain of Boats. On my left, equally serious, sits Morris-Eyton, who came two terms earlier, along with another big, podgy, pasty-faced boy. Both wear stiff collars rounded at the edges. The more senior boys wear white pointed collars. Ewbank, a scholar, is the only new man not wearing an Eton collar, exempt because of his height. Bending slightly forward, with a sagacious look, he gazes confidently up at the camera, safe in the knowledge that his equally scholarly brother is head of house. MacIver, the only one of us in the front row wearing spectacles, steel ones, sits bolt upright looking rather prim. Next to him, Drinkwater, relation of the poet, leans slightly sideways, peering forward suspiciously while, further down, Gibson, who gets by with a minimum of effort, stares expressionlessly at the camera, mouth ajar. Right at the end sits the most striking boy of the row, Malcolm Lock.

At the centre of the group stands a round oak table on which the silver cups gleam in the sunlight, subservient to the centre-piece, a handsome oval salver standing on end, testimony to Kitch as a rowing coach, to his house as oarsmen.

On either side of the housemaster are his six house monitors, but no Ruthie, for this was considered neither the occasion nor the place for a woman's presence. The Bull sits like the rock of Gibraltar, his presence massive, the huge hands and spatulate fingers clasped before him, the gaze steady and unhurried, a concentrated look of rugged determination.

The house monitors, as if taking their cue from the Bull, look stern, serious, assured and well groomed. Three of the six will lose their lives in the war, Derrick

Atkinson, D.F.C., killed in the Battle of Britain; Sammy Stockton, Scots Guards killed in action, Tunisia; John Pooley M.C., killed in action 1944. Five more face similar fates: Donald Oldham, Yates Crowley, John Bromley-Davenport, Peter Stockton, brother of Sammy, and Malcolm Lock. Their faces show no premonition of what is to come, only a serious preoccupation with the moment, all except for Peter Stockton who, as usual, has about him a perpetual air of mischief. There is one other, a gentle being standing in the back row, a top scholar, who wears a secretive, wistful look, as though seeds had already been sown which would lead him later to take his life at Oxford.

But what strikes me most, on looking yet again at the photograph, is the supreme confidence registered on the faces, in particular, of the senior boys. It is as though they are already aware that when the time comes to leave, they will have in their possession the name of a great school with a royal foundation, which will serve as a passport, a key — provided they play their cards sensibly — that will open many doors. It is a confidence bred from privilege, an assumed natural right, superiority, not to be questioned and, equally, not to be flaunted, though some of the faces already indicate clearly that they accept the former, but not the latter. Perhaps the triumphant shout of 'Floreat' and thunderous stamp of feet, followed by the extended cry of 'Salopia', which ends each verse of the Carmen Salopsiensis, has something to do with it all.

I was of course just as much a part of the system as any, and proud to have been at Shrewsbury. But deep within, I was always conscious of the yawning divide that existed between Maidwell Hall and Shrewsbury, and the Elementary School on the other side of that ugly, glass-spiked wall of 24 Normanton Road, Derby. For this reason, I have never felt much at ease with the established order of things, though must confess I have done little about it, other than occasionally tilt at authority and show an awareness and sympathy for any underdog, whoever or wherever. This is the permanent legacy of my education.

I arrived at Liverpool's Lime Street Station, prior to beginning my degree course at the university's School of Architecture, one overcast day drizzling with rain. Had I followed my instructions more carefully, I would have disembarked just outside the city, conveniently close to the university hostel, Derby Hall, a three-sided modern building of not unpleasing appearance, and saved myself a costly taxi-fare.

Allocated a small separate room in which to do my drawing, I was to share a bedroom with Basil McLaughlin, a soft-spoken, most friendly Irishman, who preferred working late into the night, so he never got to breakfast. Every fortnight a bar of golden butter arrived from Ireland, which my room-mate generously insisted I used to supplement my wartime ration. Although, like me, a freshman, there was a difference, for Basil was in his third year, having had previous experience elsewhere.

We spent our first day at the School of Architecture looking around and buying equipment, double elephant drawing boards, portfolios, T squares, set squares, paper, pencils, brushes and of course Bannister and Fletcher's *History of Architecture*. Then we were required to make sketches of a dinghy, a railway level-crossing, and any house or building that appealed to us. I made hard weather of it, scratching around with an unyielding pencil on the large white expanse of paper before me. I'd have done better using charcoal. Periodically, senior students wandered in to have a look at our work. Embarrassed, I sensed one of them at my shoulder. Without comment, he took out a pencil and quickly pulled my drawings together with firm telling strokes, made several brief, helpful suggestions and passed on. Apparently this sort of help was common practice.

Then the devastating blitz on Liverpool began and, night after night, the sirens wailed and the sinister, unsyncopated drone of German bombers circling overhead was heard, while searchlights probed the darkness and anti-aircraft batteries blasted their venom into the night. From the upper windows of the hostel we watched the exploding bombs, bursting like fiery mushrooms around the docks, the blast, despite the distance, rattling our windows. As each raid intensified, the fires grew fiercer until they became blazing infernos, casting an incandescent glow over the stricken city, lighting up our rooms. But long before then we had taken our bedding down to the ground floor and comparative safety.

We had our near escapes. A landmine fell close by and shook the hostel, blowing out many of the windows. I was returning one evening with a fellow student when we were caught in a raid. The explosion of a bomb, too close by far, drove us inside a brick-built shelter with a concrete roof. It was crowded and we both felt ill at ease, so decided to make a dash for it. We ran most of the way home, at times sheltering in doorways from falling shrapnel, until we reached Derby Hall. The following morning I passed the shelter in which we had sought refuge. The whole of one side had been blown in.

Because we were given plenty of time to complete our assignments, we tended to delay making a start. In the end, of course, there never is plenty of time, and we would finish up working through the night to get our schemes in at the appointed hour. Eventually, we'd run a bath of cold water and immerse the double elephant sheets of cartridge paper, preparatory to stretching and rendering plans and elevations. Finally, the work completed and our sheets rolled up and inserted into cartons, we'd make our weary way down to the School of Architecture in time to pin them up before ten o'clock. By the following morning the work had been marked; some sheets with a large red C for 'credit', the exceptional ones with a large red M for 'merit', the rest unmarked. I did achieve an occasional C, and once an M.

Early in the New Year of 1941 I applied to join the Fleet Air Arm and was summoned to Crewe for an interview. I did not answer their questions any too well and failed the medical board, the sight of my right eye proving defective. Rejected, the board suggested I joined the Y Scheme which entailed doing a course at a training establishment, spending a minimum of ten weeks at sea, before going on to *King Alfred* to be trained as an officer.

There remained the first-year examinations. I failed Mechanics, but scraped through the rest. We were each allotted a hanging space to exhibit our year's work, which was then inspected. Finally, it was announced who would continue as second-year students. I was allowed to go forward with most of my year.

It had, I suppose, been a fairly typical first year. I had made some friends, worked tolerably hard, drunk unwisely on more than one occasion, and played a few games of soccer for the university, once against Tranmere Rovers. By sheer coincidence one day I ran into Peter Stockton, and we dined together that same evening at the Adelphi, over-indulging ourselves as we reminisced about, amongst other things, our days at Shrewsbury. He had left Oxford and was now a lieutenant in the King's Liverpool Regiment. He had not changed. The mischievous twinkle and carefree attitude we knew so well was still present, though not for much longer; he was killed in action at Kohima attached to the Durham Light Infantry in 1944.

Whilst at Liverpool I was invited to spend several weekends with Michael Ainsworth at his home in Heswell, a fine house that overlooked terraced lawns. The family lived in some style, despite wartime restrictions, and they could not have been more hospitable. Powerfully built and ebullient as ever, his good-natured freckled face aglow with health, he joined the navy and was torpedoed in the Mediterranean serving aboard the *Hermione*. Picked up by a whaler, which was then promptly rammed by one of our own ships, he found himself again in the drink. He survived; at the end of hostilities he became a regular sailor and best man at my wedding.

But, in truth, I had grown no roots in the place and, when I came to leave Derby Hall and the School of Architecture, I had few regrets. I never really felt cut out to be an architect. It had been but an interlude, already something of the past. As to what lay ahead I could only ponder curiously. But I missed Basil's golden bars of Irish butter.

Chapter 3

Lower deck H.M.S. Foresight

THE TRAIN THAT bore me towards the West Country on that hot August day in 1941 was crowded and the journey seemed interminable. I had with me a small suitcase, and a large packet of chicken sandwiches. Fortified with my Old Salopian tie and a respectable tweed jacket, I felt ready to tackle the lower deck. At Plymouth I made my way to Torpoint ferry, crossed with others and caught a crowded bus to H.M.S. *Raleigh*, where the bulk of us disembarked and in a group walked through the gates of the camp and into the Service. Most of those around me carried only small paper parcels, some, nothing at all. My suitcase, tweed jacket and school tie seemed curiously out of place.

"This way, you lot," shouted a chief petty officer. After we had given him our names, we were directed to our various huts and told that we could get a meal at 18.00 hours.

The camp was neat, spacious and surprisingly pleasant, composed of low wooden buildings bordered by tidy grass lawns and verges. After we'd found our hut, with ten double bunks down each side, I went across to have some food, and almost immediately was accosted by a rating.

"My name's Beresford," he said recognising my tie. "I used to judge the inter-house singing competition at Shrewsbury." He was a music master at Rugby.

That night I met the rest of the hut. We were still in our civvy clothes and clearly a mixed bag. Five out of the forty odd in the hut were in the Y scheme and hoped, like me, to gain a commission.

Just before lights out, a benign, elderly pink-faced, white-haired chief petty officer, with two full rows of medals, who was to be in charge of us, introduced himself briefly.

"Just keep your noses clean while you're here, lads, and we'll get along all right," he remarked in a friendly fashion before wishing us good night.

"Silly old bastard," called out one of the Glaswegians at the end of the hut as soon as the door had closed.

"Keep our bloody noses clean, what's he fucking take us for?" and a prolonged fart preceded a burst of laughter.

It was but the prelude. My schooldays and sheltered background had certainly not prepared me for anything of this kind and, as I listened in amazement to the same four-lettered word, and a good many others, embroidering joke after joke, story after story, I could scarcely believe what I was hearing.

Finally, as another grotesque and obscene story penetrated the dark, a resonant voice thundered out, "Shut up, the lot of you, you're a disgrace."

"Sod off," came the swift retort, and there followed a moment of tense silence as the astonished hut awaited the next move. But, apart from a few comments as to what the owner of the voice should do, silence prevailed. The following morning I met the voice, another Scot, Jimmy Watson, a graduate of Edinburgh University who had been doing research work before the war.

During the next three days we drew our kit, had our vaccinations, injections and dental inspections. Squeezing into our new jumpers and bell-bottoms, and learning how to put on our collars, silks and lanyards before, finally, and with fumbling fingers, attempting to tie neat bows on our cap ribbons, made us look the novices we were. The injections and vaccinations, particularly the latter, were not so funny and the arms of those who had never before been vaccinated became badly swollen and bore unpleasant-looking scabs.

The dental inspection proved even more alarming. I had foreseen trouble here and my dentist had done all that was necessary, which was just as well. Sitting in the queue, it soon became abundantly clear that the 'Toothies' were not going to waste time doing fillings. Gums were injected and owners told to wait outside while the next man was summoned to have his tooth or teeth extracted. There was a fair amount of misgiving, particularly for those who had never experienced a dentist, and it was not surprising when one of the queue suddenly stood up and announced he'd bloody well had enough.

"Better sit down, mate," advised an orderly, "there's nothing to it," which didn't convince the rating.

The next day I was detailed off, along with another member of the hut, to cut the commander's lawn. On arrival we were each given a pair of ordinary rather blunt shears, and told to carry on. My companion found it difficult to speak, for most of his teeth had been extracted, and even more difficult to work the clippers because his arm was swollen and still giving him pain after his recent vaccination.

As we clipped away on our hands and knees, the sky grew darker and the distant rumble of thunder louder. A few spots of rain fell heavily upon our backs. Suddenly a vivid sheet of lightning, followed by a loud clap of thunder and a deluge of rain, drove us to seek shelter under the supports of the veranda. On hands and knees we watched the rain come down in sheets.

Almost as quickly the storm passed, the sun came out and the lawn glistened. I inhaled the fresh and fragrant smell of wet earth. The small area we had cut looked a good deal less tidy than the rest of the lawn awaiting our shears. I laughed aloud and glanced at my companion.

"There's fuck all to laugh about, mate," he mouthed with toothless misery, "wish I'd never joined the sodding outfit."

Peter Worth, one of the five CW candidates, who later became a submariner, was made class leader and was responsible for seeing we were on parade punctually and that things ran smoothly. The five of us got on well together and after Jimmy Watson's lead on that first night, never looked back. A friendly atmosphere prevailed and our white-haired old chief was helpful and considerate. We learnt how to march, turn-about, drill, salute, sling and lash up a hammock, and catch a liberty boat. We learnt the various parts of a ship and the rudiments of gunnery, and those who failed to pay attention learnt what it was like to double around grasping a six-inch shell.

At Stand Easy, we ate warm, freshly cooked doughnuts, and gulped down hot cups of tea. In the evenings, when it was our turn for a run ashore, we'd wander down the high leafy Devonshire lanes towards the Ring o' Bells, where we'd eat cheese and tomato sandwiches and drink rough cider.

Towards the end of the course, all the CW candidates were informed that White Papers had been taken out for them, which meant that we were well and truly embarked on a commission. Much to my surprise, I found I had come top of the class at the end of the course, something I had never achieved at Shrewsbury or Maidwell Hall.

In the last week, Michael Redgrave, who was in the next hut, organised a concert, at the end of which he sang 'London Pride' before a packed, cheering audience.

Our white-haired chief came to see us on our final night at *Raleigh* and repeated his earlier piece of advice.

"Don't forget, keep yer noses clean and you'll be all right," and then, as an afterthought, "I hope to God you'll none of you ever get into a sea action."

"Cheerful old bastard," remarked one of the Glaswegians.

"Not a bad old sod," added another. It was praise enough.

The Royal Naval Barracks at Devonport was a complete contrast to the pleasant and friendly atmosphere of H.M.S. *Raleigh*. Badly bombed in the Plymouth blitz, the petty officers' mess had received a direct hit. It was ringed by an ugly prison-like wall, behind whose forbidding iron gates, marines and white-belted ratings paced up and down, while official-looking chiefs and warrant officers popped in and out of a low red brick building. Now as Ordinary Seaman, D.J.X. 286602, I was filled with gloom as I passed through the main gates.

Our mess was one of many in a long crowded room. Down the centre, wooden pens housed the hammocks and kitbags, on each side narrow, scrubbed tables represented the messes. We found ours and stowed our kitbags and hammocks before going below to have a wash. We visited the heads and the scrawled advice, "It's no use standing on the seat, for crabs in *Drake* can jump six feet," did little to improve the general atmosphere of the place.

We were glad to escape that evening. Wandering up onto Plymouth Hoe, we ate some food at the Y.M.C.A. and filled our lungs with good sea air before returning to the barracks.

The atmosphere in that long blacked-out room was hot and full of tobacco smoke; there was no ventilation. We threaded our way ducking beneath the occupied banana-shaped hammocks and in the dim light slung our own. I lay awake and listened to the stertorous breathing, the grunts and snores and one persistent hacking cough which attracted a good deal of lurid criticism.

"You go on much longer, mate, you'll end up in a fucking coffin," and other choice pieces of advice were proffered to the unfortunate man, as the smoky atmosphere, a breeding ground for TB, penetrated his lungs. Eventually I dozed off to be woken almost at once by angry voices and shouts of, "Dirty bastards". Finally I fell asleep.

The customary shout of, "Show a leg, show a leg, the morning's fine, rise and shine — 'Eave-o, 'eave-o, lash up and stow," awoke us and, in singlets and underpants we swung ourselves out and lashed our hammocks with seven half hitches, as per King's Regulations and Admiralty Instructions, before stowing them in the pens.

At breakfast I discovered what had caused the trouble in the night. A group of noisy Belgian matelots, the worse for drink, had come in late from a run ashore, woken their immediate neighbours and angered them further by pissing on the floor.

After breakfast we would fall in for Divisions and listen as names of ratings were called out to report to the Drafting Office. Those not called would fall out into various groups and learn boat-drill, knots and splices, how to cat an anchor, or go away and row a cutter while an enormous petty officer sat in the stern sheets, his critical eye watching us as we struggled with the heavy oars. Those more fortunate got a sail in a whaler.

The day eventually came when our names were called out at Divisions and with high expectation we reported to the Drafting Office, in our ignorance most of us hoped for a destroyer. A 'battlewagon' was too impersonal, so we had heard, little more than a floating barracks. A small ship was the answer, preferably a 'Hunt' or 'Tribal' class destroyer. We got the latter.

At the Drafting Office we were ordered to report to H.M.S. *Gurkha*, lying in the dockyard. She was one of the new 'Tribal' class destroyers, and the prospect of getting away from Devonport barracks filled us with pleasure. As the time drew near for our departure, I suddenly heard my name called over the Tannoy ordering me to report to the Drafting Office forthwith.

On arrival I was informed that a New Zealander had not completed his sea-time and was to take my place aboard the *Gurkha*. Bitterly disappointed I returned to the mess and told the others my news. We hadn't known each other long, but we got on well together.

"Don't worry," said Jimmy Watson, sensing my disappointment, "you're bound to get another draft quickly."

"Lucky devils," I thought watching them leave the mess forever, lugging their kitbags and hammocks.

But, had I known it, I was the fortunate one, for on 17 January, 1942, three of them, including Jimmy Watson, lost their lives when the *Gurkha* was torpedoed by U133 in the Mediterranean north of Sidi Barrani.

Several days passed before my name, along with that of four others, was called out to report to the Drafting Office.

"You're to join the *Wolverine* right away," said the heavily built chief in a rasping voice. "She's in the dockyard."

"This is it," I thought.

She was a V&W destroyer, built during the last war. Not a 'Tribal' or 'Hunt' class, but a destroyer nevertheless, one renowned for sinking U-boat 47, the most famous of all U-boats, captained by Lieutenant Gunther Prien, who had breached Scapa Flow and sunk the *Royal Oak*.

Out of a grey sky, the thin persistent rain of the West Country hung like a pall above the blitzed city as we trudged through Plymouth Dockyard, doing our best to avoid the numerous and extensive oily puddles, for it had rained heavily during the night.

"Know where the *Wolverine* is?" we enquired of a group of dockyard maties who seemed to be doing nothing.

"Over there, mate," replied one with a nod. We headed in the direction he had indicated to find the *Wolverine* looking incredibly long, her decks deserted.

We crossed the short gangway, remembering to salute. Standing on the *Wolverine's* iron deck amidships, we waited uncertainly. There was no sign of life.

Hesitantly we walked towards the break of the forecastle to be met by a petty officer.

"What do you want?" he enquired.

"We're reporting for duty," and we showed him our draft chit which he glanced at before peering at us for several long seconds. I thought he was not entirely sober.

"Ship's paid off," he said eventually, "you'd better get back to barracks," and he carried on aft, leaving us to digest his statement.

"Interesting to know what they've got to say at the Drafting Office," I thought, as we made our way back.

But the heavily built begaitered chief at the Drafting Office was not in the least bit interested. So once again we fell in for Divisions and waited for our names to be called out and, on not hearing them, fell out into various groups to continue learning bends and hitches, boat-drill, how to cat an anchor and row a cutter, watched by the same enormous petty officer, who sat motionless, tiller under arm, like some great puffed-up toad, only his eyes, as they stared over the heads of his HO crew of oarsmen, giving any indication that he was still in the land of the living.

We did not have to wait long before the five of us found ourselves once more back at the Drafting Office.

"Right," said the same chief petty officer, when we had answered to our names. "Get your bags and hammocks and report back here in thirty minutes."

"What ship have we got this time, Chief?" I enquired tentatively.

"The *Foresight*," he replied, without looking up.

We returned to our mess, where the cooks of the day were busy scrubbing the tables in that grim room, and collected our gear. The chief was waiting for us when we returned and there was transport standing by.

Again he called out our names.

"Right, now pay attention. You're on draft to H.M.S. *Foresight*. She's up in Scapa Flow. You'll catch the 12.15 train from Plymouth, change at Bristol, Crewe and Glasgow, there report to the RTO. Right, carry on," which we did, with alacrity.

The first part of our journey was comfortable, the train surprisingly empty, so we decided to chance it and travel first-class to Bristol. We were not turned out and the five of us had the carriage to ourselves. I was able to take stock of my four companions.

Opposite me sat Gerald Oliver, a Catholic who lived at Strawberry Hill, Twickenham, in a large comfortable house. Olly, for such we called him, liked good food and comfort. He had a round, chubby red face and his cap, which sat fair and square on the top of short black hair, never looked as though it really belonged there. He was a large, friendly and likeable person. Of us all, I think, despite the fact that he had naval connections in the family, he looked the least like a sailor.

Next to him sat Ken Howard, sallow, tall and dark-haired, with a lantern jaw. Educated at Westminster he spoke with a slow deliberate, assured and slightly amused drawl. Scouts were his great hobby. He always seemed to have a Sherlock Holmes pipe in his mouth, and moved as though he had all the time in the world and never had any intention of going faster. Observing him I inwardly smiled at the thought that he might well have to move a little faster in the near future.

The other two were older and both married. Philip Dawson, an unobtrusive person of average height, worked in a bank. He possessed the most equable disposition of us all, nothing ever appeared to disturb his calm outlook on life.

The fourth of my companions, Charlie Dunn, was a short, stocky Yorkshireman, thin of hair with a jutting chin, big forehead and a mind of his own. Whenever possible he too smoked a pipe, short-stemmed with a heavy bowl. His strong North Country accent and measured, forthright manner of speech was to prove a useful counter to Ken Howard. Charlie was a good golfer and had considered turning professional, but in the end became a schoolmaster.

We sat comfortably in our first-class seats, gazing out at the passing countryside, and smoked. It was a peaceful, undisturbed ride, and I was sorry when the train all too soon drew into Bristol, and kitbags and hammocks had to be humped across to our next train.

From Bristol onwards our journey became progressively worse. At Crewe we had a wait of several hours and after a cup of tea in the canteen, we wandered off into the town. But at one o'clock in the morning Crewe had little to offer in the way of entertainment, and we were thankful once more to climb aboard the train and continue our journey north, vainly attempting to sleep in the smoky, blacked-out carriage.

The following morning, unshaven and feeling far from refreshed, we arrived in Glasgow and reported to the RTO.

"We're on draft to H.M.S. *Foresight*," explained Charlie, showing the CPO our draft chit. A moment later the chief shattered our hopes by announcing that they did not know where the *Foresight* was, or when she would turn up and, for the time being, we were to report to an establishment down Govan Road.

"Might have known it," muttered Charlie.

"Have a chance of seeing what the scouting set-up is like in Glasgow," Ken Howard drawled, and I saw Charlie glance at him keenly. "Doubt if you'll find many Boy Scouts down Govan Road," he remarked dryly.

The so-called naval establishment in which we now found ourselves turned out to have been, until recently, a doss-house for tramps. An elderly chief petty

Above: With Charlie Dunn

officer and a fat, equally elderly, three-badge killick were the only personnel of the place — 'cushy numbers' indeed.

"Stow your hammocks over there," the chief indicated, "you won't need them, you've camp beds to sleep on. Lock your kitbags. You'll be required to turn to in the forenoons, but you can have a run ashore in the afternoon and evenings. There's no pusser routine here."

This was certainly a change from Devonport. There were three other ratings and, like us, they were all awaiting news of their ships. In the forenoon we would peel potatoes, scrub the decks, polish spittoons, and enjoy an extended Stand Easy. In the afternoon we'd get out heads down for an hour or so before going into Glasgow.

The weather was cold, Christmas was less than a week away, and we were short of money. Of the *Foresight* there was no information.

One late and bitterly cold afternoon I walked into the Railway Hotel in Glasgow, discreetly climbed the stairs to the second floor and quickly found what I was seeking, a bathroom. Locking the door, I turned on the big taps and watched the hot water fill the large bath in which I soon lay, relaxed in mind and body. Our establishment had no such luxury, only a few chipped enamel bowls. Once I heard somebody try the door; apart from that I was undisturbed. Eventually I dried myself, dressed, cleaned the bath and leaving everything shipshape, opened the door to find a middle-aged woman waiting outside. Surveying me suspiciously she enquired whether I was staying in the hotel.

"No," I replied, "I'm afraid not."

"Then you've no business to be taking a bath," with which I could not disagree. I apologised as best I could and, with a stern glance and a shake of her head she passed down the corridor and out of sight. I stood for a moment, then made for the stairs. I was about to descend when a quiet, delightfully Scottish voice spoke from the recess of a doorway. "If you'll come tomorrow at the same time and go to the next floor you can have a bath. There'll be no trouble."

She was called Rosalie and as pretty as her name suggested. With her help I managed several more baths in the Railway Hotel and on her evenings off we danced to Joe Loss and his band, then playing each night at the Scala.

On Christmas Day I attended a packed Catholic church with Olly, and returned to a meal of pork and beer. In the afternoon we took Rosalie and her friend to Loch Lomond. It was a quiet, strange kind of Christmas and none of us had much money because a matelot's pay, two bob a day, didn't go far, despite the fact that you could go anywhere on the Glasgow trams for a penny.

New Year's Eve, Hogmanay, was very different. Olly and I, with Rosalie and her friend, waltzed away the last hours of the old year, caught up in a great revolving swirl of dancing couples, matelots, pongos, airmen, Wrens, WAAFs, ATSs, all moving like some great floodtide beneath the glittering chandeliers, while Joe Loss and his band played non-stop until just before midnight, when all hands were clasped and the slow sad strains of 'Auld Lang Syne' filled the air. As the last seconds of 1941 ticked away, the tempo of the music grew faster, the singing louder, till suddenly it all stopped and 1942 had arrived and Rosalie was in my arms, the dancing over.

Together the four of us walked through the blacked-out streets of Glasgow back to her home, a very humble dwelling in a very poor quarter, where most warmly were we welcomed and generously offered food and drink by her family, until Olly nodded and fell asleep. But Rosalie and I ventured forth; in the dark and narrow alleyway we clung together until the cold eventually drove us inside. At five o'clock we said goodbye to our friends and walked out into the first frosty morning of 1942.

Three days later we learnt that the *Foresight* had arrived in Scapa Flow and we were to join her right away. We caught the train to Perth, changed, and continued our journey through the night to Thurso. Going out into the corridor to stretch my legs and gain some respite from the fug of the crowded blacked-out carriage, I rubbed a part of the window clear with my sleeve and glimpsed the Highlands sliding past, shadowy and rugged, beneath a sickly moon.

A door opened and a plump girl in WAAF uniform joined me in the corridor. She too had come to seek relief from the claustrophobia of her compartment. We chatted a little until we heard the sound of a key being turned as the guard came through. He looked at us conspiratorially before announcing in a fatherly fashion, "You can go in there, Jack. I'll not be back for half an hour." And since we had no ready answer to his proposal, assuming our silence to be one of indecision, he shepherded us through the door with upraised arm adding, "I'll turn the key, you'll not be disturbed."

It may have been because we did not wish to hurt his feelings, or because it was so unexpected, or perhaps it was our inability to resist that shepherding arm — whatever it was — we now found ourselves, willy-nilly, on the other side of the door, which was promptly closed and locked.

Our new abode contained, apart from a number of heavy packages and hessian-covered bales, some loose straw and a calf. We stroked the small creature and then, sitting on the floor with our backs against the bales, made ourselves as comfortable as possible, smoked, talked, and awaited our release, which duly took place some thirty minutes later, heralded by much turning of the key in the lock.

The guard beamed at us in an even more fatherly fashion as he ushered us back into the corridor, where we bade each other farewell, before returning to our respective compartments in a further vain attempt to sleep, while the train rumbled on through the night into the early hours of the morning.

At Thurso we disembarked, unwashed and weary, a taste of staleness in our mouths.

"Put your cap on straight," a voice rang out as we shouldered our kitbags and hammocks and headed towards the steamer which was to take us across to the Orkneys.

Stowing our gear, we stood on deck and watched as two hands hauled in the head and stern ropes.

"Skipper's going to spring off astern," commented Ken Howard judiciously, puffing at his pipe. He was, of course, quite right. As the steamer gathered sternway, held only by the spring rope, her bow swung slowly clear of the jetty.

"Stop port, let go aft. Midships, slow ahead together," he drawled in his most officer-like voice, which carried a good deal too far for any of our liking and caused the odd matelot to turn and stare in disbelief.

"God help us if he's going to continue like this," murmured Charlie, distancing himself from the culprit, while the steamer, in answer to the ring of the telegraph gathered headway.

A keen easterly wind stung our faces; before long the steamer was responding to the sea's motion. I glanced at Ken who had removed his pipe and looked less sure of himself. Most of the ratings had gone below. They had done the crossing before. As we cleared Dunnet Head and steamed into the Pentland Firth, we felt the force of the sea. Altering course, the steamer began to lift and plunge and corkscrew in a sickening twisting motion, as the tide-ripped waters attacked the port quarter. It was then Ken Howard lurched to the guard-rail and was violently sick over the lee side.

Olly was next. His usual cheerful countenance had gone white and slightly yellow. Moving to the ship's rail, he retched and almost lost his cap, having omitted to put his chin stay down.

By now the big crested rollers raised and dumped the steamer on her side with contemptuous ease. Bracing ourselves, we stared in the clear northern light at the approaching islands of Orkney. Soon we were in the lee of Hoy, passing Flotta and heading up the Sound of Hoxa to enter Scapa Flow where, with a roar of cable, the steamer dropped her hook.

Retrieving our kitbags and hammocks, we stared down at several waiting motor boats, their coxswains calling up the names of their ships. Thinly we heard the cry of *Foresight* and spotted a clinker-built motor boat with sprayhood up, the coxswain balanced expertly in the stern sheets, the tiller held lightly behind him. He looked the part, nonchalant, yet alert, slim and immaculate, his cap set slightly aback, a hand up for'ard held the boat's bows and, not for the first time, I thought how raw and scruffy we must all look.

"Get a move on, down there," came the cry from above as we made our way down to the bobbing motor boat beneath, the coxswain holding her stern in by boathook.

"You for the *Foresight!*" he asked.

"That's right."

"Look slippy then."

We did our best, and then we were under way, the motor boat gathering speed, swinging in a wide arc towards a distant destroyer, one of a host of warships.

I looked at the coxswain's face. It remained impassive, head held high, eyes staring ahead. Not once did he glance down at us or speak, and I thought we might have been so much baggage. We began to close the *Foresight*, and I saw for the first time a sleek, powerful-looking ship. From the flare of her bows, 'A' gun and 'B' gun rose one above the other to the wheelhouse and bridge, forty feet above the waterline. Aft of the foremast, with its aerials and crow's-nest, were two raked funnels. In the waist of the ship lay four torpedo tubes, aft of them up on a platform, 'X' gun, then down again to 'Y' gun, and the quarterdeck, a stack of depth charges in the stern. With a kick astern the Coxswain skilfully brought the boat alongside.

Up on the Iron Deck the quartermaster glanced at us briefly, while the Officer of the Day surveyed us more seriously, but said nothing. A moment later the bosun approached and automatically we got into some sort of line.

"Right, you lot — CW candidates, I understand. We've not yet had any of your kind aboard," and he gave us a long and meaningful look before handing us our station cards and listing our mess numbers, parts of ship, action stations and duty watches. "Carry on for'ard, then," and, picking up our hammocks and kitbags, we proceeded along the waist of the skip in single file, through the fo'c'sle flat, and onto the cramped and crowded mess deck. A few curious eyes glanced in our direction, that apart we were ignored.

Across the low deck-head ran numerous pipes, grey electric cable channels and ventilating trunks, whose air was directed into the mess deck through louvres. The deck was covered with dark brown linoleum, the joints hidden by brass strips. Each mess had a bare wooden table facing fore and aft, held to the deck by iron rods. On the ship's side of the tables there was a wooden backrest, some shelving space above a row of seat lockers with twin cushions atop. On the opposite side of the tables were wooden benches. We stowed our hammocks in the netting pen, standing them upright. There was no immediate pocket space available, so we had to live out of our kitbags. Our personal effects, cigarettes, pencil, pen, writing pad, soap, we kept in our tin cap-boxes.

It was teatime. One of the cooks of the mess pierced a tin of condensed milk and emptied the contents into a large brown teapot. There was a big tin of jam, butter, a large loaf of fresh white bread, a few plates and knives, and no spare cup. My own was still in my kitbag. I felt very much an interloper as I sat down at the table.

"May I have a slice of bread, please?" I enquired of my neighbour as casually and unostentatiously as possible.

"Bread," called out my next-door neighbour uninterestedly.

"Pass the bread," said the next man.

Nothing happened. I waited and still nothing happened; until my neighbour suddenly leant forward and called impatiently up the table. "Come on, Taff, pass the fucking bread down, mate," with the result that the bread, butter, jam and large brown teapot, black with encrusted tannin to preserve the tea's flavour, arrived all at once. Somebody handed me a cup which he had just finished with, a friendly gesture. That apart I was ignored. I poured myself some tea and drank the brew, thick and strong and sweet with condensed milk, and listened to the talk.

Foresight had been in the thick of things from the start. Built in 1935, part of the 8th Destroyer Flotilla, she had begun the war assisting the escort force covering the approach to the Clyde of the Second Canadian Troop Convoy of seven British liners, and then done a short stint on the east coast before sailing to Gibraltar, in June 1940, to form Force H. At Dakar she had sunk a French submarine and a month later had taken part in the bombardment of Genoa.

Returning from operating with Force H in the Atlantic, she had gone to the assistance of the *Malaya*, torpedoed 250 miles NNW of the Cape Verde Islands. She'd been one of six destroyers escorting a vital convoy carrying tanks and stores for the Middle East when the merchantman *Empire Song* struck a mine off Cape Bon and blew up. The *Foresight* had taken off 120 survivors and, in doing so, sustained some damage and casualties.

The ship had taken part in Malta convoys fighting their way through to reinforce the island with aircraft and fuel. Closed up, guarding the flanks of *Ark Royal* and *Victorious*, under constant sea and air attack, somehow they had survived and reached the beleaguered island. On another such convoy her sister ship, the *Fearless*, was bombed and set alight south of Sardinia. It had been *Foresight's* task to sink *Fearless* after first taking off what was left of the crew. And, somewhere to the west of Gibraltar, along with four other destroyers, she had sunk U-boat 138.

Finally, in the last week of October 1941, after involvements in Atlantic convoys and in another air-ferrying operation to Malta, she was recalled to the U.K., battle-weary and scarred, to join the Home Fleet in Scapa.

It was hardly surprising that those seated around the table looked what they were, seasoned campaigners who'd seen it all, and would no doubt see it all again. Not for nothing were the ships of the Eighth Destroyer Flotilla known as the 'Fighting Fs'.

The cooks of the mess had rapidly washed up the tea-things and left the table clear for those who wished to write letters, roll ticklers for the following day, or play cards. Overhead the radio blared. Nobody spoke to me and I couldn't think what to say in order to begin a conversation.

I foraged into my kitbag for pen and paper and wrote a letter home. Then, when I couldn't remain seated any longer I went over to find Olly.

"Let's go up top and get a breath of fresh air, Olly," I suggested quietly so as not to draw attention.

"Go up top and get a breath of fresh air," repeated a matelot without turning his head, flicking his three cards face down on the table as he packed in his hand in a game of penny brag. "You'll get all the fucking fresh air you'll want, mate, before long."

I hoped nobody had heard me. I learnt at that moment it was impossible to say or do anything on the lower deck without somebody knowing.

Up on the fo'c'sle a cutting wind brought flurries of snow. We had a look at 'A' gun, climbed up onto 'B' gun deck and stood in the lee of the shield gazing at the inhospitable low rock-girt islands. There were great ships at anchor, trots of fleet sweepers, destroyers, trawlers, a hospital ship and, scurrying to and fro across the windswept, white-capped waters, small supply craft, ships' motor boats and what looked like an admiral's barge, all going about their business in the fading light.

It was too cold to stay on deck long. We went below to the warmth of the mess deck and the voice of Vera Lynn, accompanied by some of the hands, their singing interrupted by the forlorn wail of the bosun's pipe and the cry of, "Hands darken ship".

After supper I got hold of a bucket and went along to the galley to draw off some hot water for a wash. Situated along the starboard flat, the washroom was some ten feet by five feet, with basins round the side. It was tiny and congested, the sole washplace for the 120 seamen, torpedo men and stokers. Further along were the heads, five closed closets for the petty officers, seven open closets for the ratings. I left my bucket just inside the sliding door, while I went back to the mess deck to remove my jumper and collect my towel and soap. When I returned my bucket had disappeared.

"Do you know where that bucket of hot water's gone, Jack?" I asked the nearest body as politely as I could.

"Watch who you're calling Jack, mate," came the instant retort. I thought I had used a friendly term of address. Apparently not, and I didn't make the mistake again. My question unanswered, I stood indecisively and was about to go, when a heavily tattooed matelot handed me his bucket without a word. This second friendly gesture boosted my morale. But not for long.

"Don't take all that hot water," said the ship's cook as I ran off some more from the galley. I explained what had happened.

"That's all right," he remarked with more warmth.

I was woken the following morning by the bosun's pipe. Nobody took much notice so I continued to lie in my hammock. Suddenly I found myself being jerked up and down as a grey-haired three-badge killick tugged at the nettles of my hammock rope, "Wakey, wakey, show a leg, you heard the fucking pipe".

He was a sour-faced individual, lean and wizened and generally held to be the best seaman in the ship. I think he'd been detailed off by the bosun to keep an eye on us and chivvy us along. Since he was in the same mess as I was, I seemed to get the brunt of his attention. During our short spell aboard the *Foresight* he was always hovering in the background waiting to pounce and mutter, "Fucking HO, Call yourself a seaman!" whereupon he would proceed to demonstrate with brusque efficiency the quickest and simplest way to set about a job. I learnt a great deal from him, but he was never once pleasant to me. He clearly resented, and with some justification, that as CW candidates we should be allowed to gain promotion, become officers, 'pigs down aft', after having served only an absurdly short time at sea. I could see his point.

After breakfast the seamen mustered on the Iron Deck, where the bosun reported to the first lieutenant — 'Ship's company correct'— before detailing off various groups to work part of the ship, usually beginning with two cooks from each mess, followed by gun sweepers, flat sweepers, fo'c'sle party and so on. All seemed to go about their duties in an unhurried and reasonably good-humoured manner.

I found myself cleaning paintwork on the fo'c'sle. I was given a bucket, drew some softers, a scrubber and cloth, and made my way to the galley, intent on getting hot water. There I ran into old Sourface.

"You don't need hot water."

"I thought it might help to get a lather," I suggested.

"You thought. Well, don't think. Just do as you're fucking well told."

I carried my bucket and scrubber up onto the fo'c'sle and began scrubbing down the paintwork on the bulkhead of the TS room, as instructed. It didn't really seem to make an awful lot of difference and it was hellish cold, but I scrubbed hard and then wiped off the area I had done. Apart from my hands, which soon lost all sensation, I grew warm in body. At Stand Easy, I went below and drank some tea and had a smoke. A good many of the hands had already filtered through into the warm and clean mess deck well before the pipe for Stand Easy had gone. The cooks of each mess had been responsible for scrubbing the tables and cleaning their own immediate surroundings, and it all looked spotless. At the pipe, 'Hands carry on work', it appeared that a good many had suddenly found work that retained them on the mess deck. But the arrival of the coxswain soon changed all that.

"You heard the pipe," he said, addressing the nearest group, who were pretending to look busy.

"Who are the cooks of the mess here? Right, outside, the rest of you."

I continued my scrubbing. I had developed what I considered an economical way of working. Periodically I would transfer the scrubber to the other hand and, when I had scrubbed a fair area, I'd wipe it down and then take a short rest. It was during one of these short rests that old Sourface caught me 'loafing'.

"That all you've done?" I quickly picked up my scrubber and continued while he watched.

"Give it me," he said. Grabbing the scrubber, dipped it into the water before attacking the bulkhead with savage efficiency. Watching him work I felt clumsy and exposed.

"Get some clean water and more softers," and moving aft, he slid swiftly down the iron ladder at the break of the fo'c'sle and out of sight.

Two nights later, being non-duty watch, Charlie and I went ashore in a liberty boat and drank some beer inside a huge corrugated iron shed. On returning a buzz was abroad that the ship would be at sea the following morning to screen an aircraft carrier. It proved correct.

At 07.00 special sea duty men were called to their stations. In no time, we had slipped our moorings and were cleaving through the dark waters. I felt the tremor of the ship and the pressure of the wind as she increased speed. On the wing of the bridge the shutter of a ten-inch Aldis lamp clicked rapidly as a signal was flashed to the carrier, whose intermittent blinks of white light indicated she was receiving. A string of pennants flew at our yard-arm. Once outside we took up station, screening the aircraft carrier, guarding her flanks against possible U-boat attacks. The great ship seemed to be barely moving, which belied the long broad path of our wake and the high wash creaming away from each quarter. The destroyer's stem sliced into each successive wave, lifting and falling with an explosive thud, a motion similar to the sharp descent of a lift. The flare of her bows threw off the ocean in a white wall of foam and the wind drove the spray aft. Thirty thousand horsepower of engines whined, and the whole ship quivered and strained like some wild animal as she tore into the dark, rearing ranks of oncoming seas.

When the afternoon watch was piped to dinner I saw Ken take his plate of food and bucket onto the Iron Deck where he sat himself down and tried to swallow mouthfuls, only to spew them back into the bucket. I was fortunate and never sea-sick.

Charlie and I were on the afternoon watch, our part of ship masthead lookout. One glance aloft at the crow's-nest was enough for Charlie.

"I'm not climbing that bloody thing!" he remarked with forthright Yorkshire bluntness. Nor did he, and another hand was detailed off to take his place.

Before going aloft, a lookout had first to take a small wooden board, known as the 'man aloft board' into the TS room. This was necessary because should the telegraphists continue to use their electrical equipment, the hand going aloft stood a good chance of being electrocuted.

When my turn came, I handed in the wooden board, went to the foot of the mast and began to climb. The ladder was narrow, less than a foot in width and seemed to be, if anything, inclining slightly backwards, so the weight came on one's arms. Bulkily clad in sea-boots and duffel coat I climbed gingerly till I was above the bridge and experienced the full force of the wind. Glancing over my shoulder down into the black void of the for'ard chimney stack, I momentarily shuddered, before climbing the last few feet above the crow's-nest. With one hand on the ladder and the other on the mast, I eased myself round and down into the barrel which came up to my shoulders. Here I felt snug and safe. A pair of binoculars was at hand and, remembering the cardinal rule that they should first be secured around the neck, I put them to my eyes and focused on the waters ahead. From aloft, the length of the ship, looking incredibly narrow, began to heel as the *Foresight* altered course. With the seas now on her beam, the destroyer rolled heavily, and I found myself far over the water as the mast swung from side to side.

Half an hour later my relief was standing below looking up. Emerging from the protection of the crow's-nest, the wind forced me back against the swinging mast, round which I groped with my sea-boot for a rung of the ladder, grimly hanging on. However it was easier descending; once past the tall funnel and that awful gaping hole, my confidence grew. At the foot of the mast I watched my relief run aloft with expert ease.

During our short spell aboard the *Foresight* we were at sea most days, screening the big ships, once unsuccessfully searching for a U-boat reported in the vicinity, always in our ears the constant pinging of the Asdic set, a high-pitched repetitive sound — 'pee-ing, pee-ing', which penetrated every part of the ship. We were at Defence Stations, working watch and watch, four on, four off and the moment the watch on deck changed, we'd hasten below and 'crash our swedes' on any spare locker, bench, or room we could find, using our duffel coats as pillows.

It was monotonous and tiring; when those on the morning watch came off duty, they'd still be required to turn to and work ship after breakfast. The mess deck had to be cleaned, there was always work to be done up top and, if all else failed old Sourface was usually around to find some paintwork that required washing down.

When there was a make and mend we'd do our dhobying, using a metal bucket and a long yellow bar of pusser's soap, write letters, and catch up on sleep.

Our dhobying we'd take down to the boiler-room, which I never enjoyed visiting, particularly when at sea. To do so one had first to peer through a circle of thick opaque glass before lifting the hatch cover to ensure that the bulkhead door from the boiler-room below was not being opened at the same time. Should they both be opened simultaneously the pressure could cause a back-flash and endanger the stokers.

Once down in the bowels of the ship the heat was intense, the rungs of the ladder almost too hot to touch. The sight of the great boilers, with their glowing inspection windows, the whirring roar of the fans, the maze of lagged piping and pressure-gauges, the iron gratings — below which the stokers in their white singlets calmly went about their tasks entombed below the waterline, protected by a mere quarter-inch of steel — was a fearful one. It was a world in total contrast to that on the upper deck; to consider the effect of a direct hit on such an area defies imagination. I never wasted time hanging up my dhobying at sea, and would escape to the comparative freedom and fresh air up top as quickly as possible.

Nobody, apart from old Sourface, took much notice of us, and why should they have done? The ship's company had seen action and plenty of it. We'd seen nothing and had barely been aboard five minutes. We were like fish out of water, and Ken Howard didn't help matters when on two occasions he tried to convince his messmates of the value of the Boy Scout movement.

"Wish to God he'd keep his bloody mouth shut," Charlie would mutter, as fearful suggestions were hurled the CW candidate's way as to what he ought to do with his "fucking Scouts" and "sodding Scoutmasters".

The weeks passed and suddenly a buzz was going the rounds that the ship would be sailing south for a refit. When, at the end of Sunday Divisions, preceded by the order, 'Fall out the Roman Catholics', followed by the Lord's Prayer and those splendid words, 'Oh Lord God who alone spreadest out the heavens, and rulest the raging of the sea', it came as no surprise when the captain announced after we'd sung 'Eternal Father, strong to save' that the ship was sailing at 16.00 hours for Grimsby.

The cooks of the mess had prepared a tasty-looking roast followed by plum duff, and the Sunday dinner was eaten with relish, the remains scraped into the gash bucket at the end of the table and emptied over the ship's side. An air of excitement prevailed. When one of the mess offered me a tickler, I really began to feel I was one of them.

We slipped our moorings and, as one of the bridge lookouts, I watched from the wing the distant islands merge into the sea. To starboard, just visible, loomed the island of Hoy, whose massive cliffs on the far side majestically surveyed four thousand miles of western ocean. The wind blew cold and strong as we crossed the rough waters of the Pentland Firth and headed south.

At 20.00 hours the starboard watch went below, the weather deteriorating. Barely had we fallen asleep, when the bosun's pipe and the cry, "Starboard watch close up," wrenched us into consciousness. A locker had burst open and cans of food and utensils were clattering about the pitching mess deck. Pulling on sea-boots and bracing ourselves against the ship's motion, we struggled into oilskins and duffel coats, lurched our way along the canteen flat and through the blackout flaps at the break of the fo'c'sle, out onto the wet heaving deck for the middle watch. It was raining and blowing a gale, the stars hidden, visibility poor. I climbed the vertical ladder onto the bridge and reported my presence to the Officer of the Watch. The captain in brown duffel coat was seated in his chair, his presence unmistakable and dominating.

I waited until my eyes grew accustomed to the dark, then took the glasses from my opposite number and, putting them round my neck, began scanning the section off the port bow. A lookout's duty lasts half an hour.

During my spell off watch in the wheelhouse, I heard the OOW call sharply down the voice-pipe: "Hard a-starboard!' As the quartermaster spun the wheel, at the same time repeating the order, the *Foresight* heeled sharply.

"Have a look outside and see what the hell's going on," he said, lowering his voice and, at the same time, turning his head away from the voice-pipe.

I stepped outside, holding on as the ship rolled heavily. For a few moments I could see nothing. Then a faint shape loomed briefly before disappearing into the black void. 'Ships that pass in the night', I thought, re-entering the wheelhouse.

"Port 15," came the voice from the bridge.

"15 of Port wheel on, sir."

"Ease to five."

"Ease to five, sir."

"Midships."

"Midships. Wheel's amidships, sir." The quartermaster was watching the illuminated card carefully.

"Steady."

"South 30 east, sir."

"Steady as she goes."

"Aye, aye, sir."

"Full ahead together."

"Full ahead together, sir. Both engines full ahead together," and we continued our course down the east coast.

At 04.00 the watches changed and we went below. Four hours later the bosun's pipe summoned us to close up at our stations, in my case masthead lookout again.

The weather had eased somewhat, but I hung on tight as I climbed, for the ship was still bucking into a head sea, throwing back heavy curtains of spray over 'A' and 'B' guns. From aloft the scene was a sombre one, only the white crests contrasting with the grey clouds scudding low overhead. Despite the poor visibility, I quickly picked up a black vertical speck sticking out of the turbulent waters.

"Masthead lookout, bridge."

"Bridge here."

"Unidentifiable object green one-o."

"Very good."

The speck turned out to be the mast of a sunken ship; as we passed, it seemed to point a forlorn finger of accusation at us. Shortly after I spotted two more masts and promptly reported them. But this time, instead of the reassuring, "Very good," I received a curt reprimand from the OOW, "Don't report what's obvious to the bridge," which didn't really help since we'd always been instructed to report everything, no matter what or however obvious. Well — "To hell with them", and I began to speculate whether there were any acoustic or magnetic mines ahead, and what chance I'd have up here in the crow's-nest if we struck one. Probably as good as any, I came to the conclusion, until I realised I wasn't wearing a lifebelt. I learnt later that most of these sunken ships had run into mines laid by German E-boats, or dropped by air in the path of East Coast Convoys.

We entered Grimsby late in the afternoon. No sooner had we secured alongside than Posty was ashore for the mail and dockyard officials were swarming everywhere. There was a letter from home which I opened and began to read. For a while the mess deck was strangely quiet, apart from the occasional snort and expletive, as some startling revelation affected the recipient. I read with difficulty because, like that of many a doctor, my father's handwriting was atrocious, and I struggled through his letter.

Meanwhile, those going on leave had wasted no time. Within an hour the port watch, all 'tiddly' in their number ones and gripping their small brown cases, were on their way. But there was to be no leave for us. We were to be drafted back to barracks for further sea-time, and were given the distinct impression we did not deserve leave which I suppose was true, for we'd only been aboard a little over two months.

The following morning we were handed our draft chit back to the Royal Naval Barracks, Devonport. The bosun saw we were properly mustered before giving us the order to carry on. In single file, humping our kitbags and hammocks, we saluted and crossed the gangway. Transport was waiting to take us to the station. We climbed into the back of a 15-cwt truck, the engine started and we began to move. Over the tailboard we gazed for the last time at the *Foresight,* until the vehicle swung sharply round a corner and the ship was gone from our view forever.

Both watches had their leave, the *Foresight* her refit, after which she sailed on escort duty for Russia. Homeward bound on convoy Q.P. 11, the cruiser *Edinburgh* was torpedoed by a U-boat off the North Cape, her stern blown off, and taken in tow by *Foresight* and *Forester.* Attacked by the bigger German destroyers, the *Edinburgh* was again torpedoed, and the *Foresight,* though severely hit, had the task of sinking the stricken cruiser. Even so there was to be little respite for the crew. Repaired at Hull, the ship resumed service escorting Russian convoys.

In August 1942 she was once more back in the Mediterranean for yet another Malta run. Approaching the Sicilian Narrows, the convoy was heavily attacked and the *Foresight* hit by an aerial torpedo, Taken in tow for Gibraltar, she finally succumbed and met her end off Galita, sunk by the *Tartar* on 13 August, 1942.

Disappointed though the five of us were not to have completed our sea-time aboard the *Foresight*, it was indeed we who were the fortunate ones.

Chapter 4

H. M. S. Montrose *and East Coast convoys*

ONCE MORE we found ourselves passing through the grim portals of Devonport Barracks and beginning the same routine from which we had so recently escaped.

"You bastards back?" the chief greeted us at the Drafting Office, shaking his head slowly from side to side when we enquired what chance there was of a quick draft. Yet within the week our names were called out and we were on our way again.

"You're to join the *Montrose,*" he said brusquely, at the same time staring at us ruminatively before taking up his pen and beginning to fill in the draft chit.

"Wonder what run she's on?" murmured Charlie.

"We should get some sea-time in," drawled Ken Howard.

"You'll be lucky to get any fucking sea-time in where you're going," snapped the chief without looking up from his writing.

We awaited an explanation.

"Why?" enquired Olly tentatively, a puzzled expression on his round red face.

"Why?" demanded the chief, jerking his head up and handing us our draft chit, "because she's in dry fucking dock up at Rosyth, old son, that's why."

"Ah," said Olly, and Charlie groaned audibly.

"Right, carry on. Get your kitbags and hammocks," and with a final, "don't let me see you lot again," he dismissed us.

It was drizzling steadily when we arrived at Edinburgh in the grey early hours of the following morning. We had time to snatch a cup of tea at a small cafe halfway up Waverley Steps before catching the connection to Inverkeithing. At Rosyth we were informed the *Montrose* was lying in the *Hood's* dock. Shouldering our kitbags and hammocks yet once more, we finally reached our destination.

At the bottom of a huge rectangular basin lay the *Montrose* resting on a long cradle of wood. One end of the dock had a V section cut out in order to accommodate the bows of *H.M.S. Hood*, once the pride of the Royal Navy. Massive balks of timber extended from the sides of the dock, pinning her as surely as a butterfly to a board. This apart, there was no resemblance, for the 1918 V&W destroyer was a sad and neglected spectacle, and it was hard to accept she would ever look anything else.

"Better get aboard," Phil suggested, and the five of us descended the dock's damp internal steps, until we reached the narrow somewhat rickety brow bridging the gap between the dock's wall and the *Montrose.* In single file we crossed, dumped our gear on the Iron Deck and saluted. A rating hurried past in overalls, and a dockyard matey gave us a cursory glance before continuing his welding. While we stood waiting, Charlie had a quick word with Ken Howard.

"For Heaven's sake," he urged, "don't try and convert this lot to the Boy Scout movement," advice which only made Ken laugh, though he did assure us he'd do his best not to let the side down. A moment later he all but did. Taking out his Sherlock Holmes pipe, he was about to light up when the quartermaster emerged from the fo'c'sle.

The coxswain, four-square in body, who filled his worn serge uniform more than adequately, looked briefly at our draft chit, then led us for'ard onto the mess deck where we were issued with watch and quarter cards and shown our respective messes. Changing into overalls before turning to, we gathered that half the ship's company were on leave, that there was shore leave every other night for the non-duty part of the watch, and that the ship was liable to be at least another four weeks in dry-dock since, apart from numerous defects, she had bent her propeller shaft on a reef in Scapa. As though to ram home this depressing news, a sudden burst of riveting blasted our eardrums.

So the days passed and we fell in each morning and fell out, detailed off to various jobs, some of which we'd grown accustomed to aboard the *Foresight*. There was endless chipping, washing down and painting of the ship's superstructure. There were frozen sides of meat to be fetched for Tanky, the ship's butcher, and sacks of potatoes to be shouldered down the dock's slippery steps. There were guns to be tended, mess decks to be cleaned, tables to be scrubbed, whilst from below the ring of steel on steel proclaimed that the stokers were hard at it in their kingdom.

It was tedious work and didn't really seem to be getting us anywhere. Numerous dockyard maties and several women in shapeless overalls went about their tasks with minimum enthusiasm. Coils of black piping littered the decks as welders, their eyes protected from the bright acetylene flames, crouched behind their visors, seemingly oblivious to the deafening, intermittent hammer of the riveters' guns.

But for the watch aboard the evenings were pleasant, with plenty of space on the mess deck. Every other night the non-duty watch would have a run ashore, reporting back on board before 08.00 hours. There was a good Y.M.C.A. somewhere off Princes Street where we would spend the night. I even managed to sneak the odd hotel bath, but there was no Rosalie to tend to my needs. At six the following morning we'd gulp a cup of tea, before scurrying out into the dark frosty streets of Edinburgh to catch the train to Inverkeithing in time to turn to.

Then it was our turn for ten days' leave and, full of good cheer, we mustered on the Iron Deck, awaiting inspection. As always on such occasions, I was acutely aware of the regular matelots standing amidst our ranks. They possessed a professional elegance, clad in their number ones, with their neat, horizontally creased bell-bottoms, clinging jumpers, Mediterranean blue collars and tiddly bows, which no HO rating could ever hope to emulate. Despite all our efforts to be the part, we still stood out as conspicuously as ever.

"Now pay attention," the coxswain was saying, "Liberty men are warned. All leave expires at 23.59 hours…" and, turning to the officer of the day and saluting, he requested permission for "Liberty men to proceed."

Ten days later I returned aboard, one hour adrift, and was promptly put in the First Lieutenant's report. The mess seemed to think it funny and I rather suspect I went up in their estimation.

"It's the fucking rattle for you, mate," said Scouse Dowell cheerfully.

"He's right. Once in the rattle, always in the fucking rattle," chimed in his oppo, Geordie.

I was concerned, but not unduly so, for I considered my case to be a good one. I had missed my connection and had not bothered to get a chit signed by the RTO. Believing there was plenty of time to spare I had caught a train to Glasgow. Unfortunately it was late, and the connections to Edinburgh were not as good as I had anticipated, with the result that I reported back aboard one hour adrift.

I fell in with the request men and defaulters, and saw the First Lieutenant, who listened to my case, standing behind a small table.

"Captain's report," he remarked.

"On caps, about turn," shouted the coxswain.

Somewhat depressed I went for'ard onto the mess deck.

"What did you get, Sheerlegs?" for that was what I was now sometimes called.

"Captain's report," I replied.

"It's the fucking rattle for you, mate," I was cheerfully informed again, after which nobody was in the least bit interested.

The next day the Captain saw the defaulters. My name was called out and I approached the table. "Off caps," shouted the Coxswain. I hardly heard him repeat the charge of being absent without leave, for my eyes were on the man standing behind the table.

It was the first time I had been face to face with the captain of the *Montrose,* and I had hoped for a more auspicious meeting. He was thin, of average height, his uniform immaculate, his serious, rather gaunt and weather-beaten face striking.

He looked straight at me. "Why were you adrift?" he asked sternly, never taking his eyes off my face. I began to explain, but didn't get far for, turning his head, the captain spoke to the Coxswain, who promptly shouted, "Two days' pay, two days' leave, seven days' number elevens, on caps, about turn, double march."

And that was that. I hadn't even been able to say my piece properly, and I returned to the mess deck despondent.

"What did you get, Sheerlegs?" asked Geordie, grinning.

"Two days' pay, two days' leave, seven days' number elevens."

"Told you it'd be the fucking rattle, mate," announced Scouse for the third time, giving me a consolatory pat on the back, which did something to raise my spirits.

Olly commiserated, as did Phil and Charlie, but Ken, removing his pipe and smiling broadly, remarked that so far I was the only one who had been fortunate enough actually to have met the Captain. But then his turn was to come.

Once I had begun my number elevens I did not mind, though I missed the runs ashore into Edinburgh. Most of the day, with half an hour off for meals, I spent chipping and cleaning paintwork, and of that I'd had plenty of experience. I didn't rush the job, but throughout the day chipped slowly and methodically round the upper works of the fo'c'sle, keeping a weather eye open for authority.

When the seven days had elapsed, Charlie suggested we should visit St. Andrews. I had only played some dozen rounds of golf in my life, some in Edinburgh, under

Charlie's expert tuition. Although I had reached the stage where I could hit the ball, I was still a complete novice. Olly at the last moment decided to come along as well.

Arriving at the famous old golf course we promptly hired some clubs, while Charlie, fascinated by all he saw, began browsing around. "You go on and get a place in the queue," he told me, "I'll be with you in a minute." Reluctantly and feeling suddenly extremely vulnerable, I set off with Olly.

It was a handsome day and we had removed our jumpers. With growing apprehension I watched those ahead drive off with faultless ease.

"Nervous?" enquired Olly. He was enjoying himself.

"Where the hell is Charlie?" I thought, bending to tee up the ball.

Some fifty yards ahead lay a small stream; to the right, barbed wire and the sea; behind, the queue. In a glass pavilion, elderly spectators sat and enjoyed the sunshine and watched.

I concentrated on the ball, trying hard to relax and remember all that Charlie had taught me. "What the hell was he doing?" and offering up a prayer I swung and missed the thing completely, the ball merely falling off the tee. Quickly I replaced it and in haste addressed the ball again. This time I hit at it savagely, only to see it curl far away to the right, over the barbed wire, and head in the direction of the sea. "For God's sake, Olly, give me a ball," I said, appalled. Breathing another prayer, I swung again and topped the wretched thing, which flew from the tee in a series of maddening low hops, ending in the brook fifty yards ahead.

"Quick," I said, "we must move on." I was glad of Olly's company.

There was no escape. Confronted by enormous bunkers and chased by those anxious to get ahead, we hurried on our way towards the first distant green where, much to my relief, Charlie caught up with us. I watched in admiration as he tackled the rest of the course.

By now the *Montrose* was nearing completion and we had begun painting her topsides. As side-party I was working one forenoon with an enormously tall seaman, Lofty Paynter. We had been lowered over the fo'c'sle on a narrow plank, attached to lifelines looking suspiciously like old heaving lines, which I doubt would have stood our weight had they been put to the test. Forty feet below lay the bottom of the dock. A pot of grey paint hung between us. With one hand holding onto the ropes of the plank we began slapping it on. It was tricky work, since we had to lean forward to reach the ship's side, because of the bow's flare. Lofty had an enormous reach and the plank would sway precariously outwards until it seemed we would lose our footing. I think his intention was to see how far we could go before this actually happened. I tried unsuccessfully to enter into the spirit of it.

"Like being on a bloody swing, mate," Lofty would sing out, enjoying himself and watching my response.

As soon as we had finished an area he would call up for us to be lowered. Once we found our plank lowered unevenly so that one end remained higher than the other.

"What the hell's going on up top?" yelled Lofty, "we're standing on our bloody ends down here," which wasn't exactly true. A moment later it certainly was, for again they lowered the wrong end and we literally were hanging on for our lives, the plank almost vertical.

With the crew back aboard and the refit almost completed, lower deck was cleared one forenoon and told to muster on the quarter-deck. A warrant was to be read out. The ship's company fell in on both sides, the officers aft. The prisoner and escort with the Coxswain behind, faced the officers. When the Captain came on deck the first lieutenant called the ship's company to attention. The Coxswain then gave the order: "Prisoner, one pace step forward march. Prisoner, off caps," and the senior hand of the escort removed the man's headgear. Solitary and bareheaded he stood facing the captain, who read the warrant which sentenced him to ninety days' cells. Turning his head slowly from side to side, the prisoner gazed vacantly over the heads of his shipmates, seemingly oblivious of what was happening.

When the Captain had finished reading the warrant, the Coxswain barked: "Prisoner, one pace step backward march, on caps," and the same senior hand replaced the rating's cap. "Prisoner and escort, right turn, quick march."

All eyes were on the prisoner as he turned and, deliberately flouting the order, sauntered slowly off, expressing his total indifference and disdain.

"Bring that man back and march him off properly, Coxswain," ordered the captain sharply. Twice more the Captain ordered the Coxswain to bring the prisoner and escort back and make them proceed properly. And twice more he was unsuccessful, for the prisoner's attitude remained unchanged and there was nothing the Captain could do about it. With all the weight of authority against him, I had to admire the man's courage.

At last the day came when the floodgates were opened, the dock filled, the balks of timber fell away from her sides, and the *Montrose* was afloat once more in a basin of dark, oily water, its surface dotted with flotsam and scum. Towed out and placed alongside, final maintenance was completed, the engines flashed up and the ship was ready for sea trials. Ropes had been let go fore and aft, apart from a for'ard spring on which the ship was now going slow ahead. The hand surging the wire suddenly faced a riding turn, the wire jammed round the bollards, became bar taut as it took the ship's strain, and was on the point of parting.

"Ease away on that spring," shouted a leading hand.

"Looks to me as though that wire's going to part," observed Howard judiciously, peering over the ship's side and, in a voice that all could hear, "should be interesting."

"Be fucking interesting when it takes your stupid loaf with it," snapped the leading hand. "Stand back, you silly bastard," he warned just in time as the wire parted, whipping viciously upwards at the very spot where Ken Howard had been standing. We pulled in what was left of the wire hawser watched by several dockyard maties, who had been silently observing the proceedings.

That night there was no leave for either watch, so the bulk of the ship's company brought their cards, with their three written lines of numbers, and settled down to an evening of Tombola. The first to cross off a complete line won a prize. The mess deck was packed, for Tombola, like rum or duty-free tobacco, was just as much part of the naval scene. Without warning the chatter suddenly ceased and, with pencils poised, the men were ready.

"Eyes down for the line," sang out the old hand who drew the numbers and, dipping into his bag, he began to call them out, each number having a traditional name or way in which it had to be announced. "All the sevens, seventy-seven; by itself, number two; bed and breakfast, two and six; five and nine, the Brighton line; seven and six, she was worth it," until a sudden shout, "Here you are," temporarily stopped proceedings, while the winner of the line came up to have his card checked.

"Eyes down for the house," ordered the old hand once more, and he continued in his detached, unhurried manner to call out the numbers, this time for the big prize: "Royal salute, twenty-one; five, o, change hands; one and two, one dozen," until there remained just three or four men, each with only one more number on his card to cross off, concentrating intently, heads bent as the voice went on: "Kelly's eye, number one; all the sixes, clickety-click; Downing Street, number ten; unlucky for some, thirteen;" at which point the tension was broken by a snort from Joe Mul, "Here you are," and grinning all over his face, Joe got up to have his card checked, while the old hand gave the traditional retort, "And a house called," which concluded another evening's Tombola.

The next few days we underwent engine trials, until the chief engineer was satisfied, after which we took aboard stores, ammunitioned ship and practised gun drill, when I began to learn something of what was expected of a sight-setter. Finally, we slipped our moorings and sailed for Harwich to join the 16th Destroyer Flotilla.

It was the end of April 1942 and, as we steamed down the Firth of Forth, there was a feel of spring in the air. The weather was surprisingly mild and across the water the countryside looked fresh and green.

We passed the boom and entered Harwich with hands fell in fore and aft, the ship's pennants flying at the yard-arm while the wind blew our jeans around our necks and only our chin-stays held our caps on. We drew near a line of sleek, single-funnelled 'Hunt' class destroyers and, further upstream the distinctive two-funnelled V&W destroyers of the 16th Flotilla came into view. As we slid past each warship, the long high-pitched warble of the bosun's whistle brought the ship's company to attention, while the officers saluted.

Across the water the shore station was signalling fast and, in response the shutter of our ten-inch lamp clicked its acknowledgement in single white flashes. Faintly the engine-room telegraph rang. The whaler was slipped and the fo'c'sle party fell out to prepare to pick up a buoy. So far all had gone well, but now things began to happen which were not intended, nor are to be found in the *Manual of Seamanship*.

As a member of the fo'c'sle party I always tried to make myself as conspicuously useful as possible, which wasn't easy as there were always too many hands on deck, most of whom were a good deal more efficient than I was. The buoy jumper had shackled on the picking up wire. In the stiff cross wind the gap between the ship's bows and the buoy began to widen quickly.

"Get a turn round that bloody capstan," came a shout from the bridge as the three-and-a-half-inch wire hawser, full of wicked kinks and splinters, began to run through our hands and out through the bull-ring at an alarming speed.

"Fucking balls-up here, mate," grunted Geordie, avoiding an ugly bit of wire.

The situation was becoming critical because there was little wire remaining in the starboard bin.

Another angry shout from the bridge caused the officer in charge, a gentle and timid RNR lieutenant, to glance up in some trepidation, acutely aware that all eyes on the bridge were watching every move of his fo'c'sle party, just as the captain was equally aware of senior and critical eyes across the water observing his handling of the *Montrose.*

"Whaler's crew are laughing their bleeding heads off," muttered Scouse, nodding in their direction as the hands lay on their oars watching our endeavours with wry amusement.

The last remnant of wire was running out of the bin when a leading hand scattered us all and, with considerable risk to limb and a good deal of luck, managed to get another saving turn round the capstan. At once the wire tautened, the ship's bow was held and the situation saved. But immediately another developed as the full weight of the *Montrose* dragged the buoy beneath the whaler's bilge, all but overturning the boat and tipping the crew into the water. The ship's capstan rotated, drawing the bows of the *Montrose* till they overhung the buoy. The bridle was lowered and the bedraggled half-drowned buoy-jumper shackled on the length of cable and jumped back aboard the whaler. Faintly the ring of the engine-room telegraphs sounded, the ship's main engines stopped, and the *Montrose* lay to her mooring, stemming the tide.

Our first few days at Harwich were spent doing practice shoots at sea and aerial targets.

"Ever heard a gun fired?" Geordie asked with a malicious grin.

"In air raids," I replied and waited for him to continue. But Geordie was already putting on his anti-flash gear and, seeing that he had no intention of carrying on the conversation, I followed suit.

Up top 'A' gun's crew in their white hoods and long white anti-flash gloves, reminiscent of the Ku-Klux-Klan, were already closed up, the layer and trainer rotating and elevating the old 4.7-inch gun. Standing inside the gun shield, inches from the barrel, I confronted the two brass dials on which to set the range and deflection.

The ship's fire-power was controlled by the rangefinder and director, which gave the ranges to the TS, which in turn transmitted them to the sight-setters on the guns. Donning my earphones I immediately reported down the mouthpiece, "'A' gun, TS."

"TS, 'A' gun," came the reply.

" 'A' gun closed up cleared away, bore clear."

Seconds later came the order. "All guns with S.A.P. and a full charge load, load, load."

"All guns with S.A.P. and a full charge, load, load, load," I repeated to the gun's crew. At once Geordie, our loader, with his gloved hand, fisted in the fifty-seven-pound shell, while Scouse, using his ramrod and, with a cry of 'home out', rammed in the charge, a shining brass cylinder, whereupon the captain of the gun slammed the breach to with lightning finality, shouting, " 'A' gun ready for firing."

There followed a great roar and flash, the gun all but leapt from its mountings, and yellow smoke and the acrid smell of cordite filled the turret.

Faintly through the earphones my deafened ears heard the new range and deflection.

Later, when I asked Olly how he had fared, he shook his head despondently. "It's my ears," he said.

But worse was to come when we went into quarters' firing, which occurs when the director has been put out of action and it is up to the officers to estimate the ranges and deflections. These were given to Olly on 'B' gun, by the timid lieutenant RNR, the officer of the quarter for 'A' and 'B' guns, who was, as we were all well aware, in constant awe of the captain. Olly became flustered and found it difficult to hear what the lieutenant was saying between the intermittent explosions of the guns. Since I was having equal difficulty in hearing what Olly was relaying to me, I had to guess. The net result, to put it mildly, was unsatisfactory, and the shells with their maximum range of sixteen thousand yards, fell anywhere but near the towed practice targets. I don't know what happened to the officer of the quarter, but at the end of the day it was generally held that the sight-setters on 'A' and 'B' guns were as poor as piss.

The next day a lumbering old aircraft slowly towed a sleeve target across the sky for our oerlikon gunners to practise their shooting skills, the red tracer shells arcing accurately upwards towards the sleeve target. Then we were ready.

The 16th Destroyer Flotilla's task was twofold, to meet and escort convoys up and down the east coast and carry out patrols against the German E-boats, which could do thirty-eight knots and laid mines, carried torpedoes and bristled with light armament. They attacked in the dark, their low silhouettes making them almost invisible and, with their high turn of speed, they were difficult targets to hit. The enemy knew the exact route the convoys took and would lie in wait, often near a buoy, sometimes even temporarily secured to one. Their aerial reconnaissance kept them well informed of the time and direction of each convoy, which they'd attack using torpedoes before roaring off at speed for the Dutch coast. On calm moonlit nights they would attack after laying mines in the path of a convoy.

A month earlier two 'Hunt' class destroyers had been damaged, and two merchant ships sunk, when a southbound convoy had run onto just such a minefield laid off the Suffolk coast.

But bad weather restricted the ability of E-boats to manoeuvre at speed and, throughout the short summer nights their activity decreased, until September came round when, once again, it all flared up and continued through the winter of 1942-43.

During our five months at Harwich, we escorted convoys, kept a weather eye open for E-boats, experienced alarms, fired star shells, heard from afar the rumble of explosions, and saw the red flicker of tracer, yet had no contact with the enemy, apart from one occasion when a Junkers 88 popped out of the early morning mist, to roar low and lazily across our bows, exhausts flaming, its black crosses clearly visible. We were all surprised and even more so when 'B' gun opened fire and the shell exploded almost overhead.

But we got plenty of sea-time in, spending nights and days closed up on watch or at action stations. I was wearing earphones and so was unable, unlike the rest of the gun's crew, to snatch the occasional quick drag 'round the corner' in the cabouche. It was tedious work, but vigilance was essential. Always, despite the magnificent efforts of the minesweepers to keep the channels open, there lurked the menace of unswept mines.

The nights were growing shorter, but the North Sea was still a very cold spot. The old 4.7s had a half-shield with two ports and a canvas apron round the base. 'A' gun on the fo'c'sle was particularly exposed. Standing cramped inside the gun-shield for hours on end, despite sea-boots and heavy white sea-boot stockings folded over the top, long thick pants, vest, jersey, jumper, scarf, duffel and balaclava, the cold still penetrated. When, on rare occasions, we were allowed to fall out and go below, we'd stretch out on the lockers, tables, mess deck floor, or on the boards covering the capstan machinery and, to the accompanying whine of engines, roar of ventilating fans, swish of the sea surging past the ship's hull, sink into unfathomable sleep. And more often than not, no sooner had we done so, than the alarm bells would clang. Cursing our luck, we'd dash up onto the fo'c'sle to ram home and fire a star shell into the black vault of the night.

Tensely the gun's crew would peer out to sea as the first shell burst, brilliantly illuminating the dark waters, and each of us would wonder whether this time we really had made a contact, and there were E-boats lurking somewhere out there in 'E-boat Alley'. But it would prove just another false alarm and, after the brief period of tense anticipation had worn off, we'd remain closed up at action stations for the rest of the night. When the first pale streaks of dawn broke low on the horizon, and the ships of the convoy became visible, we would perk up, sip some scalding *ki* [cocoa], roll and smoke a tickler, stamp our feet and speculate on whether there'd be a make and mend, or even the chance of a run ashore. Some time in the early part of the forenoon watch, we would fall in for entering harbour and, having made the ship fast, turn to and unenthusiastically work part of ship until the hands were piped to dinner. In the afternoon we'd be free to do our dhobying or write letters, but most of us would take the opportunity to get our heads down before the boilers were flashed up and special sea duty men called to their stations. Then, with hands fell in and chin-stays down, the ship would gather headway and along with the *Windsor, Worcester, Walpole* and *Mackay,* steam down the marked channel and, in line astern, pass the boom and head once more out into the North Sea to pick up another convoy or set off on a patrol.

When we did have a chance of a run ashore, there was nowhere to go and nothing to do, for Harwich was a godforsaken place. It was hardly surprising that some of the lads would drink and then start filling each other in. The fighting grew progressively worse, until one morning a number of the ship's company, along with others of the flotilla, were lined up on the jetty, while two ratings, who had been on the receiving end, were taken round to see if they could identify their assailants. A rating had been badly hurt the previous night. Two of our crew were identified, despite the fact that the coxswain shifted the identified ratings into different positions. There were several very tough characters on the mess deck, one in particular, a huge Liverpudlian, who had done some professional boxing. He had great shoulders above narrow hips and his perpetual smile, close-cropped head of hair, soft voice and spotless attire, whether wearing overalls or number ones, created an air of menace. Though he never mentioned his exploits ashore, others certainly did. He left the ship shortly afterwards and the fighting episodes ceased.

We did a towing exercise one forenoon. Olly and I were closed up on 'A' and 'B' guns, but the first lieutenant thought that we ought to know how the exercise was progressing. With this in mind he instructed Ken Howard to keep us informed over the intercom from 'Y' gun. Howard was delighted and seized the opportunity to give us a running commentary reminiscent of a BBC commentator. I think he had in mind John Snagge reporting the Oxford and Cambridge boat-race!

"This is Ken Howard reporting from 'Y' gun,' he began in his slow drawl. "Well, here we all are and it's a lovely morning. Below me the quarter-deck is littered with wires, grass lines, a ten-inch manilla, far too many hands and, of course, the bosun, who has ordered a leading hand to fire the Schmeuly gun, and he's fired it, and the line's now snaking across to the *Windsor's* fo'c'sle and it's going to miss, yes, it has missed, and now the bosun's giving several of the hands a good bollocking," and so it went on, until the tow was eventually made fast on the *Windsor*. Then there was a pause, and I wondered whether anyone else had been listening to his commentary. Suddenly Ken started again and this time he seemed quite unable to contain himself. As the *Montrose* gathered headway, we listened to his drawled commentary grow faster and more vibrant, the words tumbling over the air:

"We're now taking up the slack, the bosun's looking concerned and well he might, we're going ahead too fast, the tow's coming clear of the water, it could well part, it has, it's parted..." and he paused, before beginning in more measured tones — "there really is the most frightful..." but he got no further because an icy voice cut in, "Howard, report to the bridge forthwith." It was the first lieutenant and now it was Ken Howard's turn to do some number elevens.

On another occasion we fired some of our 21-inch torpedo tubes, and I found myself in the whaler's crew sent to retrieve them. There was a bit of sea running. When the last torpedo was standing on its nose, plunging up and down like a porpoise between the whaler and the ship's side, with a leading hand wrestling to get a strop round the brute, it looked as though we in the whaler had every chance of being torpedoed.

It was not a highly successful exercise because we lost a torpedo. One dinner time we dropped some depth charges. The starboard watch was below deck at the time and moved fast. I was astonished at the tremendous force of the detonations. It was as though the ship's hull had been struck one mighty blow by a giant sledge-hammer. God knows what it must be like for submariners. But that night we had fresh fish for supper.

It was hands to make and mend and leave for the non-duty watch.

"All night in," remarked Geordie, "get the fucking cards out."

I joined the game of penny brag, but I could hardly keep my eyes open, and soon handed over my place and purse to Joe Mul, a Glaswegian.

"There's a few bob in it. See what you can do," I said, handing him the 'wee broon purse', as he called it.

We had an arrangement, Joe and I, that when I'd had enough, he would take my place and use what money was left in the purse. The following morning we would share the profits, if there were any. From my point of view it was a good arrangement, because now I could drop out at any time without upsetting the game, while Joe, who never had any money, was only too pleased to take over. He was a good mate to me while I was aboard the *Montrose*, and he was also a good hand at penny brag and, more often than not, we were up at the end of a session. I slung my hammock and fell asleep. The next thing I knew the coxswain was shaking the nettles of my hammmock.

"There's been a bloody air raid."

"Never heard a thing," I said. In the event of an air raid in harbour my action station was to man the strip Lewis gun on the bridge.

"Put your cap on and fall in on the quarter-deck." The following day I promptly collected another seven days' number elevens and began chipping paintwork all over again — this time at sea and having to work the dog watches.

Back on the mess deck Geordie and Scouse greeted me with their customary good humour.

"Never mind, mate, made a few bob last night," said Joe Mul handing me back my purse. "Here," he went on, offering me his tot of rum which I accepted, 'sippers.' One was either T or G, 'temperance' or 'grog'. I was the former so never 'drew', but collected threepence a day extra on my pay instead.

"Didn't we tell you, Sheerlegs? Once in the fucking rattle, always in the fucking rattle," Geordie reminded me yet again, and there now did seem some truth in the maxim.

The weather was fine, the sun hot, and my seven days' number elevens soon slipped by. I was busy cleaning 'A' gun one forenoon when a young sub-lieutenant RNVR, who had recently joined the ship, approached. His vaguely familiar face puzzled me, until I suddenly remembered where we had last met, playing cricket against each other in the

Shrewsbury-Sedbergh match. He had stayed with my Housemaster on the private side and Kitch had invited Malcolm Lock and me to have dinner in the evening. I had also stumped him and made a duck. Charles Whittle smiled and told me that he had mentioned to the captain of the *Montrose* that I played cricket.

"You're going to play with those fucking pigs down aft," remarked Geordie incredulously, "you'll be all right now, mate."

I don't remember much about the one game we played, except that I carried the baggage and I had serious cartilage trouble in my right knee, which made wicket-keeping difficult. The captain, who took the game seriously, attempted to bowl leg-breaks giving the ball a lot of air, with the result that the batsman, when he left his crease, but failed to make contact, had time to get his bat down before I could stump him. However, I managed a couple of stumpings, which, I thought, on replacing the bails, might help me get through the preliminary selection board that as CW candidates we had yet to face.

In August the ship had a boiler clean and each watch was given a week's leave. To sleep between clean sheets again, laze in hot water, wear civvies, get up late, and eat my mother's lovingly and carefully prepared meals was bliss. My father had arranged for me to see an orthopaedic surgeon, for my knee was giving me a lot of trouble.

"You've got a badly torn internal semi-lunar cartilage," the surgeon informed me. "We'll give it some treatment and try and get rid of the fluid, but you need an operation."

Far too quickly the few days passed and, at the end of the week, I bade farewell to my parents and sisters and, armed with a *crêpe* bandage, caught the train to London. On the spur of the moment I entered the Railway Hotel, Liverpool Street Station, not for a bath, but to have a meal before catching the evening train to Harwich. The restaurant was crowded and I had to wait before I was shown, with some condescension, I thought, to a table. I had barely sat down when the captain of the *Montrose* entered. Embarrassed, I wished I had gone elsewhere to eat, and hoped the waiter would not guide him my way.

He did, of course. As the captain passed, he gave me a brief but friendly nod of recognition.

We continued to escort convoys and then, suddenly and without warning, the First Lieutenant informed us we were to go before the preliminary selection board to establish whether or not we were fit to move on to *King Alfred*. The board, presided over by Captain 'D', was held aboard the flotilla leader, H.M.S. *Mackay*.

When my turn came I entered the ward-room and was told to sit down in a chair facing the board. I was asked several technical questions and my answers, I knew, were not making a good impression.

"Why should no member of a crew be abaft the after fall or before the foremost fall when lowering a sea-boat?" a commander asked, at the same time leaning forward as though anticipating a prompt reply.

I had no idea and couldn't for the life of me think up a reasonable answer. To suggest that to stand between the falls seemed the most convenient and obvious place, I thought unwise.

"Well, what happens, man, if there is a hand outside the falls and one of the falls parts?" the commander asked tersely.

I still could not see what he was driving at. The obvious retort that the whole boat's crew would at once be tipped into the 'drink' again did not seem a wise reply.

"Well, look at this pencil, man," urged the commander, thoroughly exasperated. "Imagine it's the boat and my two fingers represent the falls."

I tried hard to imagine this and, after a suitable pause nodded my head in what I hoped was a convincing manner. "Well, one of the falls parts," and he put one of his fingers down. I was fast becoming mesmerised. "What happens to the boat?"

"One end drops."

"Exactly," and he lowered the sharp end of the pencil, at the same time watching me closely. By now I was mesmerised.

"Well, what has happened?" The board waited. "Come on, man, what's happened to the chap outside the falls?"

I had no idea and felt as though I was once again back in the classroom. I knew, however, what was going to happen to me. It was the only thing of which I was certain. "Well, if I've had it," I thought, "perhaps the wretched chap outside the falls has had it too."

"He's had it," I blurted out as confidently as I was able.

"Of course he has," roared the commander and my hopes soared only to be dashed by his next question:

"Why?"

"Why? Well, because…"

"Because he's been crushed against the falls and the boat," said the commander witheringly and he sat back and looked at me, and I felt every bit as crushed as that mythical hand standing outside the falls.

There was a brief pause, while the captain of the *Mackay* looked at the rest of the board to see if anyone wanted to ask any more questions. No one did.

"Right," said the captain, "that's all."

"Thank you, sir," I replied, and left the ward-room with what dignity I could muster.

I felt now that only the captain of the *Montrose* could save the day for me.

None of us was particularly confident of having passed, apart from Ken, of course, who smiled knowingly and, in his most maddening way, announced that he had managed to answer all their questions, and found them really rather easy. In the afternoon, we were sent for individually by the captain. "You passed," he remarked dryly, but with a slight smile when my turn came, "God knows why." Perhaps the stumpings did have something to do with it after all.

In fact we had all passed, except for poor old Olly.

"I don't think I can stick much more of it," he confessed to me later on 'B' gun deck. "I could just about stand it while there was the prospect of a commission, but that's gone." He was very upset.

Above: Heavy Swell

Below: Out of Station

Above: In Convoy, fine weather

Right: Stevens, our steward, in the mess deck hatchway

"Nonsense, Olly," I said, "I'm sure they'll give you another chance." But I wasn't too sure and it wasn't much consolation for him.

We had returned from escort duty one forenoon, the hands turned to, unenthusiastically working parts of ship, I was sandpapering the mushroom head of 'A' gun, when Scouse suddenly appeared just before Stand Easy.

"Heard the buzz?"

"No."

"Scapa, you know what that means. A fucking Russian convoy."

"When are we sailing?"

"Any moment,' said Scouse, and he took out a tickler from the inside of his cap, just as the pipe went for Stand Easy.

The buzz was right. In no time, we were heading north again, burying our bows and throwing back the sea in spectacular arcs.

As we approached the islands, a thick suffocating fog engulfed the ship and I found myself doing a spell of bow lookout. We had reduced speed, proceeding slowly through a gently undulating sea. I stood right over the bull-ring and gripped the guard-rails on either side as the destroyer's bow gently lifted and fell. I could sense the slight tremor of the ship and faintly hear the engines. It was a silent and remote world. Suddenly the fog lifted for a few seconds, and a great grey shape loomed off the starboard bow.

"Ship green one-o," I called back to the bridge at the same time pointing. They acknowledged my signal. I had only the briefest glimpse of the ship before she was blanketed out by the fog, but it looked suspiciously like the *Curasao*, the cruiser which was shortly afterwards cut in two by the Cunard liner, *Queen Mary*, with the tragic loss of nearly all hands.

We dropped our hook and those of us who could got their heads down. I was on anchor watch when Sub-Lieutenant Whittle came onto the bridge and showed me how to take bearings and fix the ship's position. Only the occasional noise of the cable as the ship swung gently in the tide and the rattle of the halyards disturbed the peace.

We went to sea most days, screening the big ships as we had done in the *Foresight*, but at the back of all our minds lay the prospect of a Russian convoy. Then, out of the blue, we were informed that our reliefs had arrived and we were to leave the ship the following afternoon.

But first we had to see the ship's doc for a medical examination. He spotted my knee at once. I had removed the *crêpe* bandage.

"You've a lot of fluid there," he remarked.

"I've got cartilage trouble, sir."

"I can't send you off with a knee like that. You need treatment."

I was alarmed. The last thing I wanted was to jeopardise my chance of continuing to play games.

"My father's a doctor, sir, and knows about it. I've already seen an orthopaedic surgeon and I can have it done at home."

The surgeon-lieutenant reflected for a moment and I wondered whether I had said too much.

"Very well," he conceded, and I thanked him, very relieved. I had been finding it increasingly difficult to move about the ship, let alone climb ladders. Anything which required bending the knee was sufficient to slip the cartilage, and it was becoming difficult and painful to get it back in place.

That last evening aboard the *Montrose* I played my final game of penny brag with Geordie and Scouse, Lofty and Ginger Hill, while at my back hovered my old oppo, Joe Mul, waiting to take over. Soon I'd had enough and got up to sling my hammock, handing 'the wee broon purse' to Joe for the last time.

Lying cocooned on my back I listened to all the familiar sounds of the fo'c'sle, knowing I would probably never again sit down at the mess deck table, secretly scrutinise three cards behind cupped hands, throw pennies into the kitty, and try and bluff my way with a pair of tens.

The following afternoon it was hands to make and mend. After dinner the four of us drew our duty-free tobacco and cigarette rations, then packed our kitbags and small brown cases.

"Here, Sheerlegs, stow these in your fucking 'mick'," said Geordie and Scouse, between them handing me half a dozen packets of twenty. I thanked them as warmly as I was able and began to stuff them into my hammock.

"Gawd, mate, not like that, give 'em here," said Scouse, and he proceeded to hide them away neatly down the middle of the hammock, for I was taking over the legal amount.

It was time to go.

"Remember us when you're a fucking pig down aft," said Geordie. "And us," said Lofty and Ginger Hill.

"Good luck, mate," said Joe Mul.

"Keep the purse," I said, handing it to him with a few bob inside.

Without more ado, carrying our kitbags and hammocks we left the mess deck, went down the ship's ladder and boarded the *Montrose's* motor boat. There were only two people on deck, the quartermaster in his long greatcoat and bosun's whistle, and Olly standing sad and solitary at the break of the fo'c'sle.

Three months later I had a letter from Scouse Dowell in answer to one I had written asking him to send on my leather clothes' brush — believe it or not — and tin hatbox. In his letter, of course, he never mentioned the fact that the *Montrose* had been on a Russian convoy immediately after we had left, and that back at Harwich again she had promptly engaged two E-boats. This I happened to see in the *Derby Evening Telegraph*. There was a picture of the *Montrose* on the back page with a short account headed, A LIVELY AFFAIR OFF HARWICH. I could well imagine it all. I've no doubt the crew of 'A' gun would have described it somewhat differently. However it did somehow seem to make those long nights closed up on 'A' gun real and worth while.

But Scouse's letter brought back to me even more vividly the atmosphere of the mess deck which I had so recently left. And I knew that beneath the drinking and the fighting, the grumbling and the cursing, there existed an understanding and warmth that is not always found in the more civilised orders of society. The letter was my last contact with the *Montrose*, though I did meet Charles Whittle again, five years later at Oxford once more on the cricket field, this time in the Parks.

Scouse Dowell wrote:

Dear Ken,

I think I've neglected you for long enough and its high time I had writen you at least a few lines, but I think I told you how I like writing. I've just writen to my folks the first in 2 months, but although I haven't wrote you I sure haven't forgotten your friendship. Well Ken I'm very sorry I haven't sent on your hat box yet it was only today I found your clothes brush and now I read your letter I see you say a leather clothes brush and I can't find any as you say but I'll question the mess before I send it. Well Ken I went ashore the other night and had a decent portion of drink and I think it must have gone to my head, because I started filling in the boys I was with Ginger Hill and Joe Mul but however we are all OK now, someone hit me on the forehead with a bottle and cut it but it didn't stop me I just went ahead lashing out, but my old and faithfull pal stuck it with me Jordie and he wishes to be remembered to you he has taken over sight setter on A gun. There is one thing I must tell you and that is Olly, he is as useless as bad water and to think he expects to be an officer, if he gets through as one I think I'll escape to jerry. Well Ken I haven't much to say except I'll send on your hat box in five days time so for now cherio and all the Best.

Your Pals Scouse and Jordie

I never got my hatbox or leather clothes brush, but Olly, I am glad to say, did get his commission.

Chapter 5

H.M.S. King Alfred *and* H.M.S.Dolphin

So ONCE AGAIN we headed across the turbulent waters of the Pentland Firth bound for Thurso and, from there, onward by train to Pompey. We were down below when Charlie, who was examining our draft chit, suddenly announced, "This thing's not been dated," and he handed us the chit before lighting his pipe and puffing tobacco smoke into the stale atmosphere which did little to help Ken's stomach. "I've been thinking," Charlie continued, "why don't we take a couple of days longer getting to Pompey? The train stops at Perth. We could slip off and arrange to meet two days later. It would give us a couple of nights at home. I can't see anyone would be the wiser."

"I'm not so sure," remarked Ken, "it seems risky to me," and he beat a hasty retreat up top as the steamer slid into a deep trough and rolled heavily.

"What d'you two think?" Charlie asked us. The prospect of a couple of nights at home was sufficiently persuasive.

"But I'm not sure Ken will agree," Phil added.

"Then we'd better find out," said Charlie, and the three of us went up on deck to discover Ken, as anticipated, leaning over a guardrail.

"We've decided to give it a go. Are you game?" Charlie asked him.

He looked up, managed a faint smile and a bit of a nod before leaning over the rail and retching again.

"That settles it," said Charlie.

"Poor sod," muttered Phil.

In the early hours of the following morning the train drew into Perth. At once carriage doors began opening and ratings crossed the platform, heading for the canteen. There were a couple of POs hanging about on the platform. We sat and watched.

"There's just one PO out there now,' said Phil, dropping his voice.

"Right," said Charlie, "if he disappears we'll make a dash. Have a look outside and see where best we can dump our gear and keep out of sight."

I sauntered a few yards along the dark platform, as though stretching my legs. I sensed the petty officer watching me. I didn't need to go any further, for I had spotted a place we could make for and hide, on the far side of the urinals. I strolled casually back and briefed the other three who were keeping their eyes on the PO. The ratings had begun to emerge slowly from the canteen. "Hurry along there," shouted the PO and began moving towards the door to round up the rest.

"Now," said Charlie and, lugging out kitbags and hammocks, we made a concerted rush along the platform and hid behind the urinals.

It was madness, for we could easily have been caught and jeopardised our future. Waiting tensely we listened as carriage doors banged, the whistle finally blew and, with a prolonged hiss of steam, a jangle of couplings and several powerful snorts, the train drew slowly out of the station.

"We've burnt our boats now," pronounced Ken Howard, "we might as well get a cup of tea ourselves from the canteen," — a suggestion the rest of us deemed unwise. Instead, we hung around, keeping out of sight, until eventually we caught a southbound train, having agreed to meet two days later under the clock at Victoria.

When I got home I yarned with my mother and father and then slept the clock round. I did not tell them what we had done.

"As soon as you get any leave," said my father, "give us a ring and we'll get that knee seen to." Two days later, armed with a spare *crêpe* bandage and some sandwiches, I caught the London train and met the other three at Victoria.

On approaching the main gate of the Royal Naval Barracks Portsmouth, we became slightly apprehensive. But we need not have worried, for we sailed through in great style. At once we found the atmosphere and general appearance of Portsmouth a good deal more pleasant than Devonport, that is, until the following day, when we met the surgeon-commander who gave us our medical examination.

Naked, we stood in a queue, while this small, fierce-looking ferret of a commander snapped questions at us as he examined each body in turn.

"Where have you been?" he barked when my name was called.

"Harwich, sir."

"Doing what?"

"Escort duty with the 16th Destroyer Flotilla, sir."

"Touch your toes, stand up, knees bend."

The last I couldn't manage.

"Knees bend," repeated the commander sharply.

"I can't, sir, I've got cartilage trouble."

"I can see you've a lot of fluid there. Report to the sick bay for treatment and I'll see you again in a week," and he wrote something down. "Next, what's your name? Speak up."

I dressed, waited outside till he had seen everyone and then discreetly, if that is possible, knocked on his door.

"I wonder if I might have a word with you about my knee, sir," I began. "My father's a doctor..."

"I'm not interested in what your father is. And who the devil do you think you are coming in here to discuss your wretched knee? Report to the sick bay as you were told."

"Thank you, sir," I said. Swine! I thought. The perfect example of a pig down aft. However, he did once get his deserts when an over-anxious prospective officer and gentleman was told to bend down and lost control of his wind. He was sent back to sea forthwith.

Charlie Dunn, Ken Howard and Phil Dawson had all passed their medicals and were proceeding at once on indefinite leave, pending being summoned to *King Alfred*. Abruptly I found myself saying goodbye to the three of them. It had all happened so quickly and I was going to miss them. Charlie failed the Admiralty selection board and had to go back to the lower deck. The Navy missed a good officer in Charlie Dunn. Ken Howard passed, went into landing-craft and was mentioned in despatches. Phil Dawson got his commission, but was killed minesweeping right at the end of the war.

The following day I duly reported to the sick bay, where I sat and waited for a considerable time. Just when it was nearing my turn to be summoned, a sick bay attendant announced that we were to return at 14.00 hours.

Ignoring his comment, I went through to be confronted by an RNVR surgeon-lieutenant about to leave, who promptly asked me what the hell I thought I was doing.

"I'm sorry sir, but I've a badly torn internal semi-lunar cartilage. May I have a quick word with you, please?" And before he could say no, I pulled up the leg of my trousers and showed him the knee.

"Who sent you?"

"The surgeon-commander, sir," and I explained the circumstances as quickly as I could, adding that my father was a doctor and I was hoping to get the knee seen to at home.

"Not a chance. If the surgeon-commander ordered treatment here, then that's it. Come back this afternoon. We'll fix something up and see how it responds."

I was no further on. My only hope now was the Divisional Officer and I successfully requested permission to see him. A rather sad-faced lieutenant-commander RN, a submariner, listened patiently, asked a few pertinent questions and granted me three days' leave. "What happens then is your concern."

I telephoned home and was operated on in twenty-four hours. My father at once notified the principal medical officer, who instructed me to report back as soon as I was fit to travel. Ten days later I did so and at once ran into trouble at the main gate.

"You're to report to the surgeon-commander," said the master-at-arms. Under escort I was marched to the surgeon-commander's quarters flanked by two white-gaitered ratings. I knocked. "Yes," I recognised the voice instantly. The commander looked up and immediately his face was suffused with anger. "I ordered you to report for treatment and told you that I'd see you again in a week. You've deliberately disobeyed my orders."

"My knee's much better, sir. I've had the cartilage out."

"I know you damn well have, and I'll have nothing more to do with you. Get out."

I was escorted back to the main gate where I requested and was granted permission to see the principal medical officer.

"End door on the right," said a sick bay attendant in answer to my escort's enquiry.

A benign-looking white-haired surgeon-captain, with a florid face, was seated at a desk. He pushed his chair back and I saw how big he was as he came round and sat down in an easy chair, indicating that I should do the same.

"What's your trouble?" he asked, and I told him my story to which he listened without interrupting. When I had finished he asked to see both knees. "You've a lot of wastage there," he said, comparing the quadriceps.

"I'm very anxious to get it right, sir, so that I can continue to play cricket and football."

He wasn't interested in football, but I quickly learnt that he was a keen cricketer, had kept wicket a bit and once played on the Common at Shrewsbury. Right from the start he made me feel thoroughly at ease. I watched him now as he thought for a moment: "Well, I can see how keen you are to get that knee right as quickly as possible," and he leant forward, "I think two weeks' leave should do the trick," he concluded, getting to his feet.

I wondered if I had heard correctly. In disbelief I watched as he wrote me out a liberty ticket there and then at his desk, before looking up and handing it to me.

"Come and see me when you report back. If your knee's all right, I'll give you your medical clearance for *King Alfred*."

It was difficult to express my gratitude, though I did my best. What a difference. Here was no 'pig down aft', I thought, as I was escorted back to the gate.

"You've been a time," said the master-at-arms.

"I'm off on leave again when I've got my pay and ration card."

"What d'you mean, 'Off on leave'?"

I showed him the pass which he glanced at before handing it back.

"Then you'd better carry on."

One hour later I was on my way home for a further fourteen days' leave.

At the Derby Royal Infirmary I was given physiotherapy by a slightly stocky, pretty Irish girl with raven hair, a charming, soft voice and a tilt to her nose. We went out together on several occasions in the short time available, returning to her bed-sitter, where she gave my knee more expert massage, which did it much good until her very presence and touch became so tender and intimate that we would end up in each other's arms, locked together in long passionate embraces. But that was as far as it went. Reluctantly we would part and I would bicycle home in the early hours of the morning, up the long incline of Uttoxeter Road, a ride that proved highly beneficial to my knee and helped convince the Pompey M.O. at the end of those fourteen days that I was now fit to proceed to *King Alfred*.

First, though, I had to report to Mowden, a preparatory school in Hove, requisitioned by the Navy. After we had been there a week, we faced a selection board of three admirals, to decide whether or not we were fit to proceed to Lancing College and *King Alfred*. It was the same board that poor Charlie had failed to convince. I was asked the old stock question of why I wanted to be an officer. Shrewsbury and the topic of games, cricket in particular, seemed to do the rest.

A bus conveyed us to Lancing College, the senior Woodard school that stands on the spur of a Sussex down. It was early October. As we passed the Red Lion and approached the old wooden tollbridge that spanned the River Adur, we caught sight of the great grey pile of gothic buildings and huge soaring chapel that dominates the landscape.

Our short time at Lancing was intensive and not much fun, for there was always the possibility of failure and having to return to the lower deck. We now wore white cap ribbons and gaiters. Divisions were held each morning and we would be summoned in turn to march our classes past Commander Maclean, RN, who, standing on a white-railed brick platform, took the salute, standing erect and lean, red-faced and immaculate, white cuffs showing extensively. We were instructed in navigation, gunnery and torpedoes and, within the cloistered precincts, reminiscent of an Oxford College, practised semaphore and flashed signals to one another with Aldis lamps. In the school dining hall, beneath a splendid timbered roof, five hundred CW candidates sat down at long tables with white cloths and Wrens at our backs to wait upon us, while the officers ate and surveyed the scene from a raised dais at the top of the hall.

We learnt that the letters, O.L.Q., stand for 'officer-like qualities'. The more serious CW candidates, who tended at every opportunity to demonstrate they possessed these qualities in abundance, particularly at mealtimes, brought out the worst in some of us, who would make such requests as: "Would you mind passing the fucking salt, mate?" We slept in the boys' dormitories, using double bunks, and at night mounted guard around the college grounds and buildings.

One brilliant moonlit night towards the end of the course I found myself stationed at the top of the Masters' Tower. Sharp shadows cut cleanly across the steep pitched roofs. Below lay the quadrangle with its cloistered flint surroundings and grass lawns. To the south the sea, a glitter of silver, washed the flat sandy beaches where, but for the RAF, Hitler might have put into effect Operation Sealion and attempted the invasion of these shores.

I gazed out at the flat expanse of Shoreham aerodrome and the distant Norfolk Bridge, beneath which the river flowed seaward, enfolding the sleeping town, the tower of St Mary's standing proud, the squat Norman tower of St Nicholas, just visible in the moonlight, as it had been for the last thousand years. Several miles to the west lay Worthing, while almost at my feet the folds of the Downs rolled gently inland to Chanctonbury. I leant on the low parapet, breathed deeply the sharp night air, and delighted in the moonlit surroundings. The sound of my relief clattering noisily up the last stone steps of the Masters' Tower brought me back to reality. For once, I wished he had not come to spoil a tranquil moment.

King Alfred, the low buildings on the sea-front of Hove in which we now found ourselves, could not have differed more from the lofty ones we had just left. We seemed to live perpetually underground, which was not really surprising because our new dwellings were previously the Hove Corporation underground car park.

Each morning we would emerge at a rush to attend Divisions. An intimidating gunnery commander would lie in wait, spy a victim and, with arm extended, roar, "Come here, that man," whereupon the unfortunate CW candidate would have to take the parade. I always ensured that I never got caught by keeping my head well down and hiding in the midst of that mad morning dash.

By far the most enjoyable part of the course was the practical side of ship-handling. Using an old tug in Shoreham harbour, we were taught how to spring a ship off, come alongside and turn a ship short round, each of us taking command in turn. Least enjoyable were the final examinations, when I felt once more I was back at school being put to the test.

We had already visited the tailors and been measured for our naval uniforms, when at last the results were announced and most of us, to our great relief, learned we had passed. A few, though, had failed — God knows what happened to their newly ordered uniforms — and one or two borderline cases still had to present themselves before a final board, a thoroughly nerve-wracking experience, having got so far.

Right at the end we were asked to state what branch of the service we would like to join, but were warned that it was unlikely we would get our choice. Not wanting to join a battle wagon, and not particularly keen to go back to destroyers or into Combined Operations, I would have liked to have joined Coastal Forces and served aboard an ML or MTB. But the latter was out of the question as a high standard of navigation was required, and my marks in the examination had been anything but high. There was another choice, to volunteer for Special Service, for which one had to be under a certain age and pass a stiff medical examination. Without giving the matter another thought and, forgetting the cardinal rule of the lower deck, never volunteer, I handed in my name.

Two days later, as newly-fledged sub-lieutenants, we were sent on leave. I headed for Brighton station, proud of my new uniform with its single wavy strip of gold braid, which for wartime economy extended only halfway round the cuff. I climbed aboard the Brighton Belle, found a corner seat in a first-class carriage and lit a cigarette. Contentedly, I watched the Sussex countryside slip past, until heavy drops of rain slashed diagonally across the carriage window and obscured the view. Discreetly I felt with my fingertips the smooth doeskin material of my new uniform, so different from the rough serge of the one I had recently worn as Able Seaman, D.J.X. 286602.

My leave nearly up, I was due to report to H.M.S. *Dolphin*, the submarine base at Gosport. Before doing so, I called on old friends of the family, and there met a slender and lovely girl, whose shapely figure, gentle voice and uncomplicated manner bewitched me completely. I soon discovered she worked in Nottingham as a physiotherapist, her brother was a pilot in the RAF and the family lived in the Vale of Evesham, where they owned a fruit farm. Immediately I was certain of two things — I had to see her again and time was not on my side. Yet, when the moment came to leave, I still had not found sufficient courage, nor the opportunity to say my piece. Only at the last moment and with beating heart, I took the plunge and asked whether she would like to meet me in London: "If I can manage it," she said with a quiet smile, "I'd love to." Her name was Biddie and I had met the girl I would marry.

The following day I reported to H.M.S. *Dolphin*, where we were given another medical examination, stiffer than the previous one we'd undergone at Portsmouth, but a good deal more pleasant. The submarine depot was small compared with the great naval establishments of Plymouth and Portsmouth. There was a friendly, relaxed air about the place and the food was excellent.

To begin with, we were given a short talk on what was required of us. We were to practise diving until competent, when we would be transferred to the west coast of Scotland to begin the next stage of our training. For security reasons we were not told what lay in store for us. The general opinion, that we were destined for midget submarines, did not particularly seem to concern us at the time, perhaps because it all appeared too remote and unreal.

We started diving immediately. The tank was twenty-six feet deep. Some ten feet down, the words: 'Blow your ears', printed on the sides of the tank, reminded us that eardrums could burst. Standing around the instructor, clad in swimming trunks, with our cylinders of oxygen, tubes and mouthpieces, nose-clips and goggles, we listened as he instructed us how to use our D.S.E.A. sets: "And when your ears begin to hurt, hold your breath and blow out. You'll hear a click. Right, in you go."

I went over the side intent only on getting to the bottom. I got there all right and immediately experienced a good deal of pressure on my ears. The instructor came swaying towards me, pointing and mouthing words which I could not understand. Feeling I ought to be doing something, I began fiddling nervously with the tap on the oxygen cylinder, turned it on too much and promptly sailed to the surface. I went under again, this time more slowly. The warm water closed over my head and, as I gently sank to the bottom, I began to breathe more steadily and purposefully. For several days we continued and practised escaping through an escape hatch fitted with a twill trunk, a stout canvas cylinder, normally housed around the edge of the escape hatches in a submarine.

I never felt confident beneath the water, never completely at ease and free from tension. At the beginning of the second week we were shown how to escape from the two-man chamber which could just about hold two men with D.S.E.A. sets on. The chamber was entered through a side hatch which was then shut and flooded by turning a valve. After a time the water stopped rising because of the air inside the chamber being forced upwards to its highest point. By turning a small valve in the centre of the top hatch the air was vented and the hatch could be opened. Once inside the chamber, I had to fight a feeling of overwhelming claustrophobia as the water rose slowly until we were submerged. When the chamber was flooded, the air vented and the pressure equalised, we turned the wheel above our heads, opened the hatch and surfaced in the top tank.

Then we went through the escape tank individually. The heavy door shut behind me. Through the circle of thick glass I was aware of the instructor's face. I turned on the flood valve and watched the water level begin to rise, felt it creeping up my thighs and fought down another wild surge of panic as it reached my chin. My teeth gripped the mouthpiece tightly and then my head was under and, immediately and quite inexplicably I lost control of my mouthpiece. Instead of replacing it, I panicked. Desperately trying to hold what breath remained in my lungs, intent only on escape, I pushed at the unyielding hatch overhead, failing to equalise the pressure, my mind now a complete blank. In desperation, lungs bursting, I stood before the inspection window, frantically trying to indicate my plight, peering through flooded goggles as my mouthpiece, dangling at the end of the tube, emitted a bubbling stream of oxygen. At that moment I knew it was over and I was not going to escape. Then, as if a huge burden had been lifted, a bright light was all about me and I was being swept peacefully away on a great floodtide, happy and carefree, my mind tranquil and clear, with one thought uppermost: 'How will the Admiralty explain my death to my parents?'

The next thing I knew I was outside the tank retching and gasping my way back to life. An officer was present and, when I had regained my senses, he advised me to go through the tank again, advice I felt unable to follow.

Later, summoned by Captain 'S', I was asked whether I wished to continue the course.

"No, sir," I replied without hesitation. He made no attempt to dissuade me, but accepted my decision.

It had been entirely my fault. Fortunately the instructor was able to drain the tank I was in.

Our prediction of what lay in store proved half correct. From H.M.S. *Dolphin* the class went up to the Western Isles, and there on a Scottish loch were trained for special service in X-craft, four-man submarines, and for charioteers, two-man torpedoes — which we had *not* expected. Unpleasant though my experience in the tank had been, it was nothing compared with what the class might have to face.

My next port of call was the Royal Naval College, Greenwich, with its magnificent painted ceiling. I did an astro-navigational course and was none the wiser at the end. From Greenwich I went to Troon, a Combined Operations base in Scotland where we were introduced to Mark III Landing-craft. We practised beaching on the Isle of Arran, going through the routine of dropping the kedge, lowering the door and getting off the beach before the tide left us stranded high and dry, undesirable on an enemy shore. From Troon we went south again to Calshot, another Combined Ops establishment on the Solent, where we seemed to spend our time marching to and from lectures, the most memorable of which were those on gunnery.

In the front row of the class sat Sub-Lieutenant George Pessell, nodding his head as though in agreement with every word that was being said, every so often taking pinches of snuff. The gunnery instructor, an overweight chief petty officer, regaled us with unending and detailed accounts of his numerous and amorous escapades the world over, since joining the *Andrew* as a boy seaman. Delivered with speed and gusto, in a hoarse rasping voice and choice use of metaphor, he was a born raconteur. At the conclusion of each story he would rub his hands together, thrust his head forward and leer down at us awaiting our response, which George would provide by taking a pinch of snuff and remarking in his cultured manner: "Most interesting, Chief, a most interesting story."

On one occasion the door opened just as our gunnery chief was describing an extraordinary and lascivious weekend spent in the company of a New York millionaire's daughter. An elderly commander RN entered. Without batting an eyelid chief broke into the rapid procedural jargon for clearing a jammed oerlikon, with one up the spout. For several minutes the commander stood in the doorway, listening and observing, then nodded his approval and left. Whereupon, quick as a flash, the chief took up the story from where he had left off, concluding with another wicked leer, wag of the head, and final comment: "Bloody marvellous she was, absolutely bloody marvellous."

"Most interesting," said George again, nodding his head and taking a further pinch of snuff, "another most interesting story, Chief."

While stationed at Calshot I met Biddie again, this time in London. Too quickly our few hours together slipped away. On Sunday we spent the afternoon at the Grosvenor Hotel tea dance, before I caught the train to Southampton. As it turned out, we only managed to snatch one more weekend together, and that with difficulty, since I had been drafted to the 21st LCT Flotilla at Saltash, which was standing by to sail for the Mediterranean. But they were the happiest thirty-six hours of all, though our walk to the station was tinged with sadness, for we knew it to be our last.

It was a warm early evening in late May, the trees in blossom: 'The glad green leaves like wings, delicate-filmed as new-spun silk,' softened the harsh scars of the city as we made our way along the streets, a clear sky overhead. Waterloo was crowded and we had to thread our way in single file along the platform until we found a first-class compartment. I put my green pusser's suitcase up on the rack and then rejoined Biddie.

"D'you want to wait?" I asked her inadequately. She smiled and her hand sought mine.

"I'll write," she said, and we stood saying little, until the whistle blew when I took her in my arms. Doors were banging. There was a general stir everywhere. The whistle blew again and I climbed aboard quickly and sat down. An army captain leant out of the carriage door and blocked my view just as the train began to pull out. Through the window I caught one final glimpse of Biddie, then she was gone, lost in a sea of faces and a swirl of smoke. It was two and a half years before we saw each other again.

Chapter 6

Landing-craft

I JOINED THE 21st LCT Flotilla as assistant officer to Lieutenant-Commander Snagge, RNVR, the flotilla commander, brother of John Snagge, the well-known BBC commentator. We were part of a squadron under Commander Beatty, RN, consisting of three flotillas, each of twelve ships. The fourth and fifth flotillas, already on their way to the Mediterranean, were Mark Ills and had taken part in the disastrous raid on Dieppe. The 21st Flotilla, made up of new Mark IV Landing-craft, had been formed to replace those lost during the raid.

On a sunny afternoon in May, when I reported to Lieutenant-Commander Snagge at the shore base in Tamerton Foliot, I found myself confronted by a middle-aged Etonian of serious mien with a distinctly 'pusser' approach.

"Come outside," he said. As we walked in the pleasant leafy garden he began talking about his priorities, highest of which was to ensure that the 21st Flotilla became the best in the business. "I intend, Shearwood," and he spoke with resolution, "that the 21st LCT Flotilla shall have the efficiency and fighting qualities of the Royal Navy.

I nodded and murmured something in agreement, though what I had previously heard and seen of Combined Operations and its somewhat casual, carefree approach made me doubt whether such intentions, however laudable, were remotely realistic.

Three days later I was drafted to LCT 582, skippered by Lieutenant Johnny Harrison. A motor boat conveyed me to the landing-craft, one of twenty-four, lying together in trots of four on the north side of the Iron Bridge at Saltash.

"Joining us, sir?" asked the quartermaster, after I had clambered over the guard-rails onto the quarter-deck of 582: "Skipper's in the ward-room," and I followed him round the tall funnel, just as the skipper emerged from the wheelhouse.

"Snagge's assistant officer?"

"Yes," I said.

"John Harrison," and he shook my hand, "welcome aboard, come and meet Number One."

Pleasant-featured, smart in appearance, of medium height and build, his decisive, confident manner immediately gave me an impression that here was someone who knew exactly what he was about. I followed him through the wheelhouse and into the wardroom, where I met the first lieutenant, Bill Russell, seated at a small folding table. It was Stand Easy: "There's some tea coming up," he said, shaking my hand, at the same time indicating that I sit on one of the bunks.

"You know we're off to the Med any moment," said the skipper, sprawling on the other bunk. "Ever stood a watch?" He was observing me with a slightly amused expression. Before I could reply the steward entered with a tray of tea.

Through the open door of the ward-room I could see into the wheelhouse, the polished voice-pipe leading down from the bridge, the shining engine-room telegraphs, the compass and, dominating everything, the big wheel with its brass midship spoke. The sound of voices broke out on deck as Stand Easy came to an end and the hands went about their work.

"Be a good idea if you had a look around," suggested the skipper, getting up and reaching for his cap. "I'm going ashore, Number One, to find out whether or not this Ogo's coming. We're supposed to be having an ocean-going navigator join us for the passage out," he explained to me, putting on his worn cap, its crown and laurels tarnished: "How's your navigation?"

"Well," I began, "I've just finished an astro-navigation course at Greenwich." I did not elaborate.

"That's fine, you'll be able to use the sextant and help with the noon sights," and before I could dissuade him from further suggestions, he went out through the wheelhouse. My eventual use of the sextant did not turn out to be what he expected.

It was the first time I had set foot aboard a Mark IV Landing-craft. As I began looking around I found it increasingly hard to think of 582 as anything other than a flat-bottomed, ugly steel barge, with a great shovel of a bow and a tall single funnel abaft a box-like construction of ward-room, wheelhouse and bridge. One hundred and eighty-seven feet long with a beam just under forty feet, 582 had a draught of three feet for'ard and four feet seven inches aft. Her loaded displacement was five hundred and eighty-six tons. Twin five hundred-horsepower Paxman Ricardo diesels gave her a maximum speed of ten knots. Her complement of twelve comprised two officers, a petty officer motor mechanic, two stokers, a coxswain, signalman, two gunnery ratings and three seamen.

I wandered up for'ard and climbed the short vertical ladder onto the starboard fo'c'sle, a narrow platform, similar to the one on the port side. Below me the ten-ton door slanted upward, secured by dogs, winched up by two wire hawsers. As a further precaution the door had been welded up for the passage out. All of fifteen feet wide, the great blunt bow, shaped like the front end of a wheelbarrow, was sealed off from the tank space by watertight doors. I wondered how such a craft would behave in anything of a head sea. Down the centre of the tank space, an area capable of carrying six Churchill tanks, or nine Valentine or Sherman tanks, were non-return valves which allowed the water shipped in heavy weather to escape. Since the tank space was open to the elements, and the freeboard on either side was barely six feet, they looked less than adequate. Beneath the tank space and along the catwalks was a series of ballast tanks providing buoyancy, which could be flooded, or pumped out to adjust the trim of the craft. To port and starboard of the watertight doors were enclosed winch spaces, where the hands lowered and wound up the door. On either side of the tank space narrow catwalks from the break of the fo'c'sles ran aft, sloping up to the stern quarters. Halfway down the port catwalk was a food locker, another on the starboard side contained ship's stores. A flotta net was secured to a wooden platform. A single wire guard-rail was the sole protection, not a place to be caught in bad weather, I thought.

Across the after end of the tank space was a wash place to starboard with some basins and buckets, and down a narrow uncomfortably low four foot high tunnel on the

Above: KAS on the Bridge of 582

Below: Bad Weather

port side, three heads, two for the crew, one for the officers. The central section directly beneath the bridge and wheelhouse was the soldiers' accommodation—the pongos' shelter, below which were the fuel tanks and a breathing valve that filled the space with diesel fumes. Not surprisingly, in the months to come the pongos' shelter was rarely used by troops, who preferred to remain in their vehicles. To increase the range for the passage out, the hold was half-full of forty-gallon oil drums, from which fuel had to be pumped daily into the main tanks, using a semi-rotary hand pump.

The after part of 582 housed the crew's quarters, engine-room, ward-room, wheelhouse and bridge. A fixed lean-to ladder by the side of the wheelhouse led to the top of the ward-room, where one climbed two steps up and over, and two steps down and into the bridge. A five hundred-gallon water tank was secured to the deck on the starboard side, giving fourteen days supply of fresh water. One of the forward wing tanks had been proofed and filled with fresh water, providing a further month's supply. The water, like the fuel, had to be pumped by hand from the far end of the catwalk — a hazardous task in rough weather. Our sole armament, two oerlikons, one on each quarter, pointed their long thin barrels up at the sky. A kedge anchor hung over the stern, secured by a short length of chain, fed through a bull-ring and shackled to a three-inch wire hawser which led to a winch drum. An electric capstan did the rest. Two engine-room hatches either side of the ward-room, two Carley rafts, ready-use ammunition lockers, ventilators, coils of rope, fenders, heaving lines and, right aft, a hatchway that led to the mess deck below, completed the scene. Overhead, as though bestowing a mantle of distinction upon this humble Mark IV Landing-craft and her crew, a clean White Ensign flew from the masthead.

We slipped our moorings on the second of June 1943. In line astern the 21st and 26th LCT Flotillas got under way, safely negotiated Brunel's bridge and headed down the Hamoaze. Passing Devonport dockyard, the craft threaded their way through the twisting narrows by Mountwise, left Drake's Island to starboard and entered Plymouth Sound, where twenty-four Motor Fishing Vessels were waiting to join the long column of landing-craft heading seaward. Off Rame Head the LCTs formed four columns of six in line abreast, while the MFVs took up a similar formation astern. Out ahead, the commodore's ship, a Boom Defence Vessel, sedately began to lead the way while, bringing up the stern, two ocean-going tugs followed in the wake of the convoy, a comforting presence for those who might face engine problems.

All that day the distant coastline of Cornwall slipped past in sunlight, as the convoy of fifty-one small ships headed gently sou'west at a steady five knots, visibility good, fleeting clouds in a clear blue sky, the sea calm, our spirits high. I passed through the wheelhouse where an able seaman, his legs planted wide, was at the wheel, steering partly by compass, partly by keeping 582's bows on the stern of the ship ahead, which he could see through the open porthole before him. Up on the bridge the first lieutenant was on watch talking with the Ogo, a rather tall, serious-faced lieutenant RNVR, a solicitor by profession. Resting my elbows on the edge of the bridge, I leant from the outside and watched. We seemed to be dropping astern. Bill Russell thought so too and pressed a button at the side for an increase of fifty revolutions. I thought I could detect an increase in the tempo of the engines. "One buzz, up fifty revolutions, two buzzes, down fifty," he explained, as we began to close the ship ahead.

I was down below at the start of the first dog watch enjoying a cup of tea with the Ogo, who made no bones about the fact that he'd much prefer to be elsewhere than in a landing-craft heading towards the Atlantic, when the coxswain knocked on the ward-room door and announced: "Skipper wants you on the bridge, sir."

"You can take over for a bit," said Johnny Harrison firmly, when I had climbed into the bridge. He gave me the course, explained what I already knew about the up fifty down fifty stuff, and then left me to it. I was both surprised and pleased that he had shown such confidence in me. In fact there was very little that I had to do other than press the button a few times. The hand on the wheel did the rest keeping 582 on course, not difficult in the slight swell we were experiencing.

The bridge, four-sided and completely square, was dominated in the centre by a binnacle and compass on a raised platform. There was a flag locker on the starboard side and what appeared to be a high, home-made wooden chair, adjacent to the voice-pipe, on the port side. A large covered chart table took up most of the forepart of the bridge, on which rested parallel rulers, dividers, pencil, rubber and binoculars. The lookout, elbows supported, focused his telescope on the commodore. I ducked beneath the canvas hood and had a look at the chart, picking out the major headlands we had passed, the Gribbin, Dodman, St Anthony's Head and the Lizard. I estimated we were now some fifteen miles south of Land's End and, putting the binoculars round my neck made out the black speck of the Wolf Rock lighthouse and just visible, the loom of the Scilly Isles.

"There's a hoist up," announced the skipper one hour later, hastily clambering into the bridge. Seizing the binoculars he focused them on the commodore: "Alteration of course," and he began calling out the flags to the lookout, who pulled them from the lockers, bent them on and hoisted the halyard. Johnny Harrison was quick, he seemed to have eyes in the back of his head, and I suddenly felt well and truly caught out. Glancing around the convoy we appeared to have the hoist up before any of the others and I commented on the fact, I felt it was the least I could do.

"I wasn't a bunting-tosser for nothing," came the prompt retort, his binoculars still focused on the commodore: "Hoist's down," he called to the lookout, who quickly hauled the halyard down, unbent and stowed each flag in its locker. Slowly the convoy began to swing westward.

"Starboard ten," said the skipper down the voice-pipe.

"Starboard ten, sir," came the quartermaster's reply from below: "Ten of starboard wheel on, sir."

"Midships."

"Midships ... Wheel's amidships, sir."

"Steady."

"Steady, sir. 210, sir."

"Very good, steer 215."

"Steer 215, sir." The fifty small ships faithfully followed the squat shape of the Boom Defence Vessel out front, while to starboard the sun began to sink. Soon scuttles were being closed as the hands darkened ship.

Before turning in, I spent another hour on the bridge with the first lieutenant, who was married with a small son. An accountant by profession, Bill Russell was an unassuming person who, as number one, went about his business with a quiet, almost apologetic air. It was a clear starlit night. 582 lifted and fell in the moderate swell which was increasing, and the hand on the wheel, steering now by compass only, needed to work at it more. Every so often the bow would begin to pay off and it required checking early, for the landing-craft did not respond easily to the wheel.

"You're taking the forenoon watch, I understand?' he remarked. "Happy about it?"

"I think so," I said, nodding.

"Skipper's taking the middle, Ogo the morning. If you've any problems you've only got to give a shout down the voice-pipe. The crew are in three watches. A stoker below and three up top, one on the bridge, one on the wheel, one on deck. They take it in turns. If I were you I'd get some sleep. Starboard ten," he said bending over the voice-pipe, "ease to five," I heard him say as I climbed out of the bridge.

Day two dawned ominously. We had rounded the Scilly Isles and begun heading into the Atlantic, giving the Bay of Biscay a wide berth. Above us, a sullen ceiling of low clouds threatened, and the long beam swell, increasing all the while, was having its effect on the four columns of landing-craft as they struggled to hold a steady course.

"Morning!" the Ogo greeted me when I clambered into the bridge for the forenoon watch. "Weather's not too good." He gave me the course and waited a minute or two while I grew accustomed to the conditions: "Right, all yours," he said and disappeared.

For the next four hours 582 was in my hands, more or less, with the support of the lookout, a cheerful chubby young Scot, a pusser signalman. The landing-craft lifted, tilted steeply, then slipped sideways down a long, dark green slope to the clatter of parallel rulers sliding across the chart table. Suddenly I became aware that we were uncomfortably close to the ship ahead and I could not understand how I had failed to anticipate the situation.

"Half ahead together," I called.

"Half ahead together, sir," came the reassuring voice from below.

"Both engines half ahead together, sir," and the distance between us and the ship ahead widened as we fell back. Relieved, I glanced over my shoulder to discover that the ship astern had pulled out to avoid ramming us, its blunt bow lifting and plunging, perilously close, threatening our starboard quarter.

"Full ahead together, Quartermaster," I called in considerable alarm.

"Full ahead together, sir." The engine-room telegraphs clanged,

"Both engines full ahead together, sir," and, little by little, we drew ahead.

"They're signalling us, sir," called the lookout as he leant over the side of the bridge acknowledging the semaphore coming from the LCT astern of 582.

"What's he saying, Bunts?"

"Message, sir: 'Are you inviting us aboard for a drink?'"

"Make back: 'Apologies. Yes, in Gib.' What's he flagging now?"

" 'If we ever make it,' " reported the signalman.

An extra large swell suddenly lifted and dumped 582 into a deep trough, the bows swung alarmingly to starboard, and we began heading in the direction of the next column.

"Port twenty."

"Port twenty, sir. Twenty of port wheel on, sir."

Gradually 582 began to respond.

"Ease to ten."

"Ease to ten, sir. Ten of port wheel on, sir."

"Midships."

"Midships, sir. Wheel's amidships."

"Keep her at that, Coxswain," and once again we were back in station and I could breathe more easily.

Of course, much depended on the helmsman's ability to anticipate the swing and counteract it early with opposite wheel. But it would not be an extravagance to state that few ships were more difficult to handle in a seaway than a Mark IV Landing-craft, nor more difficult to capsize or sink. Full of watertight compartments, they wallowed in bad weather like half-submerged planks of wood. Their real danger lay in a head sea when they could, and did on occasions, break in two. Unlike a 'proper' ship, which would attempt to stem the sea in bad conditions, a Mark IV Landing-craft would be far better off lying abeam of the weather, as I was to experience later.

Several times during that first watch I was aware of the skipper below watching from outside the wheelhouse. Once he came onto the bridge to deal with a signal hoist. Other than that he let me get on with the job, and his bit of a smile and nod gave me more confidence than any words could have done.

Towards noon the Ogo came up onto the bridge to take his sight. Shafts of sunlight had begun breaking through the clouds and, as though to herald his appearance, the sun burst forth into a clear patch of blue sky. I watched as he handled the sextant, thankful that I had nothing to do with the proceedings. He seemed for the first time to be enjoying himself and did not contain his delight when the commodore's hoist went up at noon and he found he'd got it right. "Spot on," he announced and disappeared below. And spot on he was for the next few days.

By day six the glass had fallen, the sun had disappeared behind scudding clouds and the wind was increasing to gale force. The convoy, barely making headway, wallowed in the big seas which lifted the LCTs and MFVs, sweeping them up, before tossing them down into deep cavernous valleys of liquid grey. Peering over the bridge, we watched the crest of each uprearing wall of water bear down upon our port side before sweeping us up, dumping 582 beam on, burying her starboard catwalk, forcing us to wedge ourselves in and hang on as best we could. For long seconds the LCTs would disappear from sight, hidden in the great troughs as the convoy lost station and broke up. Through the night the two tugs stood by, assisting those who had fallen back with engine problems, one of which was 581. Struggling on one engine, the other had overheated, they were eventually picked up and taken in tow, hazardous for those working on deck up for'ard. In no time the tow parted. For what seemed a very long night the crew of 581 were alone on a heaving ocean in pitch darkness and a gale of wind. It was the night an MFV lost a man overboard.

Years later, chatting over a drink with an ex-RAF navigator, 581's young first lieutenant recalled the events of that night and the passage out.

"Was that in the first week of June 1943? A convoy of landing-craft and what looked like small fishing boats?"

"MFVs," remarked Jimmy Danson, nodding.

"I remember it well," said his companion: "We'd been detailed off to keep an eye on you. Did you know there was a U-boat following you on the surface? We attacked, but it got away."

Dawn found the convoy scattered far and wide, and it took the early hours of daylight for the stragglers to reassemble. But though the wind was now dropping and much of the anger had gone out of the storm, no hand yet ventured along the catwalk and, when the engine-room mechanic went for'ard to work the semi-rotary pump for the daily top-up of the fuel tanks, he went down the tank space.

Early that forenoon watch the commodore signalled another alteration of course, and slowly the convoy wheeled round, lurching and rolling in an uncomfortable cross swell. But the sun was out, and the crew were cheerfully enjoying the warm dry decks as they went about their business. Soon one of the hands came up with a mug of tea. I sat in the high chair, one hand on the side of the bridge, drank the strong hot brew and breathed deeply. I felt king of the castle. As far as the eye could see the ocean sparkled and the grey sombre tones of the past forty-eight hours were now lit with patches of green, purple and flashes of white, as the crests tumbled in the sunlight.

"Morning, sir," I heard a cheerful voice say from behind me.

"Good morning," and I turned to see Stoker Jones in a clean singlet leaning over the after side of the bridge.

"When will we get to Gib, sir?"

"About another six days," I told him, whereupon he suddenly and inexplicably launched into an account of how he had once been in the glasshouse, doubling at attention, awaiting food, when a guard snapped at a prisoner alongside him, who was smiling in eager anticipation of his first square meal since coming out of solitary confinement: "Wipe that bleedin' face off your smile." The unfortunate man laughed aloud and promptly found himself back in solitary again and without his food.

"Bit hard," I said.

"They were bastards, sir. That the sextant?" he asked indicating the box at the back of the chart table.

Right: Stoker Jones

Below: From left to right:
Chief Motor Mechanic Rose,
KAS, Geoffrey Leeds, Stoker Neild

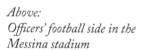

Above:
Officers' football side in the
Messina stadium

Right:
Stevens observing the German,
whose smile soon vanished when
he was relieved of his binoculars.

I took it out to show him, unwisely allowing him to handle it. 582 lurched and between us we dropped the wretched thing.

"Don't worry, sir," he said as he saw my face, "I'll take it down, put it in a vice and straighten it up. Leave it to me, sir."

I had little alternative. "Well, for God's sake, be quick! Any minute the navigator will be up to take his sighting for the noon day position.

Several minutes later he was back: "All mended, sir," he said cheerfully, handing me the sextant, which I hastily returned to its box.

Shortly afterwards the Ogo appeared and set to work with the sextant. Promptly at noon the commodore hoisted the convoy's position, and immediately I saw a puzzled expression creep over our Ogo's face: "Funny," he murmured, shaking his head, at the same time beginning to check his figures. "Can't understand it, simply can't understand it," he muttered again, and indeed for the rest of the passage, he simply couldn't understand it.

The convoy had now altered course to the east and begun the final approach to the Straits. The sun shone and the weather held fine. But on the eleventh day, the wind freshened strongly and the convoy found itself battling against steep head seas. 582's huge shovel of a bow lifted and fell with shuddering force, flinging sunlit arcs of spray back over the bridge. Every so often a sea broke over the door, inflicting enormous strain on the after end of the tank space as 582 staggered up to face the next wave. Looking down from the bridge, the whip of the tank space was alarmingly evident; it was as if we were standing on the end of some enormous spring board. Once, and for one fearful long moment, 582 buried her bow completely, and this time it really did seem she was not going to make it. But she did, surfacing slowly, wearily shaking herself free of the dead weight of water, somehow managing to survive the next onslaught. On several occasions we heard the heavy sliding door of the wheelhouse being flung back, and the tense face of the Ogo peered for'ard to see whether 582 really was beginning to break in two. Far astern of the convoy the two ocean tugs were busy assisting a straggler which had broken in two. The tugs salvaged each half and towed them into Gibraltar where they were welded together.

Gradually the wind eased, a hot sun emerged, and we made a landfall, as Spain came up on the port hand, Africa on the starboard. With Cape Trafalgar to port, bearing due east some twenty miles, we passed Tangier and Tarifa, sailed through the Straits of Gibraltar, and finally entered the Mediterranean on the fourteenth day. By then the wind had fallen away to nothing. Ahead stretched a glittering sea beneath a cloudless canopy of blue. To starboard the coast of North Africa shimmered in the heat, to port the lighthouse of Europa Point and the great Rock came into view.

"Look slippy, Mac," said the skipper to our bunts, "Commodore's got a hoist going up," and he began reading out the alteration of course. "Hoist's down," he announced, but the signalman, now on his toes, had beaten him to it once again. For the last time, the convoy swung slowly round in the wake of the Boom Defence Vessel and headed for Gibraltar.

With hands fell in fore and aft, in tropical kit, we entered harbour and secured alongside one another in trots of six.

"Finished with engines," called John Harrison down the voice-pipe.

"Finished with engines, sir," came the coxswain's reply. The telegraphs rang, the diesels faded, and silence struck us.

Our stay in Gibraltar was short. We refuelled, topped up our fresh water tank, and sent a party ashore to replenish our food store. Our Ogo had wasted no time. Wearing a white shirt and shorts, white stockings, shoes and white cap cover, he emerged from the wardroom carrying his green pusser's suitcase and, for the first time since he had been aboard, I thought he looked really happy. "Well, back to U.K.," he said, shaking the skipper and number one by the hand, "But I'll tell you one thing, I never again want to sail in one of these contraptions. But good luck to you all. One other thing. You need a new sextant. Bloody thing's defective," and picking up his suitcase he clambered across the landing-craft alongside and disappeared ashore.

"Obviously must have got his figures wrong," remarked John Harrison dryly, "In any case we shan't be using a sextant much out here. If we do," and he cast a quick amused glance in my direction, "you're the expert." I didn't pursue the subject.

The Rock was as spectacular as I had expected. In a way, the war seemed hardly to have affected Gibraltar, though a buzz was around that the Italians might be involved in underwater activity. There was no blackout, the town was full of shops and bars, the narrow streets chock-a-block with forces in white and khaki shorts. Gharrys, open, four-wheeled cabs dashed up and down Main Street, and still the most popular articles of clothing to purchase were silk stockings — the convoys to Gibraltar were known by some as 'silk stocking runs'.

"You're to join 614," John Harrison informed me with customary brevity, on returning from a meeting with Lieutenant-Commander Snagge and his commanding officers: "We're sailing shortly. Better pack your bag and hammock."

I was genuinely sorry to be leaving 582 and said so when saying goodbye to the skipper and number one.

"Leaving us, sir?" enquired Stoker Jones, who had just come up from the mess deck. I nodded and climbed over the guard-rail onto the next craft.

"Good job we straightened that sextant, sir," he added, handing over my suitcase.

"Yes," I said, "It certainly was. But I think it would be better, Jones, if you didn't mention the matter again."

"Leave it to me, sir. Good luck, sir."

"Thanks," I said, and continued my way across several more LCTs before eventually boarding 614.

My new commanding officer, Norman Rutherford, skipper of 614, leader of the 21st Flotilla, was tall, bearded and thin to the extent he looked in need of a square meal. When I arrived on board he was talking with the coxswain, a tough-looking individual with a round close-cropped head and a rasping voice, who looked like an awkward customer. Spotting me out of the corner of his eye, the skipper broke off his conversation and approached: "You're the Assistant Flotilla Officer, I take it. Better come and dump your gear in the ward-room."

I soon learnt that my new CO was married, had done some professional acting, and was a stage director in peacetime. I found him easy to talk to and warmed to him at once. The steward came in with tea. Shortly after Lieutenant-Commander Snagge, who had his own cabin below in the pongos' shelter, came up and joined us. He was slightly bow-legged, and his long white shorts above pale nobbly knees seemed to accentuate the fact. He gave a quick nod in my direction and then began talking earnestly with the skipper.

Late that afternoon we slipped our moorings, assembled outside Europa Point and got under way, destination Algiers; out front was the same old Boom Defence Vessel that had led us safely so far. With four officers aboard and the Atlantic behind us, watch-keeping became a pleasant prospect. Soon the sun went down, the hands darkened ship and a slight chill filled the air. On either side and astern the low profile of each landing-craft faded into the summer night. As flotilla leader, our station was immediately astern of the Boom Defence Vessel, its faint light just visible abaft the funnel. A gentle swell barely disturbed the sea's surface. Before turning in I stood by the guard-rail and listened to the soft swish of water running down the LCTs side. It was a tranquil moment. Later I had no need to wedge myself in on the narrow bunk before falling asleep.

It happened quickly.

I slept well, breakfasted and went up top to relieve the skipper. Three enjoyable hours of the forenoon watch slipped by. Each hour I sent the lookout down to read the log, the distance cruised I laid off on the chart. That at least I could manage. A mug of tea came up and I lit a cigarette, inhaled, and pressed the button for an increase in revs; there was little else I had to do other than savour the scene. Steadily the convoy proceeded at six knots in perfect station. I folded my arms on the edge of the bridge and watched several seamen aboard the Boom Defence Vessel ahead of us go about their business.

She had a low rounded stern, her topsides tumbling inboard. One of the hands, clad in a singlet, probably from the galley, came out on deck, tipped a gash bucket over the side and stood idly staring across the water. Overhead a brilliant sun beat down out of a deep blue sky upon a sea of an even richer hue. It was a spectacle that in peacetime many would have paid to view from the deck of a liner. An officer moved to the wing of the bridge, lifted his glasses and swept the convoy with his gaze. That was the last picture I had of the Boom Defence Vessel. The explosion which followed was cataclysmic.

It tore the air apart, and momentarily blue became grey, as what had been a ship was blasted upward into myriad particles. A rain of debris showered down, pitting the surface of the sea ahead, forcing us to duck beneath the sides of the bridge. "Starboard ten," I called a moment later.

"What was it?" asked Norman Rutherford, hastily climbing into the bridge, closely followed by the flotilla officer.

"A mine?" suggested the latter.

"Could have been, sir. Midships."

"Midships, sir," came the coxswain's voice.

"I'll take over," said Norman.

The crew below, who had come up top quickly, now stood staring silently at the black circle of oily flotsam, scattered in the midst of which planks of wood, what looked to be part of a Carley raft and several kapok life-jackets floated forlornly, sole evidence that seconds before there had been a ship and a crew. The limpet mine planted in Gibraltar had done its job.

By nightfall we made Algiers just in time to experience an uncomfortable air raid. We donned tin hats, closed up on the oerlikons, but left the firing to the big guns of *Aurora* and *Penelope*. Dwarfed by the shipping around us, with a limited arc of fire, we would have done more harm than good had we started to bang away at the invisible targets overhead.

Twelve hours later, along with three other unimpaired Mark IVs, we crept in line ahead along the North African coast, the soft night broken only by the spluttering of our diesels from the single high funnel abaft the bridge. Far astern the sky glowed as Algiers was subjected to another attack.

Crossing the Gulf of Tunis we found ourselves converging on a huge, heavily laden convoy. It was a question of whether we should hold our course and pass ahead, which we could do all right, though perhaps without a great deal to spare, or play safe, alter course and pass astern of the convoy. We chose the latter, correctly as it turned out, since a destroyer immediately began flashing us, requesting we keep out of their way. As we drew near the great lumbering merchantmen, sporadic firing broke out and suddenly every gun in the convoy opened up at a line of black specks heading towards us. In seconds the sky became criss-crossed with tracer and pitted with bursts from the big guns of the escort. As was customary, the enemy had picked off one ship at the rear of the convoy for special attention. Huge geysers of water erupted around her and momentarily hid the ship from view, yet somehow she emerged, unscathed, steaming sedately forward as though nothing had happened. Within a minute the attack was over. It had all happened so quickly. No ship had been hit. We lit cigarettes, wondered whether they would come again, and remained at action stations. Ten minutes later there was a repeat performance and again it was a ship on the edge of the convoy, a tanker, that was singled out. This time the enemy came in much lower, released their bombs and wheeled sharply to avoid the full fire-power of the convoy, to which we contributed our small share. The last aircraft took the full brunt of the barrage and, as it banked steeply and pulled away, a long trail of black smoke poured from its fuselage. It was losing height fast when we lost sight of it.

Darkness fell as the four landing-craft rounded Cape Bon. Towards the end of the first watch we heard the ominous drone of aircraft again, and listened uneasily as they passed overhead to bomb the convoy. Shortly, and well astern of us, streams of tracer began floating lazily upward and a great red burst shot high into the night, subsided, and then glowed persistently like a red hot ember. In the silver light of a half moon it seemed impossible that the four landing-craft would escape detection. Unconsciously we spoke and moved quietly about the ship, careful to show no glimmer of light. One plane flew so low we could see the great black shape clearly as it roared overhead and disappeared into the night. But when the middle watch took over all was quiet; the four LCTs sailed on undisturbed, to beach on Sliema Creek in the early morning.

Malta was very hot, the reflected light glaring to the eyes. There was plenty of harsh evidence to remind us how much the people had suffered. But, despite the occasional air raids, the island had seen the worst. There was now a bustle and fresh spirit abroad as preparations were made to open the offensive on Europe.

Lieutenant-Commander Snagge, who had gone up to the base on arrival summoned me the following morning to join him at Phoenicia, the Combined Operations base. With regret and some misgivings I gathered my belongings and left 614. My new job was to record the movement of landing-craft on a long blackboard and keep contact with what was happening in Sliema. As yet more craft piled into Malta my board became crammed with numbers. I did not enjoy what I was doing and found it difficult to share in my commanding officer's enthusiasm, a fact of which he was aware. Shortly before the invasion of Sicily took place, an incident occurred which finally sealed my fate.

I was standing before the blackboard trying to keep an up-to-date record of craft movement, when I heard the door open. I was feeling far from well and no doubt looked scruffy. The room was oppressively hot. I turned and found myself confronted by Rear-Admiral Lord Louis Mountbatten in full whites. In attendance were Commander Beatty and Lieutenant-Commander Snagge. I stood uncomfortably to attention as the Chief of Combined Operations glanced at the blackboard, gave me a quick — I thought not unsympathetic— smile and departed. Ten minutes later I was summoned and given my sailing orders — to report forthwith to LCT 614, as First Lieutenant:

"And I hope you'll prove a more effective number one than Assistant Flotilla Officer," concluded Lieutenant-Commander Snagge.

"I shall do my best, sir," I replied, more than pleased at the prospect of being afloat again and serving under Norman Rutherford.

The decision to invade Sicily had been reached only after considerable discussion between the British and Americans on how best to defeat the Axis. The Americans had no wish to expand or continue the war in the Mediterranean. Attacking Sicily and then the mainland of Italy meant committing men and resources in what would, in their eyes, soon become a major campaign in a secondary theatre. Their proposal was to withdraw all forces from the Mediterranean to the United Kingdom, and prepare for a massive invasion of north-west Europe. However, to put this into effect would have taken at least a year — probably a good deal longer — and would have merely sustained the British view that the time was not yet ripe. It was far better, argued the British, to invade Sicily, then Italy, and so continue to stretch the Axis, in particular the German forces while, at the same time, to begin preparing for a second front in Western Europe. The one thing the Allies did agree on was that it should be a 'Europe First' strategy, then deal with Japan.

At Casablanca, in January 1943, Churchill and Roosevelt, along with their military advisers, met to decide the matter. The Americans stuck to their guns, the British to theirs. Finally the Americans acquiesced in an invasion of Sicily, and the Combined Chiefs of Staff named General Eisenhower as the Supreme Allied Commander in the Mediterranean.

Four months later, a conference in Washington met to decide what to do after Sicily had fallen. It was agreed that all operations beyond Sicily should be considered only in terms of whether they facilitated and expedited the invasion of north-west Europe. On this basis the Americans accepted the elimination of Italy from the war as a prerequisite for re-entry into Europe across the Channel. In the final analysis the future Allied strategy would depend in large measure on whether the enemy in Sicily collapsed entirely or resisted fiercely. But the die was cast.

Ninety miles from Cape Bon, some sixty miles from Malta, slightly larger than Wales and barely two miles from the Italian mainland, Sicily has long been a stepping-stone for invaders — Romans, Carthaginians, Moors, Vikings and Normans. A rugged, mountainous island, the Coronie range in the north-east is dominated by Mount Etna. The coastal roads are good, but the interior ones, narrow and poorly surfaced, wind upward, round sharp curves and steep gradients to medieval towns, their streets designed for mule carts and pedestrians. On the northern coast precipitous cliffs face the sea. The only flat area lies around Catania, where fleets of Italian and German bombers took off from the nineteen airfields to attack Malta convoys and force the British to abandon their traditional sea-route between Gibraltar and Alexandria. Malta alone, beleaguered, repeatedly bombed and isolated, had survived. It was now from Malta, along with a host of shipping from North Africa, that the 21st and 26th LCT Flotillas sailed to play their part in Operation Husky, the invasion of Sicily.

July 9 1943 dawned fine but, as the day wore on, the wind began to freshen. 614's tank space was loaded with trucks and troops. Two army officers were sharing our ward-room. H-hour was 02.45 and the two flotillas of LCTs were to land on a sector of beach at Cape Passero. The commanding officers had been briefed and warned that high casualties were expected. Norman spoke to the crew briefly and put them in the picture, omitting the bit about casualties. More reassuring, the cover was considerable. Beside the escort vessels there was to be a cruiser and escort force to work close inshore in support of the army, while to the east of the whole operation a great covering force of battleships, fleet carriers, cruisers and destroyers lay waiting for the main Italian fleet, should it decide to intervene.

As the time approached for sailing, I sent for the coxswain and told him to have the fo'c'sle party stand by to get the door up.

"Right, sir," he said, but instead of carrying on, asked if I would go up for'ard. Puzzled, I followed him down the tank space and into the starboard winch space.

"Here's to the landing, sir," he said, producing the best part of a bottle of vino and pouring out two full cups of the stuff in the dim confines of the winch space.

"To the landing," I replied with scant enthusiasm, knowing full well I was showing a lack of wisdom. Irritated that I had got myself into such a situation I drank the vino as quickly as I could.

"Right," I said, exerting what authority I had left, taking the bottle before he could refill the cups, "get the door up, Coxswain."

"Aye, aye, sir," and I watched him as he set off back down the tank space to muster the hands. Then I ditched the bottle over the side.

A regular sailor in peacetime, a professional, the coxswain was in his mid-twenties, a leading seaman, who knew the ropes. He was no easy person to have dealings with. And just like old Sourface in the *Foresight*, he never concealed his disdain for landing-craft and HO ratings, let alone HO officers.

From up on the deck I watched the door rise slowly, the wire hawsers creaking as they took the strain.

"Let go, for'ard," I heard Norman call from the bridge, and the headropes were quickly pulled in and coiled down. The engine-room telegraphs rang and 614 slipped astern off the hard at Sliema. By 09.30 we had passed the boom and taken up our station. Operation Husky had begun.

The morning was sunny with a strong wind blowing from the north, causing a steep head sea. Already our door was lifting and hammering into the waves, flinging spray back over the tank space, causing the troops to seek refuge in their vehicles. The conditions, wind a good force seven, were far from ideal, and some of the troops were already sick.

I climbed into the bridge where two army officers were watching Norman maintain station in the difficult conditions, when one of the engines suddenly stopped and we began to fall back: "Find out what's happening below," said Norman, judiciously stroking his beard, a habit I was to grow accustomed to when difficulties arose. But Murray, our motor mechanic, a Scot, had already come up to explain why he had shut down the starboard engine, which was overheating badly. "Can you do anything about it?" the skipper asked.

"Needs stripping down, sir, and we've not located the trouble. It will take time."

I watched Norman as he pondered the situation. We were now astern of the convoy and making no headway on the one engine. The weather, if anything, seemed to be worsening. To put about now with a following sea we would make the short distance back to Malta all right. With shore base facilities available we might well be away again in a few hours. His mind made up he turned to our bunts. "Make to the commodore, 'Starboard engine out of action. Impossible to make headway in present conditions. Request permission to return to Malta for repairs'." The shutter of our Aldis lamp clicked away and I saw a look of concern come over the major's face.

"They're flashing us," said Norman as a ten-inch lamp winked in the distance.

" 'Permission granted'" read out our bunts.

"Starboard thirty,' called Norman down the voice-pipe. "Sorry, Major, there's no alternative."

"Understand," he said, with a wry smile, "we're in your hands."

"Better start stripping the engine, Murray," Norman advised. With the sea astern, we limped back to Malta.

Six hours later we were under way again. The weather had moderated and we made good headway through the night. Shortly after noon we sighted Cape Passero. As we drew near the south-east coast of Sicily, all eyes were fastened on the scene ahead. Liberty ships lay offshore surrounded by landing-craft. Beyond them we could make out Mark IVs and IIIs, LSTs lying bows on to the beach, which was dotted with troops and vehicles. To and fro like water beetles, the new amphibious vehicles, DUKWs, scuttled across the water up onto the shore. Apart from the distant rumble of gunfire, all seemed quiet. I went for'ard with the fo'c'sle party and as we closed the beach, a lorry's engine burst into life, followed by others, as the Eighth Army veterans prepared to go ashore. We nosed our way into a gap between two landing-craft, there was a slight jolt as our bows touched, then we lowered the door. In a matter of minutes our tank space was empty.

"Where the bloody hell have you been?" A voice boomed across from an LCT to starboard of us. I began to explain, but was cut short by a sudden outbreak of gunfire, as two low-flying enemy aircraft roared overhead, dropped their bombs and disappeared, almost before we had time to move.

"Happens every so often," said Bill Barnet, first lieutenant of 536 when we had recovered our composure, his round face wreathed in smiles.

"What's it been like?" I asked.

"All right," he replied, "apart from the odd air raid, very quiet."

"Get the door up, Number One," Norman called from the bridge, at the same time going astern. For the next twenty-four hours, we ferried supplies ashore before moving up the coast to Syracuse, which had fallen on the first day to the British Fifth Division. Only Catania now remained and the rugged terrain that lay in the path of the Eighth Army, as they pushed their way up towards Messina, the prime objective, whose capture would bottle up the Axis forces.

But if the seaborne landings had been successful and relatively unopposed, the airborne landings had proved disastrous. Bad weather broke up the formations as they flew from North Africa and, although one hundred and thirty-three planes and gliders reached Cape Passero, many of the pilots were unable to identify the release point. Out of a hundred and fifteen gliders set free, more than half fell into the sea. No more than fifty-four landed in Sicily, and of these only twelve were near the landing-zones. Eight officers and sixty-five men of the Airborne Brigade seized and grimly held onto the Ponte Grande bridge until they ran out of ammunition and were overrun. The advancing column of British infantry and tanks recaptured the bridge intact, routed the Italian opposition and entered Syracuse. By now the Italians were thoroughly demoralised and it looked as though the advance to Messina would not be too difficult. But the battle for Catania proved otherwise, for the Hermann Goering and Fifteenth Panzer Grenadier Divisions were far from demoralised.

Syracuse we found blisteringly hot. We quenched our thirst as best we could. I squeezed huge ripe lemons into tepid water sweetened with plenty of sugar. Our living conditions were basic, to say the least. The mess deck was ventilated by two small portholes, one on either side. Fuel for cooking and hot water came from a coal galley situated on the port side of the crew's quarters. We had no bolts of canvas with which to make awnings, no fans, no refrigeration, and we washed and did our dhobying in buckets. Yet our lot was infinitely preferable to that of the soldiers who, somewhat oddly, seemed to prefer their lot to ours.

From Syracuse the 21st Flotilla, along with the 26th, moved up to Augusta Bay, where we continued to ferry supplies ashore from the transports, while cheerful, grinning Basuto troops unloaded us. Every so often during the day enemy aircraft, coming in low so as to give no warning, attacked the beaches, releasing their bombs then racing back inland before any guns could be brought to bear. It was a hit and run affair, mostly unsuccessful, though our Basuto troops would disappear into thin air at each raid, taking progressively longer to return to their unloading. I can't say I blamed them.

But at night the centre of the anchorage was bombed with monotonous regularity and, at the end of a day, the LCTs would push off and select the safest part of the bay in which to anchor. We would go as far away as possible from the big warships and merchantmen, and drop our hooks close inshore in two or three fathoms of water. Each night Norman would take 614 across to the north-west part of the bay, and there secure alongside Norman Smale and Bill Barnet in 536. We would swim in the warm water and the crew would do their dhobying and talk with the crew of 536 leaning on the guard-rails. Later Bill would come over to 614 and we'd have a drink and a chat, while the two Normans got together in 536's ward-room. Night would fall, a degree of coolness would set in and we'd get our heads down. Around midnight the guns would begin firing. Both ships' companies would assemble on the quarter-deck for the early morning performance, which would last on and off till dawn. It was a vivid, at times awesome spectacle, as the night, lit by numerous flares and full of criss-cross lines of red tracer floating lazily upward, was shattered by the blast of naval gunfire and the thump of exploding bombs. Eventually the flares would flicker and burn out, and temporarily we'd feel comparatively safe under the mantle of darkness. But not for long, for soon more clusters were bursting overhead, lighting the sky, revealing the black silhouettes of ships anchored in the bay, making us all again feel naked and exposed to the enemy above.

A sudden increase in the tempo of gunfire brought cheers from the two crews, as a bomber burst into flames high overhead and, like some fiery comet, plummeted earthward. Each night the raids continued until, on August 5, Catania fell. By then the evacuation of Sicily had started. The Italians, by agreement, crossed the Messina Straits first, while the Germans contained the advancing British and American forces.

As for 614, with three other landing-craft we were given orders to push on up the coast to Catania. On approaching the port in line astern, we were suddenly attacked by two FW 190s. Bob Knott in 601, bringing up the stern, took the full brunt of the attack, his craft and crew disappearing completely as the sea erupted around them. Yet somehow they managed to emerge unscathed. The enemy had caught us completely unawares, coming out of the sun and disappearing as quickly, flying low over the water and inland, while belatedly and vainly we fired our oerlikons after them.

Gently we nudged alongside. One of the hands jumped ashore and took the head-rope. A strange silence prevailed, and devastation lay everywhere. Right from the onset Catania had been subjected to repeated air and naval bombardment, in particular from the fifteen-inch guns of *Warspite*. A final frontal assault had freed the town, but at great cost.

By now the other three landing-craft were secured alongside, with the crews chatting together. From out of the ruins, children began to emerge, warily at first. Thin, barefoot and ragged, they approached in expectation, their hands thrust forward in the suppliant manner of beggars, their dark eyes sad and worldly, watched in the background by old men and women, their bent shoulders draped in black shawls: *"Mangiare, signor, mangiare,"* the children cried and, when that did not succeed: "You want *signorina? Bella signorina. Si, signor?* I take you." They were cries we were to hear more than once in the months to come.

I had struggled through a plate of dehydrated potatoes and corned beef hash (it was either that for supper or egg powder served in the form of an omelette) when Norman returned from a meeting with senior naval and military personnel. The four COs had been briefed on a landing that was to take place in the immediate future. Chucking his hat on one of the bunks, he handed me a large brown envelope and poured himself a gin. "Better have a look at it," he said.

I took out several pages of type, headed 'Operation Blackcock'. There was a knock on the ward-room door and a rating entered with another plate of hash, 'tinned dog' as it was more commonly known. While Norman ate unenthusiastically, I read through the operational orders and my heart quickened.

The general gist was that the four landing-craft were to take aboard a commando unit and a squadron of tanks from the British 4th Armoured Brigade, and land them at Cape d'Ali on the morning of 16 August. An ML would lead us up the coast, the military objective, to cut off the retreating Germans and head for Messina. Feeling anything but confident, I got up, went up top and fetched a chart from the bridge. Spreading it on the ward-room table we soon located Cape d'Ali, just north of Scaletta: "Barely fifteen miles from Messina," said Norman, stroking his beard.

MGBs had been going up at night attempting to counter the steady flow of Italians escaping across the Straits. But the immensely strong coastal batteries around

Messina prevented bigger warships operating in such restricted waters. No matter how much British Wellingtons and American B-17s bombed the port, the evacuation still continued. Indeed there seemed no immediate and effective way of preventing the Germans from escaping, other than by another amphibious landing behind the lines to capture Messina and the evacuation beaches. With this in mind Operation Blackcock was conceived.

The following morning the rumble of tanks and shouts of command gave us due warning that the military had arrived and it was time to load up.

Taking tanks aboard a landing-craft from a quayside is no easy exercise, as we soon discovered. As a necessary precaution we kept both engines running to counteract 614's being pushed back from the quayside while the first tank drove up and over the door's leading edge. Despite our head-ropes, this was always a possible danger when using the door as a bridge onto a quayside.

In line astern, 614 leading, the four landing-craft followed the sleek ML up the north-east coast of Sicily at a steady six knots. To port, the volcanic slopes of Etna swept gently upward before soaring steeply to the summit, ten thousand feet above, where wisps of smoke spiralled into the blue haze. A slight breeze had sprung up, blowing steadily from the south, ruffling the sea's surface. From across the water, though barely audible, came the boom of guns. The commandos were resting where they could find space, some smoking, some sprawled on their tanks gazing at the rugged coastline, until it merged into the sea as the sun went down, their minds no doubt preoccupied with what lay ahead.

Our two oerlikons were manned, but there was no sign of enemy aircraft. Darkness fell and with it a false sense of security. Towards midnight we passed Taormina. Two hours later it was time to go in. In line abreast, the four LCTs headed for the shore. Using binoculars, elbows supported on the chart table's cabinet, Norman searched the coast. A low continuous rumble of gunfire filled the air, inland the sky was lit by intermittent flashes.

"Ah," he murmured as a faint line of surf came into his view: "Better stand by, Number One."

I went down the bridge ladder onto the quarter-deck where the crew were grouped in watchful silence round the capstan, and checked the kedge was ready to let go. The coxswain was on the wheel.

"Fo'c'sle party, up for'ard," I ordered and we proceeded along the starboard catwalk. The four ratings jumped down into the tank space, opened the watertight doors with difficulty and manned the winches. I climbed the vertical ladder and, with one foot on a bollard, leant on the guard-rail, feeling exposed and anything but comfortable as we closed the shore. I heard Norman sing out to let the kedge go. There was a growl of engines as the tank started up. I shouted to the hands in the winch spaces to start lowering the door. We seemed to be coming in too fast. The door was almost down as we surged up the sand. It fell with a thud and immediately the first tank was on its way. A sudden blast of gunfire to the right split the air, then the troops were running in the wake of the tanks up the beach. It was over in a matter of minutes. Clambering quickly down into the empty tank space, I heard Norman shout to get the door up. There was no need, for it was already on its way. With the kedge coming up and both engines going full astern, we drew clear of the beach. I hurried aft with the fo'c'sle party and checked the kedge was secure, before joining Norman on the bridge. We had swung round and were heading out to sea. From the flashes and the sound of gunfire the Fourth Armoured Brigade were engaging the enemy, and again I felt thankful I was a sailor and not a soldier. I found Norman bending over the voice-pipe calling for an alteration of course that would take us back down the coast: "All right?" he asked.

"Fine," I replied, as an explosion, quickly followed by several others, rolled across the water.

"That's not gunfire, that's demolition. They're blowing the road, and just look at that," he said, turning and gazing up the coast as a spectacular display of red tracer began weaving low patterns across the Messina Straits: "Plenty going on up there." He had seated himself on the high wooden chair again, and was looking ahead through his binoculars: "Better get your head down, Number One. I'll give you a shake in a couple of hours," and I left him to it.

When I took over, the sun was well up. Mount Etna's stupendous black peak lay off our starboard bow, smoking gently. Although weary, I felt a sense of relief and satisfaction, as though I had achieved something.

"Morning, sir," said one of the watch who had come up to relieve the lookout, at the same time handing me a cup of tea: "Went all right, sir, didn't it? But I wouldn't be one of them bloody pongos, sir."

"Nor would I," I assured him and lit a cigarette. Inhaling deeply I sipped the strong tea and, delighting in the early warmth and beauty of the morning, reflected on the past events.

We had been tested, by no means severely, for no harm had come our way. But it had been an experience, one we had shared and, if nothing else, it would bring us closer together as a crew.

As it turned out, Operation Blackcock proved ineffective because the German withdrawal had already passed Cape d'Ali on the evening of August 15. The tank crews and commandos we had landed in those early hours of the 16th had run up against the tag end of the German rearguard and been held just north of Scaletta. When night fell, the Germans began their final withdrawal to Messina, allowing the British to advance within two miles of the port. But, as dawn broke on the 17th, a demolished bridge across a deep ravine halted further progress.

By 06.35 on 17 August, the Axis evacuation of Sicily had been completed. Nearly 40,000 Germans and over 70,000 Italians had escaped across the Messina Straits into Italy. It had taken thirty-eight days to end the struggle for Sicily.

Chapter 7

Italy, Vibo Valentia and Salerno

A MASSIVE BOMBARDMENT by six hundred British guns across the Straits of Messina preceded the Allied invasion of Italy — Operation Baytown. But, apart from a few alarming eruptions in the water ahead, more than likely shells from our own batteries, there was no answering fire as we closed the Calabrian coast, that third day in December 1943, to put ashore on the beaches near Reggio the 5th British and 1st Canadian — and one Etonian, Geoffrey Snagge.

Most of us were aware of our flotilla officer's ambition to be aboard the first LCT to beach and then set foot on occupied Europe. To his dismay however, he was detailed off by Rear-Admiral McGrigor to take charge of the loading at Riposto. Somehow he had won the day and persuaded the rear-admiral that the 21st LCT Flotilla required his presence more than Riposto did, and once again he was back aboard 614. As we neared the shore in line abreast, Norman called for an increase in revs; forging slightly ahead of the rest of the craft, he ran 614 gently up the shelving beach. Even before the door was fully down, Geoffrey Snagge was on his way, striding purposefully across the ramp to step foot on the Italian mainland, his ambition fulfilled.

To everyone's relief, no panzers, mines or barbed wire entanglements awaited the troops. By evening, the toe of the peninsula was occupied to a depth of more than five miles. Then the German resistance stiffened as they began their withdrawal up the coast, blowing the roads and demolishing the viaducts and culverts.

For four days and nights every available landing-craft ferried the Eighth Army across the Messina Straits, the crews snatching food and sleep when they could. Despite the fierce currents, wherever able we beached without using the kedge in order to save time. As many as eight times a day we crossed the straits, some craft working on a single engine. Returning from one such crossing, our flotilla officer, who had been at the base in Messina since the Reggio landing, came aboard and informed Norman and me, with a good deal too much enthusiasm for my liking, that another operation was pending. The COs were summoned and briefed. We fuelled ship, took aboard troops and massive rolls of wire mesh and, joining a varied assortment of landing-craft, headed through the neck of the straits out into the Gulf of Gioia, to take part in Operation Ferdy. Later that night we heard on the radio that Italy had surrendered. In a funny sort of way it didn't seem to matter much. The Germans were still there; *they* certainly had not surrendered, as we were shortly to discover.

The operational plan was to land the 231st Infantry Brigade at Vibo Valentia, a small harbour up the coast, in order to cut off the retreating Germans and prevent them reinforcing their armoured troops drawn up around the beaches of Salerno. Captain Black, RN, commanded the naval force, and Brigadier Urquhart, who later commanded the Airborne Division at Arnhem, the 231st Brigade. Their headquarters' ship, LCI 263, sailed in company with seventeen LCTs. In addition there were fourteen LCIs, split into two groups, each LC1 towing two assault craft. In support was an LCG and an LCF, some fifty-five craft in all. Two LSTs were to arrive off the beaches at 05.30.

The night was dark, but fine, a hint of autumn in the air, sufficiently chill for duffel coats. Off our port bow, thirty miles to the north, lay the arid peaks of the Lipari Islands, Salina, Panarea, Vulcano and, just visible, the faint glow of Stromboli. In Greek mythology they were the home of Aeolus, King of the Winds. Some time in the night we passed Cape Vaticano, impossible to distinguish against the black background of the hills. Perceptibly it began to lighten.

"Any idea where we are?" came a cheerful voice from across the water. The army exchanged uneasy glances, as well they might, for they were entirely in our hands. Norman and Snagge ignored the request and continued to gaze at the shore through binoculars: "There's the light," said Snagge and Norman trained his glasses in that direction.

In the grey light of morning we closed the shore, steep hills to our left and a long breakwater flanked by wooded heights to our right. We went in early to get the tracking down for the transport. It seemed quiet enough, ominously so, I thought, as we reached the shore and lowered the door. But, unknown to us, all was not going to plan; the commandos had landed nearly two hours late and three miles from the correct place. Also, unknown to us, the Germans were already occupying the hills above Vibo Valentia.

The troops were wasting no time rolling out the matting, watched by the hands who hung about uneasily, glancing up at the hills, along the shore and out to sea, from where some of the landing-craft were approaching. Norman and Geoffrey Snagge, leaning over the side of the bridge, were also watching and waiting, as was the quarter-deck party clustered round the capstan. We were all watching and waiting and wondering. And then it came, cutting the stillness of the morning, as a high-velocity 88-millimetre shell exploded in the harbour. What followed next was frightening, to put it mildly. The Germans were firing down from our left, and the fact that we had beached nearest the gunfire seemed to our advantage. Doing our best to conceal our desire to get to hell out of it as quickly as possible, we waited for the troops to finish their work, assisting where possible until finally the tank space was clear and the last of the army personnel, a cheerful captain, thanked us for the trip, had wished us well, and walked ashore.

Quickly we slipped astern, the door still coming up, swung round and headed seaward at full speed. Immediately we came under fire, shells bursting abeam, ahead, and in the air. This is it, I thought in a curiously detached way, standing by the starboard oerlikon. I remained rooted to the spot, in the firm belief that were I to shift my position by so much as the slightest movement, the spell of imaginary security I had woven would dissolve, and shrapnel would slice me down. I heard heavy explosions break out to starboard as the LCG opened up with her two 4.7 guns, taking on the enemy batteries and drawing their fire. I was aware of the deck vibrating and smoke pouring from our funnel. I glanced astern. Norman was taking evasive action as we thrashed along, faster than it seemed possible a landing-craft could go. Down below Jock and his two stokers were doing their stuff, doing it so well that the port engine never really recovered. Then we were over the worst and out of it. I don't suppose we had been under fire for more than a few minutes, but it had seemed an eternity. The crew began to emerge warily from below. Cigarettes were lit and we stared in silence across the water at the LCG now taking the full brunt of the enemy's fire.

For thirty-eight minutes LCG 12 engaged the German batteries, drawing their fire and enabling the rest of the landing-craft to escape from the beach. Though hit several times and with one engine put out of action, she still continued firing her two guns. I went up top and joined Norman and Snagge on the bridge. Both had their binoculars trained on the LCG when a shell hit the bridge, killing all the officers and a number of the crew. Now in desperate straits, with no one in command, extensively damaged, both guns out of action, still under heavy fire, Ordinary Seaman T. H. Hills came to the fore and took the crippled LCG out to sea and safety. For such coolness and bravery he was awarded the Conspicuous Gallantry Medal.

We headed back down the coast to Messina, thankful to be out of it, but Operation Ferdy was far from over. No sooner had LCG 12 withdrawn than the monitor, H.M.S. *Erebus*, arrived on the scene and opened up with her two fifteen-inch guns, silencing one of the shore batteries. But the beach still continued to be shelled, and the two L.S.Ts standing offshore were unsuccessfully dive-bombed, though an MTB was sunk and Rear-Admiral McGrigor wounded.

When LST 65 was eventually called in, she was hit repeatedly and set on fire. The CO, Lieutenant-Commander Smith, RNR, increased speed, charged the beach, extinguished the fire, and cleared his jammed doors with a bulldozer. Quickly they got the guns ashore and into action, helping to relieve what was fast becoming a critical situation. The LST was hit repeatedly and abandoned on the beach. The other was more fortunate and beached safely much later.

There remained LCT 702, last of the 21st Flotilla to go in, skippered by Lieutenant Harry Rothwell, a jovial, heavily bearded, piratical-looking character from Accrington. He and his number one, Sub-Lieutenant Bill Palmer, had been instructed to stand off until further orders. They had been loaded up in Messina with cargo of high octane and ammunition. For safety's sake, they had been ordered to keep well astern of the assault force on the passage to Vibo Valentia.

All morning they had waited and watched the harbour being shelled, the reek of high octane hanging in the air, their minds focused on what lay in store when it was their turn to be called in. At last a motor launch approached and the officer in charge instructed them to proceed into harbour: "We are desperately short of fuel and ammunition," he explained apologetically through his loudhailer before wishing them good lock.

They got under way and almost at once came under fire. Attempting evasive action their luck held until, reaching the harbour entrance, they were hit above the waterline in the engine-room. Flashed up by Aldis lamp, the Beach Master directed them to a hard where they lowered the door and secured with headropes. Still shells continued to burst in the harbour, some so close to 702 that the Beach Master signalled Harry and his crew to come ashore and find cover. They did not need telling twice and the crew took refuge in shell craters. When night fell and things eased somewhat, the army unloaded their lethal cargo and the crew returned aboard.

At first light the Beach Master requested Harry to take forty wounded soldiers — some very bad indeed — out to the hospital ship lying offshore. Carried aboard on stretchers, they were laid gently on the deck of the tank space, while the crew watched silently.

Flying a large Red Cross flag — which was just as well, for shells were still falling — 702 left harbour, this time unscathed, made contact with the hospital ship five miles out and came alongside. At once medical officers and orderlies came down into the tank space, did what they could for the wounded, two of whom had died, and then regretfully informed Harry they were unable to take aboard any more casualties since the hospital ship was crammed to capacity: "But we'll notify Messina so they'll be prepared for your arrival."

Ten hours later 702 entered Messina; the wounded were quickly taken ashore and, after a night's rest, Harry and his crew were on their way to Malta for repairs.

No sooner had we returned to Messina than Snagge was ashore and back with news that we were sailing for Salerno. "Apparently things are going badly," he announced briefly. It had not gone all that well at Vibo Valentia, I thought, as we took aboard troops and trucks and prepared to leave harbour.

Twenty-four hours later, the distant rumble of gunfire filled our ears again. Soon the sky ahead was pitted with black specks, the tethered balloons evidence of the huge concourse of shipping awaiting us in the Gulf of Salerno. It was September 12, three days after the initial landings, which the Germans under Kesselring had fiercely opposed. The American general, for some extraordinary reason, had refused to make a preliminary bombardment, relying, despite persistent advice to the contrary, on the element of surprise. The initial assault, beneath a brilliant moon and a calm sea, had proved all but disastrous, for the Germans, aware of what was about to happen, were prepared and waiting, and from the start it had been touch and go, as General Mark Clark's men came under intense fire. The shoreline bristled with light and heavy machine-guns, interspersed with quadruple 20mm anti-aircraft guns, their barrels depressed on the American infantry, while 75mm and the dreaded 88mm guns fired from emplacements in the sand-dunes. In support, platoons of tanks and Panzer Grenadiers launched counter-attacks. From the foothills, batteries of mobile and self-propelled artillery fired down on the beaches and landing-craft. The decision to have no preliminary bombardment proved to be a dreadful error.

Flashed up and instructed to secure alongside one of dozens of Liberty ships lying in the huge anchorage several miles out in the Gulf, we began taking aboard ammunition, loading up the trucks, ferrying them ashore, working round the clock, running the gauntlet of low-flying attacks during the day, high-flying attacks on the centre of the shipping at night. Once, a thick smoke-screen enveloped and all but choked us when we were lying on the beach, forcing those on deck to wear gas-masks — it was the only time I ever put one on, and pretty ineffectual it proved. The alert would go, though more often than not the sole warning would be a sudden outbreak of gunfire, followed by a deafening barrage, as every ship in the gulf blazed away at enemy planes streaking across the sky, chased by long lines of tracer and bursting shells. Frequent though these raids were, they never lasted long and, surprisingly, most of the German fighter bombers seemed to get through unscathed.

On another occasion, enemy planes swept low along the shoreline, taking us all by surprise, dropping their bombs too close by far for anyone's liking, particularly our unloading party of Basutos, happy sorts, who suddenly decided they'd had enough and disappeared ashore — very sensibly, I thought — though Snagge didn't share my view.

"Can't have this," he said, strapping a revolver-belt round his waist. Almost before the next raid had begun, he was up on the door guarding the exit to the beach. Equally quickly the unloading party, aware but quite undeterred by the figure up for'ard, jumped over 614's side and waded ashore, and there was little our flotilla officer could do about it, other than greet their smiling faces on return with a few words of rebuke.

Assigned to another Liberty ship and with a fresh lot of empty trucks in the tank space, we found the *Howard Marshal* lying anchored four miles offshore on the outside of the anchorage. After repeated shouts from our fo'c'sle party: "Up top, up top," and a few misses with our heaving lines — which irritated Norman, who was having some difficulty bringing 614 alongside in the strong wind — American sailors eventually emerged from above, took our ropes, and we made fast, astern of a Mark III LCT unloading the Liberty ship's for'ard hold. In heavy nets, crates of mortar shells were swung over the Liberty ship's side, lowered and stowed in the empty trucks by the troops.

Stand Easy over, I left the ward-room and went out to see how things were going. Snagge had gone up on the bridge. A rope ladder hung down the ship's side reaching our quarter-deck.

"See if you can get some fresh bread," Norman suggested. I was halfway up the narrow ladder, when gunfire broke out and a line of ME 109s roared overhead releasing their bombs. I was down a good deal faster than I was going up.

"Bit close," said Norman, tugging at his beard. Most of the crew were on deck, some smoking, all of us waiting tensely to see whether that was it for the time being. It usually was. Flanked on one side by the great steel wall of the *Howard Marshal*, and consequently unable to fire our oerlikons, we felt about as helpless and vulnerable as a sacrificial offering tethered to a stake.

There was a shout from above. "Captain," the skipper of the *Howard Marshal* called down: "I'm gonna shift. We're getting picked off." A fair enough comment in the light of what had just happened.

"If you move into the centre you're more likely to get hit at night," advised Snagge from the bridge.

"That may be your point of view, Captain, but I shall let go your ropes all the same," insisted their skipper.

"They badly need ammunition ashore," argued Snagge in vain.

"Start up the engines," Norman ordered Murray. When our head and stern ropes had been cast off from above, we made for the distant shore, our trucks half full of ammunition.

Towards midnight a long and heavy high-level air raid began. Still on the beach we donned tin hats and watched the slow descending flares light the scene, the red tracer drifting lazily into the night sky while the guns of warships and merchantmen flashed and thundered up at the enemy overhead. In the midst of it all, an explosion, volcanic in its magnitude, rocketed into the night: "Some poor bugger's bought it," said a member of the crew. We learnt in the morning it was the *Howard Marshwl.*

On 14 September things were going badly ashore. The Germans had created a salient dangerously near the beach, and the American general was considering evacuating the troops. Admiral Hewitt, RN, had urgently requested the Admiral of the Fleet, Cunningham, to send heavy ships to bombard the mainland.

At dawn the following day, the battleships *Valiant* and *Warspite,* escorted by destroyers, came up from Malta. Later in the afternoon, lying two miles outside the shipping, her silhouette unmistakable, *Warspite* began firing broadsides, her eight massive 15-inch guns hurling shells inland nearly a ton in weight, up to a range of 18 miles. It did the trick, forced the Germans to keep their heads down, and restored American morale as they renewed their efforts to capture Altavilla.

But there was a penalty to pay, for the Luftwaffe immediately intensified their attacks on the shipping. There was also a rumour abroad that the Germans possessed a radio-controlled bomb.

Throughout the following morning a series of enemy raids swept over the Gulf, keeping the AA crews on their toes. We had come off the beach in the early afternoon and were threading our way through the merchantmen, searching for our next assignment, when another attack began. It was then, when the guns' crews were once more heavily engaged, that rumour became fact. Fifteen thousand feet overhead five FW 190s, each carrying a glider bomb, were approaching their target, the *Warspite.* Of the four guided missiles released, two scored direct hits on the thirty-eight thousand-ton battleship, while two burst close to her hull. We could see the great ship clearly as a cloud of smoke enveloped her. Slowly she turned and headed seaward, but with two thousand tons of water aboard, her boilers collapsed. Taken in tow by two tugs and with an escort of five destroyers and three cruisers, she eventually made Malta. Strangely, the Luftwaffe did not follow up their initial success. As for *Warspite,* she was repaired and later served in the Normandy landings, while *Valiant,* after a short bombardment, sailed for Malta later that same day.

We continued to unload, running from ship to shore, until ordered to take aboard Bren carriers and infantry and land them at Maiori, a fishing village to the north of Salerno where US Rangers and British commandos — the latter had landed at Victri seven miles south of Maiori — were having a rough time. On the short passage up we passed seaward of the veteran monitor, H.M.S. *Roberts,* lying astonishingly close inshore, her two fifteen-inch guns firing salvoes. Like fiery comets the shells were exploding in the rugged hills inland, where the Germans were fiercely countering the American and British attempts to capture the high ground over Salerno, and to secure the mountain passes leading to the highway into Naples.

By September 20 the Battle of Salerno was over and on October 1 the Allies were in Naples. But by then we were back in Messina, Snagge ashore, and we were ferrying the military across the Straits to Reggio. Winter was approaching, the weather worsening. The watertight doors had been damaged and would not close. Crossing one morning, with the sea rough and the tank space crammed with transport right to our 'bows', the great door suddenly fell with a shuddering crash and water poured aboard. It was a nasty moment, particularly for those in the foremost vehicle, who found themselves confronted by a gaping void, the sea washing around them. In seconds the troops were out of their trucks and standing on the catwalks, staring in disbelief at what had happened. Reducing speed immediately, Norman brought 614 slowly round and we headed sluggish and low in the water for Messina. Once back, it took several hours and a good deal of ingenuity to raise the door. From my point of view, it was a good thing Geoffrey Snagge had not been aboard, for it was my responsibility to see that the door was secure when raised. That the 'dogs' were bent and no longer functioned was no excuse. I had assumed, and not checked, that the winch party had secured the brakes on the drums. Since leaving England we had successfully lowered and raised the door a hundred times and more without incident. Norman did not criticise me — he seldom did — and I learnt a lesson.

We got under way again, crossed the Straits and continued doing so until well into November — and I always kept an eye open for Homer's legendary whirlpool. Once, when the current was strong and the sea rough, the overfalls to port took on a glassy quality, the surface of the water circling and swirling in a most sinister fashion. Could this have been Ulysses' Charybdis? I like to think so. On the Italian side of the Straits of Messina lie the other trap for those ancient Greek sailors of the *Odyssey* — the rocks of Scylla — hurled down at them by the one-eyed Cyclops. Were the rocks, I wonder, but huge boulders flung from the erupting bowels of Etna?

By now we were often running on one engine only, the other was breaking down with increasing regularity. Finally it packed up altogether. After the flotilla engineer had examined it, drunk most of our whisky and advised a major refit, we were ordered to sail forthwith for Malta and given a Byms trawler as escort. It was a passage none of us would forget.

It was a murky old day when we set forth the following forenoon in the wake of our escort, a shapely vessel with a high freeboard. None of us was particularly sorry to be leaving Messina.

Rounding the point on our surviving engine, leaden clouds low over the hills above the ruins of the harbour, we headed down the familiar coastline, the wind strong, the sea turbulent, but our spirits were high at the prospect of Malta and all the things awaiting us, fresh grub, all nights in and runs ashore.

In vain Norman and I searched the shoreline with binoculars for Cape d'Ali, where we had landed commandos of the 4th Armoured Brigade back in August. Soon we came abeam of Taormina perched high on the cliffs, in the background the slopes of Etna sweeping upward to its snow-capped summit, stark beneath a dark, ominous sky, and all the while the wind was increasing, conditions worsening.

We struggled on down the Sicilian coast, past Catania, Augusta and Syracuse, the land barely visible in the gathering storm. Approaching Cape Passero we altered course for Malta. But that was as far as we got; for now we were gripped in the teeth of a full-blooded gale, encountering weather against which we could make no headway. The seas were steeper, more relentless than the great Atlantic rollers we had met on the passage out, and it was all the coxswain could do to keep 614 from broaching. Indeed the whole landing-craft so shook, shuddered, and bent her back that it seemed she would break in two at any moment. I caught Norman's eye as he tugged at his beard: "We're not going to make it," he said, more to himself than to me. Turning to our bunts who, in anticipation, had already taken his Aldis lamp from the chart table, "Make to the escort — 'Impossible to proceed. Request tow.'"

"Stand by," came the reply.

I left the bridge. With three seamen, I went for'ard along the tank space, for safety's sake, and clambered onto the narrow starboard fo'c'sle where we hung on grimly to the guard-rails, one moment lifted high, the next plunged deep into a trough. I would have felt a good deal happier had the 'dogs' functioned, for the door was under fearful strain, scooping aboard green seas, our blunt bows staggering to lift the dead weight before despatching the water back into the tank space, from where it eventually escaped through the non-return valves. The wind and heavy driving spray lashed our oilskins, forcing us to turn our heads, shield our faces, and hang on more tightly than ever. A man overboard in such conditions was unthinkable. Nor did I believe a tow was possible.

Our escort meanwhile had fallen back and was keeping station off our starboard bow, though just ahead, for we were yawing wildly. We watched a small group on the quarter-deck of the pitching trawler preparing the tow. A petty officer pointed a gun in our direction, and we heard a faint muffled bang borne on the wind, as a line fell across our shoulders. Quickly we hauled it in and the attached grass, at the end of which was bent on the tow itself, a huge ten-inch manilla, joined to a wire hawser and a further length of manilla. Hauling in the grass, striving to keep our feet on that narrow heaving platform, we fought every inch of the way to get the manilla aboard and secured to the bollards.

No sooner had we succeeded, than 614 was swept broadside to the seas which now broke onto the catwalk, cascading into the tank space. But at least we knew she was safe from breaking her back in this predicament. The escort, burying her bows and lifting her stern high, began to take up the slack. The tow straightened, the wire hawser emerged from the waves, became bar taut and, with a sudden jerk, parted, its two ends whipping into the air before disappearing beneath the frenzied surface.

We hauled in what was left of the tow, then made our way aft down the flooded tank space. While the hands took refuge in the wheelhouse I joined Norman on the bridge. "It'll never work," I shouted above the wind, a comment he acknowledged with a brief nod.

The escort was flashing us again, this time requesting we bring 614 round into the seas, a hopeless task, as well we knew. "Make back — 'Not possible'," Norman ordered tersely.

Slowly the trawler began turning in an endeavour to keep us company. As she came beam on, a sea lifted and rolled her so far over that for one desperate moment it seemed she would bury her bridge. There was an urgent flurry of white beneath her stern as she increased speed and fought her way back into the teeth of the gale. Through the fast fading light her lamp began winking. "Impossible to stay with you. Good luck."

"Make back — 'Understand. See you in Malta'," instructed Norman, and with that we parted, each forced to go our separate ways into the black hell of that howling wilderness. Like a log awash, 614 wallowed, little by little, towards the east some fifty miles south of Cape Spartivento, while our escort, stemming the seas, headed for Malta. That was the last we saw of each other.

None of us will forget that night. We wore life-jackets, though God knows what use they would have been. We lost both flotta nets, a Carley raft and the starboard hatch cover. The seas, running express and level with our bridge, bore down on us, their crests hissing and threatening in the dark as they broke against our sides, flooding the tank space.

Yet somehow 614 rose to stagger on, the watch on deck in the wheelhouse, the rest below, all of us wedging ourselves against the savage, unpredictable motion of the landing-craft, while up on the bridge the shriek of the wind, the roar of the sea and the pitch blackness of the night engulfed us. It seemed endless.

But when that first glimmer of light appeared low in the east, it was sufficient to lift our spirits. As dawn broke fully to expose a desolate heaving expanse of grey, no land was visible to the eye, no ship in sight. But the anger had gone from the wind and the sea was beginning to subside. By the middle of the forenoon the clouds were breaking up, and shafts of sunlight and patches of blue sky were colouring the sea. Soon we were able to turn and head for our destination. Late that night we entered Malta and beached on Sliema. Then we slept.

Our stay in Malta turned out not as we had hoped. The racket of riveting and the general discomfort of being in dry-dock, coupled with the fact that most of us had lost some, if not all our 'rabbits', despite warnings to keep personal possessions under lock and key, did not help. To make matters worse, I fell ill with Malta Dog, a form of dysentery, which I had also contracted prior to the Sicily landing.

It was a relief to all when we came out of dry-dock, but for me short-lived, since Norman, on returning from a visit to the base, announced out of the blue that he was leaving 614 immediately, "I've been given command of a Flak Ship," he said, placing his cap carefully on the ward-room table, "LCF 26."

I congratulated him, but my heart sank at the prospect of change, for I liked Norman and we had got on well together. I still recall his bearded, slightly pinched face peering over the bridge, and his extraordinary belly flops from the LCT's side as we swam on those hot evenings in Augusta Bay before the night air raids began. Oblivious to the crew's watching eyes, he would launch his tall, thin, astonishingly hirsute body into the air, his legs and arms outstretched, resembling some flying ape, hitting the surface with a resounding smack.

"Lieutenant Bungy Williams is taking over, but I've not met him, so I can't tell you much." Like most actors, Norman had read my thoughts and knew how I felt.

Bungy arrived that afternoon. He had begun life as an air gunner in the Fleet Air Arm and then joined H.M.S. *Campion*, working out of Liverpool with the 36th escort group on Gibraltar convoys. His first command was a Mark III Landing-craft picked up in the Clyde. Coming down the west coast they experienced a severe storm in the Irish Sea. More fortunate than several others whose craft had sunk beneath them, Bungy and his crew made Milford Haven and safety. He was not so lucky during the Sicily landings when he lost his Mark III LCT. Outwardly shrewd in appearance, yet with an amused, slightly quizzical expression, and a twinkle in his eye, he gave an impression of competence without being over-serious.

In dry-dock we'd had stanchions fitted on the bridge and quarterdeck, in order to rig awnings for the summer months ahead. As Bungy wandered around informally meeting the crew, he suggested to me we might begin making the awnings now.

"Be a good idea. I think we should start painting ship as well," he added, looking about him. He was right, of course, nothing of that kind had been done since leaving England.

At the end of January 1944, looking spick and span and with our new awning over the bridge, we sailed for Naples.

The passage was uneventful, the weather, for the time of year, kind. We did not put into Messina, nor did I see Charybdis or Scylla. We spotted the wrecked LST lying on the beach off Vibo Valentia, crossed the Gulf of Salerno, now devoid of shipping, and stared long and curiously at the island of Capri. Rounding Castellammare we headed for Naples, its magnificent sweep of bay dominated by Vesuvius. But we were to see little of the place, being destined for elsewhere — Anzio.

Chapter 8

Anzio, Elba, South of France

IN THE EARLY HOURS of 22 January 1944 the first wave of assault craft had gone in after rocket ships had blasted the Anzio beaches clear of mines. Operation Shingle had achieved almost complete surprise. By the following day, vehicles and stores were safely inside the beachhead, very different from Salerno. But after that things began to go drastically wrong.

Nobody explained to us why there had to be a landing at Anzio. All we picked up was first-hand evidence from our colleagues who had been up there and returned for a spell of rest on the Isle of Ischia.

"Bloody awful," said Ian McNab, whose Mark III had been hit, "shelling, bombing, radio-controlled missiles, the lot. They sank the destroyer, *Janus*, and the hospital ship, *St David*. And there's Anzio Annie, a bloody great thing on rails that comes out of a tunnel near Rome, fires a fifteen-inch shell into the harbour, and disappears back before the RAF can get at it."

The truth of the matter was that the Italian campaign had become a stalemate. It was hoped that the landing at Anzio, conceived by Churchill, might break the deadlock. The Allied offensive had ground to a standstill on the two rivers that blocked their path, the Garigliano and the Sangro. Behind these rivers the Germans had rapidly improved the defences of the Gustav Line, which stretched across Italy from the Aurunci mountains to Ortona, from the Tyrrhenian Sea to the Adriatic. A landing behind this line would present the Germans with a serious threat, for whichever way they moved would leave the way open for an Allied breakthrough. If they defended against a frontal attack, the Allies in Anzio would be able to advance on Rome; if the Germans counter-attacked against the landing at Anzio, the Gustav Line of defence would be weakened. That, in broad outline, was the theory. One further fearful obstacle lay in the path of the Allies. The road from Naples to Rome passed through the Gustav Line beneath a mountain, whose name was to become synonymous with the war in Italy — Monte Cassino.

We sailed from Naples in daylight and made our way up the Tyrhennian coast, none of us looking forward to what lay ahead. Night had fallen when we passed the front line. Over to starboard we could see the flash of gunfire inland. Forty miles further on, the familiar specks of barrage-balloons and shipping unfolded; eventually the port of Anzio came into view. As we drew near we saw the extent of the damage.

We began at once to ferry supplies from ship to shore, while every so often the Germans bombed the anchorage and harbour. Several times a day a great deafening blast shattered our nerves, as Anzio Annie loosed a shell into the vicinity. We'd listen and sometimes catch the sound of the next shell being fired. Seconds later there'd be another whoosh, and explosion, and that would be it for the time being.

It was a testing time for all of us, and one of our crew temporarily lost control and disappeared ashore. He quickly found it no place to be and was glad to be back aboard.

Inland, the Allies were fighting a long bitter battle to hold the bridgehead. Initially the way had been wide open for an unopposed advance on Rome. But General Lucas, the American, was cautious, remembering his experiences at Salerno, where his troops had nearly been driven back into the sea. His aim at Anzio — from the start he had never been in favour of the operation — was to establish the bridgehead before extending his lines of communication. This was not Churchill's or Alexander's intention, and eventually the American general was relieved of his command. He may well have been right, but his caution gave Kesselring time to organise a counter-attack with great success, penning the British and Americans into the bridgehead, so that it quickly became another stalemate, the troops fighting a static form of trench warfare in cruel winter conditions.

Day and night we continued to ferry in supplies, mostly ammunition or high octane, only too glad to rid ourselves of the stuff and get out of harbour as quickly as possible.

Once we were assigned to take aboard food and NAAFI stores. This was a bonus every landing-craft looked forward to, since it provided an opportunity to supplement one's own food stocks. The night was a cold and dark one, full of wind and rain, and we had to double up our head and stern ropes, since we were surging and banging uncomfortably against the side of the American Liberty ship despite our fenders. The supplies in wooden crates were lowered quickly in rope slings and dumped unceremoniously into our tank space, causing many to split open revealing their contents, tins of food, turkey and other meats, as well as pineapple, peaches, beer and cigarettes. By dawn our hold was full of American stores, infinitely preferable to the British offerings of 'tinned dog', spam, powdered egg and VE cigarettes.

Bungy had chatted with me beforehand and decided we should top up our own food supplies, "But only in moderation," he warned, "and they must not touch any spirits or make pigs of themselves — though mind you," he added, with a grin, "if you spot a bottle of Scotch lying around, I don't see why we shouldn't help ourselves to a drink. Anyway, have a word with the coxswain," which I did.

"Don't overdo it," I instructed him. "You can put aside a bit of stuff that's sculling around and a few tins of beer, that's all right, but on no account is anyone to touch the whisky or gin. Is that quite clear, Coxswain?"

"Aye, aye, sir," he acknowledged in that gravelly voice I had grown to know so well and dislike, "Just leave it to me, sir." I should have known better.

We were in the ward-room eating our lunch, anchored off Yellow Beach the following day having offloaded our cargo, both of us enjoying a plate of American tinned turkey, as were the crew, when the quartermaster knocked and informed us that an army officer had come aboard and wanted to speak to the captain. "He's got two redcaps with him," he added, which all but caused Bungy to choke on a piece of turkey.

"Tell him I'll be out in a moment."

"Aye, aye, sir."

"What the hell do they want?" said Bungy, reaching for his cap, "See if you can find out what you can."

I followed Bungy through the wheelhouse and went down onto the mess deck: "There's an army officer and two redcaps up top," I told the crew. "You haven't stashed away a lot of stuff, have you?"

"Better not take them down the port locker," said the coxswain after a lengthy pause.

"Why?"

"There's some crates of gin down there, sir."

"Good God," I exploded. "Have you taken anything else?"

"Better not take them down the starboard locker, sir," said the coxswain.

"What's down there?"

"Crates of whisky, sir."

"Bloody hell. Anywhere else? Anything down here?"

"No, sir."

"Anything in your kitbags, your lockers, anywhere down here?"

"No, sir."

"Anything in the engine-room, the bilges?"

"No sir," said the chief motor mechanic.

"That's it?"

"Yes, sir."

"Right. So I can show them everything except the port and starboard lockers."

"Better not show them into the food locker up for'ard, sir," said Salmon the cook.

"Oh, for Heaven's sake, what's up there?"

"Crates of food and beer, sir."

I could say no more, but went up top with a sinking feeling. The army captain and his two redcaps were hanging about on the quarterdeck. Bungy was in the ward-room: "They want to search ship," he said, and I told him the bad news.

"We've had it then," he said quietly and with considerable concern, "Well, you'll simply have to show them around and try and avoid the port and starboard lockers." I nodded and went outside.

"Right," I said to our three unwanted visitors. "Follow me." I took them down onto the mess deck and made the crew open their kitbags and lockers, and did as thorough and prolonged a search as possible. I took them into the engine-room and opened up the bilges. I took them into the pongos' shelter and the extra cabin. I showed them the paint locker, coal locker, washroom and every conceivable space I could think of, staying clear of the port and starboard lockers down the catwalks.

"Well, that's it," I said, coming out of the pongos' shelter.

The army captain was looking down the length of the tank space: "What's up there?" he asked.

"The winch spaces."

"Can we have a look?" He had been pleasant enough, though I can't say I liked the look of one of the redcaps.

"Of course," I said, trying to appear unconcerned, and we walked down the length of the hold and entered the dark empty starboard winch space. As we emerged, the redcap

I had taken a dislike to had, of his own initiative, looked into the port winch space.

"There's some stuff here, sir," he called out and my heart sank. He had found some crates of tinned food.

"And what's behind that door?" enquired the army captain.

"Our food stores," I told him.

"May I have a look?"

"Of course," and I sent for Salmon the cook who had the keys: "Open the door, Salmon," I instructed him. Momentarily he stared at me, his mouth ajar, "Open the door, Salmon," I repeated and this time he did, clearing a path with difficulty to reveal a locker chock-a-block with more American goodies — and that was that.

The military police proceeded to make an inventory of the stuff and then departed, no doubt to make their report to NOIC, Anzio. I joined Bungy in the ward-room and I could see how angry and upset he was.

"At any rate we managed to steer clear of the port and starboard lockers. They didn't find the whisky and gin," I told him.

"No, thank God," he said and promptly sent for the coxswain.

"You were given strict instructions, Coxswain, by the First Lieutenant to take only tins of food that had come adrift, from boxes that had broken open in the process of loading."

"Yes, sir."

"Then how do you account for those boxes up for'ard in the port winch space and the food locker?"

"We didn't realise we had knocked that much off, sir."

"Oh, come off it, you realised what you were doing when you took those crates of whisky and gin down the port and starboard lockers. You were told specifically on no account to touch any spirits."

"I know, sir, but the First Lieutenant did tell me we could knock off some stuff."

"Within reason, Coxswain, as you well know, and only from crates that had split open."

"It wasn't much, sir, when you think we had a whole tank space full. You'd hardly notice it."

"Well, somebody bloody well did, Coxswain, and reported it," and Bungy gave him a long hard stare: "Right, you may carry on."

"Aye, aye, sir."

"A lower deck lawyer if ever there was one," said Bungy quietly as the door closed.

That night, still anchored off Yellow Beach, we ditched thirteen crates of whisky and eleven crates of gin, and I've no doubt they are there to this day.

The following morning we were called into harbour. The illicit pile of crates, testimony to our misdeeds of the previous night, lay stacked between the two winch spaces at the far end of the tank space. From the bridge it was impossible not to be aware of them, and we both agreed that the pile seemed somehow to be smaller, the number of crates to have diminished somewhat.

"You don't think that bloody coxswain's been at it *again?*" said Bungy as I climbed out of the bridge to go for'ard and lower the door.

We continued ferrying in supplies, but no more NAAFI stores. Making our way out to the anchorage one day, we were caught in the path of a sneak low-level air attack. We saw the bombs falling, small, black, evil-looking objects, and it seemed inconceivable that they would miss us. We threw ourselves down as they exploded astern, causing 614 to lift and shudder violently. Shaken, we got to our feet.

"That was close," I said, joining Bungy on the bridge.

He nodded, "I rather hoped they'd hit us," he said with a wan smile, and I knew then, if not before, the extent of his concern.

A week later a court of enquiry was held in our ward-room. We were warned that anything we might say would be taken down and used in evidence. Bungy made a brief statement, and I was asked why I had not discovered the crates when I had carried out rounds, which in our present circumstances was as absurd as it was unreasonable. The Coxswain was then sent for and, when questioned, explained that he had been told they could take some stuff.

"Who told you that you could take some stuff?"

"The First Lieutenant, sir." I watched it being written down.

The cook was sent for next, but he didn't know anything, nor did the rest of the crew who, almost before they had entered the wardroom, were shaking their heads and denying knowledge.

Finally the court asked to see the scene of the crime, and we all filtered down the tank space and squeezed into the port locker. Peering into the winch itself, the senior officer suddenly plunged his arm into the workings and, as though plucking a rabbit from a hat, pulled out a bottle of whisky which he handed to my commanding officer without a word. They were not unfriendly towards us.

"Well, that's it," said Bungy when they had gone, "there's nothing we can do about it, but await the findings," and he opened our newly acquired bottle of Scotch and poured out two stiff drinks.

Unlike the other LCTs and crews who were in due course recalled to Naples to enjoy a spell at a rest camp on the Isle of Ischia, we stayed on through February and into March, no doubt in our minds that it was to do with the NAAFI stores.

Throughout February the Germans fiercely attempted to pierce the bridgehead at Anzio, and very nearly succeeded. But by March they had begun to dig themselves in and prepare for the spring offensive, which they knew was bound to come. On the 15th of February Monte Cassino was heavily bombed which, ironically, gave more effective cover to the Germans who, after 350 tons of bombs had fallen on the monastery, moved forward to occupy the ruins in force, preventing the 15th Allied Army Group from joining up with the Anzio beach-head until late May. Consequently both the Gustav line and front at Anzio remained static.

The harbour was bombed regularly. Anzio Annie continued at intervals to emerge from her railway tunnel and deliver her salvo while the troops, existing in holes, kept their heads down and waited for winter to pass and a breakout from the beach-head to begin.

At last, towards the end of March we were recalled, though not before a final odd incident. There had been one of those short, sharp, air attacks, over almost before the guns could be brought to bear, when a lone plane was seen approaching several seconds later. The oncoming aircraft took the full brunt of the flak and was shot down. The pilot baled out and we watched him fall, waiting for his chute to open. It never did. A strong buzz quickly went the rounds that we had shot down a Spitfire. But when the body was recovered, it proved to be that of a German pilot. The following day we sailed for Naples.

The findings of the court of enquiry pointed a finger at the First Lieutenant and Coxswain of 614. I was summoned before FOIC Naples, reprimanded and informed I was to be transferred to another landing-craft, none other than 582. For Bungy it was a great relief that the matter was now over, for myself, I felt fortunate to be joining Johnny Harrison and his crew again. The coxswain of 614 went elsewhere.

The first person I met on boarding 582 had to be Stoker Jones, who was leaning over the guard-rail clad in his customary white singlet. He seemed to know I was coming and expressed no surprise. "Welcome back, sir," he said, taking my case, and I followed him into the wheelhouse.

"Thank you, Jones," I said and entered the ward-room.

"I hope you've bloody well brought a bottle or two of Scotch with you," Johnny Harrison greeted me in his usual forthright manner. He knew all about the court of enquiry and I immediately felt at home.

We remained in Naples throughout April. The previous month Vesuvius had erupted violently and was still belching forth smoke and molten rock, while overhead a cloak of grey enveloped the surroundings, shutting out the sun. I saw *Tosca* twice at the San Carlo Opera House and wandered the narrow, malodorous and poverty-ridden streets off the Via Roma, draped with washing hanging from windows overhead. On several occasions I visited the Orange Grove, an officers' club, high up and overlooking the bay, where British and Americans drank and chatted noisily to the strains of 'Lili Marlene', sung by a strikingly voluptuous woman reputed to have been the mistress of one of the German High Command. And all the while Vesuvius brooded menacingly above that great curving coastline that stretches from Naples to Castellammare and onward across the blue sea to the Isle of Capri.

May brushed aside the last bitter weeks of winter and, with the sun once more warm on our backs and spring in the air, we sailed in a convoy of Mark IVs and IIIs to Porto Vecchio on the south-west coast of Corsica. There we dropped our hooks in calm, secluded waters, surrounded by pale yellow cliffs and rugged mountains.

The great offensive by the Fifth and Eighth Armies to break the Gustav Line began towards midnight on May 11th. By the 23rd, the British and Americans had penetrated the German defences around Anzio and the approach to Rome lay open.

Prior to this, plans had been made to deceive the Germans as to where and when the attack was to take place. One of these involved repeated reconnaissance flights to the north of Rome, to create an impression that an Allied landing was imminent in the vicinity. With this in mind, two flotillas of LCTs headed across the Tyrrhenian Sea for Civitavecchia, in the hope that our presence would lead to a German withdrawal of troops from their front lines.

In fact we had no sight of the enemy and whether or not the dummy run on Civitavecchia had any effect we were never to know. I suspect not. Returning in fine weather — most of us had our heads down — the long column of LCTs filed past the flagship in which Rear-Admiral Troubridge — his grandfather had been Nelson's Flag Lieutenant at Trafalgar — now stood on the bridge awaiting the ceremonial pipes that were his due. He never received them. In no time the commanding officers were informed that the Rear-Admiral was far from pleased with what he had witnessed. Apparently one landing-craft had passed flying the ensign upside down and another flew no ensign at all. One had a meaningless hoist at the yard-arm, while several had dhobying strung across the quarter-deck. One LCT passed by with no sign of life at all, whereas another actually did pipe the admiral, but it was clear to his experienced ear it was not done with a bosun's whistle. We were promptly summoned forth again and made to pay our respects properly this time, with hands fell in fore and aft and the long shrill pipe of the bosun's whistles in our ears.

We pushed on up Corsica's east coast to our next port of call, Bastia, where preparations were under way for an amphibious attack on the island of Elba — Operation Brassard. On 17 June, Mark IVs and IIIs sailed in convoy with a force consisting of the 9th French Colonial Infantry Division – reinforced by the Bataillon de Choc and French commandos – transported in British landing-craft. Destroyers, gunboats and coastal forces covered the operation. On this occasion we carried mules and Ghoums, fierce-looking fighting men from north Africa, clad in long robes; in charge were two French officers. In addition two French nurses joined us, much to everyone's delight. At the head of each column of craft was an HDML with paravanes streamed to sweep the approaches. As we drew near, a mine bobbed slowly down between the columns of landing-craft, to be despatched by a burst of oerlikon fire from the end LCTs.

All morning we lay offshore waiting our turn to be called in. The two nurses, when not in the ward-room, spent their time up on the bridge watching the movement of craft, a thick pall of smoke hanging over the shoreline, the noise of battle in the air.

The initial landings took place at first light in the Golfo di Campo on Elba's south coast. It was known that a heavily armed German flak ship lay alongside the short, low-walled jetty of Marina di Campo, guarding the sector of beach where the French were to land. The intention was to put the enemy craft out of action with a boarding party of RN commandos. Fifty of them, in two LCAs, were to approach the seaward side of the jetty and, using ladders, storm the wall and capture the enemy ship. Unfortunately, it all went horribly wrong because surprise was lost. The first assault craft was hit and ran onto rocks close to the jetty. The second, under heavy fire, got alongside the jetty and boarded the craft. After hand to hand fighting, the Germans abandoned the flak ship, which was detonated from the shore, killing twenty-seven commandos and wounding many others.

The initial attempt by LCIs to land their Senegalese troops encountered a hail of phosphorus shells, mortar and artillery fire, and they were forced to withdraw. Eventually, under cover of a smokescreen and heavy fire from the support forces, a landing was effected, led in by HDMLs, one of which, 1301, was hit, killing the CO and wounding the first lieutenant. When it was the turn of the first group of LCTs to land, their escort, LCF15, struck a mine and sank. Heavy fighting continued until the battery on Ponto di Campo was captured by the Bataillon de Choc. By 07.30 four battalions of infantry were ashore and had made contact with the Bataillon de Choc and the commandos. By 14.30 the village of Marina di Campo was taken and we were called in to land our mules and Ghoums.

Approaching the small land-locked bay, flanked by cliffs, the rumble of gunfire reverberated round the steep wooded hills, as the battle proceeded inland. An LCI passed us by, heading seaward, smoke pouring from a hole in her side. The two nurses stared in silence. We beached and lowered the door alongside 581. Bearing their enormous loads our mules trotted ashore, leaving behind a stinking and fouled tank space. I heard the skipper of 581, Les Baxter, shout to his number one up for'ard to get the door up. Detailed off to take casualties, they had been on the beach for some time while their surgeon-lieutenant RNVR, an Egyptian who had sailed with them, established the casualty situation ashore.

At the last moment when all the stretcher cases and walking wounded were finally aboard, and everyone was impatient to get away before their luck ran out, one of the Ghoums, head bandaged, walked across the ramp onto the beach, lifted his robe and relieved himself.

"What the hell's going on?" Les Baxter called out again to Jimmy Danson.

"He's having a crap," he shouted back, pointing to the squatting figure on the beach.

"Well, tell him to bloody well hurry up," came the reply.

"See you in Bastia," said Jimmy, as 581 slipped astern, though not without the Ghoum, I'm glad to say.

Alongside the wrecked jetty lay the scuttled German Flak ship. Threading their way across the congested beach, a file of German prisoners approached, escorted by Ghoums. A scuffle broke out as a guard, for no apparent reason, struck one of them with the butt of his rifle. They looked resigned and dejected as they crossed 582's ramp and entered our tank space. It was the first time we had come face to face with the enemy.

Within two days the Germans had been driven into the northeast corner of the island and all organised resistance ceased, though the Bataillon de Choc continued mopping up operations in the mountains, and they did not take many prisoners. Entirely a French-organised assault, it was ill-conceived, badly planned, with no preliminary softening-up process. Yet again the element of surprise had been relied upon; as at Salerno, it had not come off. The casualties were high, and Operation Brassard was a grim and costly affair. In retrospect, it is hard to find any justification for the invasion of Elba; the island presented neither threat nor obstacle.

Once more it was back to Messina, not a place I particularly liked, for the blitzed port had little to offer those seeking a run ashore. But there was mail awaiting us and the prospect of a spell of leave at Taormina, a prewar haven for Europe's rich. I went first, taking some of the ship's company with me. I stayed in the San Dominico hotel perched high on the cliffs of Taormina overlooking the Mediterranean. There was a balcony to my bedroom and, across seventeen miles of water, the toe of Italy shimmered in the midsummer heat. Over my shoulder Etna sprawled like some giant pyramid, rising majestically, dominating the landscape, its summit melting into a blue heaven. Far below the enchanting rocky islet of Isola Bella lay contentedly in calm water.

The havoc of war had left Taormina untouched, but the town at the foot of the cliffs suffered severely. The retreating Germans had blown the winding coastal road and done it so effectively that a wide stretch had disappeared completely and the cliff fell sheer into the sea. I recalled Operation Blackcock and the explosions heard on the night we landed commandos at Capo d'Ali.

All too soon our stay in Taormina came to an end, though not before I had climbed up one night and visited the Greek theatre, its circular tiers of stone seats and broken columns softened in moonlight. I clambered down, crossed to the west side and for several long minutes gazed through the ruins of an archway at the sleeping Mediterranean, the coastline of Sicily stretching towards Catania and distant Augusta. 'A ship, an isle, a sickle moon.' When I turned and headed back to the San Dominico I felt enriched.

Before sailing to Castellammare, officers and ratings of the 21st and 26th Flotillas played a football match against each other on the grassless surface of Messina's football stadium. The officers lost, 3-1, the biggest cheer of all coming when Lieutenant 'Knocker' White, CO of LCT 587, noted for his remarkable inability ever to come alongside without demolishing every guard-rail in sight, was well and truly flattened on the bone hard ground, to the delight of several ratings standing on the touch-line.

It was mid-July. For the next three weeks we lay on the beach at Castellammare, our doors down, while Vesuvius smouldered across the bay and a grey sulphurous cloud hung over Naples. And every night, despite many a good resolution to stay aboard for a change, when the sun went down, we would meet ashore to eat and drink too much in a dark, unsavoury cavern of a place, lit by candles. It was as well we sailed on August 13 to take part in the Allied landings on the south of France.

It was clear that our skipper was unwell when the convoy eventually got under way. We were a small part of an invasion fleet of 880 ships. Not long after sailing, Johnny Harrison took to his bunk, having asked me to stand his watch and take over. It was pleasing to think that he felt able to leave 582 in my hands — not that he had much option!

At the end of the afternoon watch — I had already taken most of the forenoon — I popped down to see how things were. He appeared to be asleep but, as I turned to go, he suddenly asked if all was well.

"Fine," I assured him. "And you?"

"Not very good. Can you carry on a bit longer, Number One? Give me a call if there's any problem." I assured him I would and left him with a fresh glass of water and a bottle of aspirins. He looked far from well.

The weather was sultry, the sea calm and I had an easy time station-keeping. Throughout the second dog watch the far-off flicker of lightning and distant rumble of thunder warned us of what lay ahead; sure enough, when night fell we ran into an electrical storm of awe-inspiring magnitude. Jagged spears of lightning stabbed at us repeatedly with dazzling intensity, momentarily lighting up the convoy. Twice during the night I sent the lookout down to see how the skipper was faring. He seemed to be sleeping through it all. Torrential rain eventually washed away the storm in the early hours, the sky cleared and the stars came out. I carried on and stood the middle — for me the worst of all the watches, when I usually reached the nadir. But when dawn finally broke and the lookout brought up yet another mug of tea, and the sun rose steadily in all its splendour, my spirits lifted and I felt hopeful once more, ready to face another day, despite having been on the bridge for twenty hours and more. The skipper recovered sufficiently to take over halfway through the morning watch, though not before we had entered the Bonifacio Straits, between Sardinia and Corsica, passed safely through the swept channel, and headed for the coast of southern France, to take part in Operation Dragoon.

Originally the landing on the south of France was intended to coincide with D-Day in Normandy and, from the beginning, Churchill had vigorously opposed it, preferring to continue the advance up Italy into Europe. But the Americans, who by now dominated the Western Alliance, won the day and Churchill was forced to give in, but insisted the code name should show how he had been 'dragooned' into it.

The landing itself met little resistance. Perhaps the Germans shared Churchill's view that such a landing was pointless and therefore unlikely. There was the usual host of shipping lying offshore and congestion on the beaches. From several miles out a French battleship was shelling deep inland as we drew near the Cote d'Azur and landed our cargo of American transport and troops on the beach of St Tropez. The only danger I was to encounter was entirely of my own making. I was passing through the wheelhouse one evening several days later, when the massive form of Stoker Nield accompanied by the small neat figure of Stoker Jones passed the open wheelhouse door, carrying sacks: "Where are you off to with that lot?" I asked them. I had a pretty good idea.

"Going to get rid of our rabbits, sir," and they explained how they had found a safe contact ashore where they would dispose of them profitably. Sensing their opportunity might be about to disappear, they suggested I should come along and dispose of my own. Over the months, as indeed many of us had, I had come by 'rabbits'. Whatever possessed me I shall never know but, on the spur of the moment, I gathered up my few spoils of war and went with them.

The light was fading fast as, with considerable misgivings, I followed the two stokers across the beach, threading our way through the maze of vehicles until we reached the coastal road, on the far side of which a low wall concealed a ditch. With mounting apprehension I sat on the wall alongside Stoker Jones, our two sacks between us. Twenty yards further down I could just make out Stoker Nield doing business with a man in a car, its engine running. Suddenly from out of the dark the unmistakable presence of two military policemen bore down on Nield. There was a burst of engine and the car sped off, leaving the huge shadowy bulk of Nield sandwiched between the two MPs. With quick presence of mind Stoker Jones dropped our two sacks into the ditch behind us. Incapable now of movement or thought I watched Nield and his escort approach.

"What's your name and ship, sailor?" asked one of the MPs, taking out a notepad. They were Americans and armed.

"Leading Stoker Simpson, LCT 305," said Nield, giving the false name and ship with complete assurance.

"And you, sailor?"

"Stoker Wells, LCT 305," replied Jones with equal conviction.

"Report back to your ships, sailors," said the redcap, and 582's two stokers evaporated into the night, leaving me on my own.

"Right, sir, I must ask you to come with us," said the American MP respectfully, as the other, shining his torch on the two sacks in the ditch, began climbing over to retrieve them. It was now or never. In desperation I turned, took to my heels and bolted. I heard a shout and the sound of following footsteps as I sprinted across the road and onto the beach, running as I had never run before, darting in and out of stationary trucks, aware that my pursuers were armed. I reached 582; with two enormous bounds, I leapt out of the tank space onto the catwalk, knocking my shin painfully as I did so. Dashing up the ladder onto the roof of the ward-room, I collapsed on my camp bed, where I lay, breathless, staring in the dark at the awning above, cursing myself for the folly of my action.

Presently I heard footsteps coming up the ladder: "You all right, sir?"

"Just about," I said.

"Pity we lost our rabbits, sir."

"Yes," I replied. Bugger the rabbits, I thought.

"We'll bring you up a nice cup of tea, sir," said Nield.

"Thank you," I said. Neither of them was in the least bit perturbed.

Early the following morning, Johnny Harrison reported ashore and, to my great relief, returned to announce that we were sailing forthwith to Messina. "Get the engines started, Number One," and I did not need telling twice, for uppermost in my mind was the thought of another court of enquiry. Quickly the hands raised the door and we slipped astern off the beach to join a small group of LCTs. Three hours later we were battling with a *mistral*, the wind howling about our ears, the seas steep and breaking. To make matters worse the starboard engine was giving trouble. Yet somehow our chief motor mechanic, Rose, and his two stokers, Nield and Jones, kept the thing going until we made the sheltered waters of Ajaccio. We learned later LCT 373 had sunk with the loss of all hands and two other craft were overdue.

We spent three days in Ajaccio, then continued our passage to Messina, only to run into more trouble with the same engine, which this time broke down for good. Unable to keep up with the convoy, the skipper signalled the senior officer, Lieutenant-Commander Valasto, requesting assistance. LCT 397, the only Mark III in the group, was detailed off to stand by and give us a tow. The weather was overcast, the sea moderate. Towing is never an easy exercise, particularly when two landing-craft are involved. Fortunately 397's skipper and our own were both excellent ship-handlers. They needed to be. With fenders out, both crews on deck standing by, 397, rearing and rolling, skilfully closed our starboard fo'c'sle, close enough for a heaving line to be slung across with a length of rope attached, followed by the tow itself, a three-inch kedge wire which we fed through our fairlead and secured round the bollards. So far so good. As 397 took up the slack, we began once more slowly to gather headway, the two crews hurling ribald comments at each other across the water.

By late afternoon the weather had steadily deteriorated. 397 had paid out more of her two hundred fathoms of cable. The convoy was out of sight, the weather worse. When night fell the tow broke, and we went for'ard down the tank space and up onto the precarious pitching fo'c'sle to ditch the remaining bit of wire hawser which had parted by the fairleads. It was fast becoming a situation comparable with the one I had experienced a year earlier aboard 614, when our escort, the Byms minesweeper, left us to wallow through the night in the troughs south of Cape Spartivento. However 397 had no intention of abandoning us and signalled she would stand by and try again at daylight.

When dawn broke the sea presented a desolate face, but 397 was still with us, though but a speck on the heaving horizon. The first attempt by Lew Hemming and his crew to sling a line across our fo'c'sle nearly ended in disaster. Tossed contemptuously about in the heavy seas, we watched 397 approach. As they finally drew near enough to get a line over, it suddenly became apparent to those on deck that a collision was imminent. Only by the grace of God and an emergency burst of both engines was Lew Hemming able to avoid smashing into us. Indeed 397's quarter-deck and our fo'c'sle were so close that the heaving line could almost have been passed by hand. Clinging on and, at the same time, attempting to haul in the wire cable, was hazardous work for our fo'c'sle party. It was also pointless, for no sooner had we secured the tow than it parted, as most of us expected it would.

Towing in such conditions was out of the question and all that day 397 stood by, keeping well clear of us, heading into the seas, while we rolled our guts out between the crests of the waves, the tank space awash. Every so often, in order to maintain contact, Lew Hemming brought 397 round and, in doing so, risked being swamped. A Mark III, unlike a IV, has a much deeper tank space, with no non-return valves, but pumps, well known for their inability to cope in heavy weather, evident when a number of Mark IIIs foundered in the Bay of Biscay, homeward bound to take part in the Normandy landings.

Throughout that second day it continued to blow hard; when night fell we once more lost contact with each other. But at last, on the third day, the clouds started to break up and the sea to moderate. By noon, still keeping his distance, for there was a considerable swell running, Lew Hemming signalled his intention to cross our bows, towing a coir with a life-buoy attached, in the expectation that it would drift close enough for us to pick up with a grapnel. It took several attempts, but in the end it worked and we got under way. This time the tow held and when I came up for the middle watch the sea had flattened and the stars were shining overhead: "All yours," said Johnny Harrison. As he left the bridge I sent the lookout down to bring up a cup of tea. Leaning against the top of the chart table I watched the tow rise gently out of the water, felt the tug as the wire tautened before falling back into the sea, and I marvelled that conditions could change so quickly.

By mid-afternoon we sighted mountains off our port bow and altered course towards them, eventually fetching up in the lee of a curving headland, on the north coast of Sicily, where we slipped the tow and anchored in calm waters. While the crew of 397 hauled in the wire hawser yet once more, their Aldis lamp began flashing, requesting permission to come alongside for the night. It was the least we could do for them.

Over a bottle of whisky in 582's tiny ward-room we met our two benefactors, Lew Hemming and Ken Burbidge, for the first time. Lew, friendly and voluble, had left school at fourteen to earn a living. He had joined the RNVR and in August 1939 had been called up and sent out to Egypt to serve as an ordinary seaman aboard a minesweeper operating from Port Said. Within a year he had been drafted to the *Malaya*, a battleship on Malta convoys, and was aboard her when she was later torpedoed in the north Atlantic. Somehow they made New York, where the crew were promptly detailed off to man and bring back to the UK a number of the fifty American lease-lend destroyers and coastguard cutters. In one of the latter Lew returned, and continued to serve doing convoy work until recommended for a commission.

Ken, his First Lieutenant, had been an ordinary seaman aboard the battleship *Duke of York* and knew what a Russian convoy was all about. A year younger than Lew, he was a buoyant personality with a friendly, carefree disposition, who could find a laugh at the worst of times: "What the hell do we bloody well do now, Ken?" Lew would ask his number one, and invariably got the same reply: "Full ahead both and fuck the consequences."

Both had taken part in the Sicily and Italy landings, gone in early at Salerno, and been in the thick of it. Ken at the time was first lieutenant of 346, a Mark III skippered by Frank Butler. With an engine out of action, they were caught in the great storm and swept broadside onto the waves. Unable to turn and head out to sea, their craft was swamped, driven onto the beach and wrecked.

Lew was CO of 397, one of three landing-craft carrying a squadron of Sherman tanks manned by the Royal Scots Greys. From twelve miles off the beaches of Salerno, they followed the tall funnel and squat shape of a Mark IV, which was to land ten minutes ahead of the three LCTs. It never happened. The Mark IV, which had aboard the regimental guides, struck a mine and sank. In line astern, Lew now led the other two LCTs in to the beach. As they drew near, flares began to fall. Suddenly, as though someone had pressed a button, the enemy opened fire along the shore line. Above the chaos and blast of bursting shells and exploding bombs, the Beach Master hailed them from an assault craft, instructing Lew to land further down the beach. Obeying orders, Lew promptly brought 397 broadside on to the shore, followed by the other two craft, and immediately the three came under heavy fire. Without hesitating, he swung 397 round again and headed for the beach, presenting less of a target. Before the second LCT could follow suit it was hit repeatedly, caught fire and sank. Rapidly closing the shore, 397 surged up the beach and dropped the door.

The five Shermans and five 3-ton Bedford trucks, each hitched to a tank, were manned and ready to land, their engines revving in anticipation, filling the tank space with fumes, only to find that the bulldozer up in the bows had got jammed against the LCT's sides and was blocking the exit. It took precious time and cool heads to inch the heavy blades clear. But for the accuracy of the naval bombardment, in particular from the destroyer HMS *Laforey*, engaging the German batteries from 800 yards, until forced to withdraw after being hit five times, 397 would have faced a similar fate.

Towing their Bedford trucks, all five Shermans roared their way ashore, leaving 397 to pull off the beach and head seaward, out to the crowded anchorage six miles offshore where, like the rest of us, they spent the next ten critical days working round the clock, unloading and ferrying in the sorely needed supplies.

There had been one further incident at Salerno that Lew recounted to us that evening in 582's tiny ward-room. They were lying alongside an ammunition ship taking aboard crates of mortars and small arms ammunition. It was a night of frequent air raids, the sky lit by red tracer and flares, the crack of ack-ack guns and exploding bombs in their ears. Lew was in the ward-room with John Simon, his number one, when one of the crew, close to panic, reported that a bomb was dangling over the hold suspended by wire. The two officers vacated the ward-room at some speed. It was indeed a bomb. They could see that the wire, caught on one of the cross members spanning the tank space, went up and over the freighter's superstructure. If ever there was a threatening and evil-looking device, this was one, as it swung gently above the crates of ammunition.

"Keep the crew aft," Lew instructed his number one, and began climbing the ladder that was hanging down the freighter's side. The hands did not need instructions, they were already as far aft as they could get.

Up on the merchantman's deck — it was a British ship — Lew grabbed the first seaman he saw: "Stand by that wire and for God's sake make sure nobody touches it or we'll all be goners."

"What's the trouble?" demanded the ship's captain, arriving on the scene. Briefly, Lew explained the situation while the captain peered down into 397's hold.

"Well, what are you going to do about it, mister?" he asked.

"I don't know," said Lew honestly.

"It's a job for our DEMS rating. He's the man for this," said the captain, turning to one of his officers, who promptly sent for the rating.

The gunner was an old RN seaman in charge of the freighter's 4.7 inch gun, one who had seen it all over many years. Unhurried, he followed Lew down the ladder onto 397's deck, where he stood for several long seconds studying the bomb carefully: "Looks like some anti-personnel device, some sort of parachute bomb," he concluded, shaking his head slowly: "Well, sir, should be no problem. You can give me a hand, sir, but first we will need some pliers, sir," and he climbed down into the tank space and waited while Lew found some pliers. Together they made their way across the crates of ammunition until they were directly under the bomb. Carefully they piled the crates one on top of the other, until they were level with the fearful object.

"Now, sir, I'll hold it, and you break the wire, sir." He spoke slowly and calmly as though they had all day, ignoring the fact that another air raid had begun. The wire was not easy to part; in his nervousness, Lew could make little impression on it. After a few seconds watching the CO of 397's futile efforts, the old seaman could stand it no longer: "Here, sir, you hold the bomb, but try not to drop it, sir." In seconds he had worked the wire back and forth sufficiently to part it. "Right, sir, we'll put a rope round it first, then lower it overboard." Carefully they manhandled the bomb up onto 397's catwalk and gently lowered it over the side. Lew breathed again, the old seaman gunner gave him a nod and climbed back up the ladder, the crew reappeared, and the work of loading 397 with its lethal cargo continued. Lew was awarded the Distinguished Service Cross, but not specifically for that incident.

By now we had finished the bottle of whisky.

Chapter 9

Greece, some Adriatic antics and back to U.K.

FORTY-EIGHT HOURS later our stormy passage from Ajaccio finally ended when we fetched up in Messina, having crawled along the northern shoreline of Sicily on our one good engine, but this time in fine weather. Mail was awaiting us, for me two letters from Biddie and an anthology of poems from my father. In no time the 'plumbers' were aboard and working on our defective engine. We also learned there was a serious outbreak of poliomyelitis ashore and deaths had occurred. A strict quarantine was imposed on the naval base and all shore leave was cancelled. We were advised to be as hygienic as possible, wash our hands before meals and, if feeling at all unwell to report to the sick bay.

The seriousness of the disease — the thought of a person being incarcerated in an iron lung had always held a particular horror for me — was brought home to us when 582 was detailed off to bury at sea a naval officer, the latest victim. On a calm forenoon, in the middle of the Messina Straits, we lowered the ensign, shut down our engines and drifted silently on the current. In our ears, almost as though aware of the occasion, was the gentle sound of the sea, the sigh of the wind, and the chaplain's words, as he read the last rites, until the final splash signified that the body had been committed to the deep. It was a relief for all of us when the engines started up and we headed back to Messina. It was an even greater relief to learn that we were sailing to Greece the following day with four other members of the 21st Flotilla. It was October 1944; unknown to us, British troops were landing in Greece.

I was on deck when we approached the port of Piraeus and sighted the Acropolis standing proud five hundred feet above sea level, the Parthenon etched against the sky, magnificent and breathtaking, as befits one of the greatest jewels of Western civilisation.

Later I visited the ancient citadel of Athens, saw at first hand the massive Doric columns of the Parthenon, the delicate and graceful Ionic order of the Erechtheum, its porch of Caryatids, draped figures of maidens serving as columns. We had studied Greek and Roman architecture in that first year at Liverpool, drawn elevations and sections of a Greek temple, pored over Bannister and Fletcher and other sources, to discover what a cornice, frieze, architrave, abacus, triglyth and metope really was. Now I could see it all, could touch the great broken marble columns, tread the worn steps and look out across the Saronic Gulf. I visited the Acropolis once more and knew, despite its effect on me, I would not pursue my studies at the school of architecture when hostilities were finally over.

As was customary, none of us knew why we had been sent to Greece, though we quickly discovered that British troops were embroiled in a civil war, fighting the communist guerilla forces of ELAS in the streets of Athens.

Part of the explanation of this stemmed from the restoration of the monarchy in 1935, when General Metaxas became head of the Greek government and, a year later, dictator, holding the country in an iron grip. Parliament was dissolved, the press rigidly censored, trade unions no longer allowed, and secret police operated. All features of a democratic state disappeared as Metaxas and King George II became objects of popular hatred, opposed by bands of communist guerillas, the largest being the National Popular Liberation Army — ELAS.

By the spring of 1941 it became evident that Greece was now of strategic value to Germany as a base for operations in the Middle East. By April the Germans had entered Athens and the king and his government escaped to Crete, and eventually to London.

When the Germans finally pulled out of Greece, civil war still continued as the communists strove to gain control. Neither the king nor his prime minister, Papandreou, found this acceptable. Nor did Churchill, who backed the king in the name of democracy — although his record was anything but democratic — by sending British units into Greece to oppose a takeover by the communists. Tension grew throughout October and November. By Sunday, December 3, fighting had broken out in Athens. For nearly six weeks a bloody struggle ensued, and the capital all but fell to the communists.

Apart from the usual business of unloading and ferrying supplies, we took aboard Gurkhas from the Fourth Indian Division. It was the first time we had met these soldiers, famous for their courage and their *kukris*, each curved blade broadening towards a point, wicked-looking knives which they used unhesitatingly on night patrols, sometimes decapitating the enemy.

We landed them to the reverberation of gunfire inland and watched them scurry up a narrow street in single file. As we withdrew, fighter aircraft flew over, firing rockets, the missiles clearly visible, speeding in a downward slant towards their target. We heard later that one of the Gurkha officers had been killed.

We met the Gurkhas once more, this time transporting them up the Aegean to Volos. It was a rough, wet, winter's passage. Apart from the pongos' shelter, the Gurkhas had little comfort and suffered seasickness. The crew did what they could for them, which was not much. But the Gurkhas showed their gratitude after we had put them ashore by returning with hot curry and rice for the hands, while Johnny Harrison and I were invited to a meal by the two officers who had shared our ward-room, one of whom had in his possession a fishing rod and a shotgun. He took me in his jeep with a couple of Gurkhas in the back up into the snow-covered foothills above Larissa, laughing aloud — perhaps he saw my face — as we skidded round bends at speed. I was thankful to be safely back aboard 582.

On our return passage to Piraeus a freak storm sprang from nowhere, the wind ripping our bridge awning to shreds. But for the skill and experience of Lieutenant MacPherson RNR, CO of LCT 563, in peacetime skipper of a Scottish deep-sea trawler, we would have been in serious trouble. Skipper Mac, as he was known to all, had survived Dieppe and been mentioned in despatches. A professional, admired and respected for his seamanship and carefree attitude, he did things his way, whether afloat or ashore, and to hell with red tape and authority. He was a tonic and great help to the less experienced RNVR skippers. Now, in the gathering gloom and turbulent seas, he led the two landing-craft towards the line of breakers barely visible at the foot of an inhospitable coastline. Somehow he found the entrance and safety of a small fishing community on the east side of the island of Kimi, where we sheltered for a day and night, bartering tins of food and supplies for fresh vegetables and wine, before pushing south again.

Another Christmas had come and gone. Churchill and Eden arrived in Greece for an unsuccessful attempt to stop the fighting. We swung compasses in the Bay of Salamis, continued to ferry various cargoes, bales of newly printed drachmas on one occasion, until finally a truce was negotiated on 13 January 1945, the civil war ended, and we were able at last to visit Athens.

Then, without warning, we found ourselves without a skipper as Johnny Harrison was granted immediate compassionate leave on the death of his father. The crew, I know, were sorry to see him go. I certainly was.

Our new CO, a reasonably tall, well-built lieutenant, with a ruddy countenance and the hint of a smile, had a cast in one eye. He seemed pleasant enough, but it quickly became apparent that he had a drink problem, and a serious one at that. We first had evidence of this when approaching the shore to take aboard trucks and army personnel. I was up for'ard, the door well down, when our new CO rang for full ahead. We gathered speed dangerously, surged up the beach and scattered the waiting troops, who were not amused.

The climax came late one evening when he entered the wardroom, stared at me for several long seconds in a curiously detached manner, and then announced in a quiet voice that he was going to kill me. I was never quite sure which eye to look at, and he made no attempt to elucidate when or how he proposed carrying out his intention. But his expression and the calculating way in which he spoke was alarming. He stood watching me closely, awaiting my reaction, amused, half smiling, and red in the face. I decided to ignore his comment and got up to go, fully expecting him to obstruct me. Once outside the ward-room, I climbed over the guard-rails onto LCT 595 lying alongside, whose CO, Lieutenant Robbie Roberts I knew well; we had visited the Acropolis together and had our photograph taken sitting on the steps of the Parthenon. I have it still. I explained the situation and asked if he would give me a berth for the night, to which he agreed. The following morning I returned aboard 582. My new CO never mentioned the incident, but I felt very uncomfortable in his presence. Unknown to me, Robbie had reported the matter to the NOIC Piraeus, Lieutenant-Commander Pottinger.

Two days later, with three other members of the 21st Flotilla, we sailed in line astern for Messina. Shortly after arrival our CO disappeared ashore, and that was the last we saw of him. It had been a brief, disturbing incident. Nearly half a century later I received a letter from Lieutenant-Commander Pottinger — Potts, as he was known — and it throws some light on the matter. He wrote:

Dear Ken,

Our paths did not cross very often in the Med, but of course I remember you well, particularly in Greece. I set up a landing-craft base in Piraeus in November 1944 as FO 96 with barracks, engineering shop, sick bay etc.

You were then number one to your new CO on LCT 582. However he was an alarming psychopath as you discovered. I had encountered this with him before at Messina when the naval Padre told me he had been approached by your new CO's then number one in a state of anxiety arising out of his CO's nightly routine of sitting in the ward-room holding a live hand grenade, pulling the pin out then replacing it over and over again. The same unstable sadistic behaviour he displayed in Greece.

I sent Doc Shepherd to see you, whose net advice was that you should sleep in separate cabins.

When you left Greece, I wrote to Commander Snagge CLCT telling him that your CO was dangerously psychotic and should be removed from his command and receive treatment. So far as I know this was done. Peter Bull wrote to me about my report. I kept his letter which I should like to show you — but I can't lay my hands on it.

In the early years of MLCA your CO attended the annual dinners, but after one or two drinks, his manner became unacceptable to the rest of us. He is still alive which may inhibit you in referring to this horrid experience in the book you are writing on your navy days in the Med.

Changing the subject, how about your Anzio Court Martial? or rather Court of Enquiry? I spent four months at Anzio on and off and I vaguely remember being detailed off by NOIC to serve on such a Court as Senior Officer LCTs. I think it had something to do with NAAFI cargoes but I may be wrong. As an ex-LCT skipper, I knew all about not muzzling the oxen that trample the corn — but I do not recall any details of that Court. Your account would be of interest to me.

There is really room for a proper history of our LCT story in the Med. Peter Bull's book told a little of it — but I doubt if our story will ever receive full justice. Over the last 40 years, you may have noticed that I have written up this and that in the *Bulletin* — mainly light-hearted. I have the historian's instincts but, now 82, not the urge to do the job.

Anyway good luck with the book.

Yours sincerely,

M. C. Pottinger ('Potts')

I was now a Lieutenant, the wheel had turned full circle and I suddenly found myself in command of 582 with a crew I knew well. All we lacked was a first lieutenant and, when he reported aboard I knew at once we would get on well together — we still do.

Sub-Lieutenant Geoffrey Leeds had begun life as a Midshipman. By no means tall, he had a wide, generous smile, surprisingly well-informed views on a range of subjects, and a knowledge and love of music which was hardly surprising, since his father was a distinguished organist on the music staff at Eton. Above all he possessed a splendid sense of humour. The only slight irritation he ever caused me was an apparent inability to close the drawer beneath his bunk without trapping one of his garments, a small enough matter in itself, but unavoidably noticeable when living in such confined quarters. He had spent the first eighteen months in the Mediterranean with Z Squadron operating from Kabret. Until recently he had been first lieutenant of a Mark II Landing-craft, running supplies from the Italian mainland across the Adriatic to Split and Dubrovnik.

For some time the 21st had been under a new flotilla officer, Geoffrey Snagge, now Commander Snagge, having been promoted to squadron commander. Very fat, very funny, and very nice, I first met our new flotilla officer at a meeting of COs prior to sailing for Ancona. Educated at Winchester — he told me later how much he disliked the place — Peter Bull had been a professional actor before the war. Like the rest of us he had served on the lower deck in a destroyer, gone through Lancing and *King Alfred*, been drafted into landing-craft, and ended up in command of a flak ship. He was a person who made people laugh, and he did so in his books, particularly the first, *To Sea In A Sieve*, published soon after the end of the war, which began: 'I had better make it quite clear that the sea was not in my blood and I took jolly good care that my blood was not in the sea'. He stood before us now, his ample girth clad in an enormous pair of white shorts: "I don't think," he began in that rich resonant voice, the last word heavily stressed, "that there's anything too awful cooking for us in Ancona. As far as I can gather you'll be running supplies between Yugoslavia, Albania, and Greece. We'll sail in two columns and I shall take passage — if I may use that expression — with Lieutenant Candelot, whose ship I know is unrivalled for its luxury and cuisine". He caught my eye as we left: "How's your nice Mr Manchester getting on?" He always referred to Geoffrey as Mr Manchester.

It was early April 1945. For the first time in two years I was able to lie and soak in one of Ancona's hot public baths. That luxury apart, I found the place had little to offer, although the crew seemed to find plenty, particularly our steward Stevens, a Cornishman, who took the best part of a day recovering from one of his alcoholic runs ashore. As predicted, the majority of LCTs were ferrying supplies to Yugoslavia, except for us and three others, who were retained for Special Duties, a phrase none of us particularly liked the sound of, least of all Peter Bull. For several days there had been a buzz going the rounds of some hair-raising scheme involving Popski's Private Army, a small mobile fighting force of jeeps that operated behind enemy lines, answerable to no one, led by the legendary Colonel Popski. Perhaps it was mere coincidence that, of the four landing-craft Peter chose for the occasion, three of the COs played his sort of bridge.

Under a strict aura of secrecy, the four LCTs, 535, 614, 617 and 582, loaded up one night with troops and two Beaufort guns in each tank space and sailed for Corsini just before first light in the wake of sweepers. When eventually we reached the little harbour via a canal, an extraordinary sight met our eyes. Scattered around were rubber tanks and rubber lorries and an imitation hard made out of canvas. It was part of a plan to deceive the enemy into believing that another landing was imminent, which would force the Germans to redeploy their troops and aid the Allied advance and the capture of Venice.

Each morning the fake tanks and lorries were moved about and the drooping gun barrels reinflated. There was even a genuine tank that rumbled its way around at intervals. It seemed to us highly unlikely that the Germans would be beguiled into thinking that four LCTs and a few LCAs constituted a real threat, though they might have been deceived for a while by the smoke-screens put up whenever a reconnaissance plane flew overhead.

So we played bridge in the evenings and the crew whiled away the hours painting ship and speculating on what lay ahead and how much longer the war would last. For leave we went to Ravenna, where I visited the church of Sant' Apollinare in Classe, famous for its beautiful sixth-century Roman mosaics. One night some of our crew, returning from shore leave, fell out with the military by attempting, unsuccessfully, fortunately, to deflate one of their rubber tanks — Stoker Jones played his part.

But the next day there were much more important things to worry about, for Peter Bull had been suddenly summoned to Ravenna and given instructions for the coming operation. We were to stand by to make a fake landing below Venice. This was to take place as soon as the enemy's naval and aerial activity ceased to focus on Corsini. He was informed, somewhat apologetically, by Lieutenant-Commander Power and Captain Turner, that there would be no sweepers to clear the way, but two MLs would escort us up the coast.

"We can only hope," said Peter, after he had returned and formally briefed the army officers with us, and we were assembled in the seclusion of 535's ward-room, "that the Germans will continue to visit us on the sea and in the air and, as far as I'm concerned they can even drop the odd bomb or two provided their aim's not too accurate, otherwise, gentlemen, I very much fear that 'Operation Careless' " — as he now called it — "will take place. What about some bridge?"

And for the next few nights there was plenty of activity at sea and the odd reconnaissance plane flew overhead during the day. Then there was an ominous lapse for twenty-four hours, and instructions were received from NOIC that, if another quiet night ensued followed by a quiet day, 'Operation Careless' would take place that night.

Our sessions of bridge became more frenzied. In the middle of Peter's bid of five no trumps, doubled and redoubled, we heard the sound of gunfire. Hurrying out on deck, flashes and streaks of tracer lit the night sky. "Well, that's put paid to that," said Peter confidently, and we returned to our game of bridge in which Peter went 2,000 down, happily paid up, and we all had a good night's sleep.

The following morning he went ashore with a spring in his step and met the NOIC Corsini.

"Well," NOIC greeted him cheerfully, "looks as if we are all set for tonight," a comment which so stunned our flotilla officer that he did not even quibble about the pronoun.

Above: Peter Bull, D.S.C., my former commanding officer, in 1947

"What about all that activity out at sea last night?"

"What activity?" asked NOIC.

Apparently he had heard nothing and signalled Lieutenant-Commander Power at Ravenna to that effect. Seeing that it was useless to argue, Peter borrowed a jeep from the army and tore up to Ravenna as if his life depended on it, which it probably did. Fortunately Power had received another report from a different source which contradicted the Corsini signal, and the operation was cancelled, much to everyone's relief. Several days later Venice fell.

Back in Ancona we loaded up with grain, though without the cover of tarpaulins, and sailed for Venice. Five miles from our destination the wind freshened strongly and, within an hour, we were in the grip of a *Bora*, fighting our way into steep successive seas funnelling down the Adriatic, exploding over our bows with shuddering force, drenching the top sacks of grain. "Think we can make it?" I asked Geoff. He smiled ruefully, as 582 lifted and lurched violently, causing us to hang on. We did make it, but only just, the final bit proving an interminable struggle.

For the previous week and longer I had felt inexplicably weary and low and, consequently, despite a keen desire to do so, was unable to enjoy the historic charm of Venice, though the extraordinary skill of the gondoliers, as they swept their ornate craft effortlessly along the narrow waterways and round impossible bends, left a lasting impression on me.

Back in Ancona once more we took aboard a cargo of high octane and made our way up the coast to Ravenna. I was resting on my bunk, trying to rid myself of the lassitude that now seemed to be with me permanently, when the quartermaster reported that I was wanted on the bridge: "The first lieutenant, sir, says there's a small craft approaching from the north."

"Tell him to challenge it and summon the non-duty watch," I said, getting wearily to my feet. Unknown to us, the Germans had surrendered and ordered their ships at sea to proceed to certain points, or surrender to the nearest British ship, which explains what happened next.

By the time I reached the bridge, the small craft, still some distance off our port bow but closing us fast, had hoisted a white flag. The non-duty watch, sensing that something was afoot, were already on deck, the guns uncovered and manned. So far so good, though only one of our two oerlikons would bear effectively. The strange craft, which bore some resemblance to a small MGB, stopped two hundred yards ahead of us. Watching through binoculars, I counted eight aboard, one of whom was also having a long look at us through glasses. It was an odd feeling and I wondered what his thoughts were. Altering course towards them, I stopped within thirty yards. Neither gun would now bear: "We'll get them to come alongside," I said to Geoff. "Stand by to take their lines," and we waved our intention. Slowly the small enemy craft gathered headway and approached 582's port side, its engines rumbling powerfully.

It occurred to me, rather too late in the day, that despite their white flag, they could easily lob an explosive into our tank space, and that would have been the end of

Above: The German MAS boat coming alongside in the Adriatic

Below: Bunting hoisted on V.E. Day, the Adriatic

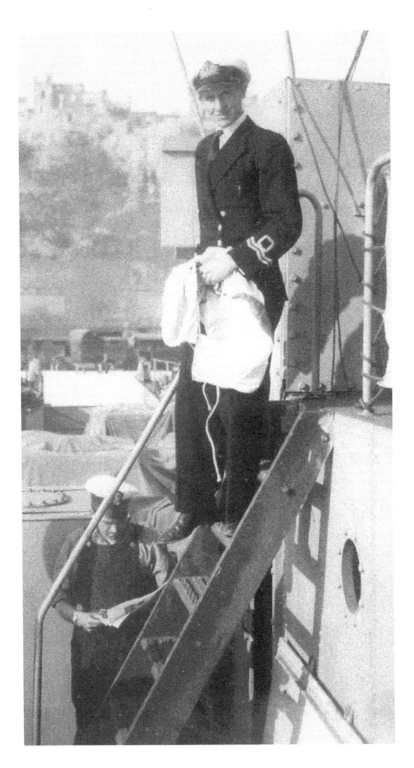

Above: KAS at Ancona

us. The only other armament we possessed was a tommy-gun — goodness knows how or why — which Geoffrey somewhat unconvincingly pointed at the Germans while our hands took their ropes.

What happened next was astonishing to say the least. In no time our crew were being offered and accepting bottles of God knows what and exchanging greetings with the eight Germans manning the craft, which we learnt later was an Italian MAS boat capable of fifty knots. Momentarily I stared down in disbelief at a scene that was more like a reunion of old friends than a confrontation of foes. Geoffrey, still waving his gun in their direction — I learnt later it had no ammunition — was doing his best to control a situation that was fast getting out of control. When I saw Stoker Jones receiving yet another bottle, I decided it was time to act: "Stand back, the lot of you, and stop taking any more of those bloody bottles. Number One, prepare to take the boat in tow."

I had no sooner tried to stamp some authority on the scene, than I was aware of a presence climbing into the bridge. Turning, I found myself confronting a tall, good-looking German officer, round his neck a large and splendid black case of binoculars. So this was the man I had seen watching us. Ignoring me completely, he moved round the compass binnacle to the chart table, picked up a pair of dividers and began measuring off distances. The sheer effrontery of his behaviour astonished me. I could only assume that, having witnessed what was going on below, he had summed us up as a worthless bunch, slipped aboard amid the chaos, and made his way round the quarter-deck and up onto the bridge. His ostentatious arrogance filled me with anger and a determination to put him in his place at once.

I called for Stoker Neild to come up immediately. A pick-and-shovel man in peacetime, immensely strong and formidable in appearance, he was the man I wanted.

"Get this man off the bridge, Neild," I instructed him.

"Aye, aye, sir," he said, heaving his massive frame up and into the bridge: "Out!" he ordered the German officer, who by now had emerged from beneath the chart table. He was a good deal taller than either of us. "Out!" Neild repeated more loudly this time, jerking his thumb and head and, at the same time, giving the German a good shove in the back with one of his huge tattooed arms — he was clad in the customary stoker's white singlet.

"And, Neild," I said when he had got the German out of the bridge, "you can take those binoculars off his neck. I'm having them."

"Aye, aye, sir," said Neild, warming to the task, "Off!" he demanded sharply, tugging at the black binoculars' case. Reluctantly the German officer handed them over. He was not smiling.

"Thank you, Neild,' I said, "now take him down and put him back aboard where he belongs."

"Aye, aye, sir," said Neild again, gripping the German by the shoulder in one of his enormous fists, and I watched him escort his captive down the ladder, round the quarter-deck and onto the catwalk, where he deposited the man unceremoniously back into the MAS boat. Several hours later we towed the boat into Ravenna and handed them over to NOIC. Where they had come from we never found out, but we assumed it was from Trieste, which Tito and his partisans had entered. I've no doubt they thought it better to fall into our hands than his.

Returning the following day, the official VE day, we hoisted all our bunting and 'spliced the main', but without a great deal of enthusiasm. News of a passage home was what we wanted to hear more than anything else, for it was our third summer in the Mediterranean.

Several times we ran up to Trieste, but found the port a bombed, inhospitable place. The only occasion I went ashore for a brief look I wandered round a corner and into a street full of armed partisans. I beat a hasty retreat back aboard, but not before a volley of firing broke out, followed by more, apparently to celebrate Tito's birthday.

Back in Ancona once more, by now wondering whether I would ever feel well again, I reported ashore to find out what our flotilla officer had in store for us. Inside Peter Bull's office was a large blackboard with ships' numbers under extraordinary headings such as, "Ships that want to go to Venice," "Ships aching for Trieste," or, "*Lazy* ships who want to stay here." Beneath the numbers were little bits of information like, "Stoker gone to cells," "Divers down and won't be up till Tuesday," or "Cheats at bridge, but good sound grub on board."

"And where would you and Mr Manchester like to go next, Ken, apart from home?" said Peter, who was looking at me closely. "Are you feeling all right?" he asked.

"Not really," I admitted.

"You'd better see the MO, I think you may have jaundice." He was right. Within an hour I had bade farewell to 582 and was on my way to the 71st General Hospital at Loretto.

At the end of the first week, Geoffrey came to tell me that the 21st was sailing for Messina. He brought me some mail which raised my spirits. But jaundice is a depressing disease, and the fact that 582 was going depressed me further.

Among the few possessions I had taken with me were a photograph of Biddie and a bundle of her letters, the clear unsophisticated writing that I had grown to know so well, sloping optimistically upwards. Rereading them, speculating on the future, and recalling past events of the last two and a half years, helped me while away the hours. Towards the end of the second week I was transferred to a surgical ward, since the hospital was closing down. Among the wounded was a sapper blown up on a 'teller' mine, a South African Spitfire pilot from Windhoek, a Russian who spoke some English and was, I suspect, one of Popski's Private Army, and a naval officer wounded aboard an HDML. There was also a wild army captain who had overturned his jeep one night during a run ashore with Dickie Hobson, first lieutenant of 601, and now lay with most of his limbs encased in plaster. They had both done their best to persuade me to join them on that occasion. Had I not felt so ill I would certainly have done so and no doubt ended up in the 71st, irrespective of jaundice.

During daytime the ward joked and pulled the nurses' legs. But the long, lonely hours of the night bared the soul and revealed the suffering. Once a cheery voice called above the groans: "The hounds are out again, nurse," which brought a few chuckles while the night staff did what they could to ease the pain.

Discharged from hospital, I flew down to Catania in a Dakota, hitched a lift up the coast to Messina, and reported to Peter Bull. At his insistence, I spent several days ashore at the base recuperating, sharing his room before rejoining 582 and sailing for the Suez Canal. "I'm giving you a third officer, Lieutenant Tony Oatway. He's a nice person and it will help with the watch-keeping." It certainly did and I was grateful, for I still felt far from well. Four hours on and eight hours off was a very different kettle of fish from four on four off.

We sailed in two groups, 582 in the second lot with Peter Bull in charge. The weather was fine and several times the six LCTs hove to, while the crews jumped overboard and swam in the warm calm sea. We put into Tobruk and found the harbour full of wrecks, one of which, so the lurid buzz quickly went the rounds, contained Italian prostitutes. Of all films, *The Desert Song* was showing in the local cinema and Peter insisted on our popping in to see it. We pushed on to Alexandria, where copies of *Lady Chatterley's Lover* and other not so daintily titled books were brought alongside for sale early each morning.

At Port Said we were consigned to a rat-infested berth by a supercilious staff officer, who said he could not understand why such useless derelicts were sent there. Our flotilla officer excelled and endeared himself to us even further when, on receiving a signal to: 'Put rat-guards on ships', accordingly deputed a rating from each ship to do the job. The first lieutenant of 535 quickly put him wise as to what a rat-guard meant when he produced some round tin guards for the ropes.

And, all the time, at the back of our minds we had a nasty feeling we might yet find ourselves joining the flow of traffic moving to the Far East. But when special heads began to be erected on the sides of our quarter-decks, we felt sure that our ships were about to be handed over to the Indian Navy. Any further doubts were removed once and for all on August 15th, when Japan surrendered, following the destruction of Hiroshima and Nagasaki.

The heads completed, we moved down the Canal to Kabret, a desolate place, not improved by the spectacle of landing-craft, many whose numbers we knew well, lying neglected and bereft of fittings.

We were to make one more short passage down the Canal to Bur Taufiq to deliver a Mark III LCT without a crew, which we had no option but to 'tow' secured alongside. To make it all the harder, once more only one of our engines functioned. To keep her on a straight course, we carried between ten and fifteen degrees of port wheel. Forced to avoid oncoming ships going west, and to give way to those going east, so alarmed and disconcerted was our pilot that he threw in the towel and left the task of handling 582 to Geoffrey and me.

The following day we returned to Kabrit and there paid off one Landing-craft Tank, HMLCT 582. Flat-bottomed, ugly and battered though she was, her guard-rails bent, her topsides rusty, nevertheless she meant something to us all as we looked at her for the last time, shook hands and said our goodbyes.

The crew's journey home was long and tedious. Packed into two landing-craft, they were taken back up the Canal to Port Said and transferred to a stinking meat boat. Five days later they reached Toulon, and there spent two days in a transit camp.

Before boarding the train to Dieppe, each was presented with a jeep seat cushion, and it did not take long to discover why. The old German carriages had wooden benches and, for the next thirty-six hours the crew of 582, along with hundreds of others, sat and slept four to a bench until they reached Dieppe, boarded a cross-channel packet, and finally landed in Newhaven. I regret that I never saw any of them again, though for a time I heard from one or two, in particular Stokers Jones and Neild, and Chief Motor Mechanic Bill Rose, who became a policeman. But the memories remain, the good and the bad, uppermost of mine are of a friendly ship's company that had got on well together. A happy ship, so the old saying goes, is an efficient ship. I think we were the former, if by no stretch of the imagination the latter. But we had got by, in our own peculiar way, and done what we had to do.

Geoffrey to this day reminds me of his astonishment on first seeing me paying the crew. "And how much would you like?" I'd ask each member, for I knew they could work out the amount they were due far better than I could, and it worked. Above all, though not always in accordance with King's Rules and Admiralty Instructions, a pragmatic approach and a sense of humour prevailed aboard 582.

On one occasion, when under sailing orders, our ward-room steward, Stevens, requested permission for an extension of leave, which I granted him to within an hour of sailing.

"Make sure you are back well in time, Stevens," I warned him.

"I will, sir," he assured me.

When we came to slip our moorings and raise the door, Molloy, our coxswain, reported Stevens adrift and it made me angry. The door was already up and we had hauled in both headropes and were about to go astern, when Able Seaman Stevens was sighted staggering incapably along the hard: "Get him aboard as quickly as you can," I shouted to Geoff up for'ard.

"Right," he called back and lowered the door sufficiently for the hands to reach over and haul our drunken steward inboard. From the bridge I watched him being supported down the tank space by two of the fo'c'sle party and taken below.

The following morning I sent for him; I was still angry. "I gave you special extra leave, Stevens. You knew perfectly well we were under sailing orders and assured me you would be back on time. Why weren't you?"

"Had a bit too much to drink, sir."

"I know you damn well did, but that's no excuse," and I gave him a long hard look: "Well, that's the last run ashore you'll be having for a while, Stevens. Right, carry on."

For the next week Stevens's face, as he tended to our needs, grew longer and more miserable, until I could bear it no more.

"Geoff," I said one morning, thoroughly exasperated, after Stevens had closed the ward-room door having bought up our breakfast on a tray. "I don't think I can stand that expression on his face any longer. Have you noticed, even his shorts seem to have a hangdog look about them?"

"Yes," said Geoff, chuckling, "I have. So what are you going to do about it?"

"Only one thing I can do. Let the blighter go ashore again."

"I thought you'd say that," said Geoff, laughing aloud.

"Stevens," I said when he came in to clear our breakfast things away, "you can leave those for the time being. Now," I said, looking at him sternly, "I cannot stand that look on your face a moment longer and, for God's sake, man, hitch your shorts up, they're below your knees." For one moment I caught Geoff's eye and barely contained smile, while our defaulter did his best to carry out the order: "Now then, Stevens," I continued in as serious a vein as I could muster: "I've given the matter some thought, and I've decided to grant you leave when we return to Ancona. But," and I paused and stared at him long and hard: "don't ever let me down like that again. D'you understand?"

"Yes, sir," said our steward, his face lighting up.

"Right, you may clear away the things."

"Aye, aye, sir," and, as he left the ward-room carrying his tray, there was a spring in his step, even his shorts seemed to have taken on a new lease of life.

"Well, you've certainly made him happy again," remarked Geoff with a broad grin. Whether or not he approved of my action I am not sure but, as ever, he was a great support, even though he still seemed incapable of shutting his bunk drawer properly.

After a brief spell in a single huge camp-site surrounded by sand, Peter Bull, Geoffrey and I left for Cairo to stay in the Continental Plaza Hotel. Ramadan was in full swing. Outside our bedroom windows an open-air cinema blared forth into the early hours. Each morning when we left the hotel, the same tall, distinguished-looking Arab greeted us in immaculate English, enquiring whether we would like to be shown round the *bazaar*. "Not today, thank you very much," Peter would reply, and the three of us would head off to Groppy's and have coffee and ice-cream, then visit the Gezira Club. In the afternoon we would swim in the pool out at Mena House near the Pyramids.

Peter and Geoffrey flew home first and I found myself on my own for a few days. Then it was my turn. With Bill Smith, a first lieutenant of the 21st Flotilla, I boarded a Short Sunderland flying-boat to find all seats occupied by passengers returning from India. So we made ourselves as comfortable as possible in the mail and baggage compartment. When the seaplane touched down in Augusta Bay, those who wished to were allowed to go ashore, but only for a short while. I stayed put, but Bill decided to have one final run ashore, which nearly proved disastrous. At the last minute, he arrived back very drunk. For a moment, it looked as though the captain of the aircraft was not going to allow him aboard. But he relented. With considerable difficulty and some embarrassment, I got Bill back amongst the mail bags and luggage, where he lay sprawled out and oblivious to the roar of engines as the great seaplane surged across the waters of Augusta Bay and lifted once more into the air.

He was still half seas over when we landed in Poole harbour. It was raining steadily. Together we caught the train to London. He looked pretty rough when we parted at Waterloo: "Better have a bit of a spruce-up before you get home, Bill," I suggested, as we shook hands. He gave me a wry smile. That was the last I saw of him. I heard later that he had gone into the Metropolitan Police Force.

Feeling weary and in need of a wash myself, I headed for 26 Palace Court, Bayswater, where Biddie lived and worked, doing her physiotherapy at Great Portland Street Hospital. I rang the bell and waited, curious, keyed up, wondering how easily we would bridge the gap of the last two and a half years. When the door eventually opened, I was informed that she had left to look after her father who was ill. Disappointed, I caught the train home to be reunited with my family. Then I slept the clock round.

It was on a railway station that I had last seen Biddie, and it was on a railway station that we met again. Full of excitement, I watched the train draw in and, with one final great sigh, grind to a halt. For what seemed an eternity I searched vainly for her in the crowd. Then, as the platform started to clear, I spotted her looking around, case in hand. I waved and she caught sight of me and waved back. Unsure of myself, I walked towards her, wondering whether this lovely creature approaching really wanted to see me again after all this time. She looked so beautiful, I could hardly believe my good fortune. She told me later that her first thoughts on seeing me had been how thin and ill I looked. "Hello," I said.

"Hello," she replied gently, smiling.

I did not kiss her but took her case. Putting my arm round her shoulder, I shepherded her out of the smoke and grime of Derby Midland railway station. Back home I could see immediately that my father had fallen for her; my mother was more circumspect, but grew to love Biddie. Unfortunately, no sooner had we arrived than there was an urgent call from Evesham to say that her father's illness had taken a serious turn for the worse. At my parents' insistence we took a taxi and arrived at the Lodge in the early afternoon. It was a big house, one of the really old houses of Evesham, the great chestnut tree in the front and beeches on the lawn already displaying hints of autumn.

Biddie's brother met us. It was the first time I had seen Flight-Lieutenant Robert Rowland. Granted compassionate leave, he had been flown back from India, where he had served in 671 RAF Glider Squadron before being seconded to a communication squadron in Burma. As I listened to them talking it became clear how ill their father was. Later that afternoon the three of us drove to Cheltenham where I met Biddie's mother. While her son and daughter visited their father, I stayed and talked with Mrs Rowland who, from the start, insisted I call her Winnie. We got on well together and I felt quite at ease even when she suddenly asked me candidly, "Are you serious, Ken?"

"Yes," I replied, without hesitation.

"Good," she said, and that was all. Nothing was said about the future and not for one moment did I think she was trying to bring me to the starting-post. But, deliberate or unconscious, it had its effect. It was what I wanted to hear. After chatting with Biddie, we decided to get married. The following morning, having chosen an engagement ring, the two of us alone went to see her father.

146

Above: Biddie's parents,
Bob and Winnie Rowland

Right:
All Saints Church, Evesham,
January 19th, 1946

"That's the second good choice you've made," he said to me after Biddie had shown him her engagement ring.

Desperately frail and ill though he was, his voice still had the rich resonance of one who has known the great oceans, sailed before the mast, sung shanties out on the yard-arm and rounded Cape Horn. The night before he died, the picture of the *Pythomene,* a four-rigger in which he had been second mate, fell from the walls of the Lodge, shattering the glass. That was the first and last time I saw Bob Rowland. I only wish I had known him better and had heard at first hand what it was like to be aloft in a gale of wind.

On leaving school at sixteen, with good academic qualifications, he went to sea. Five years later he came ashore, rented several acres of land and began growing vegetables. His venture quickly proved successful, for he was shrewd and hard working and, in 1903, he bought Oxstalls, a farm on the bend of the river Avon, for the sum of £10,000. Declared medically unfit in 1914, he continued farming throughout the war years, when he met and married Winifred Harrison Smith who worked at Oxstalls during the summer months and nursed in Birmingham during the winter.

It was down by the river at Oxstalls that Biddie spent her early childhood, the farmhouse lit by oil lamps and candles, the newspaper collected every morning by the cowman after it had been chucked from the train, which puffed and rattled along the single track to Birmingham. Cherry orchards, plum trees, fields of strawberries, and acres of vegetables surrounded the house and garden. There were days when the mist hung low over the river, and days when the Avon froze, and the meadows were white and beautiful, and the ploughed acres of soil lay hard and dark beneath a mantle of frost. There were cows with calves that she knew must never be approached, and the great bull chained in its own domain. There was the rich smell of the cowshed where pails of milk, white and frothing, were poured into tall churns, before being loaded onto the milk float. There were family picnics in the hayfield, and rides, she and her small brother sitting on the back of the dray, legs dangling. More than once they stood and watched in silent dismay as a frightened, bellowing cow was dragged from the river with ropes. But the most vivid of all her childhood memories were of the huge shaggy-fetlocked carthorses, Bumble, Fairy and Captain, upon one of whose broad bare backs she would be lifted up to plod gently onward, seated high above the world.

My final posting was Senior Officer Landing-craft Dartmouth. I had a motor boat at my disposal, so I could keep in contact with the numerous LCTs lying in trots up at Dittisham, in quiet waters and wooded surroundings. It was a 'cushy' number on which to end my time in the Navy.

We were married on January 19th, 1946, at All Saints Church, Evesham. There was a light fall of snow on the ground. Robert, in RAF uniform, gave Biddie away. She carried a bouquet of locally grown Arum lilies. As she approached, I thought once more how lovely she looked. Michael Ainsworth was my best man and Peter

Bull, Geoffrey Leeds, Bill Barnet and several others from the 21st Flotilla were present.

"Would you like us to bring swords and form an archway?" Peter had asked waggishly — we were still all in uniform.

Our honeymoon was brief and not altogether successful. We stayed at The Wensleydale Heifer, out on the Yorkshire moors, in near-arctic conditions, and both of us had a touch of flu. With some relief we returned to Dartmouth and our top-floor flat, from where we could see the ferry and the mouth of the Dart. At night, the lamps on the other side of the river shone brightly, and small craft burned their red and green navigation lights as they passed upstream. The flat was quiet, disturbed only by the occasional sound of a hooter, the quiet beat of the ferry engine, and the distant noise across the water of a late train .

Early in February I was ordered to report to Lowestoft for demobilisation. Most of the day had been spent going through the dreary routine of medicals, form-filling, and waiting in queues until, with Biddie's help, I finally chose some 'demob' clothes, which included a trilby hat.

Outside it was cold and raining steadily when we set off back to our hotel. Approaching a cinema we paused to see what was on. From what we could gather the film concerned a Cornish fishing village during the war and, on the spur of the moment, we decided to see it.

At least we would be out of the wind and rain. It proved a worth while decision, for *Johnny Frenchman*, with Francoise Rosay in the lead, we found delightful.

Back at the hotel, situated right on the sea-front, we stood for a moment before going in, listening to the sound of surf. The night was black, the wind blowing hard from the east, straight off the North Sea. "On nights like these," I said to Biddie, "we escorted convoys up this part of the coast," and I thought of the *Montrose* and Geordie and Scouse Dowell, and those cold and long nights closed up on 'A' gun.

Later, lying in bed listening to the sea, I had no clear picture of what I was going to do. My total assets appeared to be some newly acquired clothes, about £900 in the bank, and a sweet wife. The thought of returning to Liverpool was not agreeable. Endless studies interspersed with attempts to satisfy examiners presented a gloomy prospect. My mind wandered back over the day's events, beginning with the final medical inspection and ending in the warmth of a cinema watching a film portraying Cornish luggers and their crews fishing out of a small harbour flanked by great cliffs. Sea and wind, demobilisation, Liverpool University, peace, marriage, somewhere in there lay our future and, with such thoughts, accompanied by the rattling of the window as gusts of wind hit the panes, we fell asleep.

Chapter 10

The Coral

OUR LANDLORD and his wife, Mr and Mrs Ball, were a kindly couple who took a parental interest in our early days of marriage. My wife was a beginner at cooking, and we fed at times on toast and dripping, which my mother sent us. She thought it might come in useful, she said.

One particular evening Biddie attempted a treacle tart. From the start it had an unpleasant look about it, not improved when it slipped from the plate and lay, a soggy mess, on the floor. The alternatives were dripping toast or a meal out, and the decision was reached with little difficulty. Who knows? Had the treacle tart been a success, our venture might have languished there. As it was, we went out for a meal, and that was when I met George Allen.

The pub was noisy and crowded and we had to squeeze our way through to the bar where most of the landing-craft officers were grouped, talking vigorously, awaiting their drinks and demobilisation with equal eagerness. For a wedding present they had given us a handsome silver inkstand in the shape of a capstan, a present we treasured.

Over in a corner I recognised Robert Ballantyne, DSC, and Larry Osteler, a couple of naval friends and, further away, one of the few army officers in the room, an acquaintance I'd got to know slightly, Guy Greville. We jostled our way towards him and he greeted us with a nod. Lean, poker-faced and laconic, with a dry wit and plenty of self-assurance, he had finished the war in the Far East. He and his wife, Mary, had three children and an old, very large, green Daimler. Like me, he had only recently been demobilised.

We had both briefly discussed the future and, on several occasions, Guy expounded various ideas on how to make a living; so far his strongest and most consistent belief was that fishing was the answer. I enquired if he was any further on with his fishing plans.

"A little," he said. "I think there's money in it. There are plenty of surplus Admiralty craft coming onto the market. Tomorrow we're going to run over to Bath and get some information on the matter. Why not come along and bring Biddie? Anyhow, give me a ring if you can."

He left shortly afterwards and we both got up to leave. As I moved towards the door, a soft voice informed me that its owner knew just where I could find a boat and where I could catch the fish. I turned, and found myself confronted by a small man, gazing intently through steel-rimmed spectacles. His face was tanned and he wore a seaman's sweater under a navy blue reefer jacket, on his head a black beret worn at a rakish angle. He drew heavily on his cigarette, smiling constantly, his crafty brown eyes watching me closely as he awaited my reply. He had clearly overheard every word of my conversation with Guy.

"Oh," I said, slightly taken aback, "where would that be?"

"Mevagissey, and there's a boat for sale that would just suit you and me." He paused, observing the effect of the last two words. Apparently he was mate of an MFV lying on the other side of the river, whose crew was about to be paid off.

"All right," I said, as we got outside where it was raining hard. "Meet me here tomorrow night and we'll have a talk. By the way, I don't know your name."

"George Allen, me dear," he replied and, after introductions had been made, he disappeared into the night, while we climbed the wet, steep road and even steeper stairs up to our top-floor flat.

"What did you think of George?" I asked Biddie as we lay in bed.

"Bit foxy," she replied, which seemed to sum him up exactly. "Are you really going fishing?"

"I don't know. We'll see what George has to say about it. Would you like to be a fisherman's wife?"

"Yes, I think I would," she replied, and fell asleep.

But I lay awake for a while, the window slightly ajar, still pondering on the future, listening to the sound of rain and the occasional rustle of the curtains. The last ferry had crossed long ago. It was very quiet.

The following day the big green Daimler carried us all to Bath. Guy and I discussed boats, and it quickly emerged that he was thinking in terms of a large boat, one of the big MLs or an MFV, and was prepared to pay a much bigger sum than ever I could afford. Neither of us had considered the question of gear. Guy still stuck to the notion of trawling; I don't think either of us appreciated there were other methods of catching fish. The visit to Bath proved fruitless, and Guy announced his intention of going to Brixham to see whether he could buy a Brixham trawler, which he did eventually.

That evening we were both rather tired after our trip and I went down alone to meet George Allen, while Biddie stayed behind to prepare a late bite of food. George had already arrived and, in his quiet manner, asked me what I'd like to drink. We chose a secluded corner of the room and talked about my visit to Bath and George's family, as though shy of what was really uppermost in both our minds — fishing.

"Well," said George at last, when I had asked him to give me some honest and down-to-earth views on the prospects of fishing, "they're making a good living at Mevagissey, the fish are fetching a good price and I see no reason why you and I shouldn't make a living too. The boat's there, waiting..."

"How much?" I enquired.

"£700, I think, is what Cyril's asking," and he went on to extol the merits of the Coral; she was not an old boat, she was strongly built and easily handled by two men. We would need pilchard nets, a dog and spilter line, and he assured me that I would have no trouble in picking up the ropes. He would show me the way.

"You make it sound easy, George."

" 'Ess, me dear," he said, warming to his subject. "It's not too difficult and in the summer months we can always do a spot of plummeting for mackerel in the early morning."

I listened to his soft persuasive voice outlining the future, and couldn't deny that I found it a much more attractive alternative to Liverpool. The next step was to visit Mevagissey and see the boat, and I suggested there and then we should go the following day and George agreed on the spot.

As we got up to leave, he suddenly mentioned as an afterthought that the *Boy Don* was for sale.

"She's the boat they used in the film *Johnny Frenchman*," he added.

I glanced round sharply. "Good gracious," I said, "we've just seen the film."

"You have?" he remarked. "Well, it was made at Mevagissey." And, for a moment, I was once more back in the warmth of the Lowestoft cinema, watching shots of a wild and rugged coastline, charmed by a fishing village set so naturally into those splendid cliffs. Where better, I thought, to begin our married life?

Excited, I hurried home, where Biddie had prepared coffee and sandwiches. She watched my face expectantly.

"We'll go," I said. And I told her about my talk with George and how *Johnny Frenchman* had been filmed at Mevagissey, which excited her as much as it did me. She looked crestfallen when I announced I thought it better that, for the first cursory visit, George and I should go alone. But I assured her that I'd make no decision, buy no boat. We would make a full visit together later in the week.

By noon the next day George and I reached St Austell, where we caught a bus and set off on the last lap of our journey. I was not impressed with what I could see of the town, but later I was to grow fond of the place. First impressions are seldom accurate.

The bus, almost empty, rattled on for another twenty minutes until we came to Pentewan and the start of a long hill.

"There's the Black Head and Fowey Light," said George as we ground to the top of the hill and motored freely down the other side and into Mevagissey.

We climbed out, crossed the small square with its war memorial, and turned right, past the post-office. George had a nod for everyone, whilst I did my best to appear casual and normal. For these were the people among whom we were intending to live; if our venture was to prosper, it was imperative we should be accepted by them. We were going to need all their goodwill and help. We passed by the workshop of William Hunkin, Mevagissey's engineer, and came to the inner harbour. It was high water, the luggers and toshers at their moorings. A punt with three men standing was being slowly sculled through to the outer harbour. We continued along the quayside towards Edwards' store, where a row of fishermen in faded smocks and jerseys were seated on two benches, their backs to the old stone wall of the lofts, smoking, chatting, observing, missing nothing. As we approached, their heads turned. The one on the end removed his pipe and emitted a stream of tobacco juice from the corner of his mouth. He was a huge, overweight figure of a man, with a flat cap on his big brown head. For a moment I caught his eye and slightly amused expression. I was soon to see much more of him. George meanwhile had stopped and was studying a boat.

"There she is," he said, "that's the *Coral.*" Lying a short distance from the quayside was a twenty-seven foot, half-decked St Ives gig. I could see at a glance, from her good beam, her fullness on the waterline and the fine lift to her bow, that she possessed the qualities of a staunch sea-boat.

I would have liked to have gone aboard her there and then, but I could feel the eyes of the fishermen on my back, and they were no longer talking. I was relieved when George broke the silence by suggesting we should go up and meet his wife.

The Allens lived on the north side of the harbour, at the end of a terrace of cottages sheltered from most of the winds. We were met by Mrs Allen, who at once ordered us to sit down at the table, where bread, jam and cream lay spread out on a white tablecloth. It was the first time I had tasted Cornish cream since 1939 and it was as good as ever. As she moved busily about the room attending to our wants, she fired questions at her husband and made brief, pithy observations which showed such a shrewd assessment of our venture that, if I had not appreciated a certain underlying sense of humour, I would have been considerably alarmed. As it was, I was somewhat taken aback.

"Be you really going to buy that boat?" she asked me and, before I had time to reply, added with a laugh, "because if you are, you must be daft. How much is Cyril asking?"

"I'm not sure," replied George, "but I've heard tell £700."

There was an explosive snort from Mrs Allen. "That's a tidy bit of money — what are pilchards fetching?"

"Three-and-three a stone," George replied.

"You are going to have to catch a lot of fish to get that back."

"Cyril's doing well enough in her," said George.

"Yes, but Ken here's not Cyril, and he doesn't know what he's about."

"He'll learn," said George.

"He'll have to," said his wife, glancing sharply at me.

I sat quietly listening, feeling rather stupid, for I know that much of what Mrs Allen had said was true. She was a realist. Her hostile attitude towards this venture sprang from a deep suspicion of the sea and her knowledge of the difficulties of wresting a living from it. Since she was born and bred in Mevagissey — her husband was a Plymouth man — she could not understand how someone from up country could come along and imagine that by owning a boat he could earn a living at fishing, when he had never caught a fish in his life. To add fuel to the fire, her husband intended joining the venture. Despite all this, her concern was genuine and when we left to return to Dartmouth she wished me well.

"Have you anywhere to live?"

"No," I replied, and at once she offered to go and see Mrs Church who lived in a terraced house up at Beach Road.

Three days later the three of us set out for Mevagissey, and once again we walked into the square, past the post-office and William's workshop, and through to the inner harbour. More than ever I was aware of the glances, and could imagine the community discussing our venture with interest and some amusement. I had little doubt that what I had in mind was now known throughout the village.

"Do 'ee like it, Biddie, me old dear?" said George.

A glance at her face told me that Mevagissey had come up to her expectations. She wanted to be shown the *Coral*, but I could only bring myself to point her out briefly. We could not stop and examine her carefully, I said, because it would all look so obvious what we were about. Somehow I did not want this. I felt embarrassed.

We wandered past the old lifeboat shed and slipway to the outer harbour where the luggers were lying ready for the night's pilchard driving. Three-quarters of the way along the quay we turned right, and climbed the steep steps of the cliff leading up to the green field above Polkirt Hill. At the top of the steps we paused to rest and looked down on the two harbours. Across the water the old Watch House proudly surveyed the long arm of the quay that led to the entrance of the outer harbour and Mevagissey Light. Tucked behind the Watch House on the eastern corner of the inner harbour lay Frazer's boatyard and, perched on the cliff above, the white coastguard station and mast. It was a fine, windy day, with great splashes of blue sky and long white clouds racing away, reflecting their passage on the sea.

Across the outer harbour, a punt with five-gallon drums of fuel aboard was being slowly sculled out to a lugger. The man stood in the stern, effortlessly stroking his oar in a sideways figure-of-eight motion. I made a mental note that I must learn how to scull, for I could see that rowing was out of place in such a community. On top of one of the inner harbour walls a string of pilchard nets lay stretched, drying in the wind, having first been barked and tarred. Lying alongside the lighthouse quay two long-liners were unloading their catches onto lorries, the chatter of their crews distinctly audible as they worked at speed.

We gazed seaward, at the great sweep of headlands, Penare Point, the Black Head, its round hump thrusting seaward, St Austell Bay curving round to the Gribbin with Fowey headland caught momentarily in sunlight. Further on, the vague shape of Looe Island could be seen and, just visible, the distant Rame. Even as we watched, the sunlight moved along that splendid coastline of cliffs, touching each headland.

In spite of the strength of the wind, George assured me that the boats would be going out tonight, for the wind was offshore and in the lee of the land there would be no sea to speak of. It was the easterly wind that was bad for Mevagissey, a fact I was to learn from experience in the near future.

We walked down Polkirt Hill, and called in at the post-office, where we had left our cases. The genial Mr Clarke beamed and greeted us warmly.

"Come and see us when you've got settled in," he called over the counter.

We carried our suitcases up Cliff Walk, past the coastguard station, till we reached the green field that I had seen from the other side of the harbour. We stopped to get our breath and peered over the wall and down the great cliffs. I would have stayed longer, but George was anxious to hand us over to Mrs Church. In any case, I had important business with Cyril Hunkin, and the sooner that was settled the better.

We followed the line of the cliffs till we came to Beach Road, and Ranelagh, the first in a row of twentieth century houses looking across the bay to Chapel Point. We pushed open the low swing-gate. Before there was time to knock, the door was opened by a tiny white-haired lady, who peered up at us over the rim of her glasses. Behind stood her husband, bent and smiling.

"Come in, my dears," she welcomed us, "are you going to have a cup of tea as well, George?"

He shook his head, "I'll be back at six to fetch Ken."

Mrs Church began by showing us our room downstairs and then the bedroom.

"The last person who slept here," she said, indicating the double bed with the feather mattress, "was Françoise Rosay. Did you ever see a film called *Johnny Frenchman?*"

Yet once again it struck me, more forcibly than ever this time, that there does seem to be some fortuitous pattern to life.

"Well, I'll leave you to unpack," we heard Mrs Church say, "and there'll be a cup of tea when you come down."

We thanked her and walked over to the bedroom window. The bay was full of shifting colours. Across the grass we could see the top of the coastguard station and, in the far distance, the low headland of Chapel Point stretching out to sea, its three fine distinctive white houses caught in the winter sunlight.

Just before six George called and took me down to Number Two Chapel Street, where Cyril Hunkin lived. His wife opened the door and we entered *a* room heated by an open range. Cyril was friendly from the start and asked me how I liked Mevagissey.

"Very much," I replied.

" 'Ess," he said. "It's a handsome place, especially in the summer. Are you going to live here?"

"I want to," I said, "if I can find a boat," and I asked him whether he was thinking of selling the *Coral* and, if so, what price he was asking.

"Seven hundred pounds," said Cyril, still smiling, "but I'm not particularly anxious to sell. We've been doing very well of late with the dogs. Landed four hundred stone today."

A more business-like approach would have been to offer him a lower figure. But I've never been any good at haggling, it goes against the grain. I wanted the *Coral*, so I bought her for the price he asked. Although I learnt afterwards I had paid a high price, I was never to regret my investment.

As I wrote out the cheque for seven hundred pounds, I thought it wise at least to enquire about the state of her engines.

"They're in good condition," Cyril assured me. "She's had a reconditioned Thornycroft Handy Billy put in this month, and there's nothing wrong with the Kelvin. The *Coral's* a sound boat and I'll give you any help I can," he added.

He was still smiling when we left, a smile that concealed a sharp mind.

So that was that, and I suggested to George that we should now go and have a proper look at the *Coral*, since it was low water and we could walk out to her moorings. I was glad it was dark, for there were not so many eyes around. There was only time for a cursory glance at the boat, for the tide was on the make and had nearly reached the *Coral*. Indeed we had to leave in a hurry to avoid wet feet, but at least I had been aboard her, seen her engine-room, fish-berth and small cuddy up for'ard. Tomorrow I would take her out.

I bade George goodnight and climbed homewards, with half a moon to light my path. Above the coastguard station I paused to look over the cliff wall. The night was clear. Up off Fowey the lights of the fishing fleet were twinkling. The wind had eased as I turned and walked across the grass up to Beach Road.

My first thought on waking concerned my dress. I possessed some leather sea-boots and a thick white polo sweater. With a pair of old flannels tucked into my sea-boots I suppose I did not look too bad. Biddie assured me that I looked the part. I was not so sure.

With a wave and as jaunty a step as I could muster, I set off across the field and down to the harbour. All went well until I reached the cliff path, where my leather soles began to slip on the steep gradient. To make matters worse, the sea-boots were stiff, the leather almost new. With each step I took, I sounded like a guardsman on parade.

My God, I thought, they'll know I'm on the way; and sure enough, as I reached the first wall overlooking the harbour, there they were, a group of them leaning over the wall, gazing down at the inner harbour, their arms resting on the top. With one accord their heads turned to discover what on earth was coming their way.

"Good morning," I said as I passed.

"Mornin', Cap'n, morning," they replied. How dearly I would have liked to lean against that wall and talk with them! But I had not yet earned that privilege. We would have to go through a period of inspection while they watched to see what we wanted, what we intended, what we were like.

I carried on down Cliff Walk to the quayside, hoping George would be about, for I had no idea what to do next. I passed Pawlyn's store and, to my relief, saw George, complete with black beret, waiting under Edwards' store.

"No more lyin' abed now, old son," said George, looking at his watch. His remark slightly irritated me, for I was anxious to make a good impression from the start.

Cyril had been fishing for J.B. Edwards, and it was assumed that I would continue to do the same.

"Come and meet J.B.," said George, and I followed him up the steep dark wooden stairway, smelling of tar, and turned left through a door into an office.

J.B., elderly, white-haired and affable, was one of the three Mevagissey fish merchants, Pawlyns and Robins the other two.

"So you'm goin' fishin'?" he asked, with friendly amusement creasing his face. His daughter, Jean, who worked for him, I could see was interested in our conversation.

"Yes, I hope to," I replied.

"It's hard work, you know; long hours and often not much money in it. Have you got any gear?"

"No," I replied, whereupon George mentioned that we were going to buy a fleet of pilchard nets that afternoon.

"He'd better have Cyril's old loft, it'll be handy with her moorings just underneath. Has he got any fishing gear? He'll need a smock, sea-boots and an oilskin, we can fix him up with those."

"He'll also need a permit for a thermos." said Jean.

Apparently these were so scarce they could only be obtained by this authority. "And don't forget to tell your wife," added his daughter, "that you are entitled to extra rations of meat and cheese."

Once out of his office we turned left. Mounting several more steps, we entered Cyril's loft. A fisherman's loft is a fascinating place, a dark confusion of lines, ropes, nets, old sails, spars, dan buoys, tubs of dog-line and, over all, the clean, pervasive smell of tar. Cyril's loft was not particularly well served by the window, but I found that all the lofts were poorly lit. Mine, if anything, was better than most.

Directly overhead was another loft, owned by Edgar Husband, skipper of the *Margaret:* I could hear snatches of their conversation as they moved about. Outside the weather was still fine, but the wind was freshening from the east, and I gathered from what I could hear that it was unlikely the boats would be going out, as it was 'giving bad weather', an expression I was to hear many times.

"Let's go aboard," said George, "we'll use Cyril's punt." I made a mental note that a punt was the next thing I would need to buy. Once more I could feel eyes watching us, as George sculled the short distance to the *Coral's* mooring.

"Unship the legs," said George, "I'll start up the Handy Billy," and he passed me a spanner.

I wasn't clear how she was moored. There was a narrow three-foot piece of wood lying on the deckboards of the net-room, from each end of which a short length of rope joined a chain which passed through the fairleads fore and aft and was secured inboard.

George had started up the Thornycroft and now came for'ard. He tossed the narrow length of wood overboard and called to me to let go the for'ard piece of mooring chain while he let go aft. With a splash the boat was free. Taking the wheel, George put her astern. Then with a kick ahead and the wheel hard over, we were under way, passing several toshers, twenty-foot one-man local boats, threading our path through moored luggers in the outer harbour, till we reached the harbour mouth, with Mevagissey Light on our starboard hand.

"You take her," said George, "and I'll start the Kelvin."

So, for the first time, I took the small wheel of the *Coral* and looked ahead over her blunt, uplifted bows to the Black Head and the Gribbin. I felt the keen easterly wind on my cheek. Taking a deep contented breath, I knew I had made the right decision.

I heard George muttering below, then suddenly the outer engine raced into life, spluttered and died away. Surfacing with an oil can in his hand he began filling it with petrol from a tap off the Thornycroft's main tank.

"I'll prime her again," he muttered, disappearing below. Several seconds later the Kelvin burst into life once more, and I felt the boat thrust ahead and lift her bows. With both engines full ahead we motored splendidly into the easterly lop and, as we cleared Chapel Point and opened up the Dodman, I could see the sea breaking on the Gwineas rock. We turned our heads as the *Coral* hit a sea, sending spray over the boat, so I brought her round and headed towards the Gribbin, taking the weather on our beam.

Above: Biddie

Above: Mevagissey Inner Harbour

Below: The Outer Harbour

Twenty minutes later I handed over the wheel to George, for I wanted to have a look at the engines. Mechanically ignorant, I found them noisy and intimidating. Kneeling in the confined engine-room, the smell of paraffin, petrol and general stench of rotting fish in the bilges hit me in the face. I could not help speculating on the difficulty of doing even the simplest job at sea, such as clearing a blocked jet or changing a plug. With some relief I got to my feet. Standing in the engine hatchway, I leaned on the cover and breathed good clean air again.

The sea was breaking at the foot of the Black Head as we headed for Mevagissey Light. On the top of the cliffs I glimpsed the end house of Beach Road, and suddenly felt ravenously hungry. Approaching the harbour entrance, George switched the Kelvin over to petrol, and stopped her as we entered the outer harbour. With the main engine silent and the Handy Billy eased down, we chugged quietly into the inner harbour to pick up our moorings.

That afternoon I purchased my fleet of pilchard nets from Gordon Barron. I bought six of them at twelve pounds a net, and paid two pounds for the corks and buffs. That was when I first met Peter Barron, and I remember his face as clearly today as though it were yesterday. He was mending a net, strung up in the dark loft, having first trimmed the edges of the torn hole with his pocket knife. Threading his wooden needle in and out, he deftly built up the square meshes, completing the repair on a perfect square. How he had worked out the initial trimming so that this should come about I never understood. I caught his eye as he smiled. Gentle of manner, snowy-haired — and there was plenty of it — his honest, wise and kind face, full of humour, revealed a lifetime of patience and an unassumed dignity that shone through like a beacon.

In the evening, as we were to do on many occasions, Biddie and I strolled to the cliff edge and looked out over the bay. Far below we could hear the surf breaking. It suddenly occurred to me that we might bring our belongings down from Dartmouth by sea. It would save money, give me an opportunity to get to know the *Coral* and, provided there was no bad weather, offer a pleasant passage up the coast. George was amenable and we decided to go. It was the end of February.

We fuelled the *Coral* and took aboard an extra thirty gallons of petrol and paraffin in five-gallon drums. Biddie made sandwiches and although we took a thermos flask of tea, we carried fresh water for the primus stove.

By seven o'clock we had cleared the harbour and were on our way. The wind was still in the east and blustery as we set course for the Rame, bumping and sliding across the easterly seas off our starboard bow. Momentarily, before she sank deep into a trough, the *Coral's* exhausts would gurgle with delight. The sun shone, the sea sparkled, and every so often a wave slapped the bow a friendly blow, sending spray over the boat so that we could taste the salt on our faces.

George and I decided to give the boat a wash-down while Biddie took the wheel. I gave her a course to steer, and she soon understood that it was inadvisable to chase the lubber's point.

We took up the bottom boards and cleaned the channels through the boat's timbers which were blocked with pilchard scales. As I chucked down buckets of water, George swept the bilges of fish scales, oil and slime, and got her a good deal cleaner. Finally we pumped her out until she was dry. Standing in the net-room I glanced up at Biddie, who was sitting on the engine-coaming, steering a good course and enjoying herself.

"How do 'ee like it, me old sweetheart?" called George.

"Very smelly," she shouted above the engines, grimacing.

I nodded and glanced down at the *Coral's* timbers. She was strongly built and had spent some time in the Scilly Isles. Ideally constructed for crabbing, she needed more draught for netting and lining. I was to hear the fishermen remark more than once that the *Coral* was a good boat, but she'd flap like a skate in any weather and wouldn't easily ride to the lines or the nets. Most of the Mevagissey boats were much deeper-draughted, with the result that they held steadier in the water and responded better to their mizzens.

We had been running for three hours and had passed Looe Island, when we decided to have some food. George produced a large Cornish pasty and began to tell Biddie how Charlie Hicks baked them in his hundred and twenty-year-old oven.

"Just prepare your meal, Biddie, then carry it down on a tray and Charlie will cook it for you."

We had some sixty miles to cover, and I estimated we would not be at the mouth of the Dart for about ten hours. The wind was still strong but the weather was fine and looked settled. By noon we were off the Rame with the Eddystone Light away to starboard. As we crossed Plymouth Sound a destroyer was coming up on our starboard quarter. George was at the wheel and Biddie was standing up for'ard, leaning against the bulkhead, her elbows on the foredeck. I could see the ship was approaching at a good fifteen knots, rapidly overhauling us. I glanced at George and mentioned the fact that the destroyer was closing us fast. If we held this course we would either just cross her bows or she would cross ours.

"I should haul off, George," I suggested.

"It's our right of way," he replied, and said something about two points abaft the beam. I looked again and saw now that she was very close indeed. I could not believe he would still hold his course.

I gave a shout, but it was too late and for one moment I thought the destroyer was going to cut us down.

As it was, she swept ahead of us so close that we met the waves beneath her flaring bows. I heard a voice from the bridge shout something, glimpsed sailors in the waist of the ship pause in their duties and stare, and then she was past and we were being thrown about by her wash.

I felt annoyed, for it had been an unwarranted risk. I should, of course, have taken the wheel, but I was going to have to work with George and trust his judgement. Nevertheless I was shaken.

By now we had opened up Start Point. I knew there was a race off this headland and had a look at it through my binoculars. There was little doubt that there was some lumpy water ahead. As we drew nearer, I told George it would be advisable to give the point a wider berth. But once again he insisted on holding his course.

Above: The Coral, baiting up in the Inner Harbour

Above: George Pearce slinging a thorn-back ray into the fish berth

Below: Sam and I clearing and baiting up the line

"I don't like it, George," I said, still hoping he would alter course.

"It's all right, me dear. There's no point in adding another three or four miles by going outside, and you're not scared of a bit of sea." I made no reply and we motored on in silence.

Biddie was still up forward, only her shoulders were outside the boat.

"Hang on," I shouted as we neared the race. Then we were in it and a most uncomfortable ten minutes followed, while lumps and chunks of water hit the boat from all angles. But she was a stout craft and, apart from giving us all an eyeful of spray, she bounced her way through.

I should, once more, have insisted on going well outside, but again I held back. This was not the Navy, where the captain is answerable to his lords and commissioners, the Admiralty, but a fishing boat with a skipper answerable to no one but the owner, in this case, me. I had to learn from George and the last thing I wanted was for him to feel I was questioning his every move.

By five o'clock we were entering the mouth of the Dart. There was our flat and the old ferry crossing the river. We shut down the Kelvin and motored upstream, past the Royal Naval College, till we rounded a bend and sighted the trots of landing-craft, of which I had recently been Senior Officer.

We made fast the *Coral* and climbed aboard the outside landing-craft, to be greeted warmly by officers whom I knew. After a wash and a meal, and we'd been shown somewhere to sleep, it was nostalgic sitting and chatting again in a Mark IV ward-room. But this was a life I had left forever and in a strange way I felt closer to the sea aboard the *Coral* than I had ever felt as a rating or an officer.

The following afternoon we took the *Coral* down river to call on Mr and Mrs Ball and collect our belongings. They insisted on our staying to tea. Her husband had spent all his life at sea in cable-laying vessels. I brought him a pound of leaf tobacco, which he apparently enjoyed more than anything else. Then we did some shopping.

It was dark when we began to carry our goods and chattels down to the *Coral*, where we stowed everything in the net-room, lit by the fishing lights. We had secured the boat near the Customs Office in the midst of numerous other small craft.

I started up the Thornycroft myself, feeling confident, having received some useful instruction that morning from one of the landing-craft motor mechanics.

"Knock her in," shouted George after our line had gone. No sooner had we begun to move than we fouled our propeller on a rope. Seizing a gaff, I was just able to reach some vertical wooden steps and pull her stern into the side.

The next few minutes were by no means enjoyable. With George and Biddie holding the *Coral* clear of my head which was between the boat and the jetty. I went down the wooden ladder up to my thighs in the water to see if I could do anything. There was no chance of my reaching the propeller, but quite a fair chance of having my head crushed.

Weary and fed up, I emerged from the cold water and climbed aboard the boat.

"We'll start the Kelvin." Primed generously, she fired first go.

"Knock her in," shouted George. As I bent forward over the Kelvin to tighten one of the priming valves, there was a sudden bang and I was thrown forward, hit my head against the engine-room deck-head and broke the light bulb.

"What the hell's that?" I called, knocking her out of gear and emerging from the engines.

"I don't know," said George, and small wonder, for the fishing lights were still on. I switched them off and peered into the darkness. All I could pick out were vague shapes of boats. As far as I could see, everything appeared to be all right. Whatever we had hit, it had done us no damage.

"Better get out of it," said George, and I put the engine ahead again and carefully we motored clear of any more obstacles and up the Dart to the landing-craft. We would plainly not be able to sail the next day for Mevagissey; the *Coral* would have to be beached to free her propeller.

The following morning I was lying half-awake when I was suddenly jerked to full consciousness by the ominous words, "Is the owner of the boat FY63 aboard?"

A rating came down and told me there were two men on deck who wanted to see me. I dressed quickly and went up top.

"Good morning, sir. Is that your boat alongside?" asked one of the customs officers.

"It is," I answered.

"I believe you were moored outside the Customs Office last night and left shortly before nine o'clock."

"Yes, that's right," and waited for what I knew would come next.

"Did you hit anything?"

"We hit something," I replied.

"You certainly did," they said in unison, "one of our boats. If we hadn't heard the bang and come out she'd have filled up and probably sunk. We were just in time to shift her pegs over and list her damaged planks clear of the water. We've brought her up for you to have a look at."

There was no doubt that we had somehow hit her fair and square, on the waterline, but I was surprised we had done so much damage.

"Well, come and have a cup of coffee," I suggested. Considering the circumstances, they were extremely genial. It was decided that they should obtain an estimate from the boat-builders. It cost me £48 and I paid up that day, never questioning the estimate or considering insurance. Although the boat was insured, it was not in my name.

That afternoon we beached the *Coral* on the Dart's wooded banks and freed the propeller. She lay in thick mud, which made walking difficult and the task of freeing the half-buried propeller far from easy. But we got her free and floated her off by teatime. In the evening we took some officers upriver to an inn in the *Coral*. We had sandwiches and beer and talked till closing time.

By six o'clock the following morning we were on our way down the river. It was a cold, beautifully clear morning, and the *Coral's* decks glistened with dew in the early morning light. Ahead of us lay the mouth of the river and the open sea, a pale grey and calm.

There was hardly any movement as we set course for Start Point, a course which I was determined would take us well outside the point this time.

Our passage home could not have been more fun. The sun shone, there was not a cloud in the sky, and the sea was calm the whole way down. We lit the primus and boiled a kettle and made a pot of tea. We lay full length on the *Coral's* warm deck, drank and watched the distant coastline.

Suddenly we were startled by a shout from George. "Gannets," he cried, pointing over the starboard bow. "There they go."

We saw them for the first time, their wings folded, plummeting vertically into the sea, sending up small splashes. We soon came to distinguish these birds from seagulls. Gannets are torpedo-shaped, bigger and their wings are tipped with black, but apart from these distinguishing features they always appeared to me to look much whiter against the sky. To the luggers' crews out pilchard driving, the sight of these beautiful birds circling over an area of sea is as exciting as ever, for it is a sign there are fish about, probably shoals of pilchards in the vicinity, and the fleet will head towards them eagerly.

Gannets will gorge themselves until unable to take off. As the boats draw near, the birds in fear regurgitate their food, leaving evidence of what they have been feeding on — sprats or pilchards.

More than once aboard the *Montrose* I had been called a gannet, though never in quite such polite terms. In fact, because of my hearty appetite, I was denied any mess savings. But it had been well worth forgoing them to satisfy my hunger with a good hunk of bread and jam between watches.

We had come down with the ebbtide and were entering the harbour by three o'clock that afternoon, having made an excellent run. There was just enough water in the inner harbour for us to moor the *Coral*. We would have to wait till the evening, when the inner harbour would be full, before we could bring the *Coral* alongside and offload our belongings.

We said goodbye to George and made our way home. We walked up Cliff Walk and found several fishermen were still leaning over the same old wall, watching and talking. As we approached they turned.

One of them spoke. "Have a good trip?" he asked.

"Yes," we replied. He was small and seventy years old, with the bluest of eyes. He was well turned out and wore his cap straight on his head; his coarse blue serge trousers were neatly pressed and his thick-soled boots highly polished. His name was Willie Rolling and I was to see much of him in the future.

"Missus enjoy it?" he asked.

"Yes, it was lovely," replied Biddie.

They were now all watching us with friendly interest.

"We saw lots of gannets coming down," I remarked.

"Whereabouts did you see 'em, me old dear?" asked Albert, skipper of the *Pride of the West*, one of the oldest boats in the harbour and, like the *Zona*, without a wheelhouse.

"Most of them were between Looe Island and Fowey."

"Then you'd better get them nets aboard," said Bill Rolling, Willie's son, and they laughed.

"We're going to put them aboard tomorrow, all being well."

"Proper job," they all said, "proper job," and we continued our way up to Beach Road, weary but happy and full of good sea air, feeling that, despite one or two tricky episodes, the *Coral* really did belong to us now.

Biddie and I on Hemmick Beach, Cornwall, 1946

Chapter 11

A night of pilchard driving

EARLY IN MARCH we put our nets aboard the *Coral.* J. B. Edwards had lent me his lorry to transfer them from Gordon Barron's loft to the boat. Standing on the back of the lorry, George and Gordon hauled the six nets down over the roller that lay across the open doorway in the wall of Gordon's loft high above. There seemed to be an incredible amount of it and, despite the lightness of the fine Egyptian cotton, the nets weighed heavily.

Along the top of a pilchard net, one hundred and twenty yards long, lies the headrope to which the nets are attached. Corks are fixed into the headrope at short intervals. At longer intervals, are strops, three-fathom lengths of rope with a coble at the end. This is simply a bunch of corks tied together, which helps to hold up the nets in the water. We had seven buffs, white, inflated, balloon-like objects about twice the size of a football, which also serve to support the nets and give an indication of their lie.

The meshes in a pilchard net are a little under an inch square, and the nets lead out from the boat in one straight line and hang down in the water to a depth of forty to fifty feet. The fish swim into the net and are caught by their gills in the meshes. Two men can shoot the nets with little difficulty in a boat like the *Coral,* but I remember on one occasion a fisherman in a tosher going out and shooting his nets single-handed. It was a Sunday and his partner, on principle, would not go to sea. Luggers with their bigger crews work twenty nets.

When shooting nets from a lugger, one of the crew mans the wheel and attends to the engine, one shoots the headrope, the other the leech. The fourth member is on hand and ready if there's an emergency. Sometimes a coble will get fouled in the net-room, in which case the headrope must be held while the coble is cleared, easy enough in fine weather, not so easy when it's blowing half a gale. An accident at sea happens quickly: if a line or a net takes charge, a man can be injured or, at worst, lost overboard, swept away into the darkness without warning. Weighed down with oilskins and sea-boots he has little chance.

As I stood watching George and Gordon, I realised how little I knew. It was the first time I had ever set eyes on a drift net, and I knew nothing of how they worked. I had never even seen a pilchard. But I would soon learn, for that night we were going out pilchard driving for the first time, and perhaps might even earn some money.

The term pilchard driving originates from the feud between the seine-netters and the drift-netters. Long before drift nets had come into use, pilchards had been caught in great quantities by seine nets. In one year alone it is recorded that 3,500 tons of pilchards were exported from Mevagissey. But from the beginning of the nineteenth century the number of drift boats began to increase, and great was the enmity between the two camps. In 1839 several of the drifters were brought before the justices for shooting their nets too near the shore, contrary to an Act of Parliament of 1662, which laid down that no fishing was to be within a league and a half of any cove in Cornwall from the first of June till the last of November.

But there was no stopping the increasing number of drifters in spite of the seine-netters' strong opposition, and repeated accusations that the drifters were breaking up the shoals and driving the pilchards away. "Pilchard drivers" was their bitter cry, and the name has stuck.

It was high tide when we brought the *Coral* alongside the lorry now parked conveniently on the quay's edge, and began hauling the nets down from the back of the vehicle into the *Coral's* net-room. I manned the headrope, George was on the leech.

"Not so fast, Ken," he said softly, "there's a good deal more leech than headrope; and don't put the headrope all in a bunch, spread it out alongside the engine-room bulkhead."

When we had finally hauled the six nets aboard, I took hold of two empty five-gallon drums of petrol and paraffin, and climbed onto the quay to walk to William's and get them filled.

"Take Cyril's punt," George called after me. Cyril had kindly allowed us to use his punt until I had obtained one. I jumped aboard the *Coral* again.

"I don't think I will, George. I can't scull," I said awkwardly. He gave an understanding nod.

"You'll have to learn," he said. "We'll both go. I'll scull and you can watch."

We put the five-gallon drums aboard the punt and George sculled her across to William, the engineer, while I stood in the bow and watched the seemingly easy figure-of-eight movement of the oar.

It was the first time I had met William. He had a large round face, and his quick intelligent eyes missed nothing as he worked at his bench, his thickset body encased in a greasy, faded, one-piece boiler suit, on his head a flat cap, on his feet heavy boots. The only time I ever saw him without a cigarette was when he was in the process of removing one and lighting another. For all his great bulk, he moved with remarkable agility. Standing at the workbench, its surface littered with tools and bits of engine parts, he worked at an astonishing speed, and could lay his hand unerringly, despite all the clutter, on any tool or part he required, while his alert mind handled the constant flow of questions and demands made by the fishermen as they came and went.

He broke off from his work at his bench, wiped his hands on a rag, rolled a half-smoked unlit cigarette across his mouth, and began to fill our drums.

"Going out tonight?" he asked, giving me a keen look and, before I had time to reply, he was busy answering a question from one of the Lakemans who was standing in the doorway. I often wondered whether William made any money, for although he worked very fast and all hours of the day, he charged very little for his labour.

We fuelled the *Coral,* put her to her moorings and went back home. I had acquired from J.B. an ordinary fishing smock, long fisherman's thigh boots, and a stiff yellow oilskin, all in one piece, which reached to my ankles. I had bought, in addition, two pairs of blue dungarees. After an early cup of tea I waved Biddie goodbye. With a tin of food under my arm and a thermos in my right hand, I set off for my first night of fishing. I felt a good deal less conspicuous in my sea-boots, blue dungarees and brown smock, in spite of their newness.

When I reached the quay, men were still emerging from the narrow streets and alleyways which led down to the inner harbour, where the crews were assembling in small groups, chatting amongst themselves. Some of the crews, standing in their punts, were already being sculled out to the luggers lying in the outer harbour. The steady beat of a diesel broke out, followed by others as the boats began to get under way.

George had pulled Cyril's punt alongside and we were about to go down into the boat when a thickset, barrel-chested fisherman came over and spoke to me. I found him difficult to follow, for he talked at such speed and very earnestly.

"Now look 'ee here, me old Cap'n, you've got a shallow-draughted boat there, so pump her out as you haul your nets aboard, otherwise you'll get water into your fly-pans which will wet your magnetos and stop your engines." I had barely time to nod, let alone speak, before he went on: "They're giving easterly and it may blow a bit later, so my advice to you, old Cap'n, is to stick with the fleet."

I was touched by Charlie Pearce's advice; it was, I felt, not only sound, but given with a clear desire to help. I glanced across at George and knew that he had not approved of Charlie's remarks.

"Let's get aboard," he said, and we climbed down the steps and into the punt, which George sculled the short distance to the *Coral*. We unshipped the legs, started the Handy Billy and, when we had cleared the inner harbour, the Kelvin. It was five o'clock, with not much daylight left as we passed Mevagissey Light. The boats ahead of us were making towards the Gribbin.

I took our tins of food and stowed them up for'ard in the cuddy, the tiny fo'c'sle which contained our twelve-volt battery and two shelves, where one man could shelter, but hardly two. I closed the sliding door and looked up. There was nothing ahead but open sea. The rest of the boats were now off our port bow, heading away from us on a northeasterly course. I clambered aft. Standing in the engine-room space, leant forward and asked George why we were not following the fleet.

"I know where they are tonight, Ken," he said, with quiet conviction, and continued on the same course, his hand on the wheel, peering through his steel-rimmed spectacles over the *Coral's* bow, oblivious of the fleet disappearing in the other direction.

"Yes, George," I said. "But Charlie's last words were to stick with the fleet."

"Never mind what Charlie said. We'll run down and have a look on the other side of the Dodman."

"Forecast's not too good."

"Leave it to me, old son," said George.

So I did. But I was far from happy. Once again I was faced with the dilemma of whether to insist and take charge or give George his head. Apart from the fact that

Above: Willie Rolling: 'fingers before forks!'

Below: Inner Harbour, 1946

I had never seen a pilchard net shot or hauled, and consequently would have to rely entirely on George, there was the additional difficulty that we would be coming in by night and I was unacquainted with the coast.

I glanced astern. We were now on our own, well to the south of the fleet which was fast heading in the opposite direction. We passed to seaward of the Gwineas buoy, its doleful, intermittent bell warning of the hazard that lay to starboard — a great granite beast of a rock that rose menacingly from the sea, around its base the flash of surf. Ahead of us the huge rounded mass of the Dodman loomed in the fading light.

"That's a headland you want to give a wide berth," said George, "particularly when it's blowing sou'westerly and the tide's on the ebb."

"Like Start Point," I murmured, more to myself than to George.

We motored on across Veryan Bay, but saw no gannets. Two miles off Nare Head, George brought the *Coral* round: "We'll shoot here, Ken. Shut down the Kelvin." With the main engine silent and the Thornycroft eased back, we slowly nosed our way round till we were before the wind and sea.

The first white buff hit the water with a smack as we began to shoot the nets, George on the headrope, myself on the leech. In order to keep the net square, I had to shoot the net faster than George. At times he gave the *Coral* a kick ahead to keep enough way on the boat and to ensure the nets were lying in a straight line; occasionally he would pause and hold onto the headrope while the weight of the boat pulled the nets out.

Shooting the leech was not difficult, but one had to keep going. I was sweating when we shot the last net overboard. George went aft, lit and hoisted our masthead lamp while I took for'ard the boatrope, the line that is attached to the headrope of the end net, and passed it through the fair leads before securing it. Slowly the *Coral's* bow swung round into the wind and sea and we lay to our nets, both engines shut down. Daylight was gone, the stars were hidden by low clouds. To the east it looked black and the wind had increased.

"We'll eat," said George and we took out our tins. Leaning against the boat's side, we peered into the darkness and drank our tea. Occasionally we talked, but for the most part just watched the gulls as they floated up and over the seas, emitting quiet squawks, occasionally taking off to flutter and settle further down the headrope. It was as though they knew what was to come and were saving their energy. George drew heavily on his cigarette and the glow revealed his eager, aquiline features. I began to whistle softly.

"Damme, what be 'ee about?" he said. "Do 'ee want to whistle up more wind?"

The boat gave a sudden lurch as a sea lifted her more quickly and passed on its way. It was as if the *Coral* was tugging impatiently at the nets, and I wondered when we would begin to haul them. It had started to rain and visibility was closing down. George must have had similar thoughts, for he began putting on his oilskin. I had difficulty getting into mine, for it was brand new and very stiff. But once inside, no matter how much water came over the boat, I knew I would remain dry, for I was encased from neck to ankles.

We shipped the roller, over which we would pull the nets inboard, on the starboard side, the side from which all fishing boats operate their gear unless trawling.

"We'll hoist the mizzen," George called out. "You start up the Handy Billy." She fired first time and I turned to give George a hand. The sail was almost up.

"The bloody halyard's jammed," he muttered. "Here, catch hold of it and give a hand." Even as I did so there was a sudden twang, the halyard parted and the gaff crashed onto the boat's counter and into the sea, narrowly missing us both. Cursing, we leaned over the plunging stern of the *Coral* and, with difficulty hauled aboard the spar and the heavy bit of canvas sail, stowing it as best we could. The idea of passing another halyard, even if we had one, through the sleeve and trying to hoist the mizzen was not in either of our minds.

"Now, look," said George, "it's best if you haul the headrope and I'll haul the leech. But whatever you do watch out you don't foul a coble strop. Just keep her bows up to the nets and knock her out of gear if you look like riding over a coble."

So my task was to haul in the headrope, attend to the wheel, give the boat a kick ahead when necessary and knock her out of gear if there was too much way on. By leaning over into the engine-room I could easily reach the gear lever.

"Right," said George, "knock her in," and he cast off the boatrope and, lying back, pulled it in, hand over hand, till he came to the headrope which he handed on to me and we began hauling the nets, George up for'ard on the leech standing on the fish-berth hatches, myself on the headrope alongside the wheel and engine. I gathered in the strop of the first white buff and tossed it into the net-room.

As the net came up and over the roller, the pawl hit the ratchet, creating a fast, metallic clicking noise. I soon found that it was all too easy to snag and tear the net on this mechanism.

"Watch out for that coble," George shouted above the screeching flock of gulls that materialised out of nowhere to hover over the net, their wings beating the air, close enough almost to fan our cheeks.

"Here they come," shouted George, "see 'em, Ken?" Looking down into the water lit by the fishing lights, I saw for the first time the silver pilchards caught in the meshes, watched the fish hanging from the net as we hauled it over the roller, some of them falling lifeless back into the sea to be swooped on and devoured by the frenzied gulls. The strident clamour of the birds never ceased while the nets were being hauled.

"Knock her out," I heard George shout as I retrieved a coble and slung it into the net-room. Reaching over, I pushed the lever into neutral and, lying back on the headrope again, continued hauling it over the roller. After we had pulled in several more cobles the bow began to pay off once more, for there was no mizzen to help keep us up into the wind. I leant over, knocked her in, gave the wheel a few spokes to starboard and the hauling became easier once more. "Few here," shouted George standing on the hatches of the fish-berth, giving the leech a good shake, scattering the pilchards into the fish-berth beneath him, before dumping the small, heavy 'splat' of fish into the net-room, where it lay quivering and glittering beneath the fishing lights.

"Knock her out," he called to me again and I pushed the gear lever back into what I thought was neutral and put the wheel amidships. In fact I had gone through the gate and knocked the engine into reverse.

"Is she out of gear?" shouted George. "Look out, man, she's going astern." Grimly hanging onto the headrope with one hand, I reached down into the engine-room and pushed the gear lever ahead. Working at such slow revolutions, with the shrieking of the gulls in our ears, made it difficult to detect whether the engine was in or out of gear. Gradually the strain on the headrope eased once more as the boat came up into the wind, and we continued hauling.

We did so for the next half hour but there were few pilchards about. Even so, the gulls, despite the scarcity of fish, still hovered overhead in clamorous expectation. Steadily the wind increased, the night wet and black. There were now white caps to the seas which hissed as they raced away into the darkness. My arms were aching and I began to wonder what on earth I had let myself in for. Once more the bows were swinging away from the lie of the nets, and I felt the dead weight of the headrope as it began to slip through my hands.

"I can't hold it," I called out to George, as the boat yawed and fell away in the seas.

"Give her a kick ahead," he shouted and somehow, still hanging onto the slipping headrope, I managed to open up the engine and put the wheel over. Slowly the boat came up into the wind. Even as she did so there was a sudden ominous bang on the bottom of the hull.

"That's a bloody coble we've caught," said George, "cut the strop from the headrope, Ken, and don't, whatever you do, let it go overboard or we'll foul the other prop."

Grabbing a bait knife, I severed the strop and secured it. That completed George took the headrope for'ard and with difficulty got a turn round the cleat on the foredeck, so that the *Coral* lay, once more, to the nets.

I looked across at George. "What do we do now?" I asked. We had no mizzen and no Thornycroft. There were still four nets to be hauled and the weather was deteriorating. I glanced around to see if I could spot any boats. There was nothing to be seen, only the whistle of the wind and sound of the sea filled the black void of the night; even the cry of the gulls had lessened. We could have started up the Kelvin and run her on two cylinders, but I was unaware of this, and George did not suggest — I think rightly — that we should attempt to do so. Had we fouled the Kelvin we would have been in serious trouble.

"Right," said George, clambering into the net-room. "Let's get these nets in. We'll haul them from here." Leaving the wheel, I climbed over the bulkheads and joined him in the net-room.

It took us two back-breaking hours heaving them over the roller, standing unceremoniously on the nets and fish, while the boat rolled beam on to the sea, and the gulls shrieked their derision at the unprofessional manner in which we were hauling our gear. Eventually we got the four nets inboard, dumped in a dreadful heap beneath us.

For several minutes we rested, our wet yellow oilskins glistening under the fishing lights. Most of the gulls had departed, but a few remained, emitting occasional squawks as they hovered over the boat, before slipping sideways, into long silent glides to vanish into the night. "I'll start the Kelvin," said George. While he did so, I pumped the *Coral* out. It surprised me how much water we had taken on board. I heard the main engine splutter and fire on two cylinders before bursting into life on all four. We switched off the fishing lights, opened up the Kelvin and, with our navigation lights burning brightly, George brought the *Coral* round. Standing in the engine-room hatch I watched the compass-face lit by a shaded bulb. We were heading on a northeasterly course. It was raining steadily, the visibility poor. George was wiping his glasses. The easterly seas were growing and there was more anger in them now, but the *Coral*, splendid sea-boat that she was, rode them buoyantly.

"Can you see the Gwineas Light?" called George. We had been coming some time. Using the binoculars I had taken from the skipper of the German MAS boat during our brief encounter in the Adriatic, I picked out the faint, intermittent flash of the buoy.

"Off to port, George," I said, pointing. After wiping his glasses yet again, he peered vainly in the direction I was indicating.

We motored on, rounded Chapel Point and opened up Mevagissey Light. Though barely visible, it was a most welcoming sight. Fifteen minutes later we were off the entrance, George had brought her round, and we were preparing to run in through the harbour mouth. On either side the seas were breaking against the harbour walls. Lifted up and thrust forward by successive waves, the *Coral* drew near the entrance. We were all but home and dry when it happened.

The Kelvin stalled. Suddenly we were powerless in the grip of the sea, still several boat-lengths from safety. There was little time at our disposal. If the bows swung off we would be driven against the harbour wall. My immediate thought was to get an anchor over and see if we could hang on. But George had other ideas. "Grab hold of that sweep, stand on the nets and try and keep her bows heading in," he shouted.

But it was hopeless. I had no purchase with which to use the sweep, and it was all I could do to keep my feet as I stood balancing precariously on top of the nets, facing the oncoming seas, which would either pin us onto the harbour wall or sweep us into the safety of the outer harbour. Turning with the sound of breaking seas around us, I saw, to my intense relief, that we were going to make it. In those brief, vivid moments, with the wind and sea astern we were swept silently past Mevagissey Light into the calmer waters of the inner harbour.

I felt very tired. Neither of us spoke. George took the sweep and slowly sculled the *Coral* into the inner harbour, where several crews stared at us curiously as they shook the pilchards from their nets. We picked up our moorings, secured the boat, and sat down in the stern sheets.

"Let's have a cup of tea," I said, and George lit a cigarette.

We drank in silence and I felt the peace of the harbour. Around and above us the cottages slept.

"Did you put any paraffin in the Kelvin's tank?" George asked.

"No," I replied, "I didn't."

"Well, she's either got a blocked fuel pipe from the main tank or she's out of paraffin. It's unlikely both her jets would be blocked at the same time."

He took hold of a broom handle and dipped it into the Kelvin's main tank. It was empty. By failing to fill that tank we might easily have lost the boat and our lives.

"Let's get to work," said George, and neither of us mentioned the incident again.

We unshipped the roller from the starboard side and shipped it across the forward bulkhead of the net-room. Standing on either side of the fish-berth, we began to pull the nets over the roller and shake out the pilchards. This was hard work and entailed not only keeping the net square in a confined space, but a great deal of arm and wrist movement. In order to free individual pilchards which could not be unmeshed by more vigorous movements, we would insert our fingers through the meshes around the head of the fish and a quick flick of the wrist would make the pilchard fly clear of the net.

When the fish were more thickly meshed, we would shake the heavy net up and down, smacking it against our oilskins. The movements need to be quick and vigorous, otherwise, with any quantity of fish, the job would never be finished. But, although speed and vigour are essential, a net needs reasonably careful handling, particularly if it is an old one, when rips soon develop into large holes.

It took us two and a half hours to clear our six nets of about thirty-seven stone of pilchards. When the last net had been cleared, we replaced the deck-boards of the fish-berth so that the pilchards were not exposed to the gulls, and pulled the nets back over the roller into the net-room.

The tide was still on the make. The rest of the boats had long finished and gone home. We took off our oilskins, pumped the *Coral* out, closed up the engine-room, switched off the fishing light, put on the legs, climbed into the punt and went ashore.

With our food tins under our arms, we walked together up Cliff Walk. We were the last to finish, and I was thankful that few had seen us come in. Below us, the harbour lay shrouded in rain and deserted. Halfway up I said good night to George and continued along the steep path, past the coastguard station, which had an easterly gale warning black cone hoisted, till I came to our field. Before I left the path I peered over the wall down at the breakers far below. I could now feel the full force of the wind, and the thought that only a few hours back we had been fishing somewhere out in that black void was indeed a sobering one. I remember thinking with some dismay of what lay ahead if this night was a sample of the future.

I walked up the short path and pushed open the porch door. I took off my sea-boots, their black surfaces dotted with pilchard scales, and closed the door against the noise of the gale. I switched on the hall light and glanced at the clock. It was five to four. We had been eleven hours in the *Coral*. Very tired, I groped my way in darkness up the stairs to sink into the feather mattress.

"How did it go?" Biddie asked sleepily.

"All right," I said, and fell asleep.

Chapter 12

Willie Woodbine and Uncle Dick

IT BLEW HARD from the east for the best part of a week, and no boats left the harbour. I was glad when I came down at ten o'clock to a cup of coffee and a late breakfast that it was still blowing a full gale, for I had no wish to go out again that night.

My hands and fingers were painful, for the net had inflicted little cuts around my nails and, when I had used my hands to wrench the occasional pilchard which refused to be shaken out, I had crushed the lifeless body and been pricked by fish bones as sharp as needles. Looking at my hands, I saw that already the fingers looked larger. I put this down to the constant opening and shutting of the hand as I grasped and pulled the headrope. Later I found that this was true. My fingers became spatulate and my grasp powerful. The palms of my hands grew tough and hard and, while fishing, were never free from tar stains.

George had not yet arrived when I reached the quay, so I sat down on the bench opposite the *Coral* and waited for him. Several fishermen passed by and gave me the odd nod of recognition. The sky was leaden and the boats were at their moorings, safe in the inner harbour. The *Coral* was surging at her chains, the two seagulls on her foredeck seemed to be enjoying the motion. Her hull was a dingy white, and I thought I would paint her a different colour at Easter.

I looked along the quay for a sight of George. There was no sign of him, but I spotted the small distant figure of Willie Rolling unhurriedly rolling along the quay. I watched him approach, pausing to chat with some of the crews busy unloading their catches of the previous night. I wondered if he would speak to me, and was delighted when he stopped.

"Did you do anything?" he asked, a twinkle in his very blue eyes.

"Well," I replied, "I believe we caught about six or seven baskets full."

"Have you landed your fish?"

"Not yet. I'm waiting for George." I watched him carefully remove his cap, take out a packet of Woodbines and extract a cigarette.

"Got a light?" he asked, replacing his cap containing the Woodbines. I told him I did not smoke. He went over to one of the others sitting on the bench, to be handed a box of matches and thrown a remark which I couldn't quite catch. They laughed as Willie Rolling turned his back to the wind and cupped his hands over the flame.

Known to all as 'Willie Woodbine', I really believe a proffered Woodbine meant more to him than anything. He used to mend my nets and would never take any money, but merely growled in a friendly fashion that Woodbines were what he wanted. So I fed him Woodbines as he worked, and rewarded him at the end with a packet or two. It was terribly cheap payment for one who was a skilled and recognised expert.

He tried teaching me how to mend a small hole, but I never mastered the art, though I could just about repair a single mesh or 'shank'. He would string the net over a line in the loft and discover a great rent, which he would then repair and I would watch. His eyes were none too good, but he would take out his penknife and, with unerring accuracy, start to trim and shape the meshes until the hole was the right shape to begin repairing. I never fathomed how he knew exactly when the hole was the correct shape.

He would wind the black cotton round his wooden needle and with deft movements begin the repair. I watched each mesh grow symmetrically and effortlessly until the hole gradually closed. Now came the part that never ceased to amaze me. The original hole might have been several feet square but, little by little, the rent in the net would close until only a small hole was left He would finish this on a perfect square and then, like a cricketer who had scored a century, he would take off his cap. Here the resemblance ceased, for out of the cap he would produce a Woodbine. I would congratulate him and hand him a packet of Woodbines. He had been mending nets for fifty years but he still seemed to enjoy my congratulations. George had by now joined us.

"Still giving easterly," he remarked. The fishermen agreed with nods and grunts.

He peered up at me from under his black beret.

"We'll need some baskets,' he said. We went over to the yard under J.B.'s office, where the fish were weighed, cleaned and boxed, before being loaded onto lorries and taken to St Austell station. We collected seven baskets, and then brought the *Coral* alongside the quay. A basket of pilchards, not quite filled to the top, weighed six stone. While George scooped the fish up with what resembled a dustpan, but with a much longer lip, I walked over to William the engineer to get some fuel.

His workshop was crowded. William himself was surrounded by fishermen chatting and watching as he worked at his bench.

"Be with you in a minute, Ken," he called out. I was astonished that he had spotted me. I was also aware of being under scrutiny.

"Go out last night?" he asked, giving me a keen but friendly glance as he took my two drums, leaned over and began filling them with paraffin. Before I had time to reply, he was busy answering questions fired at him as others sought his help and advice. "There you are," he said, replacing the caps, then scribbling the cost down in a small, grubby-looking account book before returning to his workbench.

I carried the heavy cylindrical drums along the quayside, my spirits high, pleased that he had called me by my Christian name.

Meanwhile George had filled six baskets with pilchards. We carried them together up to the weighing machine in the fish store, to be met by Waller, who weighed the baskets with unbelievable speed, using his hands to scoop up the pilchards from the tops of those baskets weighing over six stone, and throwing them into a separate basket, which he weighed last. Six and a half baskets of pilchards stood by the weighing machine, totalling thirty-nine stone of fish. They were giving 3s. 3d. a stone for pilchards, so our night's work was worth £6. 6s. 9d.

Out of this would have to be taken our petrol and the various shares. It is customary for the owner of the boat to take one share for the boat, one for the nets and one for himself. Some skippers of luggers take a half of the week's taking and then share the rest. We did not go out again that week, so I split the amount with George, after deducting the cost of fuel. I told him that in future I would only take two shares to his one, as I had much to learn and would need all his help.

I still had a good deal of gear to buy and the following days of bad weather were useful in this respect. I bought a pram with the name *Babs* written across the stern. As prams go, she was well-proportioned, clinker-built, broad and sturdy. At the time, punts and prams were difficult to find and expensive to buy. The pram cost me £20, and J.B. sent one of his lorries to pick her up. We gave her a coat of paint and put her in the water.

I rowed to the outer harbour one afternoon to practise sculling. There was a shallow notch in the centre of the transom where I rested the oar. Seated, facing the stern and holding the oar in both hands, I began to waggle it in a sideways figure-of-eight movement. Almost at once the oar jumped out of the groove. But, after practising a while, I found I was able to propel and manoeuvre the pram. Next I tried to scull standing up, holding the oar in both hands and facing aft. This was easier, for the oar tended not to jump out of the groove so readily. Finally, I stood facing for'ard, and practised sculling with one hand on the oar, in the manner in which all fishermen scull their punts. When I felt sufficiently confident I, tentatively and with some satisfaction, sculled back to the inner harbour, secured the boat and climbed up the steps onto the quay, where a row of elder statesmen were seated on the benches beneath J.B.'s office, surveying the scene and, no doubt, my sculling. Feeling the novice that I was, I gave them a bit of a smile and received a nod or two in return. As I turned, one of the elders got to his feet and came slowly towards me.

"Takes a bit of practice learning to scull properly, old Cap'n, but once learnt never forgotten." I noticed he did not lift his feet much as he walked, no doubt his joints were stiff and painful. "You've picked it up quickly," he said and, adjusting my step to his, we proceeded slowly along the quayside.

He wore his cap straight, but pulled well down over his eyes, so he had to hold his head back in order to see ahead. With his lower jaw thrust forward, he looked like a rather weather-beaten old bulldog. I never saw him hurry and I seldom saw him without his hands in his pockets, yet for all that he represented a quiet authority and his words were heeded. His name was Willie Barron, known to all as Willie Wish. We stopped outside Pawlyn's store and I could sense he had something more to say.

"You were in the navy and you had your own ship?"

"Yes, if you can call a landing-craft a ship." I said.

He thought for a moment and then continued: "The insurance agent was asking us whether you could handle a boat. We told him you could, so you can insure the *Coral* at a fisherman's rate." I thanked him warmly.

"It's nothing, old son. But look 'ee here, I'd like to see you get another man alongside o' you." He thrust his jaw still further and nodded his head to emphasise his points. "George Allen's all right, but it would do no harm to ship an extra hand. Three in the boat would be better than two," and he began to question me about the other night, shaking his head in concern at my answers. I did not want George to take all the blame, and told Willie that I could at least have checked the fuel in the tank myself.

"Next time, old man, you stick with the fleet," he said emphatically, "and if anything goes wrong there'll be someone there to give you a hand."

"I certainly will," I said, and we parted.

The following morning I had my introduction to Uncle Dick. I was up in the loft making up some line with George, to the accompaniment of constant chatter, bursts of laughter, and occasional thuds from the loft above, inhabited by Edgar and Peter Husband and their crew. The two brothers owned a lugger, the *Margaret,* and each of them possessed an infectious sense of humour. Edgar, in particular, saw the funny side of life, and walked with a slight, arrogant sway of the body from foot to foot, typical of a seaman.

After a while we heard the door above open, and the sound of footsteps coming down the wooden stairs to stop outside our door. There was a rattle of the latch and Edgar entered, followed by his brother.

"Ken been over and seen Uncle Dick yet?" he asked George. He spoke quickly, his eyes full of merriment.

"Not yet," said George, "but I'm just going over."

"Ken coming?" asked Edgar.

George was nonplussed. I had no idea what they were talking about.

"If he's going to be a fisherman, he must come and see Uncle Dick," said Edgar, now highly amused. "It's the dole, old man," he explained, when he saw I was still in the dark. "We call the dole Uncle Dick. Six and eight a day if you are married, and you may be in for a week or more. You can't turn down two pounds a week. If the weather's too bad, you sign your card and collect your money at the end of the week. You'd better come along with us and sign on, old man."

So I joined the dole queue, and was introduced by Edgar to a Mr Richards, Uncle Dick himself, who gave me a slow, rather weary smile and seemed to have no objection to my signing on. As for Edgar, I found him splendid company, nobody's fool and his ever-buoyant manner a great tonic.

In the evenings Willie Rolling would come up to Beach Road, ask how the missus was, and smoke a Woodbine. He was busy trying to teach me how to mend a small hole, and always brought a piece of net with him. When I had gone wrong, a not infrequent occurrence, he would glance across at Biddie and remark: "Fetch a basket of eggs, missus, and a big stick." We then gave him a cup of tea, which he would drink with noisy enjoyment. He would ask questions and chuckle to himself a great deal before abruptly announcing that it was time he went. I would slip a packet of cigarettes into his hand; I invariably had a supply of Woodbines in store in packets of tens, for he preferred these to twenties because they fitted more neatly into his cap.

He never thanked me. It would not have been right to show gratitude. The Woodbines were a bond between us. As I walked with him across the green field to the coastguard station, where I bade him good night, I found his silent companionship a soothing nightcap. Biddie would be waiting for my return and together we would go and lean against the cliff wall, and breathe the salt air of the night before going to bed.

The weather continued bad for the rest of the week, but there was plenty for us to do. There were hooks and lines to be bought and made up, and wooden tubs to be painted. There were dan buoys to be constructed, and we would need bait-knives, gaffs, grapnels and creepers. For the last three items we went to see the blacksmith.

Albert worked halfway up Polkirt Hill. Like all craftsmen, he loved his job. He would mould the metal with strokes as sure and deft and fond as though he were shaping a pat of butter. It was fascinating work to watch. He would place a piece of metal in the fire and turn on the electric fan. In no time at all he would take it out, and golden sparks would fly as the ringing tap-tap of his hammer shaped the metal. He held it up, looked at it, thrust it back in the fire and spoke a few words. Out it would come again, and this time it would be bent over the anvil, tapped gently, held up and carefully scrutinised. When completely satisfied, the blacksmith would plunge the hot finished article hissing into a bucket of cold water. Albert always had more work than he could manage, and would grumble in a good-natured way that it was all becoming too much for him. Such pressure never showed in his work.

Towards the beginning of the second week in March, the weather had fined down sufficiently for the boats to go out again. The near disaster of that first night was no longer fresh in my mind. I looked forward to shooting the nets and catching more pilchards. We continued fishing throughout March and I learnt a lot during this time. In my ignorance, I had imagined that fishing took place mostly in the daylight, which was far from being the case. The bulk of the work, particularly when pilchard driving, is done at night. When the lining season came round, I was to find that, although we hauled the line during the day, we would leave harbour in the early hours of the morning.

Our catches varied from as little as fifteen stone to several hauls of thirty and forty stone. After that first night out, the price of pilchards dropped to two shillings a stone and remained at that price all the time I was fishing.

The evenings were growing lighter and the fleet would leave harbour two hours before nightfall, sometimes earlier, and search for signs. Occasionally we would have word that gannets had been seen off Fowey, or that the Polperro and Looe men had been having good catches. Often, though, there were no signs and, after motoring around, the luggers would finally get their nets overboard in the hope that they had chosen a good bit of water.

From now on we stuck with the fleet and followed what they were doing. Passing a lugger during this period of search, we would get the occasional friendly wave and shout. I could see the man in the wheelhouse, his head and shoulders framed in the window gazing intently ahead. One would be leaning against the mizzen watching out astern, another up for'ard scanning the sea and sky, while the fourth member of the crew would be down below tending the galley stove and brewing up tea.

"Might as well shoot here,' George would say eventually and we would hoist the mizzen, shut down the Kelvin and, using just the Handy Billy, begin shooting the nets, George on the leech, I on the headrope.

On fine nights when the nets were all out and both engines silent, a deep peace would descend over the boat. Only the sound of water lapping against the hull, and the occasional flutter of wings as a floating gull rose to settle further along the nets, broke the silence. Lulled by it all, we ate our food, drank our tea, and gazed across the water at the distant lights of the fleet, burning more brightly as the night closed down. To the west, the Dodman had long since been swallowed up, but the round shape of the Black Head and the Gribbin to the east were still visible. For a while we rested, George smoking, I dozing. Towards midnight, when the lights of Charlestown and St Austell had gone out and the last train down from the north had crawled like some yellow caterpillar through the darkness, we donned our oilskins and started to haul the nets.

Quite often on these nights we would shoot the nets twice, for at this time of year the fish were scarce and thin in quality compared with the winter pilchards. 'Winks' they were called, and the fishing was known as 'winking'. At other times we would haul in a few cobles to see if any fish were going to net and, if they were, we might decide to leave the nets in the water for most of the night. But when the moon was up and full, the fish would not go to net until it had set.

When the weather was kind Biddie would accompany us, which amused the fishermen. On a still night the crew of the *Margaret* would hail us, and Edgar Husband's voice would sing out across the water, "Is the missus aboard?"

The fishermen insisted that Biddie brought us luck and, oddly enough, we always did seem to do better when she was out with us. She loved these occasions but, when we were lying to the nets and there was a bit of a swell, she found the motion of the boat uncomfortable. However, provided she did not have to tend the primus and kept up in the bows, clear of the smell of the bilges and engine fumes, she was fine. We had hand-lines in the boat, and would fish off the bottom, until it was time to start and haul the nets.

One evening George suggested we should ship another hand, Sam Ingrouille. Sam knew nothing about fishing. He had spent twenty-three years of his life in the Royal Navy, had survived Russian convoys and the war, and ended up as a Chief Petty Officer. He now wanted a job to augment his pension. A Channel Islander himself, he had married a Mevagissey girl, and lived at the western end of our road.

I went to see him and liked him immediately. He was very tall, thin and cadaverous and gave a deep impression of integrity and dependability. I asked him if he would come with us and at once he said he would.

"Fine. Can you come along tonight?"

"Yes," he said, and so Sam joined us.

Shortly after his arrival I bought another three nets, so that we now had nine in the boat. The weather was settled and we continued 'winking' throughout April, but not with a great deal of success, for the fish were scarce. When our night's work was done we would walk along the quay, split up, and make our way home. Halfway up Cliff Walk I would pause. Leaning over the wall, I'd look down at the harbour, where some of the crews were still shaking out their fish.

On one such night I heard a great deal of excited chatter coming from the crew of a lugger entering the inner harbour, so I stopped and watched them pick up their moorings. I knew by now that this was the *Pride of the West,* an old boat without a wheelhouse whose crew were renowned for their talking, led by Albert Hunkin, who talked faster than any person I have known, constantly repeating a phrase in order to make his point. It was Albert who insisted that boiling water on a primus was always hotter than 'they 'lectric kettle jobs'! And when his wife sent him shopping he'd tell them, "Don't 'ee give me what I ask fer — give me what I want."

At sea on calm nights their ceaseless chatter could be heard across the water, until it reached a crescendo as they discussed whether or not to shoot their nets. When silence reigned we knew they were of one accord and were getting their nets overboard, after which they would retire below to drink their tea and carry on their conversation. It is difficult to imagine what it must have sounded like in such a confined space. Several hours later the chattering would break out again as they came on deck to haul their nets.

On one occasion Albert and his crew were just passing Mevagissey Light, arguing amongst themselves as to whether there was sufficient water in the inner harbour to get alongside and land their catch, when the tiller swung hard over and jammed on a fish-box. In seconds the boat veered to port and hit the lighthouse quay head on. If their chatter had been considerable before, it now reached unprecedented heights. I never did discover what the helmsman was doing at that precise moment.

However, all was well and when, next morning, we gathered round to see what damage had been done to the *Pride of the West,* Albert and his crew were in great form, patting the eighty-year-old hull and repeatedly assuring us that no real damage had been done, though it would be necessary to scarf a piece onto her stem.

They were a splendid crew. As I now watched them clamber over the boat's side and into their punt, they never ceased talking. Once up on the quay they stood in a little group, still talking, Albert nodding as hard as ever, before eventually dispersing. A happy crew, the *Pride of the West,* and I left them to continue up-along-Cliff, feeling the happier for having watched them.

Towards the end of April we decided to take the nets ashore and give the boat a good clean-up and a coat of paint. We had not yet finished making up our spilter line, but our dog-lines were ready. During this period I had one or two altercations with George, which eventually led to our parting for the summer. As things turned out, it was to his advantage as well as mine, for he missed a poor summer's fishing, and I was taught lining by a first-class Mevagissey fisherman. George joined me again the next winter, and by that time I had learnt much and had gained experience to make the decisions when they were necessary. But I always liked the three of us to decide together as far as possible when and where we should shoot our gear.

Sam and I beached the *Coral* on the little shelving sandy beach alongside the old lifeboat house in the outer harbour. Listing her over, we scrubbed her bottom with brooms and sand before giving a coat of red lead to her keel and bottom planks. We had to do this on successive days, since only one side could be painted at a time, but the rest of the *Coral's* spring painting could be done at her moorings.

Biddie helped in the painting, but not on the hull. She was given the job of red-leading the deck-boards, which amused the fishermen, who would remark to me that the missus was making a 'proper job of it'. We painted the *Coral's* topsides a bluish-green, and inboard we painted her white. With her red-brown decks and her newly painted hull, she looked handsome.

Easter was approaching and a few visitors were beginning to wander along the quayside in the warm spring air. It felt as though summer were just round the corner and there was a feeling of expectation. But two problems were looming, which had to be faced. The first concerned accommodation. Mr and Mrs Church had warned us that we would have to leave at the end of May, because they let their house during the summer months. We had made enquiries, but without success. Mary Husband temporarily came to our rescue and said she would take us in for a couple of weeks, but after that we still had nowhere to go.

It was becoming a distinct worry, until one day we found an anonymous note in our letter-box, telling us to telephone a certain Mevagissey number. We did so at once and were told, to our great surprise, that we could have a flat for the whole summer at a most reasonable figure. It turned out to be just what we wanted, with a small garden and plenty of room. We never found out who did us this good turn, despite enquiries.

Our second problem concerned me a great deal. Neither Sam nor I were capable of fishing with dog-lines. I needed, as Willie Wish had told me, a top-grade fisherman, and no top-grade fisherman was going to jump at joining a boat with two novices aboard. I was aware that some of the fishermen were discussing my problem, Willie Rolling, Willie Wish, Peter Barron, Edgar Husband all had our interests at heart, and this fact and Biddie's quiet assurance that something would turn up sustained me. There was little that I could do but wait and see what would happen. Then, all of a sudden, our problem was solved. It was Willie Rolling who came up one evening to break the news to us.

"George Pearce will go with you," he said without any preamble and I gratefully gave him the usual packet of Woodbines, which promptly disappeared into his cap. We were relieved, to say the least, and Biddie poured out cups of tea.

Later, when I walked with Willie across the field, he suggested that I should give George Pearce half the boat's share, for he was, as Willie put it, a really good man. I had little doubt that Willie and others had engineered it all, and I felt a warmth for him as I watched his small figure, with its rolling gait, go steadily down past the coastguard station and out of sight.

On the way back I called in at Sam's house and told him the good news. I was invited in and given yet another cup of tea and a piece of home-made cake.

That night Biddie and I sank into the deep feather mattress of our bed, easy of mind, for our two problems had been solved. We now had somewhere to live for the coming summer and, more important still, a top-grade fisherman had agreed to join us as crew and show us how to work a dog-line.

Chapter 13

George Pearce and dogging

As HE LEANT comfortably against the wall, he appeared to me a veritable Falstaff in the flesh, a great Humpty-Dumpty of a man, on whose bull-like shoulders sat a round head, and to whose ample paunch clung a long grey sweater. His cap was flat and sat slightly on the back of his head. His eyes were a quizzical blue and shrewd, and he chewed a plug of tobacco continuously, turning his head occasionally to emit a stream of spittle from the corner of his mouth — they called it 'gobbing'. It was with distinct apprehension that I approached George Pearce, for I suspected he was a man of few words.

"I hear you would like to come with us, George," I ventured. It was, however, as I had feared, for he looked at me, said nothing, and there resulted one of those awkward pauses in which the lead has to be firmly taken and something has to be said. It was clear that George was in no way embarrassed, so I began again. "I'd be very grateful if you would join us."

This made a sharper impression, for he turned to gob again and murmured something I could not catch. I suggested he might like to come and see our gear and added that the loft would be open all morning, to which I received only a curt nod, followed by another stream of spittle, in the face of which I beat as dignified a retreat as I could muster.

Once I had gained the sanctuary of my loft I sat down on a wooden box and, peering through the window down into J.B.'s yard, felt far from confident. The meeting with George Pearce could not have been more awkward. I began to wonder if I had not made a grave mistake in parting from George Allen. Sitting wrapped in increasing gloom, I was startled by the abrupt entrance of Edgar Husband and at once I felt better.

"George Pearce is a very good man," he remarked immediately. "He'll put you right and he knows what he's about."

I was grateful indeed for this news and told Edgar that, after my first conversation with George Pearce, I was beginning to wonder whether something had gone wrong, perhaps George never had any real intention of coming with us. At this Edgar laughed out loud, and no sound could have been more reassuring.

"Of course he's coming with you, and you've got a damn good man in George," he assured me. "He's a damn good man," he repeated, still laughing.

Edgar had a habit of screwing up his eyes when he laughed and it was the most infectious laugh and comical expression imaginable. He would make some preposterous statement, speaking very quickly and with a perfectly straight face, but it was too much for him and, unable to contain himself, he would screw up his eyes and laugh silently till the tears ran down his cheeks. Edgar and his brother Peter were great leg-pullers, but there was never any malice in their fun. I was to have many laughs with them and they were clearly intrigued by the *Coral's* activities.

Together we went over to see Uncle Dick and, on the way back I popped into Roland Billing's to have a cup of coffee and a crab sandwich. Apart from the fact that I have never tasted better crab sandwiches, I enjoyed chatting with Roland about football. He kept goal for St Austell and Cornwall and was a good player. He talked about the Mevagissey football team, so I told him I would like to play for the side next season.

When I returned to the loft I found the door open and George Pearce examining our gear. "You haven't finished making up these dog-lines," he grunted. Turning his head, he emitted a dark stream of tobacco juice which hit the floor with a splash. I wasn't sure what he had said so I gave a non-committal answer, which seemed to satisfy him. George Pearce was never easy to hear or understand, for he invariably had a plug of tobacco in his cheek when he spoke. I knew he was irritated when I asked him to repeat himself, so until I got the hang of things I was constantly misunderstanding him and sometimes doing the opposite of what he intended.

That afternoon we finished making up our dog-lines of 3,000 hooks, each of us working 1,000 hooks. That completed I locked the loft door, and went into J.B.'s office to order six stone of pilchards for baiting the line the following day.

"Going to put your dog-line aboard?" he enquired.

"Yes," I replied, "and George Pearce is joining us."

He nodded, and I could tell he was pleased about that. I bade him good night and walked home. It was pleasant to sit, tired and relaxed, watching through the window as the light slowly faded over Chapel Point. Next week we would no longer be here, for our time was up. We were moving down into the harbour to stay with Mary Husband for ten days before going to our new home. We were going to miss this splendid view, but there were other things which would compensate for it. Having a bathroom was one. At Ranelagh we had to make do with a tin tub filled with kettles of hot water in which we washed before our sitting-room fire. Mrs Church had been most friendly towards us. Her husband was a remarkable old man, well into his seventies, who, most mornings of the year, regardless of wind and rain, would venture down the precipitous cliff path to the beach below and collect firewood. He never failed to bring back something. Biddie won his admiration by bathing on occasions, but I did not attempt to compete. My time in the Mediterranean had ruined what pleasure I had ever taken in bathing around these shores.

The following morning we collected our six stone of pilchards and salt, and began cutting up the bait aboard the *Coral*, slicing each pilchard into five or six pieces before sweeping them with the blade of the knife into boxes of salt. Periodically we would pause and sharpen the bait-knives on a carborundum.

My first attempt at cutting up a pilchard produced an angry snort from George Pearce, as he saw me inexpertly sawing through a fish.

"You're not cutting a loaf of bread," he grunted turning his head to gob over the side, before showing me how to cut a pilchard into four or five pieces with clean sweeps of the knife. I tried again and met with success. Sam, who had been watching discreetly, also got the hang of it and eventually we got our bait cut up and salted.

Next George showed us how to bait up the dog-line, setting our tubs at a convenient height so we need not stoop. We had five tubs of line to bait and each tub contained three hundred and fifty fathoms of hemp line with six hundred hooks on it. The hooks, at the end of eighteen-inch 'stops', were secured to the main line at regular three-foot intervals.

Taking a tub each, we tipped the lot out. With our empty tubs alongside we began baiting up. The hooks were a good two inches in the shank and each bait was hooked and with a quick twist hooked again, so it would not drop off. When the first piece of line was coiled into each tub, a short length free of hooks was left hanging over the edge, so that it could all be joined together into one long line before being shot. The baited hooks were laid one on top of the other along one third of the inside of the tub.

George worked swiftly and deftly, every so often turning his head to gob over the *Coral's* side. Well before Sam and I had completed baiting our lines, George was well on his way baiting up the fourth tub. Together Sam and I baited up the sixth tub. Finished at last, we covered the tubs with tarpaulins, weighted down in order to protect the baits from rain and marauding gulls — I once saw one caught on a hook and it was not a pretty sight.

Finally we carried down the two big dan buoys, their flags drumming in the wind, and the two baskets of dan line, eighty fathoms in each basket, with the two creepers made by Albert lying on top.

"Have you ordered the six stone of bait and salt for the morning?" George asked me. I assured him I had. "Got enough fuel aboard?"

"I've topped up both tanks and we've an extra five gallons of petrol and five of paraffin." I had not forgotten that first night out. "When shall we start?" I asked him.

"Be down at four," and he gave us both a sharp glance before heading off towards the Ship Inn.

Sam accompanied me up-along-Cliff, for it was not that much further for him to go.

"Well," I said when we reached Ranelagh, "we shall know what we are in for tomorrow."

"We shall indeed," he replied, "and so will George."

"See you at four," I called after him as he walked on to his home at the end of Beach Road.

Willie came up that evening, but would not come in, so I strolled with him back across the field. I felt he wanted to reassure me, but I knew he would never wish me luck — no fisherman would ever make such a comment, for these were a superstitious people, and I quickly learnt that one word — 'rabbits' — must never be mentioned. Indeed, in the not too distant past, should a vicar be spotted on the quayside, the men would return home immediately and not put to sea. Even now there were crews who would not begin the season, or put their gear aboard, on a Friday. Sunday, for many, was, without compromise, the Sabbath, to be kept holy. During my short time as a fisherman, I do not once recall seeing a Mevagissey woman down on the quayside; perhaps the old superstition that women brought men bad luck when they were about their boats still prevailed in 1946.

The alarm went off at half-past three, and I was loath to leave the enveloping warmth of our deep feather mattress. I dressed quickly while Biddie made up a thermos flask of tea. My grub, a pasty, a hard-boiled egg and a piece of cake was ready in my bag. It was time to go.

"Good luck," she said.

"Better not let Willie hear you say that," and I kissed her goodbye.

I made my way down-along-Cliff, past the coastguard station, pausing above Frazer's Yard to look down at the old Watch House, the lighthouse and outer harbour, where the luggers lay, grey shapes anchored out in the 'pool'. Over on Polkirt Hill the lights of one or two cottages shone wanly. Below me, figures were moving along the quayside, engines spluttering into life, punts being sculled across the inner harbour, their crews standing, some silent, some chattering, the dark hours of that early morning alive with the sound of boats preparing for sea.

Sam was already down, but George had not yet arrived, so we collected the basket of bait and box of salt and pulled the *Babs* alongside the steps.

"Here he is," said Sam.

"Morning, George," we greeted him and received a gruff grunt in reply as his massive figure clambered down and stepped aboard the punt, in which the three of us now stood, while George sculled the short distance out to the *Coral*. It never ceased to amaze me that the pram bore our weight, for George was all of sixteen stone and more, Sam was six foot three, and I was six foot.

While Sam stowed our grub up for'ard, I opened up the engine-room hatches, switched on the petrol, primed the Thornycroft and swung her. She started easily and I closed the hissing priming valves.

"Go astern," called George as Sam let go our moorings. I did not wait for George's "Knock her out" but gave the *Coral* a kick ahead. We were under way, motoring through the outer harbour with several others. Once past the light I started up the Kelvin and our first day of dogging had begun.

Approaching Chapel Point I remembered I had not switched the Kelvin over to paraffin, so quickly opened the tap and closed the petrol feed. George had not noticed. We passed well to seaward of the Gwineas buoy, its light flashing, its melancholy bell tolling in the moderate swell, and I recalled again that first night out and then deliberately put it behind me as we motored on.

Gradually in the east a faint streak of grey heralded the dawn and I felt the better for it. To starboard the Gull Rock and Nare Head were visible and the distant headland of St Anthony was slowly emerging. Standing in the engine-room and leaning over the hatch cover I glanced at the compass. We were heading west by south. George had hoisted his great bulk onto the top of the engine-room and was sitting by the wheel, steering, wedging himself in with one thick thigh boot thrust against the gunwale.

Sam, meanwhile, had begun cutting up our six stone of pilchard bait so I squeezed past George and went for'ard to lend a hand.

"Give 'em plenty of salt," said George. "Dogs like salt bait and if there's a spell of bad weather and we're in for a bit, the line's all right."

He seemed satisfied with our efforts because, after that piece of advice, he paid us no more attention. Taking out his pipe he filled and lit it. I was not sure what had happened to the tobacco he had been chewing, presumably it had dissolved and gone over the side.

"All right, Sam?" I enquired. We had finished cutting up the bait and were leaning on the foredeck gazing at the splendid coastline, the distant Lizard clearly visible off our starboard bow.

Before he had time to reply the Kelvin started to falter and lose power. "Have a look at the jets," advised George as I clambered past him and knelt in the confined space of the engine-room. Groping round the side of the Kelvin with my left arm, my body pressed against the hot engine. Using an adjustable spanner, I loosened the for'ard jet sufficiently to unscrew it with my fingers. It came away with a spurt of paraffin. Still holding the small jet I tried with the same hand to turn off the feed to the carburettor. I succeeded in doing this, but also in dropping the jet down into the bilges.

"Got it?" came an impatient bellow through the open hatchway above and, looking up from my kneeling position, I saw George's great round face peering down at me.

"Nearly," I lied weakly.

"Well, is it blocked, man? Is the bloody thing blocked?" Fortunately, before I had to confess that I had lost the 'bloody thing', he had disappeared.

Praying hard, for the chance of finding the jet was small, I groped round the side of the engine and plunged my hand down into the slime of the bilges as far as I could reach. There were plenty of pilchard scales and one or two fish-hooks and suddenly I felt something small and hard. It was the jet all right and I breathed a sigh of relief.

I got to my feet, stiff from the awkward position in which I had been working. "Here we are, George."

He took the jet, held it up to his eye, then put it to his lips and blew a great juicy blast through the tiny aperture. Without a word, but with a keen glance, he handed it back to me. I replaced it, tightened it up with a spanner and, surfacing, switched on the fuel. I wiped my hands on some engine-room waste and, leaning over the side, watched the intermittent splash of the exhaust quicken to an even flow as the for'ard two cylinders fired.

Sam who had been watching from his distant and enviable position up for'ard gave the thumbs-up sign. George glanced round and gave me a slight nod of approval, took his pipe out of his mouth and gobbed over the side. But that slight nod delighted me because I detected a momentary flash of distinct amusement in those shrewd blue eyes.

By now we were well to the west of the Manacles, between the southern Black Head and the Lizard. George had been altering course a good deal, glancing frequently at the coast until he had got his bearings and was in the position from which he wished to shoot the line.

"Shut down the Kelvin," he ordered. Leaning over into the engine-room he knocked the Thornycroft into neutral, at the same time calling Sam to pass one of the dan buoys. Swiftly he bent on the dan line, then with a quick glance astern at the coast and compass, he lifted the dan buoy over the side and lowered it into the water, calling me to go ahead. As the *Coral* gently gathered way, with a flinging motion of his right arm he shot the eighty fathoms of dan line in a flat arc from out of the basket.

"Knock her out," he shouted, slinging the empty basket up for'ard. Picking up the creeper onto which the dog-line was attached, he lowered it into the water and began shooting the line due east before the floodtide. "Knock her in," he called, sending arc after arc of baited hooks flying through the air. "Knock her out," I heard him shout, as the boat gathered too much headway, glancing at the compass and round at the dan buoy now some distance astern. Satisfied, he continued shooting the line with that rhythmic movement of his right arm, flinging the flying hooks overboard as though sowing seed. As he came to the last hundred hooks in each tub, Sam would bend on the next tub of line to be shot, pushing it in front of George after first pulling away the empty one.

Three tubs had been shot when several hooks fouled in the fourth tub. Quickly knocking the engine into neutral I watched George struggle to hold the taut line and with astonishing speed clear the entangled hooks and stops. A bait knife was always at hand to cut the stop of any offending hook that failed to clear.

By now I could anticipate when to go ahead and when to knock the engine out of gear and forestall George's orders. Half an hour later the last bit of line was shot overboard and the second creeper, the end of the dog-line attached to a fluke, was on its way to the seabed. In no time George shot the last eighty fathoms of dan rope and, lifting the second buoy over the side, dropped it onto the water. The whole line of three thousand hooks now lay stretched along the bottom, anchored by the two creepers, marked on the surface by the two dan buoys. As we motored slowly back to the western dan we ate our grub. The time was half-past eight. Overhead the sun broke warmly from behind a high cloud and touched St Anthony's Head and the white lighthouse at its foot. There was plenty of blue sky about. Two big tankers lay anchored off Falmouth. Fishing boats, distant specks, were dotted around the horizon, one not so far off, its outline visible. "Looks like the *Margaret* over there," said George, nodding, at the same time throwing the remains of his tea over the side. "They'll be working six thousand hooks and have three and a half miles to haul." Using his penknife, he cut himself a plug of tobacco, put it into his mouth. Donning his faded, worn yellow oilskin he began hoisting the mizzen. Sam had put on his black naval oilskin, but there was no need for me to follow suit, since my task was to tend the engine, mizzen and wheel in order to keep the *Coral* up to the line, while George did the hauling facing aft standing on the fish-berth hatches, Sam alongside him.

With only the Thornycroft slowly turning over, I brought the boat starboard side to the western dan. Leaning over, George lifted it and the white bladder aboard and began to haul in the dan rope, coiling it swiftly into the basket until the rope was up and down. Putting it across his great shoulders he broke the creeper out of the seabed, hauled it up, unbent the line from the fluke and began the haul.

Stemming the tide, keeping the *Coral's* bows up to the line I peered over the side to see green shapes slanting down into the dark water. "Go ahead," called George, as he pulled in the line hand over hand, until the first few dogs came up over the gunwale to be quickly unhooked and sent spinning into the net-room, which we now used as a fish-berth. Effortlessly George removed each fish. I watched closely as he handled dog after dog, catching hold of the stop with his left hand and twisting the hook out of their mouths, which made a slight grating noise like a tooth being drawn. Suddenly he stopped hauling.

"Always catch hold of 'em when you're handling dogs by the back of the head," he said, holding up a big one, "otherwise you'll get pricked," and he showed us the vicious spur on the foreside of each dorsal fin. "They can make a nasty mess of your wrist," he warned, despatching the creature with a flick of his wrist into the fish-berth.

The dogs, varying in size from two to three feet, resembled miniature sharks, grey, streamlined and sinister with unwinking green eyes and flat underhanging mouths. A number of starfish, 'five-finger-Jacks' came up which George wrenched off and tossed into the water. "Never touch these," he said, dangling a gurnard, its spines erect on head and body, and he thrashed it against the side of the *Coral's* gunwale so that the ugly red-tinged fish dropped off the hook.

While George hauled, sometimes calling me to go ahead or knock her out, according to whether the line was slack or taut, Sam cleared and coiled the line into an empty tub. Both stood alongside each other facing aft.

A big twenty-pound brown-backed huss came up, its sides pale, its twisting body covered in large black spots, which George promptly chucked overboard. "And there's no market for these kind of dogs," he said, gripping a 'row'ound' by the middle so that its tail could not coil round his arm. "They've no spur, but they've got a hide like sandpaper," and it too went back into the water. "Haul in on your sheet," he said, glancing up at the mizzen. "Right, knock her in," and he continued to haul the line and Sam to clear and coil.

"Gaff," said George and, glancing over the side, I could see a triangular shape in the water coming to the surface. "Their mouths can crush a broom handle," and he gaffed the big, ugly thorn-backed ray and, with a quick twist of the T hook, capsized the hook before sending the ray into the fish-berth.

I could see George leaning back, pulling against something that was heavy on the line. "Skate," he said, "you can feel its weight when they go broadside on. Here he is."

Using a gaff each, I helped George lift the huge fish aboard, where it lay ponderously on the hatches, hissing its life away as it slithered down into the fish-berth. Steadily George continued hauling the line which still contained plenty of dogs.

"Ease your sheet," he called to me yet once more. Having done so, I turned, just in time to see him reach over and gaff a six-foot conger. Fascinated, I watched as he slashed the stop near the conger's mouth making no attempt to retrieve the hook. "Knock her out," he shouted again, glancing in my direction with a hint of amusement in those blue eyes: "Never let one of them get hold of you," he warned, using the gaff to steer the writhing monster into the fish-berth.

I wondered whether George would let us have a turn at hauling the line, but he showed no such inclination and I thought it unwise to offer our services. By simply watching him at work we were learning a lot.

"Never try and haul one of these out of the water, they've soft mouths and will drop off the hook," he explained. "There's his mate swimming up behind. Gaff him first," and, leaning over, I gaffed the unattached turbot and then George gaffed the one on the line. We caught several more turbot that day and still the dogs came up thickly.

"Knock her in, knock her out; ease your sheet, haul in on your sheet; starboard your wheel, ease your wheel;" so it continued for the best part of four hours, until finally we came to the eastern dan, which George lifted aboard, then hauled up the creeper, unbent the line from the fluke and the haul was over. It was one o'clock.

I was feeling tired and Sam looked as though he had had enough, but not George, who seemed none the worse for having pulled the entire length of line.

"Start the Kelvin," he called, nodding to me. Stationing himself alongside Sam, he tipped out one of the tubs of line and after first 'gobbing' into the tub — he always did this before he began baiting up — he shoved a tub of line in my direction. "You can bait up as well as steer, and you might as well lower the mizzen," he added with a nod and another gob over the side and what I thought was a bit of a smile.

With both engines at full speed I headed for the Dodman, visible in the clear light. The wind had freshened strongly from the northwest and every so often spray came over the bows as we punched our way home.

Standing by the wheel, steering and baiting up, I glanced occasionally at George and Sam facing me across the net-room. Sam was a slow, methodical worker and I could see he would never go much faster. His movements were deliberate and to every one hook that he baited, George did two. They could not have looked more different, George squat and massive in his yellow, faded oilskin with a bit of scarf wrapped round his neck, Sam tall and lean, his old trilby pulled well down over his angular face, his body protected by a black naval oilskin. He looked very tired and was getting the worst of the weather by being on the windward side of the boat. I did my best to avoid the short steep seas, but every so often one would hit the *Coral's* bluff bow, sending a curtain of spray clean over the boat, dousing Sam, wetting my face and beating a tattoo on the front of my oilskin before running down onto the top of the petrol tank over which I stood.

It seemed to take a long time to reach the Dodman. Before me an ominously large pile of hooks and line lay awaiting baiting up. I was about halfway through. Sam had about the same amount still to bait up. But George had already finished his tub of line and was well on the way to completing a second one. Throwing an occasional glance over his shoulder to see how we were progressing, he seemed impervious to the spray and not in the least weary, in spite of the fact that he had been working the hardest of us all. He quickly cleared, baited the hooks, and coiled the line with skilful ease, chewing his tobacco, gobbing over the side at regular intervals, saying little, but missing nothing. He had not a great deal of patience when things went wrong, but I knew that beneath his gruff exterior lay a kind heart and, provided he was home in time for a beer, he seemed prepared to tolerate our lack of knowledge and ability.

By half-past four we had entered the outer harbour and brought the *Coral* alongside the lighthouse quay, where J.B.'s lorry was standing ready for us to offload our fish. Baskets were slung down, the net-room hatches were removed and George, standing in the fish-berth, chucked the dogfish two at a time into the baskets, while Sam and I hooked the ropes onto each handle, before signalling Tony up on the quayside to hoist away on the little motor crane. When all the dogfish had gone we sent up the baskets of ray and turbot and the conger in a basket on its own. The latter, still alive, had got its teeth into a dogfish which George dealt with by standing on the conger's stomach, which made the fish, not surprisingly, release its quarry. Finally, there remained the skate. These were sent up singly, the hooks on the crane's rope being inserted into the skate's mouth.

"Go on," said George. "Go and see 'em weighed, we'll put her to her moorings," and I climbed the steps up onto the lighthouse quay.

"Got a few dogs, Ken," said Tony, who drove J.B.'s lorry. He was always friendly and helpful and invariably in a great hurry. "Hop on the back."

We drove along the outer harbour quay and into Edwards' store, where Waller and Tony whipped the baskets off the lorry and Waller weighed the dogfish first. Then he weighed the basket of ray and conger, and finally he put the great skates flat on the weighing machine.

"Bit of 'huffy' here," said Waller pointing to the half full basket of turbot. I had no idea what he was talking about and told him so.

"Well, it's like this, old man," explained Waller. "If you get a lobster or a turbot or a crayfish or two, they fetch a lot of money, so instead of the usual sharing system, the money is split evenly between the crew."

I thanked him for the information and watched as he quickly wrote out a chit and handed it me. We had caught just over a hundred and fifty stone of fish. Delighted, I went out and joined Sam and George on the quayside, who had just put the *Coral* to her moorings. I showed George the chit and mentioned the word 'huffy'. He gave a slight nod, said nothing, but I could tell he was pleased and so was Sam.

"What time tomorrow, George?" I asked.

"Be down at four. Have you ordered the bait and salt?"

"No," I admitted.

"Well, you'd better," and then he added, "I've left a turbot aboard for you to take home for the missus," and with that he was gone. I watched him go up the narrow alleyway, his massive figure rolling away in his white sea-boots, both hands thrust deep into his pockets, his red food tin under his arm, a splash of colour against his pale blue, much washed smock.

"I know where he's bound for," said Sam. "The Ship Inn."

"Better get back aboard and finish baiting up that fifth tub of line," I suggested. "I'll get the fuel, you order the bait and salt."

It was half-past six when we finished our first day of dogging. Once home, I gave Biddie the turbot, took off my sea-boots and sank into an armchair. It was then I realised how weary I was. I drank a cup of tea and thought with dismay of four o'clock next morning when we would start up our engines and repeat the whole performance. Gradually my tiredness eased and I sat relaxed, listening to the wireless, waiting for the weather forecast.

Barely had my head touched the pillow than I fell into a deep, velvet oblivion, only to be wrenched back to consciousness by the harsh metallic clamour of the alarm clock. For a moment my heart sank, my spirits plummeted. I was filled with that same feeling of dismay I used to experience when summoned by the shrill piping of the bosun's whistle, or the rough shake of a messmate to turn out for the middle or morning watch. But once up and about it soon evaporated.

There was a fine drizzle and sea mist as I quietly closed the small iron gate behind me and set off across the field. Below I could hear the steady beat of engines. When the sleeping harbour finally came into view, a lugger was already heading out through the mouth of the harbour, while overhead the white beam of the lighthouse probed the darkness.

I was first down, so collected the basket of bait and salt. By then George and Sam had arrived. Sculling out to the *Coral* we climbed aboard, started up the Handy Billy, and got under way, towing the pram which we anchored out in the 'pool' since it would be low water when we returned.

Once more we headed sou'west and while Sam and I cut up the bait, George steered. "*Margaret* caught seventy stone yesterday," he announced cryptically after we had been coming some time. This was news indeed, for Edgar and his crew worked twice our number of hooks. I was busy thinking how well we had done the previous day, when his next remark brought me swiftly back to earth. "You can have a go this time," he said, giving me a hard look.

We motored on for another two hours, until George, who was steering and casting occasional glances at the land to check his bearings, shut down the Kelvin and nodded at me to start. I lifted the dan over the side and began shooting the line. Several times a hook fouled which, with Sam's assistance, we cleared. Apart from that, I managed to shoot the lot overboard under the close scrutiny of George, who said nothing, though when I lowered the second dan onto the water and the line was finally down, he gave a slight nod of approval in my direction. It was recognition enough.

Motoring slowly back to the first buoy, we ate our grub, resting as best we could, gazing out over the placid water at the distant coastline now bathed in sunlight, until it was time to start the haul. Slowly George brought the *Coral* alongside the first dan buoy which I lifted aboard and handed to Sam.

Hauling and coiling in the eighty fathoms of dan line, it was quickly up and down. With my knee against the gunwale, I leaned back until, with a jerk, the tension of the rope lessened.

"Creeper's aweigh," I called.

"Well, haul it up then. Haul the damn thing up," said George testily.

Soon I could see the fish down below. As the creeper came out of the water, I handed it to George, who quickly unbent the line and passed it back to me, "Pull steadily," he said, as the first dogfish came up over the gunwale, twisting and turning. I grabbed at it with my right hand, conscious of those two spurs. I missed the creature and grabbed at it again.

"Get hold of it, man!" shouted George.

At the third attempt, more frightened of George than the fish, I gripped the dog by the back of the head with my right hand, experiencing its cold, coarse skin. With my left hand I grasped the shank of the hook between thumb and index finger, at the same time holding the line with my right hand. Then, with a quick twist of both hands, as I had seen George do, the hook came free, making that slight grating sound, and I sent the fish spinning through the dark hole of the net-room to land on the *Coral's* bottom boards with a dull thud.

I had handled my first dogfish. Here came the second. I could see plenty more on the line as it slanted downward through the clear water. Gradually I became more adept at handling the dogs and was able to look around and throw an occasional glance at the squat, massive figure of George tending the wheel and engine, waiting for a tub of line to bait up. Alongside me Sam stood, head bent, slowly and methodically clearing and coiling. Suddenly I felt the line tauten and become fast.

I held on grimly, aware of Sam's nearly full tub of line on my right-hand side. There was a distinct possibility of the line taking charge and the hooks running through my hands. Something had to give.

"Turn up on the line," I heard George call, as it started to slip through my hands. But, before Sam could come to my aid, I felt the line jump and break out, enabling me to continue hauling once more. I caught George's eye.

"Must have fouled something," I suggested.

"Line's over some 'hitchy' ground," he grunted.

"What do you do when that happens?"

"Hang on," he retorted.

There were not so many fish as yesterday, but enough to keep me busy. After a while I could feel there was something heavy below and said so to George.

"Skate probably."

Deep down I caught sight of a vague triangular shape. Then the line came in more easily again and I thought he had gone, but he was only swimming up with the line and not resisting. I could now see him clearly, a huge bat-like creature. Again he lay broadside on and I probably pulled too fiercely, for again he broke free.

"Lost him!' I said.

"Pull more steadily," advised George.

In fact I had not lost him, for the great fish promptly swallowed another bait and it occurred to me that the skate could neither be afraid nor hurt. Leaning over, George gaffed and dragged the fish up onto the net-room hatches, where it lay making that strange hissing sound I had heard earlier.

By now my hands were sore, my arms and back were aching and I was working more slowly. I was halfway through pulling the third rub of line, when George knocked the engine out of gear and clambered across the net-room. Without a word he took over the line and I took over his position in the stern, steering and baiting up. Despite his enormous bulk he moved with surprising speed and agility.

Shortly after one o'clock the line was all in and we were homeward bound and, by mid-afternoon, back alongside the lighthouse quay unloading our fish. Before going in to watch the catch weighed, I filled up the *Coral's* tanks. Then, climbing up the steps onto the quay, I sat on the back of Tony's lorry and, with both arms resting on the two empty fuel drums either side of me, we motored round the outer harbour and into J.B.'s store where the baskets of fish were promptly put on the scales. We had caught seventy-two stone in all, mostly dogs, a few ling, ray and skate, no turbot this time.

I ordered the bait and salt for the following morning, picked up the two empty five-gallon drums and set off for William, the engineer.

"I'll give you a lift back if you hurry up," called Tony.

"All right, Ken?" William asked, stooping to fill the drums with petrol. Rolling a half-smoked unlit cigarette across his mouth, his eyes were amused and alert as ever. With difficulty, for they were heavy and awkward to grip, I carried the two five-gallon drums, one on each arm, along the quayside to the lorry.

"Put 'em on the back and hop aboard," I heard Tony shout and he drove me out to the lighthouse quay, where I found just enough strength to carry the drums down the steps and hand them to Sam.

We took the *Coral* out into the 'pool' and anchored her fore and aft, for it would be low water when we came down the following morning. Then we finished baiting up, climbed over the side and sculled ashore.

For the rest of the week we met at four each morning, motored off for two to three hours, shot and hauled our line, motored back, baiting up all the while, finishing around six in the evening. They were long, full days and I would return weary and satiated with sea air to a quiet welcome from Biddie. During those early days I must have been a dull companion in the evenings, for I was physically incapable of anything but dozing in a chair as the fatigue of the past fourteen hours overcame me. Biddie was a great support for she was ever patient, understanding and encouraging, never demanding.

J.B. paid me on Saturday and in the loft I shared out the money with Sam and George. We had not done badly, having caught three hundred and ninety-seven stone of fish and, when the expenses of fuel and bait had been deducted, there were some forty pounds to share. Sam received ten pounds and George and I fifteen pounds apiece, for I split the boat's share with him. I was never to earn as much again when dogging, although we worked just as hard.

Above: Biddie in 1947

Chapter 14

Spiltering with George Pearce

THAT WEEKEND we moved down to Mary Husband's. She lived just above the harbour on the north side, less than half a minute's climb from the quayside. No cars could reach this snug little alley with its whitewashed stone cottages, thick, irregular walls and small windows, a sure protection against those wild winter nights when the wind came thundering in from the sea to seek out every sheltered nook and cranny. Some of the cottages were still linked by passages, relics of the days of smuggling, when contraband was run up to the cliff-tops and dispersed inland. An archway led into a small courtyard which once contained nets and lines and salted fish for the winter months. Her front door lay just inside to the right. We knocked and Mary Husband herself opened the door and invited us in.

We found ourselves at once in the main low-beamed eating and living room. In the centre was a fair-sized rectangular table around which were six chairs. Two easy chairs stood on either side of the fireplace. In one of these crouched an old man, poking the fire. A settee lay up against the window, an upright piano stood against another wall and a small sideboard ran along the fourth wall.

"I'll show you your room," said Mary Husband. She breathed heavily as we followed her up a narrow flight of wooden stairs. "I've put you in here," she panted, opening a door at the top, and left us to it.

The room was small and the two narrow beds did not look very comfortable. I had noticed a peculiar smell down below and I could now smell it in our bedroom. I suddenly felt depressed and shut in and with difficulty opened the single tiny window.

Biddie, however, was quite unperturbed and assured me gently that Mary was a dear. "After all," she pointed out, "Mary has taken us in and she's charging us very little."

I knew she was right and felt better as fresh sea air seeped in through the open window. I suggested we had a walk round the village before the shops closed.

We bought a few things we needed and I noticed how friendly everyone was towards Biddie. I could see they accepted her and were ready to help her as the fishermen helped me. We wandered back along Church Street before making our way out past the old lifeboat-house, along Lighthouse 'Kay', until we reached the steep steps cut into the cliff leading up to the sloping green field at the top of Polkirt Hill. There we lay on the grass and looked across the bay to the Black Head, the Gribbin and distant shape of Looe Island just visible. The sun was hot, the sea a-glitter, the view as handsome as could be. Half an hour later we got to our feet, walked down Polkirt Hill, along Fore Street and into St George's Square where we ran into Peter Barron.

"I hear you're staying with Mary Husband," he began. "The missus and I would like you both to come and have tea with us one weekend." We thanked him.

Back in Mary's living room a late high tea was being prepared. The old man still crouched over the grate, but there were now two others in the room, a man and a child. Mr Close had a facial paralysis, which made his speech very difficult to understand. He had injured himself severely when he slipped and fell on his back climbing up a wooden pile at low water in Looe Harbour. He owned the *Manxman*, a small lugger which fished for him. He had been up at Oxford and would talk to me of pre-war university days. I liked him; he had courage.

The child was a girl of ten, who had been evacuated during the war and now seemed to live permanently with Mary. She had one maddening habit, which she indulged throughout the day, even during mealtimes. She chewed bubble-gum, with which she made sharp little explosions. I could put up with it during the day, provided I did not inadvertently put my hand on a piece of gum which she had left lying around. But to spot her suddenly, in the middle of a meal, pop a piece of half-chewed gum into her mouth, a piece which had been sticking conveniently on the dining table, and contort her mouth in such a way as to produce yet another sharp explosion, I found difficult to ignore.

Mary seemed indifferent to it. I suppose by now she had grown accustomed to the explosions. Nor did the old man worry, but then he was deaf and heard little, except when Mary ordered him to stop poking the fire, which invariably sent him into a paroxysm of rage and reduced Mary to silent heaves of laughter. Mr Close, however, liked it as little as I did, but he was too fond of Mary to say anything. I could see she was a great support to him, for under her easy-going roof he could live a normal life, close to the two things he loved most, the sea and his boat.

Those days we spent under Mary's roof neither of us will forget. We quickly learnt that cats were responsible for the smell which pervaded the cottage. There were three or four of them, enormous creatures, which would leap onto the kitchen table with silent grace and crouch defiantly amongst the unwashed pots and pans, dishes and cups. I have but to close my eyes to see Mary of an evening sitting upright on the left side of the fireplace, a cat stretched across her lap, the old man hunched in his chair on the opposite side of the hearth holding his palms to the fire, while Biddie and I sat on the hard sofa and Mr Close read *The Telegraph* spread out on the table. Every now and then the crack of bursting bubble-gum punctured the conversation followed by Mary's request: "Go to bed, Peggy." Suddenly, and to my distaste, for I am no cat lover, and consequently had been keeping a wary eye open, a great furry creature would land on my lap and sink its claws into my thighs, as I moved with instinctive revulsion.

Mary was a very big, overweight lady who moved slowly, resigned to the fact that her breath was short and her feet painful. She had plenty of fair hair and a full round face, smooth and unworried. She was placid and benign; the cares of the world — and these she had certainly experienced — had left no mark upon her, for she refused to bow to them. Her movements were slow and deliberate as she puffed and padded her way around in slippers, but her mind was quick and active. Sitting of an evening in her straight-backed chair, gazing into the fire with a cat stretched motionless across her knees, its head up and eyes closed, did she even bother to listen to the conversation going on, I wondered. I was soon aware that she not only did, but joined in with a will.

It usually began with Mr Close commenting on something he had just read in *The Telegraph* whereupon Mary would query his comment — often I suspect deliberately — smiling broadly to herself and nodding her head as the *Manxman's* owner lengthily and somewhat testily disagreed. She had a good sense of humour, at times an impish one, particularly when she teased the old man until he would brandish the poker in her face causing her huge frame to shake with seismic gusts of laughter.

Her brother, Joe, would come up most evenings. He was a tall, heavily built man, who invariably wore a blue serge suit and an old flat yachting cap which he never took off indoors. Mary would give him a cup of tea and piece of cake and he'd sit upright, looking remarkably like his sister, smiling, but saying little.

We continued dogging, experiencing days when the weather was 'wisht', bad, and the tubs of line slid all over the place as the *Coral* rolled and plunged in the seas. I learnt what effect the tide had on the line and how important it was to keep the boat heading into the tide in case it be swept away from the line.

"You can see it now," said George, nodding at the buoy which was leaning over, hard pressed by the rush and weight of water as we drew near to pick it up. When the moon was full and the spring tides at their highest we did not go to sea.

One Friday afternoon as I steered the *Coral* through the outer harbour after a long day of dogging, George announced that we would start spiltering the following week. Tired, but content at the prospect of a restful weekend ahead, I walked home.

I awoke next morning at a civilised hour and, keeping a weather-eye open for the cats, ate an unhurried breakfast seated at a table instead of hauling a line aboard a pitching small boat some fifteen miles offshore.

When I later reached the loft entrance I met Winston Barron, genial as ever, and Edgar Husband who were standing chatting.

"George and Sam are up in the loft waiting for their pay," Edgar greeted me. "They've been there these past two hours and George is becoming impatient as it's getting near opening time."

I laughed and went up the wooden steps of the loft into J.B.'s office where his daughter, Margaret, paid me our week's earnings. In fact, when I entered the loft George and Sam had not even arrived. When they did, half an hour later, I shared out the money. Along with Sam, I brought the five tubs of dog-line ashore and began removing the hooks, storing them in a large tin. The lines we would hang out to dry before taking them over to Joe Furze to be barked and tarred in preparation for another season.

George meanwhile was working on the spilter line, which is shot in the same way as a dog-line, the difference being that the spilter line is thinner, it has the same number of hooks, but they are smaller and set closer together. The shank of each hook is little more than an inch long with a flat piece at the end, over which the stops are secured with a clove hitch.

In the afternoon we walked up to Beach Road, climbed over the stile and in single file went down the precipitous path to the beach below. The tide was out;

while Biddie bathed I lay on my back and watched the white clouds drift slowly overhead. Not once had either of us felt the slightest regret at our chance encounter with George Allen which had brought us to Mevagissey.

On Sunday we went to tea with Peter Barron and his wife. They welcomed us into their tiny parlour and plied us with scones and cream and cups of strong tea. They showed us photographs of their son and talked about fishing and how it had been good during the war, but very bad at times between the wars.

"We're putting our spilter line aboard," I told him.

"'Ess," he said, "I heard you were. You'll find it a fiddly old job to begin with and a bit tedious. It's longish hours, but you'll soon get the hang of it and you've got a good man in George Pearce. He'll show you what 'tis all about."

"You must come again, my dears," said Mrs Barron as we went down the steep steps of her front door and into the crooked, narrow little alleyway that led to Mary's cottage.

Despite the cats and the sharp bubble-gum explosions, the smell and the incredible muddle in the kitchen, we had grown attached to this strange household and its varied occupants. Time did not matter, speed of movement was inessential and unlikely. Meals were never hurried affairs which began and finished at certain times, but leisurely occasions when lots of tea was drunk and Mary, at regular intervals, would pad slowly from the direction of the kitchen, breathing heavily and carrying a large brown pot of freshly made tea.

All Monday morning we worked hard finishing making up the spilter line, breaking off only to visit Uncle Dick. In the afternoon we collected a basket of mackerel from J.B.'s store to bait up the spilter line. Mackerel was more expensive than pilchard bait and cutting them up required greater skill. Holding the mackerel by its head and placing it flat on the bait board, we would insert the knife below the gills and with one clean sweep down the backbone, cut off a fillet. Turning the fish over we did the same to the other side, leaving two fillets of mackerel. These were then cut straight down the middle, making four narrow strips of mackerel which in turn would be cut into six or seven pieces, producing twenty-four or so baits from one mackerel.

I enjoyed cutting up mackerel, for the fish were much firmer than the soft pilchard and I soon found I could fillet them without even looking at the fish, simply by the feel of the blade running down its backbone. The hooks were baited in the same way as a dog hook, but being smaller, it was more fiddly work.

Willie gave us a hand during the afternoon. By five o'clock, we had finished baiting up and put the tubs aboard the *Coral*. I fuelled the boat, checked the oil, cleaned the plugs and jets and went ashore where we arranged to meet at 3.30 the following morning.

I was in bed by nine and woken at three by the alarm. I dressed quickly, filled my thermos flask with tea, picked up my tin of grub and stepped out of Mary's front door into total darkness.

I felt the wind on my face, heard it sigh and fall, only to regain strength quickly as it buffeted the thick, uneven chimney breasts and heavy stone-slated roofs of the huddled cottages. I knew if we went out today we should have a rough old time of it, for I now had enough knowledge to know at once what it would be like at sea from the direction and strength of the wind inshore.

When I got down I found that no boats had yet gone out, though most of the crews were gathered on the quayside. I joined Sam and George sitting on the benches alongside the entrance to our loft and watched the various groups, dark figures moving beneath the yellow pools of light thrown by the odd lamp scattered around the harbour. Some of the crews walked out along the north sea-wall to have a look at it. They were waiting, unsure of the weather.

All at once their indecision was shaken by the noise of an engine starting up, followed by the slow, deliberate beat of a diesel. At once eyes were focused on the dark shape of a lugger as it headed slowly into the outer harbour, its masthead and navigation lights burning brightly. It was the signal for action. With one accord the crews sculled out to their boats, started up their engines and got under way.

Well before we were outside the Gwineas we had donned our oilskins. Under the fishing light we began cutting up the bait. We spoke no words, for that hour before dawn is not much of a time for conversation. I wondered what George and Sam were thinking as they stood facing aft, wedged in against the motion of the boat, steadily cutting up the bait. George had handed over the wheel and given me a south-easterly course to steer. We finished cutting up the bait and relaxed as best we could for the next hour and a half until we reached the fishing grounds. Dotted around the horizon, boats were heading in the same direction.

Dawn was a grey affair with low scudding clouds and plenty of wind. I had to watch out that I didn't give Sam and George too many dousings, for the seas bore down on our starboard bow, the wind every so often whipping spray across the boat.

Looking around I recognised some of the luggers accompanying us. There were a number of toshers — one-man boats who motored the eighteen miles offshore to shoot and haul their lines singly.

Three hours after leaving Mevagissey Light we shut down the Kelvin, having reached the fishing grounds, a sandy patch on the seabed some five miles square, where the whiting come for a short spell during the summer months.

The boats had begun shooting their lines, all in the same direction and more or less in a long row. I watched as George manoeuvred the *Coral* into a good position, a fair distance from the nearest boat. This was important, as I was to learn later, for if the tide was strong and we were too close, our line could easily be swept down and foul that of another boat, an appalling prospect.

It was gone seven o'clock when we finished shooting the line and began motoring slowly back to the western dan buoy, eating our grub on the way. I steered the *Coral* up to the plunging buoy which George lifted aboard. In came the eighty fathoms of dan line, up came the creeper with the spilter line attached, and the long pull began.

At first the fish were scarce, but gradually they began to come, mostly whiting, with here and there an odd ray or turbot, ling or monkfish, an extraordinarily ugly fish with a short body and a huge mouth, capable of holding a small football. The merchants paid us five and six a pound for the creature. George pulled steadily, periodically calling on me to go ahead when the line was fast on the bottom. He had great strength and would hold onto the quivering line waiting for it to jerk free. He seemed to concentrate harder when this happened, and even stopped chewing. Suddenly the line would break free and he would gob over the side and give me a stern look, as though I had somehow been responsible. So we progressed, George hauling, Sam steadily clearing his line and baiting up, whilst I kept the *Coral* heading into the tide, baiting up when I could, periodically glancing over the side at the slanting line of fish.

"*Gaff,*" George shouted as a fine turbot came up.

After a while George called me to have a go and I soon found the thin line cut into my fingers despite changing grip. Seeing my discomfort, George handed me his own finger stalls, simple things home-made from an old rubber inner tube.

The line must have gone over a field of starfish. For a short distance, there was one on every hook which I quickly removed, flinging them overboard. Every so often a gurnard would come up on the line, which, with a quick flick against the gunwale I shook free of the hook. Some of the fish, big cod and ling, floated up on the line seemingly lifeless when they neared the surface. It was as though they had given up the struggle. Looking down I saw a three pound-lobster coming up.

"Don't pull him out or he'll drop off," warned George and, leaning over with a basket, he scooped up the lobster. We caught the occasional sole and a few dogfish, which now felt excessively hard and rough after the soft, silky feel of the whiting.

At last, after what seemed a long time, the dan buoy was alongside. It had been hard work and my fingers were sore, despite George's rubber stalls. We started up the Kelvin, ate some grub, had a drink and got under way, clearing and baiting up the line for the following day. The seas were now on our port quarter, lifting us up and thrusting us homewards. It was gone noon when we headed for the coast, not yet visible. There was no break in the low ceiling of clouds overhead; to the north a slanting grey curtain of rain joined sea and sky. The weather looked bad and I was glad we were homeward bound.

I now appreciated what Peter Barron meant when he said spiltering was tedious. As I tipped the line out of the tub onto the deckboards and peered at the great black pile of uncleared line, with its tangled mass of little hooks, their stops wrapped round the main line, it appeared an endless task. The very thought that this had to be cleared and baited before finishing the day's work was daunting.

It took much longer than clearing and baiting up a dog-line. For one thing, a spilter hook is not as easy to get hold of as a dog hook. Again, we seemed to lose many more hooks in spiltering, all of which had to be replaced. Finally, there was the stop's maddening habit of wrapping itself round the main line. Seeing me slowly and laboriously struggling to unwind such a stop, George quickly showed Sam and me a simple, efficient method, which involved hanging the hook on the mainline, then holding it in front of one's chest, and spinning the line in the opposite direction.

As I stood baiting up these interminable hooks, it didn't take me long to work out that if I baited a thousand hooks and took ten seconds over each one, nearly three hours would pass before I finished the job. This would not be too bad, but it also became equally clear that by the time I had replaced and cleared the hooks of the leathery pieces of mackerel bait, baited them up and coiled the line down in the tub, my average time per hook would be nearer fifteen seconds and probably more, taking me every bit of four hours to finish baiting up the line.

We usually arrived back between half-past three or four in the afternoon. Once inside the harbour, there were the fish to be taken ashore and weighed, the engines to be attended to, fuel to be fetched, the boat to be washed down and pumped out and, on top of everything, at least another hour or more of baiting up to be done, before the work was completed. Sam and I would be fortunate if we were on our way home by half-past six. The secret, of course, is to waste not a second of time, but seize the line and work at it without a stop, without pausing to talk or look up, making sure that the replacement of hooks and untangling the line did not take much longer than the actual baiting of a hook.

It fascinated me watching the silent speed, dexterity and concentration of the crews as they baited up their lines. Each one of them was racing the clock, all intent on getting ashore and home as soon as possible.

It was well past six before Sam and I completed our first day of spiltering. George by then had long since finished and in all probability was enjoying his second pint in the Ship Inn. Each of us took a few whiting home for supper.

I opened Mary's front door, took off my sea-boots and went into the living room, where I found Biddie writing a letter at the table. Over in the corner the old man sat crouched over the fire. I held up the whiting in front of her.

"Hello," she said, smiling. "Like a cup of tea?" and, taking the fish, disappeared into the kitchen where she handed them over to Mary.

The wireless was on and the weather forecast was just beginning. I leant wearily against the upright piano and listened. I noticed the old man in the corner was trying to catch the forecast as well, for he too had once been a fisherman. Everyone listens to the weather forecast in a fishing village, for on it so much can depend. The clear, concise voice of the announcer filled the room: "Viking, Cromarty, Forth, Tyne, Dogger..." I waited, and then it was our turn — "Wight, Portland, Plymouth. Strong south-easterly winds increasing to gale force..."

I had heard enough.

I drank the hot tea which Biddie brought in and went upstairs to wash and shave. The sore places on my hands smarted when I put them in the warm water.

After supper we strolled down to the harbour. Everyone knew the forecast and it was generally considered that no boats would go out tomorrow. We walked out along the north quay.

"The cone's up," I said to Biddie, glancing up at the coastguard station perched on the cliff edge.

"That means a gale?"

I nodded. Already the seas were breaking heavily against the outside walls of the quay, rolling in through the outer harbour which was now empty of boats.

On the way back we met Sam. "They're giving an easterly gale," he remarked.

"Have you seen George?" I asked.

"Yes. He said there was no point in our coming down. All right, Biddie?" he enquired before going on his way. We both liked Sam.

Halfway up the cliff we paused and leaning on the wall looked down on the inner harbour. All the boats were at their moorings and beginning to surge restlessly. A few visitors wandered disconsolately along the quayside. Even the gulls seemed subdued. The wind was freshening and there was a chill in the air as we turned and made our way back up to the cottage. For the next forty-eight hours it blew an easterly gale and no boats went out. In the last two days we had caught some whiting, but not in any quantity.

We moved that weekend into the bungalow which we had rented up to the end of September. This was our first taste of living on our own. Here we had no landlady to watch over us, nor did we have to share our sitting-room. This was ours and we basked in our privacy. Apart from a fair-sized sitting-room, three bedrooms and a kitchen, we had the luxury of a bathroom. Above all, there were no cats.

Sunday night was dark and cold and we wondered what the weather would be like at three o'clock the following morning. Some of the boats were going out even earlier so that it appeared to be developing into a race to reach the fishing grounds first.

I awoke before the alarm. Leaning over, I pressed the button to stop it ringing. I lay quietly for a moment, listening to the wind stirring the rambler rose that framed part of our bedroom window. The weather didn't sound too good. I slipped out of bed, made a quick cup of tea and gave one to Biddie, who was by now awake. It was time to go. In my sea-boots and smock, with a scarf round my neck and my tin of food under my arm, I felt very much the primeval hunter going forth, as I leant over the bed and kissed Biddie's warm cheek.

Sam and George were waiting, having collected the basket of bait. Without more ado, we sculled out to the *Coral* and started the engines. For the first hour little was said as we cut up the bait. Dawn was sullen and overcast as we began shooting the line. The forecast had predicted the weather would improve later in the morning. Motoring slowly back to the western dan, it looked as though it was already beginning to brighten. Over to starboard, Nipper Lee and his crew had begun hauling their line. It struck me that we were closer than usual to the next boat. I noticed that the tide was ebbing strongly because our line floated down and away from the *Coral*. Suddenly the sun broke through the clouds and the sea sparkled. Peering over the side, I could see we had a good few whiting on the line.

We always kept some baskets aboard the boat into which George now chucked the whiting. We had filled three baskets, about eighteen stone, when I happened to glance across at Nipper Lee and was surprised and not a little alarmed to see how close we were getting to his boat. I glanced at George who did not seem particularly concerned, though I could tell he was aware of the situation.

I continued baiting up, tending the wheel and engine, while the gap between the two boats steadily closed. Nipper and his two crew, Abe May and John Gill, were watching us closely and, when I saw them hand their line round their stern and begin hauling in on the port side, I knew real trouble lay ahead.

I caught Sam's eye. "Looks like we fouled their line," he remarked, a comment which brought no response from George but an immediate retort from Nipper Lee, which confirmed our worst fears. "You've bloody well shot over our line, George," he bellowed, waving his arm at us to clear off, which was hardly possible in the circumstances.

We were now no more than a boat's length apart and the two lines could be seen horribly entwined and with plenty of whiting wrapped round them as they slanted into the depths.

"What the hell do you think you are doing, George?" called Nipper, more calmly this time, which merely produced a scarcely audible grunt from George and a stream of tobacco juice over the side. He seemed quite unperturbed. It was of course entirely our fault, having shot our line uptide of Nipper's boat and too close.

It fell to George Pearce to do the clearing for us, which he tackled fearlessly and skilfully, while Sam and I did what we could to help. Using a bait knife, I leant over the side and cut free many a taut offending stop, gaffing what fish I could before they floated away on the tide. Since I was steering and working the engine I had to take great care that the *Coral* did not collide with Nipper's boat.

Disentangling that dreadful mass of hooks and fish wrapped round the two taut lines presented a temporary, though awesome, task for George and Nipper, particularly when every so often a hook flew dangerously through the air. But they set to with a will and got on with the job until eventually the lines parted and we were able to haul them separately once more. I tried tactfully to discover what George thought about it but, apart from remarking that Nipper seemed a bit put out, I got little from him.

Overhead the sun shone, the wind had fallen and the weather looked more settled as we motored home. We brought the *Coral* alongside the quay opposite J.B.'s fish store, collected a dozen baskets and prepared to land our fish.

"I think we ought to give Nipper a couple of baskets of whiting," I suggested to George and Sam.

"If you want to," said George dryly, but not ungenerously, for I could detect a twinkle in his eyes. I looked at Sam who nodded. "It could do no harm," he said, and together we carried two baskets of whiting along the quayside to where Nipper and his crew had secured their boat.

"Here you are, Nipper," I said, "I'm very sorry we fouled your line."

"George should bloody well have known better," remarked John Gill, looking up at us as he continued baiting his line and Abe May nodded his head in agreement.

"That's all right, Ken," said Nipper, as he accepted the baskets. "These things do happen. It could have been worse."

I stood on the quayside looking down at them as they baited their hooks with astonishing speed. I felt awkward, for I didn't know what to say.

"Yes," I said, after a moment or two of silence, and turned to go. Suddenly I heard Nipper call after us.

"You got a few yourselves, didn't you?" And, as I turned, I could see by their faces that they were now rather amused over the whole affair and had forgiven us.

I returned to the *Coral* and began to bait up my line.

"Were they pleased?" asked George.

"Yes," I replied. "They seemed to be."

"So they bloody well should be," said George, as he finished baiting up his line.

On the way home that evening I ran into Edgar, who had long ago finished and was now on his way down to the quay.

"What be you doing today?" he asked, and then he began to laugh long and silently. "Did George shoot over Nipper Lee's line?" he managed to ask at last.

"He did indeed," I replied, "and I hope I never see such a sight again. Into the bargain, George wants us down at two-thirty tomorrow morning."

At this Edgar bent forward, put both hands on his knees and rocked in silent laughter. I couldn't help laughing myself.

All at once he straightened up, his face momentarily serious.

"Never mind, old man. You get along home and have your tea."

"I think I'd better," I said. "It's six o'clock now and that damned alarm will be going off in a few hours' time."

"Yes," he said, "it will," and this seemed to make him laugh harder than ever. I never tired of Edgar's company and humour.

All August we fished hard, leaving harbour at half-past two in the morning and, sometimes, if the weather was 'wisht', later. It was on those occasions, when the elements looked uncertain and no one was prepared to make a start, that I wondered what the hell I was doing endeavouring to earn my living as a fisherman. While the crews strolled slowly up and down, chatting, or leaning against the old walls of their lofts, philosophical, resigned, I would sit on one of the benches, my back against the wall, eyes closed, arms folded, saving my energy, and thinking of the warm bed I had just vacated and the long hours that lay ahead. Eventually an engine spluttered into life and we would put to sea.

We continued spiltering throughout that summer of 1946 and, apart from one fine week, the weather was foul, our catches meagre. But we savoured that week of fine weather, for there is nothing better than being on the water, with the sun warm overhead, the sky clear, the sea calm.

Sometimes Biddie came out with us and I wondered how George would react when she was aboard. He could not have been nicer, and took a delight in handing her the odd raw scallop to eat. We used to get quite a few clinging to the line, which George would prize open with his bait knife, clean away the inedible part, before handing her the gleaming shell with the white scallop in the centre.

Sharks on one occasion attacked our line, their heavy tugs indicating to George they were down there seizing the fish. We had a pole in the boat with a metal spike lashed to the end. Two thresher sharks swam up attacking the whiting. Going to work with our home-made spear, I prodded at the sinister streamlined creatures until they disappeared with a swirl back to the deep.

Too soon those few hot days were over. The wind went round to the sou'west, cloud and rain prevailed and we knew no more the calm sea and blue sky of that sole week of summer.

One evening our neighbours, Jimmy and Beryl Earl, invited us in for a drink. They had a friend staying with them, Bill Hurrell, who was considering buying a boat and fishing for his living.

"It struck me," said Jimmy, "that you'd be just the man to take Bill out and show him the ropes."

"Of course," I replied, "he can come whenever he likes."

"Tomorrow?" suggested Bill.

"Fine. Better bring some grub. I'll pick you up at twenty past two."

There was plenty of wind the following morning, and I was in two minds whether to warn him that the weather did not look good and the forecast was poor. Eventually I decided to say nothing, deeming it better that he should see the realistic side of fishing before plunging in and buying a boat, as I had done. He was waiting and eager to go.

"This is Bill," I said to George and Sam, who were already down on the quayside, having put the basket of bait aboard the punt. Sam shook his hand, but George could only manage a slight nod and some unintelligible words before making his way down the steps and sculling us to the *Coral.*

The wind was still sou'west. As we cleared Chapel Point, I let Bill have a go on the wheel, giving him a course to steer which, after a minute or two of guidance, he managed successfully.

"This is the life," he sang out, clearly enjoying himself, causing George to look up sharply and give our man at the wheel a long, incredulous stare, before continuing cutting up the bait.

Dawn broke angry and red, the grey, white-flecked sea sombre and uninviting. But our newcomer was still in good spirits, laughing out loud when the odd sea slapped our weather bow, sending spray over the foredeck. Two hours later I took over the wheel as we were approaching the fishing grounds while George and Sam prepared to shoot the line. I shut down the Kelvin and suggested to Bill that he go up for'ard where he would be out of the way, but in a good position to see what was happening. I wondered how he would fare, for now was the telling time when the boat, barely under way, began to pitch and roll and slide all over the place. Well before the first rub of line was shot, Bill was leaning over the side, retching violently, and there was nothing we could do for him.

For three hours we hauled our line, while the weather steadily deteriorated and the rain beat down on our oilskins. At last we approached the eastern dan.

Leaning over, Sam grabbed the lurching flag stick and lifted the buoy inboard. Quickly I started up the Kelvin and we got under way. While Sam took the wheel, I clambered across the net-room and fish-berth to see how Bill was faring.

"All right?" I asked him rather fatuously. He nodded, attempting a smile. He looked very far from all right and I left him leaning on the foredeck, to continue clearing and baiting up my tub of line.

It was high water when we got back and secured alongside. We had four baskets of whiting, a basket and a half of cod and ling, and a few ray.

As for Bill, Sam and I had to help him ashore where he stood unsteadily.

"Will you be all right?" we asked him. He nodded, thanked us and set off slowly and shakily along the quayside.

We landed our catch, finished baiting up, moored, pumped out, fuelled the boat and went ashore.

"Is he coming tomorrow?" asked George, with a mischievous twinkle in his eye.

"Poor sod will think twice before he goes fishing again," Sam remarked.

Bill Hurrell had picked a bad day for his initiation. Perhaps it was intended that he should go no further with his ambition. I couldn't help wondering whether I would have bought the *Coral* had I undergone a similar experience. I heard later he had spent several hours on his bed recovering.

Through Jimmy Earl I was asked to play cricket for St Austell. Willie Rolling happened to turn up when I was going through my cricket gear which I had sent for.

"Does he know what to do with all that stuff, missus?" he asked Biddie.

I kept wicket that Saturday for St Austell. Their ground was not particularly attractive but I enjoyed my games with the club. They had a left arm spinner, Ted Griffiths, a generous cricketer who was to play for Cornwall. He gave the ball plenty of air and could spin it viciously, particularly when delivering his chinaman, as I soon discovered. On more than one occasion I misread the spin, going the wrong way behind the sticks, causing a broad smile at the other end, as the ball beat the bat and me and went down for byes. He still managed to smile when I missed a simple stumping chance, such was his good nature. I much enjoyed keeping wicket to Ted and achieved some satisfying stumpings and catches off his bowling.

Towards the end of the season we played Gorran Cricket Club, who rightly regarded themselves as champions of eastern Cornwall. They took their cricket seriously, peering out from under baggy blue, Australian-style cricket caps. It was then I first met Archie Smith, their tall, left arm medium-fast bowler who played many years for Cornwall. He was an impressive person, all of six foot three, broad, upright and powerfully built, who would look one fair and square, with a face that was strong and sunny. As he caught the ball at the bowling crease in his big left hand, he gave me a brief, comprehensive glance, and I noticed, to my astonishment, that a net covered his blonde hair. All the time I knew Archie, I never heard anyone mention his hairnet, though in county matches the Dorset crowd used to get at him a bit, he once told me.

I watched him as he turned. After a short, smooth run-up, he delivered a quick, good length ball outside the off stump, which moved in with his arm and clean bowled a middle order St Austell batsman. We were in trouble. Apart from a few balls bowled at me before going in, I had not held a bat in my hands for five years. Determined to get my head down, I concentrated on each ball. In doing so, enjoyed a splendid battle with Archie Smith. I got the better of him, but not without a fair share of luck and by the end of the day had scored an undefeated sixty and we had won the match.

Afterwards, I was asked by one of the Gorran players whether I would be interested in playing for them next season. Their ground, he pointed out, was a good deal nearer to Mevagissey than St Austell.

Both our families paid us a visit before the summer was over to see how we were faring. They made no enquiries about how long we intended continuing our way of life. They were clearly interested in what we were doing, somewhat astonished and, no doubt, a little concerned, but they kept their counsel and gave us their support.

We had other visitors that summer — one in particular, Bill Barnet, first lieutenant of 536. Naturally, we reminisced, recalling those nights when our two landing-craft anchored alongside one another in Augusta Bay, Sicily, as far as possible from the merchantman and warships, which were the focus of nightly air attacks. Bill came out with us on several occasions and had a taste of spiltering. Like the 'other Bill' he was fine when the boat was under way but, when shooting and hauling the line, the change in the *Coral's* motion proved too much for him.

I was now in possession of the first of many second-hand cars, a 1929 three-wheeler Morgan, which gave us nothing but trouble from the start.

With Bill Barnet navigating, we set off early one Sunday morning for South Molton in Devon to collect a black Labrador pup from a litter we had seen advertised in a local paper.

The journey began badly when I stopped to fill up the tank and found I had left my petrol coupons behind. Fortunately the garage proprietor accepted our promise to send them to him. Then, a lead on one of the two plugs on the open twin-cylinder engine out in front came adrift and had to be fixed. Finally we had a puncture.

It was late in the afternoon when we eventually made our way down the narrow, twisting lanes flanked by high hedges, until we reached our destination, a gracious, grey-stoned house overlooking an extensive terraced lawn. There was no gate or any form of enclosure, just the house and the lawn sloping down to a retaining wall of stone. The entrance was up a short drive at the side of the house. We knocked and were ushered into a long, low room whose windows reached almost to the floor.

"I'll be with you in a minute," said the lady and promptly disappeared. There was a black grand piano at one end, antique furniture, one or two heavily framed oil paintings and a big open fireplace, with shelves of books on either side. Time had stood still in this peaceful, fine old house. Through the windows we could see a black Labrador and her litter come gambolling onto the lawn, a young girl in attendance.

"They've never been inside a house," said the lady on her return. "We've fed them on milk and the haunches of rabbits."

I thought it highly unlikely we would follow suit.

"Come and meet them!" We followed her through the French windows out onto the lawn. "You wrote in your letter," she continued, "that you wanted a dog with a big head and big paws. Well, there he is," and she pointed him out to us.

He was indeed the biggest of the litter and seemed the most timid and docile of them all.

"I'll get you his pedigree," said the lady and, while she did so, Biddie went over and gently lifted him up which he seemed to accept, perhaps aware he was in safe hands.

Church bells were ringing for evensong when we climbed into our red three-wheeler and set off for home.

Our return journey to Mevagissey must rank as one of our worst. Bill did not help matters by suggesting a short cut. It, of course, proved no short cut. Apart from getting hopelessly lost, it nearly cost us our lives. 'Steep Hill' read the notice. Although I changed gear, the Morgan was still gathering momentum as we approached the corner at the bottom.

"Put your brakes on," bellowed Bill.

"They are on," I shouted.

"Take it wide. Take it wide," he boomed. What he meant I'm not sure.

Somehow we negotiated the bend, only to find the road dipped even more steeply, down towards a few cottages, then rose as steeply on the other side. With the engine backfiring we careered down the narrow lane, roared past several couples at the bottom enjoying a quiet Sunday evening chat, and shot up the other side only to lose power almost at the top and start sliding backwards. Our chain had come off.

"Stop her," shouted Bill.

"Can't," I said irritably and swung her stern first into the hedge.

"Are you all right?" I said, turning to Biddie, sitting patiently in the Morgan's cramped space at the back, holding onto Kim, for that is what we had decided to call him.

We clambered out and with difficulty manhandled the Morgan backwards down to the bottom of the hill, where the three of us stood looking dejectedly at the wretched machine, not knowing what to do next. I became aware of a pair of eyes watching us.

"You be in a bit of trouble then, mister?" asked an elderly man standing at the gate of his cottage.

"We certainly are," I said. "Our chain's come off."

"You got any tools?"

"No," I replied.

"You got a jack?"

I shook my head.

"Nice little fellow you got there," he said, nodding towards Biddie, who was clasping Kim in her arms, and I thought how natural and lovely she looked. I think he thought so too.

"I'll get my son to have a look at it and see what we can do."

He returned shortly, his son carrying a bag of tools. We watched as they jacked up the Morgan and set about replacing the chain, the son lying on his back underneath the three-wheeler. It was a dirty, awkward job.

"That should be all right," said the son, eventually getting to his feet and wiping the oil from his hands.

With difficulty I managed to persuade the father to accept a pound note. Heaven knows what we should have done without their help; certainly we would not have got home that day. They watched us get into the three-wheeler and start off. They were still watching as we reached the brow of the hill.

By nine o'clock we were in familiar country and had only a few more miles to cover. I had driven carefully, using the engine to slow down, for there was little response when I used the brake pedal. It had begun to rain heavily and the three-wheeler had no hood. It was now that our last mishap occurred when we were going up a hill. The throttle was on the steering wheel and I used my thumb and forefinger to operate it. Suddenly, as I pushed it wide open with my thumb, the wire became detached and the cable hung loose. I passed the wire casing quickly to Bill.

"Pull out the wire, Bill," I called and at once the engine, which had nearly stalled, picked up and we got to the top of the hill.

"Easy, Bill, easy," I said and he pushed the wire in and our speed decreased.

"Bit of a hill coming up, Bill. Give her the gun," and he pulled feverishly at the wire and the three-wheeler responded, motoring up the hill. "Right, slow her down," and he obliged by poking in the wire again. So we proceeded in this madcap fashion, drenched with rain until eventually we reached Mevagissey and home.

I sold the three-wheeler shortly after it had played its most annoying trick of all — it caught fire. I had been cranking the little beast unsuccessfully when smoke began to appear from under the dashboard. I dabbed with a rag ineffectually, only succeeding in touching a red-hot wire and burning my fingers. I disconnected the battery and the smoke died down. That was enough. I got rid of it for £70 — £20 less than we had given — and neither of us was sorry to see it go.

The spiltering season was drawing to a close. The weather had been bad throughout, the fish far from plentiful. We were out spiltering one day, the sea calm and oily, when a thick fog without any warning enveloped us. It was as though the three of us were alone in a white world of our own. Somewhere on our port side a foghorn was blowing persistently and with increasing power.

"Get the foghorn," said George, and Sam got out our small trumpet-shaped foghorn from the fo'c'sle, handing it to George who put it between his lips and blew a resounding blast. He was hauling the line at the time, but had stopped and was listening intently. He blew again and there came a deep booming answer from an unseen ship that seemed uncomfortably close.

"Here," he said, thrusting the foghorn towards me. "Blow it." I wanted to lean over the side and dip the mouthpiece into the sea and cleanse it of George's tobacco spittle. But I had neither the courage nor the time.

"Blow it," he ordered tersely, and I blew it, making a noise not unlike a child blowing a tin trumpet at a Christmas party. A great blast of a foghorn replied.

"Bloody close," murmured Sam, and I blew once more, more successfully this time. Again came a great answering blast, but this time from our starboard side. The ship had passed and we had not seen her. Out of the wet whiteness engulfing us came a series of rollers from the wash of the unseen ship to rock the *Coral* gently.

We looked at each other, continued our work and no one spoke.

Three days later George Pearce left us. We had been out fishing in poor weather. The wind was sou'west and strong and there was a steep sea running as we neared home. On the way we passed a naval frigate proceeding slowly and rolling heavily. I saw Sam watching her closely. It must have brought back memories of his twenty-three years in the Service.

We entered the inner harbour and picked up our moorings. Suddenly, without a word of warning, George seized his tin of food, lowered himself over the side into the pram and pulled himself ashore by means of the painter. He never turned, but simply walked away and disappeared up Jetty Street.

Sam and I looked at each other. "What's up with George?" he asked.

"No idea," I replied. "But I think he's finished with us," and I was right.

We continued baiting up our lines and I wondered what this new turn of events would mean. At first I was very worried because the fishermen had taken the trouble to find a good man for us and now we had lost him.

But gradually it became clear to me that there was not a great future for George if he stayed with us. The spiltering season was over and some of the boats had already hauled their nets aboard and were starting pilchard driving. On the credit side, George had taught us a great deal about lining, and I suddenly felt I would like to finish the week spiltering by ourselves. It would be interesting to see if we could do the job without the aid of *a* professional.

We finished baiting our lines and took George's two tubs up into the loft. Having satisfied ourselves that the *Coral* was shipshape, we went ashore after agreeing to meet at 2.15 the following morning.

When I got home I told Biddie that George Pearce had suddenly and without a word left us.

"What an extraordinary thing," she said. "I am sorry, I liked George and I shall miss his scallops."

I stroked Kim's head while I told her of our plans to see the week out on our own.

"Can you manage?" she asked. "I'd come with you, but we can't very well leave Kim by himself for all that time." I agreed and added that it was time we had a go at it ourselves.

We did not do too badly for the rest of the week. We both knew what had to be done. Although we were slow, we shot and hauled our line and caught a few fish. I shot the line while Sam steered and pushed the tubs into position. We took it in turns hauling the line. On our first day on our own we caught four baskets of whiting, two baskets of dogs and a few ray and ling and three turbot. We had done as well as one or two others, even if we were the last to finish.

Sam was a good companion and most conscientious, but too slow for George's liking when it came to hauling and clearing the line. I had got the hang of it, felt comfortable doing the job, and George was happy to let me do my fair share of hauling, but not Sam. His slowness was accentuated by his three deliberate and separate movements as he caught hold of the fish, unhooked it, and finally despatched it into the fish-berth. George would do all three in one quick, fluent movement, making it look easy. But then George had been doing it all his life, and I was much younger than Sam.

As I watched him now, steadily and methodically hauling in the line, going his own pace, I knew exactly how exasperated George must have felt, and I was sorely tempted to call out: "Come on, Sam, let's hurry up and get the bloody thing inboard!"

Friday was our last day of spiltering. As we motored slowly back to the eastern dan, I watched a great bank of ominous clouds massing over the Lizard and Falmouth.

"Take a look over there, Sam," I called to him. "Doesn't look too good," he replied. I glanced around. There were few boats to be seen.

"Best get to work quickly," I said. As I hauled the creeper up, I could feel the wind increasing. There was no doubt we were in for a blow.

For an hour I pulled the line hard and then handed over to Sam. We were not catching many fish and perhaps it was as well because the weather was getting worse. After a while I took over again from Sam. Eventually we had the line in, and not before time. I started up the Kelvin and we ran helter-skelter for home, driven forward by the gathering storm. Whenever a bigger sea ran down on our port quarter, we would ease the *Coral* away in the same direction as the wave, like a boxer riding a punch, and then bring her back on course again.

We approached the harbour, the black storm cone hoisted above the coastguard station. As we passed Mevagissey Light, I glanced briefly over my shoulder at the dark sky and grey, sullen sea, flecked with white horses, and suddenly I felt glad that we were in, and this was Friday, and the spiltering season had ended. I paused on the quayside and looked across the inner harbour to the Watch House.

The summer was over. The boats were straining at their moorings before the rising gale. Against the dark sky a few gulls, their cries carried away on the wind, swooped down on the defenceless luggers. I stood for a moment longer, weary but enchanted, before turning to go home.

Chapter 15

Catherine, Mevagissey football and a night of storm

Walking away from the crease one Sunday afternoon — having been caught on the boundary of the Gorran cricket field after playing a wild, wayward stroke — I heard a voice say jocularly, "That wasn't a very good shot for someone wearing a Saracens cap."

That was how I met the Warden of St Edward's, Oxford, the Reverend Henry Kendall, previously a housemaster at Shrewsbury where he had been educated. Saracens are members of the Old Salopian cricket club, and he had recognised my cap.

It turned out to be another fortuitous meeting. It was the end of September, we were on the move once more, but had no idea where to go. Chatting with Henry Kendall, having removed my pads, I casually mentioned that we were looking for somewhere to live.

"You can have my cottage in Portmellon if you like. Five shillings a week all right?" It was an offer we gratefully accepted.

A rubicund clergyman with an alert mind and a quick, lively sense of humour, he invariably wore a battered old trilby, the brim turned down fore and aft, owned a seaworthy twenty-seven foot motor yacht, the *Mongoose*, and, in the summer months, invited friends and boys from St Edward's down to his cottage in Portmellon.

Our new three-storey home was different from anything we had experienced. Built at the turn of the century, set in the middle of a single row of four attached houses facing seaward, it was no more than twelve yards from the beach. The accommodation was basic, but there was plenty of room and it proved to be just what we wanted. As Henry Kendall had explained, it was a holiday home and never intended to be lived in during the winter months, when it could be 'a bit wild', he explained.

The front door, protected by a rickety old glass portico, led onto a concrete forecourt, shielded from the road by a low wall. On the other side of the road was a thick four-foot-high wall, whose base the sea reached even at neaps. But at spring tides the sea rose to the level of the road and, when the wind was easterly and blowing, the road was impassable and the houses threatened.

Portmellon faces south-east, lying at the head of a small cove, its sandy beach a mere forty yards across. Several fishermen's cottages perch on the north side of the cliffs around it, their grey walls weathered as their rock foundations. In one of these lived Edgar Husband's brother, Peter.

On the other side of the cove, at the foot of Bodrugan Hill, all but adjoining our row of four houses, was Mitchell's boat-building yard, where Biddie and I would often wander in and watch the 'chippies' at work. We never ceased to wonder how Percy Mitchell managed to build such fine boats in such ramshackle sheds. Even more astonishing was how he ever got them out of the shed, across the road and into the water. But he did and, when it was known he was about to launch a big boat, people would come from Mevagissey to watch. He was a large, heavily built man, slow of movement and speech. His words were sparse, but to the point and seemed to come from deep within him. He possessed a slow, winning smile, and was as strong in his beliefs as the great balks of timber stacked around his yard.

The other boat-builder was Will Frazer of Mevagissey. Physically quite different from Percy Mitchell, he was slight of build, quick of movement, and his face, full of humour, was lined and creased heavily when he smiled. It was not difficult to distinguish between their boats. Percy's were like himself, solid, fine, bilgy boats, with a good beam and bluff uplifted bows. Will's were slighter, with slender bows and shapely sterns and quarters, which gave them a fair turn of speed. Well-known and respected, they both built splendid boats and were craftsmen at their work.

The walk from Portmellon into Mevagissey took us ten minutes. It was one we never tired of. It began when we passed the empty, black-tarred old inn on the left, its windows shuttered against the storms, and ended when we reached the brow of Polkirt Hill. There we would pause. Leaning on the wall, look down at the fleeting purple shadows of clouds and catspaws racing over the water, we would gaze across the bay at the Black Head and Fowey Light, the latter so often caught in a patch of travelling sunlight. Further up the curving coastline Looe Island was sometimes visible and on very clear days we might even see the distant Rame.

By now the pilchard season had begun again and Sam and I had put aboard seven nets to start with. I found it a pleasant change handling a headrope once more, after all those hundreds of fiddly old spilter hooks, and together we managed all right for the first two weeks. The weather was kind and most nights we would shake out the pilchards at sea as we hauled the nets over the roller. But one night, when we were up off the Gribbin and had caught a few pilchards, the wind, which had been freshening steadily, suddenly grew fierce, the sea turbulent, and we found ourselves struggling to get the nets aboard. With relief we approached Mevagissey Light, motored through the outer harbour and picked up our mooring.

We drank some tea and then set about shaking out the pilchards, in wind and rain. As we shook and thrashed the heavy bunches of slippery, silver net against our oilskins, I discussed with Sam shipping another hand. After what we had just experienced and, with winter coming on, we agreed it would be a sensible move. But who would want to join two novices?

"What about George Allen?" I suggested. "He's not working at the moment," said Sam. "It's worth a try," I said.

It had gone one o'clock in the morning when we decided to pack it in, go home and come down and finish shaking out the nets after we'd had some sleep. The rain had ceased, the clouds were breaking up and a few stars were shining, though it was still blowing hard when we set off in opposite directions, Sam up to Beach Road, I to Portmellon.

Above: Winter 1947

Below: Our house in Portmellon, second on the right, facing some stormy weather

Later in the morning we landed our catch of just over ten baskets, some sixty stone of pilchards, at two shillings a stone worth a little over £6. The wind had gone away and the weather had fined down sufficiently for the boats to go out that night. Going up Jetty Street, I ran into George Allen as he was about to enter the Mevagissey Social Club.

"Hello, George," I said.

"Hello, m'dear," he replied softly, "how are you doing?"

"Not too bad. Caught sixty stone last night."

He drew heavily on his cigarette, smiling, looking as crafty as ever, his brown eyes peering up at me through those steel-rimmed spectacles. He was wearing the same old black suit and black beret that he had worn at our first meeting in Dartmouth. Good old George, I thought and could not help smiling.

"What's funny?" he asked.

"Nothing, George," I said. "Nothing at all. I was wondering whether you'd give us a hand with the nets?"

He took a last long drag at his cigarette, making a slight hissing sound as he inhaled the smoke deep into his lungs. I waited for his reply, watching as he flicked his cigarette into the gutter, emitting a long cloud of smoke.

"All right, m'dear." he said. "When shall we be going out? Tonight?"

I nodded.

"What time?"

"Half-past four," and, with the briefest of nods, he disappeared into the Mevagissey Social Club.

George was already aboard the *Coral* when I got down later that afternoon.

"I see he's back with you again," said Willie Rolling, approaching me, and I slipped him a packet of Woodbines which he promptly placed under the peak of his cap.

"Well, you should know a bit more about it now, mister. How many nets are you working?"

"Seven," I said, "we're putting two more aboard," and he nodded his approval, gave me a brief smile and rolled slowly off along the quay.

I let George take the *Coral* out of the harbour. Watching him peering ahead over the small wheel, following the general direction the other boats were taking I thought of that first night out together and how near we had been to disaster. This time I had no qualms and George made no attempt to take a course different from the fleet's.

He was good company in the boat, an excellent raconteur. As we lay to our nets during those long nights, he would talk imaginatively and knowledgeably about the fishing between the wars, when the luggers sailed for the Wolf Rock in search of the pilchards, landing their catches at Newlyn, living aboard their boats during the week, shooting their nets alongside crews from Plymouth, Looe, Polperro and Mousehole, from St. Ives, Newquay and Padstow. At weekends the Mevagissey men would catch the train to St Austell, and then the bus back to Mevagissey.

Catches in those days were counted, not weighed. Holding three pilchards in each hand the crews would throw them into the baskets — maunds as they were then called

— counting as they did so. When they reached forty-one, the next man would sing out 'tally', instead of forty-two, and the maund would contain two hundred and fifty two pilchards. The skipper and the foreman kept the 'tally' up on the quayside where the maunds were hoisted and finally loaded onto waggons and taken away. The crews were paid a pound a thousand pilchards and had to give back two hundred fish on every ten thousand caught.

"Know why it's called the Wolf?" George asked, his cigarette glowing in the dark. "Because there used to be holes in the rocks," he went on, "and the pressure of tide and wind set up this weird howling noise. It served as a warning to ships until the wreckers went out and filled them in."

He spoke of times when the sea's surface was smooth and oily, giving off a distinct fishy smell, a sure sign that shoals of pilchards were about. Then sharks and dogfish could do great damage, particularly the dogfish which would swarm like frenzied rats, attacking the pilchards, tearing the nets, their green eyes glinting beneath the fishing lights.

"And you can lose nets if you're not careful," he said, and explained in vivid terms how it had happened one winter's night when he had been crewing aboard a lugger.

"We were up inside the Eddystone and Rame Head in fine weather. I was up in the bows looking down over the stem, when we ran into a living whirlpool of pilchards, the bubbles coming up like sherbet water, millions and millions of them," and he paused, turning his head. "Hear that?" he said, and the three of us listened as the stillness of the night was broken by a series of splashes, like the sound of running water, as fish broke the surface. "They're about," said George softly, "we'll leave 'em down for another hour," and he continued his story.

"We got the nets over fast that night and, even as the boat swung head to wind, we could see the headrope begin to dip beneath the surface. We didn't need telling, but manned the spring rope, hauling it in inch by inch till we came to the headrope, and that was all there was of it. The whole net had been torn clean away by sheer weight of fish, and sunk," and he paused to roll and light another cigarette before continuing.

"One boat that night lost all its nets. They had shot too many and by the time they came to haul them they were up and down, stretching vertically from the boat's stem to the bottom. There was nothing the crew could do, other than watch the skipper sever the spring rope with one stroke of his knife, losing the lot — his fleet of nets and catch. We were luckier," he mused. "After a great struggle, we managed to get the rest of our nets inboard and, my God," he added softly, "they were white with fish."

He talked of how the Mevagissey men always put their herring nets aboard in early December and sailed for Plymouth, where, for as long as could be remembered, the herring had come in December and January. Being a Plymouth man he knew all about this, recounting how boats from as far off as Yarmouth and Lowestoft had sailed for the West Country, and alongside the Cornishmen fished the waters from the Start to Plymouth, as many as two hundred boats.

"Round Wood Jetty, Coal Quay and Sutton Harbour, the luggers moored in rows ten deep, while the big East Coast boats berthed over by the Barbican," and he explained how in 1934 some Plymouth boats had trawled in Bigbury Bay, when the herring had been on the point of spawning and the effect on the shoals proved disastrous.

"1937," he said, "marked the end of the herring fishing in the West Country." And with those words we switched on the fishing lights, started up the Handy Billy, hauled in on the spring rope and began once again to pull our nets over the roller, while the gulls, arriving from nowhere, hovered and swooped above the *Coral's* fishing lights, a white cloud fanning the air, their penetrating cries ceasing only when we had pulled aboard the end net — the flitter net.

Early in October I played my first game for Mevagissey in the St Austell and District Junior League of Cornwall. The pitch lay high above the village, at the top of Tregony Hill on the way to Kestle, situated on a sloping, uneven field overlooking the bay.

I had been made captain, goodness knows why, for though it was known I played cricket for St Austell and was equally keen on soccer and wanted to play for Mevagissey, nobody knew whether I was worth a place. I suspect the club chairman, Major Barton, who lived halfway up Bodrugan Hill had something to do with it. However it came about, I felt honoured and, although my recollection of most of those games remains hazy, I remember a few of them clearly, and one person in particular — Catherine, an eccentric lady, who became a great supporter of mine.

Seated at her open window overlooking the corner of the inner harbour, she would watch the men passing below, going in and out of William's workshop. Whenever I went to get some fuel, or seek William's advice on some engine problem, I could never escape her eye or comments.

"You played a wonderful game, me beauty. You did, you played a wonderful game," she would call vociferously from her window above, to the amusement of those below and much to my embarrassment, because more often than not I was only too aware that I had far from played 'a wonderful game'.

"We'll try and win next time, Catherine," I'd call up to her before beating a hasty retreat into the safety of William's workshop.

Catherine lived for her football and it upset her when the Mevagissey team lost, which it did rather too often that season. Along the touchline, the sea in the background, the fishermen stood chatting and shouting ribald encouragement. Major Barton, the chairman, who was as responsible as anyone for keeping the club going, stood slightly apart. Every so often, as though he were back on a parade ground, would bellow forth, "Well played, Mevagissey".

But it was Catherine who stole the limelight, as she took up her usual position on the halfway line, at times advancing onto the pitch to exhort the Mevagissey players even further with her own choice words of encouragement.

"Come on, Charlie. You show 'em. Well played. Oh, you dirty bastard! Yes, you did. I saw you. Referee, referee." By now she was well and truly on the pitch, egged on by the supporters. "Why don't you stop him, ref, and blow your bloody whistle? No, I won't get off, ref." She always did, of course.

One Saturday she went a bit too far. It was a cup match and a tough one and we had lost by a penalty. When the final whistle blew, Catherine was ready. Clasping a large lump of mud, she ran at the referee and I saw her missile go sailing past his head. Not content with her near miss, she aimed a kick at his backside. The referee did not wait for more and Catherine was left, disconsolate, a solitary figure, standing in the centre of a muddy pitch, shaking her head.

"Never mind, Catherine," and I went over to give her a pat on the shoulder. She brightened immediately.

"You played a wonderful game, me old beauty."

"Oh, I don't know about that, Catherine," I said.

"Yes, you did, you played a wonderful game." As we walked towards Biddie who was waiting on the touchline, Kim came bounding up to greet us.

But the matter did not end there, for the committee decided that something had to be done to protect referees on the Mevagissey football ground from further assaults of this kind, and Catherine was temporarily banned from watching home matches.

The following week we played away, but the week after I found myself once again spinning a coin on the Mevagissey pitch. The game had not been in progress for more than a few minutes, when strange noises were heard coming from the hedge behind the supporters. All heads turned in time to see Catherine struggle through the hedge to the cheers and laughter of all, save Major Barton, who could only stand and watch with a look of concern. She wasted no time and began at once to urge on the home side.

"Come on, Mevagissey. You show 'em how to play. Go on, Billy Moore. Oh, you dirty devil, yes, you did. You did it on purpose. Referee ..." and so it continued until the final whistle blew. This time her cup was full, for it was one of the few games we won that season.

On another occasion we played somewhere inland, a carpet of snow on the ground, an icy wind blowing the length of the pitch. We were four down at half-time and changed ends to battle against the fierce wind and driving snow. The opposition were top of the league and by far the better side and, with the wind at their backs, we soon found ourselves overwhelmed. It did not help matters when our right-back suddenly left the pitch and headed off towards the wooden shed in which we had changed. I pulled back a forward and the game proceeded. Several minutes later another player decided he'd had enough and was on his way, sprinting towards the shed. This was no wavering in the ranks, but a rout. All of a sudden, as though someone had given the order — I certainly had not — we ran for it, the lot of us, as hard as we could go, straight for the wooden shed and shelter, laughing our heads off, watched by an astonished opposition and referee, not to mention their few supporters.

A minute later the door was opened and an angry voice asked what the hell we thought we were doing.

"Tell 'em to bugger off," came the helpful advice from Billy Moore who was standing with a towel round his waist.

"Are you going to finish the game or give us the points?"

"Give 'em the points," shouted everyone, "and shut the bloody door." Fortunately Catherine did not come to our away matches.

They were happy footballing days, full of humorous incidents and characters. I still remember that Mevagissey side and most of the names, in particular Billy Moore. He was our centre-forward, a highly intelligent player, stocky and strong, difficult to get off the ball, for he screened it well and could turn and take on defenders.

Later, when I was captain of the Oxford University side, I brought the team down to play two early season matches against Cornwall. We won both of them and a crowd of Mevagissey and Gorran men came over to watch the game played at St Blazey. The following morning I took the side over to meet our old friends and see the harbour and the boats.

"He never could do any bloody good for us," said Edgar Husband to some of the Oxford players.

"Well, he's not much good for us," said Donald Carr, who was later to captain Derbyshire at cricket and an England touring side to Pakistan.

"Have you seen Catherine?" a voice called out.

"Not yet," I said, "but I'm going to."

I found her in great form and she told me how well the Mevagissey side was doing.

"We're coming down in the holidays, Catherine," I said, "and I'll bring my boots."

I did bring them and played one game for Mevagissey which we lost and, as I left the field I knew only too well that I had played a far from 'wonderful game', despite Catherine's assurance to the contrary.

The New Year of 1947 dawned stormy and cold, and there were few nights when we could safely go to bed without putting up the shutters. We bought a Willys Jeep, though not before William had come with me to St Austell and checked it over. The jeep had a steel roof, with wooden sides, but no doors. One of Percy Mitchell's men made and fitted two wooden doors for us, with small, sliding windows. There was plenty of room for Kim, and we could pile any amount of stuff into the back of our new vehicle, which proved tough and reliable.

At the end of January neighbours arrived. Ted Doust and his daughter took up residence in the end house next door to us. He had been stage carpenter at the Stratford-on-Avon Memorial Theatre and had bought the house with a view to retirement and taking in a few guests during the summer months to help pay the bills. Bent and rather breathless, he shuffled slowly around with a perpetual look of concern on his face. His daughter, Jo, on the other hand, was the exact opposite and never allowed her father's anxieties to rob her of her naturally cheerful disposition. She had two wire-haired terriers which went with her everywhere.

Sometimes of an evening, father and daughter would come over for an hour and Ted would sit staring into the fire, while Jo talked to Biddie with the two terriers at her feet, watched by Kim, who sensibly kept his distance. Outside, if it was high water, the thud of waves hitting the sea-wall could be heard, followed by the heavy patter of spray striking our shutters.

"Sounds bad," Ted would mutter, turning slowly in my direction. I had not the heart to tell him how much more serious a south-easterly gale on a spring tide would be. But then neither had we yet experienced such conditions. We had tasted wild days, when the road was impassable for a time, but never a full gale, from the south-east, when the crested seas, caught in the bottle-neck of Portmellon would come roaring up the cove to explode against the wall protecting the road and our four houses.

Before moving in, Ted had decorated the house from top to bottom in preparation for the coming season.

"Think we can leave the shutters down tonight?" he'd ask me, breathing heavily as he sat on the thick low wall that separated our two cottages.

"Yes, I think we'll be all right tonight, Ted," I'd assure him, and he'd nod and give another long glance at the sea, before shuffling into his house, looking slightly less worried.

Then the snow began to fall as the severe weather of 1947 set in, bringing chaos, hazards and hardship to cities and towns, in particular to isolated rural communities.

But we found our walks into Mevagissey more enjoyable than ever, for the curving coastline, now capped by snow for as far as the eye could see, stood out brilliantly on clear, sunlit days. At the top of Polkirt Hill we would pause, as we usually did, and gaze down at the harbour. The snow lay thick on the decks of the boats and roofs of the cottages and the whole scene had a still quality, of breathless enchantment. But the nights on the water were cold and we pulled the nets with plenty of vigour. Around us the sea lay black and uninviting, and the white tops of the cliffs, etched sharply against the night sky, appeared much closer than they actually were.

Kim thrived in the snow, plunging into a brook on one occasion and breaking the ice. He loved the water and was not afraid of a rough sea, though he did not enjoy the one time he came out with us in the *Coral*.

The bitter wind kept up in the north-east, snow continued to fall, roads froze, and the boats faced a spell in harbour. We kept our fire going as best we could, supplementing our coal ration with drift-wood off the beach, and any odd bits we found lying around Percy Mitchell's yard.

One clear cold night, when the stars shone brightly overhead, we went perhaps a bit too far. Coming across a thick six-foot balk of timber, buried in the snow, we staggered back with it, to place one end in the fire, leaving the rest protruding into the room. As it burned, we pushed it further in, withdrawing it from the fire when we went to bed. It lasted for several days.

"Percy Mitchell seen that bloody great thing?" enquired Peter Husband, unable to contain his laughter. Even our next-door neighbour could not resist a smile when he saw it.

Few cars now ventured into St Austell and most of the roads in and out of Mevagissey were impassable. But I was still able to keep going in the jeep and taxied several people to St Austell, as well as carrying coal and supplies to inaccessible houses. With the jeep's low-ratio gear and four-wheel drive, there was no hill we were not prepared to tackle. I carried hessian sacks and a shovel, both of which we used on occasions, particularly when going round the steep bend at the top of Bodrugan Hill. I enjoyed the challenge.

One Sunday we journeyed to Dartmoor, to see what it looked like in such conditions. It was a hazardous and foolhardy venture because we might have broken down. But, in the end, the journey was worth it, for the sight before us was magnificent. The bleak, white, penetrating silence of the moor, stretching for as far as the eye could see, lay tinged beneath a pale winter's sun. It had an awesome beauty.

That severe winter of 1947 seemed to go on forever. The battleship, H.M.S. *Howe*, came and anchored offshore, its presence dominating the bay. I took Biddie and the Bartons out to look at the great ship. Circling her on that wintry morning, I nearly fouled my mizzen on her boom. For a while we motored around, looking at the cliffs, stark and black against the white landscape. But all the time my eyes were drawn to the massive warship, and the hands going about their business on the upper deck. Across the water came the long shrill whistle of the bosun's pipe and memories of the lower deck came flooding back.

On Saturday we played the *Howe's* football side, up on our impossible frozen pitch at the top of Tregony Hill. We lost, despite Catherine's vociferous support, which amused our opponents, particularly their supporters, who pulled her leg constantly and egged her on. But it was all in good humour; even Major Barton was seen to laugh at times.

The *Coral* was originally built as a crabber and the fishermen had several times suggested that what the boat required was a good strake around her, which would give more freeboard and security. I thought it sensible to have it done while there was not much doing in the fishing. But neither Percy Mitchell nor Will Frazer could do the job at once. At Will's suggestion I went to see Alfie Cloke, a shipwright, whose son played in the Mevagissey side. He started and finished the job within the week, putting a seven-inch strake around the *Coral's* side, scarfing a piece into her stem and building it up. He made an excellent job of it, and the *Coral* looked an even better boat when it was finished.

At last the weather turned warmer and the great thaw began, a depressing spectacle, when the crisp brightness of snow turns into the grey, wet, slush of a thaw. The very air itself loses its intoxication, and the spirit wilts with the melting snow, until the colour and shape of the countryside become once more apparent. But the winter of 1947 had lasted a long time, and everyone welcomed the warmer weather.

For a week the boats sought the pilchards up around Par Bay and off the Gribbin. One night in particular I remember. The sea was calm and most of the boats had shot their nets. Across the water came the chatter of voices: "That's the *Pride of the West*," said George, as we drank our tea and ate our grub, leaning against the *Coral's* side. The moon was in its first quarter and shining brightly as we lay to our nets for five hours, periodically hauling in on the spring rope to have a look, but few fish were going to net. It was gone one o'clock in the morning when we began the haul, shaking out barely ten stone of pilchards. Motoring home, we moored the *Coral* in the silent inner harbour, and sculled ashore.

I felt at peace with the world as I made my way back to Portmellon. The moon had disappeared, the night was clear and there was no wind. It was very quiet. I paused at the top of Polkirt Hill. Leaning on the wall, I looked across the bay. The distant boats were still there, fishing outside the Gribbin, their masthead lamps flickering flecks of gold in the night. Far off the intermittent light of the Eddystone flashed its warning. Turning, I headed on, the stillness broken only by the singing of the telephone wires overhead, and the steady beat of a distant engine.

Later in the morning, when I came down to land our meagre catch, I was surprised to find most of the crews still hard at work shaking out their nets.

"You left too early last night, old man," observed Willie Rolling, who was standing beneath J.B.'s office, chatting with Cliff Nichols and Winston Barron.

"If you'd stayed another hour," added Edgar, who had joined us, "you'd have had a hundred stone and more."

His comment dismayed me for I knew he was right, and we should have remained with the rest of the boats. I watched Willie Rolling light his last cigarette, cupping both hands round the flame, before discarding the empty packet over the quayside. I caught Edgar's eye.

"Got his packet of Woodbines, Ken?" he asked me, his face creasing with laughter. I had, of course, and handed Willie his packet of ten, which he promptly tucked beneath the peak of his cap.

"Fish often go to net when the moon goes down," Willie explained, his blue, rheumy old eyes surveying me.

"Yes," I said, "we should have stayed," and I turned to go, feeling even more disconsolate.

"Never mind, old man," said Edgar, laughing aloud, "you'd better take the missus with you next time," and at once I began to feel better.

During the first week of February, the thaw, followed by heavy rain, brought flooding to the back of our houses. The water continued rising, creeping towards our primitive bathroom on the ground floor at the rear of the house.

On 7 February the wireless gave out, "South-east wind increasing to gale force." By three o'clock that same afternoon a full gale was blowing straight into Portmellon. More ominously there was a huge sixteen-foot-eight-inch spring tide. By five o'clock the wind was driving a curtain of fine spray against our upstairs windows, whipped from the crests of oncoming seas. We were having a cup of tea in our darkened living room, for the shutters were already up, when Percy Mitchell called round.

"You're for it tonight," he said and we watched him do what he could to shore up the outside door of our rickety old porch. We offered him a cup of tea, but he would not stay.

"Hope you'll be all right?" and he gave us a slow smile.

"It was good of him to come," said Biddie.

"Jolly good thing we were not burning that balk of timber," I added.

Around six o'clock heavy spray began to hit the house, and there was still three hours to go before high water. One hour later we heard the first thud, as a sea hit the wall, followed by water drumming heavily against our wooden shutters. We ate our supper round the fire, which hissed indignantly, as the sea began to find its way down the chimney. All of a sudden the lights went out. Fortunately we had a hurricane lamp which I eventually lit after a good deal of groping around in the dark for matches and paraffin. The fire was now out, and a steady dribble of dirty water crept from under the grate onto the floorboards, where we had rolled back the old bit of carpet.

"There's water coming under the front room door!' Biddie called as I dealt with the stream of chimney water. We only had a dilapidated soft broom in the house which was worse than useless. I opened the back door to find flood water lapping the doorstep.

By eight o'clock the house was shaking alarmingly from the explosive thuds of the waves. We decided to have a look at what was going on from the top floor. I eased the sash window down a bit and was immediately met with a stinging sheet of spray.

I was determined to see what was happening. In that brief interval before the next wave hit the sea-wall, I took in the scene. There was another great thud as a wave smashed against the wall and, just in time, I slammed the window shut before the pane was struck by a torrent of spray. I was astonished the glass had not shattered.

What I had seen in those few moments showed me how serious the storm was. The road, covered in swirling water, deep enough to envelop a car, had filled the forecourt up to our porch door. I thought, though I could not be sure, that I had seen a breach in the sea-wall.

Our ground floor was now awash. Despite our efforts to stem the flow, water poured in under the living room door and down the chimney. To make matters worse, flood water had found its way into the bathroom and was lapping round the lavatory pedestal and bath. The house shook alarmingly from the continuous battering of the waves, the noise was thunderous, and still thirty minutes remained before it was high water.

There's nothing more we can do," I said to Biddie, "we might just as well go to bed." Followed by Kim, we made our way up the stairs, carrying the hurricane lamp to our small room at the back.

For the next two hours we lay and listened to the storm and the noise of water cascading down onto a corrugated iron roof at the back. There were times, so severe was the assault, when our room and two narrow cast-iron beds shook so much, that we feared the worst had happened. Eventually, as the tide receded and the noise lessened, we fell asleep.

We woke early, as daylight began to penetrate our room. Peering out of the back window, I could see that the flood water seemed to have risen but the wind had dropped. We dressed quickly and went downstairs. The living room, if anything, looked worse than it had the previous night. I pulled on my sea-boots, Biddie her Wellingtons. With some difficulty, we pushed open the door into the porch. Like some drunken spectator, the outside door hung loosely on one hinge, surveying the shingle and debris covering the porch floor and forecourt. We crossed the road, strewn with sand, stones, seaweed and shingle, and joined several locals who were standing examining the breach in the sea-wall.

"You survived then," a voice greeted us.

"Never believed the sea could do that much damage," added another. Out of the corner of my eye I saw Percy Mitchell approaching. He stared long and hard at the extensive damage.

"I think we ought to go and see how Ted and Jo are getting on," Biddie reminded me quietly. Approaching the house we saw that their front door was wide open.

It was, in fact, more than wide open. It had gone. The sea had swept through the hall and passageway taking the door with it. We found father and daughter in the kitchen at the back of the house. She was surprisingly cheerful and greeted us warmly. Even the two terriers accepted the presence of Kim. But Ted was in the throes of despair, and nothing we could do or say could help. Not even when the electricity suddenly came on, and we were able to have a hot drink, were his spirits raised.

"Decorated from top to bloody bottom and all for nothing," he groaned, shaking his head forlornly.

We learnt later from Peter Husband that the sea had come over the quayside of the inner harbour.

"But the *Coral's* still there," he said reassuringly.

By ten o'clock it was high water once more and, although the wind had subsided, there was still a big sea running, making the road impassable one hour either side of high water. Throughout the day people walked over from Mevagissey and Gorran to see the damage.

In the afternoon Willie Rolling came to see us and had a cup of tea. He could not keep his eyes from wandering over the living room.

"Come and see our bath," I suggested, "it's almost afloat."

"Must have been a bad night, missus," he said, several times over, chuckling to himself all the while. When he got up to leave I gave him a packet of Woodbines. Carefully he took from his wallet a photograph of himself, which he gave us. I have it to this day.

We watched his small figure rolling up the hill towards Mevagissey before crossing the road to lean on the sea-wall and gaze. By now the tide was far out, the wind freshening. "Could be in for another rough night," I said to Biddie, as a flash of sunlight pierced the grey, scudding clouds. For one brief moment the wild surface of the sea seemed to smile in acknowledgement. Then, just as quickly, as though such a shining display was out of keeping with the occasion, the sun vanished, and all was as before, sombre and wild.

It took another two days for the seas to moderate and the wind to lessen. On one of these nights a car foolishly attempted to run the gauntlet and pass through Portmellon half an hour before high water, when the sea was already starting to sweep across the road. The driver, hopelessly mistiming his run, was caught by a wave and swept sideways off the road onto the shingle at the side of Ted Doust's house. Soaked and shaken, the man and his wife crossed Ted's forecourt — his front door had been replaced by nailed planks — climbed over the low wall into our forecourt and banged on our shutters.

Three hours later, when the tide had receded sufficiently, I was able to get the jeep onto the road, and haul their car out of the shingle.

Chapter 16

'There's a dog in the sky'

"PLENTY of gannets in the bay." Peter Husband announced in his usual breezy manner one Sunday afternoon.

"Going out tonight?" I asked him.

"No," he replied, "but some boats are."

Sunday was still treated by many of the fishermen as a special day, a day to go to church, to walk the quay in Sunday best and enjoy a cooked dinner with the family.

The following morning we learned that the boats which had gone out the previous night had caught a lot of fish. "Plenty of sign," the word went round, "plenty of fish."

We shot our nets that Monday night up off Polperro and caught eighty-six stone of pilchards, finishing work in the early hours of the morning. Throughout the week we did well. By Thursday, we had landed another hundred and thirty stone of pilchards, bringing one week's catch to over four hundred stone, our best to date. But shaking out that last haul I had found exhausting. Before beginning the work, we would ship the roller athwart the boat, have a cup of tea and a brief rest. Then, with George and I on the leech, and Sam on the headrope, the three of us would pull the net, thick with pilchards, out of the net-room and over the roller, shaking and thrashing the dead weight of slippery net against our oilskins, sending the silver captives cascading into the fish-berth beneath us. Not all the fish came free, invariably a few remained obstinately stuck in the net. These we cleared by inserting our fingers into the meshes, flicking, shaking and plucking them free, until the first bit of the net was cleared and we were ready to haul up the next part and repeat the performance. All night we worked, clearing the nine nets, breaking off occasionally for a short rest, up to our thighs in pilchards, our legs warm in our thigh boots, as though wrapped in blankets. Throughout those long hours, though I concentrated physically on the task of unmeshing the catch, I tried to remain mentally detached. Finally, shortly before ten o'clock on Friday morning, after fuelling, washing down and pumping out the boat, we landed twenty-one baskets of pilchards and agreed to be down on the quayside at three o'clock that afternoon.

Pausing briefly outside J.B.'s office to watch several crews still hard at work clearing their nets, I heard a shout from overhead. Edgar and Peter were standing at the open front of their loft overlooking the harbour.

"Going out tonight?" they called down. "Yes," I replied.

"Bit of a dog in the sky," said Edgar. "Bit of a what?" I asked.

" 'Dog in the sky'," repeated Edgar, screwing up his eyes and looking towards the sun. "See that small rainbow in a ball just outside the sun? We call it a dog in the sky, sometimes a gulch."

I shielded my eyes and saw it, but could see little resemblance to a dog. "What's it mean?" I asked.

"Means we're in for a bad time of it, old man," said Peter. "It's a sure sign of poor weather."

I glanced again up at the sky and the sun. It was watery, the atmosphere hazy with here and there a few wisps of white cloud. There was a distinct chill in the air and the wind moaned softly down from the north.

"What's the forecast?" I asked.

"Not too good," said Peter. "The wind's gone round to the north, by tonight it'll be easterly. They're giving force six, increasing eight."

"If you're going up to the Rame tonight," said Edgar, "you want to watch your step. Stick with us. If the fish are there, run 'em in and don't leave your nets in the water too long."

I drove home in the jeep, weary but thoughtful. Biddie, I knew, had wanted to come out with us during the week, but because of the distance and the hours involved, I thought it unwise and discouraged her. Certainly after what Edgar and Peter had just said, the coming night was out of the question.

"How did you get on?" she greeted me.

"Fine," I said giving her a kiss, before ungallantly washing my hands and face and staggering up the stairs to fall asleep almost immediately, just as I had done so many times when coming off watch during the war.

Four hours later Biddie woke me with a cup of tea. She had got my tin of grub ready and my thermos filled.

"We shall be at it all night," I told her, climbing into the jeep. She looked the very picture of health, standing there with Kim by her side, serene and beautiful. I was glad she had him for company while I was away. Sometimes, unbeknown to me, she walked over early in the morning with Kim and saw us at work, shaking out the nets. At other times she caught sight of us from the cliff-tops returning from sea, easily recognising the *Coral* when she was still some distance off. As the boats approached, circled by gulls, she would assure me later that the *Coral* was the prettiest of them all, with her distinctive turquoise sides, topped by her black strake, her bluff uplifted bows, shoving the water out of her path as though eager to be home.

On the way in I picked up Peter Husband and parked the jeep on the quayside opposite Winston Barron's house. A lot of crews were already aboard and preparing to move off.

"See you up at the Rame," called Peter, as I went down the steps and joined Sam and George who were in the pram waiting to scull across to the *Coral*. While Sam unshipped the legs and George prepared to let go the moorings, I started up the Handy Billy. Well before reaching the harbour mouth I had both engines going. Once past the light, we set an easterly course for the Rame, in the wake of a number of boats ahead of us. Already there was an easterly lop. Just as Peter had predicted, the wind veered to the east, though as yet there was no anger in it. But the hazy light blue sky of the morning had given place to a grey overcast ceiling that had all the signs of deteriorating weather.

"Bit of a dog in the sky this morning, George," I remarked casually.

"I saw it, old son," he said, "I saw it. Be all right as long as the weather holds."

I watched as he deftly rolled a cigarette. Up in the bows Sam too was in the process of rolling himself a cigarette. He took much longer than George nipping off the stray strands of tobacco and carefully replacing them in his tin. Each of us, aware we were in for a long night of it, settled down and retired within our own thoughts.

A string of boats was following. Leaning into the engine-room I opened up the Thornycroft. The Kelvin was already at full throttle. Glancing over the side I checked the flow of water from both exhausts and tested the fishing and navigation lights. George had meanwhile given the pump a few strokes until the ugly sucking noises, indicating the bilges were dry, produced the usual stench of rotting fish.

Three hours later we were abeam of Looe Island, barely visible on our port side. The wind had freshened steadily, the light was fading. Seven miles off our port bow the Rame thrust its headland into the sea, to starboard lay the Eddystone rocks and lighthouse.

For another hour we motored on. One by one, the Mevagissey luggers overhauled us. As they passed us by I was able, with the occasional help of George, to identify them: the *Ibis, Margaret, White Heather* — nicknamed the *Silent Night,* since the crew would never divulge what they had caught or where they had been — and the *Pride of the West,* doubtless chattering their heads off. The *Zona, Guide Me, Vera, Christobel, Little Pearl* and *Fairy* followed, all heading on a course that would take them between the Rame and the Eddystone.

As we drew near I had a long look through my binoculars at a scene I shall never forget. A host of boats from Polperro, Looe and Plymouth were circling, searching for a berth, preparing to shoot their nets. Some, I could see, were in the process of getting their nets overboard, some had already shot them. Everywhere masthead lights dipped and danced and glittered. Overhead the white shadows of scores of gannets soared and swooped, before folding their long, black-tipped wings and, like the first drops of rain heralding a downpour, plummeted into the sea.

We wasted no time, found some space, shot our nine nets, hoisted the mizzen and shipped the roller. Then we ate some grub and drank our tea, wedging ourselves in against the pitching motion of the boat, as the seas lifted the *Coral,* their crests breaking with a sinister sibilance as they passed us by.

"We'll have a look," said George, and Sam from up for'ard began to haul in on the boat rope, passing it to George, while I started up the Thornycroft and gave the engine a good kick ahead, to keep the *Coral* up to the nets.

"Plenty of fish," observed Sam, peering over the side. We had only pulled in a few feet of net, yet already the fishing light revealed the glitter of silver, deep beneath the surface.

"Better get 'em in," said George, passing me the headrope, before clambering across the net-room to join Sam on the leech.

Immediately, as I leant back on the headrope and felt the weight of the net, I knew we were in for a long, hard haul. I gave the boat another good kick ahead and turned the wheel a few spokes to starboard. At once the haul became easier and the net came over the roller with plenty of pilchards. Quickly I eased down the revs and put the wheel amidships, before the boat rode over the net and it fouled the propeller. I had not forgotten that first night of pilchard driving.

For the next two hours we sweated away, hauling in more fish than we had ever caught before. By the time we had got the fifth net in, the boat's motion had become heavy and sluggish, so we paused briefly to pump her out, and not before time, for there was an uncomfortable amount of water in the bilges. The seas had grown bigger, the wind stronger and the nets more heavily laden than ever. For a short spell we hauled up a heavy 'splat' of thick horse mackerel. They were too large to get firmly enmeshed by the gills and, as the net came out of the water and over the roller, a number fell back into the sea to be swooped upon by the gulls.

Weary and near to exhaustion, we began to haul in the end net and at once it was evident to us that this was going to be different. I found the headrope had suddenly become bar taut and some of the near cobles were bobbing under the water. It was as though a great force was dragging the net to the bottom and, glancing over the side, I saw the reason why. Slanting down in the water was a solid wall of silver.

"White with fish," I had heard the Mevagissey men say on occasions and now I knew exactly what they meant and how easy it would be to lose nets and catch.

I believe we all thought the task that now faced us was beyond our powers. But, bit by bit, we sweated and struggled, and fought to get that last net in, gradually winning the day, hanging on grimly as the boat pitched and rolled, then seizing the right moment, leaning back and, with all our remaining strength, heaving the net up and over the roller, unceremoniously dumping great piles into the net-room, until it was heaped high and the job finished.

Trembling with fatigue, I switched on the engine-room lights, to find the deck-boards covering the propeller shafts awash, the water almost up to the half circular pans protecting the fly wheels.

"Hell of a lot of water in the boat," I called to the others, but George was already pumping hard.

When we had topped up the fuel tanks, no easy task in a pitching boat, Sam retired up for'ard, George took the wheel and I stood in the engine-room, leaning on the hatch cover, experiencing the warmth of the engines beneath me. On through the night the *Coral* slogged and laboured her way, burdened with nets and catch and low in the water, every so often, rolling so heavily, she all but buried her starboard gunwale. But for that seven-inch strake she would have shipped water.

Three hours later we were off Fowey Light and the Gribbin. The tide was on the flood, the sea confused, the waves steep, as wind and sea competed against tide. But ahead Mevagissey Light beckoned reassuringly, over to starboard loomed the round hump of the Black Head and, just visible, far off to port, the flash of the Gwineas buoy caught the eye. Inland, the distant lights of St Austell, Charlestown and Par, shone wanly across the water.

By 2.30 in the morning we had tied up, shipped the roller across the net-room and begun shaking out the pilchards. Eight hours later we landed our catch, put the boat to her moorings and sculled ashore. I climbed into the jeep and drove back to Portmellon to find the house empty. Leaving my sea-boots in the porch, I sank like a sack of potatoes into an armchair and, peeling translucent pilchard scales from the backs of my hands, weariness overwhelmed me. My mind, as though detached from my body, relived the night's work.

We had been at it for nineteen hours. The *Coral* had covered nearly fifty miles. We had worked on through the early hours of the morning until the dawn broke and the sleeping village slowly came to life. Scattered around the inner harbour, the crews were still hard at work, the air full of the noise of clicking rollers, as the men worked silently, ruthlessly, smacking their nets against their oilskins, sending pilchards flying thick and fast into the fish pens, all with one end in view, to finish the job as quickly as possible. Every so often a burst of chatter broke out, from one lugger in particular. It was, of course, the *Pride of the West*. However long and hard Albert and his merry men worked, their chatter never ceased.

Towards the end, when we had brought the *Coral* alongside the quay to offload our catch, Waller had come across a couple of times to see how much longer we were going to be.

"You'd better hurry, Ken, or you'll not be ready for the kick-off," he had remarked quite seriously on his last visit. I hope I managed a smile, but my mind was intent on one thing only, shaking the last pilchard out of the last net.

When we had finished and Tony had brought the lorry alongside and taken away sixty baskets of fish I went to watch the catch weighed, while George and Sam put the *Coral* to her moorings. Finally Horace handed me the chit on which was scribbled 273 stone of pilchards and 86 stone of mackerel.

"I couldn't possibly play today, Horace," I told him. "I'm whacked, though I hate to disappoint Catherine."

"All right, old man," he had said, "I'll tell 'em."

I sat and mused for a moment or two longer, then drifted into oblivion. It was late Saturday morning.

I was rudely awakened by Kim's nose.

"Hello," said Biddie, her face aglow, her hair windswept, "We came over and watched you for a while, but didn't want to disturb you." It was so typical of her approach which had been such a help during the past months. My response was probably little more than a weary grunt and a smile.

In fact all the boats had done well that night, and some of the luggers had caught over six hundred stone, though unfortunately Jim Behennah and his crew lost three nets, carried to the bottom by sheer weight of fish.

We continued pilchard driving, but never again had such a catch. On one still night, when we were lying to our nets and Biddie was aboard the *Coral*, we heard a shoal of fish breaking the surface.

"Sometimes you'll hear them on a calm night making a sound like a running brook," the fishermen had told me. As we listened, leaning against the boat's side, peering out over the surface of the sea, the black hump of a whale rose slowly out of the water and with a snort spouted a jet of water into the air. "See him, Biddie? See the old hog?" said George.

I was down on the quayside, having fuelled the *Coral* and pumped her out, for we'd had some heavy rain overnight, when Winston Barron and Willie Wish approached me.

"My God!' said Willie, "there's some great vessel of a boat just come into the outer harbour. The skipper aboard is asking for you."

"Is she a Brixham trawler?" I enquired.

"She is, old man. D'you know the boat?"

"I think I know the owner," I replied.

I was right. It was Guy Greville and I was delighted to see him again. He wanted to buy something in the village, and together we visited the shops where we ran into Biddie outside the post-office. The three of us had a cup of coffee in Roland Billing's cafe, before going aboard Guy's Brixham trawler secured alongside the lighthouse quay. She was indeed a fine boat. He had bought her from the author, A. E. W. Mason, who had fitted her out luxuriously below. Currently trawling out of Fowey, he was not meeting with much success. He did not know the bottom and he had lost some gear. But if he was discovering that fishing was hard, skilled work and, in his case, far from lucrative, outwardly he gave no sign. He was still the same person, quiet, assured and as poker-faced as ever. We cast off his ropes and watched as he got under way, motored through the harbour entrance and headed towards the Gribbin. He had only one hand aboard and I admired his courage, even if it was perhaps a little unwise to take on a boat of this size. I saw Guy and his family once more over at Fowey, and learnt that he was contemplating buying an old steel steamship and carrying coal up the coast. He was very confident about it, though in fact it did not materialise. I never saw Guy again; I believe he went into the mushroom-growing business.

In April Sam left to start fishing with George Furze, so I was back where I had begun, fishing the *Coral* with George Allen. For three weeks we continued pilchard driving and then it was time for George to leave and start work on the small clinker-built motor boat he had recently bought to take out passengers and do a bit of plummeting. For me it was time to start painting the *Coral* again.

But our most immediate problem was to find somewhere to live during the coming summer months and once again we were fortunate. Henry Johns, a crabber, who lived in Gorran Haven and bicycled in to Mevagissey each day to fish aboard the *Pet*, an old half-decked lugger, tipped us the wink that one of the cottages on Bodrugan farm was empty.

"Go and see Leo Kendall who owns Bodrugan and he might let you have it for the summer; he's living at Trewollock."

We wasted no time and went to see the owner.

"Yes.' said Leo Kendall, looking at us curiously though not unkindly. I could see he was a man of few words. "You can have the cottage for the summer," and he gave us the key.

So, one morning in the middle of May, we piled everything into the jeep and began our fifth and last move, up to Bodrugan. The cottage was semi-detached, one of two, at the top of Bodrugan Hill overlooking the bay. There were five small rooms, three up and two down. There was no electricity, no gas, and the water had to be pumped from an outside well. At the back of the cottage, hidden amidst nettles and brambles stood the 'privy', a rickety wooden contraption with the door hanging loose, in which roosting hens had left their mark. It was quite inaccessible and, as far as we were concerned, its use was out of the question. The kitchen contained an old-fashioned range which we struggled in vain to light until Ivy, who lived next door with her aged parents, came over and rescued us. In no time she had it going. But it was soon clear to us that the kitchen range was not going to be the answer to the cooking problem. So we took the jeep into St Austell and purchased, besides pots and pans, bed and mattress, another primus stove and a small tin oven to put on the top in which we could cook a joint. We also bought an Elsan loo and the necessary chemical. On the way back we picked up a worn though colourful red carpet from Mevagissey to cover the stone floor of the living room.

In the evening we lit a fire, for there were plenty of bits of wood around, and it burned surprisingly well in the small high grate. The yellow light of the paraffin lamp gave a warm glow to the room. Later we climbed the narrow wooden stairs and undressed by the light of a hurricane lamp. Through the open window the night air smelt fresh and sweet. Above the water hung a bright, crescent moon and, away in the distance, the intermittent white light of the Eddystone winked and blinked its warning to ships.

Chapter 17

To new fishing grounds

WITH THE HELP of Biddie and one or two jovial comments from the fishermen about the 'missus doing a proper job', we gave the *Coral* a coat of paint. It was springtime, the hedgerows full of wild flowers. I had played my last game of soccer for Mevagissey and had been asked to play cricket for Gorran. The ground was only a mile from our cottage, opposite the village school, which Anne Treneer wrote about so delightfully in her book, *School House in the Wind*.

I was once more back to square one, without a crew, and uncertain of what to do in the coming summer months.

"You don't want to go spiltering again," Edgar and Winston Barron said to me one morning, advice with which I readily agreed. "If I were you, old Cap'n," they went on, "I should do a bit of plummeting in the early morning and run the 'red lips' during the day. Take visitors round the bay for an hour, let 'em catch a few mackerel. Be a much easier way of life for you." It made me think. It certainly sounded an easier way to earn a living and already there were a number of visitors about. So I talked it over with Biddie and we decided to give it a go.

The following morning, having secured the *Coral* alongside the quay in the inner harbour, I watched from aboard the boat the visitors drifting slowly past, every so often calling out, but with some embarrassment, "Want a trip? Like a trip round the bay?" And when the tide was low I did the same, lying off the lighthouse steps in the outer harbour along with the toshers, until it was my turn and I collected enough passengers to make a trip financially worth while. Twelve was generally considered the maximum number to take aboard. I had no Board of Trade certificate, carried no lifebelts, not even a fire-extinguisher. The passengers stood up for'ard, leaning their elbows on the foredeck, while others sprawled on the fish-berth hatches, or stood in the net-room from which I had removed the central hatches. They seemed happy enough, particularly when they caught a few mackerel.

For a week I ran trips round the bay and caught a basket of mackerel in the early hours and made a bob or two. But I did not enjoy the business of touting for trade, for want of a better expression. It was Biddie who suggested an alternative, running sea trips to Fowey, Polperro and St Mawes. It was a better way of getting there than by bus and nobody was doing it from Mevagissey. We had leaflets printed and distributed them to the Trelowen Hotel and guest-houses, having first consulted with the fishermen what I should charge. Seven shillings a head for Fowey, twelve shillings for Polperro, and fifteen shillings for St Mawes was their advice.

The summer of 1947 turned out to be a glorious one; day after day, week after week, long hours of sunshine, ideal for being on the water. I remember one of those trips in particular. I was taking a full boat-load of passengers to St Mawes. The weather was fine, the wind up in the north. As we cleared Chapel Point, a short sea broke against our port bow, sending a sheet of spray across the *Coral* causing some discomfort and concern to the passengers. I quickly decided to change my plans and motor up to Fowey so the wind and sea would be astern of us on the return passage, rather than find ourselves heading into it on the longer return passage from St Mawes. I explained this to the passengers and they were happy to go to Fowey instead. Halfway across the bay one of the passengers asked if I would stow his camera in a safe place.

"Of course," I said, handing over the wheel to Biddie, and went for'ard to put the man's camera on the small shelf in the cuddy.

Approaching the Gribbin we had a bumpy old time of it and I had to ease back the engines as we ran into a series of short, steep seas. Finally rounding the Cannis rocks, we entered Fowey, came alongside and offloaded our passengers, having agreed to pick them up again at three o'clock in the afternoon. We were about to cast off when the owner of the camera came hurrying back along the pontoon to reclaim it.

"Right you are," I said, "I'll get it for you." Going for'ard, I bent down to open the hatchway into the cuddy. To my horror I found that the camera had jumped off the shelf into a bucket containing some tar — not much, but enough. For one brief moment I stared down at it in total dismay.

"I'm dreadfully sorry!' I said retrieving the dripping camera, "I'm afraid it has fallen off the shelf into a bucket of tar. It must have happened when we hit that rough bit of water. It's entirely my fault."

"That's all right," he said calmly, "It can't be helped."

However, I knew only too well it could have been helped, and said so. "I'll try and clean it with petrol and, of course, you must let me know what I owe you."

"You don't owe me anything," he replied, "and it's not your fault," and with that generous utterance he left us.

We let go our ropes and motored off to pick up a buoy. Then for the next hour or so Biddie and I attempted to clean the camera, repeatedly dipping it into petrol and drying it off. But no matter how much we did so, tar still seeped out. It proved a hopeless task.

When we got back to Mevagissey, running before a comfortable following sea, I collected the fares, except from the owner of the camera. He was the last to leave the *Coral* and would not do so until he had paid his seven shillings. He came out with us twice more, once to St Mawes and once to Polperro and, despite my attempts on each occasion to pay something towards the loss of his camera, and not to charge him for the trips, he would have none of it.

So, those warm summer days passed and, at the weekends, I played cricket for Gorran on their high, picturesque, sloping ground, with Gorran church tower in the background, and the distant white sunlit china clay hills clearly visible on the far side of St Austell, looking like some lunar landscape. To the north-west, across green fields and woodlands, lay Polmassick, Grampound, Probus and the road to Truro.

A wooden Nissen hut served as a pavilion and Archie Smith's wife, Doreen, together with Peg and Goodie Whetter, and Cath May, provided the cream teas, and very good they were in those days of austerity.

The Gorran side was largely composed of farmers, six in all. Stan and Howard Whetter, both farmers close on fifty, gnarled and weather-beaten as two windswept trees in a Cornish hedgerow, along with Ernie Liddicoat who owned the Gorran garage, stood their ground in the field, sticking out the occasional boot when a ball sped their way, too fast by far for them to bend and stop. Les Rowse, another farmer, a steady opening bat who was to play a couple of times for Cornwall, and Jack Hurrell fielded alongside me in the slips, while I kept wicket. Jack, who talked a lot, was full of wit and humour, and shrewd in his judgement and knowledge of the game. Joe Grose, a medium-pace bowler, who moved the ball appreciably and also played once or twice for Cornwall, and Harold and George Bunney, both competent cricketers, were the other three farmers in the side. Bill May completed the team.

Led by Archie Smith, who flew with the RAF during the war, the team was a happy mixture of old and young, who got on well together. Archie was a splendid captain, who bowled fast-medium left arm, round the wicket in swingers, sometimes bowling over the wicket, occasionally throwing in a slower ball, varying his pace, thinking all the time. Every so often he would send down a really fast ball using his considerable height and strength. He was also a forceful bat, with an upright stance, a high back-lift, who played well off his front foot, hitting through the line of the ball with the full face of the bat. He made his runs quickly.

Most of the pitches we played on that hot dry summer were lively, some alarmingly so, in particular those of Fowey, St Minver and Rock. Over at Rock, Archie went out to inspect the pitch with Harry Champion, the home captain, before spinning the coin.

"This looks a bit dodgy, Harry," said Archie, to the Rock skipper, who had to agree.

"I'll tell you what," said the latter, "we'll play across the pitch," and the stumps were promptly shifted and a new pitch marked out there and then, at right angles to the existing one.

But, of all the grounds we visited, two particularly I remember for their lovely setting. Lanhydrock, seat of the Lord Robartes family, and Boconnoc, the prettiest of them all, ringed by woods out of which deer wandered to graze in the long grass surrounding the outfield, totally unconcerned at the cricket going on. It was on the Boconnoc ground that one of the Gorran players challenged the umpire, when he had been given out L.B.W. halfway down the wicket.

"I couldn't have been out L.B.W.," said the batsman.

"No," said the umpire, "I'm not giving you out L.B.W. I'm giving you out for obstructing the wicket-keeper." There was no answer to that one.

One afternoon I was driving back to Bodrugan when I saw the Reverend Henry Kendall standing outside his cottage in Portmellon. I stopped the jeep and got out to talk to him. That short conversation changed the course of our lives.

"Are you going to try and make a living from the sea for the rest of your life?" he asked me.

"I don't know," I replied truthfully.

"Why don't you try and get up to one of the universities? As an ex-serviceman you are entitled to a grant. At any rate, I should think about it."

I did. I thought long and hard about our future. After talking it over with Biddie, we agreed it was unlikely I would ever make a fortune at fishing. We had tasted a way of life, experienced a little of what was involved, and enjoyed being part of a fishing community. But, deep within me, I doubted whether I had the resolve to be a fisherman forever. My capital had run out, I would require another hand to work the *Coral* in the winter months and, although we had been generously accepted, helped, and made welcome, I was still a novice. During the war the fishermen had made good money, though under restricted and often hazardous conditions. Since the end of hostilities, the price of fish had fallen. To make any sort of a living meant long hours at sea, often for scant reward, in what was already a declining industry.

There were twenty luggers fishing out of Mevagissey in 1946, but it was still possible to imagine what it must have been like at the turn of the century, when up to a hundred luggers hoisted their tanned lugsails and, getting out their great sweeps when there was not enough wind, laboriously made their way through the outer harbour and into the bay for another night of pilchard driving up off the Gribbin.

So, with mixed feelings, I decided to heed Henry Kendall's advice. I had long discarded the idea of returning to Liverpool University and pursuing a degree in architecture. Where to go was the problem and what to read. Well, why not start at the top, I thought, and wrote there and then to several colleges at Oxford and Cambridge, applying for a place to read History that coming October. I chose History not because I had been any good at it, far from it, but because it was a subject I could prepare for on my own, or so I thought. If pressed to justify my choice, I would argue on the lines that some knowledge of the past is surely essential if any sense is to be made of the present. The responses were prompt and brief — the colleges were full. It was disappointing, but hardly surprising. Then, I suddenly recalled that Shrewsbury had some connection with Brasenose. Tim Singleton, a contemporary of mine in Ridgemount, had gone up to B.N.C. having been awarded something called a Heath Harrison, and there had been others too. Of course, there was not the slightest likelihood that I would gain an award, but the connection was worth a try. So, as a last resort, I wrote to the Oxford college.

I decided this time to give a brief, but more detailed account of my past and what I was now doing. When I had finished the letter I showed it to Biddie.

"D'you think it's too much of a good thing?" I asked her. The letter was longer than I had intended.

"No," she said, "it's fine. Send it off as it is," and I did so.

Three days later, going into Mevagissey, I met the postman and asked if he had any letters for us. He had; there was one from the principal of Brasenose College, W. T. S. Stallybrass. He wrote:

Dear Sir,

I am obliged to you for your letter of the 28th of May. The College is, of course, extraordinarily over-full and admission is very highly competitive, but if you would care to come up for our College Entrance Examination on July 1st and 2nd, we would be very pleased to examine you. Would you please complete the enclosed College Entry Form? I do not of course at present know whether you are exempt from Responsions.

Mevagissey brings up happy memories to me.

Yours sincerely,

W. T. S. Stallybrass

I was intrigued by the second and third words of his last sentence and wondered whether he had been out fishing and suffered somewhat. At any rate this was the most hopeful reply to date. The door had not been politely but firmly shut in my face. However, the prospect of a College Entrance Examination I found daunting. My academic career had been anything but distinguished. It was only at the second attempt that I had attained the necessary number of credits in the School Certificate for matriculation, which did exempt me from Responsions. But what on earth, I wondered, would I have to do for this College Entrance Examination? However, there was hope, so I wrote back at once to W. T. S. Stallybrass, saying that I would very much like to sit the College Entrance Examination, but that I feared the results would be dreadful. "I have not sat an examination for six years, apart from one on gunnery in which I scored five out of a hundred," I wrote.

By return of post I heard again from the Principal:

Dear Mr Shearwood,

Thank you for your letter of the 2nd of June. You should not worry too much about the Entrance Examination.

Allowances will be made for the fact that it is a long time since you have done that sort of work.

Yours sincerely,

W. T. S. Stallybrass

I also heard from the Ministry of Education, to whom I had previously written, asking whether I would be entitled to a grant. Their reply was, I thought, rather ominous. After quoting from the government pamphlet P.L.120 they wanted to know why I wished to discontinue my career as an architect at Liverpool University and study for a History degree. They ended by explaining that they could do nothing until they had received definite confirmation that I had been accepted by a university. Things were moving, but my chances of getting into Oxford still appeared remote.

The sun shone continuously throughout June, the wind blew gently down from the north and, over calm waters I ran my trips to Fowey, Polperro and St Mawes.

I found that I was now seeing less of the fishermen. They were just as friendly and helpful, but I was working on my own and, although I enjoyed 'running the red lips', I missed the massive form and grunts of George Pearce, the soft singsong voice of George Allen spinning his yarns, and the sight of Sam Ingrouille, tall as a lamppost, a trilby on his head, a weary look of resignation on his face, as he began clearing yet another heap of tangled line and hooks. Above all, I missed that exciting moment when the creeper was in sight, the line visible, slanting away to the bottom of the sea. It is a moment of drama which never palls, for each man knows that on that line or in those nets, hang his pounds, shillings and pence — his living. Whether or not there are plenty of fish on the line or in the nets, few comments are made. It is a philosophy, bound up with the fact that fishermen for generations have experienced the hardship of toil and poverty and, being naturally superstitious, as are all who wrest their living from the sea, will never tempt Providence by an unguarded word of enthusiasm, or disappointment, let alone a prediction of what might, or might not be on the line or in the nets.

My pounds, shillings and pence now sat, or stood in the *Coral's* open fish-berth and net-room, chatting, leaning against the boat's sides, gazing out across the water at the distant coastline. They were a cheerful catch, easy to handle, easy to offload and made me quite good money. But it was not the answer to our future.

Walking along the quayside one Wednesday morning, I stopped to join a few visitors, who were watching the crew of a lugger in the process of landing their catch. She was the *Ibis*, registration number FY118, a well-known boat, forty-two feet overall with a beam upward of thirteen feet and a draught of six foot six. She was built by Percy Mitchell, in 1930, for the Lakeman brothers, Eddie, Archie, and Dick, renowned and respected fishermen.

They left harbour at six o'clock on Monday evening, and had been away long-lining for the past thirty hours. Having shot their ten drift nets and caught sufficient bait, twenty-five stone of pilchards, the lugger headed on into the night, south-east by south, the crew cutting up the pilchards and baiting the long-line, twenty great baskets of it, each basket containing three hundred and fifty hooks on four hundred fathoms of line. They went sixty miles off and shot their line over the Hurd Deep, more commonly called the Ray Pits, where ray and skate swim in abundance. The line, all eight thousand fathoms, lay stretched along the seabed, seven thousand hooks attached to it, marked on the surface by four ten-foot dan buoys, anchored on the bottom by creepers, very similar to a dog-line, but on a far greater scale.

At half-past nine on Tuesday morning they began the long haul. The weather remained fine, the tides were slack, and the going was straightforward. By 4.30 in the afternoon, the line was all in and they were under way, homeward bound, the crew clearing the hooks, coiling the manilla line down in the centre of the huge baskets, each one of the three hundred and fifty hooks, stuck into the cork, bound round the top outside edges of the baskets. In the early hours of Wednesday morning, they passed the light, and secured alongside the quay in the inner harbour.

I watched for a little while longer, as the four of them worked silently, economically, getting on with the job, making it all look easy, which was hardly surprising, since they had been doing it for a lifetime. These were the men I would have to measure up to, compete with, if I were ever to become a successful fisherman. As I caught Eddie Lakeman's eye, he gave me a brief nod and greeting. "All right, Ken?"

"Fine," I said.

It made me feel good. As I turned to go, I felt several pairs of eyes switched in my direction.

My old CO, Peter Bull, came and stayed with us for two long spells during that hot summer of 1947. He was fascinated by our way of life, made a great fuss of Kim, was very fond of Biddie and, from his tiny bedroom window, he could see, across the bay, the lights of Charlestown, Polruan, and the Eddystone. He brought with him the manuscript of his first book, *To Sea in a Sieve*, which I read with huge enjoyment. Later, his old schoolfriend, the actor, Nick Phipps, joined us. He had just written the script of *Spring in Park Lane*, which became a successful and delightful film. They had much in common, though not in physique.

"Remove the fat man," came the shout from a member of the audience one night in the West End, when Peter was playing the part of Pozzo in Samuel Beckett's *Waiting for Godot*.

We wondered how Nick, very tall, lean and elegant, would like the cottage, still more the camp bed, not to mention the Elsan and the primus stove. Somehow he survived the first night with us, though I suspect the pills and medicines surrounding his camp bed had something to do with it.

We ate our meals round an antique gate-leg table we had found in Penzance. We have it to this day. For seats we used three five-gallon petrol drums, and two upturned fish boxes. Cliff Nichols in Mevagissey sold us an old rocking chair and that was about the extent of our furniture.

In the evenings, we drove the jeep down to Hemmick or Caerhayes, where Peter, Biddie and Kim swam, while Nick and I lay on the warm sand and listened to the murmur of the sea, letting the world go by. At other times, after supper, we would wander past the old house of Bodrugan, empty and neglected, on down the narrow, overgrown footpath, past Old Wall's Cottage, lonely and crumbling with age, until we reached Colona Cove, protected on the east by the low rocks of Chapel Point. There on the small sandy beach we sometimes found cattle standing motionless in the shallows.

Early one morning Peter attempted to make us a cup of tea. "Having a little trouble with the primus," he cheerfully called up from below. He had filled the stove with methylated spirits instead of paraffin.

By now I had heard again from Brasenose, enclosing the timetable of their entrance examination.

"We shall naturally expect you to take a General Paper, a History Paper and a French Unseen Translation."

They concluded by saying they would be obliged if I would let them know what period of History I was going to offer and, whether it was English, or European, or both.

The period should cover not less than a hundred years. After a hurried consultation, it was unanimously decided that the Tudors and Stuarts were the answer.

"I think you'd better get hold of a book," Peter suggested.

I had heard from some source that Mrs Clarke, wife of the postmaster in Mevagissey, was interested in history.

"Yes, my dear," she said, when I went to see her, "I've always enjoyed the subject. I've a book that gives a general outline. Take it by all means."

The outline was general all right. Lying on the *Coral's* warm deck while my passengers were ashore, I browsed through the two hundred-odd pages that covered the lives of the Tudors and Stuarts. "Had a good day?" Biddie greeted me when I got back. "Know all about the Dissolution of the Monasteries?" Peter enquired.

"And all those wives of his, not to mention the Reformation," added Nick, chuckling.

At the end of June we set off for Evesham, where I left Biddie and Kim at the Lodge, while I went on to Oxford. I took with me enough for two nights and, of course, Mrs Clarke's history book, which I looked at the night before the examination.

On July 1st I sat three papers. The examination room was full of candidates who looked an earnest and confident bunch of young men. In the morning I wrote a French Unseen Translation. I knew the meaning of few of the words, but by guessing and, with the help of a generous next-door neighbour, when the Examiner twice left the room, I managed to get something down on paper. In the General paper I was faced by a number of questions. I remember one that I attempted: ' "Faithful study of the higher arts softens the character and preserves us from savagery." Discuss this view of the moral and social value of art.' God knows what I wrote, but I thought how Edgar would have laughed had he seen me attempting it.

The History paper proved a disaster. Mrs Clarke's book was found sadly wanting, as was I. In vain I searched for a question I could write on. Eventually I found one on Wolsey: 'Do you consider that Wolsey played a brilliant, but essentially futile, part on the European stage?' It did not help much. I handed in my single page well before time, glad to escape from the earnest scratch of pens and sight of candidates bent over their scripts, writing their heads off.

It was hot outside and I felt in need of a cup of tea. I bought a paper, found a cafe in the Turl and had a wash. Then I wandered in the late sunshine, down the busy High Street, crossed Magdalen Bridge and walked along Iffley Road, until I came to the Oxford University football ground. I retraced my steps up the High towards Carfax, where the traffic was heavy and the roads seemed to flow in all directions. I turned right and headed off down the Broad, aptly named, past Balliol and Trinity Colleges, paused to look through the windows of Blackwell's bookshop, before crossing over to enter Radcliffe Square, where the circular mass of the Camera, flanked by Brasenose, the Bodleian, All Souls and St Mary's church, dominates the scene with its towering dome.

I should, I suppose, have been more concerned about my papers which, I was only too aware, were worthless. But it did not worry me all that much. The result, whether I went to Oxford or not, was no longer in my hands, it never really had been. It certainly did not stop me from having a good night's sleep.

The next morning we were interviewed. I was rather looking forward to it. When the time came, I was called into a panelled, mellow room with long windows and heavy curtains. I was asked to sit at a table, around which several dons were seated, presided over by the principal, Dr Stallybrass. As I faced him down the table, I got the impression of a heavily built man with a kind face.

"Mr Shearwood, you were in the Navy during the war?"

"Yes, sir," I replied.

"Would you tell us briefly what you did?"

I had no problem doing so.

"And since the war you have been fishing for your living?"

"I have," I said.

"What sort of fishing?" a voice enquired.

For the next five minutes or so, I told them about my experiences and enjoyed myself.

"Why do you want to come up to Oxford?" another asked me. I found that not such an easy question to answer and for the first time felt slightly exposed.

"Thank you, Mr Shearwood," I heard Dr Stallybrass say. "We will let you know the result in the course of the next few days."

I got up from the table, thanked him and left the room in a happy frame of mind, despite that last question.

I drove back through the Cotswolds to Evesham. The following day, I set off for Cornwall with Biddie and Kim.

Three days later, I came in from an all-day trip to Polperro. It had been very hot, no wind, the sea a sheet of glass. I could feel the glow of the sun on my face and arms.

Kim heard the jeep and, as I got out, came bounding from the cottage, followed by Biddie.

"Hello," she said smiling, "there's a letter for you from Oxford."

"Is there?" and my heart quickened. "Now we'll know one way or the other."

I gave her a kiss on the cheek and hurried inside. The letter lay on the table. I picked it up, looked at it for a moment, then opened it.

Dear Mr Shearwood,

I have much pleasure in informing you...

I read no further.

"It's fine," I said, "they've accepted me."

It was wonderful news and we were both excited.

"You must have done well," said Biddie.

"I certainly did not do well," I replied. "It must have been the interview that got me through."

Years later, 1963 to be precise, Eric Collier, one of the dons who had interviewed me on that occasion, writing about that interview in the college magazine, *The Brazen Nose*, in an article entitled, 'Admissions Procedures of the Past', wrote:

The marks gained by the successful candidate on this occasion are still preserved in a tutorial file, but they constitute one of those journalistic confidences, rather than violate which the Editor of this magazine would prefer to suffer a long term of imprisonment.

In fact he did give the game away when he wrote and asked my permission to quote the account of that interview which I had recorded in *Whistle the Wind*. In his letter he said:

I may disclose, incidentally, that after I read your book, I looked up my examination records and found I gave you delta for History, with the comment that you appeared to know none. But you did a respectable General Paper, and that, combined with your close resemblance to a former pupil of ours, whom we greatly liked and was killed in the war, got you in! — I may add that we never had any regrets at our decision.

The fact that we were now definitely leaving Mevagissey and returning inland to live upcountry and out of sight of the sea saddened us.

"There are always the holidays," I said to Biddie, "we shan't lose touch."

That evening we went into Mevagissey and called on Willie Rolling. He was eating a kipper with his fingers. "Fingers before forks," he said to us. When he heard we were going, he was upset, but brightened up when I slipped a packet of Woodbines into his hand.

"We shall come back, as often as possible," said Biddie.

"We've not gone yet, Willie," I added.

The next morning I was on the quayside with Biddie and Kim, preparing to take some passengers to St Mawes. Word had got round that we were leaving.

"Well, missus," said Willie Wish, swaying from one leg to another as he approached, peering up from under the peak of his cap, his jaw thrust forward, courteously addressing Biddie first, "so he's going to Oxford University. Well, I'm very pleased for both your sakes."

"I'm going to have to sell the *Coral*, Willie," I added ruefully.

"Never mind, old man," he said, "what we've got to do is find you a buyer. You leave that to us. We'll find a Joe all right."

"I hear you are leaving us," said Winston Barron.

"Is it true?" said Edgar, coming up. "Have you told Catherine, Ken?"

"Not yet," I replied.

"You'll have to tell her, old man."

Later that day, returning from St Mawes, the Kelvin began making an ominous thumping noise and I had no option but to shut the engine down. When I had moored the boat I went to see William in his engineering shop. "Be with you in a minute, Ken," he said.

Despite his great bulk and heavy boots, he was surprisingly nimble as he clambered over the *Coral's* decks and knelt in the confined space of the engine-room. "Your main bearings are worn. The prop shaft will have to come out," he informed me.

This was our second summer in Cornwall and I was now eligible to play for the county. I had been making runs and keeping wicket for Gorran and, to my delight, was invited to play for Cornwall against Devon at Mountwise. Archie was also selected and together we travelled in the jeep to Plymouth. I had a good day behind the sticks and scored seventy in the first innings. It was a high-scoring match which ended in a draw. I was to play once more for Cornwall against the Royal Navy.

Meanwhile, Gorran had gone from strength to strength that season and come top of the Eastern Cricket League. Troon, who had won the Western Cricket League, were our opponents. The final of the Western Morning News Cup, to establish who were to be the league champions of Cornwall, was played at Camborne, on a hard fast wicket, before a sizeable crowd that stretched round the ground. Gorran lost the toss, had a torrid time of it in the field, faced a total of well over two hundred to win the match and were bowled out for exactly a hundred runs, of which I scored fifty and, in doing so, broke the headlight of a parked car.

So the long hot summer days of 1947 passed by and the time was fast approaching when we would have to pack up our few belongings and go. I still had not sold the *Coral*, despite advertising. Willie Wish, however, did not seem the least bit worried when I told him of my concern.

"We'll find a Joe, old man," he assured me, and he did. One late afternoon in September, I had come home after an-all day trip to Polperro and was sitting in the rocking chair, wearily pushing myself gently backwards and forwards with my stockinged feet, my eyes closed, when I was roused by a knock on the door. It was Willie Wish.

"Come in and have a cup of tea," I heard Biddie say. "No, missus, I'm not staying. Just come over to tell Ken I've found a Joe. Be down on the quay tomorrow at half-past nine and ask seven hundred and twenty pounds for the boat," he told me as I got to my feet.

I did my best to persuade him to stay, but he would not even allow me to run him back to Mevagissey — Willie was nearing seventy. "Remember, seven hundred and twenty," he repeated, with that air of authority he possessed, "you'll get it, old man. Goodbye, missus," and, with the briefest of nods, he turned and set off slowly down Bodrugan Hill back to Mevagissey.

The following morning I arrived promptly to find Willie Wish already down on the quayside, talking with two men, who were looking at the *Coral* on her moorings. As I approached I could see one was clearly a fisherman, the other I assumed to be the buyer — the Joe.

"Good morning," I said and, shaking their hands, I introduced myself while Willie wandered away, though not before he had given me a knowing look.

"Well, shall we go aboard?" and I sculled them out to the *Coral*.

"What are your engines like?" asked the one I imagined would work the boat.

"Fine," I assured him. "I'll start them up and you can have a look." I watched as he knocked both engines in and out, opened them up for a second or two and checked the exhausts.

"Seem all right," he said to the other man, at the same time giving me a nod of approval.

"D'you want to go out for a trial run?" I asked.

The two looked at each other. "I don't think it's necessary," said the prospective buyer.

While I shut down the Kelvin and Handy Billy, the two men clambered for'ard over the net-room and fish-berth, to remove the hatches and inspect the bilges.

"What d'you want for her?" asked the buyer eventually.

"Seven hundred," I replied.

While the two men conferred in the bows of the *Coral,* I pumped out the bilges for something to do.

"Give you six hundred and eighty, cash," said the buyer from up for'ard.

"All right," I said, "I'll accept that," and he clambered aft, produced a wad of notes and paid me there and then.

I don't know why I did not ask seven hundred and twenty as Willie had advised me. Perhaps it was because I felt the *Coral* owed me nothing or, more probably, because I was only too glad to have found a buyer.

"Better get some fuel aboard," said the new owner.

"Weather's handsome," said the other. "We can take her down to Mousehole now."

Once ashore, we shook hands and then I took a long last look at the *Coral.* Her fine, blunt uplifted bow seemed to look me straight in the face, as though I had deserted her, and I rather felt I had. I turned and walked away with a distinct feeling of loss, for the *Coral was* no longer ours.

Willie Wish was hanging around outside Pawlyn's store. I guessed he had been keeping a close eye on what was happening and would want to know how things had gone.

"All right, old man?" he asked me.

"Yes," I replied. "Sold her for six hundred and eighty pounds, Willie."

"Did you ask seven hundred and twenty?"

"No," I admitted.

"You'm a damned old fool then," said Willie Wish. "If you'd stuck out you'd have got your price. Still, I'm glad for your sake you've sold her."

I tried hard to persuade Willie to accept forty pounds, for he had found a buyer and saved me a lot of money as well as worry.

"Take it, Willie," I said quietly, but nothing I could say or do would make him change his mind. I glanced at the *Coral* once more. The two men were busy filling up the tanks in preparation for their passage to Mousehole.

"Thanks, Willie," I said, "thanks for all your help."

"That's all right, old man." I left him standing on the quayside. Slowly and thoughtfully I drove back to Bodrugan Cottage.

"Come on," I said to Biddie after I had told her what had happened, "let's go to the Dodman and look at the *Coral* on her way down to Mousehole." We took the jeep to the top of Hemmick and then walked to the Grooda and on to the Dodman.

It was a wild and wonderful day, the wind well up off the land. The sea lay blue beneath us. White horses whipped up by the stiff breeze, danced in the sunlight, and purple catspaws, fickle dark shadows, scurried hither and thither across the surface of the sea. While Kim hunted around in the deep bracken we waited for the *Coral*. We waited for the best part of an hour, but she never came. She may have put back into Mevagissey and set off later. We never found out and I never enquired. There we stood on that bright, breezy day on top of the Dodman and waited for the *Coral*, but she never came. She had gone from our lives forever.

We decided to leave at the end of September. There was a week to go. Willie Rolling helped me dispose of my nets and lines. My smocks, sea-boots, oilskins, gaffs, creepers, grapnels and Aldis lamp I gave to Edgar and George Allen.

We spent the last week saying our goodbyes. Although Oxford was an exciting prospect, we both knew how much we would miss the warmth, humour and kindness of this Cornish fishing community. It was a way of life we would never experience again but one we would not have missed.

Our last night in the cottage was a strange one. Everything had been packed up, and what little furniture we possessed Leo and Phyllis Kendall had allowed us to store in the big old farmhouse of Bodrugan they were shortly to inhabit. All that remained were our suitcases, a few pots and pans and two primuses which stood on the stone floor below.

We climbed the steep narrow flight of wooden stairs for the last time. The night was a clear one, peaceful, beautiful, and we stood at our bedroom window and looked at Fowey Light as it winked at us across seven miles of dark water. The fleet was up off the Gribbin, pilchard driving, their masthead lights, flickering fireflies in the dark, as the boats lay to their nets. A sliver of moon hung low in the sky and, far off, the Eddystone Light flashed faintly. Vividly I recalled that night up at the Rame, when the gannets plummeted down and our nets were heavy with fish. The beam of a car's lights as it reached the top of Bodrugan Hill jerked me back to reality.

Around midnight, I became conscious of strange noises coming from below. Kim, who slept at the foot of our bed, was on his feet and restless, aware that something was happening. My immediate thought was that the sounds must be coming from the adjoining cottage. For a while there was silence and then the noises broke out again, this time waking Biddie.

"What's going on?" she asked in alarm.

"I don't know," I replied quietly, far from happy myself. "Whatever it is, I think it's best we leave well alone."

We lay and listened. It was just as though every so often someone was rummaging amongst our pots and pans and other bits and pieces we had placed on the stone floor ready for packing the jeep in the morning. I had little doubt now that it was not next door. Eventually the noises ceased and we dozed off.

Just before first light Biddie awoke to the sound of footsteps coming up the stairs. For a fleeting moment she thought it was me until she realised I was by her side. Tensely, she listened as the footsteps reached the top of the stairs, passed our door and entered Peter's room. "Someone's just come up the stairs," she said softly, "and gone into Peter's room."

Kim was aware of something too and was on his feet again, and restless. I propped myself up and, straining my ears, listened intently, until I could almost hear the silence.

"Are you sure?" I whispered.

"Certain," she said, and I did not doubt her.

But we heard nothing more and, as the first grey light of dawn stole into the room, we fell asleep, and awoke to bright sunshine.

Highly intrigued, we pushed Kim out first and followed his tail-wagging hindquarters down the steep, narrow wooden staircase. A quick glance around told us nothing had been disturbed. Everything was exactly as we had left it the previous evening. No explanation could be found for the strange noises we had heard in the night. Breakfast over, we went next door to say goodbye to the elderly parents of Ivy.

"Were either of you up in the night?" we asked them gently. The old lady shook her head vigorously, while her even older husband smiled and said nothing. But then we never did hear him say anything.

"Did you hear any noises?" Again she shook her head and gabbled a few incomprehensible words, for she suffered from a serious speech defect.

I filled her bucket from the pump for the last time and then we said a warm goodbye to them both. There were tears in the old lady's eyes.

No sooner had we started packing up the jeep than the man from the insurance turned up.

"Good gracious," I said, before he could get a word in, "you're just in time to give us a hand," and at once he found himself busy helping to carry our possessions from the cottage to the jeep, till we were packed and ready to go.

"I heard you were going," he said, "and wanted to catch you before you left, to ask if you would like to increase your policy?"

"Well, one good turn deserves another, but only by a very little," I warned him.

By now Ivy and her husband were there to see us off. The old lady joined them and we could see her old man peering through the window.

So, with a wave from the four of them, we started up the jeep and drove slowly away, down Bodrugan Hill to Portmellon, past Percy Mitchell's boatyard and the four houses that had survived the great storm, past Black Cottage and on up the steep, winding cliff road to Mevagissey. At the top of Polkirt Hill we pulled in for one final look down at the inner and outer harbour.

Below us we could see the *Margaret* and the *Ibis*, the *Christobel, Pride of the West, White Heather, Little Pearl* and others. They were all there. All except the *Coral*. She had gone.

I let in the clutch of the jeep and plunged down Polkirt Hill. I felt Kirn's heavy head rest on my shoulder, as we drove through the village of Mevagissey and away, up and over the hill, towards new fishing grounds at some place called Oxford.

Chapter 18

A first tutorial

WITH DIFFICULTY we eventually found somewhere in Oxford prepared to take a couple with a big black Labrador. Our new abode was not amidst dreaming spires, but out at Botley above a fishmonger's shop. A short flight of concrete steps led up to the front door. We rented a sitting-room with a double bed and shared the kitchen and bathroom with the landlady and her husband, who played the double bass and drank. They had an eight-year-old son whose strange behaviour sorely taxed his mother's patience until she became exasperated and began shouting. It was not an ideal situation, but they were friendly and accepted us until they discovered Kim sleeping on our bed when we were out. Instead of telling us, they put some sort of preventative powder on the eiderdown which did nothing to deter Kim, but got onto our pyjamas and caused us a night of considerable irritation and discomfort. So we began our time at Oxford.

I remember very well that first tutorial with Kevin O'Hanlan, a tall, highly intelligent Irishman, for it proved a most disquieting affair. Attired in our short commoners' gowns, we sat upon an enormous settee covered in a loose fabric of gold hopsack and listened as Edgar Stanley Cohn outlined the course of study for the term, gave us a bibliography and advised us what lectures to attend.

"Of course, we expect that you've done some reading and know the background of what we are about to study," he remarked casually, standing before his elegant fireplace in a room lined with books, its mellow old walls and ceiling panelled in oak.

I hastily nodded my assurance but I found his words neither comforting nor particularly easy to hear. Stanley Cohn had a habit of speaking in low musing tones, almost as though we weren't there. And then, without warning he would break off, glance down as if suddenly aware of our presence once more and smile benignly.

He was a small man, dark and slightly Jewish-looking, and when he smiled his eyes narrowed, his mouth curled upwards and his whole face creased in puckish humour. He wore a hound's-tooth brown jacket, dark flannels and neat suede shoes and he rocked gently to and fro, his heels on the hearth, while he stared thoughtfully over our heads at the long windows overlooking the quad.

"Well," he said at length, addressing O'Hanlan, "I think you'd better write an essay this week on the..." and I watched Kevin's aquiline features as he scribbled something down on paper.

Then it was my turn and, although I could hear his voice, for the life of me I could only distinguish one word, Northumbria. I pretended to be writing it all down, for I had not the courage to ask him to repeat himself.

"Right," he said softly, dismissing us with the slightest of nods and another brief smile, and we got up to go.

Outside the door I followed Kevin down the narrow spiral steps.

"Did you manage by any chance to catch the title of my essay?" I asked him as we went out into the sunlit quad.

He shook his head. "Something to do with Northumbria, I think."

"Yes," I said, "I got that bit too."

"Well, we've a whole week to do it in," he remarked cheerfully as we parted.

But I found it difficult to see what difference a week or even a year would make to the predicament in which I now found myself.

Several afternoons that week I spent at Iffley Road striving for recognition in the soccer trials held for freshmen. Those interested had written a short account of their previous performances for Colin Weir, the Oxford captain and goalkeeper, who stood all of six foot six.

As far as I was concerned the trials were not a success, for I found myself playing at left-back, a foreign position, and marking a neat, fleet little right-winger, Jimmy Potts, who was to play for England.

At half-time, Laurie Scott, the current England and Arsenal right-back who was coaching the university side that year, spoke to us and told us what we were doing wrong and what he was looking for.

I saw Rob Tillard, Wykehamist and regular army captain in the 60th Rifles, who had played with fearless ferocity — unwittingly he was to help me in the not too distant future — listening attentively and noticed a short stocky player whose hair was silver-grey, Tony Pawson. Slightly behind Laurie Scott, watching the proceedings closely, his grey eyes hooded and unwinking, stood the honorary treasurer of the OUAFC, an old Blue, a fair, curly-haired man in a raincoat, a cigarette in his mouth. He was Dr Harold Thompson MA, FRS, a fellow of St John's College. I was acquainted with only one other person in the changing-room, Tony Peet. He was the secretary of the OUAFC; we'd met that summer playing cricket together for Cornwall against Devon.

The mood was very competitive and not particularly enjoyable and I returned disconsolate to Botley and Biddie.

Three days before my next tutorial I decided that there was no alternative but to visit Stanley Cohn and find out the title of my essay. So, mustering my courage, I climbed the spiral staircase at five o'clock one dull afternoon and knocked on his door. I heard a muffled voice call out and I entered.

Stanley was reclining on his enormous settee, the warm glow from a solitary lamp lighting the pages of the book he was reading. He glanced at me over the top of his spectacles.

"I'm extremely sorry to trouble you," I began, still standing in the doorway, "but I didn't quite catch the title of the essay you set me."

"Oh," he said, frowning slightly, "I've set a number of essays over the past few days."

I nodded and waited uneasily.

"Well," he said at length, "you'd better write something on..." and I watched his lips moving, drank in the scene as though mesmerised and heard his words as from a great distance, and then his voice suddenly tailed off and he picked up his book and began reading again.

"Thank you very much," I said, coming to, and backed out of the room.

Outside the door I stood for a moment, appalled. Exactly as before, I had caught only that one wretched word, Northumbria. I was no further on. I considered knocking on the door and saying, "Look, I'm very sorry, but I simply cannot hear what you are saying; would you please speak up and tell me again what you want me to do." But my courage failed me and, with sinking heart, I retreated slowly down the steps and out into the quad.

I visited the Camera and tried to find out all I could about Northumbria. The following day I wrote my essay in our bed-sitting-room.

At the appointed hour we entered Stanley's room and sat down. For a moment or two our tutor studied us reflectively.

"Well now, O'Hanlan, let's hear what you've written," and Kevin gave the title of his piece of work and began to read.

I listened to the words of his essay with mounting apprehension for, though its content meant little to me, it nevertheless sounded impressive.

When he had finished, Stanley nodded his approval and asked one or two questions which Kevin answered confidently.

Then I could feel Stanley's eyes turned in my direction.

"And what have you got for us?" I heard him say. Taking the bull by the horns, I mumbled a few incoherent words and at the end let fly in a firm voice my single trump card, "Northumbria" and, without waiting, began to read. As I came to the end of my first page Stanley moved over to the window.

I read on, my discomfiture increasing at every word, until at last I finished.

Stanley did not return to his usual see-sawing stance before the fireplace. I half turned in my embarrassment. He was still standing gazing out of the tall window.

At last he spoke, his voice low, but this time I heard him clearly.

"I think that might safely be committed to the flames."

I looked at the empty fireplace and folded my worthless sheets of paper in two.

But I caught just a flicker of amusement as I got up to go which gave me some slight consolation.

Nearly every afternoon we would train at Iffley Road and there was usually a Centaurs' match, which was well organised by Jim Hornby, for those not playing in the university side.

I made friends with Jimmy Potts, who was married to a charming girl called Toni, and David Carr, who had been badly wounded in his right arm while serving with the Royal Norfolks in Normandy. Despite eighteen months in plaster and an eighty per cent disability pension he played football and cricket most effectively. Both were reading History. When travelling to away matches we would discuss the subject in a jocular fashion — in my case it couldn't really be in any other manner — and they were always curious to know about the current essay I was doing. Much later Jimmy Potts was to be of considerable help to me.

Another who played in those early Centaur games was Denis Saunders, a tall, gentle soul who came from Scarborough. He had long thin legs and seemed to have all the time in the world to collect and do what he wanted with the ball. Despite his big feet he had immaculate control and I never saw him bettered in the air. I also never knew a player with a calmer disposition.

And, as each Tuesday morning came round, sitting on the big settee alongside Kevin O'Hanlan, I would read out my essay to Stanley and, when the ordeal was over, repair to Fuller's or the Kardomah or the Kemp and drink a cup of coffee and breathe a sigh of relief.

I attended two lectures. On the first occasion Vivian Hunter Galbraith, a fine old gentleman with magnificent white locks, was lecturing on the Anglo-Saxons. There was such a crowd that I had to sit on the floor, my discomfort slightly ameliorated by the fact that I was inconspicuous. I recall one of his sentences, he repeated it several times, as he pattered to and fro on the dais, shaking his mane from side to side. "Anglo-Saxon justice was nothing less than unmitigated barbarism", and I quickly wrote it down in my notebook, feeling that I had at least achieved something.

The second lecture I attended, given by W. A. Pantin, was on church history. This was an embarrassing experience for, unlike the first, there were no more than half a dozen people in the lecture room and I felt exposed. Not infrequently I caught the lecturer's eye and, whenever I did, I tried to look knowledgeable, and ever so slightly inclined my head to assure him that it was all going in. He was quick and competent but as I had no basic framework of history to which to relate his words, I found it all quite meaningless and nothing went in. So I repaired once more to Fuller's and drank yet another cup of coffee. Those were the only two lectures I attended during my three years at Oxford.

The term was rapidly drawing to a close when, going into the college one morning, I found in my pigeon-hole at the porter's lodge a card from Tony Peet to say that I had been selected to play for the university on Saturday against Epsom at centre-half, since Rob Tillard had elected to shoot pheasants that afternoon. So I promptly hastened back to tell Biddie the news because I had almost given up hope of being selected.

It was a good time to come into the side. There were only five more matches to go before we met Cambridge. Of the seven games already played, the Oxford side had won only once, beating the Corinthian-Casuals. They had lost to the Army, Bromley, Oxford City and to selected sides from Tottenham Hotspur, Arsenal and Wolves. It was my chance.

I remember very little of the match, except that we won 4-1 and Colin Weir and Dr Thompson — who came to all our matches and was known to us as Tommy — seemed reasonably satisfied with my performance.

The following Tuesday, 18 November, we played a very strong FA side captained by Leon Leuty, the Derby County and England centre-half. There were two other First Division players on view that day, Len Goulden, the England and Chelsea inside-forward, and J. McCue of Stoke City. Leon Josephs, Phipps, Hopper, Stroud and

Topp were all then, or later, amateur internationals. My task, to mark Ron Phipps of Barnet and England, was not as difficult as Rob Tillard's, for he had to mark the cultured Len Goulden. Mark him he certainly did, particularly his ankles, as Len, in all good humour, testified later.

After the game I asked Leon Leuty how he coped with Tommy Lawton in the air. "Tommy?" he said dryly, "You go up with him, but you don't win it often."

On the first Saturday of December 1947, we met Cambridge at Champion Hill, Dulwich, and were decisively beaten. When they came out they looked business-like and confident in their light blue shirts, white shorts and light blue stockings.

On the day they were the better side. Norman Kerruish, Hubert Doggart, Barry Abbott, Doug Insole and Trevor Bailey were all good players. Trevor Bailey, in particular, caused us a lot of trouble, cutting inside and outside our left-back, sleeves flapping, rapping the base of the upright late in the second half and crossing the ball dangerously to his powerfully built inside trio of forwards. Despite a good performance by Colin Weir in goal and some fine individual attempts by Tony Pawson and Jimmy Potts to penetrate the Cambridge defence we lost the game 2-0.

But I thought at the time, and so did some of the papers, that the outsanding player of either side was Denis Saunders. Elegant and poised, he did everything possible to set things going for us.

Two days later, our disappointment behind us, we all met at Euston Station to catch the boat-train for a tour of Eire and Northern Ireland. We played the Bohemians first in Dublin. Then we went on to Derry City, where the crowd behind Colin Weir pelted him with mud balls and anything else they had to hand, all of which he ignored with noble and lofty disdain. In a match that should have been cancelled but, in fact, inexplicably went on for one hundred and ten minutes in dense fog we beat the Irish universities. I left before the final game at Cliftonville to captain the Old Salopians against the Old Reptonians in the first round of the Arthur Dunn at Repton, a match which the Old Salopians won convincingly, despite the balding head of Dickie Sale, the Derbyshire cricketer, who did his best to stem the goals.

And so I came home to Biddie and Christmas at Derby, and the New Year at Evesham. I had taken a pile of books with me and plenty of resolution, but somehow the days slipped quickly by and, in no time, the Hilary term was at hand.

Chapter 19

Tommy's plan

BACK ONCE MORE in our room above the fishmonger's shop out at Botley, I found, on going into Brasenose at the start of our second term at Oxford, that I had been given a new tutorial partner, another Irishman.

Martin Moriarty was a humble soul, with a certain passive acceptance of life which gave him an air of vulnerability. He spoke in moderate tones, each word carefully selected. He was not tall. His face, rugged and seamed, had the quality of one who had seen much and learnt to endure patiently. Before coming up to Oxford he had worked for a publishing firm in America and had a tenuous connection with the radical movement. We soon discovered we had something in common, a mutual apprehension of our weekly confrontations with Stanley Cohn.

Martin, it seemed to me, lacked confidence. He would always denigrate his intellectual capabilities, which were considerable, with a quick wry smile and a slow shake of his head. In fact, he had literary style, a critical mind and was widely read. I knew that he had nothing but his grant to live on and that books meant more to him than anything. He managed his affairs quietly and never complained. Looking back, I now realise how much of a struggle it must have been for him. It was only many years later that I discovered how different his background was from that of the average undergraduate of those times. From an elementary Roman Catholic school he had won a scholarship to the local grammar school, headmastered by one Arthur Hope, a Brasenose man, a fact that came up at his interview. He was forty when he came to Oxford and we were to see much of each other in the next three years.

The new Oxford soccer captain for the Hilary term of 1948 was John Tanner, a Carthusian who had already played as an amateur for England and Huddersfield and, under him, we began to build our side.

John was an independent cove, unpretentious and neat in style and looks, his freckled features even, his smooth dark hair never out of place on his round head. I had met him first in that memorable Shrewsbury versus Charterhouse match back in 1938 when we knocked in ten goals to their one. The second time I met him was in an Arthur Dunn match against the Old Carthusians at Charterhouse in 1946. Biddie and I had come up from Cornwall and I remember the game well.

John played at outside-right and destroyed our left flank. I was drawn from the middle, time and again, to cover the left-back. His technique never varied. He used sheer speed to beat his opponents and he certainly had this most valuable of assets. He would take the ball up to an opponent, show it to him and make his break when in striking distance to do so. On one of the many occasions he had rounded the back, I went across, obstructed him and he fell.

"That was unnecessary," he remarked, picking himself up, and I agreed with him. We lost the match.

Our last match of the season was against Bournville Athletic in the Midlands. I cannot remember whether we won or lost. I recollect that Tony Pawson — he was to become the world fly-fishing champion — had to rush away immediately after the match without a bath to catch the boat for a fishing holiday in Ireland. Sitting in the train on the way back to Oxford, Tommy began to tell us about his plans for entering a combined Oxford and Cambridge eleven to play in the FA Amateur Cup Competition.

"That's if we can get permission!" He ruminated, coughing for quite five seconds as though to emphasise his point. "Won't be easy," he reflected, "there'll be a lot of opposition," and regarding us with those brooding, calculating eyes, he began to explain what these difficulties were.

To begin with, to enter for the FA Amateur Cup, a club had to have its own registered ground. His proposed new club had no ground of its own. The Grange Road pitch at Cambridge belonged to the university rugby club, so it looked as though it would have to be the Oxford ground at Iffley Road.

Then there was the question of gaining exemption from the earlier rounds of the Amateur Cup which otherwise would have to be played before December. The Oxford and Cambridge match is not played until early December. Throughout the preceding months of the Michaelmas term each university has its own standing fixtures given up to preparation for this game. In Tommy's eyes it was vital that we have this exemption. I thought at the time, though, that it was extremely unlikely that the FA Amateur Cup Committee would grant us such a request because it seemed to be asking an awful lot.

"What's the club to be called?" someone asked.

"Well," said Tommy, after another long cough and much falling of ash — he'd seldom remove the cigarette from his lips — "my wife has thought of a name, she suggests we use the combination of the Oxford Centaur and Cambridge Falcon and call the club Pegasus, the winged horse of classical mythology,"

After a moment's pause to consider his words, we all thought it an excellent idea. Then, lighting another cigarette, Tommy sat back and gazed thoughtfully out of the window, while the train rattled on towards Oxford.

Towards the end of the term we learned we were to have a child and the prospect delighted us. Once again we faced the same old problem of finding somewhere to live. We also had an even bigger problem, a financial one, for we had nothing in the bank. My grant was a little over £300 a year which did not go very far. The £680 I had received from selling the *Coral* had dwindled away. I had no other resources. It was Biddie's mother who came to our rescue. She had been left some money, of which three thousand would eventually be ours. She let us have it now. After a good deal of searching, we found Laburnum House in Woodstock, for exactly this amount. The house was three centuries old, at the end of a row of tall semi-detached houses set back on the left at the top of the steep incline which one approaches when heading north for Chipping Norton.

There was a big open fireplace in the sitting-room. The tiny kitchen had French windows opening onto a narrow path flanked by a tall uneven stone wall. An ancient apple tree grew alongside the house. The pathway served as a right of way for two elderly Welsh spinsters who lived with their snappy pekinese dogs at the back of our house. Above the kitchen was the bathroom. When the wind blew from the north, the branches of the old apple tree brushed against the window-panes of this small, weird-shaped room with its thick, crooked walls. There were two bedrooms on this floor. Through a latched door and up another steep and narrow flight of stairs two beamed attics served as bedrooms. From one of the windows facing north could be seen the great column on which the first Duke of Marlborough stands in high, solitary splendour, surveying the acres of his palace, Blenheim. Beneath the kitchen and down a short steep flight of steps lay the cellar. On entering the front door one came straight into the hall which was big enough to use as a dining-room. It was our first home and we grew very fond of it.

That Easter holiday, after we had moved into our new home, we went back to the West Country to see our old friends down in Mevagissey. How good it was to be with them once more and see at night the Mevagissey fleet of pilchard drivers, their fishing lights, scattered specks of gold, flickering in the darkness of the bay. You never see them now.

I'd taken my football boots with me in expectation of a game and, sure enough, the committee invited me to play that Saturday.

Eagerly we drove up Tregony Hill and along the narrow familiar twisting lane, the high thick hedgerows full of primroses, the small stunted hawthorn bushes prickly and white as snow, till we came to the preposterous, rough, sloping field set above Mevagissey, where the players were already assembled. They handed me a green and yellow shirt, number five, which I slipped over my head before running onto the pitch. There were shouts of encouragement from the fishermen on the touchline, and particularly from Catherine, who gave me a great welcome, "You show 'em, me beauty," she shouted as I ran onto the pitch. I was fit and confident and determined to show them that I really could play a bit.

Ninety minutes later, when the final whistle blew and we had lost the match, I was not so sure that I had achieved my objective. By the middle of the following week I knew for certain that I had failed because a note arrived from the committee politely informing me that they thought it better to keep the team as it was and hoped I would understand.

A week before the start of the summer term of 1948 I was invited to attend the early nets in the Parks so that the powers that be could assess the cricket form of the newcomers, as well as the established. Keeping wicket, my enjoyment was not particularly enhanced by Garth Wheatley, a keeper and Blue himself, who stood behind my net and remarked caustically, "Snatching a bit, aren't we?"

I did not impress them and was not chosen for the trials. But I played a lot of cricket, becoming an Authentic and later a Harlequin, whose colourful cap Douglas

Jardine wore when captaining England in the famous bodyline Test matches in Australia — a cap to which Trueman in later years would refer as a fucking jazz hat.

Sometimes of an afternoon, if it was sunny and warm, Biddie and I would go to the Parks and watch Tony Pawson, the captain the Oxford side, hook, cut and glide with praiseworthy control, now and then nudging the ball into the covers to scamper for a quick single, for he was no exponent of the off-drive. He had some good players in his side: Philip Whitcombe — who twice clean bowled Len Hutton that season and played for the Gentlemen — Hafiz Kardar, a future captain of Pakistan, Clive van Ryneveld, a future captain of South Africa, Geoffrey Keighley of Yorkshire, Tony Mallett of Kent, and Hughie Webb, who hit an unbeaten 145 against Cambridge at Lords that summer.

There was also the enormous Australian, Jiker Travers, the Oxford rugger captain. During one net practice in the previous season he had been bowling to the left-handed New Zealander, Martin Donnelly. Donnelly, playing with classic abandon and contemptuous ease, was eventually struck on the pad by one of Jiker's deliveries.

"Ow's that?" he let fly with a stentorian nasal shout.

"Not owt, you big bum," came the even more nasal and emphatic reply from his wife who, unnoticed, was approaching the nets while out walking in the sunshine with her children.

It was the summer that Bradman's Australians came and went with the Ashes, their side at Oxford captained by Lindsay Hassett, the only team that year to defeat Tony Pawson's eleven. Of the nine county sides played, Oxford had beaten Middlesex and Somerset, and drawn with Gloucestershire, Yorkshire, Hampshire, Warwickshire, Lancashire, Sussex and Surrey. Finally, at Lords, just to round it all off nicely, Cambridge had been defeated promptly at three o'clock on the last day by an innings and eight runs, despite Doggart, Dewes, Insole and Bailey.

We went to a May Ball at Pembroke College, not one of those all-night affairs, and enjoyed ourselves hugely. In the still, early hours, we jogged slowly through the slumbering city back to Woodstock in our little old box-like Morris Minor, which we had acquired after selling the jeep. As we let ourselves into Laburnum House, Kim came forward and greeted us with sleepy warmth then returned to his slumbers in the kitchen. Before climbing the narrow stairway to snatch a few hours' sleep we made ourselves a cup of tea and sat and watched through the French windows as the first streaks of dawn imperceptibly lightened the darkness outside.

And every week Martin and I would meet for our tutorials, and somehow I'd manage to get something down on paper to read out. I would go into the Camera and sit for an hour or two and try to work, or browse at Thornton's, or Parker's, or Blackwell's, those excellent bookshops in the Broad. But I found it heavy going and knew I was making little headway. In the end I'd seek out all the conclusions and summaries that I could find, to obviate ploughing through the lengthy bibliographies we were given.

Often of an evening Martin would come out and have supper with us, and later I would walk with him to the stop outside Roadnight Carter's antique shop where we'd gaze through the window at the old bits and pieces inside, chatting while we waited for the last bus back to Oxford.

So the summer days passed and our first year at Oxford came to a close with a Commem' Ball at Brasenose, an all-night affair this time. It was enjoyable enough, chatting, eating, drinking and dancing our way through the night hours but, by 5.30 in the morning, we were glad to set off for home. Tony Peet, Jimmy Miskin and Michael Morton, all to become lawyers, Jimmy the Recorder of London, came out with their girls to have breakfast with us, which Tony Mallett and his wife-to-be, Vivienne, set about cooking with a will. Since it was a lovely morning we took our plates of eggs and bacon and hot cups of coffee and sat on cushions in the sunshine outside the front door of Laburnum House, the girls gay in their finery, their chatter every so often drowned as an early lorry struggled up the hill.

Eventually we said goodbye to our friends who, climbing into two rather battered-looking cars, set off for Oxford. We watched till they were out of sight and then turned to go in. The sun was well up and hot, the sky cloudless. It looked as though it was going to be another perfect day, a fitting start to the long summer vacation.

Chapter 20

Oxford versus Cambridge, 1948

I RESOLVED TO DO some serious reading that vacation, my intention to achieve a comprehensive grasp of Anglo-Saxon history, embracing all those basic facts and events that Stanley Cohn had so rashly assumed I knew at that first tutorial. I consoled myself that at least I was now aware that 'Anglo-Saxon justice was nothing less than unmitigated barbarism' and remembered that Stanley seemed particularly interested in something called the Writ of Praecipe.

But at length I closed my books. Climbing into our 1932 Morris Minor, Kim in the back with my cricket bag, we set off once more for the West Country, where I played several games of cricket for Gorran and went pilchard driving in the *Margaret* with Edgar and Peter Husband and their crew, which included George Pearce.

"Never mind about Oxford University and its soccer side," shouted Edgar over his shoulder to me in the wheelhouse, at the same time lying back and hauling in the headrope, "Starboard your wheel, come on, keep her up to the net, man," and, pausing momentarily, he glanced swiftly round at the lights of the rest of the fleet before hauling in again. "You never were any damned good for Mevagissey soccer. You know very well you only had one damned supporter and that was Catherine," and he shook with silent laughter. "Never any damned good at all," he said, even more emphatically than before, and he laughed so much that he had to cease hauling, while George Pearce on the leech emitted a great snort of mirth. Turning his head, he sent a stream of tobacco juice across the boat as he thrashed the heavy net against his yellow oilskin, the silver pilchards showering into the fish-berth. All the while, the gulls hovered, a white cloud over the boat shrieking their derision, the beat of their wings all but fanning our faces as the black dripping net, shimmering with fish, came up out of the water and over the clicking roller. At such moments it didn't really seem to be very important that I knew so little history.

Towards the end of September I received a letter from Archie Smith, asking me to go down and play for Gorran in the cricket final of the Western Morning News Cup.

It was a difficult decision to make. I had already begun soccer-training and we were preparing for a pre-season tour of Cornwall. The October term was threatening and I knew I must get down to more reading because there were Collections — informal examinations at the start of a term — to be faced. I'd played only a few matches that season for Gorran. There was the expense of a long train journey and I could well go the whole way down and not score. Above all it meant that a regular player would have to be dropped from what was the most important match of their season.

I wrote and explained all this. Back came a letter from Archie saying that they had held a committee meeting and decided to pay all my expenses. I wrote and thanked them profusely but still felt I should not go. Back came another letter saying that I could have a taxi all the way down at their expense. Finally Archie telephoned and it was all I could do to stick to my guns. I was very touched. I had a great affection for the little Gorran cricket club with its Whetters, Hurrells and Bunneys, and all the others that kept it such a force in the eastern league of Cornish cricket.

Unfortunately they lost that 1948 final of the Western Morning News Cup and I still have a long letter from Archie telling me of the match and explaining that if I had kept for them they would have won. Who knows? All I do know is that I enjoyed my cricket with Gorran as much as any that I played.

Going into Brasenose at the start of the new term I called on Eric Collieu, my tutor for the foreign period, 1789-1870. A slight man with a thin, sensitive face and a sympathetic manner, he spoke beautifully, his voice quiet, his words carefully selected, each pause significant, each sentence smooth, faultless and delivered with disarming thoughtfulness. I liked him very much from the start.

I don't think my essays had improved much, but I began to enjoy reading about the French Revolution though, the more I did so, the more complicated it seemed to become. With Stanley we tackled some political science, in particular Aristotle, Hobbes and Rousseau. We discussed the teleological approach, the problem of 'ought', and why man is born free, yet is everywhere in chains. I saw a glimmer of light.

Most afternoons I'd catch a bus, or walk down the High and over Magdalen Bridge to Iffley Road where we'd do our training. Twice a week we'd play a match and afterwards have tea upstairs, served by Ben Standen, senior common room steward at Corpus and his wife. Tommy would buttonhole the local press and comment, not always as discreetly as one might have hoped, on the afternoon's performance.

I grew rather fond of the pavilion at Iffley Road, which was a homely, off-white, stuccoed architectural monstrosity, but the ground was excellent. The pavilion was equally ugly inside, but when the weather grew cold, we'd have a big glowing coke fire in the changing-room which did something to compensate for the splintery floors, the two huge Victorian baths, antiquated showers and row of basins stained with age and use.

There, on a match day, standing on the balcony at the top of the pavilion, in belted mackintosh, trilby tilted slightly over one eye, Tommy would watch the proceedings with all the wariness of a Chicago gangster. Those plans he had first spoken about some seven months back, when returning in the train from playing Bournville Athletic, had now been realised.

At a meeting held at the East India and Sports' Club in St James' Square, London, on 2 May 1948, Biddie's birthday, representatives of Oxford and Cambridge, with members of the Corinthian-Casuals in attendance, met and formed the Pegasus Football Club, its object, 'the encouragement and improvement of Association Football at the universities of Oxford and Cambridge by the formation of a joint team'.

In principle, Pegasus sides were to be selected from members in residence at either university, but the constitution granted the selection committee a right to call upon players who were in residence during the previous season. Tommy, the founder and inspiration, became the first honorary secretary; the Rev. K. R. G. Hunt, of

Corinthians, Wolverhampton Wanderers and England fame, the first president, A. G. Doggart, the first honorary treasurer. A committee was to include the captains of the university football teams, and the secretaries of the Oxford Centaurs and the Cambridge Falcons.

There was no money in the bank or in sight and, until matches were played, the only income was from the 2s 6d life-subscription payable by the joining members. Nor was there any support to count upon. It was just a belief, little more than a dream cherished by Tommy and several others that this new club, this winged horse of mythology, Pegasus, might fly to the very heights of amateur soccer and, in so doing, stimulate the game in the schools and universities.

But there remained the difficult question of exemption, and preliminary enquiries at the FA had not proved very hopeful. Understandably there were those who thought that new entrants for the competition should prove themselves before any sort of exemption be granted. Nevertheless, despite this lack of unanimity, the FA Amateur Cup Committee, considerably influenced by Mr Andrew Ralston, to whom Tommy had sent a long and detailed memorandum, decided to grant Pegasus exemption until the fourth qualifying round which was to be played at the end of November. They further empowered the new club to ask its opponents to defer the tie until a week after the varsity match.

We had drawn the Athenian Club Enfield at home in the fourth qualifying round, the match to be played at Iffley Road, Oxford. Enfield agreed to postpone the date only provided the match was played on their ground and not at Oxford. We had no alternative but to accept, and I do not blame Enfield one bit for what they did.

And so, throughout that term, Tommy could be seen up on the balcony, often with his wife, Penelope, at his side, or down with us in the changing-room, smoking, plotting, coughing; laughing one moment, the next planning, with deadly intent, some Machiavellian counterstroke against occasionally real, often imaginary enemies of his beloved winged horse. And when his prophecies of doom reached outrageous proportions and we would laugh outright, he would pause and regard us in some astonishment before remarking with slow deliberation and knowing shakes of the head, "Well, don't say I didn't warn you. You'll see, you'll see I'm right." And, maddeningly, he often was.

And he was up there now, of course, not only as treasurer of the OUAFC, but as secretary of Pegasus, very much aware that just a week after the 1948 varsity match, a team would have to be selected from the two university sides to represent Pegasus against Enfield.

Meanwhile the Oxford side had improved steadily and towards the end of November, when we played an FA eleven, it was settled. I had a difficult task that afternoon marking Charlie Vaughan, the Charlton Athletic centre-forward. Playing at centre-half for the FA, I saw for the first time Vic Buckingham of Spurs, a most cultured player who seemed to have all the time in the world to contain the speed of John Tanner and distribute the ball. Derek Richards, at right-back, had to contend with Finchley's outside-left, George Robb, who later turned professional and played for Spurs and England against the great Hungarian side of 1953.

Eventually, after a good deal of early experimenting at full-back and inside-forward, the side was ready for the annual combat with Cambridge. We had a good goalkeeper in Roy Lenton, who, though a little on the short side was agile and confident, catching the ball early and quick to come off his line. Derek Richards, though he had sound control, was vulnerable against speed and would use every wile in the book, and some that were not, to contain his winger. Geoffrey Pass on the other flank was tall and dependable, but again a little slow on the turn. Our half-back line was the same as in the previous year. Denis was playing as skilfully and calmly as ever. I could read the game and usually hold the middle, while Rob's endeavour, if anything, had become even more ferocious. Tony Pawson, now at right-wing, John Tanner at centre-forward and Jimmy Potts on the left wing were our three match-winners. Dick Rhys at inside-left could take on a defence while Stanley Heritage at inside-right, good in the air, collected and worked the ball unceasingly, looking for his players all the time.

It was an excellent, well-balanced side and, on 4 December, on the Spurs' ground at White Hart Lane, before a crowd of 12,000, we defeated Cambridge 5-4 in a gripping match.

Cambridge had M. J. Hardy in goal. At back A. R. Butterfield and Mike Bishop, a huge, fearsome Reptonian who was to become a doctor. In midfield, Cyril Tyson, a tiny, stocky and very competent half-back, whom I was to see much of later as a schoolmaster, Ralph Cowan, an excellent centre-half, dominating in the air, and W. R. Sheret. In their forward line they had E. R. Jackson at outside-left with Hubert Doggart inside him, big, awkward, high-stepping and snorting all the while as he bore down on any ball he considered his. T. McGurk at centre-forward was elusive, and quick off the mark, giving the ball early and going fast for the return. At inside-right, Doug Insole, the Cambridge captain, was a heavy, deliberate sort of player with a tremendous shot in either foot, who'd get hold of the ball and hold it; outside him, Johnny Dutchman, leggy, tall and dangerous, was a footballer through and through.

As we came off, when the final whistle was blown, the crowd gave both sides a great reception. It was auspicious that it should have been such an excellent match. Of those who had played, eleven would, in a week's time, be doing battle with Enfield.

Above: Commem' Ball, Brasenose 1949

Below: Tommy, John Tanner, KAS and Donald Carr on a wet day in St John's College

Chapter 21

A spreading of wings

BIDDIE had not watched the match. Though fit and well, she had been advised not to attend, which was just as well because four days later, on 8 December, early in the morning, Paul was born.

We had arranged for a nurse to come and stay. Everything seemed prepared. Her mother, Winnie, was staying with us and we were to notify the nurse as soon as was necessary, which we did. Then everything went wrong. It was a long labour and at four o'clock in the morning on the third day, Winnie urged me to summon the doctor despite the nurse's assurance that all was well. When the doctor, hastily attired, arrived twenty minutes later and went upstairs he was down almost immediately asking if my wife had ever had fits. "No," we both said, shocked.

"Well, then, you'd better ring for an ambulance," Seeing my concern, he added, "I don't think your wife's in any immediate danger, but I'm worried about the child."

I was very alarmed. I lifted the receiver and flashed the operator. There was no reply. It was an old telephone. I flashed again. There was still no reply. I heard a lorry rumbling up the hill and then, unable to wait any longer, rushed out to the Misses Parker's house at the back of ours and banged on their door. Astonished, they allowed me to use their telephone, their white pekinese snapping at my heels.

In surprisingly quick time a very old ambulance arrived with two young attendants, who seemed no more than boys. Somehow they got Biddie down those impossible stairs on a stretcher and set off for the Radcliffe.

As if in a nightmare, with Biddie's mother sitting beside me, I drove the eight miles into Oxford following the ambulance. Forewarned, the hospital staff was ready and waiting. A little later, halfway up the stairs of the maternity wing, I don't know how I got there, I met our doctor, who reassured me and disappeared up the stairs again. I was too bewildered to say anything and went down and walked outside, oblivious of the cold winter morning, while Winnie sat inside and waited. After what seemed a very long time the doctor came down and told us that Biddie was under anaesthetic and we had a fine healthy son.

Quite exhausted we got into the car and drove back to Woodstock. In the afternoon I returned to the hospital and peeped at Biddie through the glass doors of the darkened room where a nurse sat by her bedside. She had suffered from eclampsia and I was told that it was important that she be brought back to consciousness very carefully.

The same day Pegasus played their first match against the full Arsenal Combination side and won 1-0, the winning goal coming from a header by Barry Abbott, the Cambridge centre-forward of the previous year, from a cross by Tony Pawson.

After the match, the selectors, Guy Shuttleworth, John Tanner, Doug Insole and Tommy, having canvassed opinions, selected the side to play against Enfield.

Surprisingly, they brought me in at centre-half and moved Tony Peet to left-back, dropping Geoffrey Pass at right-back for Ralph Cowan. I say surprisingly, because I thought Cowan, the Cambridge centre-half, was a better one than I was. He was taller, more accurate and commanding in the air, and a much better distributor of the ball. I was probably faster, as good positionally and as hard, but little more than a purely destructive stopper, and I believe it was in that capacity that they selected me for the fourth qualifying round of the Amateur Cup. I could not make up my mind as to whether I should play, so I went to talk it over with Tommy.

"You might just as well," he said, after careful consideration. "There's nothing you can really do," which was quite true. So I took his advice and played.

John Tanner captained Pegasus that afternoon and the match was televised.

At half-time the score was level. As we sat sipping our tea, saying little, there wasn't one of us who didn't know we now faced a formidable task. Tommy came round and spoke a few words of encouragement but I could see he was worried. We needed a professional to take control, reassure us, give us some quiet words of advice, lift some of the weight from our shoulders. There remained forty-five minutes to prove ourselves and vindicate the FA Amateur Cup Committee's decision to grant us exemption. If we failed now there would be no exemption next year, and that would mean the end of Pegasus and Tommy's dreams.

The referee's head appeared round the dressing-room door. "It's absolutely crucial that you score an early goal," said Tommy, as we went out for the second half. Ten minutes later Enfield scored. As the ball was brought back to the centre I felt a sudden wave of panic well within me, which I tried hard to dispel by looking fixedly at the opposing centre-forward, who, alert and ready for the kick-off, was watching the referee, waiting for the whistle. I tried hard to rid my mind of the fact that they were ahead now and would fight like hell to keep their lead. Who wouldn't? My heart thumped. I felt dismay and forced myself to keep calm and not worry about the time factor. But it wasn't easy. The sharp blast of the whistle did the trick.

And then there came one of those turning-points well on in the game, an incident that I recall most vividly. Jack Rawlings, their powerful international inside-right, after a lot of Enfield pressure, broke through ominously and hit a tremendous shot from well outside the penalty area. It passed me close by, going too fast to intercept. I just had time to turn and watch, a helpless spectator, as the ball flew low and true towards the right-hand corner of our goal. It was on target all the way, the final nail in our coffin. I had no doubt of it, nor had anyone else as I afterwards discovered. And then, impossibly, Ben Brown was diving horizontally to his right and, instead of turning the ball round the corner, caught and held it clean as a whistle. I for one, thanked the Almighty as we breathed again.

Reprieved, with less than a quarter of an hour to go, we suddenly began to play a bit. Tony Pawson and Jimmy Potts, taking on their backs, opened up the middle for John Tanner's quick thrusts. Twice he broke clean away and scored typical goals, using his speed and driving the ball home low each time. He was a deadly finisher and watching from defence I always felt that if he could get his shot in, with either foot, it would usually be thereabouts. Seldom would he hit one over the top. Finally a penalty sealed it for us, Doug Insole crashing the ball home. Then the whistle blew and it was over.

As I shook hands with their centre-forward and saw his dejected face, I felt for him; it could so easily have been the other way round. But then, that's cup football. It's a cruel business, a case of sudden death, them or us, ninety minutes of tension at the end of which you're in or you're out, either on top of the world or lying at the bottom, sprawled in an abyss of gloom. This time it was us.

So we went through to the first round proper, having won, on reflection, the most important cup-tie Pegasus ever played.

Tommy was in tremendous form as I drove back with him and Penelope in their Wolseley, which Tommy drove extremely fast, as he always did. On the way we stopped to see some friends of his and I can see him now, all beaming smiles, a drink in his left hand, his right arm flung protectively round some female shoulder as, bending slightly, he expanded on Pegasus and how the lady in question must come to the next match. And so, into the car we climbed again and went on to Oxford, even faster, where I was able to peep through the window at Biddie who was asleep, a nurse by her side, before going out to Woodstock.

I talked at length on the telephone with my father and he stressed the importance of Biddie's being kept very quiet and not quickly dismissed from hospital. I attempted to put all this tactfully to the specialist without causing offence and was informed with courteous gravity, "You can rest assured, Mr Shearwood, your wife will not leave here until she is completely well."

A week later we were told she could be taken home and eagerly I drove in from Woodstock early one cold December afternoon to fetch her. We had a great log fire burning merrily in the open fireplace of our sitting-room and the house was warm and welcoming. As we brought the tea in, I saw Biddie seated by the fire suddenly begin to shake violently. There was nothing we could do to stop the *rigor* and eventually I carried her in my arms upstairs and sent for the doctor. She had a temperature of over 104° and was ill for the next few weeks with acute pyelitis. They were trying days. We owe much to both our mothers, who came to the rescue and looked after us all so well.

Before, throughout, and after that Christmas of 1948 Biddie was far from well, but it was very good to see our son in his cot beside her and know our family was complete. Kim, too, would spend a lot of his time lying quietly on the landing upstairs. And, at nights, when the December winds blew cold round the house, we'd listen to the sound of approaching lorries rumbling up the hill, hear them change gear as they came to the steep bend, then draw away past the Maryborough Arms, where they'd change gear again before heading on towards Oxford.

I did no reading. There was no real excuse for not doing some, but there seemed such a lot to do about the place. And, little by little, as the days went by, Biddie steadily grew stronger, but it was a slow process. A gale of wind finally blew the old year away, and caused the branches of the ancient apple tree to rattle the bathroom window-panes.

On New Year's Day Pegasus played Headington United and won 3-2. The following week we defeated Barnet on their ground 4-2. Now we were ready for our next opponents, Smethwick Highfield, a Midland side whom we had drawn in the first round of the Amateur Cup, the match to be played at Oxford. We made one change from the side that had played Enfield, bringing Hubert Doggart in for Barry Abbott. We won 4-1, John Tanner scoring three, Doug Insole one, and the size of the crowd and measure of support astonished us.

We awaited our next opponents. When the third round was announced, we knew we faced our stiffest task to date: Willington, from the north, who had been finalists in the last season before the war (and were to win the cup in 1950). Before taking them on we travelled to Merthyr Tydfil to play a Welsh FA side and lost 3-2. It was a hard game in every sense of the word and, when the final whistle blew, their centre-forward, who had a face of granite and a handshake of steel, growled some fierce unintelligible words of Welsh which I wasn't sure sounded all that complimentary. But it was good preparation for Willington.

On the day we made two changes. John Tanner was injured, so Barry Abbott came in again at centre-forward and Geoffrey Pass took over at left-back from Tony Peet who had gone into the Colonial service. Ninety minutes later we had beaten Willington 3-2, our goals scored by Stanley Heritage, Barry Abbott and Tony Pawson. As the crowd of nearly seven thousand streamed contentedly away down Iffley Road and across Magdalen Bridge, we sat, tired but delighted, in the changing-room which was now suddenly full of people all talking at once.

Tommy was going round laughing, telling us he'd told us so, coughing his head off, then retreating into a corner with Harvey Chadder and Graham Doggart, his face suddenly serious, with no smile now, for he was seeing where nobody else could, to far beyond the horizon where unseen and terrible dangers lay in wait for us all. But he couldn't keep it up and, once more all smiles, he disappeared up the stairs and began to commiserate with the Willington officials and players, who weren't in the least bit keen on being commiserated with.

A stocky, beaming supporter, inarticulate with excitement, had somehow got into the changing-room and was going round cutting off segments of orange for us with a penknife, his hand shaking so dreadfully that on accepting the proffered piece one was liable to severe injury. His name was Chedder Wilson. We were to see much of him and his oranges in the future.

Upstairs in the midst of the noisy, jostling tea-nudging throng, Sir Stanley Rous, Secretary of the FA, and our president, the Reverend Kenneth Hunt, stood talking together, the latter a head and shoulders above everyone else, apart from Colin Weir. I found myself alongside a distinguished elderly gentleman, who spoke quietly and most knowledgeably about the game. In the years to come — Guy and Helen Pawson seldom missed a cup match — I was to find their unobtrusive presence and wise counsel a soothing antidote to those tense moments before and sometimes after a match when all has been lost and there seems nothing worth living for.

So on we went into the fourth round of the Amateur Cup, one of the last eight remaining clubs left in England to go into the hat for the quarter-final draw.

By Monday we knew who it was to be, Bromley, one of the strongest sides in the country, at Oxford. And suddenly the name of Pegasus was on everyone's lips and wherever we went people were stopping us and talking to us and wishing us luck and saying they were coming to the game.

We had a fortnight in which to prepare, the Oxford contingent training at Iffley Road, the Cambridge one at Grange Road. There was no question of our getting together and working things out as a unit. We had no coach, so no tactics were laid down. It was term-time and both universities were still playing, so it was not possible to have a match before the quarter-final took place. Added to all this there was doubt about John Tanner's fitness. Barry Abbott had played very adequately for us. He was big, strong and good in the air, if a little predictable. But John had the happy knack of scoring goals and in the end it was he who played.

Of the team that was finally selected, eight of us were resident at Oxford, three at Cambridge. The die was cast.

Just under twelve thousand people packed into Iffley Road that last Saturday of February 1949 to watch the cup-tie with Bromley, a record crowd for any Oxford sport.

By one o'clock a hundred coaches had converged on Oxford bringing the Bromley supporters. Everywhere buses, cars and crowds of people were streaming towards the ground. Arriving early, we watched the scene from the changing-room windows facing the pitch, around which four temporary stands had been erected. Long before three o'clock, the ground was full. The referee came in. There were five minutes left. Nothing had been said. We had joked and laughed and talked as we changed, but not about football. We were keyed up. There was much at stake. Now it was time to go.

As we emerged a roar greeted us and shouts of, "Come on, the Pegs!", "Up the Pegs!", "Come on, the Lillywhites!" cries that were to become so familiar now came from all around the ground.

There was another roar, not so loud, but significant none the less. Bromley were coming out in their hooped blue and white shirts and black shorts with white flashes down their sides. I took a good long look at them and I thought they appeared a thoroughly professional lot.

Guy Shuttleworth was shaking hands with Charlie Fuller, the Bromley international centre-half and captain, and then we were off.

I could tell at once that they were good because they began to move the ball around effectively and confidently as one would have expected from a side with four current England players in their midst and more to come.

I'd studied my opponent, big George Brown, their international centre-forward, who already had 73 goals under his belt that season. I quickly discovered that he screened the ball well and moved wide and deep for crosses. I found him particularly good in the air and I determined not to let him get on the back of me.

Things were going well. We were coming at them on the flanks, both Tony Pawson and Jimmy Potts worrying the Bromley backs with their speed and skill.

But soon it became apparent that we had a problem on our hands. John Tanner was limping. Whenever he tried to accelerate, his injury was obvious to all. It was a serious blow because it took the pressure off Charlie Fuller and gave him time to move forward and create.

Then, after twenty-five minutes had passed, Tony Pawson, from a corner, dropped an away swinger into the far part of the six-yard area where Stan Heritage found space and headed an excellent goal. Our elation was short-lived, however. Five minutes later, Bromley had equalised through George Brown.

But then *their* elation was short-lived. Within two minutes, we were ahead again.

A quick, retaliatory break down our right by Pawson found Bromley's defence stretched and Potts scored, putting us in the lead at half time.

As we sat in the changing-room, sipping our tea, I cannot recall any constructive advice being given. But there was plenty of encouragement, not least from Chedder Wilson, who had somehow got in and was going round armed with his orange and that lethal penknife.

Five minutes after the restart Bromley drew level again, through Tommy Hopper, their England inside-right, who, seizing upon a loose ball, hit an unstoppable twenty-five-yarder. Now, aided by the strong wind, our opponents began to pressurise us in earnest. Their style of play differed from ours. We tended to push the ball about more and keep it on the ground. They tended to use the long ball, sweeping it out to their wingers or thumping it up the middle to George Brown, whom I found increasingly difficult to hold in the air.

And then it happened. A dangerous swirling cross came over from the left and I went up for it. Even as I jumped I knew I had mistimed it badly. I knew also that Brown was right on the back of me and the roar of delight that rose from the Bromley supporters told me the bad news; he had made no mistake.

But they weren't ahead for long. Again Cornthwaite could only parry another fierce cross from Tony Pawson and John Tanner was on hand to make the score three all.

Five minutes from time Bromley took the lead through Martin, their outside-right, and now things were really desperate for us. Even so, we weren't finished. Jimmy Potts, from some twenty yards out let fly with his left foot and hit the upright. An inch to the right and we would have been level again. Nor was that the end of our challenge. Right on time a brilliant bout of short passing brought our forwards and wing-halves swarming into the Bromley penalty area. A fierce cry for 'hand ball' rose spontaneously from the crowd behind the goal.

But the match was over. We were out. As I shook hands with George Brown, I knew exactly how the Enfield centre-forward felt.

It remained but to ponder on what might have been and wait for the press reports on the morrow. There was naturally a strong sense of anti-climax and disappointment, the taste of which seems always particularly bitter on waking the following morning. But it all passes and we had much to be thankful for and to look forward to.

Tommy had proved his point beyond doubt. We had won the respect of the amateur world of soccer and would gain exemption next year. The press said some very nice things about us all. Despite my mistimed header I was favourably compared with Charlie Fuller and there was mention of international honours for some of us.

As for Bromley, they went on to play at Wembley before a crowd of 93,000 and won the Amateur Cup of 1949.

And Pegasus? Why, we had spread our wings and taken flight.

Above: Iffley Road, Quarter-final Amateur Cup 1949.
Pegasus 3 Bromley 4.
A contest in the air with George Brown

Chapter 22

Aspects of amateurism

WELL BEFORE the spring of 1949 Biddie regained her health and strength and we were able to walk together once more in the grounds of Blenheim, pushing Paul in his pram, accompanied by Kirn.

That Easter I went with the Oxford side to Holland, where we stayed in Amsterdam at the Hotel Krasnopolsky. There we took part in a tournament comprising the now-famous Dutch side, Ajax, Le Stade Dudelange from Luxemburg, the Swiss side, Biel, and us.

On paper it looked rather formidable. And in practice it certainly was. To make matters worse, John Tanner, who had played in an Arthur Dunn match just prior to the tour, had again been troubled with the same injury which plagued him in the Bromley cup-tie. Since we were short of forwards and Tommy was anxious that we should make a good impression in our first match against Biel, he persuaded John to play, much against his inclination, having first taken Denis, Tony and me aside and given us his considered opinion that Tanner was becoming neurotic.

In the light of events we did well to draw with Biel, but John, who somehow got through the game, ruptured the quadriceps of his right leg so badly that the muscle never properly knit together, but built up round the side of his thigh.

There was much muttering of 'nicht fair play' overheard later that night from the Swiss contingent — staying in the same centrally heated oven of an hotel as us — who had sampled Rob at his most ferocious.

Walter Crook, once captain of Blackburn Rovers, now the Ajax coach, gave us all the help he could. But, in the end, we were no match for Ajax, who won the tournament while we finished with the wooden spoon. On the last evening, all four teams sat down to a big dinner at which Tommy made a speech in German that was not only well received but did a little, I thought, to compensate for our somewhat undistinguished performance.

So the season ended and we returned to England and the summer term, feeling more than a little weary, none more than Denis Saunders.

As I had been in the previous year, I was invited to attend the early cricket nets, this time with more success. The new Oxford captain was the South African, Clive van Ryneveld, and coaching in the nets was George Pope.

"Watch for the back of his wrist. He can't bowl a googly without showing it," said George, seeing I was having difficulty keeping wicket and spotting Clive's 'wrong 'un'. "Well, watch his elbow then," he called from the bowler's end, as I went the wrong way again. "He can't bowl a googly without bending his arm," and he came down behind the net and read each ball that Clive bowled. He could read and play the spinners as well as anyone in the country.

I first met George when he'd bowled to me in the Derbyshire nets in the late 30s, when the county had such players as Tommy Mitchell, Stan Worthington, the two Pope brothers, George and Alf, Dennis Smith and Harry Elliot, to mention a few of that championship side.

As boys we would go down in the Easter holidays and be coached by the Derbyshire players under the eagle eye of that dour, terrifying little old cricketer, Sam Cadman. He would wear an old-fashioned cap with a small peak which did nothing to hide a fierce face, mottled and purple. I was happily walking one fine morning in 1938 down the long unattractive approach to the Derbyshire cricket ground with a friend, John Keatinge. I suppose, to be more accurate, we were just sauntering along on this occasion, carrying our bats and pads over our shoulders.

Suddenly Sam Cadman, looking like an enraged Mr Punch, assembled the Derbyshire players. With his hands on hips, roared in our direction, "You just take your time, gentlemen, don't you trouble to 'urry yerselves." We hurried then all right. I went straight into a net, where I had a most uncomfortable half-hour trying to obey Sam Cadman's repeated instruction to, "Get yer foot to the ball, get yer head over it", as I strove to play a young and lively fast bowler, Bert Rhodes, who eventually changed to a leg spinner when Tommy Mitchell gave up.

John Keatinge was at Maidwell Hall with me and was to become Senior Commoner Prefect at Winchester and win a scholarship to Cambridge. He never reached the university; he was killed near Caen in 1944 when the turret of his tank received a direct hit from an 88-millimetre. He had just gained his commission and was serving as an officer with the Second Armoured Battalion of the Irish Guards.

George Pope did all he could to help me in those early Oxford nets. Before he left, he assured me that I should get into the side. How much influence he had I'm not sure, but I was selected to play against Gloucester in the first match and fared none too badly. I caught two, stumped two and made 28. But I still found Clive van Ryneveld's googly difficult to read, so to facilitate matters, he gave me a prearranged indication of when he was going to bowl it.

I played in the next match against Worcester and then, out of the blue, I had an invitation to go as one of three reserves on an FA tour to the Channel Islands, the first since the war. I was in a quandary. The FA side was a strong one, containing four top professionals, Len Duquemin of Spurs, Jim Taylor and Joe Bacuzzi of Fulham — the Fulham side had just won the Second Division Championship — and George Curtis of Arsenal. Both Len Duquemin and Jim Taylor had been capped for England. Denis Saunders and Jimmy Potts had been selected to play and were going, so I would have company. The tour was from 7th May to the 12th, bang in the middle of the next match against Leicester. I sought Tommy's advice and he urged me to go on the tour as he thought it would stand me in good stead for an amateur cap. So, after informing Clive, I decided to go, hoping that it would not jeopardise my chance of getting back into the Oxford cricket side.

Unfortunately, the FA lost the first match against Jersey, and the selectors, not unnaturally, decided to keep Jim Taylor in at centre-half for it was imperative that the FA put up a better show against Guernsey, which they did, winning narrowly.

Our trainer, Jack Jennings, advised me not to go on and play out of position for half a match, which was what it would have meant. So, heeding his advice, I sat on the touchline for both matches. On reading the paper I discovered that Ian Campbell, who had come in as wicket-keeper, had scored 43 against Leicester. When I read, a little later, an article in the *Daily Telegraph* stating that Oxford could well have a trump card up their sleeve in Ian Campbell, a big, bold hitter, I knew I'd had my chips. Apart from two enjoyable sea-passages, the presentation of a small replica of a Channel Island urn, and my dubious assistance to Joe Bacuzzi in judging a beauty competition, I neither achieved nor contributed very much to that tour.

I never got back into the Oxford side, though I made a few runs, including a 65 out of 140 for a strong 'A' eleven against Jim Swanton's Arabs.

Jim Swanton, as everyone knows, is a big, dominant character. In 1949, as cricket and rugby correspondent of the *Daily Telegraph,* he wielded considerable influence at Oxford and, to me, epitomised the establishment in these two sports.

I remember particularly one evening having coffee in the top room of Vincent's Club when Jim came in.

"Tell me now, Ken," he began, his presence filling the room, "what's all this I hear about Pegasus?"

I don't think that he meant to be patronising, but he knew and I knew that for many years soccer had not had the same status at the universities as rugby and cricket, and in this context I felt he was having a slight 'dig', and I felt irritated. "Well, Jim," I said, "it's a club composed of Oxford and Cambridge players who have just been knocked out of the quarter-finals of the Amateur Cup before the biggest crowd that has ever watched a match in the history of Oxford." He looked at me for a moment.

"Quite something," he said with sonorous amusement, and somehow that did it.

"Yes," I replied, now truly nettled, "it was. And what's more, Jim — who knows? Perhaps one day we might win the Cup and, if we do we shan't be playing at jolly old Twickenham, but at Wembley, the premier stadium in the world, so you'd better come along and see for yourself."

"I will indeed," said Jim with another deep chuckle which promptly started me off again.

"It's about time cricket took a leaf out of soccer's book because otherwise the game's soon going to be as dead as a dodo. You want to have a knock-out competition on an over basis with a cup final at Lords so that the crowds can come and take their shirts off and wave their rattles and banners and shout and enjoy themselves." And this time he laughed me out of court, assured me with the utmost confidence that it would never happen, and promptly bought me a drink.

I wanted to go on and say a lot more, but it would have taken too long. In the end, I would probably not have made my point. However, I hope the reader will bear with me now if I digress for a moment to reflect on just why soccer in 1949 did not have the same status as rugby and cricket at Oxford and Cambridge. The short and immediate answer, of course, is that in soccer the professional had got under way and the amateur had been outpaced. But that is only to state the obvious and ignore the great part that the amateur has played in the game. So briefly, back to the beginning.

From the 1860s to the 1880s, the amateur clubs such as Oxford University, the Old Etonians, the Old Carthusians, the Wanderers, the Royal Engineers, the Swifts and Clapham Rovers, reigned supreme, winning the FA Cup regularly between 1872 and 1883, the last victory of all in that year going to the Old Etonians. After that the great amateur clubs of the south never again got their names on the trophy, for the FA Cup's entry had increased in that first decade from 15 to 100 clubs. The professionals had arrived; from then on it was to be their cup.

However, this was by no means the end of the matter. In 1893-4, the amateur was revived and given a new interest by the institution of the FA Amateur Cup. In that first final of 1894 the Old Carthusians beat the Casuals. In the following year Middlesborough, the same Middlesborough we know today, but then amateur, beat the Old Carthusians. The Carthusians won again in 1897, but after that, apart from the victory of the Old Malvernians over Bishop Auckland in 1902, the old boy sides disappeared even from this new competition.

So, as the years passed, the old boy clubs and the universities, who had been the founders and once masters of the game, superseded by professionalism, now found themselves in competition with a 'new' type of amateur, the working class player as opposed to the middle and upper middle class. And, feeling that the Amateur Cup had become the be-all and the end-all for certain types of club, sixteen of them banded together in 1903 to form their own exclusive old boy competition, the Arthur Dunn Cup.

There were now three strata in the game: the professional; the school, university and old boy type of player; and the working class amateur, the 'shamateur', who was paid.

Upon this developing scene the Corinthians made their great impact and contribution to the game. Founded in 1882 and composed of old boy and university players, they became the most powerful side in the country. Had they entered the FA Cup there is no doubt that they would have run away with the trophy more than once in those days when the rest of the amateur clubs had fallen behind. But Rule 7 of their constitution reads: 'the Club shall not compete for any challenge cup or prize of any description whatever'.

So strong were these Corinthians that, in 1894, their complete side represented England against Wales at Wrexham, winning 5-1. Perhaps the most famous victory of all was their 10-3 defeat of the full Bury side, the FA Cup holders, on 5 March 1904, Bury having beaten Derby County 6-0 in the final.

In 1923 the Corinthians altered their rules and entered the FA Cup for the first time, but without much success. The most sensational and thrilling game they played was against Newcastle United in the fourth round of 1927, having previously beaten Walsall 4-0. Fifty-six thousand spectators in the old Crystal Palace ground saw the cream of the amateur game, leading by one goal with fourteen minutes of the match left, lose 3-1 to the cream of the professional world, who were at that moment leaders of the League First Division. But by the 30s the slide was well on and all the glory that was Corinth had crumbled away, a sad end to a great saga.

Somewhere along this line, the soccer public schools and Oxford and Cambridge were very slow to adopt a more professional approach and seek advice from their new masters. I am tempted to suspect that, particularly in the 30s, the distinct working class connotation of soccer had something to do with it. Most public schools had cricket professionals to help in the coaching, but then the amateur in cricket was still in command, captaining his county and country, for command still remained, as it did in most walks of English life, an amateur occupation. And rugby? They have never had any problem in this respect. In 1949, abhorring professionalism, they set their own standards, their own ceiling, an artificial one, but truly amateur. And this was the crux of the matter. The perfection of rugby as it then stood is a myth. Association Football, by its professionalism, has left rugby behind in the fullest exploitation of the game as an art. Here lies the great difference between soccer and rugby as played at their top levels.

To imagine in 1949 that an Oxford or Cambridge soccer Blue might possibly be selected for the full England professional side was as absurd then as it would be today. Yet, an Oxford or Cambridge rugby Blue has always had every chance of playing for his country. Had one, over the years, compared the standard of soccer and rugby as played in the public schools and universities, there would have been little difference one way or the other.

In the mid-20s, and throughout the 30s, there was a new development. A number of schools turned from soccer to rugby, a trend originating from Cyril Norwood's proposal to the Headmasters' Conference that all schools should change to rugby. In 1929 he followed this up with an extraordinary attack on Association Football in his book, *The English Tradition of Education*, in which he wrote:

> When rugby becomes 'rough' or 'unfair', the game is ruined; it is one of its many merits that it can only be played by those who are in the real sense of the word gentlemen. It is a test of character.

> There are those, however, who would raise the claims of the rival code of Association Football as the best, because at present it is the most popular game, and who deplore the fact that more and more schools desert association for rugby on the ground that it is bringing class distinctions into a national game. Association football is a good game, but it is not so good a game as rugby for the education of boys; it does not require the same speed, endurance, courage or chivalry. It has, as a game, been almost entirely ruined by the professionalism which dominates it, and professionalism is the complete antithesis to the English tradition of sport.

> What is to be desired in the interests of the true athletic tradition of the

country is that more and more schools should take up rugby, prove themselves morally and physically fit to play the game in the spirit in which it should be played, and never on any consideration whatever allow a breath of professionalism to come into it.

Of course, those in education are bound to have their own views on the relative merits of soccer and rugby as a school game, though it is astonishing that even today the choice of rugger is often justified on grounds of expediency, thirty boys to a pitch instead of twenty-two!

However, I cannot help but feel that somewhere lurking behind Cyril Norwood's dogmatic and harmful assertion, lies a deep sense of alarm that soccer had been so eagerly and successfully seized upon by the mass of the population. J. B. Priestley, in his book, *The Edwardians*, writes critically of that large section of the upper middle class who, both before and after the First World War, preferred rugby to soccer, because the 'latter game had been enthusiastically adopted by the working class'.

The social implications of the relation between the two games are there for all to see. It is not surprising therefore that the universities in the 30s and the 40s — middle-class to the core — made rugby their game. Fortunately soccer has succeeded in losing its class connotation. In the words of A. J. P. Taylor, it has proved to be 'the most democratic game' which 'united all classes'. Perhaps we at Oxford in 1949 couldn't so clearly see this process in operation and felt unjustifiably patronised by the rugby pundits.

Against this background Pegasus emerged.

Good cricketers were ten-a-penny at Oxford and Cambridge during those years. To mention but one, D. B. Carr in 1949 scored nearly five hundred runs in his first three matches against Leicester, Gloucester and Middlesex, and three years later the Cambridge side contained no less than six Test players. There was never any question of either university not being able to hold their own in the world of professional cricket, so very different from the university soccer situation.

The explanation for this is that there are far fewer professionals in cricket than in soccer and the opportunities to play cricket are not equally distributed. Middle-class boys are well equipped and well coached, first at their preparatory schools, then at their public schools, where the conditions and the coaching advantages are infinitely superior to anything that the state schools can hope to offer. Another indisputable fact is that it requires money to play cricket, thus putting the game beyond the reach of naturally talented working-class boys, always, of course, excepting those in Lancashire and Yorkshire, who reach the game through their distinctive league system. Had there been more facilities, money, and coaching available, as well as a more realistic approach at the top — akin to those counties already mentioned — the standard of English cricket would have risen and the amateur been eclipsed, just as surely as he had been in Association Football.

I kept wicket a few times for the Derbyshire second side. Towards the end of June 1949, I played my one and only first-class match for the county against Gloucester down at Bristol. I found myself staying in a different hotel from the rest of the team, along with the two other amateurs in the Derbyshire side, David Skinner, the captain, and Laurie Johnson.

As for the match — it was a disastrous affair and we lost by an innings and one run. My contribution, a single crude blow for four off Tom Goddard, promptly caused the Gloucester captain, B. O. Allen, who was fielding at silly mid-on, to belch loudly, whereupon I was bowled the next ball. Before going out to field, Andy Wilson, the Gloucester wicket-keeper whom I had played against earlier in the season, gave me some advice.

"Don't get caught standing too close up to Copson and Jackson," at the time considered by the professionals as two of the fastest and best seam bowlers in the country. "Stand well back," he advised, "the ball tends to keep low out there."

"Thanks," I said and heeding his advice stood well back to Les Jackson who was opening the bowling.

The first ball came through fast and low, bouncing awkwardly in front of me, as did the next ball.

"Bugger this," said Cliff Gladwin at first slip, "better get up a bit."

"Andy Wilson advised me not to get too close," I said, as discreetly as I was able.

"Never mind about that," said Cliff, moving up several paces with the other two slips, until we were, I thought, uncomfortably close.

The fifth ball of the over found the outside edge of Tom Graveney's bat and flew like a rocket between Cliff and me. Without a word we retreated to where we had just been, while Tom Graveney went on to make a lot of runs.

However, the crowd did get its money's worth once when a swarm of bees descended around the fiery head of Bill Copson who, flailing his arms and using fearful expletives, set off at an astonishing rate for the pavilion, urged on by cries of "Windy ... windy!" from a delighted crowd. I was invited to play in the next match against Kent, at Ilkeston, but declined because we had tickets for a Commemoration Ball.

Looking back on it, I now rather regret that I did not take the game more seriously, though I would not have enjoyed the extraordinary segregation of amateur and professional that was still in existence. But I had too much on my plate. I was a married undergraduate with a child. I'd already played a great deal of football and cricket at Oxford and there was a good deal more football still to come, it was my first love. And always, nagging away quietly at the back of everything, was the fact that in nine months' time I had to sit my Finals.

I tried hard to work seriously that long vacation, sitting in one of the rooms at the top of the Lodge, the big old house where Biddie's mother still lived and where we stayed for most of the summer.

Through the open window I could hear the distant sound of tractors and see across the Vale of Evesham to the tower on top of Broadway Hill. I read and noted and put in the hours, but I seemed to make no headway. As the days and weeks slipped by, my efforts served only to make me increasingly aware of my appalling ignorance and how short was the time that lay ahead.

Chapter 23

The one-year rule

REFRESHED FROM a short holiday in the West Country we returned to Woodstock in September 1949 to learn that Denis Saunders was in the Osler Hospital at Headington with chest trouble.

I rang Tommy at once.

"Hello." His voice was as flat and expressionless as ever.

"Ken here."

"Ye-s." He never made the running in a telephone conversation.

"How's Denis?"

"Well," and there followed a good deal of coughing at the other end. "I'm afraid he's not at all well." He spoke in solemn, measured tones, his words almost a drawl, his Yorkshire inflection unmistakable. "He'll certainly not play football this year and I think it's very unlikely he'll ever play again."

"Oh dear," I said.

"Yes," said Tommy, "it's all most unfortunate; we'll just have to wait and see," and he began coughing again.

"And how's Penelope?" I asked.

"Oh, she's all right... but I've not been at all well."

"I'm sorry to hear that, Tommy." I smiled, this was routine stuff.

"And I'm not at all happy about the way things are going with Pegasus. I'm convinced we've got to get rid of this one-year rule if we're ever going to do anything as a club. Still, we'll talk about all that later. You and Biddie all right?"

"Yes, we're fine."

"That's good... G'bye," and, before I could reply, he hung up.

I went into the sitting-room and sat by the fire we had lit, for the evening was chill.

"Any news about Denis?" Biddie asked.

"Not really. He was X-rayed and they found a spot on his lung. It's now a question of rest and treatment."

"Poor Denis," she said.

I nodded and began to think how much we would miss his quiet personality and skilful control in midfield. And then I considered Tommy's words about the one-year rule, which had first been questioned at an extraordinary general meeting of the club, held on Saturday, 9 April 1949, when the club still had no rules.

It came up again shortly afterwards when Tommy received a letter from the wife of the club's president, dated 26 April, in which she wrote:

April 26th 1949.

Dear Dr Thompson,
My husband is still in bed after his pneumonia and so will be unable to attend the meeting

on Saturday. He wants me to say that he feels very strongly that the rule of qualification for only one year after going down should be altered at once, otherwise the club will die a natural death in a very few years. He asks me to ask you if you will convey his congratulations to the team upon the magnificent start they have made.

With kind regards,
Yours sincerely,
C. May Hunt

On the 27th the Reverend Kenneth Hunt died.

Two days later, the committee met at the East India and Sports' Club where Graham Doggart took the chair and spoke of the very sad and unexpected death of our first president. After this it was agreed unanimously to invite A. H. Chadder to become the new president until the next Annual General Meeting. Then Tommy read out the letter he had received from Mrs Hunt. The cat, so to speak, was well and truly out of the bag.

There followed long, earnest discussions on the eligibility of players. In the end, what was clearly and rather painfully emerging was a steadily growing difference of opinion concerning the question of the one-year rule, which Cambridge and the Corinthian-Casuals wished to retain and Oxford wanted to abolish.

Such was the situation at the start of the Michaelmas term of 1949.

We played our first match of the season against Aylesbury Town on a bone hard ground. Jimmy Potts had taken over from Denis Saunders as captain of the Oxford side. I was secretary, not a very effective one, though it was not altogether my fault, for an injury put me out of the game for six weeks.

I had gone up for a ball and received a severe blow on the side of my head; I think it was an elbow. I recall a bright flash and momentary bewilderment. I was able to carry on all right and went home with nothing more than a considerable swelling and a dull ache.

The following day I still had a headache. Feeling listless and tired, I went down to Iffley Road in the afternoon to train and perhaps get rid of it that way. It was raining hard and I did a few laps to start with. As I jogged slowly round behind the goal a ball came over and automatically I went up and headed it back on to the pitch. It shook me considerably because the ball was wet and heavy.

When I awoke next morning my headache was no better and I could not sleep. That afternoon the doctor called and I was examined and told I had concussion and was to stay in bed. Two days later I was still no better and sleeping badly. I began to wonder whether perhaps I had something worse than concussion and with this in mind I turned to the *Home Book of Medicine* to see what light that could throw on my condition. Reading the chapter on head injuries and the brain, my consternation mounted in leaps and bounds till finally I came to the conclusion that I was suffering from nothing less than a brain tumour.

"What do you think's the matter with me?" I asked our pleasant but rather serious Wykehamist doctor when he called the second time.

"I'm not sure," he replied truthfully.

"Could it be a tumour?"

His eye caught sight of the *Home Book of Medicine* lying on the floor at the side of our bed and suddenly he was not amused. "So you've been reading that stuff," he remarked, frowning.

I nodded and smiled weakly. "But why doesn't this headache go?"

He looked at me gravely for a moment, and somehow I rather wished I had not asked him.

"You could have a blood clot," he said quietly.

"Good God," I said, now thoroughly alarmed.

"I'm going to send you by ambulance this afternoon to see a brain specialist. I shouldn't worry if I were you," he added.

But then, of course, he wasn't me and I certainly did worry. I worried a great deal, bemoaning my fate and predicting to my long-suffering wife that this was it and I probably would never make the return journey.

"Of course you will," she assured me, as I was lifted into the same old ambulance that had conveyed her to the Radcliffe nine months earlier.

At the hospital I was taken on a stretcher and put behind a curtain on the other side of which someone was either having a baby or some sort of fit. My heart beat madly and my imagination ran riot as I lay and listened and suddenly I wasn't at all sure whether I had a headache or not. After what seemed a very long time they wheeled me away to have my head X-rayed. Then I was trundled back to my curtained compartment where I was asked some more questions and eventually allowed to go. Greatly relieved, I was just being pushed back into the ambulance when somebody rushed out and said they wanted to re-examine me.

So once more I found myself back in the curtained-off area. "We'd like to see you tomorrow," said the man in the white coat when he'd finished his examination and then I was taken out and pushed finally into the ambulance.

That night, propped up in bed, I slept very little and my headache was severe.

The following morning I was duly carried off again to the Radcliffe where this time I saw the chief 'nutcracker' himself. He examined me quietly and with immense authority which impressed me deeply.

"You've got a bruised brain, Mr Shearwood," he said when he'd finished. "It will take time. Could be a few days, could be a few weeks, could be even longer. Just like any other internal bruise it will eventually disappear. When it does you can carry on quite normally."

"I can play football?"

"Yes. As soon as it goes you can play. But until it does, stay at home and take things quietly."

Very relieved, I thanked him and was carried on a stretcher back to the ambulance.

That evening the telephone rang.

"How is he?" asked Donald Carr.

"He's fine," said Biddie, "they've X-rayed his brain and found nothing there."

"What — nothing at all?" remarked Donald, incredulous and delighted.

"No, nothing at all," she assured him, which startling piece of news promptly spread through Vincent's and elsewhere.

For four long weeks I suffered a severe headache and crept about the house feeling ill and weak and thoroughly wretched. The nights were the worst. I could do no reading. Tommy, Jimmy Potts, John Tanner and others came out to see us and tell me how the Oxford side was faring. And, as the days and weeks passed, I began to wonder if I ever would play again. Then, one night, I fell into a deep sleep and when I woke it was as though my head had suddenly been released from the grip of a steel band.

"It's gone," I said to Biddie, "it's completely gone. I feel a new man."

"I know," she said, coming into the room with Paul in her arms. "I watched you sleeping, you've had a really good night."

I put on my dressing-gown and went down and made a cup of tea.

I had just over three weeks to get fit before we played Cambridge, so I began training straight away. I also began trying to catch up on my work. Eric Collieu had been in touch and insisted that I was not to start unless I was really feeling all right. I never told him just how much his kindness meant.

By the beginning of December I was fit again and ready to play against Cambridge at Tottenham where this time we drew. The match had hardly begun when I received a severe blow on the head trying to win a ball in the air and, just for one awful moment, I wondered if there was not to be a repeat performance, but all was well.

Jimmy Potts, who had already won a cap for England, had a very good match, jinking away on the flank, nibbling at their defence, but I knew I had not particularly distinguished myself. For Cambridge, Ralph Cowan played beautifully at centre-half and I admired his mastery. But there was little doubt we missed the cool influence of Denis in midfield and when the final whistle blew I felt we were fortunate to have drawn the match.

Later that afternoon an Annual General Meeting of the Pegasus FC was held at the Public Schools Club and there the rules of Pegasus were discussed and amended to read as follows:

All members shall be eligible to play for the club, but it shall be the policy of the selection committee to choose primarily those players who are either resident in their university or who went down the previous season. It shall be clearly understood that the Corinthian-Casuals FC shall have the prior right to request the services of players who have been down from the universities for more than one year and who are members of both clubs, in the event of the selection committee wishing to play them. The final decision rests with the player himself.

Much was to hinge on that last sentence.

Five days later Paul celebrated his first birthday and, before we knew it, Christmas was upon us and another year was drawing rapidly to its close — but not before we had spent the last few days on a football tour based at Torquay, in preparation for our next venture in the Amateur Cup. The club had played only three matches since our defeat by Bromley the previous February.

The tour began with a win against the Amateur Football Alliance at Finchley. I had badly turned my ankle and could not play in this game. But at Barnstaple, where we lost 3-1 on the last day of 1949, I strapped it up and captained the side. I should never have played. The ankle was thick and full of adhesions and I sweated every time I touched the ball with my right foot, let alone tackled. That night, donning our dinner jackets, we danced, in my case, hobbled, the Old Year out and the New Year in.

The following morning we gathered round a billiard table with Tommy, Graham Doggart, and Harvey Chadder, to discuss tactics. There was a good deal of talk and demonstration with billiard balls, which became not a little out of hand, particularly when one of the Cambridge contingent hurled the pink across the table to jump the pocket, narrowly missing Tommy, who had to be persuaded later that it was not an attempt on his life.

I suggested that we should appoint a professional coach who should dictate policy.

"We never had a coach," said Graham Doggart, smiling, his manner gentle and courteous as ever. I never saw him put out. He and Harvey Chadder had played at the end of the great Corinthian era, the latter marking and holding Hughie Gallacher, the famous Scottish international in that Corinthian versus Newcastle United cup-tie of 1927 played before fifty thousand spectators. But I could not see the logic of Graham's statement and suggested again that if we had a coach it would neutralise any differences of tactical opinion among the players and he could advise on the selection of the side. Tommy had that old foxy look about him and I could see he was not going to commit himself. Not surprisingly, we got nowhere.

When I got back to Woodstock, Biddie worked on my ankle and I was able to play against Morris Motors in the Oxfordshire Senior Cup, a match which we won by six clear goals.

A week later we met Erith and Belvedere in the first round of the Amateur Cup on their ground. Of all pitches that I have played on this was the stickiest and heaviest. In such conditions the ball had to be whacked about; too much of the short frilly stuff courts disaster. That day we tended to play some of this and very nearly paid the penalty. Only a single goal by Tony Pawson kept us still in the Cup. As the game wore on, it became a physical effort to lift one's feet from the cloying mud. Our forwards were small and we relied on the strength of Doug Insole and the skill of Norman Kerruish to spray the ball about. Above all, we missed the penetrating thrust of John Tanner, who was injured. At the end I was so tired I could hardly pull myself aboard the bus.

The following Saturday, before a capacity crowd on the Oxford City ground — the Iffley Road ground was having a running track put round it and being resurfaced — we defeated Erith and Belvedere in the replay 5-2, Potts and Tanner scoring two apiece and Insole one.

In the second round we drew Walthamstow Avenue away — a really stiff hurdle — and Doug Insole, who had played for Walthamstow, was able to give us a lot of information about the London side. But on the day it availed us nothing. Despite an early goal by Tanner, we lost 3-2 and were out with a bang. Once again I had allowed Turner, their centre-forward, to get on the back of me and score with his head from a Lewis cross.

I had played against Walthamstow two years earlier when on tour with the Yorkshire Amateurs and marked Doug Insole. My chief impressions then, and now, are of the skill of this semi-professional side, but the ugliness of their ground, dominated at one end by a great towering block of flats — which did nothing to alleviate my sinking spirits as we made our exit from the Amateur Cup of 1950 on that bleak afternoon at the end of January.

But we still had something to play for — the Oxfordshire Senior Cup — and this we went on to win, defeating Chipping Norton 5-0 in the final, though only after a replay. Both games were played on the Iffley Road Rugby Ground to accommodate the large crowd. It was our first trophy.

Chapter 24

Finals

BARELY FIVE months now remained before I sat my Finals. Only too painfully I was aware of the fact. The very thought of entering those grim Examination Schools and writing for twenty hours and more sent shivers down my spine and filled me with alarm and despondency. My scalp literally prickled when I reflected how little I had done, how little I knew, how much lay ahead.

I'd been gently reminded of the last fact by Sonners — Dr W. T. S. Stallybrass, the Principal of Brasenose College — at that first Collection in 1947, when every undergraduate appeared in the hall before the Principal and Fellows to hear his tutor report publicly on his progress.

I met Sonners only once more, this time informally on a week's cricket tour in Devon with the Strollers, his Brasenose side of undergraduates. I remember the tour chiefly because, celebrating after making 80 against Sidmouth in the first match, I was apprehended, along with Tim Whitehead and Nevill Acheson-Gray, the following evening in the village of Beer by a friendly and bucolic member of the Devon constabulary. I was charged with having purloined a 'shrub in a tub' and driving it away on the bonnet of my jeep — a charge I could not, in all honesty, deny.

Later, when facing a belligerent and slightly alcoholic Sidmouth sergeant of police, who began with a long and lurid account of what Sir Archibald Bodkin, the magistrate, would have in store for us at the local bench, the six legal brains of the Strollers, who had accompanied me to the police station, rose magnificently to my defence. Summoning their wits and using every conceivable form of legal jargon, they so impressed the astonished and bemused sergeant that in no time a compromise had been reached, all was forgiven and the undamaged 'shrub in a tub' duly conveyed once more on the bonnet of my jeep back to its proper place of residence by the side of the Sidmouth Hotel's front door, with abject apologies to the management.

Tragically, on 29 October 1948, Sonners mistakenly opened the carriage door when returning on a late London to Oxford train and fell to his death, an accident attributed to failing eyesight and extreme fatigue.

Now, two years later, I faced Hugh Last, Sonners's successor, at my last Collection before Finals, and was reminded once again how much lay ahead, how short was the time that remained. It was a warning I acknowledged with as much assurance as I could muster, in a vain attempt to hide my acute embarrassment and feeling of real despair — for at that stage I did not even know for certain which king succeeded which.

I was faced with two alternatives. Carry on as I had been doing, nibbling away at the subject but never getting anywhere, or make one great assault on the work. I decided on the latter and made my plans.

First, I determined that each day I would write down exactly the number of hours and minutes that I had sat reading. My target was to work six hours a day without exception. If I could do more, so much the better, but on no account was any day to be missed, Sundays included. I would start at seven each morning, do two hours before breakfast, have a break, do another two between ten and twelve and a couple more between two and four in the afternoon. That left plenty of time to find several hours more in the day if I felt like it. But above all the routine must never be broken. On paper it looked easy.

Next, I had to organise an up-to-date but minimum bibliography that would cover the syllabus thoroughly. I had no time to read round the subject. Every corner must be cut. Here Martin Moriarty was a great help and so were Tony Pawson and Jimmy Potts, the latter particularly, for he generously allowed me to borrow his book of essays for a week, each essay beautifully written in immaculate longhand. I wanted to copy them all out but it would have taken hours and there just wasn't the time to spare. So I called on our solicitor in Woodstock and asked if I could borrow his secretary to type them out.

"She's doing rather a lot of work for me at the moment," he said, "but I can get them done for you."

"Within a week?"

"Yes."

"Then go ahead."

Back they promptly came, typed in triplicate, complete with a bill I had not bargained for. £26! A lot of money in 1950.

I decided to do all my work up in the attic, seated by the window, from where I could perhaps gain some solace and inspiration from the distant statue of Marlborough. I began the assault immediately on our return from the New Year tour.

Each morning the alarm went off at half-past six and well before seven I was up in the attic doing the necessary reading to cover the first paper of English History.

At first my task seemed insurmountable, but gradually I got into the swing of working and ever so slightly I began to make some progress. But there were often ugly moments of black despair when I felt I was getting nowhere and the centuries of reading that lay ahead stretched interminably. At such times I would get up and go for a walk or take a bath before going back to the books.

And ever so gradually I found I was beginning to enjoy my work. When, at the end of each day I came to write down the exact hours and minutes I had sat reading, I even began to feel slightly virtuous!

A genuine six hours of reading and noting I quickly discovered took some doing, but in no time I was managing eight hours a day and more, only easing off on a Saturday if I had a match. Even then I would manage several hours in the morning and probably an hour or two in the evening. Sundays were no exception, for I was determined that I would have not one day's rest until the examinations were over.

Soon I actually looked forward to climbing the steep and narrow wooden stairs at the start of each day. As the mornings grew lighter, the birds sang earlier and the first green shoots of another spring appeared, there came hope and a growing confidence that despite the acres of reading that still lay ahead, I might yet digest the pile of books that surrounded my chair in time to pass my Finals.

At most weekends Martin Moriarty would come out and we'd discuss the Chartists, the Docker's Tanner and Keir Hardie as we walked along the road that leads north to Chipping Norton. I learned much from Martin, who was a specialist in the early days of the labour movement.

I never went near the Parks or opened my cricket bag. As I sat on the top of the bus on my weekly tutorial visit to Oxford, I'd take from my inside pocket a packet of white postcards that I always carried with me, on which I had made neat precis of all Potts's essays. These I would read, committing to memory, only putting them away when the bus reached the tree-lined Woodstock Road, for then I liked to look down at the big square houses, their gardens now colourful and summery beneath the various shades of fresh foliage.

I read, noted, and re-read Rousseau, Hobbes and Aristotle, until I understood something of the philosophy and flaws of their arguments. And the more I worked the more virtuous I felt until I could almost feel the halo about my head! I had now reached the stage when I wanted to put myself to the test. I no longer feared the examination. In fact, I looked forward to it.

May was drawing to a close. John Tanner, much to his disgust, had got a Third in History and was now working at the Oxford Appointments Board. I knew he was mildly curious about my result. I hadn't seen much of Denis Saunders, but the news was encouraging. Donald Carr was making runs in the Parks and Ben Brown, who had got a first in science, was now doing research work at Oxford. Tony Pawson, who had just missed a first, was teaching at Winchester, without much enthusiasm; Rob Tillard had returned to his regiment with a Third in History. Several times Jimmy and Toni Potts came out to see us with their year-old daughter, Janet. While our two wives pushed their respective offspring in the park, we'd talk history and I'd impress Jimmy by giving him detailed and analytical answers to various questions he'd put to me about subjects on which he'd written essays.

"You seem to know quite a lot," he said, astonished, unaware, of course, that I possessed copies of all his essays, which I had memorised. He was extremely able and those who knew about such matters considered he'd get a First. They would not have been quite so confident in my case.

June arrived and I made my final plans. I decided that each day I would have a taxi into Oxford and a taxi back and I organised my revision in the following manner.

The evening before each examination day I would revise between eight and ten for the following afternoon's paper. Promptly at ten, come what may, I would pack up and go to bed. On examination day the alarm would go off at half-past five and I would be at work well before six, revising for the morning paper which began at 9.30. Biddie would bring me my breakfast on a tray and I would work as I ate. At half-past eight the taxi would arrive and I'd set off sitting at the back still working. A friend had arranged that I should have a room at his digs in Longwall Street, conveniently close to the Examination Schools. A cold lunch would be laid ready for me when I came out at 12.30. I would then work through the lunch period revising for the afternoon paper which started at half-past two and ended at half-past five. That completed, I would return to the digs in Longwall Street, where the taxi would be waiting to drive me back to Woodstock.

So came the first day of the examinations and, dressed in a blue suit, white tie, commoner's gown and mortar-board, I kissed Biddie goodbye, climbed into the back of a big comfortable old Austin and set off for Oxford. On the way in I glanced through Sayles's *Foundations of Medieval England,* and had a look at a couple of Potts's essays. As a last minute stand-by I had taken with me a thin little book entitled *History Helps* — not found, I hasten to add, in any of the university's libraries!

My friend and host, Michael Wrigley, a very tall, erect and assured Harrovian, who went into the Foreign Office, greeted me with his customary air of benign condescension. I'd kept wicket to his fast bowling on occasions, when he displayed a splendidly cavalier approach to the game that appealed to me. He had a whirligig action — all arms and legs and an uncanny adroitness at dropping the easiest of slip catches, at the same time making them appear the most difficult. But he hit the jackpot all right in 1949 when he took eight New Zealand wickets for fifty-one runs.

"All ready, Shearwood?" he now said, looking down at me with that amused, slightly twisted grin of his, "know all about the Anglo-Saxons?"

"I know that their justice was nothing short of unmitigated barbarism," I replied.

"Very impressive too," he said, laughing and showing me my room where I dumped my books. "I've laid on your lunch and a stiff gin — we shall both need it." Then we set off down Longwall Street, the high stone wall of Magdalen College mellow and bright in the June sunshine. Dodging the High Street traffic, we reached the other side where serious-faced undergraduates in short gowns were converging from all directions on the open doors of the Examination Schools. We entered the building and joined the general scrimmage. "See you later," said my companion above the hubbub and I went up the broad stairway and into the examination room where I found my desk. Glancing round, I caught sight of Jimmy Potts. I saw no one else that I knew. And then we were off. I picked up the paper and began to study the twenty-three questions, of which I had to answer four.

Three hours later I handed in my paper and emerged blinking into the sunlight. I ate my lunch, drank my gin, and revised hard for the afternoon paper.

"Time we went," said Michael, still grinning away, and we walked the short distance back to the Examination Schools.

At 5.40 I climbed into the back of the waiting taxi and closed my eyes. I was very tired but satisfied, for I had not disliked the two papers and felt that I had coped adequately with the eight questions I attempted.

"How did you get on?" Biddie greeted me when I got back.

"Not too bad," I told her, sipping a cup of tea before taking a bath. At seven I had supper. When I had finished, I went up top and worked till ten when I promptly went to bed.

All week I kept this up, working twelve hours a day and then suddenly it was over and we were drinking champagne at the top of Vincent's. That night I went to bed early and slept for twelve hours. When I woke I had a feeling that I should be up in the attic working, for the sense of purpose that had motivated me for the last five months was still active. I felt slightly flat.

I felt also that I had passed, for I had found none of the papers beyond my powers. In fact, I had quite enjoyed doing them, particularly those on political science. My family too had played their part nobly, Biddie by her quiet, unfailing support and undemanding nature, Paul by never keeping me awake at night during the examinations, something which could have proved disastrous. For several days I felt drained and I could not forget the books and the attic.

Weeks later, some time in July, when I had long forgotten all about the examinations and what I had written, I was called by the Examining Body for my viva. Sitting outside, waiting to be called, dressed once again for the occasion in blue suit, white tie and gown, I felt somewhat apprehensive though, at the same time, intrigued. All the work that I had done had now become something of the past, almost unreal. The night before I had glanced through some of the books in the attic for an hour or two, but the spark had gone. I had written the papers and, as far as I was concerned, they were either good enough or they weren't.

When I went in I was asked to sit at the centre of a long table facing a group of dons and one woman. They were in no hurry and I could see they had my papers before them. I cannot remember a great deal about that viva, but I do remember that they asked me what the Chartists wanted and I was able to give them all six of their demands. Then I was questioned on Paper 3. It was about something I had written on Gladstone and Disraeli and I found myself in some difficulty, my plight made no easier by the presence of the distinguished historian, Miss Hurnar, a cousin of Stanley Cohn, who sat opposite me, one elbow resting on the table, eyes closed, hand to brow in what I could only suppose was an attitude of prayer or great suffering, I suspected the latter. And then I was thanked politely, God knows for what. Rising awkwardly, I walked to the door and closed it behind me.

Now there was only the waiting for the lists to be put up in the Examination Schools to see who had got firsts, seconds, thirds, the rare fourths, and fails.

I was not particularly worried. I had done what I could, so I just forgot all about it, opened my cricket bag and played for Blenheim Palace, the side I had captained the previous season.

One evening I was playing cricket for the Brasenose side of college servants, somewhere in the Oxfordshire countryside, trying to keep wicket in the gathering twilight. At last, as the stars were emerging, we finished the match and adjourned to the village pub. Chatting and drinking our pints of beer, I suddenly saw my old friend, Charlie, making his way towards me through the crowded little room with outstretched hand.

"Congratulations," he said, "you've got a Third."

"I have?"

"You have!' he nodded, smiling and twitching his nose. "I've been and verified it. Your name's there. It's all quite true. Now drink up and I'll get you another," he said, making his way to the bar before I had time to reply.

Good old Charlie, I thought. He'd no need to have done it. He had watched all our Pegasus matches and that's how I met him. He had also been a great help to me when I had been short of money, taking me with him on jobs clearing houses, drawing up lists for the big auction sales which were to follow, joking about the various items, twitching his nose at great speed like some frightened rabbit sensing danger, as he skilfully sorted through piles of pictures, books, chairs, curtains, carpets, kitchen utensils, telling me, as he did so, what this would fetch and that wouldn't. During the lunch breaks we'd often talked of Pegasus and on occasions I had spoken to him about my academic fears.

Somehow that afternoon he must have heard that the results were out and gone down to the Examination Schools to see whether I had passed. He rang Woodstock immediately and told Biddie the good news. She told him that I was out playing cricket for the college servants., but was unable to tell him where, so he had promptly gone to the Lodge at Brasenose college and found out. Good old Charlie. I hope he reads this book. We all had a few drinks that evening.

"You've passed," said Biddie delightedly when I got back. "You've got a Third."

Then we made some telephone calls.

"Let's go down to Cornwall," I said that night, "I want to smell the sea again."

Two days later we set off for the West Country.

Chapter 25

On the way

EARLIER THAT YEAR I had applied to the Oxford School of Education to do what is called a Dip Ed and been accepted. I had as yet no real plans for the future, though Colin Weir had sown some seeds when tentatively sounding me out as to whether I would be interested in going to teach at Lancing College. What really appealed to me about taking a Diploma in Education was that it gave me another year at Oxford and the chance to play some more football and captain the university. At any rate, on the credit side, I now had an honours degree in history, if only a third, with which to face the future.

Returning from our holiday I immediately went up to White Hart Lane with Stan Heritage, the Oxford secretary, to meet the Tottenham player, Vic Buckingham, who was to help us in the forthcoming season. Over lunch it was agreed that he would coach us on Mondays and watch our mid-week matches. The physical fitness of the side he intended leaving to us, which was quite right.

Vie was tall, good-looking, debonair and charming. I could see, as he coached us that season with his own brand of amused, casual authority, that he was enjoying himself every bit as much as we were enjoying his coaching. He would laugh quietly at our awkwardness as he worked with us, correcting and encouraging, watching closely and assessing us shrewdly. He wanted us to play it simple and quick, push and run stuff, give and go, our wingers coming right back and collecting the ball from defence, everyone playing a part and taking responsibility. "This fellow Ramsey at Tottenham," he would say, "he's so good at taking responsibility. Even in the six-yard area he'll want the ball and try and start something going. He's as slow as an old carthorse, but what a player, what positional sense, what a good passer of the ball."

When each session was over, Stan and I would discuss with him the selection of the side for the mid-week match, which he would come down and watch.

We had a lot of difficulty finding a goalkeeper and tried, amongst others, two cricket Blues, Christopher Winn and George Chesterton. Chesteron, on his one and only appearance against Wolverhampton Wanderers, was forced to retrieve the ball five times from his goal. In desperation, Vic brought the England and Spurs goalkeeper, Ted Ditchburn, down to try and help us find a keeper. In the end we plumped for Bernard Boddy who had played the previous year at back. He had a good eye, was big and strong and had what we thought sound hands.

When the side was finally selected, four Salopians were included, John Clegg, Dick Rhys, myself and Miles Robinson, chosen in place of Derek Richards. It is never a pleasant business dropping an old Blue but, on balance, I thought Miles was the right choice. He was not as good a player on the ball as Derek, but he was bigger, stronger and faster and, I thought, better equipped to contain the threat of the Cambridge right-winger,

Roy Sutcliffe, who was to play for England. To our great delight, Denis Saunders was well and able to play again. He had gradually eased himself back into the game and was as good as ever. With Gordon McKinna and Denis, future England players, we were strong in the middle of the field. Up front we had two good wingers, John Clegg and Donald Carr, and a very experienced player at inside-right, Stan Heritage.

But Cambridge, too, were strong in midfield, with such players as Reg Vowels, Ralph Cowan, their captain — both to become internationals — and Jimmy Platt. They had a couple of good inside-forwards, Jack Laybourne — later to play for Spurs — and Peter May, the future England cricket captain. The Light Blues would be no push-over.

The match was played again at White Hart Lane, the sides coached by two Tottenham players, Vic for us, Bill Nicholson for Cambridge. Both coaches hoped we would play it the Spurs way, give and go stuff, simple and quick. In fact the football that afternoon was too tense, the marking tight, and the contest became a dour battle, with no goals scored at the end, and no quarter given.

It was my fourth and last varsity match and I chiefly recollect an incident towards the end of the match which our opponents felt had robbed them of a goal. In the heavy conditions Bernard Boddy fumbled a close-range shot from Lionel Boardman and in a trice the Cambridge winger followed up and banged the ball out of his groping hands into the back of our net. Immediately our goalkeeper fell flat on his face and remained motionless. It was difficult to know quite what was wrong. I tried to get a response and find out if he was injured. Or was he just mortified by what had happened? Our Man with the Sponge, Leslie Laitt, was on his way out, trilby on head, running through the mud. Cambridge meanwhile had taken the ball back to the middle and were lined up, impatient to start again. There was no doubt in any of their minds that they were now one up.

"Kicked it out of his hands, ref," said Leslie, arriving on the scene and puffing indignantly at the referee, Mr J. H. Lockton, who seemed momentarily at a loss at what to do or say, "kicked it out of his hands he did," and, bending over the recumbent Boddy (excuse the pun), he held a wet sponge to the back of his neck.

"I know," said the referee testily, and he signalled to the Cambridge players to return the ball, which did not please them one bit.

And then Bernard began to stir and after several moments rose shakily to his feet. Leslie Laitt left the field, I took the free kick from the goal-line, and play resumed. Twenty minutes later the match was over, a goalless draw.

"The magic of a cold sponge and silver-tongued oratory had saved the day for an Oxford side that began on its toes but ended on its heels," concluded *The Times* correspondent. But I ought to remind the reader that Geoffrey Green, besides being a Salopian, was also a Cambridge soccer Blue.

The following morning, Sunday, the customary Pegasus meeting was held and Tommy and Graham Doggart were appointed to the selection committee for the season 1950-51. Then Graham dropped a bombshell by proposing that players

Above: Alf Ramsey between Jimmy Potts and Ralph Cowan after a friendly played between Pegasus and the full Tottenham Hotspur side prior to the Wembley Amateur Cup Final of 1951

Below: Highbury, semi-final of the Amateur Cup 1951.
Pegasus 1 Hendon 1. Ben Brown about to take the ball off the foot of Stroud.

selected for the coming tour should be limited to those in residence or for one year thereafter, his proposal seconded by Peter May.

At once Tommy strongly opposed the proposal, pointing out that, apart from any other considerations, a few senior players had held themselves available for Pegasus rather than playing in cup-ties for other clubs. Whereupon Graham at once withdrew his proposal and the meeting ended with Denis Saunders being appointed captain for the coming season.

I was present at that meeting, as I was for many others, and could see how wide the rift was growing. Graham Doggart, a Cambridge and Corinthian player, naturally had many friends and connections with the Casuals and was in an unquestionably difficult position. His son, Hubert, had just come down from Cambridge. The Cambridge contingent, led by Doug Insole, was coming out into the open more and more as supporters of the one-year rule. Sadly and, inevitably it seemed, a major difference of opinion over the interpretation of the rules and future of the club was becoming a chasm too wide by far for any bridge to link the two universities. In all sincerity, Graham believed that the Cambridge point of view was the right one. With equal sincerity, Tommy and the Oxford contingent believed that, unless the club used its resources to the full, Pegasus would never make the necessary impact to stimulate the game at the universities and, as the Reverend Kenneth Hunt had so bluntly predicted in his letter, 'the club would die a natural death in a very few years'.

This was the position when we set off on the New Year tour of 1951 with a party of eighteen players, twelve from Oxford, six from Cambridge, plus wives and officials, to play three matches against Winchester City, Salisbury Town and Jersey with Vic Buckingham, much to my delight, as the club coach.

We beat Winchester City, lost to Salisbury and ended with a fine win against Jersey, when Johnny Dutchman scored four goals and John Tanner one. In the heavy conditions the side 'clicked' and Vic Buckingham was delighted. I had particular cause to remember the Jersey centre-forward, Le Mesurier, who had been with West Bromwich Albion for a spell and was sharp and mobile. I stuck to him closely — perhaps too closely — because, backing into me to make good a ball laid at his feet, he brought his elbow back into my midriff with a short vicious jab that knocked the stuffing out of me for a minute or two.

But, in all, it was a very successful tour. When we got back — Biddie had come on tour with me — the telephone rang, almost as soon as we opened the front door of Laburnum House, and there was Jerry Weinstein on the other end wanting all the news.

Jerry was at Brasenose. Having taken a good degree in Jurisprudence, he was reading for a BCL. I'd really got to know him that Michaelmas term when he was reporting our matches for the *Isis* magazine. I liked him at once. As a Japanese interpreter in the Far East during the war, he had caught polio, which left him severely crippled. Black-haired and blue-jowled, tinted glasses bridging heavy Jewish features and wearing a long airforce officer's overcoat, he would limp slowly and lopsidedly across the High, grim of visage, holding the oncoming traffic at bay with stick aloft, occasionally stopping to tap the bonnet of any car that ventured too close. Once he was safely across his features would suddenly break into a huge grin, engaging and infectious. He had come to Oxford as a scholar from St. Paul's. He was fluent in four languages, had a rapier mind, witty and devastatingly fast. Since he was unable to play, he watched and wrote with insight about the game and not only contributed a great deal, but became as much a part of the Pegasus scene as anyone.

"Gosport will be no push-over," I heard him say, "I've watched 'em and they've a useful centre-forward, Albert Mundy. He's turning professional for Portsmouth at the end of the season. You'll need to mark him tight. How's Tommy?"

"Pretty good form."

"Might pop over and see you tomorrow evening."

"Why not have some supper?" I suggested, and he accepted.

Ten days later, having defeated the Home Air Command, we travelled to Portsmouth. After lunching together, we caught the ferry across to Gosport to begin our next venture in the Amateur Cup along with sixty-four other clubs. A mighty close affair it turned out to be as *The Times* made clear in its opening paragraph:

> Pegasus reached the second round of the FA Amateur Cup competition when they beat Gosport Borough Athletic at Gosport on Saturday by four goals to three, but they scarcely took to their wings in doing so.

"Well," said Tommy, when it was all over and we were on our way home, "I think we were very lucky." And that week he sent out a notice to twenty-four players advising them of the need for maximum fitness, which had seemed in question, against Gosport and not to underestimate Slough Town, our next opponents on 27 January.

Jerry Weinstein drove Denis Saunders, Donald Carr and me to the game in his black Hillman, especially converted for his needs. He drove fast and generally well, but on this occasion not quite well enough. I was sitting in the front.

"You're driving too close to his tail, Jerry," I said.

"D'you want to walk?" he retorted, which made Donald laugh. The road was narrow and winding and Jerry was impatient to pass.

Suddenly, the car in front, which was being driven irritatingly slowly, braked sharply and, equally suddenly, Jerry jammed on his brakes and we skidded gently, but inevitably, into the back of the car ahead, to the sound of breaking glass. There followed a moment of silence, broken by some barely controlled laughter, as we watched Jerry indicating with his stick the damage inflicted on his car, at the same time angrily addressing the other driver whose vehicle appeared to have escaped any real damage.

"That was a fucking disgraceful piece of driving if ever there was," said Jerry, getting in again, after addresses and insurances had been exchanged. "And if you say, 'I told you so', Shearwood, you can bloody well get out and walk to Slough," which made us all laugh out loud.

As we drew near Slough, however, we became increasingly preoccupied with our own thoughts. I was thinking of Clements and what I knew about him as a centre-forward from the report we had been sent. I began to sweat slightly, anticipating the game and the movements of the man I would soon be marking for ninety minutes. Then we were at the ground; there was Tommy and Graham and Harvey Chadder and Sir Stanley Rous, and I caught sight of Denis Compton, who had come to report the match and lots of friendly Oxford faces in the crowd outside the ground. Inside the cramped changing-room Leslie Laitt was putting out our kit with trilby still on head. He was never without it and some of us, Jerry in particular, were of the opinion that he wore it in bed.

Over six thousand watched our unchanged side defeat Slough Town 3-1, all four goals scored in the first twenty minutes. Denis Compton wrote:

> It was half an hour of incident-packed football. Slough had no counter to the speed of the Pegasus attack. Tanner was fast, and his two goals were beauties and Dutchman opens up the game and is a good forward. But the Pegasus defence is not so sure and confident and, though it looked better after the interval, one felt that a top class attack would have riddled it earlier on. It is here where changes will have to be made if Pegasus are to go forward, and they can win the cup if the defence is tightened up.

Coming out for the second half we heard, above the noise of the crowd, the pleasant strains of the Eton Boating Song, sung by a group of college boys who had come over to watch the match. It became our theme tune and we were to hear it on many more occasions.

After the match the three of us again drove back with Jerry to Oxford, stopping to have a meal on the way. Much later, entering Oxford, we passed the road where Leslie Laitt lived and decided to pull up. A ladder lay outside; a light was on upstairs. Carefully, though somewhat unsteadily, we placed the ladder against the front of the house and Donald, singing the Eton Boating Song, began to climb. Halfway up, the window opened.

"Hello, Leslie," said Donald.

"Is he wearing his hat?" enquired Jerry from the foot of the ladder.

"You'll wake the neighbours," warned Our Man with the Sponge, good-humouredly, "you'd better come in and have a cup of tea."

Before the three of us parted that night we telephoned Tommy from a public call-box.

"Ye-es," came the guarded drawl.

"Swing, swing together," we sang down the phone and waited for a response.

"Well," he said, his deliberate slow response completely ignoring our singing, "I've been giving the game a lot of thought and I don't think we're going to get much further unless we do something about the defence. I'm not at all happy about Ted Bowyer. He's a very nice fellow, but he's not the answer. And I'm still very concerned about the club's constitution and the one-year rule. There's a great deal of hard thinking to be done. I don't think any of you quite realise the sort of difficulties that lie ahead."

"Swing, swing together," we sang back and there was a slight chuckle at the other end followed by a bout of coughing.

"It's time you three went to bed," he said and hung up.

"At any rate, Tommy's in his usual fine form," said Jerry, emerging last from the call-box.

We were drawn away to Brentwood and Warley in the next round. Neither Tony Pawson, who had pulled a muscle, nor I could play. I had eaten something that had disagreed with me and felt ill and weak and very disappointed. I was just about fit enough to travel to the game with Jerry and watch the match.

Ralph Cowan, who had already won a cap for England, took over at centre-half and held the defence together brilliantly.

It was a match memorable for the dreadful conditions. Two goals down at half-time, we again failed to adapt to the heavy mud, tending frequently to pass short and square. But for twenty minutes of the second half we pressed strongly and Potts reduced the lead after a Sutcliffe-Tanner move. Then the minutes began to tick away fast until there were only ten of them left and onlookers could do little more than hope. The equaliser came with a pass from Tanner, and Potts was through to score. Suddenly Brentwood disintegrated, as can happen sometimes when a side has sensed victory only to have it wrenched from their grasp. For the last five minutes we had them by the throat and could have scored several times. Sutcliffe got our third and winning goal with a clever lob. For the second time in three years, we had reached the quarter-finals of the Amateur Cup.

Yet again, we were drawn away from home but, in a way, this cup-tie was at home, for we'd drawn our neighbours, Oxford City, who, in the previous round, had defeated the redoubtable Crook Town in a replay.

Immediately the coming game was the talk of Oxford. It was Town versus Gown. Not quite — five of the Pegasus side were from Cambridge.

"You can do it — of course you can," said Doug Margetts, friend and staunch supporter, who lived not thirty yards down the road from us and had never missed a match. Doug worked at Morris Motors, getting up every morning well before five. He was a small wiry man who cheerfully accepted life's lot. He didn't seem to need sleep because he never went to bed before midnight. He made a great flat plywood flying horse attached to a pole which came to all our matches. "Up the Pegs!" he would greet me, and we'd discuss the prospects for the next game. I'd get tickets for him and his friends from Tommy. Often of a morning his young daughter would come and play with Paul. They were a very kind family.

That Easter I started my term's practical teaching at the Woodstock Secondary Modern School, a low, prefabricated building. It was very convenient and I felt it was the only really valuable part of the educational course I was doing. The theory of education is a splendid-sounding phrase but has little bearing on the practical business of teaching a class — as I soon found out.

The headmaster of the school, Percy Thompson, was a diminutive Yorkshireman, full of personality and vigour and a great cricket enthusiast. He had kept wicket in the

Yorkshire League and proudly showed me his broken fingers. One morning I was teaching a big class, well over thirty, girls one side, boys the other, trying to give them some idea of what the French revolution was all about, when the door opened and in walked Percy.

"Aye," he said, looking at the blackboard curiously, where I had written a few names: Lafayette, Mirabeau, Danton, Robespierre, "what have you got up there, Ken, the runners for the 3.30?"

"Oh, we're just doing a bit of history," I told him.

"Aye, now let's see," he said, taking over and addressing the class. "Who's best batsman in't world?"

"Bradman," came a voice from the back.

"Can't hear," Percy pretended, leaning forward and putting his right hand to his ear.

" 'Utton," came a few more voices.

"Still can't hear you."

"Len 'Utton," came the concerted shout.

"You're right," said Percy. "Now then, which county did he play for?"

"Yorkshire," came the prompt reply.

"Right again," said Percy. "And who were Yorkshire's great enemies?"

"Lancashire," sang out the class, warming to the subject.

"And didn't they each have a flower for an emblem? I think the girls could answer this one."

"A rose," whispered several shyly.

"A rose," repeated Percy, "and wasn't there once a war called the War of the ... ?"

" ... Roses," roared the class.

"Right again," said Percy triumphantly and, turning to me and dropping his voice, "Got the idea, Ken?" and he went out and left me to it.

I learnt a lot at that school and was greatly helped by the geography master, an excellent teacher, who had been a chief petty officer in the Royal Navy. I wasn't in the least surprised to learn that shortly afterwards he was appointed a headmaster.

I used to sit in and watch the technique of the masters when I wasn't taking a class myself. There was a young Scot who couldn't keep order at all and he asked me if I would mind not attending his classes, a request to which I readily acceded.

The master who took the metalwork classes, however, had no trouble in keeping order. I would stand talking with him while the class got on with their work, banging away at the metal until some of them began to wander about and get up to mischief, believing their master's attention to be elsewhere — which was very far from the case.

"Jenkins," he would shout abruptly, "what the hell are you doing with that bloody hammer?" and he'd glare at the offender for several long seconds before continuing talking, his eyes alert.

Suddenly he'd break off again. "Just a minute," he'd say, lowering his voice, "just look at that little bugger over there." Moving stealthily forward, he'd catch the unsuspecting boy a fourpenny one, which made the rest of the class titter until they felt his eyes turned in their direction. Coming back poker-faced he'd give me a wink and carry on talking as though nothing had happened.

The most skilful teacher I've ever listened to was the mathematics master. He was a veteran and an artist and a lesson to anyone in how to use the voice. It was a to and fro business. He'd put a simple fraction on the board and build it up from there with questions whispered to his riveted audience. He never hurried, he never raised his voice and he never lost their attention. He knew his trade and they knew he did.

I was in the common room one afternoon doing some marking, when the geography master entered. "There's a parson and two ladies outside who are asking to see you. Apparently they're something to do with the Oxford Educational Authority and have come to hear you teach."

"Well, they're out of luck!' I said, "I'm not in."

"I think you'd better go and see them," he advised. So I opened the door and went out.

Across the hall a parson and two formidable females wearing spectacles were standing together, talking. As I approached them, the concern on my face — I learned this afterwards — caused the parson, the Very Reverend Jerry Weinstein, to begin shaking uncontrollably with laughter while the two females, also Brasenose undergraduates, unable to contain their serious expressions any longer, followed suit.

"We'd hoped to catch you teaching," said Jerry. "We were going to sit at the back of the class and ask you one or two awkward questions."

I enjoyed that term's teaching at Woodstock and, whenever I ran out of words, a not infrequent occurrence, I'd get straight onto the subject of football, and Pegasus, and who was going to win the Cup. I couldn't really go wrong.

There was a tremendous demand for tickets to see this all-Oxford fourth round cup-tie. Letters signed 'Disgusted' and 'Bitter Sweet' appeared in the local press from some of the unsuccessful applicants.

Tony Pawson failed a pre-match fitness test and John Tanner had a groin injury. So Roy Sutcliffe kept his place at outside-left, Jack Laybourne came in at inside-right and Johnny Dutchman moved to centre-forward. I took over again at centre-half and Ralph Cowan moved to left-back. In the Oxford Green 'Un, Syd Cox had this to say:

> After a thrill-packed first half, in which the honours were even, Oxford City fell away against Pegasus in the quarter-final of the Amateur Cup before a crowd of 9,500 on the White House ground this afternoon.

So we reached the semi-final — and Tommy was delighted, but not for long.

Chapter 26

Two semi-finals

BEFORE WE played the semi-final against Hendon at Highbury the Lent edition of a Cambridge university magazine, *Light Blue*, came out, in which Doug Insole wrote a long, highly critical article on Pegasus, giving his views which, at the time, I could appreciate but not share.

Naturally there followed a good deal of talk within the club. Tommy, of course, was at his best, confiding his concern to us at Oxford that the article was a deliberate attempt to sabotage the semi-final. "I've a good idea who's behind this. We've got to have a meeting as soon as possible." He loved meetings. And when Denis gently suggested that perhaps it wasn't really as bad as he was making out, Tommy peered over his spectacles at him in disbelief for several seconds, before remarking with slow gravity, "Sometimes. Denis. I think you're very naive," which made us all laugh, except for Tommy, who indulged in much coughing, shook his head knowingly, and lit another cigarette.

We had three weeks in which to prepare for the semi-final and each day we trained at Iffley Road, using the new running track, mingling with the Oxford athletes, Roger Bannister, Nick Stacey, Chris Chataway and Philip Morgan, who was doing a Dip Ed with me and was in the same tutorial group.

Roger Bannister would burn his way round the track where he eventually achieved the four-minute mile. I tried running with him on one occasion for some fifty yards, matching his stride, and was amazed at its length. Chris Chataway, on the other hand, was short and stocky and we all felt that he would not get very far. We were wrong.

Nick Stacey, an Etonian with a splendidly affected voice and a delightful manner, was a most lovely runner and he'd take us in line abreast for short sprints up and down the track in front of the pavilion.

"Now we are completely relaxed," he'd drawl gently as he ran with us and we'd jog along letting our arms and hands flap limply at our sides. "Now we're really beginning to open up a bit." And finally he'd urge us, "Come on, let's go," and surge effortlessly ahead, drawing smoothly away like a Rolls-Royce leaving behind a row of old 'bangers'.

Most of them had watched our matches and were great supporters of Pegasus. I had hired out Potts's essays to Nick Stacey for a small sum. Donald Carr had a copy and, come to think of it, I'm not sure that he ever paid his fee. The essays were already becoming a sought-after acquisition for those not so strong candidates about to embark upon their History Finals.

Entering the main doors of the Arsenal Football Club we climbed an impressive broad stairway of thick blue carpet, at the top of which stood the tall figure of a commissionaire, medals and all.

From the main stand we had a look at the pitch, a smooth muddy waste, ironed flat, the lines broad and white, with just a vestige of green at the edges. Already a big crowd was gathering.

Vie Buckingham was talking with Jack Crayston and Tommy was deep in conversation with the Pawsons.

"You'll have to be on your toes today, Ken," Tommy warned.

"He'll go in the bag," I assured him. I always carried my kit in an old Gladstone bag.

"I hope you're right," he said, looking his most melancholy. "You know Stroud's turning professional after this season." I nodded, and was suddenly more aware than ever of the old butterflies in my stomach.

"Good luck," said the Pawsons.

Our changing-room was spacious and first-class, the tiled floors heated. While we changed, Vic Buckingham wandered round and had a few words with each of us in turn. He was by far the most relaxed person there — except perhaps for Leslie Laitt who, hat upon head, was giving John Tanner some massage.

When we ran out, the smooth wet mud bore the imprints of our studs. The conditions were going to be very heavy and I thought of Erith and Belvedere and hoped that we wouldn't start playing it around too short.

Denis lost the toss and right from the start Hendon showed that they intended to get on with the job. A touch from Stroud, their centre-forward, to their inside-right, Phebey, resulted in a low sweeping pass straight to Avis, the Hendon left-winger, a tall gifted player, but very left-footed. At once he took the ball up to Johnny Maughan, our right-back, teased him for a moment, then slipped past. Within seconds, we were a pawn down and in dire trouble.

I stuck with Stroud who had moved into our penalty area in line with the far post and didn't go out to Avis because Jimmy Platt had come back fast and was containing this threat. John Dutchman had picked up the Hendon inside-left. Suddenly Avis accelerated on the outside of Jimmy Platt, winning space to drive a hard low centre from the bye-line across the edge of our six-yard area, which Stroud met quickly. I went with him but he had the advantage of me in timing his run. Somehow I just got a leg out to block his deflection and in the ensuing scramble Ben Brown got hold of the ball and cleared our lines.

The reader may well wonder how I can recall such a detail of a match that was played all those years ago. I think most players can remember certain incidents in important games, but no more. For a picture of these cup-ties I have taken extracts from the press, in particular from Geoffrey Green's reports in *The Times*.

There was one more incident in that semi-final against Hendon that stands vividly etched on my memory. This time it happened right at the end of the match and once again the threat came from Avis.

The Hendon left-winger had given Johnny Maughan a most difficult afternoon and with only two minutes remaining he was still at it. This time he had wandered inside, picked up a pass and was weaving his way through the appalling mud towards the centre edge of our penalty area. I cannot remember where Stroud was; I think he'd dropped wide to the right and I had let him go. At any rate I found myself confronting Avis, knowing full well that this was a tackle I could not afford to miss. He was working the ball back onto his left side, turning to set it up for a shot with that lethal left foot. I knew I dared not leave it any longer. I committed myself and went into the tackle. As I did so, he flicked the ball to one side. Down he went, all six foot and more of him. Immediately the whistle blew and the referee was pointing to the penalty spot. "Sorry," he said quietly, coming across. I was standing just in front of where the kick was to be taken. "I've no alternative." I could only manage a nod. It was a desperate moment.

I watched Dexter Adams come up and clean the ball with his hands before placing it carefully on the spot. I saw him wipe his right boot against his stocking. He didn't hurry. He seemed quite composed. I glanced at Ben Brown, research chemist and doctor of philosophy. So did twenty-six thousand five hundred spectators, who were strangely silent. I hoped the Hendon and England centre-half would try and place the kick with a side-footed shot. It might give Ben more of a chance. Instead he came in fast and true, and fair blasted the ball with tremendous force, high and slightly to the left of Ben, who got a fist to it and sent the white ball soaring high over his crossbar for a corner, which we survived. Then the final whistle blew.

The following morning the press was full of it. Harry Ditton wrote:

WONDER SAVE FOILS HENDON.

From every point of view the FA Amateur Cup semi-final at Arsenal Stadium was worth going a long way to see. It had everything — excitement and thrills galore, and academic skill which often left us spellbound in admiration ...

Alan Ross was also impressed:

Pegasus and Hendon, each of whom have reached the semi-final of the FA Amateur Cup for the first time in their history, drew yesterday in the drizzle and mud of Highbury. Despite the conditions, however, no one who saw the game will quickly forget it, or is likely to grudge the result.

The quality of the football on a treacherous surface was remarkable. Though Hendon were the stronger, more polished team a truly magnificent display by Brown in the Pegasus goal earned his side a replay. Not only did Brown bring off nearly a dozen brilliant saves but, in the closing minutes he put a penalty from Adams which, though not far wide, was going with great force, over the top...

Geoffrey Green wrote:

THE FINAL DRAMA

Only four minutes of life remained when all at once Dutchman, the mainspring of the Pegasus attack, sent Tanner away on a quick burst through the middle which ended with an infringement on the centre-forward and a free kick to Pegasus some 30 yards from the Hendon goal. Dutchman took it, slashing a low shot with all his power into a packed goalmouth. As it sped by, Tanner, with outstretched foot, got a touch to divert the ball into the far top corner past the helpless Ivey, and Pegasus, amidst a bedlam of noise, by some miracle were level.

But the last drop had yet to be squeezed from the afternoon. Two minutes from the end, Avis, in a quick Hendon riposte, was brought down by an unbalanced Pegasus defender as he dribbled his way cross the penalty area. Penalty. Brown faced Adams across twelve yards of mud and across an ocean of silence in which the beat of one's heart was like the jangling of an alarm clock. Adams moved to the kick and suddenly there was Brown twisting to turn a fast shot to his left, head high, away and over the bar. The world seemed to shift on its axis. Umbrellas waved and hats flew in the air or were pressed down about their owner's ears. And when soon the final whistle brought blessed relief Brown and Adams were seen to shake hands and seal a moment that had been theirs alone.

HENDON — R. Ivey; P. Lynch, M. Lane; L. Topp, D. Adams, W. Fisher; J. Westmore, A. H. Phebey, R. Stroud, G. Hinshelwood, R. Avis.

PEGASUS — B. R. Brown; J. Maughan, R. Cowan; J. Platt, K. A. Shearwood, D. F. Saunders; H. J. Potts, J. A. Dutchman, J. D. P. Tanner, J. S. Laybourne, R. Sutcliffe.

We had a week's respite to gather our wits and consider how best we could strengthen the side to deal with Hendon in the replay the following Saturday at Selhurst Park.

The all-round ability of our opponents was abundantly clear. In attack Avis had been a thorn in our flesh and it was thought expedient to switch Johnny Maughan to left-back and let Ralph Cowan, such an accomplished player, look after Avis. Then there was the question of whether or not Tony Pawson's ankle was strong enough. It was touch and go but, in the end, he played. Donald Carr came in again at inside-left in place of Jack Laybourne who was preferred when the going was heavy, as at Highbury. With his accurate left foot Donald could find Tony Pawson with long cross-field passes from left to right. He wasn't as busy a player as Jack Laybourne, nor as strong, but I think at the time he possessed more guile for that particular position.

And so, with two new faces up front, Jimmy Potts left playing on the left and the switching of our two backs, Hendon now faced fresh problems and a different team, a fact which Tommy did not release to the press, only announcing the changes just before the kick-off.

We left our London hotel and drove by coach to Selhurst Park accompanied by several wives, Tommy and Graham, Vic Buckingham, Harvey Chadder and Jerry and, of course, Our Man with the Sponge, Leslie Laitt. Having eaten an early lunch of boiled chicken, we drove through the streets of London, listening on the radio to the rich voice of John Snagge recounting the 1951 Boat Race. Cambridge were in the lead and the going was very rough. Suddenly John Snagge's voice took on a new pitch of excitement. "My goodness, Oxford are in trouble, they're shipping a lot of water, I think they're sinking." Much cheering from the Cambridge contingent. "Yes they're sinking... the Oxford boat is sinking, the crew are sitting up to their waists in the water." More cheers. "They're swimming, the whole of the Oxford crew are now swimming, this is really quite extraordinary," and the rest of his words were drowned by the laughter and cheers of our five Cambridge players.

"I reckon Tommy suspects Doug Insole's hand in all this," said Jerry in my ear, as we drove on in high fettle towards Selhurst Park.

Unlike at Highbury, the main entrance to the Crystal Palace ground in 1951 was marred by a great ugly facade of corrugated iron and a huge bank of open terrace on the far side. To compensate, the day was fine and the ground conditions firm, quite different from the previous week, and I thought it would suit us better. Promptly at three o'clock we began the battle all over again, this time with a strong wind at our backs.

Immediately we saw how Hendon had countered our team changes by switching Stroud to outside-right, his international berth, in an attempt to exploit Johnny Maughan. Within six minutes, their move had succeeded and Stroud scored. Ten minutes later Tony Pawson equalised and at half-time we were still level, one apiece.

It was the bitter blow that struck us two minutes after the start of the second half that I found so demoralising. One of the Hendon forwards ran the ball well over our bye-line and cut it back to Avis who, spotting Ben Brown already moving out of his goal — unwisely anticipating a goal-kick — shot into our empty net. It seemed incredible that neither the referee, who was well up with the play nor the linesman, particularly, had seen that the ball had gone over, but these things can happen.

We didn't say anything; there was no point. We all felt plenty, particularly Jimmy Platt. The ball was already back in the middle. Ralph Cowan was exhorting us, calling for the ball and, coming forward to attack, committing the Hendon defence, before slipping the ball to Tony Pawson. Denis too, quite unruffled, kept collecting, pushing and prompting our left flank, forcing Pat Lynch and his men to play more and more defensively. But no goal came. 2-1 down and with just six minutes left we were still pressing desperately, but Geoffrey Green, in his last two paragraphs, can capture those final moments far better than I can:

> Two minutes after the change of ends Avis, dubiously retrieving the ball from the bye-line, put Hendon into the lead again with a long swirling shot into an unguarded net against a Pegasus defence that had relaxed and stopped, expecting the decision of a goal-kick. Hendon, with a sharp wind behind them, now seemed set for Wembley, and they would probably have won their place there, too, but for a great diving save by Brown to Avis, turning the winger's shot on to his post and away for a corner.
>
> But Pegasus now arose to touch the heights. Driven on by the unhurried Saunders and by Platt, the restless terrier, Dutchman and Carr sprayed their passes into

attack, left, right and centre. For half an hour they took complete control, but Hendon, with Adams outstanding, packed their defence solidly. For them the top of the hill was almost within reach when suddenly Pegasus with wings outstretched, soared past, away, and over the blue horizon. This was the stuff dreams are made of, and poor Hendon were left bowed before an intangible, irresistible force.

PEGASUS — B. R. Brown; R. Cowan, J. Maughan; J. Platt, K. A. Shearwood, D. F. Saunders; H. A. Pawson, J. A. Dutchman, J. D. P. Tanner, D. B. Carr, H. J. Potts.

HENDON — R. Ivey; P. Lynch, M. Lane; L. Topp, D. Adams, W. Fisher; J. Westmore, A. H. Phebey, R. Stroud, G. Hinshelwood, R. Avis.

Chapter 27

Wembley

"CHAMPAGNE for anyone who wants it back at 100 Piccadilly," announced Bush O'Callaghan, bursting into our changing-room like some swashbuckling pirate of the Caribbean.

Bush was a Harrovian and a man of considerable wealth. His chief occupation was horse-racing and he was determined to play a hundred cricket matches a season. He was short, stout, had a thick moustache, a great belly of a laugh and didn't give a damn. He invariably opened the batting and struck the ball ferociously, planting his left foot imperiously down the wicket. I once had the uncomfortable experience of being driven by him at a hundred miles an hour down Piccadilly in his Bentley.

He'd been a gunner in the 49th West Riding Division. During a break for rain whilst playing with him for the Frogs at Oxford in one of his many matches, I learned from our captain, Mike Singleton, how, on a certain nerve-wracking occasion in Normandy, he'd been shelled by Bush's battery and forced to take refuge beneath a wrecked German half-track that lay by the roadside.

However, Bush never denied his unofficial success in the liberation of the Benedictine monastery at Fécamp. And when the monks decided they'd sold just about enough bottles of Benedictine to him, he promptly rustled up a three-tonner full of sugar, a commodity the monks were very short of, and business proceeded at an even brisker pace than before.

Jim Swanton was amongst the gathering sipping a glass of champagne and I asked him if he was coming to Wembley.

"Couldn't possibly miss the opportunity of seeing you play there, Ken," he assured me.

"Give you a Dover sole if you beat the Bishops," said Ken Pitts, our fishmonger, the following day back at Woodstock.

"Are you coming?" I asked.

"We'll be there," he replied.

And so, it seemed, would the whole of Oxford and those who couldn't go would be watching the match on television or listening to it on the radio. Throughout the country there was an astonishing display of interest. As the final approached, the press began to make their forecasts.

Our opponents, Bishop Auckland, had beaten Evenwood, Shildon, Whitby Town, Walton and Hersham in a replay, and Bromley, and on the whole were thought to be the favourites. David Williams wrote:

> Their attack is probably the best in the country. This asset plus experience should be the winning factor.

Right: Tommy

*Below: 'Bush' O'Callaghan
and Biddie en route for
Wembley*

Harry Done, in the *Evening Standard*, also considered them the favourites:

Yet the majority of the 100,000 spectators will be hoping that Pegasus can spring the greatest surprise of their remarkable career. Pegasus have caught the imagination by their tremendous fighting spirit and victory for them would complete the most romantic story in amateur soccer. I expect Auckland to win, but if a replay is necessary it will take place at Middlesborough.

Harry Ditton, under the headline, 'THIS SOCCER SIDE HAS A MISSION, concluded:

Those with the best opportunities of judging the strength of the finalists believe the trophy will go North again. I will only suggest that it should be one of the greatest finals ever and, if Pegasus produce their top form and the 'Bishops' still prove their masters, then the North will deserve the cup.

Rather endearingly, Raymond Glendenning remarked:

Even if the Combined Universities side, Pegasus, don't beat Bishop Auckland at Wembley they will still be my football team of the year.

And under another headline, 'PROUD PEGASUS', someone had this to say:

Who would you name as the soccer team of the year — Spurs, Blackpool, Newcastle or Preston North End? Well, mine is Pegasus — the amateur club that has done more than your Arsenals, Aston Villas or Prestons to raise the prestige of the game.

General interest in the unexpected triumph of this three-year-old soccer baby is so great that there had been an increased rush on the tickets for the final against Bishop Auckland at Wembley on April 21st, and Stadium officials are already forecasting that the 93,000 record attendance for the Bromley-Romford clash the year before last will be broken. All seats have been sold out and only 2s. standing tickets remain. Bishop Auckland will face the battle knowing that the sympathy of the country outside of their own supporters will be behind the varsity men, because with the fading of the old Corinthians, soccer has become the poorer.

If Pegasus can lift the trophy, let us hope that there will be such a revival at Oxford and Cambridge that one day Pegasus will have a team to appear in the FA Cup Final.

Norman Ackland expressed a slight preference for Pegasus and I heeded, in particular, one of his sentences:

A lot depends on the ability of Shearwood to hold McIlvenny.

Dennis Roberts wrote:

Two amateur footballers, Denis Saunders and Harry McIlvenny, will shake hands before 100,000 people at Wembley Stadium on Saturday; then will begin an amateur match that could not be rivalled in interest anywhere in the world.

Geoffrey Green summed it all up in his long article beginning:

The meeting of Bishop Auckland and Pegasus at Wembley Stadium this afternoon clearly promises to be the most interesting FA Amateur Cup final for many years. The fact that a record crowd for an amateur match of 100,000 people, among them the visiting South African cricketers, will be gathered together in the stadium to see the game — every square inch of space has already been claimed — supports this.

Attack is Pegasus' true *métier*. Now they take their place on the national stage of Wembley without once having played on their home ground at Iffley Road, Oxford, and famous Bishop Auckland, for all their history and experience, will need to go to the final whistle no matter what the score.

We had a month to prepare for Wembley and began by playing a reserve side, which included Jimmy Platt and Johnny Maughan, against Cambridge Town away and lost 0-1.

The following week we lost again, 2-3, to Sutton United, on their ground, with eight of the side that had played against Hendon. Sutton's winning goal came from a free kick hit through our badly lined-up wall, giving Colin Weir — Ben Brown was playing for England against Scotland at Hampden Park — no chance.

I was driven to the game in Leslie Laitt's car, with Tommy sitting in the front, Denis, Donald, and myself at the back. Leslie owned a Morris Oxford, registration number FLO, which he nicknamed Flossie and tended with loving pride and care. Overhead it was drizzling steadily.

"Take the next left turn, Laitt... No, left," said Tommy. "Never mind. Go on and take the next one."

The traffic was heavy, cars hemming us in on either side.

"Now," said Tommy, "you can pull over to the left. Now. Quick, man. You're too late."

"I couldn't get in!" explained Leslie.

"You can now — look out!"

The bus in front had stopped suddenly and, braking sharply, we skidded along the tram-lines straight into its backside.

"God," said Leslie.

"Get over to the left and you can take this one coming up," said Tommy, as the traffic began moving again, oblivious of the incident.

"It's a one-way street," said Leslie desperately.

"Then take the next," said Tommy irritably. "If you don't get a move on, Laitt, we shan't make the kick-off."

We did however — just.

"Never mind, Les," said Denis, as we surveyed the damage, "it could have been worse."

"A fat lot he cares," said Our Man with the Sponge, looking disconsolately at the back of Tommy, who was fast making tracks towards the main stand.

On the Saturday before the final we defeated Moor Green 2-1 with what was to be the Wembley side, except that Colin Weir kept goal in place of Ben Brown, who had a damaged thumb.

Finally, with three days remaining, we played an hour's practice against the First Division leaders, Spurs, out on their training ground at Cheshunt. Once again, Colin Weir had to deputise for Ben Brown, while Roy Sutcliffe came in for John Tanner and promptly scored within thirty seconds. But at the end we were 3-1 down which wasn't bad, considering they had eight of their regular side playing. Observing Alf Ramsey at right-back I could see what Vic meant. He was slow all right, but his telling use of the ball and positional sense could not be faulted.

So, barring last-minute accidents, the final side was selected, the same as that which had defeated Hendon. Eight players were from Oxford, three from Cambridge. Seven came from grammar schools, four from public schools. All except two, John Tanner and Tony Pawson, were still in residence.

Looking back on it now, I believe our strength lay in a blend of maturity, ability, intelligence and humour. Several of us had been through the war and seen active service. Most of us had done other things before going to university. Our average age was on the high side, Tony Pawson, John Tanner and I were all on thirty. When things had gone badly and we found ourselves up against it, these extra years of experience had already proved a valuable asset.

Our ability, too, had been recognised because we could now boast four internationals, and it looked as though there would be more to come.

With a doctor of philosophy in goal, a couple of near firsts on each wing, not to mention two third-class bachelors of arts at centre-forward and centre-half, Vic Buckingham could afford his comment to the press, "I can reach their feet through their minds."

Finally, there was the humour of it all. Tommy with that perpetual bee in his bonnet that the club was being sabotaged. Leslie Laitt, "I'm not going to be spoken to like that", refusing to treat Ralph Cowan and retiring from the mud-bath of Highbury in high dudgeon because, in the heat of battle, we'd reprimanded him for examining our right-back's leg, when it was really his arm that was in question.

All this and a lot more produced a blend, sufficiently strong and resilient, upon which I always felt we could draw when the chips were down and the going tough.

On Friday afternoon we paid a visit to Wembley and looked at the pitch. It was in beautiful condition. As we wandered over the immaculate turf, the Bishops arrived to do the same. We didn't make contact but I've no doubt each of us cast an appraising eye at the other. We could spot Bob Hardisty's balding head, but I wasn't sure which was Harry McIlvenny. There'd be plenty of time to make his acquaintance the following afternoon.

We spent that night, Biddie and I, at 100 Piccadilly, Bush's flat, and a strange thing happened in the morning. We were looking at our host's fine collection of bird photographs, when a barrel-organ which had been playing outside suddenly broke into the Eton Boating Song. Was it an augury?

While Bush looked after four of our wives, the team lunched together and then set off by coach for Wembley. Tommy, cigar in mouth, was in expansive mood, while Vic Buckingham, brown trilby set jauntily and coat flung characteristically across his

Left:: Vic Buckingham

Below: Oxford 0 Cambridge 0

shoulders, was full of relaxed confidence. When the great twin towers eventually came into view, I think it all set us thinking. But not for long because, true to form, we immediately lost our way and ended up in a builder's yard at the back of the stadium, with Leslie sitting in the front directing operations and Tommy momentarily concerned lest it be some last-minute piece of sabotage. So we finally made it to Wembley, the great doors opened and we drove right in.

The changing-room, with its long narrow windows, spacious and light but strangely impersonal, lacked the friendly atmosphere of Highbury or White Hart Lane. We had plenty of time to change. Our kit, which Leslie had already begun to put out, was new, our white shirts carrying the bold insignia of a light blue horse flying against a dark blue background. There were hundreds of telegrams to greet us. I personally received twenty-three which included five from former colleagues in Mediterranean landing-craft, one from the Gorran Cricket Club, and one from the Mevagissey Football Club. A great wealth of goodwill seemed to surround us.

I did not feel nervous any more about this game. Perhaps, if anything, less than before. After all, we had arrived and were nearly at the end of the race. It's those early matches that are so often the more nerve-wracking, when drawn away on a small and hostile ground against an unfashionable, but competent, side that had fought its way through the early qualifying rounds. Then, things sometimes go wrong and Wembley can seem a thousand miles distant. But now the stage was set, the sun shining, a great crowd gathering. This was what we had been playing for, this was what Tommy had planned and hoped for. There was nothing to fear, everything to enjoy. We were prepared and ready for the final test.

"Listen now," said Vic quietly, holding up his hands as though giving us his blessing, "you each want the ball, every man jack of you, so be prepared to have it and take responsibility, right from the start. All right?" He looked at us quizzically for a moment, still completely relaxed. "Good luck, then," and we went out into the tunnel, lined up alongside Bishop Auckland and waited for Tommy and the FA officials to lead us out. We could hear the band playing and the crowd singing and then we were off and walking side by side with our opponents up the slight gradient of the tunnel out into the sunlit stadium — and what a sight and sound greeted us both.

There is plenty of time as one walks out and lines up yet again to see and savour it all and I had a good look round at that vast Wembley crowd before shaking hands with Lord Wigram, the official guest. There was also time for a few last-moment thoughts of what lay ahead.

We were well aware of the threat Bob Hardisty constituted and had made our plans to contain him. We decided to let him come and not bring Donald Carr back specifically to play defensively. Then, after gaining possession, we'd quickly exploit the gap behind and find Donald. Otherwise, we'd continue to play just as before, with the accent on simplicity and speed, adopting Arthur Rowe's maxim, "Make it simple, make it quick", endeavouring always when possible to give the early ball and not give it away.

We knew, too, that if we supplied our forwards we had three who could take on the opposition and beat them: Tony Pawson and John Tanner by sheer speed, Jimmy Potts, more by guile than speed. At inside-forward, Donald Carr and John Dutchman could both open the game up. They had shooting power too. In the middle Denis would quietly take control and set things going, while Jimmy Platt, small, neat and explosive, would never be out of the game for a second. Ralph Cowan, at right-back, was adept at turning defence into attack, linking with Tony Pawson, often receiving the ball back, then looking up and finding John Tanner or pinpointing a long cross. On the left, Johnny Maughan, very quick into the tackle, could match any winger for speed. Finally there was Ben, who never called, never spoke, and never got ruffled; it was just not in his nature. We understood each other. He knew what I was going to do, though some might dispute this. I knew what he was going to do. If I could protect him from the centre-forward I would. If he could help me, he did — with quiet and graceful efficiency. I felt a great confidence in having such players around me.

Now the ball was in the centre, the clock showing three, the curtain lifting. Then the whistle blew and the game began.

Of that Amateur Cup Final I recall little. Only the last dying moments stand out with any clarity. Ben, in conceding a corner, had collided with an upright and suffered a severe cut above his left eye.

"That needs stitching," said Vic Buckingham, who had run on and was examining Ben's eye.

"Come on, Vic," urged Arthur Ellis, who was to become such a world-famous referee.

"Anyone would think it was a Cup-Final," retorted Vic, sticking a piece of plaster over Ben's eye.

"And isn't it?" said Arthur, as Vic retired behind the goal to squat amongst the photographers and watch as we faced that final corner.

It was the Bishops' last chance and well they knew it, as they came swarming into our penalty area, putting us under great pressure.

I stuck close to McIlvenny, but could sense the lurking menace of Hardisty lying deep outside the far post, waiting to come in over our backs, timing his run in one last desperate endeavour to head an equaliser. But Denis was there too.

And then the ball came across, a soaring out-swinger, and up we all went, the danger lifted and, as we broke from the penalty area, the final whistle blew.

Two policemen were chasing a frantic red-faced figure who was striving to reach us, gripping an orange in each hand, waving his arms and shouting in delirious incoherence. But Chedder Wilson, most loyal of Pegasus supporters, did not, on this occasion, escape the arms of the law and was firmly but cheerfully deposited back whence he'd come.

We climbed up the steps to receive the Cup and our gold medals. I was surprised at how low the ledge was that protected us from a twenty-foot drop. It struck me at the time how easy it would be to topple over. And then we went down onto the pitch again and were photographed with Denis seated on somebody's shoulders. I had another good long look round at it, savouring a moment I thought I would not see again. When eventually we left the pitch it was still a perfect afternoon.

Back in our changing-room there was a popping of corks, a lot of people and a lot of chatter with Tommy ecstatic, Jerry, leaning on his stick, peering delightedly through his dark glasses, Graham Doggart and Harvey Chadder quietly going round congratulating everybody, Vic joking, Ben having his eye attended to, but not by Leslie who was busy, hat upon head, collecting up our gear.

We climbed into the bus, the doors of Wembley swung open and we drove with the cup through the thinning crowds back to the Great Western Hotel where we bought the *Evening News* with its headline: PEGASUS WIN TITANIC AMATEUR CUP. Then we changed into evening dress and went on with our wives and girlfriends to the Mayfair Hotel for dinner and dancing.

I felt in great form — we all did. A waiter hovered in the wings.

"A drink, sir?"

"Yes," I said, "that would be nice. We'll have forty-eight sherries."

"Forty-eight sherries, sir?"

"That's right."

"Very good, sir. Sweet or dry?"

"Better make 'em half and half."

"Very good, sir. And shall I credit them to your account?"

"I think probably not. Pegasus Football Club would be the better bet."

"Very good, sir."

It sort of set things going.

Geoffrey Green proposed the toast of the club with the Cup gleaming in the centre of the top table. Amongst the many nice things he had to say was a warning that we were about to face our most difficult time, keeping on top.

The following morning, such was my vanity, I bought every paper I could lay my hands on and revelled in the tremendous press we received. It was quite astonishing.

Great black headlines in the national papers greeted us: '
WONDERFUL PEGASUS, I SALUTE THEM ALL' — 'PROUD PEGASUS REVIVE PAST GLORIES' — 'MODERN CORINTHIANS SERVE UP CHAMPAGNE AT WEMBLEY' — 'PEGASUS SHOWED THE SPURS TOUCH' — 'THRILLING AMATEUR CUP FINAL VICTORY' — 'PEGASUS AMATEURS MADE LEAGUE STARS LOOK LAZY' — 'THE BEST THING THAT'S HAPPENED IN SPORT FOR YEARS', while the whole of the back page of the *Sunday Graphic* told the story in pictures. So it went on.

Geoffrey Green had this to say:

The FA Amateur Cup found a new resting-place on Saturday when a record crowd for the final of the competition, 100,000 strong, saw Pegasus gain a great victory over famous Bishop Auckland by two goals to one at Wembley Stadium. The trophy forthwith goes into residence, *in statu pupillari*, at the very heart of the Universities of Oxford and Cambridge, and in so doing has perhaps satisfied the desires of a sentimental majority.

The story, in fact, moved towards its finale on the sunlit and shaded stage of Wembley with a balanced and measured tread. In retrospect it would seem somehow to have been inevitable. This was but the last drawing together of the stray ends, the process of tidying up to provide a rational climax to all the emotional upheaval amidst the mud and the rain of earlier passages. Pegasus, without having to draw fully upon their resources of spirit and will, by their technical skill alone strode to a wider victory than the score will ever reflect.

BISHOP AUCKLAND — W.N. White; D. Marshall, L.T. Farrer; J.R.E. Hardisty, R.W. Davison, J.Nimmins; J.W.R. Taylor, W. Anderson, H.J. McIlvenny (Captain), K. Williamson, B. Edwards.

PEGASUS — B.R. Brown; R. Cowan, J. Maughan; J. Platt, K. A. Shearwood, D.F. Saunders (Captain); H.A. Pawson, J.A. Dutchman, J.D.P. Tanner, D.B. Carr, H.J. Potts.

Then Biddie and I returned to Woodstock where, on Monday morning, I collected my Dover sole from Pitts, the fishmonger.

Chapter 28

End of the one-year rule

OUR LAST TERM at Oxford began with an early cricket match in the Parks which was brought to a sudden close by a fierce hailstorm that drove all before it, whitening the ground in seconds.

A month later there was no such relief from a match of immense tedium played against Notts beneath a cloudless sky and burning sun. Oxford made a big score in their first innings, and then Nottingham decided they'd have some batting practice for the remaining day and a half and began with an opening stand of 284. For most of that day few balls passed the bat as Simpson headed towards his double century, yet each ball had to be concentrated on and studiously covered. Eventually, his partner, Giles, misjudged his shot and got a touch. Fortunately my gloves were in the right position and I caught him standing up.

Denis Hendren and Frank Chester umpired the game. Towards the end, Denis, at square leg, removed his handkerchief and dabbed his eyes, at the same time glancing across at his illustrious and rather formidable colleague, Frank Chester, at the bowler's end, causing him to shake with laughter. When the last over began and the Oxford field was scattered to the far corners of the earth, the scoreboard read 578 for 7. And, just to liven up proceedings still further, Charlie Harris, who had scored 66, carefully took guard twice.

I suppose my real priority should have been to work hard for the examinations that were coming up for my Diploma in Education. I had a thesis to write, something about the purpose of education which I managed to complete with the aid of Colin Weir. But I simply couldn't take the examinations seriously. Colin had also been instrumental in getting me a teaching post at Lancing College.

I had, some months previously, gone down to Lancing for an interview with the headmaster, Frank Doherty, and been offered a job.

"Well," the head said, drawing heavily on his cigarette and inhaling deeply. He always used a holder and I never saw a cigarette smoked faster. "I've got no room for you on my staff ... but, er ... I'm going to have you. You can teach maths? To the bottom form, of course," he added, seeing my hesitation.

"Oh yes, I think I could manage that."

"And you'll take over the cricket from Colin? Well then, that's settled. We shall look forward to seeing you in September."

Our biggest problem now was selling Laburnum House and finding accommodation in Lancing because the school could not help us over this.

So we advertised our house in the *Oxford Mail* and *Oxford Times*. Eventually, having shown round an assortment of people, on each occasion hurriedly stuffing everything out of sight yet suffering such comments as, 'How nice it could look', we sold the old house for what we had given for it and with much regret.

One June day I set off for Sussex with Jerry Weinstein to see if we could find a new abode. I had arranged to pick Jerry up at seven in the morning.

"Don't be late," I warned.

"Am I ever late?" he replied.

The following morning, on the dot of seven, I called for him and found him still dressing.

"Bloody hell, Jerry, I thought you were never late."

"Go and buy a *Times*," he retorted, "I'll be with you in a minute," and I did as I was bidden.

Now a 1936 Ford Eight was never a particularly spacious vehicle and by the time Jerry had opened his *Times* and begun reading, half covering me and the steering wheel in the process, there wasn't much room for driving. When he eventually emerged from behind his paper I saw that he had not shaved and quickly resolved that it would be better not to show him the school this time, a resolution which was promptly scotched by his next observation, "A small public school of ecclesiastical temper on the South Downs, I believe Evelyn Waugh described it in *Decline and Fall*. Well, I'm much looking forward to seeing it."

"I doubt if we'll have time, Jerry."

"We'll bloody well make time, mate."

To which I made no reply, but smiled and drove on towards Lancing and the south coast.

It was the thought we would once more be living by the sea that made the prospect of teaching at Lancing such a pleasant one.

The day was bright and sunny, the white clouds drifting lazily overhead, as we drove through Henley-on-Thames, out of Oxfordshire, on through Surrey and into Sussex, until we saw the South Downs ahead and spotted a signpost to Brighton. Threading our way through the town we reached the sea, turned right at the first pier, motored six miles along the front to Shoreham, until we finally came to the old wooden tollbridge spanning the Adur. The tide was well up, the river at its widest, sweeping in broad curves up the valley towards Steyning.

We paid the sixpenny toll and drove across the bridge, before us, perched on a spur of the Downs, the great chapel and school buildings dominating the scene.

"Some small ecclesiastical building!" observed Jerry dryly, peering through the windscreen. I could see he was impressed.

We visited an estate agent in Lancing and were shown several properties. One I fell for immediately, a pleasant, small bungalow, at the top of a hill, close to the Downs and close, but not too close, to the college. I liked particularly the sitting-room, which was half-panelled in oak and had a low latticed bay window, with an uninterrupted distant view of the sea.

This is the one, I thought, as I drove back to the agent's office where I paid a deposit. The bungalow cost three thousand pounds, exactly the amount we had paid and received for Laburnum House.

"Now," said Jerry, as we set off once more, "we'll go and have a look at the school and meet your future employees."

"Yes," I said, with some hesitation, glancing at his unshaven visage, "I suppose it's sensible now we're down here."

Parking the car at the top of the drive beneath the dining hall, we walked towards the broad flight of steps by the side of the headmaster's study and, precisely at that moment, he chose to appear.

"The head," I murmured to Jerry, unsuccessfully hoping Frank Doherty would not see us. But he did, and recognised me.

"Hello," he said, stopping.

"Hello," I replied, as we approached him. "Just come down to find somewhere to live ... May I introduce Jerry Weinstein," adding as an afterthought, I can't think why, "Jerry's my legal adviser."

"Hello," said Frank Doherty, a little curiously, I thought, while Jerry, shifting his stick to his left hand and, with a fearful unshaven leer, peered lopsidedly at the headmaster through his dark glasses at the same time shaking his hand.

We ran into Colin Weir who took us up for a cup of tea in the common room. Opposite me someone was reading *The Times*. Suddenly I was aware of being watched and, looking up, caught sight of pale blue eyes before the paper shifted sideways again.

"Who was that behind the paper?" I asked Colin when he saw us off.

"That was the Reverend Henry Thorold, our assistant chaplain."

"Ah," I said. "He seems inquisitive."

"Yes," said Colin, "Henry doesn't miss much." With that we set off back to Oxford.

It was well past midnight when I got back to Woodstock and opened the door of Laburnum House, to be met by Kim and Biddie, who had heard the car and come down in her dressing-gown.

"How did you get on?" she asked, smiling, her manner quiet and gentle as always. "Did you manage to find somewhere?"

"Yes," I said and over a cup of tea I told her about the bungalow and showed her the agent's pictures and details.

"Looks nice," she said, "but I shall miss this old house."

"I think you'll like 'Clovelly'," I assured her, "and we can see the sea."

We drank our tea and got up to go to bed. Faintly, I caught the sound of a distant lorry approaching from the north, heard it change gear and start the slow climb, till it reached the top of the hill, where it changed gear once more and, gathering speed, drove past our front door and on through Woodstock.

In June, the Cup side played a cricket match against Cowley Works on their ground. I was batting in a net when Graham Doggart, the treasurer of Pegasus as well as president of the Corinthian-Casuals, approached the side of the net. "How easily you play games, Ken," he said quietly, a remark that gave me much pleasure.

"By the way," he went on, "there's a small matter of forty-eight sherries that seems to be unaccounted for."

"Ah," I said, "I remember." We arrived at a very fair compromise.

More important by far than those forty-eight sherries was a meeting held the previous day at St John's, Oxford. It was an occasion when views were aired on the future of Pegasus — Tommy's in particular. Throwing his cards on the table for all to see and have minuted, he made it clear that, despite the enormous public support and interest now shown throughout the country in Pegasus, the current difficulties and problems with the Corinthian-Casuals over the interpretation of the one-year rule still existed and needed to be resolved.

I caught Denis's eye and we could not help smiling as Tommy, casting an occasional glance at our treasurer, talked seriously about sabotage within the club, his voice measured and deliberate, analytically presenting his views, breaking it down, spelling it all out as if we were attending one of his lectures on infra-red spectroscopy in structural diagnosis. The fact that Graham Doggart now had a foot in both camps, Tommy maintained, was proving detrimental to Pegasus.

Graham replied quietly, but firmly, that in no sense had he ever acted against the interests of Pegasus and disliked the suggestion of sabotage.

Matters were drawing to a climax. A revised version of the club's rules was drawn up for submission to the committee and, through the latter, to an extraordinary general meeting of the club to be held in October.

In fact that meeting never took place. Graham Doggart had contracted a serious illness and was no longer able to continue as our treasurer. At the annual general meeting, held at the Public Schools Club, on December 8, 1951, the revised rules were presented and accepted, twenty-nine members voting for and none against. All members in future were now eligible to play for Pegasus. The one-year rule no longer existed. It was a turning-point in the club's short history.

Two other matters were agreed upon, over which there was no dispute. Vic Buckingham, our splendid coach, was to be presented with a dispatch case — I like to think it was made of leather — as a token of gratitude for all his help, and Leslie Laitt given an honorarium of ten guineas. If nothing else, we were truly an amateur club.

So the summer term wound down and our time at Oxford came to an end. I had sat the examination for a Diploma in Education. I am not sure to this day whether I passed or failed, I rather think the latter. But I had got through the practical side of the course, teaching in Woodstock's secondary modern school. The headmaster, Percy Thompson, bless him, had seen to that and assured me I had nothing to worry about. "Aye, you'll make a good teacher, Ken," were his parting words.

All that remained now was to bid farewell to our friends in Woodstock. Finally, closing the front door of Laburnum House for the last time, we set off for Lancing.

Lancing

Chapter 29

Lancing

I BELIEVE in Providence, I always have, though it sometimes seems to be an irrational conviction.

I was never cut out to be a fisherman and I was certainly never cut out to be a schoolmaster, nor ever had I any particular intention of becoming one; yet, here I was back once more at Lancing.

Throughout my schooldays I was little more than a cheerful nuisance — my last lesson at Shrewsbury I spent sitting at the back of the form dressed as a parson with a dog collar — until the master could stand it no longer and drove me from the room. Always occupying humble positions in lowly forms — the mark system ensured that all failures and successes are well labelled and known to all — gave me, perhaps, one advantage, an instinctive sympathy for the academic underdog and an awareness that encouragement is a schoolmaster's most precious gift, something that never seemed to come my way, though I've no doubt that was largely my own fault.

I was down to teach History, English and Maths. The first two subjects I could cope with, but Maths was going to prove a problem, particularly geometry. So I rang Blackwell's in Oxford to enquire whether, by any chance, they had a 'Key' to all the geometrical riders in Durell, the book I was to use.

They hadn't, a voice said, but they could get me one.

"Would you do that, please, and get it off to me as soon as possible? I'm in dire need of it."

"Who shall we send it to?"

"Ken Shearwood, Lancing College, Sussex."

"The Pegasus centre-half?"

"Yes."

"I watched all your matches, sir."

"You did?"

"I certainly did. Great they were. Are you going to continue playing?"

"I hope to — if the headmaster will allow it."

"You must persuade him, sir. At any rate, I'll get this sent off to you as soon as possible," and I thanked him.

I managed to postpone the teaching of geometry for three whole weeks, concentrating on arithmetic and algebra, often getting stuck, but learning on the way.

Right in the middle of the front row was a 'know-all', who was, in due course, to become a doctor.

"When are we going to start doing some geometry, sir?" he would ask with regularity.

"All in good time," I'd reply, for the book with the answers had still not arrived.

At last it came and we embarked on a week of geometry, starting at the beginning and, for a while, know-all seemed satisfied. And then he suddenly fired a broadside at me.

"Can you do any question in this book, sir?"

"I wouldn't be teaching you if I couldn't," I replied dismissively, hoping this would shut him up.

"Can you do this one, number six, on page one hundred and eighty?"

"Of course, but you wouldn't understand it. You'll probably none of you ever get as far on as that while you're here." They waited expectantly. My desk was well above their heads so they couldn't see my small flat book, which held the solution to my troubles.

For a few seconds I put on a studious frown as though working it out, whilst discreetly finding the answer to the problem on page one hundred and eighty. Then, with as much nonchalance as I could muster I turned towards the blackboard and began to write it out. It was as meaningless to me as it was to them, but know-all seemed satisfied, at least for the time being.

But gradually I grew a little too confident, with that small book tucked up my sleeve, so to speak, and would take a problem which I hadn't prepared beforehand and, looking up the answer begin to write it out on the blackboard. I did this on one occasion and, when asked to explain part of the solution by know-all, found I was unable to do so.

"You can't understand it?" I said, looking at them with feigned astonishment.

"No, sir," said know-all of the front row, grinning delightedly, "we can't, sir. Can you?"

"Of course," I said, laughing. "Look here, I'm not going to do everything for you. I've written the blasted solution out on the blackboard. It's quite clear. You've got some preparation for me tonight," — at Lancing it's called Evening School — "you can use your brains for a change and work it out for yourselves. It'll do you good."

Later that night, over several glasses of sherry down at the Sussex Pad, the late Parnell Smith clarified the solution for me, not for the first time. A Cambridge mathematician in his late sixties and a veteran of schoolmastering, Parnell was very small, wore stout black boots, once commanded the Corps at Lancing, stood as a Liberal candidate, saving his deposit, and played a more than shrewd hand of bridge. He smoked innumerable cigarettes using a long holder and his hand shook so badly that his straight line drawn between two points on the blackboard was famous. He had kindness, a fine command of the English language and, despite experiencing more than his fair share of sadness, possessed a splendid sense of humour. He told me stories about the school, particularly of his time under the late headmaster, Cuthbert Blackeston, who was forced to leave. A huge scholarly man, he had been a housemaster at Eton and was known as 'The Blacker'.

"He'd break wind a lot," Parnell would reminisce, "and I remember once passing him in the lower quad carrying a number of toilet rolls in his cassock which he held before him as though it were an apron. 'Parnell', he said, 'this is a damnable disgrace.'"

Apparently, he had that morning received a letter from a parent complaining that their son's behind had been singed. Promptly flying into one of his uncontrollable rages he had begun a searching investigation which soon revealed the source of the complaint. In the old 'groves' — lavatories — at Lancing, there was no individual flushing system, but disposal was by means of a trough running beneath each pan. A group of boys had lit some paper boats — miniature fire-ships — and set them on course to float down the trough, their flames damaging those seated about their morning business.

On another occasion The Blacker assembled the whole school and staff and, with shaking head and quivering jowls, thundered forth, "Your private parts are sacred. I will not have you meddling with them."

Parnell's close colleague, Putt, short for Puttock, another Cambridge mathematician, also well turned sixty, would also come to my help. He'd been a boy at the school and only had the use of one arm. Apart from his time at Cambridge, he had spent most of his life at Lancing and, despite his disability, rolled his own cigarettes, played a good game of tennis and had represented the school at cricket. He would polish off *The Times* crossword and was a stickler for punctuality.

The school was peculiar in that it had a resident doctor — Gordon Crisp — who lived on the premises and was dedicated to the place. He had to be, for he was paid a pittance. He was a big, warm-hearted man with an ugly, rather jaundiced face. He hated all cant and was something of an authority on ancient civilisations. He once gave Patrick Halsey, housemaster of Fields, an old Etonian, an injection which took such effect that, by the middle of the morning, his vision was blurred and he could hardly move.

"Well, Patrick," said Gordon, studying the stricken housemaster. He had a loud, emphatic way of speaking. "It's quite clear what's happened; we've given you too damned much of the stuff. We'll know better next time."

The following day Patrick recovered. Gordon's patients always seemed to do so. One year several boys had their appendices removed, and so did Patrick Halsey. However, Patrick's operation, much to Gordon's delight, was performed in the school sanatorium which had its own operating theatre.

"The last thing I remember seeing as I went under," said Patrick, "was Gordon bending over my stomach and I had a horrible feeling that he was about to perform the operation himself."

It was an elderly common room and a friendly one and I liked my introduction to Lancing. The school had a relaxed atmosphere and the headmaster had the respect and liking of his staff. Common room meetings were blessedly short, and the headmaster would address everyone as Mister, though, on informal and private occasions, he would always use our Christian names.

We didn't see a great deal of him. He was usually in bed by ten. He'd had a difficult stewardship because the school was evacuated during the war to Ludlow and, not unnaturally, numbers had fallen. His immediate task was to get the place back on its feet again and he was succeeding. But it had taken its toll and he was tired now and ready for retirement.

Left: Sanderson's Memorial

Below left: Vanessa above Gorran Haven

Below right:
Paul and Vanessa in the
'Duckling'.

Yet, to see him about, one had little doubt that he was the headmaster because he walked with a measured and erect authority, his handsome face serious beneath a full head of iron-grey hair. In short, he was impressive, a man you would look at twice.

Tommy had written a detailed and informative letter to him about the purpose of Pegasus, ending with a request for me to be allowed to play for the club during the coming season. When I went to see Doherty about the matter he could not have been nicer. "Provided you make up the work you can certainly play." I noticed the ash on his cigarette lengthen as he drew heavily through the holder, inhaling deeply. "How's it all going?" he asked, looking at me steadily, his face rather too grey and heavily lined.

"Fine," I assured him.

Just as at the Woodstock school, when things became a trifle tedious in form, we'd get onto football and Pegasus.

"Did you win, sir?" they'd ask on Monday morning, and off we'd go. And towards the end of the week it would be a question of, "Who are you playing on Saturday, sir?" and we'd be off again. But, in the interim, we did some work and I never had another peep out of know-all.

Just as Geoffrey Green had predicted, it wasn't going to be easy keeping on top. We lost our first game of the season 4-5 playing with a certain frivolous ease.

"Shall I take it with my left foot or my right?" I enquired of Denis before doing something about a free kick awarded to us just outside our penalty area.

"Oh, get on with it," said Denis, "and kick the bloody thing."

So I took it with my swinger. My left foot miscued abysmally and the ball found its way to the much surprised Leyton centre-forward who promptly shot and scored.

Ben Brown patiently retrieved the ball with an imperturbable smile, taking it all in his stride, as was his wont. Denis gave a wry grin, John Tanner looked, I thought, a trifle tight-lipped, while Tony Pawson chuckled his head off on the right wing. Fortunately I couldn't see Tommy.

In the Cup we were drawn away against Kingstonian, a London side, and the match was to be televised.

That our opponents should have won this cup-tie in the first twenty minutes there was no doubt, least of all in the minds of the Kingstonian players, in particular their centre-forward, Whing, who was to play for England. They hit the upright, they smacked the crossbar, they had us going all ways. We seemed to have no time to start things going. And then, right against the run of events, Peter May scored with his head, and then John Tanner scored, and scored again, and yet again and they were finished. Throughout most of the second half we were on top. But the breaks had been ours and frustrated Kingstonian lost their confidence and became desperate.

Towards the end I was shadowing one of their forwards closely, while concentrating on the play that was going on around the Kingstonian goalmouth, when I received a sudden back-heeled hack on the shins which, fortunately, struck my guard. I felt sorry for him and not in the least bit angry because I could well understand his feelings of frustration.

It was the same player — and on this occasion I did feel angry — who gave me a sharp shove in the back as I went up for a corner early on in the game, when Kingstonian were putting us through the mill, causing me to miss a ball that was clearly mine. They scored, but fortunately the referee, helped no doubt by my whoop of indignation, had spotted the incident. The television commentator, I learnt afterwards, had spotted it too.

So we got through that first round by four clear goals, a score that did not reflect how fortune had favoured us. We'd been forced to make three changes from the side which had played in the Cup Final. Miles Robinson, who had played cricket once for Sussex and claimed the wicket of Cyril Washbrook, took over the left-back position from Johnny Maughan, who was in the process of becoming ordained. Peter May filled the inside-right berth, since John Dutchman wished to play for the Casuals, and Roy Sutcliffe took Donald Carr's place at inside-left. Donald was vice-captain of the MCC which was touring in India and Pakistan.

Of the newcomers, Peter May, tall and gangly, took up intelligent positions and was good in the air. Roy Sutcliffe, who had played before, of course, was a direct runner, more suited to the flanks where he had some freedom and a measure of protection from the touchline. But I thought we missed the guile of Donald Carr and the all-round ability of John Dutchman.

Before we travelled north to play our next opponents, redoubtable Crook Town, we flew to Switzerland, taking with us our wives and our new coach, the England centre-half, Reg Flewin, captain of Portsmouth. We stayed at Lausanne and played two matches, against Schaffhausen and Malley.

Against the former — having first viewed the Falls of the Rhine — we lost 4-1 on a pitch that was icebound, a veritable skating rink. It was impossible for defenders to turn, and Schaffhausen, with their forwards moving early onto balls that were held judiciously before being laid in behind our defence, beat us comfortably.

After seeing the New Year in, followed by some training next morning and a tactical discussion in the evening, we defeated Malley 5-0 and with a splendid headline tucked under our belts — *'Brillante demonstration des champions d'Angleterre amateurs'* — flew back to England and promptly gave a very far from *brillante demonstration* against Wealdstone the week before the second round of the Amateur Cup.

We met on Friday afternoon at King's Cross station. Seats had been reserved for us. We all knew this was to be a hard one and for the last few days my mind had been full of it. Crook Town were of the same calibre as Bishop Auckland and Willington, competent and hard to beat — doubly so on their own ground. I caught sight of Guy and Helen Pawson, who were travelling up with us, and went across to talk to them. Jerry was leaning on his stick, talking to Denis. Tommy, of course, was looking worried. He had some cause to be. He caught our eye and came towards us, his overcoat turned up, his shoulders hunched, a faded Blue's scarf round his neck, brown trilby tilted, a cigarette in the corner of his mouth. "They're going to miss this train if they leave it much longer," he announced with grim certainty, shaking his head and coughing. The Cambridge contingent, Ralph Cowan, Peter May, Roy Sutcliffe and Jimmy Platt had failed to arrive. "They were told to be here..."

"It's all right, they're coming," said John Tanner, as Roy Sutcliffe came bursting through the ticket-barrier slightly ahead of the others.

"Got held up, Tommy," he explained bluntly, puffing and grinning.

"Well..."Tommy began, but there was no time to hear his further comment because the whistle was blowing, doors were banging and we climbed aboard. Very shortly the train began to move.

"Bridge?" enquired John.

"I'm not partnering Shearwood," announced Jerry.

"I suppose I'd better," said Tony.

And we got the cards out and began to play.

I always enjoy travelling to an away match. It tends to bind a side closer together. It certainly did in our case, because unless we were on tour, we were never together as a unit. The Oxford and Cambridge contingents trained separately, while Tony Pawson, John Tanner, Denis Saunders and I had to do our own training. We met once a week in the changing-room, and perhaps for a brief moment after the match. A long journey such as the present one gave us an opportunity to get to know each other better. We'd discuss everything under the sun, from the one-year rule to the splitting of the atom, for hadn't we two scientists in our midst, a legal mind, undergraduates past and present, even a couple of schoolmasters to toss ideas around? It was amusing and stimulating.

"Four hearts," called Tony.

"Double," said John.

"Redouble," said I.

"Bloody ridiculous," said Jerry.

Whereupon Tony made his call, which gave us the rubber, much to Jerry's annoyance.

"Who'll take penalties?" enquired Reg Flewin, just before we went out.

"I'll take 'em," said Roy, "I've never missed one."

So it was decreed.

Ten thousand watched us draw one-all with Crook Town on a ground that was wet and treacherous. They were a good side and got on with it right from the start, cutting out the frills, making direct sorties upon our goal, hitting the ball about, attacking us on the flanks, coming at us from all quarters. They scored their goal from an out-swinging well-met corner, fairly early on in the first half. John Tanner, who played very well indeed, got our equaliser. And then we were awarded a penalty well on in the second half, which Roy Sutcliffe took and hit — if he will forgive my saying so — unforgivably high over the crossbar.

"Thought you'd never missed a penalty, Roy," remarked Reg Flewin when we were once more back in the changing-room, the match over.

"That's right," said Roy, "I haven't. I've never taken one before."

It could be said to have cost us the match because in the replay at Oxford — Jack Laybourne replaced Peter May — we got knocked out on the university rugby ground before another ten thousand spectators by the only goal of the match and I felt very low.

"Sorry you lost, sir," they said on the Monday morning. "What went wrong?"

"Should have clinched it the first time," I suggested, and told them about the penalty incident.

But there were still plenty of matches to play, including one against Tottenham Hotspur Reserves which we won 3-1, and another for charity against Charlton Athletic which we lost 1-4. We were still in the AFA Cup and met Kingstonian for the second time that season in the final, on 5 May, at Griffin Park, home of Brentford Football Club. There we won by the only goal of the match.

The surface was bone hard, it was the back-end of the season and Kingstonian sought their revenge. They didn't get it, though at times they did 'play most foully for it'.

The season was over and cricket was upon us. Though we had not distinguished ourselves in the Amateur Cup this time, we'd won another, the Amateur Football Alliance Cup.

Reading through the minutes of a committee meeting held at St John's College, Oxford, on 29 March 1952, I discovered how much difficulty Tommy was having in raising suitable teams, since it had been stated at Cambridge that, in the Hilary term, in addition to the Michaelmas term, the claims of university matches should be placed before those of the Pegasus club. Before any commitments for 1952 were undertaken he wanted to know what our playing resources were likely to be. He mentioned that only two Falcons had joined the club during the present season.

At a later meeting of the committee in June, he pointed out that only one member of Cambridge University was present, Jimmy Platt. The committee recommended that Jerry Weinstein be made an assistant honorary secretary, Leslie Laitt be given his grant of ten guineas, and Reg Flewin an honorarium of twenty-one pounds.

Some of the minutes of those committee meetings highlight the innate difficulties Tommy faced in running Pegasus. Cambridge, by virtue of the fact that the seat of control remained in Oxford, may have felt isolated, but without their co-operation the club could never achieve its potential. Many clubs had invited us to play them and Tommy was rightly loath to put out weak sides. It was a very real problem and, behind it all, there lurked the feeling at Oxford that the Cambridge players were going to abide by the one-year rule. We had no concrete evidence but we had already lost John Dutchman from the cup-winning side and, earlier, Guy Shuttleworth, Hubert Doggart, Doug Insole and others. There seemed every likelihood that more would follow.

These problems apart, Tommy had his work to do. He was here, there and everywhere, lecturing, preparing lectures, popping over to America or Europe, attending meetings, then coming back and working in the laboratories till late into the night. Yet still he found time to cope with the running of the club.

He was immensely gifted, hard-working and efficient. And, being Tommy, he did not try to conceal the burden he carried on our behalf.

"You know, Denis," he once said dolefully, when travelling to an away match, "I think Pegasus is ruining my marriage."

"Oh, I don't know, Tommy," said Denis reassuringly.

"Well ... I don't think any of you fully appreciate the work that is involved."

But had we tried to lighten his load — not that we were ever really in a position to do so — he would not have wished it for, in his heart, he believed we were potentially the best amateur club in the country.

So he held on, calculating each step, informing us discreetly and sometimes not so discreetly, that there was more sabotage afoot for you-know-who, that he was not feeling very well and that he didn't know how he was ever going to carry on.

That he did, of course, was due entirely to one person, his wife, Penelope, who shared all his worries, intelligently putting them into perspective — she had a first-class mind — laughing off trivialities, welcoming us all. She kept him going, and she was as much a part of Pegasus as anyone.

My first summer term at Lancing I found delightful. The school, with the Downs rolling away westwards towards Chanctonbury at the back, and the sea glittering in the sunshine a mile distant on its southern flank, is magnificent. And it has the best of all worlds too, quick access to civilisation — Brighton, London, Worthing, Shoreham — yet stands solitary in its own flint kingdom up on a hill. No boy need wander far to house, form room, library, chapel or playing-field. The school-bell summoned us and in the summer months motor mowers cut green swathes down the quads, while masters and boys went about their business. Saint's days were frequent and welcome occurrences, for they meant a 'lie-in' for those who did not attend early Communion, and no first periods of teaching for the staff. For the more important saints, and there seemed an abundance of these that first summer at Lancing, we'd have a holiday from mid-morning.

Cricket was still the major summer game and school matches were watched by some of the staff sitting in deckchairs within the privacy of their own sheltered garden, a natural grassy little amphitheatre surrounded by rhododendrons up on the bank, As master in charge of cricket, I spent a lot of time up there watching the boys make fools or heroes of themselves, and listening to the comments of my colleagues. On one flank we were protected by the white wooden side of the school shop up which roses rambled towards low thatched eaves. Through an open window tea would be passed out to us. While we drank and chatted, wickets tumbled, batsmen came and went, until chapel summoned, evening shadows stole across the square, and stumps were drawn with the match resolved one way or the other, to the satisfaction of at least one of the masters in charge.

I played in two cricket matches for Pegasus that summer term, the first against Morris Motors, who did us proud though we beat them, the second against a Kent side at Penshurst Place, the home of the De Lyles, where the Pawsons lived in the king's wing.

There, Biddie and I spent the night with them, and very gracious it was too. I seem to recollect we won the match; we certainly didn't lose it. Indeed, I never remember our ever being beaten at cricket for, after all, we could, if need be, put out a side of county strength.

Abruptly the summer term came to a halt, the boys disappeared like a swarm of locusts and some of the life went out of the place.

Just before the term ended Frank Doherty offered us school accommodation which we really had to accept though, at the time, neither of us relished being too close to the school. Consequently the first part of the holiday was spent moving into our new abode with rather mixed feelings, for we liked our bungalow and we had barely paid for the curtains. However, we got on with the job and then set off once again for our old haunts in the West Country.

Chapter 30

Was it luck?

THERE WERE two new faces in the side which lost the opening match of the 1952-53 season against St Albans City 0-1, because Ralph Cowan and Jimmy Platt, abiding by the one-year rule, had decided to join the Casuals. Their positions were taken by two Cambridge players, Jerry Alexander and Reg Vowels.

A week later, watched by our new coach, George Ainsley of Leeds and England, we defeated Welwyn Garden City. Jack Laybourne replaced Ernest Tweddle, and Mike Pinner, a young cat-like goalkeeper from Cambridge with tremendous potential — he was to play more amateur internationals than any other goalkeeper in the country and eventually turn professional — deputised for Ben Brown.

Our new coach, George Ainsley, a Leeds United centre-forward, was a big, tall, fair-haired extrovert. We didn't attempt any new style of play, but continued as before to bring our wingers right back.

Of course we had a good knowledge of what we were trying to do, a number of us had now played together for some time. We knew each other's strengths and weaknesses. We practised no set-piece moves and didn't worry about them much. In retrospect our training was unimaginative compared with today, but we gave the game a great deal of thought and would discuss our problems in depth, gradually ironing out the difficulties. In that way we developed faith in the pattern of our play, which remained basically 'push and run' but which never, at any time, discouraged individual freedom of expression.

By the first round of the 1952-53 Amateur Cup we'd played ten matches, won five, drawn two, lost three and tried out thirty-three players, old and new.

We had one real set-to in November with the Chelsea reserves in a so-called 'friendly' at Oxford. We had a strong side out and were 4-2 up at half-time. Towards the end of the first half the Chelsea captain, Joe Willemse, marking Tony Pawson, who had already scored twice, got, as they say, well and truly stuck in.

I was marking Bobby Smith, who was to play at centre-forward for Spurs and England. He was physically immensely strong and for high balls down the middle, held me off with a back as broad as a barn door, so that by half-time I had not won a single ball in the air.

"Lie off him a bit," advised George Ainsley, "and come in with a run."

I did so, soon after the start of the second half. Sailing in high through the air, I won the ball but caught Bobby Smith in the small of the back and down he went, all thirteen and a half stone of him.

"Sorry," I said, and he gave me an old-fashioned look as he got to his feet.

"There's too much fucking sorry in this game, mate. I'm getting fucking stuck in."

"Not into me, I hope!" A plea that fell on deaf ears for, true to his word, the Chelsea centre-forward joined Willemse in what I can only describe as a battle, more bloody and infamous than any I ever experienced. Throughout the game the referee ran nervously to and fro, a fixed smile upon his face, seemingly oblivious of the outrageous fouls being perpetrated, not only now by Chelsea, I hasten to add. Eventually and, in near-desperation, he blew his final whistle and both sides withdrew, scarred but unvanquished, with the score standing at four apiece.

"I hear some of our lads had a bit of a set-to with yours the other day," Joe Meers, the Chelsea chairman, mentioned to Tommy the following week.

"Well ... I suppose you might call it something like that," replied Tommy dryly.

Two days after our 'friendly' with Chelsea, Tommy sent out a long circular in which he wrote:

> Our success at Hayes will put us in an extremely strong position, assure the success of our tour both as regards enjoyment and finance, whereas failure in the Cup would prejudice the whole future.
>
> I am sometimes accused of taking a too realistic view of the position; may I therefore for the last time draw your attention to some facts about Hayes. On the past three Saturdays they have:
>
> Won 6-0 against Redhill
>
> Won 5-0 against Clapton (away, Amateur Cup)
>
> Won 6-0 against Cambridge University
>
> They are stated never to have been beaten in the Cup at Hayes and, during the past seven years have in every season finished near the top of the Athenian League.

The circular did not mention one other ominous fact, that Hayes had convincingly defeated us the previous season on their own ground by four goals to one.

By 8 December the side was finally selected and it was decided that the Cambridge international, Jerry Alexander — he was to keep wicket for the West Indies — should play at right-back. There was some risk involved in that he had last played in that position in a floodlit match against the Wiltshire FA one night early in October. Since then he had been playing regularly at centre-half for Cambridge.

The forward line contained those same players who had played earlier against Welwyn Garden City, but it had been radically rearranged, Jack Laybourne moving to centre-forward, Roy Sutcliffe to outside-left and Bob Lunn to inside-right. Donald Carr and Tony Pawson retained their old positions at inside-left and right-wing. Ben Brown was in goal, of course, Gordon McKinna at left-back, and Denis, Reg Vowels and I made up the half-back line. Our reserves were Jimmy Crisp of Oxford, and Cyril Tyson of Cambridge.

The Times made this brief comment:

> Unlike their brothers, the Corinthian-Casuals, the Pegasus formation, which contains internationals in Brown, Saunders, Alexander, and Pawson, will be playing together for the first time this season. They will in effect be playing for time to develop an effective understanding.

We met for dinner at the Great Northern Hotel on Friday evening and later had a long tactics talk with George Ainsley, at which there was the usual constant flow of side-comment with nobody appearing to pay any attention at all. In fact, nothing that was being said was missed by anyone. It was part of our make-up, a light-hearted euphoria which prevailed during those rather tense hours before a match, which drew us closer together, concealing the seriousness of our intent, often deceiving our coaches, even Tommy at times.

It was raining the following morning, a miserable overcast day, when we set off for Church Road, the Hayes ground in Middlesex, to begin our fifth quest for the FA Amateur Cup.

"Can't think why we ever play games seriously," I confided to Tony as we bent down to put on our boots. I noticed his were far from clean. He took a perverse pride in their not being so and would show them to me with relish.

In a little over ninety minutes, always excepting a draw, one of us would have gone under. It needed only an early slip, an error of judgement, a missed open goal, a moment of panic to send us on our way. In the other changing-room Hayes would be experiencing all that we were going through. They'd be just as keyed up, just as keen to win, just as determined, just as fit and well prepared. What then would prove the ultimate factor in deciding our fate? Skill, style of play, strength — we had a big, powerful defence — speed, intelligence, captaincy, experience, character? All would play their part. But where would the edge lie?

I'm tempted to suggest that the key was somewhere between the last two factors. I felt sure, during those remaining nerve-wracking moments before going out, that we possessed sufficient character, common experience, determination and confidence in our corporate ability to withstand the inevitable moments of crisis and see us through. At any rate, our supporters seemed to think something of this kind for when we emerged they gave us a great welcome, dressed in their gowns and mortarboards, waving many a home-made banner of the Flying Horse. Then we were once more in the thick of it and the battle was on.

It was apparent immediately that everything Tommy had predicted about Hayes was correct. Right from the start we had our backs to the wall and, in the twenty-first minute, were a goal down. Twelve minutes later Hayes scored their second goal, a perfect header from a free kick, and almost immediately Gordon McKinna cleared off our goal-line with Ben well beaten.

Two goals down in an away cup-tie is not a particularly happy predicament for any side to find itself in at half-time. And there wasn't an awful lot we could do about it, apart from continuing to play football, do the things we believed in, and keep going to the end. I have no recollection of anything in particular being said when Denis took us out for the second half. As in that first match against Enfield, everything would depend upon what we could produce in the next forty-five minutes. It was up to us.

The light was very poor when we kicked off again, using a new white ball. Within a minute Jack Laybourne had been put away down the left wing and from his cross

Bob Lunn drove the ball into their net. From that moment on we pushed them back and their defence had a sore time of it trying to keep us out. But they did and the minutes ticked away alarmingly until there were only three of them left. And all the while the light was fading until it was difficult to see the length of the pitch.

I caught a glimpse of Tommy sitting on the touchline next to George Ainsley. He was leaning forward, hatless, elbows on knees, his fair head bent, looking dejectedly at the ground. In contrast, big George Ainsley was sitting bolt upright, staring intently at the play. A great noise was coming from the many hundreds of spectators. Our own supporters were doing their best, but the brave strains of their version of the Eton Boating Song were being swamped.

We were attacking again. The referee had already glanced at his watch and I wondered if the match would be abandoned. I hoped it would, it seemed our only chance. And still we pressed. I watched, isolated, from the halfway line, a helpless spectator as Roy Sutcliffe raced down the left wing and cut into the penalty area. He was going at top speed, right on target, when the ball and his feet were swept from under him and the whistle shrilled piercingly above the clamour. Vainly and desperately, Hayes protested, gesticulating against the referee, who remained a grim, statuesque figure, pointing at the penalty spot. Twice Donald Carr had to replace the ball on the spot and wait, for the Hayes players had now turned their full attention on him, and he was under great pressure. But Donald had a cool head for such occasions. Not for nothing had he played against the Australians in a Victory Test at Lords and walked out to face the bowling of Keith Miller. When eventually he took the kick, he did so with an easy rhythmic swing of his left foot, timing it to perfection, hitting the ball as though he were driving another four through the covers, giving the Hayes goalkeeper no chance whatsoever.

They were shocked and, before they had time to recover, Roy Sutcliffe scored again. Now, mortally stricken and, as though paralysed, they watched as Jack Laybourne took advantage of an unbelievably bad defensive move and popped in our fourth. As the ball was brought back and Hayes kicked off in those last dying seconds, Jack Rawlings, their veteran international, who had so nearly sunk us in that first-ever cup-tie against Enfield, turned his back on it all in bitter disgust and had already reached the touchline when the final whistle blew.

Was it luck, then, that had decided this match — good for us, bad for them? I think it would be difficult to deny that we had not been lucky. And yet nobody could say that it had been a bed of roses for us at half-time.

It is often remarked, and I'm inclined to agree, that barring injuries and the fallibility of referees, a team makes its own luck. There was certainly nothing lucky about the manner in which we had kept Hayes subjected to constant pressure throughout most of the second half, the product of which had been that last despairing tackle from behind.

Our good fortune lay in the fact that the referee had chosen not to award Hayes a penalty for a similar incident committed by one of our players in the first half.

334

There is a cruelty about such moments. Hayes had vanished. The air was now filled with shouts of 'Up the Pegs!' 'Good old Pegasus!' as our delighted supporters swarmed around us, oblivious of the home crowd filtering slowly away, turning its back upon a scene which, for them, had suddenly become as distasteful and sombre as the gloom of that bleak winter's evening.

Very shortly after Christmas we set off on a tour of the North, starting with a match against a Sheffield representative side at Bramall Lane, winning 8-1, six of the goals coming in the second half. Then we went on to Elland Road where we put paid to the Leeds and District FA 4-3, finally losing 1-3 before a packed crowd against our old foe, Bishop Auckland, their pitch covered in a thick carpet of snow. It was an excellent tour and our stay at the Royal Hotel, Scarborough, could not have been more pleasant. Tommy always saw to it that we did ourselves well on these occasions.

We knew little about our next opponents, Cockfield, except that they played in the Durham Central League and their centre-forward had been given a trial with Burnley. On the day, however, we knocked them out by five clear goals, conceding none. For the third time in five seasons, we became one of the last sixteen clubs left in the FA Amateur Cup.

On Monday morning a half-column report of our match appeared in *The Times* alongside Geoffrey Green's full-length column of the Corinthian-Casuals fine win against Finchley, and I quote his opening two paragraphs, for they are pertinent to the story:

> All good things have an end and Saturday saw the end of Finchley's great record. They had stood supreme since the season's beginning against all amateur opposition. But now for the first time in this sphere they met their masters in the Corinthian-Casuals, who gained a magnificent victory by four goals to one, before a record crowd of 10,000 people at the Oval and so reached the third round of the amateur Cup.
>
> The Corinthian-Casuals are now clearly a force to be reckoned with. Displaying all the fine qualities of attack and defence inherent in their illustrious hyphenated name, they held a distinct advantage in speed, determination in the tackle, and resilient spirit. Furthermore, by their clever blend of short and long passing, in which the point of attack was switched, they were the tactical masters who took their chances splendidly with the long game — much in the Arsenal manner. It was this ability to turn defence into counter-attack in economical moves that completely confounded a Finchley defence often caught on the wrong foot. With eight former Cambridge Blues in the Casuals' side, the shining occasion merely served to underline the revival of university football since the war.

"Well ..." Tommy confided to some of us over the weekend, looking his most gloomy, "they're now very much in the reckoning. I believe it would be utterly disastrous if we were to draw them in the next round," a pronouncement we thought perhaps a little excessive, though I've no doubt the Casuals had similar thoughts.

And, of course, as fate would have it we did draw them, slap bang out of the hat and, immediately I heard the news I got the shivers and the more I pondered it, the more shivers I got. In the middle of the week I received a cryptic typewritten postcard from Jerry, who was now at Corpus Christi, Cambridge, where he was to obtain a diploma in International Law:

```
You had better get a heavy lock for the Gladstone on the
7th. The bag will never need to be as tightly closed again as
on that day. See you Saturday. Love to Biddie, Paul, and Kim
```

Jerry was right. I'd be marking Hubert Doggart, a big, awkward and very determined customer. He'd not be easy to get into the bag. Because I knew most of their players, I at once began to play the match in mental anticipation, more as the occasion drew nearer.

Walthamstow Avenue, the holders, were still in the competition, having been held to a draw by the Athenian League champions, Wealdstone. On form, Walthamstow looked to be the most dangerous club left, for they were having a great run in the FA Cup. Drawn away against Manchester United in the fourth round, they drew one-all at Old Trafford and were the toast of the amateur game. But then the wheel of fortune turned full circle for them and they lost both their cup replays.

Generally, the London press seemed partial to the Corinthian-Casuals. Leslie Nichol of the *Express* concluded:

> One question the match will settle: Who are the present mid-century Corinthians — Pegasus or Corinthian-Casuals?

Already the game was a sell-out. The gate was limited to 12,000 to protect Surrey's cricketing interests, otherwise the Oval would have been filled.

It was strange running out and seeing at the end furthest from the great gasometer all those familiar faces. There was Johnny Dutchman moving about in that rolling professional gait, and Jimmy Platt rubbing his hands and glancing curiously in our direction. Ralph Cowan looked as classy and confident as ever. And there were all the others who had played for us: Doug Insole, Guy Shuttleworth, Hubert Doggart, Norman Kerruish, and Lionel Boardman, who was a registered player but had not played. All eight of them hailed from Cambridge; seven of us came from Oxford. It was almost another varsity match, except so much more was at stake.

Tommy had earlier remarked with characteristic bluntness to the Press: "This match should have been reserved for Wembley. The winners must play in the final."

Insole had been quoted as saying that Pegasus relied on the old men to ride the Flying Horse.

But there was no time for joking now. The gates had long been closed; the whistle had blown, and our task lay ahead; mine was to ensure that Hubert Doggart never received a ball without my closest and most destructive attention.

It proved a dire, uncompromising battle. Perhaps there were too many good players on both sides for any liberties to be taken. Perhaps we knew each other's play too well. Whatever it was, the game never quite reached the excellence that had been anticipated. I did not envy Tommy having to sit and sweat it out on the touchline for those ninety long minutes.

Afterwards, when the final whistle had blown and Hubert had gone into the bag for keeps, we sat weary and delighted in the dressing-room, while the poor old Casuals faced a weekend and more of gloom. "He played a blinder," Tommy was saying, "I thought Reg Vowels played an absolute blinder," and he shook his head in bewilderment, coughed loud and long and disappeared in the direction of the Casuals' camp.

He was right, of course. Reg Vowels had played well, very well indeed. But my man of the match was Denis, so cool and resourceful — and so thought Geoffrey Green who summed the match up in the opening paragraph of his *Times* report:

> There was only one really positive emotion that attended the clash of the Corinthian-Casuals and Pegasus in the third round of the FA Amateur Cup at the Oval on Saturday. It was that one of these brothers had to be left behind by the wayside. That Pegasus, the younger of them finally emerged victorious by one goal to none to reach the last eight of the competition for the third time in five years, was perhaps just about correct on the balance of chances. But all through a cold, sunlit afternoon one could sense the feeling of divided loyalties in a record crowd of twelve thousand strong, that lined the ancient enclosure.

He concluded:

> In the dying moments, Laybourne hit the crossbar from point-blank range, but it mattered little, for by then the pale sun had already gone down on the Casuals, and on all those who would wish to serve two masters.
>
> CORINTHIAN-CASUALS — D.J. Bunyan; R. Cowan, D.W. Newton; G.W. Shuttleworth, D.H. Eastland, J.F. Platt; N.Kerruish, D.J.Insole, G.H.G. Doggart, J.A. Dutchman, L.J.Boardman.
>
> PEGASUS — B.R. Brown; F.C.M. Alexander, G.H. McKinna; R.C. Vowels, K.A. Shearwood, D.F. Saunders; H.A. Pawson, D.B. Carr, J.S. Laybourne, R. Lunn, R. Sutcliffe.

Chapter 31

Wembley again

ROY SUTCLIFFE and John Tanner saw us through into the Amateur Cup semi-final of 1953 with a goal each in the second half, when we defeated Slough Town once again on their ground, the Dolphin Stadium, before a capacity crowd of 9,000. We had the same side out that had played against the Casuals, with the exception of John Tanner who displaced Jack Laybourne, the Cambridge player, a controversial decision and one taken only after a great deal of thought.

The selection of our sides — particularly the cup ones — had never proved easy right from the start, for however unbiased the selectors tried to be, they had always to contend with a natural and understandable dichotomy within our ranks, brought about by the very nature of our make-up, and irrespective of the one-year rule.

Our selection committee consisted of the president, three representatives from each university, one of whom was to be the captain of the university at the start of the current season, and two others to be elected annually together with the captain of the club. The secretary was always to be in attendance, and the coach — though surprisingly this was not written into the rules — was naturally consulted. Had the coach been able to attend all our matches I would have liked him to have always had the final say in selection. As it was, he could only attend a limited number of our games and so had to rely on the opinion of the selection committee.

After our defeat of the Casuals there were those who considered that Jack Laybourne should have played against Slough, for John was injury-prone and the explosive speed, on which he relied so much, seemed at times to desert him. Jack Laybourne, a Bevin boy during the war who had spent four years underground as a miner, was a different type of centre-forward, very capable on the ball, bandy-legged, neat, stylish, incisive and, though not tall, well built and determined. He was soon to play for England and once for Tottenham Hotspur. It was a difficult decision. In the end the selectors plumped for John; he played well and came up with a goal. He had, in fact, from the club's inception, scored more goals for us than any other player. So he was chosen to play against Southall, our opponents in the semi-final, the match to be played at Highbury.

The afternoon was bright and sunny, the ground bone hard, when we emerged from the tunnel just before three o'clock and ran out once again onto the Arsenal pitch to see what we could make of Southall. I had taken a measure of comfort in recalling what *The Times* had said in concluding the report of our previous cup-tie with Slough:

> Since being two goals down at half-time at Hayes in the first round, the Pegasus defence has not been penetrated in five and a quarter hours of football, while their forwards have scored 12 times. There is a warning here to the rest of the field.

Glancing across at the other end, where Southall in their red and white striped shirts were warming up, I wondered whether they had taken any heed of this warning.

Their progress so far was impressive. In the first round they'd travelled the long distance down to Saltash and won the replay. In the second round they'd disposed of Bishop Auckland, in the third, Wealdstone, who had just defeated the cup-holders, Walthamstow, and in the fourth, Romford, in a replay at Romford.

A ball came over and bounced awkwardly before me. I didn't like the look of the pitch or the feel of it underfoot. It was altogether too nobbly and sparse of grass. A day for mistakes, I thought, and thereupon made up my mind to get in fast and win the ball if possible before it bounced. I glanced at the main stand speculating where Biddie was sitting, watching along with 30,000 others. Then the whistle blew and I closed up on Parker, their centre-forward, whom I recognised from the portrait and pen pictures of their side in the official Arsenal programme.

At once the bounce was most treacherous, and a moment extra dwelling on the ball was to court immediate pressure from Southall's eager and hungry forwards. I felt vulnerable, as the report from the *Guardian* made abundantly clear:

> Southall started with a smooth competence which forced the Pegasus defence to kick wide and wildly. Shearwood, as near as makes no difference, scored through his own goal and a few moments later made an appalling back pass which should have cost a goal had not Parker stumbled over the ball and Brown thus been able to clear.

And I wasn't at all sure what to make of another of his comments:

> Shearwood is an extraordinary centre-half and his display varied sharply between the heroic and the comic. He was completely lacking in polish or constructive ability and yet, innumerable times, in desperate situations, a long leg would dart like a chameleon's tongue or a leaping head appear when all seemed lost.

But it was obvious that the man from the *Guardian* had enjoyed the match because he wrote in his opening paragraph:

> During the last few days one has travelled more than a thousand miles to watch Association Football matches. The last of these journeys was infinitely the most worthwhile because not for a long time has one seen such a virile, exciting and wholly entertaining game as the FA Amateur Cup semi-final in which Pegasus drew 1-1 against Southall here today. This was a game of rare contrasts, particularly in the football of Pegasus, which varied from moments of high adventure to ones of incipient brilliance.

As for that back pass, I remember it very clearly. It was one of those tight situations, the ball bobbing before me, needing but the most delicate of touches to Ben who had left his line. I tried to stroke it to him, conscious of the drumming footsteps of Parker hard on my heels as I screened him from the ball. Very gently I touched it — too gently — and Parker, following through, was on to the thing in a flash. Incredibly he failed to score, somehow tripping over the ball which Ben gathered calmly and without a flicker of emotion.

The encounter was fast and desperate and, with only seven minutes remaining, Southall got the equaliser. When we left the field shortly after to do battle another day the score was still one apiece. Geoffrey Green began:

> There was a duel in the sun at Arsenal Stadium on Saturday, where a gathering, 30,000 strong, saw Pegasus and Southall leave the battlefield at the end still locked in deadly combat with one goal each in their semi-final tie of the FA Amateur Cup. In truth, it was not so much a subtle duel as a resounding clash of arms with no quarter asked, and it is to be continued at Craven Cottage, Fulham, next Saturday.
>
> PEGASUS — B. Brown; F.C.M. Alexander, G.H. McKinna; R.C. Vowels, K.A. Shearwood, D. Saunders; H.A. Pawson, C.B. Carr, J.D.P. Tanner, R.G. Lunn, R. Sutcliffe.
>
> SOUTHALL — E. Bennett; T. Prior, E. Hardy; A. Merry, C. Mears, R. Sloane; J. Blizzard, J. Way, E. Parker, W. Wenlock, M. Reynolds.

The replay took place the following week on Fulham's ground, Craven Cottage, in conditions much the same as at Highbury. We'd made one change in the side, bringing in Jack Laybourne at inside-right in place of Donald Carr.

Barely fifteen minutes had elapsed when I received a severe kick on my ankle, at the same time turning it badly. There was no question of there being a foul. I had raced Parker for a through ball and stuck out my leg to block his shot, taking the full impact of his kick on the inside of my left ankle which I then somehow twisted. I knew the injury was serious; I knew also that it was something that I either had to ignore or go off. So I tried to pretend it was not there and got on with the game. At half-time the ankle was thick and shapeless and rather than remove my boot — I don't think I would ever have got it on again — I eased the laces while Leslie pressed a cold wet sponge against my sock and George Ainsley poured lead opium around the ankle.

I'm not sure how I got through that second half. It helped a lot that Parker stuck to the middle and did not work the wings, allowing me to stick with him by hook or by crook. But the pain when I ran and tried to turn was intense. It was the longest and most painful forty-five minutes of football I ever experienced. Surprisingly, Southall seemed unaware of the fact that I was injured and so missed a chance of putting me under the kind of pressure which would have exposed my physical handicap. Equally surprising, though there were mentions of the injuries sustained by John Tanner and Mears, the Southall centre-half, there was no mention of mine in the press reports, apart from one in the *News of The World*, which more than made amends with a spectacular and personal headline that did something to restore my morale, but little to improve the condition on my ankle. However, much to my great relief the X-ray showed no broken bones.

We won the match — and rightly, according to Denis Compton, who wrote:

> Pegasus fully deserved the right of yet another visit to Wembley. And their performance was even more remarkable, in that for well over half the game Tanner was virtually a passenger on the right wing.

So there it was; once more we were back at Wembley and, if selected, I had exactly three weeks to get fit for the final. It took a week of treatment to get rid of the swelling and because of the bruising, Biddie could only begin light massage at the end of it. In the middle of the second week I began to do some running and light work with a ball. Finally, with a well-strapped ankle, and, in some trepidation, I played at Iffley Road in the first round of the AF A Cup against Histon United, a match we won 4-1. Donald Carr came back into the side and Jack Laybourne took over John Tanner's position at centre-forward. My ankle pained me considerably and thickened again, but it had survived the test and there was still another week before the final.

It now seemed likely that this would be the team that would play at Wembley and John would have to miss the final. It was hard for him, but Jack was a very good player and fit. And, no doubt, recalling how John had broken down in the 1949 quarter-final cup-tie against Bromley, the selectors settled on this side that had just played against Histon.

The spring days were drawing out. Each afternoon of that last week I'd jog across the field known at Lancing as the Sixteen Acre, do some wind sprints and practise with a ball on the first XI pitch. A number from the College and the surrounding district were coming up to Wembley, and those who were not would be watching on television. I received many requests for tickets, but there were none to be had; the match was a sell-out.

And suddenly it was all happening again. We were up in London together trying to get a sound last night's sleep without interruption — not always easy on such occasions. But when, the following morning, we set off from the Great Western Hotel, Paddington, we did this time manage to avoid ending up in a builder's yard at the back of Wembley, making our way with unerring accuracy towards the great stadium whose doors once more swung wide to swallow us up, bus and all.

We changed in the same changing-room that we'd used two years before. My ankle had been strapped up on Friday by the Brighton and Hove Albion trainer because I'd once played for their reserves against Luton, a fact rather astonishingly mentioned in that now extinct national humorous weekly, *Blighty*. I still had twinges of pain, but I knew I could get through. Then it was time to go. We were in the tunnel again and, after waiting a while, walking up the slight slope and out into that vast arena beside our opponents. The sun was as brilliant, the sky just as blue and cloudless as it had been in 1951.

There, on that sunny April afternoon at Wembley, we murdered and buried Harwich and Parkeston by six clear goals, conceding none. Our opponents had previously defeated

Whitton United, Harrogate, Clevedon, Leytonstone and, in the semi-final, Walton and Hersham. But that afternoon they simply had no answer and it proved our easiest cup-tie of that year. Denis got our first goal, climbing typically high above everyone to head home a corner from Roy Sutcliffe. Davies, the Harwich and Parkeston centre-forward, was suffering from a knee injury which soon began causing him trouble. A player they were relying on, he'd been given a pain-killing injection before the match in the hope that it would see him through. But a knee injury is a very different kettle of fish from an ankle injury and he should not have played.

The Guardian summed it all up with a headline:

PEGASUS OVERWHELM HARWICH

And Geoffrey Green began with a splendid opening paragraph:

HARWICH BEATEN BY PURE ARTISTRY

Wembley in springtime is to Pegasus what Headingley and Worcester in summer once used to be to Sir Donald Bradman. The rich emerald surface now sparkling once again under the proverbial Wembley sunshine, and the steep packed curve of this amphitheatre seem to act as a stimulus on them. So it was on Saturday when an all-ticket crowd of some 100,000 saw them carry off the FA Amateur Cup for the second time in three seasons. Theirs was a mature exhibition of pure football that cut poor Harwich and Parkeston to ribbons to the tune of six goals to none and reduced them to the status of a selling plater that has strayed by mischance into classic company.

Their positional play and imaginative passing, long and short cut along the ground to the last refined inch magnified the Wembley pitch, so much space did they win for themselves. They seemed to have the ball on a string, tantalising opponents who were a yard behind the pass for most of the afternoon.

Pegasus, in fact, were a team, a single unit. To see them on this sunlit day was to admire the inner workings of some Swiss watch. Everything and everyone hung together. The mechanism worked perfectly.

The final touch came five minutes from the end. Pawson suddenly turned up on the left; Laybourne nodded down his centre and Carr stroked home the final goal to bring the widest victory ever achieved (wartime apart) by any side at Wembley. Looking back, how much history was held at the end in those last fateful minutes at Hayes last December! And now, if certain conditions are overcome, Pegasus will be seen in the FA Cup itself next year, for better or for worse.

It was a eulogistic account by any standards, bettered only on that score by what Denzil Batchelor had to say in his autobiography, *Babbled of Green Fields*, published eight years later. But he was referring to our earlier Cup-Final when he wrote:

The best football ever seen in a Wembley Final wasn't shown by Blackpool and Bolton in 1953; that must take second place to the Amateur Cup Final won in 1951 by Pegasus against Bishop Auckland.

Astonishingly he continued:

If Pegasus could have been given three seasons' full-scale training as an integral combination they would have been good enough to win the World Cup in 1954.

He had, of course, now gone much too far, but it nevertheless makes very nice reading and a fitting end to the first part of the Pegasus story.

Above: Pegasus 6 Harwich & Parkeston 0

1953 Wembley Cup final.
Pegasus 6 Harwich & Parkeston 0
Reg Vowels about to tackle; KAS following.

Chapter 32

Hong Kong

THAT SUMMER of 1953 was Frank Doherty's last at Lancing. I was sorry that he was leaving. The headmaster-elect, John Dancy, was a Wykehamist, aged thirty-three, who had taught classics for five years at his old school.

I met him first one hot afternoon in the middle of the summer term. He'd walked across the Sixteen Acre with John Handford, one of the senior housemasters, and arrived on our doorstep, shirt-sleeves rolled up, his jacket over one arm. As he limped across our threshold to be welcomed by Biddie, I saw the extent of his legacy from the polio he had had in 1949. Then for an hour we talked and I found myself, as I invariably do on such occasions, speculating more about the person than concentrating on what was being said.

The man sitting opposite me was tall and thin, tufted above the ears, otherwise nearly bald, apart from a few wisps of fair hair spanning his considerable cranium. He had a youthful and engaging enthusiasm and when he smiled, his eyes would brighten, and his expressive, highly intelligent face would light up. It was also a smile which I guessed could be switched on and off with all the significance and warning of a flashing light at sea. I noticed he had long expressive hands.

"Well?" I asked Biddie when he had gone.

"I liked him," she replied. "He seems a nice and friendly person."

"Yes, I thought so too," and we left it at that.

The next time I saw John Dancy was at the common room meeting at the beginning of the September term when, naturally, we were all intrigued to see the professional cut of his jib. We did not have long to wait.

"I won't beat about the bush, gentlemen," he began, "when I tell you that I have been appointed to Lancing to raise the academic standard." Before many of us had fully digested this piece of information, he continued, spelling it out in clear economic terms, "Life is competitive and it's going to be competitive at Lancing."

But what did rather grate on that first official occasion was his habit of referring to the staff, a number of whom were much older and considerably more experienced than he was, by their surnames. A prefix would have helped. Then we were off, the term got under way, the new broom began to sweep and some dust rose.

To stress the competitive side of life he began by intensifying the mark system. There were fortnightly orders, first half-term orders, second half-term orders, full-term orders. There were set marks, raw marks, scaled marks, cooked marks, examination marks, combined marks, until, come the end of term, swamped by lists of names, bemused by graphs, slide-rules and God knows what, we arrived at some preposterous total simply to establish who should be first and who last. It was time-wasting, educationally meaningless and psychologically disastrous, serving only to point another accusatory finger at the wretched failures and encourage the habit of cheating.

From the start our new headmaster decided to do some teaching at every level in the school to get an academic "feel of the place". He got it all right and, to his credit, stuck to it. But he was a true scholar and found it hard going at the bottom end. In a different way he found it not so easy at the top end when he took over the classical sixth from John Handford. Despite his unquestioned intellectual capacity he had not the teaching experience of the older man nor yet the wisdom that comes of years.

An incident illustrates this clearly. I was going into chapel one Friday evening, the day's work over, when John Dancy accosted me at the west door.

"Who was that singing upstairs in the new block at the end of last period?" He was aware that I taught up there; he had been teaching below.

I told him who I thought it was and gave the matter no further consideration.

The following morning the master was sent for. After being well and truly admonished for singing a hymn in Latin at the end of a period, he was told to write an apology to his colleagues for the inconvenience he had caused them and pin it to the common room notice-board.

It was an extraordinary thing to do, explained only perhaps by the fact that he'd been teaching a lower form at the time — a task that was probably driving him to near-distraction — and the sound of singing had been the last straw. The master, Donald Bancroft, was a forthright and respected Yorkshireman, a first in classics from Corpus, Oxford. He was a valuable man on any staff, who knew exactly what he was doing — a fact which Dancy later recognised when he made him his personal assistant.

Our new headmaster preached his first sermon, a lecture really, based on the teleological approach and, delightedly, I recognised what he was talking about. There is a chance here, I thought, to do myself a bit of good. But, try as I might, I never quite found the right opportunity to convey the fact that I, too, was aware of Aristotle.

But the man's enthusiasm was infectious and though he did some things which were hurtful and unnecessary, it was largely as a result of impatience and inexperience. Given time, there was much that he could and would do for Lancing and vice versa. I was particularly grateful to him because he allowed me to continue playing for Pegasus, never expecting me to go, cap in hand, to beg permission each time.

Leslie Compton, centre-half for Arsenal and England, was our new coach for the coming season in which the club played thirty matches. I played in twenty-seven of these, eleven thanks to John Dancy, in that September term when we brought a side down and popped in nine goals against the boys by half-time. We split up after that.

Prior to our first-round Amateur cup-tie with Clevedon at the end of 1953 we played two floodlit matches against Portsmouth and Watford. At Fratton Park a large crowd saw us — a goal down at half-time — lose 3-1 to their full First Division League side which included five internationals: Stephen of Scotland, Dickenson, Froggatt, Philips, and Harris of England. Against Watford in another excellent game we lost 1-2 before some 12,000 spectators.

Before the Portsmouth game I had gone into our opponents' dressing-room to get some strapping because Leslie Laitt had slipped up with our medical equipment.

"Can I help?" asked one of their players who was sitting on a medical couch swinging his legs.

"I'm looking for some Elastoplast to strap my ankle."

The man regarded me for a moment with amusement.

"Get your sock off and I'll do it for you," and he sprang lightly off the couch. "What's your job?"

"I'm teaching at Lancing."

"Any chance of coming over and doing some coaching?"

"Of course."

"Tuesday any good?" he had deftly completed the strapping.

I nodded. "Why not come and have lunch first?"

"Fine!' said the player, "I'll see you after the game then — that's if you haven't kicked us all to death," he added, grinning as I left their changing-room.

It was the beginning of a long friendship with Jack Mansell who taught me how to coach and a lot more about football. Later on his son, Nick, came to Lancing and played for the school.

On 19 December we put paid to Clevedon in the first round of the Amateur Cup by three clear goals. That Christmas we spent at Evesham with Biddie's mother, who had moved to Oxstalls, the old farmhouse on a bend of the River Avon, where Biddie had spent her childhood.

The day after Boxing Day I bade farewell to my family and set off to join the rest of the Pegasus side in London to begin our New Year tour.

We flew from Heathrow to Hong Kong in a noisy Argonaut, putting down at Zurich, Rome, Cairo, Basra, Karachi, Delhi, Calcutta, Rangoon, and Bangkok on what proved a long and tiring journey.

Disembarking at Cairo and inhaling deeply I was suddenly acutely aware once more of all those familiar smells of the war and a host of memories came flooding back. I wondered where my old Mark IV landing-craft was which we'd paid off in the Bitter Lakes, and where too was that tall dignified Arab who used to greet Peter Bull and me each morning as we emerged from the Continental Hotel? Was he still accosting the residents in that impeccable English? "Would you like me to show you round the bazaar today, sir?"

We flew on, playing bridge most of the time, once being requested — with some urgency — to evacuate the round part in the after-section of the aircraft because the wretched thing was flying tail-heavy. We talked a great deal and tried to sleep, ate unwisely at Calcutta and spent one restless hot night in Rangoon where I shared a room with Jimmy Potts.

Jimmy did things his own way — he usually did. On this occasion he insisted that there was no need to get under a mosquito net. The result was little sleep for either of us, since my companion spent what short time we had at our disposal doing

Biddie on Shoreham Beach in 1953

battle with the mosquitoes. Eventually, just when all seemed quiet, a dreadful row broke forth outside. Poor Denis was one of those who had taken food at Calcutta and, feeling dreadfully ill, staggered out into the courtyard and vomited over a sleeping Burmese. But by then it was three o'clock and time to get up, we were flying at four.

"I don't like the look of Saunders," pronounced Tommy from out of the darkness as Denis was assisted aboard the bus. "We'll be lucky to get him home, let alone onto a football pitch," he continued. We were motored to the airstrip outside Rangoon, the lights by the wayside flickering wanly across each dark threshold of the humble Burmese abodes.

As dawn broke, we soared up into a magical sky for the last lap which required a special pilot to negotiate Hong Kong's short landing-strip.

"Fasten your safety-belts, please," we were politely requested for the umpteenth time and then, after a few hair-raising moments threading our way down the hillside, we landed safely to face a battery of cameras.

In terms of playing the tour was a disaster. We lost all three of our football matches and were completely outclassed in a golf contest in which I partnered Leslie Compton against the Hong Kong champion and another who appeared almost as good. I spent most of the day on my own for I seldom, if ever, reached the green which, if nothing else, served to amuse my barefooted young caddie who each time insisted that I used the club of his choice and then proceeded to shake with uncontrollable mirth as I struck, or rather attempted to strike the ball. His innumerable excursions into the rough — the ball once almost disappeared into communist territory — never failed to produce a result.

However, we did a little better in a cricket match, and I felt privileged to captain our side. Our opponents, the Hong Kong Cricket Club, were captained by T. A. Pearce, well known in English cricket. The honorary secretary, Mr Owen-Hughes, was an Old Salopian who had already entertained us royally in his beautiful home on the summit of the island. We drew the match, declaring at 228 for 8. John Tanner, who was handicapped by an injury, insisted vehemently that Jimmy Platt should not be his runner — in his opinion he considered he did not sufficiently understand the game — and was promptly run out by him for nought, which didn't please John at all. However, Jimmy Potts then hit a very good century and I got what was described as a lively sixty-seven.

None of us slept much that first night, for the rooms were excessively hot and all night long fireworks were going off in celebration of New Year's Eve. I was still sharing a room with Jimmy Potts. Much to my astonishment, he suddenly announced late one night that he was going out to find a doctor to remove his big toenail which was giving him trouble. He returned in the early hours of the morning full of gory details and minus his big toe nail — which didn't prevent him from playing later that same evening.

We were lavishly entertained and no one was more solicitous of our welfare than a certain Tak Sing who would arrive early each morning and invite us, not unsuccessfully, to visit his shop and buy his garments. He sold us silk kimonos, black, gold-embroidered slippers. The swell-looking white pyjamas with red dragons, once worn, never quite looked the same, splitting along the seams at the slightest provocation, and fraying dreadfully.

Eventually, after a final banquet in Kowloon we assembled wearily at the Kai Tak airfield and climbed aboard another Argonaut — no mass of cameras and reporters this time to see us off — only one solitary well-wisher, our friend Tak Sing, who greeted us with unfeigned delight and stood waving his arms as we tore along the runway and soared out over the sea.

It was an exhausting tour. Several of us suffered the usual stomach complaints and we'd had no time to acclimatise. We were not only physically below par but not at full club strength, having left behind Tony Pawson, Donald Carr and Gordon McKinna. We were also ill-prepared for the conditions. It was extremely hot and the grounds bone hard. Most of us had boots suitable only for the heavy conditions of an English winter. We should have worn rubbers. The Chinese, skilful and sharp, mastered the lively ball much better than we did and were well worthy of their three victories.

"Well ..." Tommy said at the first *post mortem* after we'd lost the initial match 1-4 before a crowd of 15,000, "you've got to win the next one." And when we lost it by the only goal of the match three minutes from time he began the second *post mortem* in tones even more serious. "It's absolutely vital you win this last match." Later that evening he confided in several of us, "I sat with his Excellency the Governor yesterday and I didn't find the man at all forthcoming. The trouble is they're expecting us to win all our matches and they feel we're letting them down." It didn't much help matters when we promptly went and lost the last match of the tour 1-4 — despite playing seven internationals.

The plane banked steeply and began to climb. We unfastened our safety-belts and, sitting back, got out the cards. Two days later, 9 January, we arrived back in London, thirteen days after having set forth.

A fortnight later, this time in icy conditions, we met Gedling Colliery on their ground, Plains Road, Mapperly, in the second round of the Amateur Cup.

Our supporters, many wearing mortar boards and gowns and holding aloft on poles their flat wooden replicas of the Flying Horse, lined the roads to the ground long before the kick-off.

Gedling Colliery had played their way right through from the first round of the qualifying competition — five long months of cup-battling. Champions of Nottingham Alliance, they had only been beaten once in fourteen months. They had everything to gain and little to lose.

As for us, cup-holders, fielding ten of the side that had won at Wembley, six of whom were internationals, it was a match fraught with danger, one that seemed to have all the ingredients of the cup-tie that goes wrong — and very aware of it we all were — Tommy had made certain of that.

Right from the start it felt as though things could well go wrong because Gedling, whose training had been supervised by the Nottingham Forest manager, Billy

Walker, played with tremendous competitive spirit, meeting the ball early and tackling in deadly fashion, roared on by a crowd of 6,000. But, in the end, we scored 6 and they 1. Alan Hoby wrote:

> It was 'massacre' but, for fifteen glorious minutes, the miners' grit matched the skill of amateur soccer's top team.

At the beginning of the Easter Term of 1954, John Dancy announced to the common room that, since he wasn't sure what went on in certain areas of the school, he intended to come round and listen to us teaching. "I will," he added, "try and give masters as much warning beforehand as I can," a proposal that did little to alleviate the unpleasantness of such a prospect.

"You'll be all right, Henry," I remarked, "at least you'll be able to see him coming."

For the Reverend Henry Thorold always taught with his door wide open so that, he would explain, "I can always make a quick getaway, if need be."

I wondered what John Dancy would make of his blackboard work, which remained unaltered — most of it, at any rate — not for the term, but for the whole year. Written in his beautiful handwriting at the top was a bald statement, "Only sixty more lazy days till the end of the term", the number naturally decreasing each day. Beneath lay a coloured and carefully drawn coat of arms with the ancestral name, 'Sir Marmaduke Strickland Constable, Bart'. At the bottom right-hand corner was the only reference to work, 'Remove Classics Evening School, Prose 23' — which also would remain to the end of the year.

Henry Thorold was a scholar of Eton, had not taken a degree at Oxford, we never discovered why, was the proud owner of a vintage fabric-covered Rolls-Royce, loved good food, and resided at Marston Hall, Grantham, Lines. He taught classics his own way, interspersed with odd, irrelevant questions from members of the form.

"What car have you got, sir?"

"I have no car, sir. I have a Rolls-Royce. Keeler, sir, construe."

"I'm not quite sure what you mean, sir."

"Keeler, sir, you are an ignoramus."

"Can we have the door shut, sir?"

"There is no door, sir. Triptree, construe."

But behind this eccentricity lay a very shrewd mind and a prodigious memory. An outrageous snob, he unashamedly loved the good things of life and left those he disapproved of to go their way with a cool indifference that was without rancour or judgement. I saw him always as a medieval priest more fitted to pre-Reformation times than the twentieth century. In many ways he was good for Lancing, for he debunked much that needs debunking in the educational world.

"Flying horses, my foot, more like dumb bloody geese, if you ask me," began the *Guardian's* report, quoting an ebullient red-faced northerner's loudly proclaimed comment on our performance in the third round FA Amateur Cup-tie against Willington, played at Oxford, on the 6th of February, 1954.

Seven days later we made the long journey north for the replay only to find that the ground had been declared unfit by the referee and the match postponed.

The following week, amidst another mining community and on a wet treacherous pitch, we took them on again before a small partisan crowd of 3,500.

Our start could not have been more hysterical. In the opening seconds a beautiful low-angled cross ball laid deep behind Gordon McKinna at right-back — Alexander was unfit — found Armstrong, the inter-changing Willington inside-left, cutting in at tremendous speed to blast a glorious shot which gave Ben no chance whatsoever. At that precise moment it felt very bad. The slippery surface was making it difficult for defenders to turn, and we were stretched to our limits. Nor did it help — though it made me laugh — when, a minute later, Ben Brown drop-kicked a ball straight at the back of Gordon McKinna's head. For a split second Ben stood staring at Gordon's massive frame stretched motionless in the mud. The danger was imminent, for the ball had run loose just outside the edge of our penalty area and Ben was still out of his goal. But Denis was on hand. Racing back, he just beat the Willington forwards, only to chip the ball high and wide of Ben's reach smack against our crossbar, the rebound falling dramatically into our goalkeeper's grateful arms.

"Keep your head down next time, Gordon," I suggested, as he got shakily to his feet, whilst Ben, who had cleared his lines, was once more back in goal, surveying the scene with his customary composure. *The Times* began:

> In confident and thrustful mood Pegasus reached the last eight of the FA Amateur Cup for the fourth time of their meteoric career when they overcame Willington by four goals to two in Saturday's third round replay.

We were all delighted and, over dinner on the train home, discussed the prospects of our fourth round cup-tie with Briggs Sports the following Saturday.

"I hope to goodness," Tommy warned, "that we don't take them for granted. They're obviously a good side with an excellent record." And for emphasis he sent round a circular that week warning us against complacency, as did Leslie Compton.

On the Monday, the draw for the semi-final was made and we heard on the radio that either Briggs' or we were to meet Bishop Auckland up at St James's Park, Newcastle. But first Briggs' Sports had to be dealt with. And once more it began to feel very much as though it could all be happening again.

Unbeaten on their own ground in the Spartan League that season, Briggs' Sports were coached by Jim Paviour, the old Bromley and England amateur centre-half, and had at centre-forward a sixteen-year-old, Les Allen, who was to turn professional and play for Spurs and England.

We lunched together, that last Saturday in February 1954, and then left central London by car for Dagenham. That was the start of a lot of our troubles. We had left ourselves insufficient time. Frustrated by the traffic, we eventually arrived at Victoria Road only to find ourselves further delayed in our efforts to find somewhere to park, for the immediate vicinity around the ground was jammed with cars and people. It was quite the wrong way to approach any match, let alone a cup-tie, and we had to change at great speed in cramped conditions. There was no time to muster our thoughts, no time for Leslie Compton to say anything more than a few hurried words. When we left the dressing-room we were in the wrong frame of mind, mentally unprepared, our thoughts insufficiently focused on what lay ahead, and we were to pay for it dearly. Right from the start Briggs' Sports showed a sharpness we never matched. There was an apathy about our play that simply could not be shaken off. Towards the end, when they had scored their third goal, a Briggs' supporter sitting behind Biddie bellowed down her ear, "The bloody old Flying Horse is a goner this time!" and he was right.

But what I remember most about that cup-tie, which was watched by a record crowd of 6,500, and which turned out for us such a sad occasion, was the difficulty I had in getting to grips with Les Allen. He was always on the move, darting about, as slippery as an eel, playing slightly off-centre, dropping away and laying it off first time or, when possible, holding and turning whilst another went hunting down the middle for his through pass — which was what happened in the first few minutes.

Moving deep into his own defence and feeling he had time and room to hold the ball, I failed to go all the way with him and so was not on his back, the young centre-forward turned and, sizing up the situation in a flash, hit the ball down the centre to find Keen, the Briggs' outside-right, racing inside Miles Robinson to score their first goal. After that we were never really in the game.

When the final whistle blew I shook hands with Les Allen, wished him luck in the semi-final against the Bishops — they had been watching the match — and left the field wondering once more why anyone ever plays games which are remotely serious.

Eighteen years later I met Les Allen again when, as manager of Queens Park Rangers, he brought them to Lancing — Rodney Marsh, Terry Venables and all — to do some training on the school grounds. By then the stinging memory of that cup-tie was only something of the dim and distant past.

Chapter 33

Arthur Rowe

AT A COMMITTEE meeting held at the East India and Sports Club on 9 May 1954, Tommy announced with regret that he was no longer able to continue as secretary of Pegasus, a statement that was to mark a turning-point in the club's short history, though perhaps not appreciated by many at the time.

And at that meeting a discussion took place about the organisation for 1954-55, in which three decisions were taken. Two were obvious and sensible ones: that a second eleven be formed, and a booklet be prepared about the club for distribution to members. But it was the decision that the club should continue, that caught the eye. I can find no record of who suggested the possibility that the club might not continue, but that such a prospect could even be contemplated, as early as May 1954, cast the first real shadow of doubt over our future, a shadow that was to grow darker and more ominous as each year passed.

Five months later, at the AGM, Tommy was unanimously appointed the first chairman of the club while Ben Brown became the new secretary, with John Tanner and John Blythe of Cambridge acting as assistant secretaries for their respective universities. W. V. Cavill continued as treasurer, with W. J. Sartain as assistant treasurer at Cambridge and Jerry Weinstein at Oxford — he was also on the selection committee. Harvey Chadder remained the club's sympathetic president. Finally Denis was re-elected captain for the coming season and Joe Mercer became our new coach.

Above all else and to our great joy, we learnt in the spring we were to have another child at the end of the year. Recalling all the difficulties Biddie had experienced when Paul was born, we decided this time she should go into hospital when the time came. As the months passed she looked to me the very picture of health, calm and gentle as always, more radiant and lovely than ever.

The summer term of 1954 at Lancing passed quickly. In June, Pegasus played their annual cricket match with Morris Motors, Jimmy Potts made his usual century, Tony Pawson craftily bowled his off-spinners, while I kept wicket, aided and abetted by John Tanner at first slip who had also kept wicket for Oxford.

With the key to Durell by my side and Parnell Smith down at The Sussex Pad should that fail, I no longer feared the geometry periods and became quite *blasé* about the teaching of mathematics.

The highlight of the term was Founder's Day, when the staff sat on the dais in Great School, while the parents gathered to listen to the speeches. The chairman of the governors, Admiral Sir William Whitworth, K.C.B., D.S.O., of Narvik distinction, began with a few introductory words.

I was sitting at the back between my two sexagenarian colleagues, Parnell and Puttock, both already nodding away peacefully, when the admiral suddenly wheeled round and addressed us all as though he were once more back on the quarter-deck of

Warspite and we were his ship's company: "I would ask the staff to do one thing," and he fixed us with a fierce eye, "Maintain the object."

"What was that?" said Parnell Smith, with a start.

"We've got to maintain the object," I whispered.

"Oh," said Parnell, and promptly closed his eyes.

The Bishop of Peterborough, Spencer Leeson, spoke next and informed the parents that, as headmaster of Winchester, he'd known John Dancy well. "And I can assure you he's a very good chap. You're lucky to have him."

Finally Dancy — it was his first Founder's Day — made his contribution which included a jocular reference to the Lancing staff, that perhaps he might be able to show a few of the old dogs some new tricks.

But by then Parnell and Puttock were fast asleep.

We played thirty-four matches in the 1954-55 season, won twenty, drew five and lost nine — losing the first match of all against Walthamstow Avenue away 0-4.

I met Joe Mercer for the first time at the Royal Military Academy, Sandhurst. We were waiting to go out and Joe had said his piece. "How's your leg?" I asked him. He'd broken it very badly in a collision with his team-mate, Joe Wade, when captaining Arsenal against Liverpool in the last league match of the 1953 season.

"I don't want the lads to see it," he confided, as we began to move out, his face wrinkling in good humour. As the last man left the dressing-room he quickly drew up his trouser-leg and I saw a very nasty-looking leg injury.

We won the match 2-1 and then took two scratch sides down to play against Collyer's School, Horsham, and Lancing College, winning 10-1 and 12-0.

In the second week of October we played the Northern Nomads in the final of the 1953-54 AFA Cup, a match which I did not forget in a hurry, for I woke that day with a severe headache which I could not shake off.

"You'll be all right," Leslie assured me over lunch at Oriel College, arranged by our new secretary, Ben Brown, who was now a fellow of the college.

"It's imperative we win this one," urged Tommy, which promptly produced a spasm of intense coughing.

"Just push it around and get control of the middle," said Joe. He'd already gone round and had a few words with some of us. "And enjoy yourselves," he added as an afterthought.

My head was buzzing and I hoped that I would enjoy myself and not have too much to do in the air; it was more important still that the game would not go to extra time. But I soon found I had a great deal to do in the air and, to make matters worse, just before full time our opponents equalised. So we were forced to battle on into extra time until finally, after two hours of it, we defeated the Northern Nomads 3-2, winning the AFA Cup for the third time.

The Michaelmas term was drawing to a close. One Saturday late in November, I said goodbye to Biddie and Winnie, her mother, who was now staying with us and giving us great support, and set off for Oxford to play against the university side at Iffley Road. We had already defeated Cambridge.

I took Graham Collier with me, our new Director of Art at Lancing, to watch the match, talking ceaselessly as we drove to Oxford. Graham had found his way to the college in rather peculiar circumstances. He had been teaching at Giggleswick and had come down to visit relatives at Lancing. Wandering round the chapel after having a look at the school, he ran into John Dancy and they started to talk. By the time Graham had said his piece about extra-sensory perception, the compass-points of consciousness, the purpose of life and a good deal else, he was in and the current art master was out. Perpetually broke, he would put a gallon at a time into his ancient and thirsty Ford V8, free-wheeling whenever he could to make it last as long as possible. Long, well-groomed hair swept back over his ears, tall and lean, with an inquisitive moustache whose ends, antenna-like, twitched as mischievously as his eyes shone brightly, he had a distinction that could not be denied. He was impatient with colleagues, had rows galore and, at regular intervals, handed in his resignation which John Dancy would calmly accept, but with tongue in cheek, for Graham, above everything else, was first-class at his job.

On the way back — the side had defeated Oxford University by seven clear goals — we stopped at Guildford and had a drink. By the time we reached Lancing it was late and blowing one gale of a wind.

"Biddie's in hospital," Winnie greeted me as I opened the door. "The sea road's blocked," she explained, "so Mr Tydd very kindly ran her in by car." Bill Tydd was the school bursar who lived next door.

I rang the hospital at once but there was no news. I went to bed and lay awake thinking about Woodstock and all that she had been through and prayed that all would be well this time.

I woke early, immediately telephoned and learnt with delight that Biddie was fine and we had a daughter, born in the early hours of that last Sunday of November 1954. She was to be called Vanessa. My prayers had been answered.

The side had no particular difficulty in disposing of Dagenham, and went on to defeat Stevenage and West Auckland.

So, for the third successive year we reached the quarter-finals of the Amateur Cup and went into the hat along with Bishop Auckland, who were drawn to play against Finchley, Wimbledon against Hendon, Alton Town or Carshalton Athletic against Hounslow Town, and Wycombe Wanderers against ... you-know-who.

"It will be our first real cup test of the season," remarked Joe Mercer to the press. "If we win we can talk of Wembley with confidence."

Unchanged, we went to Loakes Park on 26 February 1955 and, on their notorious sloping ground, which fell eleven feet from one side-line to the other, with our backs well and truly against the wall, fought desperately in the mud to hang on to a goalless draw. It was one of those matches at the end of which every muscle is an ache, every step an effort. Mike Pinner was magnificent in goal, catching an unending stream of dangerous high crosses which Wycombe floated down that wicked slope, an advantage they knew exactly how to exploit.

We got away with it all right at Loakes Park. But I knew that, although our chances of success would be better at Oxford, only our best form would do. Wycombe were a very good side; they didn't stand on ceremony, but beavered away at it, content to take the quickest and most direct path to goal.

"Will you win the replay?" asked the boys.

"It's not going to be easy," I told them guardedly.

Nor was it, and we lost the cup-tie 1-2. PEGASUS GIVEN A TASTE OF THEIR OWN MEDICINE read *The Times* headline on Monday morning.

We felt thoroughly punctured sitting in the Iffley Road changing-room. Jerry, clad in his excessively long officer's airforce coat leant on his stick and, lifting his head and rolling his eyes, kept muttering, "Bloody hell, bloody hell."

"Never mind, lads, you did your best," Chedder Wilson quavered, with tears in his eyes, his hand shaking dreadfully as his knife, more lethal than ever, hacked chunks of orange for us, "There's always another season."

In front of the fire stood Tommy, his shoulders hunched, peering over his spectacles, a cigarette in his mouth. God knows what was going on in his head. John Tanner looked very serious. Harvey Chadder, our president, was quietly going round commiserating with each of us, and Joe Mercer, as upset as anyone, was doing his best not to show it. Only Leslie Laitt appeared unperturbed as, with trilby on head, he went about the business of collecting up our dirty gear.

Teas for the losers never quite taste right and when I got upstairs most of the talking was coming from Wycombe.

"Bad luck, Ken," said Helen Pawson gently, touching my arm.

"So near!' said Guy Pawson, smiling wistfully and peering sideways at me.

"Unfortunately not near enough," said Tony with a wry smile as he joined us.

And then Wycombe were suddenly leaving and we wished them luck. Presently we too broke up and went our different ways home.

I felt very tired and dispirited as I drove back alone in our old and sedate black Rover saloon. Mentally I went over the match. They'd shown more fight than we had and I wondered if my contribution had been good enough. I didn't feel that it had. I nearly dozed off and had to put the window down and breathe deeply the fresh cold air. Eventually, because I couldn't keep awake any longer, I pulled off the road and slept for a while.

Biddie had long gone to bed when I got back, so I undressed in the dark.

"What bad luck," she murmured sleepily. "We heard it on the wireless."

"They were better than we were."

"Were they? I expect you played well."

"No, I don't think I did. Children all right?"

"They're fine."

I peered briefly through a gap in the curtains. The moon was well up and I could see its light upon the sea. Then I climbed wearily into bed.

I began my last full season with Pegasus on 25 August 1955, by playing for a Southern Amateur XI against Schaffhausen at Ilford. The game was billed as an international representative match and included players from Woking, Wycombe Wanderers and Pegasus. We had met the Swiss side, Schaffhausen, on our tour back in December 1951 and lost 1-4. In 1954 Schaffhausen had drawn with Queen's Park (Glasgow) and, as part of their training for the World Cup, England played them, winning 4-2. We did well to beat them 3-1, that hot August afternoon, John Tanner scoring twice, G. Hamm of Woking once.

In September, at Earls Court, in a BBC five-a-side television tournament, Pinner, Saunders, Pawson, Scanlan and Tanner defeated Scotland 2-1, but lost to Wales 0-1. Four years earlier I had played in a similar competition at Wembley Pool where we'd ended up with the wooden spoon.

How fortunate we were that season to secure the help of Arthur Rowe to advise and coach us. He had managed Tottenham when they won successive Second and First Division Championships in 1950 and 1951 and sent us that memorable telegram at our first Wembley Cup Final, 'Make it simple, make it quick'. "Football," he'd often repeat, "is basically simple. It's we who make it difficult."

In 1954 he'd appointed Billy Nicholson as coach after his partnership with Vic Buckingham had broken up when Vic went to manage Bradford. Then his plan that Alf Ramsey should become his assistant came to nothing because Alf left to manage Ipswich Town. In the end, opposition from certain quarters in the boardroom and a serious illness finally drove him from High Road, Tottenham.

In his autobiography, *The Double And Before*, Danny Blanchflower wrote of Arthur Rowe, 'His push-and-run philosophy and the manner in which he guided the great Tottenham team of the late 40s and early 50s to such soccer delights had been a great source of inspiration to many of the young hopeful players that I knew'. And Alf Ramsey, in *Talking Football*, wrote about Arthur's profound and constructive approach to the game and its problems.

Now, to occupy himself temporarily after convalescence, he was promoting the sale of his own soccer boot, the Arthur Rowe Streamline, forerunner of the flexible soft shoe-like boots of today. Utterly direct and honest in all his views and dealings, humorous and sympathetic, he was still vulnerable and far from fit when he came to us in 1955.

At every opportunity we would discuss and analyse the game with him and he would put us wise and tell us stories about the Spurs.

"I never saw a sadder-looking bunch sitting in a dressing-room than after our semi-final FA Cup-tie with Blackpool in 1953. I felt so sorry for them, because most of that side would never get another chance to play at Wembley. They were too old," and he ran through the team: Ditchburn, Ramsey, Withers, Nicholson, Clarke, Burgess, Walters, Bennett, Duquemin, Bailey, Medley.

"We'd played so well. It was right on time. Alf Ramsey had run a ball down the line and struck it back outside the box to Ditchburn and then gone wide to collect the return. Unfortunately the ball stuck in the mud. Little Mudie, chasing hard, nipped round and just beat Ditchburn to it. After that there was only time to kick off before the whistle blew. What can you say to them? To make matters worse, one of the directors railed on and on at me about Ramsey. In the end I told him to shut his mouth.

"Leeds were the first team to deal successfully with our deep-lying wingers. We were up at Elland Road and their backs — both hard men — had been told to come all the way with Walters and Medley, however deep they dropped. We lost that one, the first in nineteen games. We also learnt a lesson. From then onwards we got Duquemin to exploit the gaps behind any opposing backs that marked our deep-lying wingers tightly.

"So much of this game is just plain common sense. Never stop thinking when you haven't the ball and, when you've got it, make sure you pass to the same shirt as your own. Have plenty of movement; supporting movement from behind, attacking movement in front. And limit your passes to thirty yards. If you're inaccurate over that distance then you can't play."

"Which just about bloody well scuppers you, Shearwood," said Jerry maliciously.

The Michaelmas term of 1955 was spoilt for most of us, certainly for me, by the arrival of Her Majesty's Inspectors. Their task was to inspect the school from top to bottom and, after a full week of it, depart and write their report, which would be sent to the headmaster. Immediately every head of department began to prepare lengthy screeds about the intentions and purpose of his department with all sorts of educational theory which was never put into practice but would, it was hoped, create a good impression on the inspectors. An inspection is also a very convenient way for headmasters to get rid of staff. It has as well, I suppose, some value in ensuring that a bad school is exposed, though, even then, I doubt whether it is entirely successful in achieving this.

What an inspection really does successfully is to disturb the natural routine, put the common room on edge and produce a good deal of toadying. The boys, of course, take it all in their stride and enjoy it.

"Ready for the inspection, sir?"

"Oh, of course, I'd forgotten all about it. When are they coming?" They might have been taken in.

"D'you mind being inspected, sir?"

"Mind? Good heavens, no. They're usually failed schoolmasters."

"We'll not let you down, sir!"

Fortunately, know-all had moved on and, in any case, I was no longer teaching maths, which was just as well. An alarming experience the previous term had been instrumental in my ceasing to be a member of the Lancing Maths department.

John Dancy had invited a number of preparatory school headmasters to meet the Lancing heads of departments and have an exchange of views in the school library.

"I'd like you to be there, Ken," he said, "since you teach the new men maths and your views might be helpful,"— an invitation that promptly sent a cold shiver up and down my spine. No *Key* to Durell's geometry could possibly get me out of this one.

On the appointed afternoon, twenty or so preparatory school headmasters sat facing us across the floor of the library and exchanges began. I kept very quiet indeed and everyone seemed to have a great deal to say. After an hour I began to think I would be all right. But not a bit of it. To my dismay, one of the preparatory school headmasters suddenly asked a general question about the way maths was taught at Lancing to the new intake. "I think Ken Shearwood is the man to answer this one," said John Dancy, leaning forward and looking sideways to where I was sitting, "he takes the new men."

My rambling response and final comment, that most seemed to find geometrical riders difficult to handle, neither impressed nor fooled anyone, least of all John Dancy. However, in retrospect, I was most grateful to that preparatory school headmaster for I was now spared from having to perform in this subject before one of Her Majesty's Inspectors.

We got through the week, the report duly arrived and, at a common room meeting, John Dancy gave us the gist of it and announced that any master who wished to come and discuss his own report could do so, "But I won't pull any punches, gentlemen," he added rather ominously.

I happened to be playing at Portsmouth that night so I decided to go and hear the worst and then I could enjoy the game.

"You're all right," said John pleasantly. He didn't refer to my report, and I didn't press him to do so. "When's your next match?"

"Tonight, against Portsmouth."

His face lit up with a smile and he inclined his head in acknowledgement. "I hope it goes well."

"I hope so," I replied and closed the door. I liked John Dancy.

We lost the game 3-6, after leading the First Division side by two goals to one at half-time, before a big crowd which had their money's worth.

Before the match, Arthur presented me with a brand new pair of his Streamline boots. "See if they'll improve your game a bit," he said, handing them to me. He wore a dark blue overcoat and a black Homburg. His hair was silver and he looked distinguished. I thought he looked better, too.

On the last Friday of December 1955, we all met for dinner at the Zetland Hotel, Saltburn, Yorkshire.

The following morning we visited Imperial Chemical Industries and saw the extent of the horrifying industrial landscape that ran parallel to a grey, uninviting North Sea. We toured a factory, saw some laboratories and in the afternoon drew 3-3 with the ICI side, Billingham Synthonia.

Afterwards we were shown a film and at 6.30 met the directors over cocktails. The dinner they gave us was first-class, not exactly true of the dance held at the Zetland Hotel much later that evening.

"Well," said Tommy, as we chatted before going to bed, "if any of you want a job, here's your chance. I can tell you now, they'll take some of you."

I gave it some thought, but decided, no.

New Year's Day came and we went on to the Royal Hotel, Princes Street, Edinburgh, playing bridge most of the way at the back of an extremely cold bus which went like a bat out of hell on the icy roads, once skidding and hitting the curb violently, knocking the cards flying — just when I had a good hand.

"Think the bloody driver knows what he's doing?" remarked Jerry, who was in charge of travel arrangements.

The Royal Hotel, where we stayed, was of particular interest to me, for it was where I had gone in 1942 as a matelot and been caught taking a free bath. With nostalgia I looked up some of the old haunts of those days, the little cafe halfway up Waverley Steps, the YMCA at the back of Princes Street where, at six in the morning, we'd eaten hot bacon baps and gulped scalding cups of tea before dashing out into the cold, dark streets of Edinburgh, to catch the train to Inverkeithing, which would get us back on board the *Montrose* just in time to 'turn to'.

Then we went on next to Glasgow to play Queen's Park at Hampden and draw the match. I knew the stadium was big, but was unprepared for its sheer vastness. Ten thousand watched, though it seemed more like five hundred.

And a very mixed press we got too, some of it extremely critical with headlines like: MISTAKES? WE GOT THE LOT HERE and:

PEGASUS? CALL THEM CAB-HORSES

It was cab-horse stuff from the university men and Queen's Park. A drab draw, a dull game with full marks only to one man — Maurice (Mike) Pinner, the English amateur international goalkeeper.

Queen's were weakened by reserves. But they would still have been too good for the men of Pegasus, who had more initials than soccer ideas, but for Pinner.

And:

Maybe I was watching in the ranks of the visitors a future Prime Minister, or a Lord Chancellor, or an Archbishop of Canterbury, but certainly no star of the soccer firmament.

Pegasus twice in postwar years have won the English Amateur Cup and, on each occasion played to a packed Wembley. English amateur football is not exactly, on yesterday's evidence, something to boast about. I reckon a team of teenagers from our secondary juveniles would do very well in the Saxon Competition.

But we got some better reports and Gordon McKinna, who captained us that day, played exceptionally well and was referred to as 'a giant of a man in the true Corinthian mould'.

Then we went south to Harrogate where we stayed in a great barn of a hotel before playing the British Police on the Huddersfield ground.

I didn't play but sat with Arthur Rowe and listened.

"Look at David Miller. He'll be over that stand and into the next county before he knows where he is."

David was fast, extremely fast. But for most of that night there was a policeman on his tail who was not only twice his size but almost as quick. And, like many a winger, before and since, David did not relish crossing the enemy's bows too often, but would make lightning tracks for the corner flag. But, to give him credit, he scored a fine goal at Hampden, cutting in at great speed and rifling a fine shot into the far corner of the Queen's Park goal from the edge of the penalty area.

Of the old hands, only Denis Saunders and Roy Sutcliffe played. Brian Wakefield came in for Mike Pinner and how fortunate we were to have him as a reserve goalkeeper. Though not as brilliant as Pinner, who had already played for England in the Olympics against Bulgaria and for Aston Villa, he was good enough later to be reserve for Great Britain in the 1960 Rome Olympics.

Newell, Walsh, Coe, Millner, Beddows, Blythe, Scanlan and Land played in that last match of the tour which we won 4-1. And there was another new Oxford forward, Robin Trimby, who played in the previous game at Hampden and was eventually to become an international.

Our journey home was a nightmare. The bus was like an old refrigerator, the roads foggy and icy and the driver, urged on by Tommy and the odd lurid comment from Jerry, had plainly lost his nerve.

Around ten o'clock at night, the bus stopped, still some 140 miles short of London, and I dropped off with Tommy, Leslie Laitt and kit, to pick up my old Rover which I'd parked to meet the bus at the start of the tour. It took us some time and much winding to get the thing started. Eventually we got it going and set off to drive the sixty-odd miles to Oxford where I was to stay the night with Tommy.

And what a hell of a drive that proved to be! For I was now the bus driver, on whom Tommy as pilot could turn his full attention. It wasn't long before I knew exactly how the real bus driver felt, and why he had lost his nerve.

With no heater in the car and wipers that couldn't shift the ice, I drove with my window down, stopping every so often to scrape the windscreen. And, all the while, ceaseless instructions poured into my left ear: "Turn left, turn right, go faster, go straight on, get over, look out, man, you're on the wrong side". I think Tommy developed cat's eyes that night and a sixth sense. He seemed quite oblivious of our dangerous skids, bumps and frequent near-misses which kept Leslie sitting rigidly attentive, frozen, and bolt upright in the back seat. We finally made Oxford at half-past three in the morning.

How nice it would have been, if only for Arthur Rowe's sake, had we been successful in the Amateur Cup of 1956.

Barnet, our opponents, were a young side, with an average age of twenty-one. Their centre-forward, Tommy Lawrence, an amateur with West Ham, had scored twenty goals to date '... but not enough', the *Express* wrote, 'to stop Pegasus winning'.

Just as Les Allen had done when Briggs' Sports knocked us out of the Cup in the fourth round of 1954, so Lawrence played deep and presented me with the same old problem of whether to be drawn upfield, or let him go, in the hope that he'd be picked up by one of our midfield men. My going left a gap behind me, staying placed an extra burden on Denis and Paddy Walsh. If one of these should fail to pick Lawrence up — and each had their opposing inside-forward to mark — the centre-forward was then free to come at me with the ball. In such circumstances I could but hope to contain him before committing myself somewhere outside the box. I did a bit of both that afternoon and had an uncomfortable match of it, creating problems not only for myself, but for my colleagues. We were fortunate in possessing a goalkeeper of the calibre of Mike Pinner, defeating Barnet by two clear goals.

On hearing the draw for the second round my heart began to beat slightly faster, for we'd drawn Wycombe Wanderers again. A glance at their playing record was enough to show that they were an even better side than in the previous year. Top of the Isthmian League with eleven wins, three draws and three defeats, they'd scored fifty goals and conceded nineteen. Just as when we'd drawn the Corinthian-Casuals in 1953, so now we knew a lot about Wycombe and that fluent, well-supported forward-line of theirs: Worley, Trott, Truett, Tomlin and Bates. Well, it was up to us to stop them, up to our completely Cambridge forward-line to score some goals.

The match was to be played at Iffley Road, on 4 February but because of frost it was postponed. When we met the following week the ground was still treacherous, with an east wind that cut like a whetted knife. Inside the old changing-room a big coke fire glowed red. Outside in the chill entrance hall the referee, a big, tall man who exuded authority stood talking to his small son.

"Would he like to come into our dressing-room and keep warm by the fire?" a suggestion the father promptly accepted. "Might do us a bit of good", I thought, showing them through the door and into the referee's room, which was off ours. "Might make him think twice and save us from a harsh decision." I should have known better.

They were out first, Syrett, their goalkeeper, in a tracksuit, their players wearing gloves and rubber-studded boots, a wise precaution. Our leather studs drummed on the hard slippery surface. There was no chance here for a defender to turn quickly and every opportunity for mistakes.

Straight from the kick-off their forwards began pressurising us, in particular Mike Pinner, harassing him as they followed through on their shots in the hope he'd mishandle. He never did. Yet so fiercely did they come at him that, on more than one occasion, the Wycombe forward ended up in the back of our net, having first had the ball whipped brilliantly from off his feet. They raided us from every quarter, laying the ball in behind our backs for their front men to run onto, measures not easily counteracted in such conditions other than by cover in depth.

Then, midway through the first half, much to our dismay, and mine in particular, John Newell brought Truett down and the big referee blew and pointed authoritatively.

Waiting for the kick to be taken I thought of the penalty Ben had saved at Highbury in those closing minutes of the 1951 semi-final against Hendon, and the crucial penalty we'd been awarded against Hayes that had sent us on our way to Wembley in 1953 — the slings and arrows of outrageous fortune.

Now not even Pinner could save us and we came off at half-time a goal down, to try and sort out our problems with Arthur Rowe.

The small boy, still warming himself by the fire, greeted his father a good deal more cheerfully than I felt like doing at that particular moment. For though no doubt the referee's decision was correct, it was also unquestionably a very tough one — they invariably are when you are on the receiving end. John Newell had never intended a foul, but had simply lost his feet and collided with Truett. Not altogether surprisingly, Ken Aston, who was later to referee the Cup Final of 1963 when Manchester United defeated Leicester City 3-1, and become chairman of the FIFA Referees' Committee, had not been swayed one least bit by my little stratagem.

The sudden hope that Peter Hancock's equalising goal gave us eight minutes from time was almost immediately dashed in our faces as the Wycombe centre-forward, Paul Bates, scored their winning goal and knocked us out of the 1956 Amateur Cup. The biggest crowd of the nine ties, 6,500, saw the exciting finish. It was my thirty-sixth and last cup-tie for Pegasus.

The drive back was interminably long, cold and depressing, the road icy, with thick fog lying in patches between Guildford and Horsham. As always on those journeys I reflected on the match. Long before I reached home I had come to the conclusion that, even if I was still required, it was time to call it a day.

Eight marvellous years of football I'd had with Pegasus and played one hundred and seventy-two matches for the club. I was ever aware of my good fortune for there were others who could have done just as good a job at centre-half, if not better. Now, like all things, the scene had changed and of the team that had just played against Wycombe only Denis and I remained from the 1951 side.

And Denis? *The Times* correspondent was correct in his estimation of him. How well he'd played. Tall and thin and as imperturbable as ever, he'd got hold of the ball with those long spindly legs and, searching, found space and time to support his forwards with telling passes and still defend, winning, as usual, most things in the air. Even then he must have been as good an amateur wing-half as any in the country.

We played out what was left of the season, losing at Cambridge in the final of the Cambridgeshire Invitation Cup 0-2 to Wisbech Town, somewhat redeeming ourselves by once more reaching the final of the AFA Cup for the fourth time — we'd already won it three times — after defeating Cambridge Town 3-2.

But our eyes — and those of many others — were now fixed on the Corinthian-Casuals, who, with their seven ex-Pegasus players, all from Cambridge, were going from strength to strength. Sheppey United, Wimbledon, St Albans City and Hitchin Town had fallen to them. In the semi-final they met Dulwich Hamlet at Stamford Bridge and won 3-1, playing for seventy minutes with only ten men, for Jack Laybourne had been carried off with a severely cut leg which required eight stitches.

Then, at Wembley they met our old opponents, Bishop Auckland and, after extra time, drew with them 1-1 before a crowd of 82,000.

Before the replay took place on the Middlesborough ground, Ayrsome Park, the Casuals' committee telegrammed Jim Swanton, Port of Spain, Trinidad, where his cricket side was touring, requesting permission that their inside-forward, Mickey Stewart, the England and Surrey cricketer, be allowed to fly home and play in the final. Unfortunately, severe head winds delayed the plane and after a dramatic rush by car from Prestwick, he arrived just too late to take the field, but in time to see his side lose to the Bishops 4-1.

What, I wonder, might have been the outcome if Pegasus and the Corinthian-Casuals had pooled their resources?

Above: Arthur Rowe

Chapter 34

Some selling, writing and coaching

ABOUT THIS time, I was approached by a small, rather old-fashioned — in a nice sort of way — clothing manufacturing firm, Burleigh Clothing, in Northamptonshire, to represent them in London and try to open some accounts with the big stores. For doing so I was to be paid three pounds a day plus my expenses.

Before Easter, I went to stay for a few days in order to learn something about the clothing trade. The firm had five hundred employees and I got on well with the two senior directors who each had their own private aeroplane. I returned to Lancing not having learnt much, but prepared to have a go. I had, at least, been measured and presented with a new suit because the firm considered it would be a good advertisement for me to wear one of their make.

Soon my samples began to arrive: a man's overcoat and lamb's-wool jacket., two men's Harris tweed jackets and Terylene trousers. There were youths' jackets and blazers, trousers and shorts. They were accompanied by numerous swatches, heavy bunches of different shades and grades of cloth, to be shown to the buyers when they had, we hoped, presented me with an order.

I went into Worthing, bought the biggest Revelation expanding suitcase I could find, and one warm day towards the end of April, bade Biddie farewell and set off by train for London.

At Victoria I caught a bus to Kensington, my huge, heavy suitcase only just fitting beneath the stairs. For my first port of call I had decided on Pontings, which I considered might prove not too swish.

I felt hot and conspicuous as I entered the crowded store and made for the lift. Nearby a middle-aged shop assistant wearing a smart black dress was demonstrating a product to a group of shoppers, working away deftly, occasionally glancing over the heads of her audience with an air of bored detachment. I watched idly until the lift doors opened. Then, as I bent to pick up my suitcase, one end of the handle came adrift and I had no alternative but to clasp the case in my arms — which didn't particularly endear me to the liftman or the occupants already packed tightly. "Men's clothing," I murmured and seconds later emerged from the lift still holding the case.

I put the wretched thing down and approached an assistant. Walking across the carpet I was vaguely aware of the muted sound of traffic pouring along Kensington High Street far below. I was thankful there wasn't much activity in the department.

"I'd like to see the buyer if possible," I stated, as nicely as I knew how.

"Mr Crawford's still at lunch. He shouldn't be long. Have you got a card?" I gave him one.

Twenty minutes later the assistant signalled that Mr Crawford had returned from lunch and was willing to see me. Clasping the suitcase once more I went towards the buyer, a short elderly man to whom I warmed at once.

"You seem to be in some trouble," he remarked, as I put the case down.

"I am, it's brand new. I only got it yesterday."

"Looks as though you've a soft rivet there," he said, examining the case. "Your best bet is to take it straight back to their place at Chiswick and they'll give you a new one. You can get there by bus."

I nodded. "May I show you what I've got?" I asked tentatively.

"I'll have a look at it. I know your firm, I've dealt with them in the past."

This sounded encouraging.

I took out the overcoat, a soft, long, very heavy dark grey crombie. I showed him the jackets and the trousers and the youths' stuff. He quite liked the man's lamb's-wool jacket. But he gave me no order.

"I'll give them a ring at Chiswick and tell them you're coming," which was nice of him. "Come and see me again," he suggested, holding out his hand.

It proved a long bus journey to Chiswick and all the while the sun shone hotter than ever. Eventually I arrived, explained the situation, unpacked my clobber and repacked it into a new case. At least I had learnt how to fold clothes. Then I set off for Victoria and caught a crowded train back to Lancing, standing for most of the journey. I made out my report and expenses and decided to try Gorringes the following day — they ran our school shop.

I had last visited Gorringes in 1930 when my mother took me there to be fitted out for my preparatory school. As far as I could see the store had changed very little. For a while I hung around watching an assistant indulging a concerned parent whose bored young son seemed to be going through much the same performance as I had done some twenty-five years earlier.

Eventually I was summoned to see the buyer, a man in his fifties who had a round, slightly florid face beneath a head of flat yellowish thinning hair. His blue eyes looked at me keenly through steel-rimmed spectacles.

I decided on a different tack this time.

"Let me put my cards on the table," I began. "I'm very much a novice at this game, only doing it part-time. I'm really a schoolmaster by profession."

He glanced at my card.

"Lancing College?"

I nodded.

"I can't do much for you at the moment, but we'll have a cup of coffee," and I followed him past the young boy who was now trying on a blazer and looking even more bored.

Mr Kenyon was friendly, he enquired about Lancing and announced that he would be down later in the term to see the bursar. He had a brief look at my samples, showed some interest in the men's Terylene trousers, but presented me with no order. He wished me good luck and told me to call again in a month.

I telephoned Harrods next and spoke to an unpleasant upper deck voice in the buying department who, on hearing of the firm I was representing, informed me with curt rudeness that we were not for them.

"And bollocks to you," I managed to get in before the phone clicked at the other end.

I went up to Whiteley's in Bayswater humping my suitcase, which this time did not have a soft rivet. I sought anonymity in the crowded store and felt more at home. Eventually, after waiting a very long time, the buyer gave me a couple of minutes and, I thought, showed some interest in the boys' blazers, but gave me no order.

I visited amongst others, Barker's, Derry and Toms, Ely's at Wimbledon, Bentall's at Kingston, and Cheesman's at Lewisham. As I sat in the last-named store drinking a cup of coffee one morning, Colin Cowdrey came in with another man. He had married into the firm and worked there.

"It's all right, I haven't got the sack from Lancing," I assured him, as he greeted me in passing my table, at the same time glancing curiously at the suitcase. "Just trying to do a little business with you," in which, needless to say, I did not succeed.

The summer term began and my merry-go-round temporarily ceased, though I managed to slip up to town occasionally to keep some continuity going.

Once, of an evening, John Dancy popped in to see us, just when two of my samples were suspended on coat-hangers from the sitting-room picture-rail. As he sipped his cup of coffee I saw him, more than once, cast a curious eye at the two ticketed garments hanging on our walls but he made no comment.

The sun shone; May, June and July came and went and another summer term slipped quietly away, leaving behind, as relics of some distant age, Founder's Day, the written sweat and worry of all those dreadful 'O' and 'A' level examinations, and a host of mixed memories to remind the leavers that their schooldays were over — to remind the rest that they still lay ahead. But, for the staff, there now stretched the golden prospect of eight glorious weeks of holiday.

We spent all August in our caravan down on the farm at Treveague, Gorran, home of the Whetters. Our field was beautifully situated, high above Hemmick and close to the Dodman. We looked across an expanse of sea, flanked by cliffs and headlands, with the Gull Rock and Nare Head standing out distinctly and the distant loom of the western Black Head visible on clear days. On bad days we'd watch sou'westerly gales gathering over the Goonhilly Downs, before driving across the dark, white-capped waters, eventually smothering our field in sea mist, while the wind shook our van and the rain beat fiercely upon the roof.

On one such day we drove down to Lamorna to visit Biddie's cousin, Susan, wife of J. H. Williams, author of *Elephant Bill,* which had become a best-seller.

It was teatime when we reached our destination, drove down a steep incline, turned into a short twisting drive and found the house, a big grey dwelling, with a heavily slated roof and deep eaves, tucked into the hillside, protected from the winter gales.

As I switched off the engine, an enormous mastiff appeared round the corner of the house and stood in front of the heavy oak porch door, confronting us.

"For God's sake, don't let Kirn out," I said, grabbing his collar, as Biddie prepared to get out and face the mastiff.

"He's all right," she said, opening the car door, "he looks a friendly old chap." I hoped she was right.

Quite undeterred, together with Paul, the pair of them approached the huge dog and made friends at once.

Our host, Jimmy Williams, a big genial native of Cornwall, opened the door and welcomed us.

"Those belonged to Bandoola," his wife, Susan, explained to Paul, who was staring wide-eyed at two enormous ivory tusks mounted in the hall.

Elephant Bill, as Jimmy was now known, had just completed another book on the life of Bandoola, his favourite of all the elephants.

As I sipped my tea, I glanced around at the paintings on the walls, the ornate silver framed photographs on the mantelpiece, and works of carved ivory and teak, mementoes of the years they had spent together in Burma before and during the war.

Later, accompanied by the mastiff — Paul saw to that — we wandered out into a garden of rockery and lavender, of fuchsia bushes and terraces of blue hydrangeas and camellias, falling steeply towards the trees at the bottom, through whose foliage, dark turquoise and purple patches of sea could be glimpsed.

"Why don't you write a book about your experiences as a fisherman?" Jimmy urged me before we left. "You've got a book there."

As we drove back to our caravan, the wind buffeting the car, I considered his advice. And the more I thought about it the more determined I became to start.

I began to write *Whistle the Wind* the following day, scribbling down the story in a cheap exercise book and enjoying doing it. I wrote whenever I could and wherever I was. Distractions around me didn't worry me in the least; I simply shut myself off. I wrote on the Brighton Belle, going to and from London as I tried unsuccessfully to sell clothes. And once, after an unprofitable call, I sat in the sunshine on a park deckchair and, forgetting the world, scribbled away for a couple of hours, using my suitcase as a desk.

Returning from that summer holiday I gained an introduction to John Lewis and saw their buyer, a Mr Tallon, who was most considerate.

One afternoon just before the start of the winter term, I called at their offices in Draycott Avenue, off the King's Road, and was given the break I had been waiting for.

"The single-weft satin lining in that jacket of yours is no good. Apart from being expensive, it threads," and he picked up the lamb's-wool jacket — still my best exhibit — and showed me what he meant.

"Now," he said, "I want you to make some sample men's jackets."

I took out my pencil and notebook and waited with some excitement and a good deal of gratitude.

"Right," he continued, having examined the swatches most carefully and given me the cloth number, sizes and price. "I want your firm to make sixteen men's

Thornproof jackets, three-button, single-vent, with a Marsdon Wilsdon lining. And then," he said, smiling and getting up from behind his desk, "provided they are up to standard, we should be able to do some business."

Delighted, I went out and found the nearest telephone box and put through the order. The firm was pleased and the following week I had an encouraging letter from one of the directors.

Two weeks later I called again on Mr Tallon knowing that the sixteen jackets had been despatched.

He was standing by the window when I went in. Turning, he shook his head and I knew the worst.

"Their make simply isn't good enough," he said. "I'm sorry," and I could see he genuinely was.

"That's all right," I told him, trying to hide my disappointment, "but would you show me where they've gone wrong?"

"Well, to start with, the lapels are too heavy and the jackets need to be more waisted. The pocket lines are not as clean as they should be nor is the sleevehead." He told me a lot else, all of which I reported to the firm.

They wrote back and asked if I would come up as soon as possible and discuss the matter with their cutter, which I did. But it was now clear to me that I was representing a firm whose articles were simply not good enough for the London market. However, I was prepared to persevere and they seemed happy that I should do so. Certainly the money was a great help, three pounds a day and expenses, irrespective of sales.

The Michaelmas term of 1956 began with the usual batch of new boys' tea parties and, as assistant housemaster to the Reverend Henry Thorold, I attended them.

Such occasions are always fraught with tension and Henry's presence ensured that the Gibbs's new boys' tea-party was no exception.

"Keep them standing," he'd say of the parents. "Never let them sit, Ken."

Around the walls of his drawing-room hung some fine paintings, a Poussin, a large sporting painting of two horses by J. F. Herring, and two family portraits by Reynolds, both looking remarkably like Henry.

When the parents began to arrive, he'd greet them with a limp handshake and a broad smile, his long fair hair swept back, his full black cassock encircled by a thin, worn leather belt extended to its last notch. Then the fun would start.

"Here," he'd say, introducing me, "is our house tutor. He is the most distinguished amateur footballer in England," a statement which caused me acute embarrassment and completely nonplussed the parents.

A little later, when one of them rashly broached the subject of work, I found myself even more heavily committed, as Henry, drawing himself up and seeming to inflate as he did so, suddenly announced to his astonished audience, "In this house we do no work, do we, Ken?" To which gobstopper I'd muster an idiotic grin of acquiescence, while Henry continued to survey the parents and their sons with smiling composure.

On another occasion when conversation was wilting — Henry made statements, not conversation — a slightly hysterical mother began relating how her nephew's housemaster at Clifton was a very keen outward-bound type of man, who organised all sorts of exciting expeditions for his boys. "Once they had to cross the Avon Gorge at night without using the bridge!' she enthused, while Henry listened saying nothing. "Don't you think it was a good idea?" she finished in near desperation.

"Yes," said Henry firmly. "A very good idea. But in this house," and he fixed her with an amused, beady eye, "we're inward-bound."

In mid-October I took Nick Evans and Graham Sharman, two of the Lancing side to watch another of our floodlit games with Portsmouth. Throughout the match the rain sheeted down and by the end we'd lost by eight clear goals.

"You're not only over the hill," announced Arthur Rowe, putting his hand on my shoulder, "you're bloody well halfway down Porlock Hill, mate."

"I know, Arthur," I replied.

In fact, it hadn't been anything like such one-way traffic as the score suggested, for the goals, most of them snap shots of tremendous power, were all beautifully hit yet could so easily have gone wide of the mark.

Before leaving Portsmouth, I called on Jack and Moyra Mansell. Jack, who played at left-back, caused us lots of problems that night, attacking our right flank, crossing a stream of balls into our box with his lethal left foot. He scored a number of goals for Portsmouth from that position.

When we set off for Lancing, the rain had lifted and the night was fine. Everything was going well until suddenly, between Arundel and Worthing, the engine began making a most alarming noise.

"What the hell's that?" I asked, slowing down and in some dismay.

"Sounds like a big end," suggested one of the boys cheerfully.

I thought so too and promptly switched off the old Rover engine. It was one o'clock in the morning. A light shone from a downstairs room in a house across the way. I went over and knocked discreetly. The door opened and I saw in the hall a policeman's helmet. We were in luck and the man kindly allowed me to use his telephone. Then I went and sat in the car and wondered how much it was going to cost.

The moon had risen and I watched wearily as the two lads kicked a tennis ball about on the empty wet road which glistened in the moonlight.

We waited a long time. Eventually a van arrived and towed us into Worthing. It was well gone 3 a.m. before we finally got back to Lancing.

I worked hard that Christmas holiday trying to sell clothes and get on with the job of writing *Whistle the Wind*, a task I found a good deal more enjoyable than the former. When I had written something Biddie would read it, we'd then discuss it and she'd remind me of episodes and encourage me to write more.

By now I had got to know the buyers much better and included several schools on my visits; Dulwich, Alleyns, and one at Reigate where an order always seemed in the offing but never quite materialised. And I seemed at last to be getting somewhere with the buyer at Barker's, Mr Edwards; but then, just as an order seemed imminent, the House of Fraser stepped in and bought the wretched store, so I had to begin all over again with a new buyer.

I did not go on the 1957 New Year tour with Pegasus which began with a resounding 7-2 victory over Harwich and Parkeston in the first round of the AFA Cup. A new centre-forward from Oxford, Martin King, scored four of the goals.

On New Year's Eve in a 3-1 floodlit win over Bury Town, the same player scored all three Pegasus goals. A week later at Iffley Road he played another big part in the defeat of the British Police by hitting a further three goals. He was small, skilful, quick and elusive. He was already playing a bit for Colchester United and was eventually to turn professional for them.

So, with a full measure of confidence Pegasus faced Romford at Iffley Road in the first round of the 1957 Amateur Cup only to find themselves trailing at the end by the odd goal in three and were out for another year.

I read the result in the evening paper and shared their disappointment. I consoled myself that at least I did not have to face that long and tiring drive home.

And once again the eyes of many were now turned on the Corinthian-Casuals, who went from strength to strength, only to lose to Wycombe Wanderers in the semi-final.

On a Saturday in early February 1957, I'd taken the Lancing soccer side to Eton and was having tea after the match when my opposite number, Tolly Burnett, casually remarked to a small man sitting opposite me, whose son Peter, now Lord Palumbo, had once played for Eton and was currently at Oxford, "Ken has a business side-line."

"Oh," said Rudolph Palumbo, "what do you do?"

"I represent a clothing firm, and I'm trying to open a few accounts for them in London," I replied, a little flippantly, handing him my card, which he looked at carefully.

"Do you know Edward Merrell of Whiteaway and Laidlaw?" he asked, looking up.

I shook my head. He continued to stare at me thoughtfully.

"I know the managing director of the Army and Navy Stores very well. I'll have a word with him. Could you manage to have lunch with me at the Savoy one day next week and we can then talk about it?"

I said with alacrity that I could. Shortly afterwards he left.

"Who's Mr Palumbo?"

"Rudolph?" said Tolly. "He might be able to help you. He's a millionaire."

The following week I duly had lunch at the Savoy with Rudolph Palumbo and on several occasions later. He was always extremely considerate and did all he could to help me.

I visited Whiteaway, Laidlaw and Co. Ltd. in the City and showed them my samples which they examined carefully, saying very little but shaking their heads frequently. "Is that one of their suits you are wearing?"

I nodded, feeling more like a fish out of water than ever.

"They should make you another. It's not good enough. A very bad advertisement. The clothing trade's a tough business," explained Edward Merrell quietly. "The cut and make of your samples are not good enough."

I telephoned the Army and Navy Stores using the introduction Rudolph Palumbo had given me. It worked like magic, but I detected a certain wariness in the voice at the other end.

I was not kept waiting long in the famous store. Very shortly after I had presented my card, a well-dressed man with a superior manner swept towards me as though he wished to get the whole matter over and done with as quickly as possible. I opened my case and showed him the lamb's-wool jacket which he bore away over his arm, disappearing behind a frosted glass door. Very shortly he was back, walking quickly and shaking his head, holding the jacket at arm's length — disdainfully, I thought — and making sinister indrawn hissing sounds.

I beat a hasty retreat to Kensington and the friendly old buyer at Pontings, who did something to restore my morale. But the truth of the matter was that I had now lost confidence in the firm and my samples.

One afternoon, I met Rudolph at the Grosvenor and drove down in his chauffeur-driven Rolls-Royce to watch his son play for Oxford in an end of season away match at Witney. Peter was a useful player but did not get a Blue. I think he was inhibited by his wealthy background and lacked confidence in his ability, which was a pity, because he was fast and direct and, with support, had the makings of a good winger.

We arrived at the ground only to find that the lad was unable to play at the last moment because of an injury. I introduced Tommy to Rudolph and after the game Penelope joined us for a late dinner at the Mitre.

Long after midnight I set off for Lancing sitting in the back of the Rolls with Rudolph, stopping first at his house in Totworth Ascot, where we arrived at two o'clock in the morning.

I was invited in for a drink. After, I set off once again in the Rolls. This time I sat in the front with the chauffeur, looking down the car's long glistening bonnet to the graceful silver emblem winging its way towards the first faint shafts of light breaking in the east. It was a drive I shall always remember, for the great car sped quietly and effortlessly along the empty road, the speedometer needle every so often creeping over the hundred mark.

When we arrived at Timberscombe the Reverend Henry Thorold's Rolls-Royce was standing outside, as upright and distinctive as a dowager duchess, its ancient body clad in fabric.

The chauffeur got out and walked slowly round the old car, smiling to himself as he examined it carefully.

"Look," I said, "why not leave yours and take that one back instead?"

We went inside and had a cup of tea. Then I saw him off.

Standing outside with Kim I sniffed the fresh air. The sun was up, the sea reflecting its golden light. It was a perfect morning to herald the start of another summer term at Lancing.

It was to prove a particularly full one, what with a heavy timetable, coaching the school cricket XI, which took many hours and playing a bit at the weekends. Towards the end of term, I received a letter from the secretary of the Lancing Town Football Club, asking me to coach them. I wrote that I'd like to do so, but could do nothing until the latter half of August. The Town were in the second division of the County League, had a flat, large ground of their own with ample parking space and a covered stand that seated five hundred. They seemed to have an abundance of enthusiasm and plenty of players.

Returning from the West Country I watched them for the first time lose the opening league game of the season. To me the main problem that afternoon seemed to lie with the captain and centre-half, a tough, fearsome-looking player who, urged on by a vociferous home crowd, never failed to belt the ball indiscriminately, and not only the ball, I might add.

After a couple of training sessions I suggested to the selection committee, which met regularly in a singularly depressing and dingy room of the Railway Hotel down in the town, that we make some changes and, in particular, drop the captain.

We won the second match but, at the next meeting, the supporters in the large railway works at Lancing presented us with a lengthy, signed petition demanding the reinstatement of the captain. To make matters more awkward still, the former captain himself turned up demanding to meet the selectors and know why he had been dropped from the first side. We explained again — I had already told him why he had been dropped as gently as possible — and, sticking to our guns, left him out of the next game which we duly won. After that there were no more petitions and we won the league handsomely and gained promotion to the First Division. At the annual dinner the players presented me with an inscribed cigarette-case, while the secretary — though more discreetly — slipped an envelope into my hand which contained a cheque for fifty pounds, which today would be worth well over five hundred pounds. I was surprised and grateful.

Pegasus began the 1957-58 season in good shape, with a profitable long afternoon's coaching session at Iffley Road under Jack Mansell. We were looking for a coach and I had strongly recommended Jack for the job. The club badly required a man who could go onto the field and actively demonstrate and inject fresh ideas and method into our training and play. We needed someone decisive to take charge, widen our horizons and select our sides. The world of amateur soccer had not stood still. Clubs were better organised, money was being paid to players and the major amateur clubs were always on the look-out for good footballers and rewarding them well. Already several of our players had been offered money to play for other clubs. If we were to keep abreast of the times we needed to plan carefully for the future. When I heard that Jack had been officially invited to come up to Oxford and have an afternoon of training with Pegasus I was pleased.

He put on an excellent session, the players occupied and interested as they worked in tight areas and small groups, gradually developing into lengthier and positive attacking patterns, with balls knocked in and laid off and players coming at defenders.

It was exciting stuff to watch, ahead of its time. For Jack Mansell, besides being a fine player, was a highly skilled, intelligent and articulate coach who knew exactly what he was doing and demonstrated what he wanted of us. Unfortunately he possessed a certain abrasive toughness of character and sharpness of tongue which tended to cloud — for some — the undoubted ability of his coaching.

Two incidents that afternoon were to illustrate this side of his character.

He had been working with the players for some time when John Tanner, who was not now playing for Pegasus, came running onto the Iffley Road ground, full of beans.

"Where do you want me, Mr Mansell?" he enquired.

"Over there until we're ready," said Jack, who was deeply engaged in some blind-side running.

He didn't mean to be curt, but such brevity didn't help.

Meanwhile Tommy, who had been watching everything most closely from the touchline, suddenly called across, "What about doing some attack versus defence, Mansell?" Tommy was to address Alf Ramsey by his surname when he was chairman of the Football Association, and that didn't help!

Jack gave a perfunctory wave of acknowledgement and continued with what he was doing.

Several minutes later Tommy called again, "Are you going to do some attack against defence, Mansell?"

This time Jack called things to a halt and turned towards Tommy.

"Doctor Thompson," he said, "we've been practising attack against defence at Portsmouth for the last eight months and we still haven't scored a goal."

Tommy said nothing.

But I knew then that this would be the last time Jack would ever be asked to coach Pegasus — and it was. And more was the pity, for he would have been so good for us, then, or at any time, always provided that he had the time and was given a completely free rein, the only way in which a coach can operate effectively.

Even so, though he was never to coach us again, we won our first seven matches against Coventry, Newbury, Oxford City, March Town, Ilford, Eastbourne and Worthing, scoring thirty-one goals, conceding ten. Martin King played in six of these games and scored twelve times.

I played in the game at Worthing and was able to have a good look at our new centre-forward as he knocked in another four. His style was economical and I was impressed by his skill as he moved swiftly forward, sleeves flapping loosely about his wrists, leaving defenders floundering in the wake of his fluent control. Trimby, Sutcliffe, Miller and Walsh all helped themselves to a goal each that afternoon making it eight. With Pinner in goal and with players of the calibre of Dougall, Harding, Beddows and Hancock to cover him, I thought the side looked good. And it needed to be, for the draw was an extremely hard one, away against Walthamstow Avenue, who had reached the first round of the FA Cup, conceding only two goals in three cup-ties against Bedford Town and Coventry City.

On the day, Pegasus were soon in dire plight and, by half-time, with the slope to face and two goals to make good, looked finished. That they survived, scoring twice in ninety seconds was a measure of their potential. In the replay at Iffley Road Pegasus defeated Walthamstow by three goals to one.

There was jubilation in the Pegasus camp. Martin King's goal was a match-winning classic and Dick Lucas, Walthamstow Avenue's coach, and their secretary, Jim Lewis, agreed that this goal won the match for Pegasus.

George Ainsley, who was now our coach again, was as delighted as anyone, and remarked to the press, "I have seen Pegasus six times since I took over this season and I am certain they are outstanding prospects for Wembley. As the competition progresses, so the side will become stronger and stronger. If we reach Wembley I am certain we will win the Cup."

George was paid a bonus of thirty pounds for helping us defeat Walthamstow Avenue and it was agreed that for subsequent FA Amateur Cup-ties, he should receive a fee of ten pounds and ten pounds for all other matches, provided the club was still competing in the Cup. There was to be no bonus for wins in rounds two, three and four of the Amateur Cup, but if the club reached the semi-final, he was to receive an additional bonus of two hundred pounds. If the club reached the final, a bonus of three hundred pounds. If the club was eliminated from the Amateur Cup he was to be paid seven pounds a match for the rest of the season.

It all looked so promising and confidence ran high as the side prepared for the next cup-tie at Iffley Road against Ferryhill Athletic, the Northern League side.

I couldn't believe my ears when I heard on the radio that they had lost by two clear goals. And, for the third year in succession, the Corinthian-Casuals did well in the Amateur Cup, losing to Crook Town in the quarter-finals this time.

Martin King played only four more games for Pegasus after that cup-tie with Ferryhill Athletic, yet still managed to score a further twelve goals. By the following season he had left Oxford to play professionally for Colchester and we never saw him again.

I played once more for a scratch Pegasus eleven against Eton when we scored fourteen goals! It was strange to recall that once their old boys had won the FA Cup.

Under floodlights at Headington we defeated Oxford City 3-0 in the final of the Oxfordshire Invitation Cup and lost in the semi-final of the Cambridgeshire Invitation Cup to Wisbech Town. Of late we were having to rely on our performances in these other cups for our continued exemption from the preliminary rounds of the Amateur Cup.

In June the committee met at the Morris Motors Athletics and Social Club, Cowley. Glancing through the minutes of the treasurer's report I noticed that Leslie Laitt's honorarium had fallen from fifteen guineas to fifteen pounds!

And then, business over, we went out into the sunshine to play our annual cricket match against Morris Motors.

Chapter 35

Whistle the Wind *and a final five-hour contest with the Bishops*

EARLY IN THE summer of 1958 I finished writing the story of my days of inshore fishing and sent the manuscript up to Peter Lewin, a literary agent, to whom I had been recommended. He wrote back:

> I think you have made an excellent job of this and it is a wonderful change to read a story of this sort with its natural charm and modesty. I think it would suit a number of publishers, but I am sending it to Rupert Hart-Davis to start with.

I felt tremendously encouraged because it had passed its first hurdle.

Towards the end of June I heard again from Peter Lewin, this time informing me that Rupert Hart-Davis wanted to publish the book, but were unhappy about the title, *A Dog In The Sky*, and felt the book was a shade long.

I was delighted with this news and so was Biddie. So also was Elephant Bill, who wrote in a warm letter:

> I must remind you, this is when you start writing another. Plant a tree, build a house, beget a son and write a book is a man's job in life I have been told.

The title certainly proved something of a problem. I had chosen the Cornish fisherman's expression for that small round rainbow which can at times be seen just outside the sun and is a sure portent of bad weather. Look closely and sometimes two 'dogs' can be seen 'mocking the sun'. Unfortunately, however, at that very moment, the Russians sent up a dog called Laika to orbit the earth which promptly put paid to this idea.

We thought of a good many other titles before eventually settling on 'Whistle the Wind'. I chose it because I enjoyed whistling to myself when fishing in the *Coral*. But I quickly learnt that it was not acceptable. "There's enough wind without you whistling," I was reminded bluntly more than once.

I visited the offices of Rupert Hart-Davis at 35 Soho Square and they couldn't have been more friendly. Over lunch, David Hughes, who was married to Mai Zetterling, told me they wished to cut some of the book and indicated parts that I should look at again — a task for the coming holiday.

When finally the summer term came to an end, we faced another move, this time into the College itself. Six months earlier, John Dancy had asked me to take over Sanderson's House. I accepted but on the condition that the school build an internal staircase and knock a doorway through from the vast kitchen, into the dining room. Dancy gave us his support, but the bursar opposed our request — bursars usually do — and the matter went to the council, who agreed that the work should be done.

Sanderson's was a very big two-storey flat in a wing of one of the school buildings, close to the boys' dormitories, house-room and studies — the latter known as 'pitts'. The front door opened into a long, well-lit corridor with a view of the sea at the far end. Two lofty rooms lay off the corridor, a dining room, and a fine, spacious drawing-room, with a panelled cedarwood ceiling, high windows on the east wall and a great mullioned stone bay window facing south, overlooking the distant Channel with extensive views east and west. Originally the Provost's room, it was the most gracious in the College.

But, and here was the first snag, apart from a small serving hatch, there was no means of getting into the kitchen, other than by going down the corridor, out through the front door, into the boys' passage, turning sharp right and sharp right again, finally entering the huge antiquated kitchen outside the main living rooms.

The second snag was far worse. In order to go upstairs to take a bath, have a rest, or go to bed, the present incumbents of Sanderson's had to leave by the front door, climb a broad flight of wooden stairs, used constantly by the boys, proceed along a passage, unlock a door and enter the upstairs accommodation which consisted of four large bedrooms and an awful bathroom. Inside there was a lidless lavatory with a wide mahogany seat and a rusty, iron-framed window which did not shut. Above the old chipped and stained cast-iron bath was an antiquated gas boiler which leaked fumes. It was depressing, to say the least.

It took all day moving our possessions into Sanderson's drawing-room which my predecessor, John Handford, who was still in residence, had kindly emptied for us. The move was made more difficult and expensive, since the van could not get under the arch into the inner quadrangle and everything had to be carried round its perimeter — which we had to pay for, not the school.

Finally, quite exhausted, we closed the door on an empty Timberscombe, hitched on the caravan and set off late in the evening for Cornwall, stopping after some hours' driving, to sleep.

Arriving in our field the following afternoon we found Bill Kennard, our pathologist friend and his family, the only other occupant. His son came running towards us. "Have you heard the news?" he called breathlessly. We had no idea what he was talking about.

"You didn't see it in the papers?" enquired his father, rather anxiously, I thought, as he came across.

I shook my head. We hadn't bought a paper that day.

"Oh dear. I'm afraid your friend Elephant Bill died yesterday on the operating table."

We were shocked and saddened.

Six weeks we spent in our caravan that holiday and then, ten days before the term began, we returned to find the house in an awful state. We hadn't been able to return earlier because John Handford, through no fault of his own, had not been able to move sooner.

At once we set about humping everything from the big room into the other rooms and a hell of a task it proved. To make matters worse, the maintenance staff were still in the process of knocking through the thick wall of the kitchen into the dining room, and there was noise, dust and rubble everywhere.

Somehow we managed to get things shipshape for the beginning of the term. There had been no decoration done in any room and I even had to fight the bursar to get a lid to the lavatory in the bathroom.

Just before the term started we entertained our first guests, David Hughes and Mai Zetterling, who was as delightful as she was beautiful. David presented us with a copy of a novel he had written called *A Feeling In The Air*, inscribed 'For Ken and Biddie — a set book for the upper sixth' and, in return, I presented him with the corrected manuscript of *Whistle the Wind*. Then we were ready for our first new boys' tea-party.

Fourteen of them there were and, apart from getting the parents' names all mixed up, in particular introducing the wrong one as an admiral, it seemed to go all right, though it's an occasion that nobody in their right senses can even remotely enjoy.

Later Henry came in to enquire how we'd got on. "Did you make your how d'ye do's and keep them standing?"

He had spent his customary first two nights with us, the first sleeping on the kitchen windowseat with our Labrador as company, the second on the windowseat in the dining room. He'd shifted his berth because the intermittent rumblings of the huge seven-foot-high ancient school refrigerator — we had no larder — and the dog's occasional visit to see how he was faring had not helped his night's rest. He was unable to use our spare room because the floor was still up.

So I came into housemastering with no preconceived ideas other than that there should be no corporal punishment by me or anyone else, that personal fagging — known as underschooling at Lancing, I hate such hierarchy — was to stop, and that our own door would be open at all times to any boy. We were fortunate in having a mature and humorous head of house, Christopher Saunders, who, in due course, was twelfth man for Cambridge at Lords in 1963 and gained Blues at Oxford for both soccer and cricket the following year. I found the job absorbing, enjoyable, full of problems, some funny, some not so funny and, by the end of the term, very, very tiring. But that's another story; my concern is still Pegasus and those closing years that were finally to mark the end of the road for the old Flying Horse.

1958-59 was the last fully recorded season in the Pegasus Minutes Book in which twenty-seven matches were played.

I took part in one of these at Iffley Road, the last time ever, when the cup-winning 1951 XI played the 1958 XI and lost 2-1 in the last minute. 'The masters had lost but not before they had given their lessons', wrote *The Times*.

Trevor Churchill was now the coach and the New Year tour took place once again in the Channel Isles where the side drew their two matches.

Drawn at Oxford against Kingstonian in the first round of the Amateur Cup, the club got through by the single goal of the match, a typically headed goal by Denis Saunders from a Sutcliffe corner.

A week later, on 24 January 1959, the same eleven: Pinner, Dougall, Harding, Hancock, Edge, Saunders, Race, Trimby, Barber, Scanlan and Sutcliffe, travelled to

Bishop Auckland and drew 0-0 with our old enemy, surviving magnificently on a cruel, rutted and frozen pitch.

The following Saturday, with one change, Grayson for Barber, the side drew again with the Bishops at Iffley Road 0-0. By all accounts Pegasus should have won comfortably, particularly since Bishop Auckland had two spells with only ten men on the field. But Pegasus missed too many chances, one of which included a penalty taken by Denis, who tried to place the kick, but side-footed it with insufficient power, giving the Bishop Auckland keeper time to palm it round the post.

If the verdict goes against them under the Hillsborough floodlights on Wednesday, Pegasus will have paid dearly for Saturday's missed chances, wrote the *Oxford Mail*

And indeed most dearly they did pay, losing to a side that on the day won worthily by the only goal of that mammoth Amateur Cup-tie scored in the fifth minute. Yet things might have been different had Pegasus not yet again missed the penalty awarded them in the thirty-third minute. This time it was Jack Dougall's turn to 'have a go', and have a go he certainly did, driving the ball high and wide of the crossbar far into the gloom of the Spion Kop.

Missing those two penalties and failing to take the chances that came our way, particularly in that first replay, cost us dearly.

Beneath the floodlights of Hillsborough, after eight years of memory and five hours of titanic struggle, the Bishops finally wiped the slate clean and took their revenge on us for Wembley 1951.

Early that March I received the proofs of *Whistle the Wind*, which I corrected and returned. By the end of April I was sent six advance copies. On 14 May, I heard from Harry Townshend, one of the directors, who wrote:

> Just a line to greet you on publication day. We have sold slightly over 1,000 copies of *Whistle the Wind*; quite a good start and I am sure that when the reviews appear it will really start moving.

The edition was only 3,500, but it did have some surprisingly good and lengthy reviews, nineteen in all — including a third of a column in the *Sunday Times* by the poet, Charles Causley.

As a family it gave us great pleasure that summer, seeing the book displayed in Mevagissey and knowing that the fishermen liked it. It has since been reprinted, and it gives me just as much pleasure to know that it is still being read by the families of those skippers, alongside whom — for a short while — I once fished for my living.

So, to the last few years of Pegasus, the events of which are not easy to piece together. The picture is blurred and only by a close examination of the minutes book — some of which is missing — and putting together what records I can lay hands on, does the end become at all clear.

On reflection, it now seems inevitable that the wheel should have turned full circle and we'd find ourselves once more back where we'd begun — an undergraduate club — but sorely pressed.

The constitutional cracks that had appeared as early as 1949, when the one-year rule had been voted out, had never healed. By the mid-50s we'd built up a mature team with a lot of experience of the rough and tumble of cup-ties, but the passage of players to the Corinthian-Casuals: Shuttleworth, Cowan, Doggart, Insole, Laybourne, Dutchman, Platt, Vowels, Alexander, Pretlove, Adams, Harrison and others, had split our forces. By the end of the 50s the average age of the team had fallen from twenty-six to twenty as the old guard of Brown, McKinna, Saunders, Pawson, Tanner, Potts, myself, Carr, Lunn, Sutcliffe, Blythe and Hancock, gradually fell by the wayside. Never was the need for unity and understanding between the two universities more essential to the future of Pegasus. But it was never to be attained.

Long and difficult committee meetings were held at the two universities. At one of these, representatives of Cambridge and the Corinthian-Casuals proposed that the committee examine in detail the playing policy of the club with regard to the reintroduction of the one-year rule and it was carried unanimously. Well before that, however, Tommy had resigned as chairman. Finally, and I could never understand why, a contract was signed to use the White City stadium as a London ground and play at least four matches on it during the 1960-61 season. It was to prove both a foolish move and a failure.

Chapter 36

With Pegasus again

I HAD NOW completed two years as a housemaster and John Dancy's initial impact at Lancing — which had brought about much coming and going of staff and had been referred to by some as 'Dancy's inferno' — had gradually softened with time as the school not only flourished but was full to overflowing. Many of the old guard had left and, at last, all those preposterous marks were discarded for a tutorial system which was infinitely preferable and beneficial to all concerned.

I was still coaching the Town — I did so for eight years, as well as coaching the school — and had got both sides playing a four-two-four formation, twin centre-forwards, full-backs wide, double cover in the centre of the back line and two link-men in the middle. I couldn't understand why other clubs, apart from England under Walter Winterbottom, were so slow to adopt this system. No one in the county league of Sussex was using it, nor were any of the schools. I asked George Curtis, manager of Brighton and Hove Albion — ex-Arsenal inside-forward — I'd been with him on that FA tour of the Channel Islands back in 1949 and hadn't seen him since — why he didn't adopt it. "You need special players," he assured me. You need special players in any system, I thought.

Before Lancing played Winchester that season I rang Hubert Doggart in the guise of a retired Wykehamist naval officer.

"Haven't been down to the place for a long while. Wondered if you'd a game of soccer coming up?"

"We have," said Hubert, "we've got a school match this Saturday."

"Splendid. I'd like to come and watch. Who are you playing?"

"Lancing College."

"Never heard of 'em. Never played 'em in my day. Are they any good?"

"Not bad,' said Hubert, "they're playing a four-two-four system."

"Four-two-four? We never used to do any of that sort of thing. Do Winchester play it?"

"No," said Hubert emphatically.

"Have you got a good side this year?"

"Yes," said Hubert, "I think we have," and he began warming to his subject. "We've got a good strong centre-forward and a very fast outside-right."

"What's the goalkeeper like?"

"Weak on crosses and a bit slow off his line, but otherwise adequate."

Gradually, without giving the game away, I drew from him a clear picture of the Winchester side.

Eventually, satisfied I had found out all I could, I revealed my identity. "Thank you, Hubert," I said and heard an explosive snort at the other end.

But he had the last laugh because, right on time, we lost by the only goal of the match. Jeremy Nichols, the Lancing captain and centre-half, who was to run the soccer at Eton — successfully, I might add — and is now headmaster of Stowe, with no pressure at all, proceeded to put through his own goal and give them the game.

I was still popping up to London whenever I could, trying hard to sell a few clothes. Once I had a near squeak. I was showing some men's Terylene trousers during one holiday, when I suddenly spotted a member of my house. "Be back in a moment," I said and quickly moved away before the astonished buyer could open his mouth. However, on this occasion, and to my amazement, I received an order for fifty pairs of men's Terylene trousers. Upon this climactic note I decided to call it a day, 'hang up', whatever one does in the clothing trade, and end my career as a part-time salesman.

Pegasus had permission to use the White City stadium and for the inaugural match, our old foe from the north, Bishop Auckland, travelled south and defeated us, 4-2. It was the sixth and last game the two clubs were ever to play, and a good one at that, which deserved a much larger crowd. As Harry Sharret, the Bishop Auckland and England goalkeeper remarked, "There was no atmosphere out there. It was like a morgue". Less than 500 watched the match in a stadium that could hold 65,000. Leslie Nichol wrote:

> 100,000 cheered the same clubs when Pegasus beat the Bishops 2-1 in the classical 1951 Amateur Cup final at Wembley. The 'gate' on Saturday amounted to around £50. Bishops had a guarantee covering the cost of the trip, which must amount to much more than £100.

One evening during the Michaelmas term of 1960 the telephone rang and out of the blue I was asked by John Tanner to coach Pegasus. I was amazed, delighted and honoured, particularly the former, for I had no FA preliminary coaching badge, though I had been repeatedly urged by Jack Mansell to get one. But time was always pressing and I was deeply involved with the town side as well as the school, and in constant touch with Jack who had succeeded Ron Greenwood as player-coach at Eastbourne United.

I first officially met the Pegasus players on 29 December, in the Great Northern Hotel, Peterborough, where we had a long talk before playing the British Police that night under floodlights. Several faces I knew, but a lot were strangers to me. There were two first-class goalkeepers in Pinner and Wakefield; three backs: Sharp, Harding and Dougall; five midfield players: Saunders, Pearce, Beddows, Hancock and Moxon; and six forwards: Jackson, Carlisle, Ogden, Race, Randle and Smith.

Pinner was an Olympic goalkeeper and had already, as an amateur, been helping out Queen's Park Rangers, as he was later to do for Aston Villa, Sheffield Wednesday, Manchester United, Chelsea and Leyton Orient — for the last club he eventually turned professional. Harding had captained the England amateur side and was now playing for Kettering Town. Saunders and Dougall were both internationals and Carlisle had played for Scotland. Wakefield, Jackson and Moxon were all to become internationals and there were five former captains of Oxford and Cambridge in the party. They looked to me a pretty good lot and I felt honoured to be their coach.

After John had briefly introduced me, I considered it wise to make clear from the start the way in which I might possibly be of any assistance to them as a coach.

I was strongly aware of succeeding such distinguished professionals as Vic Buckingham, Reg Flewin, George Ainsley, Leslie Compton, Joe Mercer, Arthur Rowe and Trevor Churchill. Under all but the last I had been a player so, at least, I had that experience to hand on. Even so, I was only an amateur, of no great distinction, and I knew, if I was to gain their confidence, I had to convince them I had something more to offer, above all, that I believed in what I was propounding and was capable of carrying it out on the field in practical coaching sessions. I explained that I had been coaching men for some years now and had been fully involved in plenty of cup football, the FA Cup, the Amateur Cup, and local Sussex cups, as well as a full county league programme in which ex-professionals could play. The experience gained had been supplemented by a close working alliance with Jack Mansell. It was this I hoped to pass on and in doing so to promote a professional approach — the only approach — since it represents above all the highest aspect of the game.

I was keen to play a 4-2-4 formation straight off that evening and after I had discussed it thoroughly with the players they seemed happy to do so, though Denis Saunders, I knew, was a little dubious and so was John Tanner. They felt we'd lose the midfield, and that it was asking too much of the link-men.

I contended that if this were so, one of the centre-forwards could drop back and lend a helping hand; so, also, could one of the centre-halves move forward to strengthen the middle or contain any oncoming threat. In the latter case it would be up to the appropriate full-back to pivot round and cover the centre as of old. And there was nothing, I argued, to stop the unengaged winger from moving inside and so helping out the midfield. Any formation should be fluid. There was strength too where it mattered most, down the length and centre of the field involving seven players, two strikers, two link-men, two centre-halves and the goalkeeper. Above all, in a 4-2-4 system one did not need to anchor defenders rigorously, but could free them. Who better to go forward than unmarked players — defenders — in particular, wing-backs?

So we put Denis Saunders into the back four to play alongside Jack Dougall at centre-half. It would take some of the pressure off him, and his skill and ability to read the game would be invaluable. Jack Dougall, the captain, an enormous chap, taller than Denis and, physically very strong, was a more orthodox centre-half. With Mike Pinner behind I thought they'd be well capable of holding the fort and winning everything in the air.

Under floodlights we drew 1-1 with the British Police on Peterborough United's ground that night and I was delighted that our goal was the direct result of Harding at left-back attacking freely. What a good player he was — so elegant and composed. It surprised me not a bit that he had captained England.

Then we travelled back to the Melville Hotel, Oxford — our headquarters for the New Year tour — talking, as usual, most of the way. It was like old times, but I missed Jerry, who was now living in Paris and had just been promoted to the rank of Counsellor of the European Nuclear Energy Commission, and Tommy, who was in America, and our old treasurer, Bill Cavill, no longer with us, who had once with booming geniality and headmaster's firmness refused Mike Pinner's demands for his girlfriend's breakfast expenses.

We did a long stint of training at Iffley Road the next day trying to develop a pattern of play on the flanks, with wingers coming at opponents and plenty of support and movement off the ball. I was particularly looking for someone who could break fast from the middle and head for the heart of an opposition. I was looking also for skill — but then who isn't?

On the last day of 1960 we travelled to the White City and defeated the Sussex FA 4-2. I knew most of their side, having watched them playing in the Sussex County League. In particular, I knew about Nigel Wrigglesworth, who was the Lancing Town goalkeeper.

'PEGASUS 4-2-4 OFF TO PROMISING START' wrote the press, concluding,

> 'Only a bold club would take the plunge like this, but if one expects boldness anywhere in football, one expects it from Pegasus.'

Then we went back again to Oxford and some more training on Sunday at Iffley Road. At the White City a week later, we drew 0-0 with a Draconian side containing eight Welsh internationals. Our defence looked good, but we needed another forward and I was trying to get hold of David Jacobs, a current Cambridge player, who I thought would fit the bill.

Before journeying to play Erith and Belvedere — our opponents in the first round of the Amateur Cup — we defeated London University at Oxford by the only goal of the match. After watching the game I was more certain than ever that we needed something extra to support the thrusting speed of Jackson, a match-winner, given the right service. So I telephoned David Jacobs again — he was playing in the Eastern Counties League — this time successfully.

I felt confident now that the side was capable of giving a good account of itself. But I knew too well the pitfalls of Erith's ground and, remembering our last cup game with the Kent club in 1950, when we'd precariously hung on to a 1-1 draw, I warned the players of the dangers they'd find themselves in if they attempted to play short stuff. "Get power and length into your passes."

Ideally I wanted the back four to by-pass our midfield, the backs to get it in early to the wingers, the centre-backs to find our two front men, who could then lay it off to the link-men. Under such glutinous conditions I hoped to bring our midfield into the game from the front and not from the back.

The referee had looked in. Time was running out. "No ball watching," I urged, as the team prepared to leave the dressing-room. "Goal-side when they're in possession and remember, no ceremony. Win it and whack it — that's the order of the day. All the best." And then they were gone and I was left with Leslie Laitt in a strangely quiet and empty changing-room. "Up to them now, Les."

"Yes," he said, unperturbably putting things into his bag. He still wore his hat, the same brown trilby.

There's not much to be said with effect in the last stages before a match. A word in an ear here and there, a bit of reassurance, but too much directive is unsettling. In any case it should all have been done before.

Sitting on the touchline I felt the old pre-match tension seeping out of me and hoped it had not shown earlier. As the two sides kicked around at each end I could see the ball was already beginning to stick, in and outside both penalty areas. John Tanner, the secretary, quietly preoccupied, was chewing his upper lip watching the scene closely. Colin Weir, team secretary, habitual dark blue scarf wound round his neck, sat tall and upright, chatting concernedly with Sydney Bayliss, our treasurer. How much these three had done for Pegasus. Tommy, of course, was in America. Then the whistle blew. Ninety minutes later we were still in the Cup, having drawn 3-3.

On Monday when the draw for the second round was announced we learnt of our tough assignment — Bromley away. But we had first to defeat Erith and Belvedere. We read also in the *Oxford Mail* of that same day a criticism of the match being played at the White City, criticism that I think we all felt was justified and understandable, for Oxford had given us such tremendous support.

For the replay we made two changes, Flann and Randle for Race and Jacobs, the latter having a septic foot. I was glad that Randle was in, for he was the type of player we were looking for, direct, very quick into his stride and with a good deal of skill. He played well that day when we won 2-0 at the White City before a meagre 800 spectators.

The match had been too close for any of our liking, but I felt that Randle's inclusion as one of the link-men had given us a good deal more thrust and chance of creating opportunities. Above all, he took some of the pressure off Jackson who was now a closely marked man. For Randle had speed and control to take on defences, though he had difficulty knowing when to release the ball. Beddows, the other link-man was a slower, stronger and more orthodox wing-half, whose task it was to win and use the ball early and support his forwards. Denis too was a key factor, for he was free to go forward and initiate attacks and plug any gaps left by abortive midfield thrusts.

But our chief difficulty lay in adapting to positional interchange and recognising the opportunity of a quick break from defence to attack.

However, there was little doubt in any of our minds that we faced a stiff task. For Bromley were top of the Isthmian League, having played twenty matches, won thirteen, drawn five, and lost only two, with 58 goals for, 29 against. But I liked the look of our side and felt we could do it. Ogden on the left was a neat player, Jackson, with Jacobs alongside, would prove a dangerous pair up front, while Carlisle on the right, if he lacked stamina, had craft. A lot would depend on Beddows winning the ball, and Randle's thrust from the middle. I had no worries about the back four or our goalkeeper, Brian Wakefield.

Very quickly the week passed and we found ourselves at Hayes Lane, and there were Helen and Guy Pawson making for a section of the main stand which had been reserved for Pegasus supporters. It was good to see them both and I chatted briefly with them before going to our changing-room.

We began unpacking our gear and suddenly those two faithful supporters, Chedder Wilson and Doug Margetts, stuck their heads round the door and wished us good luck. It was twelve years ago that we'd lost to Bromley 4-3 at Oxford when the Kent side had gone on to win the Amateur Cup, beating Romford 1-0 at Wembley. Now only Denis, aged 34, remained of that 1949 Pegasus side, and only Reg Dunmall, 38, of that Bromley side. Once again they faced each other in what *The Times* considered a 'GRIPPING TIE AT BROMLEY'.

"D'you think Pegasus will beat Bromley in the replay, sir?" the form asked me on Monday morning.

"I think we've every chance," I replied.

"What went wrong on Saturday, sir?"

"We didn't sufficiently exploit their weakness," I explained and began to tell them — it was what they wanted, of course, and plenty of it — how we'd tried to get our left-winger to run Dunmall in the second half. "It was clear early on that the Bromley right-back lacked pace and, I suspected, wind. He gave our left-winger a tremendous amount of room — using all his positional wisdom to save his legs and not commit himself. He waited for us to make the mistakes. We should have come at him, run him into the ground and buried him. Instead — and he must be given credit for it — we played it the way he wanted us to play, to the extent we even made him look good." I refrained from telling them that if we'd had Pat Neil, the brilliant Cambridge outside-left, it would have firmly tipped the scales in our favour and we'd have won the match first go.

But we still lived to fight another day and, a week later, back once more at Iffley Road, Oxford, on a gusty Saturday afternoon in early February 1961, before an official crowd of only 2,001 — nearly 10,000 less than had watched Bromley conclude our first ever venture into the Amateur Cup of 1949 — we lost once again to the same club, 2-1.

On the day we simply were not man enough for the job, and a power-headed corner in the second half seemed somehow to ram the fact home. I felt a powerless shrinking feeling as I watched the side strive for an equaliser that never really seemed within their grasp.

Driving back on my own to Lancing, I relived the game as I'd done so many others. To ease my disappointment I took some consolation in the knowledge that I'd been with the club for eight matches and we'd only been defeated once. It did something to help. I never saw Pegasus play again.

Chapter 37

Demise of the winged horse

WE WERE NOW under a new headmaster, E. W. Gladstone, who succeeded John Dancy, who became Master of Marlborough. John Dancy — we were to reap the harvest he'd sown by gaining forty Oxford and Cambridge awards in four years — had done great work at Lancing, and Biddie and I were far from being the only ones saddened by the departure of him and his family. We missed his friendship and his enthusiasm, though it once provoked Henry Thorold to exclaim: "I can stand lying, I can stand cheating, I can stand downright evil, but I cannot stand enthusiasm."

Willie Gladstone, great-grandson of the Prime Minister, did not particularly want the job because he was about to become a housemaster at Eton. The Lancing post had not been advertised and it was done under the usual old boy network. The inner ring of the HMC, the Ushers' Union, knew of someone who, in their opinion, would fit the bill, and, abracadabra, there it was, we had a new headmaster. It was one way of doing it, I suppose, but there was something slightly distasteful about it all. A few years later when the headmastership of Eton came up — it was not, of course, advertised — I decided to put in for the job. There was much speculation in the papers as to the likely candidates and the name of Willie Gladstone — he, like me, had got a Third in History — had been suggested as a possible and certainly suitable one, but for the fact that he'd only been at Lancing for a short while. So I wrote my letter:

Dear Provost,

Despite what Peterborough and the *Daily Mail* write, I feel that I'm your man. I would be most grateful if you would send me the relevant documents concerning the post of headmaster of Eton. I make this request as so far no notice has appeared on our common room notice-board. I shall look forward to hearing from you.

Yours sincerely, Ken Shearwood.

I did hear — indirectly and very shortly — because the Provost of Eton promptly telephoned Willie Gladstone, who wrote to me:

Dear Ken,

I should be most grateful if you would discontinue your correspondence with the Provost of Eton — please!

Yours,

Willie Gladstone.

Which made my hackles rise somewhat.

"The trouble is, Ken," explained Willie on the telephone, "there are so many important people concerned in this appointment that it could do our cause harm."

My hackles rose even more.

"It's all this nepotism that I so heartily dislike," I replied, with some heat. "You're bang right," agreed Willie, before hanging up.

And bang right he was about important people being involved, for Tony Chenevix-Trench, at the time headmaster of Bradfield — we'd overlapped at Shrewsbury — had to visit the Rt. Hon. Harold Macmillan, at Number Ten, before being appointed headmaster of Eton.

And, talking of Bradfield, Paul was now at this school, and I shall not forget in a hurry their new boys' tea-party because it dragged on interminably.

First, we all had to go to the school shop and buy games clothes, which I found tedious and irritating, particularly when I saw their balloon-shaped soccer shorts, which smacked of the other game. We stood in a long queue — I was told this was to help the parents get to know each other — while a stupid mother at the front held us all up as she fussed ostentatiously around her unfortunate son. The man in front of us, I discovered later he was in the Foreign Office, blew immaculate smoke-rings and fiddled so nervously with his matchbox that it suddenly exploded in his hand and, for one brief moment, it looked as though the Bradfield school shop might be burned to the ground.

By now storm-clouds were gathering fast over Pegasus. Tommy had returned from America and at the AGM in October 1961, as president, spoke his mind. The Cambridge captain had written to him saying that he intended to resign and play for Harwich FC. Furthermore, he stated in his letter that resident Cambridge players should not play for Pegasus without first consulting the Corinthian-Casuals. In such circumstances, Tommy considered it would be impossible for Pegasus to continue without proper club loyalty. The press, too, was well aware of our difficulties and Brian Glanville voiced them in *The Sunday Times* with an article headed 'PEGASUS IN DANGER':

> Is it too late to save Pegasus, the winged horse which has apparently flown too near the sun? It would be a tragedy for British football were it to disappear, for such a club can give soccer, in time, the administrators it so desperately needs.

Such was the situation when the club faced Hendon at Iffley Road before a crowd of only 1,100 in the first round of the Amateur Cup on 20 January 1962, of which *The Times* wrote:

> Although this fixture had been imbued with a certain morbid poignancy by those prophets who forecast the death of Pegasus this season, it proved to be a rousing, rather than funereal, affair, with the combined universities giving such a good account of themselves against the 1960 Cup winners that they are entitled to hold high hopes for the replay next Saturday.

But it was not to be.

Psychologically, it could not have helped seeing Mike Pinner in the Hendon goal. And he was there the following week when Hendon took ample revenge for that sunny afternoon back in 1951 when we had defeated the London club 3-2 at Crystal Palace in the semi-final of the Amateur Cup. This time at Claremont Road, on a glutinous morass, it was their day and we lost the cup-tie: Hendon 6 — Pegasus 1.

Things were rapidly coming to a head. A meeting of senior members discussed in the summer whether the club should continue. It was decided that it should. Since the club had not been granted exemption from the qualifying competition, the Oxford and Cambridge captains agreed to leave a number of Saturdays free in the Christmas term so that Pegasus could prepare and select a side for their matches.

The 1962-63 season began with a match against Walton and Hersham at the end of September, culminating in a resounding defeat by six clear goals. A week later, the side lost again to Southall away 0-2. Several more matches were played and then we got knocked out of the Cambridgeshire Invitation Cup 3-4.

Such was our short and undistinguished playing record, when on December 15, Pegasus met Windsor and Eton in the fourth qualifying round of the Amateur Cup played at Iffley Road and lost 1-3. Fourteen years ago, almost to the day, we had begun our first venture away against Enfield in the same round, knowing we had to win to survive, and the present players faced the same critical situation.

I am glad I did not see the match. The headline in *The Times* said it all: 'ILLUSTRIOUS NO LONGER — SAD DECLINE OF PEGASUS'. The end was in sight.

At a meeting of the committee held in Tommy's room in St John's College, Oxford, in March 1963, a single item was on the agenda, 'The Future Policy of the Club'. There and then the committee finally agreed: "There should be no further entries for competitive football and that the club should be put into 'cold storage'." The last recorded match that Pegasus played was on 6 April 1963, against Marston United in the third round of the Oxfordshire Senior Cup, which Pegasus won by a single goal scored by G. Clayton.

And Denis Saunders, once captain and sole remaining player of those two Amateur Cup-winning sides of the early 50s — with well over two hundred matches under his belt — was still present that afternoon at Iffley Road, playing quietly on as though determined to see Pegasus through — right to the bitter end.

So, what began as a combined football venture by Oxford and Cambridge undergraduates, inspired by Tommy, finally foundered on a difference of opinion that was apparent as early as 1949 when the one-year rule was rescinded. It created a gulf that was never bridged, a contention never resolved.

By and large, players at Cambridge — and a few at Oxford — stuck to the now extinct one-year rule and, after being down a year, moved on and played for the Corinthian-Casuals. The London club had attended that first meeting of Pegasus to discuss the formation of an Oxford and Cambridge football club, and supported Tommy in his important and successful bid for exemption. Understandably, they opposed the abrogation of the one-year rule because, in their eyes, Pegasus had now suddenly become a rival — a club that could retain university players who would otherwise have found their way to the Casuals' camp.

Right from the start it was evident that a link existed between the Corinthian-Casuals and Cambridge that was not to be found at Oxford. But then, at Oxford, there existed a link between Tommy and the university that was not to be found at Cambridge. And this was significant, for it explains why the Cambridge players tended to view Tommy differently from us at Oxford. To them, he represented the 'auld enemy'; brilliant, arbitrary, and sometimes most disconcerting. Fundamentally, Tommy was a pragmatist. His policies and his pursuit of them were not always compatible with diplomacy. But, as Pegasus soared higher and ever higher during those early years, such matters were of no real consequence for we had the world below us. Towards the end of the 50s, however, when our wings had been well and truly clipped and we were falling fast, the Cambridge players viewed the club more and more critically and the distant figure of Tommy with increasing incomprehension.

But still the real question remains — should the One-Year Rule have been abolished? Most of us at Oxford believed that it had to go and that Tommy was right and justified in striving for its abolition.

Hypothetical though it may be, Pegasus would not, I think, have survived and won the Amateur Cup in 1951 and 1953 had the club quickly lost the services of that postwar generation of players with their pre-university experience. And from our success, it should be remembered, the Casuals rejuvenated themselves and later reaped the benefit of experienced Pegasus players who helped them in their own successes of '56, '57 and '58.

What a pity it was that the two clubs could not have amalgamated in some way, sunk their differences and pooled their resources, but it was simply not practicable.

In the final count, then, no one was really to blame. The club's early demise was an inescapable fact. The real reason lay not solely with the players, Tommy, differences of opinion, problems of administration, the Casuals, or the attitude of a new generation of undergraduates, although all were contributory factors.

The real reason lay in the timing of Pegasus's inception, its growth and success, in the aspiration of men who came to Oxford and Cambridge, not as typical undergraduates, but as older and mature students, something that Tommy recognised and used to such telling effect.

Was there ever then the basis for a permanent club once this generation had gone? I don't think so, nor really did Geoffrey Green, who wrote in his book, *Soccer In The Fifties:*

Pegasus came and went like a shooting star. But in their short life they shed a bright light on the game as a whole. They were something different.

And if there is one name that has earned a permanent right to be associated with Pegasus first and foremost, then it is surely that of Professor Sir Harold Warris Thompson, Commander of the British Empire and Fellow of the Royal Society, more simply known to us all as Tommy.

As for me — have I any regrets? None — this isn't strictly true: there is just one — that I never played for England as an amateur. But then had Rob Tillard not elected to shoot pheasants on that particular Saturday back in October 1947, I might never have played for Oxford, let alone Pegasus. So who knows ... who knows?

Above: Lancing Staff 1960

Above:
A bit dressed up!
A wedding in Arundel.

Right:
Relaxing at Lancing in the
early Sixties.

Chapter 38

Sanderson's House

I HAD NOW been housemastering for eight years and Willie Gladstone had come and gone. I said goodbye to him in his study. During his six years at Lancing he had married Rosalind Hambro, inherited a title and was ready to start afresh, bringing up his family, running Hawarden Castle and his Fasque estate in Kincardineshire. He sent his daughter to Lancing for her sixth-form education and he told me later it was the best thing that could have happened to her, which pleased me, for I was more than partly instrumental in her coming to the school. He was sitting at his desk, having completed five hundred end of term reports, his work at Lancing finished.

"I haven't been a very good headmaster," he announced modestly and, with a characteristic dismissive smile, pushed back his chair and got to his feet.

I was surprised. "I don't know about that, Willie," I said, "in the final count, I don't think any of us are all that good," which made him laugh and nod and we shook hands.

That he will be remembered by some of us for abolishing the scouts at Lancing and, on retirement becoming Chief Scout, and paying personally for the last stretch of the school drive to be straightened, so it should end directly beneath the *flèche* on the roof of the dining hall, is only part of the story. By many he will be remembered as a modest, thoroughly nice man, who planted trees and enhanced the site, and who perhaps might have enjoyed being a housemaster at Eton rather than braving a career as headmaster of Lancing.

His successor, Ian Beer, was different. Educated at Whitgift and Cambridge, a Rubgy Blue, with an England cap to his credit, he had taught at Marlborough, cut his teeth as headmaster at Ellesmere and arrived at Lancing full of vigour and intention.

"What I shall do straight away," he informed the housemasters at his first meeting with us, "is visit every prep school within a radius of sixty miles," which he promptly did, speeding through the countrysides of Sussex, Surrey, Hampshire and Kent in his low-slung green MG.

The common room met him first in the Old Farm House, considered one of the best of all the independent schools' headmasters' residences. A big, impressive man, he had a floating rib, of which he was secretly proud, and bruised ears, rugby relics. It was quickly apparent to most of us that he was alert, firing questions with a seeking gaze and a slight inclination of the head as he met members of the common room individually.

Very much a front man with ambitious ideas for Lancing, he knew all about the value of public relations and never missed an opportunity to show the flag, thrusting his way forward, as though leading a Cambridge scrum into battle, the staff following in his wake, some eagerly, some not quite so eagerly. His wife, Angela, was charming and veiy pretty, and I told her there and then how much she reminded me of Susan Hampshire, who played the part of Fleur in the *Forsyte Saga*.

I was to cross swords with Ian Beer just the once. It happened at the end of his first summer term at Lancing and I have no doubt he was as tired as I was. I had gone down to the Old Farm House around nine o'clock on the evening of the last day of the term, to discuss whether a boy in Sanderson's should stay on in order to be head of school. We both agreed he should not stay on. It was not the issue. Together we walked to the bottom of the short drive. It was a warm, balmy July evening, the light beginning to fade, the air still and full of the scent of flowers. Across the field that lay opposite, four boys were approaching the stile that led onto the College drive, several yards further up from where we were standing. All were in my house.

"I wonder what they've been up to?" said Ian, his eyebrows contracting.

There was not much doubt in my mind. "I'll find out," I said and walked up to meet them. "Where have you been?" I asked as they clambered somewhat sheepishly over the stile.

"We've just had a drink at the Red Lion, sir."

"You didn't ask my permission."

"No, sir."

"You should have done."

"Yes, sir."

"You're not the worse for wear, are you?"

"No, sir." A certain indignation in their voices all but made me smile. It was clear they were telling the truth. Three of them were leaving and were house captains. The fourth boy, his hair was a vivid red, had still a year to go and should not have been there. Nor had he particularly endeared himself to me, or to his parents — his father was a commander RN — by dyeing his hair jet black just before Founder's Day. It had made him look quite extraordinary, for beneath his new head of black hair, his eyebrows shone like two red beacons. I had words with him later. We are still in touch, he is now headmaster of a school in Kenya.

Of the other three, two were identical twins, their father an admiral. Big strong boys, they could have been a handful, but they had done all right, enjoyed their time at Lancing, survived and, if not particularly academic, were fine sailors. They had that very day presented me with a handsome hand-bearing compass as a leaving present.

The fourth boy, a university candidate, academically good, if perhaps a little dull, had never put a foot wrong. I thought it rather a good thing he had stepped slightly out of line. No harm done, all part of education.

"Well, you'd better get back up to the house," I said, "and just make sure there's no trouble tonight," I added, looking at the twins.

"Right, sir, there won't be," they assured me and set off up the drive.

"Well?" said Ian, as I approached him, his eyebrows now beetling more than ever.

"It's all right," I said, "they've had a drink at the Red Lion and no more. They are not in any way the worse for wear. I'll deal with Dougie Arnold. He had no business to be there." There was a moment's silence.

"Is that all you care?" he asked, frowning in disbelief, staring long and hard at me, before turning and heading towards the porch of the Old Farm House.

Astonished, I pursued him up the drive.

"If that's all you care,' he went on, wheeling round and facing me when we had crossed the threshold, "you ought seriously to consider whether you should continue being a housemaster."

I was now not only astounded but very angry indeed and followed him into his study, where we confronted each other.

"Right," I said, "now just tell me exactly what you want and how you would handle it." I did not wait for his reply. "Apart from Dougie Arnold, and I shall deal with him, the other three have caused no trouble at all. The twins easily could have done. They are nearly nineteen, it's their last night. Yes, they've had a drink without permission, but they're not the least bit drunk. You'd think it was some great crime they'd committed," I did not mention the very nice leaving present they had just given me. But I had not finished.

"So, come on, just tell me what you would have done, what you suggest? Beat them? Give them a good thrashing?" That still went on at Lancing, though not in Sanderson's. "Expel them? Make a real issue of the matter? Make sure the school and everyone knows about it? Summon the parents? What's your answer? And I'm quite prepared to find another job. We can move on. So what do you intend to do?" I was more than angry, I was furious at his over-reaction. He had no answer and I left.

Outside the chapel the following morning he approached me with a wry smile, head inclined. "You were the one person at Lancing I did not want to get across," he said genuinely, and went on to express how upset he had been that night.

"I've forgotten it," I said, though indeed I had not nor, I'm sure, had he. But that was the end of the matter and, when I had completed my fifteen years as a housemaster, he asked me to do an extra two years.

Ian Beer did a great deal that was good for Lancing, as well as making one or two decisions that were not so good, particularly in the architectural development of school buildings, but then it is easy to make judgements in hindsight.

My philosophy in running Sanderson's was basic and simple and I like to think the house was aware of how I felt towards them, that, in my eyes, each had their own value as a person and there were no favourites. Of course, there has to be some form of hierarchy for administrative purposes, but elitism of any form is abhorrent and destructive. Every boy should be given an opportunity of experiencing responsibility, and I found no difficulty in appointing, as a house captain, a boy who was not much good at his work or games or anything else, for that matter, but was simply a thoroughly nice person. What better contribution could one make to any community? So should the boy who creates difficulties for himself and others be given the same opportunity when the time is ripe. There will always have to be a first and a last in life but, niggling away at the back of my mind, I was ever conscious of those contradictory and disconcerting words: 'The first shall be last and the last shall be first.'

Above all, I wanted members of my house to be decent and kind to one another, and those in authority to look out for and help the vulnerable. I like to reflect that Sanderson's on the whole was a 'happy ship', with a sense of humour, and I ran it rather as I had my landing-craft, waking a sleepy dormitory in the morning with a: "Wakey, wakey, rise and shine, the morning's fine, show a leg, show a leg," turning a blind eye when possible, never passing any boy in the school without a friendly greeting, and always finding time to listen carefully, drawing from my own experience and never from theory, particularly if it had anything to do with education.

The one thing I could not and would not tolerate was any form of bullying, intimidation, physical or verbal. That angered me more than anything and I made sure the culprit was fully aware of how I felt. Vigilance and regularly reminding the house that such behaviour is never acceptable, will go a long way to contain, but never completely obliterate, unpleasantness of this kind.

Homesickness is the root of most initial unhappiness in boarding schools. There are always sufferers, which is hardly surprising since most schools, Lancing included, still only allowed two exeats a term. In the early 60s I had one small, frail boy who was desperately homesick. Son of a boarding preparatory school headmaster — we are still in touch — the youngster would knock and enter our kitchen well before breakfast to announce that he had hardly slept at all. I advised his father, who lived less than an hour away, to take him home each Sunday. The boy would then, I suggested, have something to look forward to. The father, drawing from experience of homesick boarders in his own school, thought it might only make matters worse.

However, the parents decided to give it a try and it worked immediately.

For the life of me, I could see no reason why in those days there should not be regular exeats, particularly if that was what parents wanted, which, for the majority, I knew to be the case. Weekends were already becoming a problem and, by the 60s and 70s, when authority and traditional beliefs were challenged everywhere, it seemed common sense to change the rules of boarding and ease a situation that was becoming increasingly difficult to contain.

A committee from the common room was formed to discuss the matter, from which nothing new emerged, other than a unanimous decision that television was not the answer, and sets should be banned in houses. Since we were the only house to have installed a television set, and it had proved an invaluable asset, I had no intention of removing it. Indeed, at weekends it was a safety-valve, particularly for senior boys from other houses whom I allowed to come in at certain times, *Top of the Pops* being one, on condition they behaved themselves, which they usually did. I was fortunate in having a large central room in Sanderson's which could contain up to a hundred boys. It was also my classroom and conveniently close to our living quarters.

Word quickly got round that boys in Sanderson's were going out more frequently on Sundays and, at a housemasters' meeting, the headmaster, Gladstone, was happy to leave Sunday exeats to the discretion of each housemaster. In no time, five hundred boys were no longer incarcerated from Saturday to Monday morning and a freer atmosphere prevailed. Weekends at Lancing are now even freer and will become more so as parental demand for full weekly boarding inevitably grows.

Gone forever are those days when public schools — they now like to be termed independent schools — called the tune. All but the great, and they too are fully aware of the market-place, now strive fiercely to promote their institutions whenever possible in a competitive world. In crude terms headmasters are mostly concerned with selling their schools, keeping up their numbers and academic standards, and winning over prospective parents and the preparatory schools. There are registrars on staffs to help with the marketing side of things and deal with the press, careers staff, public relations consultants and impressive prospectuses to hand out and send to Europe and the Far East. There are ISIS exhibitions to attend, where schools have their own spot-lit stands, displaying spectacular coloured photographs of their buildings, chapels, spacious playing-fields, and all the other splendid new facilities that many of them now possess. I found these exhibitions, apart from the amusing spectacle of schoolmasters attempting to be enthusiastic salesmen, tedious, generally ineffective, and demeaning, all part of the new approach in which independent schools now appear to be offering a service industry which they are happy to have judged, not so much by their own standards, but by the agreed yardstick of the rest of society.

The answer to the question why parents still choose such expensive, exclusive schools, is a straightforward one. They are buying a better education, better examination results than at the local comprehensive school, and consequently a better future prospect for their sons and daughters. If this is disputed, how is it that independent schools provide such disproportionately large numbers of the *élite* in so many areas of national life? Every country has its *élite*, but the British *élite* is still dominated by the products of a tiny number of schools which make their selection at thirteen — scholarships apart — the *sine qua non* being parental valuation. It is this egalitarian undesirability of private education, which leads to such inequality of opportunity for the vast majority of children seeking education.

Over the years, inevitably, much has changed at Lancing, and generally for the better, just as it has with most independent schools, for never more intently have they had to look to their laurels. But, apart from this constant struggle to prove its worth, there exists within Lancing a distinction, a streak of humour and tolerance, a sense of the ridiculous, and genuine acceptance, indeed encouragement of eccentricity, which weaves throughout the place and makes it different and for me appealing. It was this, perhaps, that Ian Beer was referring to when he remarked in a speech: "I could never quite understand it. There was something slightly mad at Lancing when I arrived and it was there when I left". Long may it continue, say I, and recall this little incident.

At one common room meeting at the beginning of an Easter term, Ian Beer announced to the staff that a boy's report had gone adrift: "Would those of you who teach the boy please let the office have the reports as soon as possible. You all keep copies of your reports," he added.

I caught the eye of a senior housemaster — an old friend whose brothers and forebears had all been at Lancing — just as he tried unsuccessfully to stifle a laugh.

"You think that's funny," said Ian, frowning and looking across at the culprit from his position at the head of the long table.

"In a way, yes, I do," said John truthfully. Ian did not pursue the matter.

"The trouble is," John told me afterwards, "I caught sight of your face, Ken, and, knowing you never keep copies of any of your reports, I simply couldn't contain myself."

His facts were not quite right. I did for one term try keeping a few copies of house reports, until Henry gave me some sound advice.

"I never keep a copy of any report that I write," he declared, when eating with us one evening. He did not elaborate, Henry never did, though, on this occasion, he did add briefly, "If I repeat myself and it is the truth, then what does it matter?"

I knew exactly what he meant. By constantly referring back to what was written previously one can become bogged down. A report should be a spontaneous and, whenever possible, optimistic account to parents of how their son has fared during the term in question. And if it has to be a critical report, however severe, there should be some attempt to spread a ray of light at the end.

During the term we never locked up, not even at night. Parents would wander through our open front door, down the long corridor to our sitting-room, while others, when they got to know us better, would knock and enter our huge kitchen, where I think they felt at home, certainly intrigued by the great beast of a school refrigerator, by the two thick chipped and stained yellow china sinks lying side by side beneath a dilapidated gas hot water system, by the ancient gas-fire and nursing guard, above which clothes hung from a four-bar wooden clothes rail, hoisted aloft by a rope pulley.

In the centre stood a long farm table and through the high mullioned windows, the distant tollbridge spanning the Adur could be seen linking Lancing to Shoreham. It was the window-seat on which Henry had spent a restless night.

How fortunate I was to have a wife who welcomed everyone in her own inimitable manner. She was unobtrusively on the side of the boys, which was invaluable when problems arose, for her quiet listening qualities and calm sensible advice, helped me keep things in perspective and avoid hasty judgements. I once heard an elderly, much respected member of the staff say of a particular housemaster: "He judges," adding with slow shakes of his head and a sibilant intake of breath, "Never, never judge." I think I know what he meant.

My seventeen years as a housemaster were drawing to a close. They had been happy, amusing years, but I was ready to call it a day. I used to use the phone a lot, for I found it the best way of keeping in touch with parents, though not always. I had one father who would ring me up when he had drunk too much.

"I like you, Ken Shearwood," I heard his slurred voice say on more than one occasion, "I like you very much, but I don't like the way you are indoctrinating my son with all this damned silly socialist nonsense."

"Well," I said, "I like you too, and your son, but not those damned Tories."

I enjoyed meeting the parents and helping their sons, experienced the usual problems that face anyone running a house in a boarding school and, with the support of my family, survived without too much wear and tear.

Once a mother arrived to inform me that her son's grandmother, whom they had asked to keep an eye on their boy while the parents were away for the night, had discovered him in bed with a girlfriend. "He's behaving more and more like some randy spaniel, Mr Shearwood," she declared, which, observing the mother, I could understand.

There was a boy in the house whose mother, I discovered, was his sister. The police rang the school one evening to say the same boy's grandfather, who lived locally, was being hunted on the Downs for a murder that had been committed and was heading our way. We were advised to keep the boy under close surveillance.

Another parent had the firmest and longest handshake I have experienced. The harder he gripped, the more he smiled. And there was a charming, slightly batty clergyman who would drop in, usually to the kitchen, and borrow the odd fiver which he always paid back. On one occasion he successfully showed Biddie and Vanessa how to hypnotise our Labrador, Ringo, who remained thoroughly dozy for the rest of the day.

Twenty-four hours after the start of a singularly dank and dismal Easter term, the telephone rang.

"Hello, sir. Have you missed me? It's John Belmore."

"No," I said, "I can't say I have, John. Where are you?"

"Back in Ireland, sir. I simply couldn't face it. I found a rat in my pitt and my sheets were damp, so I caught the next plane back to Ireland."

"Well, thank you for letting me know, John. When are you coming back?"

"Tomorrow, sir."

"Fine," I said. "Look forward to seeing you."

John was in his last year at Lancing, lived in Castle Coole, Enniskillen and was the current Earl of Belmore.

A head of house, Broderick Munro-Wilson, came to say goodbye at the end of one summer term and presented me with a pair of suede Hush Puppies, a make of shoe that had just come into vogue and was a real fashion item.

"Always judge a man by his shoes," he remarked with a broad grin, looking down at the rather decrepit pair I was wearing. "Now you'll be well shod, sir, just like a racehorse."

Some years later, after he had gone down from Cambridge and ridden in three Grand Nationals, as well as winning the Cheltenham Foxhunters' Chase on Drunken Duck, I saw a full-length picture of him, dressed for Ascot week, that took up a complete page of one of the tabloids, with a caption in heavy black print, 'WHY GIRLS LOVE A CAD'. We are still in contact.

At the end of Christmas terms, parents were often most generous to us. Henry would usually call in and see us before he set off for Lincolnshire and the holidays.

"Have you scored?" he would ask. "Yes," I'd reply.

"Well, I have not. So I'm going to buy myself an expensive present."

Occasionally an unusual problem would crop up. Having tea with the family one Sunday afternoon towards the end of a Christmas term, a small boy knocked on our drawing-room door which was ajar and asked if he could have a word with me.

"Of course," I said, "I'll be with you in a minute or, better still, would you like to come in and have tea with us?"

He stood indecisively for a moment, hovering in the doorway before entering to kneel on the rug in front of the fire. Slightly surprised, we watched while Biddie poured a cup of tea and handed it to him and my daughter offered him a piece of cake.

The only child of elderly parents, he was a clever boy, old fashioned and distinctly odd in his ways, a boy whom I knew would be vulnerable, so we had kept an eye on him from the start. I wondered now whether this was the problem.

"Everything all right, John? No worries? Getting on in the house?"

"Yes," he replied and, reassured, I sipped my tea and waited for him to make the next move. Eventually he spoke, still gazing into the fire and shaking his head.

"The trouble is, I don't know why I did it."

"Did what, John?" I enquired tentatively, no longer reassured. He did not answer.

"Come on," I said gently, "you're beginning to make me feel nervous, John. For goodness' sake, put me out of my misery and tell me what it was that you did."

Then he told us. "I strangled Robert's three baby rats and I don't know why I did it."

"Well," I was somewhat taken aback. "We can all at times do strange things," I remarked, for want of something better to say, whereupon he looked at me, but said nothing.

"Have you told Robert?"

Apparently he had and the owner of the deceased rats had accepted the situation.

"The best thing to do now, John, is to put the whole thing out of your mind and not worry. It's all over and best forgotten."

I was well aware that my advice was not particularly therapeutic, but I did not wish to make a great thing of it and it seemed to do the trick. When he left Lancing he considered going into the church. We did not see him for a number of years and then, one day, he called on us with his wife, long after I had left Sanderson's and we were living in Shoreham. He had grown a full beard, was working in the computer world, doing well and seemed happily married.

Later, when I was registrar of Lancing, I heard that he had changed sex and was now living with another man who likewise had undergone a sex change. Out of the blue they came and had tea with us one Saturday afternoon. John, now Jennie, was wearing a long dress, her friend, Alison, well over six feet tall, wore a short mini-skirt and had long, shoulder-length hair. She had befriended John and been a great support to him during his traumatic change. We sat around the same old farmhouse kitchen table we had used in Sanderson's and chatted. It transpired that Alison had read *Whistle the Wind* and knew a number of Mevagissey skippers and their luggers, for she was Cornish-born and bred and, to my astonishment, had been coxswain of the Fowey pilot boat for ten years and knew the waters around the Gribbin like the back of her hand. Vulnerable and courageous, they could not have been nicer.

When I finally left Sanderson's in 1975 I had no regrets. I handed the house over to the man I had hoped Ian Beer would appoint. Ted Maidment was a medieval historian, an academic and choral scholar to Cambridge, possessor of a truly fine baritone voice. He had an acerbic wit, was considerably overweight, possessed a prodigious memory, an astonishingly wide and varied intellect, and played a mean and, at times, dishonest game of tennis. I partnered him more than once. "Just away," he'd call with conviction, when the ball was clearly in. And, "Must you throw the ball up so high?" he would ask Simon Prior when the lad was about to serve, "is it really necessary?" which made the two boys, Richard Cowley and Simon, both in Sanderson's, laugh uncontrollably. Ted never threw the ball up when he served, but hit a low waspish shot above the net which, if a fault, would be followed immediately by a gently struck ball that just dropped over the net. No amount of, "I wasn't ready, sir," made the slightest difference. To the boys he presented a comical sight in his long white shorts, his massive superstructure supported by surprisingly slender, well-shaped legs. He did five successful years as housemaster of Sanderson's and then was appointed headmaster of Ellesmere, from where he went on to become headmaster of Shrewsbury. Eton did their best to persuade him to go their way, but were unsuccessful. I think Ted was right to stay at Shrewsbury — it's a better school, but then perhaps I am biased.

Chapter 39

The Chapel

AT THE START of the summer holidays of 1968 — the boys had long gone home and all was quiet — I watched from my study window in Sanderson's, as Henry, on the far side of the quadrangle, packed the last few things into his huge green Rolls-Royce with its gleaming silver headlights, climbed in and, for the last time drove slowly and sedately out through the Masters' Tower, and away forever, bound for Lincolnshire and his ancestral home, Marston Hall, and I was sorry to see him go.

For some time we knew there was something amiss. He had stopped staying with us at the beginning of each term, something he had always done. "I cannot bear starting before the kiddie-winkies," he would say.

For the last few years, life at Lancing had grown increasingly sour for Henry and, as the problems of the 60s grew and dissent focused, amongst other things, on the school's religious life and its beautiful chapel, in size and splendour all but a cathedral, he had become increasingly disenchanted and withdrawn. The upheaval of the 60s and the demand for change in chapel services was more than he could take and resignation followed. No longer would we be able to listen to those short memorable sermons with their startling beginnings, 'Slumming it at the Dorchester', or 'Soup, Seven and Sixpence!' no longer hear those preposterous, though not entirely inaccurate pronouncements, 'What the young need today is some good wholesome neglect'. Henry never pretended to be a schoolmaster. It was the very last thing he would have wanted to be called. He never came into the common room, unless there was a meeting which he had to attend. Late at night he would slip in and clear his pigeon-hole when no one was about. He was a true scholar with a fine mind and a prodigious memory. "Second top scholar to Eton. I scored nought in mathematics and a hundred in Latin verse!" he once told me. Invariably he wore the same clothes whether it be the coldest day in midwinter or the hottest day in summer. I never saw him in an overcoat. He loved good food, architecture, paintings, distinguished acquaintances and, of course, anyone related to the aristocracy. To many of his colleagues his attitude to life was outrageous though, to be fair, he was never intentionally offensive. An eccentric, perhaps the last remaining squarson in England, he lived in a world of his own. If oblivious of others, he was not critical. If he disagreed with a point of view, he would never argue the point, just turn the page and, by doing so, eradicate from his mind any controversy or unpleasantness.

I remember so clearly when the conflict between the two chaplains was at its height and there was literally no communication between them, I saw him standing alone in the quadrangle outside his house one bitter afternoon in late January and decided to tackle him.

"Henry," I said, shivering in the wind despite my duffel coat, "I'm your friend. You haven't been in to see us or have a meal for a long time." There was no immediate response, so I continued. "It's just that I feel over this chapel business that what Christopher Campling wants to do with the services does seem sensible."

He stood, head raised, the wind blowing his long straggly fair hair down the back of his head and I wondered whether he was going to reply. At last he spoke.

"Ken," he said, "how would you like it if you had someone over you in football doing things which you simply could not tolerate."

"Well," I suggested, "I'd try and find a way out of such a predicament, perhaps by talking together."

I stood waiting for him to say something, but he remained silent, gazing up at the grey flint walls of his house, Gibbs's. Our conversation, as far as he was concerned, was over and that was the end of the matter. He had turned another page.

The earliest signs of change began with the departure of Wilfred Derry in 1953. He had been Lancing's chaplain during the war years when the school was evacuated to Shropshire and, in the eyes of Frank Doherty and others, he had been a good one. But, in Dancy's view, he was doing too much that was not strictly a chaplain's job, organising the Friends of Lancing Chapel, running the Book Room, the Scouts, the Estate Club and the Model Railway Society. Usually seen with a briar pipe in his mouth, good-humouredly going about his business, he would at times in chapel services perform a sort of knee-bend exercise up at the High Altar, giving the congregation a fleeting glimpse of the Scout shorts and stockings he usually wore beneath his cassock.

"I've been sacked," he announced one teatime in the common room, having just opened and read the brief contents of an internal letter from the headmaster, "I've been sacked," he repeated, with customary cheerfulness. It was a brave front. But he left Lancing a bitter man and never forgave John Dancy, whom he held responsible. Nor was he the only member of the staff to have been dismissed or who had to resign during J.C.D.'s first year at Lancing. Eight others bit the dust. Many years later, giving an address in the chapel at Patrick Halsey's memorial service, Wilfred could not refrain from making it clear to his packed congregation that he had neither forgiven nor forgotten. My sympathy on that occasion lay with Dancy who was sitting in the row ahead of us.

Wilfred's successor, Cuthbert Shaw, was a Lancing old boy, and had served in the navy. Kind and gentle, a stabilising influence, he was never one to seek change, which was a great joy to Henry, but caused some concern to Dancy. Appointing a chaplain to Lancing was the Provost's responsibility, but the headmaster had his say and John would certainly have been looking for a candidate with intellectual qualities. So it was a surprise that Cuthbert was chosen, for he was no academic, never pretended to be and quickly found himself intellectually struggling when tackling a sixth-form Divinity set, a fact of which John Dancy was soon aware.

Throughout his time at Lancing, Cuthbert was under considerable pressure to make changes in the services. But the way ahead was never clear and he quietly resisted. It was this and a general lack of agreement and support that led to a deterioration in his health and resignation in 1959. He is remembered for his warmth, sense of humour, total lack of self-importance, and for once writing a report on a boy who had left Lancing a year previously.

Christopher Campling, who succeeded Cuthbert, had also been in the navy, serving first as a coder in a Greek destroyer in the Mediterranean, then as a cypher officer on the admiral's staff aboard *Nelson* out with the East Indies Fleet, ending as captain's secretary in the *Howe* and *Ranpura*. Henry, too, had been in the Mediterranean at the end of the war, and served as a chaplain aboard a 'Leander' class cruiser. That apart, the two had little in common.

Christopher arrived at Lancing in the Easter term of 1960. Married, with a family, he had been at Lancing as a boy during the school's wartime evacuation to Ludlow, so knew about Lancing and thought highly of Wilfred Derry. Appointed by the Provost, Browne-Wilkinson, he had come through a testing, but successful, interview with John Dancy, for they had similar views on the chapel and its services. Unfortunately for Christopher Campling, before he had settled in, John Dancy was appointed Master of Marlborough and left at the end of that summer term. To make matters even more difficult for him, the Provost died in 1961, leaving Lancing's new chaplain without the support of the two main authorities.

Christopher's intention was to replace the non-communicating Sung Eucharist Service, held every Sunday morning at 10 a.m., with the Parish Communion Service, which had become the practice of the church. But there was a problem; Lancing still upheld the fasting Communion tradition. Boys could attend the voluntary eight o'clock Communion Service and make their Communion, but that meant an early rise on Sunday morning which, understandably, was unacceptable for many. Whether or not they had attended the early Communion Service, the whole school had to attend the ten o'clock Sunday non-communicating Sung Eucharist Service. Since the Roman Catholic church had relaxed the emphasis on fasting during the war years, and their example had been followed by other churches, there was no reasonable justification for the school any longer to uphold the non-communicating Sung Eucharist Service. This was the crux of the matter, the great divide between Henry Thorold and Christopher Campling.

I was aware of what was going on, but not involved, nor did I have any wish to be. But it was clear to me that Christopher was right in wanting to replace the Sung Eucharist Service with the Parish Communion.

The matter came to a head when the chaplain dropped in late one afternoon, just as I was about to leave for a housemasters' meeting, and fired a direct question at me.

"Have I your confidence, Ken?"

"Of course," I replied. "Why do you ask?"

"Because I understand I have lost the confidence of the housemasters."

"Well," I assured him, "as far as I'm concerned, you are the boss, you are the chaplain, and you have certainly got my confidence," and with that I had to hurry off to the meeting.

There was nothing on the agenda about the chapel, or the chaplain, and at the end I thought the matter was not coming up. I was wrong.

"I understand," said Willie, pushing his chair back from his desk, "that some housemasters have lost confidence in the chaplain, so I would like to discuss this matter."

After several moments of thoughtful silence, I decided to declare my hand — "I'd like to disassociate myself from what has just been said, Headmaster. Christopher Campling certainly has my confidence." Then it began to come out.

Christopher, sympathetic to what was going on in the outside world, wanted to make weekly school services at Lancing more meaningful, more relevant, words and intentions which to Henry were anathema. As chaplain, Christopher had attempted, without much success, to separate the Evensong services, giving them a different character, which the boys quickly nicknamed 'kiddies' corner' and 'Willie's waffle'. The chapel, by some, was referred to as the 'God box', but then that was nothing new. After the First World War it had been known as the 'Zeppelin Shed'. And just as many a public school chapel during the 60s became a natural cock-shy for discontent, Lancing's proved no exception. It was not an enviable time to be a chaplain, headmaster, housemaster, parent or, for that matter, anyone in authority.

Of the seven housemasters present at that meeting, four were old-fashioned High Churchmen, intent on retaining the Sunday non-communicating service. Troubled, though undeterred, by this opposition, Christopher proceeded on his way and introduced the Parish Communion Service to the consternation of the four, who were highly critical of the boys' behaviour during the new services, so much so that on one occasion two of the four housemasters walked out of a Sunday morning service which Christopher was conducting.

"It's their approach," said one of them, despairingly. "It's utterly wrong. They talk, they laugh, they show no respect. I can hardly bear it." There was a long pause.

"Yes," said Willie eventually, nodding gravely from behind his desk, "I take your point."

Henry, as was his custom, said nothing. But it was impossible to ignore his silent presence and, wisely, the headmaster, apart from looking in his direction, did not further seek his opinion. Had he done so, he would not have got it, for Henry had long since turned another page.

In the end, no solution to the impasse was forthcoming. The gulf was too wide to bridge, the inflexibility too strong. Within the common room there was a measure of indifference. The new Provost, freshly appointed Bishop of Lewes, was too busy elsewhere to be involved, but listened carefully and then agreed with

Above: The Chapel

both sides, while Willie, sympathetic to Christopher, had four housemasters to cope with, as well as several senior members of the staff who were opposed to the chaplain's changes. But opinion among the younger staff and the boys favoured what Christopher was doing.

I must confess I did not think the boys' behaviour was anything like as bad as was being made out. Yes, their approach was light-hearted and frivolous, but by no means all of them were like that and more than a few were subsequently ordained as priests. Without being too presumptuous, I suggested some reasons for their behaviour.

"I think one should take into consideration their youth and the fact that they probably feel exposed and embarrassed as they come up the nave with all eyes on them. It's a natural reaction. I don't think we should judge them too harshly. At least they are taking part in the service."

"Yes, and at what cost?" asked one of the four. "Well," I said, somewhat tentatively, "when all is said and done, is our approach always the right one? I know mine isn't." Shortly afterwards the meeting ended.

As I climbed the broad flight of steps alongside the headmaster's study leading up to the lower quad, I knew only too well that what I had just said would not have enhanced my friendship with Henry. But there was little I could do about it.

Christopher, an exceptional Divinity teacher, who produced consistent university successes during his seven years's chaplaincy at Lancing, left in the summer of 1967 to become Vicar of Pershore Abbey. It had not been an easy time for him. Eight years later he became Archdeacon of Dudley, from where he went on to be Dean of Ripon, until his retirement in 1995. Now, in familiar haunts on the Sussex coast, in sight of the sea, the wheel has turned full circle and he is back once more, Chairman of the Friends of Lancing Chapel, in contact with his old school and past friends. Author of the *Food of Love*, a book on music and faith, he wrote, *The Way, The Truth And The Life*, edited *Words For Worship*, which became an essential for all religious assemblies in schools, and was chairman of the Council for the Care of Churches.

And Henry, what of Henry? He left Lancing a year later and I am glad to say we are still in touch and good friends. He lives, of course, at Marston Hall, near Grantham, home of the Thorold family since the fourteenth century, where he has spent the years researching and writing his books on cathedrals, abbeys, priories and the English counties. They are splendidly written, his eye for beauty and knowledge of architecture as perceptive, clear and authoritative as his two old friends, John Betjeman and John Piper, would agree.

'The bell is ringing for Evensong; under the medieval gateway the path slopes gently down to the west front,' he begins the introduction to his book on *Cathedrals, Abbeys and Priories*.

And later: 'The appeal of a great Cathedral lies in its silence and its emptiness. The very stones cry out proclaiming the power and majesty of God. Let them speak, *Dat Deus incrementum.*'

Although his latter years at Lancing were not always the happiest, friends and boys in his house, who keep contact and visit him, are well aware that Henry still holds an amused yet genuine affection for the school, and his erstwhile colleagues, both ordained and lay.

Above: Sanderson's, 1970

Chapter 40

President of the Common Room

FOR TEN YEARS I was President of the Common Room, a job I found amusing and rewarding, for I had the support of a likeable and varied 'ship's company', who generally did not take things too seriously, yet possessed a spirited will and a lively sense of humour.

No sooner had I started the job than I was informed by an elderly, somewhat doughty lady, once Frank Doherty's secretary, that four retired housemasters, who, having given their working lives to the college, had retired before the government's pension scheme for independent schools had come into being and, consequently, received no pensions. "It's a disgrace," she said, "that nothing's been done by the school to help them." Three were educated at Lancing, the fourth was an Etonian. I decided to take the matter up and arranged a meeting with Nigel Ventham, who represented the common room on the school council. He also had been educated at Lancing and knew each of the housemasters well. He listened sympathetically and was happy to present their cases to the council, but he was not too optimistic about the governing body's reaction, and he was right. The council considered it would be creating a precedent and were not prepared to go further.

I then decided to put the matter to the common room and found they were strong in their conviction that something should be done to help the four. I saw Nigel Ventham again and expressed how the common room felt and at the next governors' meeting I was glad to learn that the matter was on their agenda. I was even more delighted to hear from Nigel later that the governors had decided to award each of the housemasters an annual sum, which their wives would continue to receive in the event of death. It was a generous decision welcomed by the common room.

Towards the end of the usual common room meeting at the start of the following term, Michael Power brought up the subject of our representative on the school council. "This is no criticism of Nigel Ventham, but isn't it about time we elected our own member of the common room to represent us on the governing body? It seems more sensible than the present arrangement. I wonder what others think?"

There followed a short discussion, in which no one disagreed with what Michael had just suggested and, after a formal proposition had been made and seconded, it was voted unanimously that we should elect our own man from the common room to represent us. "And I suggest," Michael added, "that Ken, as President, should be our representative," which was voted on and accepted. It all happened quickly and quite out of the blue.

It was indeed a radical move, for no other school elected its own staff member to a governing body, and few, if any, had a representative, other than their headmaster. What is more, when put to the chapter of the school and to the other Woodard headmasters, it was strongly opposed by all.

When I informed Ian Beer of the common room's decision it did not surprise me that he was initially taken aback.

"Is there something wrong with the current arrangement?" he asked, frowning heavily.

"Nigel's fine," I assured him, "there's no implicit criticism."

"Then why change?"

"Because we considered it more sensible and effective to have someone from within the common room to represent us directly, rather than an intermediary."

"And if the governing body considers the choice unsuitable?"

"They have every right to say so."

"Would the common room find that acceptable?"

"They would have to. I don't see it as a problem. I'm sure, provided there's good will on both sides and it's in the school's interest, there's no reason why it should not work." There was a lengthy pause. He was still frowning.

"And have you elected someone?"

"Yes. They want me to represent them."

"Well," said Ian, getting to his feet. "I'll have to put the matter to the Chairman. It's up to the governing body."

When I left his study, his brow was less puckered, but I could see he was still trying hard to come to terms with something he had never envisaged happening.

I never discovered what the governors' views were, but the Chairman, Sir Charles Chadwyck-Healey, welcomed me warmly when I saw him. However, right from the start he made two things clear. The governing body would not accept a representative whom they considered unsuitable and, whenever there were matters they wished to discuss in private, the common room representative would be asked to leave the meeting — both demands acceptable, and reasonable. "So let's see how it goes, Ken," he said.

By now Ian Beer had got over his initial surprise and seemed happy about the situation. However, I was soon to find myself involved in a serious problem concerning a housemaster, a man I knew well for he had once been my house tutor. He had previously been tutor to another house until a new incumbent had taken over and appointed his own man. At the time I felt some sympathy for the rejected house tutor, and it was this and the fact that he was a Cambridge classical scholar and a good academic — and, I knew, secretly wanted to be in Sanderson's — that prompted me to invite him to be my house tutor, a post he readily accepted. However, I was fully aware that I was taking on someone who possessed an absurd pomposity and, at times, a total lack of sensitivity, indeed, of common sense. But I had not anticipated the antipathy towards the appointment of some of the senior members of my house.

"Well, we shall just have to try and educate him," I informed them when they came to see me about the matter.

As individuals we were poles apart, he was elitist, traditional and conservative in his beliefs. But he could be good fun with his clever mimicry, amusing anecdotes and outrageous observations. As a family, we enjoyed his company and I know he enjoyed his time with us, though I was always wary of him and watchful. He left eventually to take over a house.

The problem arose from an incident that occurred at the top of the Sixteen Acre one summer term. Youths from the town had, at times, been coming up in the evenings to seek confrontations with any Lancing boys they might run into. On this occasion several senior members of the school spotted a group coming across the Sixteen Acre and decided to take action. It was commonly known that two members of a certain house had been given permission to keep shotguns. Their housemaster, to give him the benefit of the doubt, had jokingly remarked, "Next time those yobbos come up, give 'em a whiff of grapeshot," and gone off to play bridge. The two marksmen were sent for and confronting the intruders put them to flight, firing a volley of grapeshot over their heads, followed by a further volley for good measure.

At that very moment Ian Beer was about to get into his car having visited a member of the staff living down in Hoe Court.

"That's a twelve-bore somebody's firing," declared Jeremy McLachlan, looking across the Sixteen Acre up at the College. A Wykehamist and a countryman, he knew about such things.

"Nonsense," said Ian, who had never fired a shotgun in his life. No sooner had he spoken than another volley rent the still summer evening.

"Those are shotguns all right," repeated Jeremy. This time his quiet conviction thoroughly alarmed the headmaster, who leapt into his MG and sped up to the school where he found an animated group of boys gathered around the gate that led onto the Sixteen Acre field.

"Has anyone been firing a gun?" he asked.

"Yes," they admitted, "but only over their heads to scare them off, sir?"

"Are you out of your tiny minds?" exclaimed Ian Beer angrily. "Go back to your houses," and, climbing into his car once more, drove down to the house of the two boys, where he made them each write separate accounts of what they had done, stating who had given them permission to use the guns. He left a message for the housemaster to telephone him immediately he got back, which he failed to do.

Ian Beer had no alternative but to inform the police, who were helpful, but made it clear that should the incident be reported by any other person, they would prosecute. However, provided the school dealt with the matter responsibly they would take no action. Heaven knows how Ian managed to keep it out of the press.

The following afternoon, as I left the common room on my way to attend a sixth-form lecture, the housemaster of the two boys approached with a slight, wry grin.

"I'm just going back to my house. I wonder whether you would care to see a picture I've just bought. I know you like paintings." I was well aware of what he was up to, that he was not going to make the first move, bring the matter up and show that he was in any way concerned.

"It's not the painting you want me to see, but to discuss what happened last night," I suggested. "It is serious," I warned.

"Storm in a teacup," came the reply.

"It's not," I said. "It's very far from a storm in a teacup. The police have been informed. My advice is go and see the head at once and apologise. He's not an unfair man. Admit your folly."

"All a storm in a teacup," he repeated dismissively and we went our ways. He had not, at that stage, received the letter demanding his resignation as housemaster. That was to come towards the end of the week.

The Chairman of the Governors, Sir Charles Chadwyck-Healey, was abroad at the time, but was returning at the weekend. Several times more I urged the housemaster to go and see Beer, but he brushed any such advice aside, confident that the whole issue would blow over. I even called on his wife, who was in the kitchen, to see whether she could persuade him to go and talk with the headmaster, to no avail. There were some toilet rolls on the table, which she seized and threw at me, shouting that, as President of the Common Room, I had not done a thing to help her husband. I retreated.

However towards the end of the week, when he received the letter demanding his resignation as housemaster, his tune changed and he began talking about consulting his lawyer, taking legal advice and, if necessary, action against the school.

On the Sunday morning, Ian, who had still received no word of apology, rang up and asked me over for a drink and a chat.

"He has not been near me or offered one word of apology," and he spoke about the written and verbal complaints he had received from parents whose boys had been on the receiving end of the housemaster's temper. "I've already written him a warning letter, and now this. I really am beginning to dislike the man," he said as I left.

On Monday morning the Chairman of the Governors arrived and following a discussion with Ian Beer, the housemaster was summoned to the headmaster's study. This housemaster was someone who could and would, when so inclined, deliberately ignore the presence of another person, and he did so on this occasion, focusing his attention entirely on Ian Beer to the total exclusion of the Chairman of the Governors, who might just as well have not been present. Sir Charles was not amused.

"If your letter of resignation is not on the headmaster's desk by twelve o'clock today, you will no longer be an employee of this school," the chairman announced, his anger barely contained.

Half an hour later the housemaster knocked on the door, entered and with an ostentatious flourish of his arm, deposited the letter of resignation on Ian Beer's desk, "I think this is what you are waiting for, Headmaster," and, without so much as a glance at the chairman, swept out of the study.

At the governors' meeting that followed, just before half-term, held in the headmaster's study, I sat outside with the housemaster, for it was the governing body's wish that I should be 'prisoner's friend'. As we waited to be called in, the door opened and the headmaster emerged. Fortunately there were sufficient rooms outside for him to be apart from us, otherwise we would have made a very uncomfortable trio. Eventually the headmaster was called back and, shortly afterwards, we were summoned.

At one end of the long table sat Sir Charles Chadwyck-Healey, confronting him at the far end, a vacant chair for the housemaster. I sat on his right. Down each side of the table the full governing body was mustered.

After a moment's silence the chairman invited the housemaster to present his views on the incident of that evening. Clearing his throat and, with a glance at the assembled body, he began to speak in an unhurried confident manner. The gist was that the incident was a light-hearted affair, that there was no malice whatsoever intended, that it really should not be taken too seriously or out of context and, finally, that in the light of everything, he hoped the governors would show sympathy and consideration for an incident that was never meant to cause trouble for anyone. I caught Sir Peter Daniel's eye. I could not make out whether it showed disbelief, amusement, or amazement at what he had just heard, probably all three.

Then it was Sir Charles's turn and he did not take long or waste words. "The governing body upholds the headmaster's demand that you resign from being a housemaster. As for the incident being a light-hearted affair, that is very far from the truth. Indeed it was one that might have had the most serious consequences. You will vacate your house by the end of this half-term. I hope that you will then put this matter behind you, make a fresh start, and serve the school to the best of your ability." With that we left the room.

Mounting the broad flight of steps that led up to the lower quad, The housemaster's wife called from an upstairs window, "How did it go?"

"Predictable," retorted her husband from over his shoulder, still continuing on his way.

That was by no means the end of the story. A grammar school in the heart of the Midlands had long been closed, its buildings empty. A group of city businessmen recognised the local need, had the foresight and financial means to get the school going again and advertised for a headmaster with ability and drive. Generously, and with a degree of pragmatism, Ian Beer dropped a line to the dismissed housemaster, suggesting that he apply for the job. He did, was offered the post, accepted it and, under his skilful management, the school soon prospered.

I was watching the six o'clock news one evening, when, to my utter astonishment, I saw Margaret Thatcher, escorted by a headmaster in gown and hood, being shown round a school in the Midlands. He was, of course, you-know-who — he of the shooting incident. But once more he failed to hold the position for long. Foolishly, having done the hard work and done it well, he could not refrain from making unwise, critical observations about state schools in the vicinity, which caused such friction that he had to pack his bags and take to the road again. My father's comment, "All brains and no common sense," would have proved a fitting epitaph.

As President of the Common Room I became involved in another difficult problem concerning staff contracts, which for years the governing body, headmaster and common room had found impossible to resolve. It began with Ian's ringing me up one morning. "Ken," he said, "I'm sending up the new contracts to the common room. I'd be grateful if you'd get the members to sign and return them to my office as soon as possible."

That afternoon the contracts arrived in the masters' pigeon-holes. It was evident a major problem concerning the age of retirement had to be overcome before members would sign. It had always been understood at Lancing that sixty-five was the age of retirement and many had geared their life insurances and mortgages to this. Indeed, there had been only one example of retirement at the age of sixty over the last thirty years, and there were some of us, myself included, who had never even seen a contract, let alone signed one. In the light of this and the fact that the government was now insisting on everyone having a contract, the council decided it was time to clear the matter up once and for all and the new contracts demanded that the age of retirement should be sixty for everyone.

Not surprisingly, there ensued a good deal of heated discussion over the issue, as we drank our tea in the common room that afternoon, the majority of us far from happy at the prospect of signing away five years of salary. Standing before the fireplace, watching and listening to what was going on, the suspicion of a smile on his face, that I knew to be a sure portent that something outrageous was about to be said, was he of the 'shotgun incident'.

"Brothers," he began, addressing the common room and flourishing his contract, as he stood before the fireplace, "we must stand fast and fight the tyranny of this document, which, if we sign, will deny us five years of salary and pension rights," and he followed this up with a brilliant spate of trade union rhetoric, in the manner and voice of Clive Jenkins addressing an assembly of the ASTMS. "So, I warn you, brothers," he concluded, "what we have here," and he waved his contract high in the air, "what we have here, brothers, is nothing less than a scabs' charter," and, with a final flourish and a flick of a none too clean handkerchief, he blew his nose noisily. It made us laugh, though I'm not sure the governing body would have thought it quite so funny.

Chapter 41

A tempting offer, Lancing football and some teaching

HAVING TEA one afternoon in early July 1976, another summer term passed and gone forever, our doorbell rang and there was Vic Buckingham standing outside, smiling, tall, lean and debonair as ever.

"Good gracious," I said, only too glad to see him.

"I want you to come out to Kuwait for a year and help with the coaching," he announced before he had even crossed the threshold.

I was taken aback. "Why me, Vic?" I asked. "I'm an amateur. I haven't even got a coaching badge, though I've worked with Jack Mansell and know the professional side of things."

"I know you do," he said, "and I know your worth. I'd like to have you out there with me. The sheikh will pay your replacement, so you'll continue to receive your salary from the college. In addition, you will get ten thousand pounds and, of course, everything will be found for you both. There could be more in it. But I must know by August, so there's not much time. Think about it and let me know."

I did think about it, long and hard, and I felt most flattered and honoured to have been asked, for Vic, besides being a cultured player, was a distinguished coach who had managed West Bromwich Albion when they won the FA Cup, Barcelona when they won the Spanish Cup, and Ajax when they won the Dutch Cup, not to mention his success with Pegasus. He had also discovered and encouraged a young man, Johann Cruyff, who would mature into one of the greatest footballers Europe has ever produced. He had done it all and more.

I talked it over with Biddie and the family. Ian Beer, despite such short notice, gave me the opportunity to go. We discussed the matter with Lilian, Vic's wife, who always accompanied her husband overseas. In all honesty, she had to admit that she did not enjoy Kuwait. In the end, I declined the offer which turned out to be just as well because Biddie had to undergo an operation in September. But it was nice to have been asked.

Shortly afterwards I had another proposition put to me by two ex-pupils, James Wood and Phil Stallibrass. They asked if I would coach the Lancing Old Boys soccer side, which played in the Arthurian League, and entered the Arthur Dunn Cup, a competition which in seventy-five years they had never reached the final, let alone won. I was no longer doing any coaching, having completed twenty-one years of running the soccer at Lancing. The thought of giving the Old Boys a helping hand had its appeal and seemed to make sense, for I knew them all and their ability. So I agreed, but on three conditions: that I had a real say in the selection of the side, the style of play, and who played where; to which they agreed. When they had gone I pondered for some time on all those previous years running the football at Lancing.

Above: With Ian Beer watching a match

Below: A Lancing 1st XI soccer side, 1976.

Above: With Paul in Worthing

From the start, back in 1955, I had been determined to approach the game professionally and began by throwing away the first eleven's gear of heavy shirts and old-fashioned flannelled shorts, replacing them with the professional strip of the day. I wrote to *The Times*, which in those far-off days used to invite pre-season comments on the prospects of independent schools that: "Lancing may not be the best side, but they will certainly be the smartest turned out of all the schools," which provoked a few comments. It was not long, however, before others began to follow suit.

I invested what money I had in buying plenty of footballs and bibs, and arranged for county referees to handle the matches. We trained with a squad of sixteen, working in small groups, never playing eleven against eleven, occasionally ending up with some shadow football. The emphasis was on skill and work off the ball, doing the simple things and doing them quickly. We were the first school side to play with a back line of four with two link-men, a four-two-four formation, as I did with Pegasus. Of the two centre-backs, one was always dropping off and covering the other, a form of sweeping. We did not anchor defenders, but encouraged them to get forward into space when appropriate. If a boy was skilful enough, whatever his age or physique, we would always look at him for the first eleven. At the end of one training session in early October, a watery sun overhead, the leaves beginning to turn, I wandered down onto the lower field with Jack Mansell, where an under-sixteen game was in progress. The ball, as invariably happens when twenty-two unskilled youngsters play against each other, was being kicked aimlessly from one end to another, with no pattern or shape, rhyme or reason.

"What's he doing?" said Jack, indicating a boy on the far side, who was keeping the ball in the air, using both feet, thigh and head.

"Why aren't you playing?" we asked, approaching him.

"Mr Cooper thinks I'm selfish and fiddle too much with the ball," he explained.

"Does he?" said Jack, demanding the ball and for the next few minutes we knocked it around between us. The boy was naturally left-footed, but could use his right and showed considerable skill. He was just fifteen and came from Brazil. "Well, you'd better come and do some fiddling with us," said Jack, and the following week we put him into the first eleven, stuck him out on the left wing, where he could hold the ball, give it and go, as well as cross sweetly with his left foot. He was an asset for the next two years.

I invited professional sides down to use our facilities for training purposes. The clubs, in turn, sent their youth sides to play against the boys. During those years a number of distinguished sides visited the school, usually staying in Brighton, training on our grounds in the morning. On one occasion in the Easter term, the boys found themselves playing against QPR, with Rodney Marsh and Terry Venables displaying their skills. Malcolm Allison, fedora hat and all, brought Crystal Palace down, and Tottenham, Chelsea, Portsmouth, Arsenal, Brighton and Sheffield Wednesday all paid visits; Wednesday included Tony Kay, Peter Swan, and David Layne, who were later convicted of bribery and banned from the game.

"Bloody hell," said one of the Sheffield Wednesday players, as I showed them into the big dungeon-like changing-room of Sanderson's. "What's this fucking place?"

"A place for pigs like you," said Jack, quick as a flash. He was now coaching Wednesday under the management of Vic Buckingham.

On another occasion Joe Mercer brought the Aston Villa side down to enjoy a few days of fresh air in Brighton before playing Tottenham in the Cup. I had known him when he was coaching Pegasus. He invited me over for a meal. "Here," he said, introducing me to Derek Dougan, "is the best centre-half in England." From his great height, the Irish international — his head completely shorn, a rare sight in those days — stared down at me in curious, unsmiling bewilderment which caused me considerable embarrassment.

On their last afternoon Joe generously allowed their full Cup side to play forty minutes each way against the boys, the towering figure of Dougan leading their attack. Geoffrey Green came down to report the game and the following day *The Times* featured his account and a photograph of the play with the great chapel dominating the background. It was good to see Geoffrey again and we stood together on the touchline and talked of those epic Pegasus battles which he had described so vividly in his own inimitable style.

There were some good players in those Lancing sides, which included six who became Oxford Blues, and another, Richard Field, who played for England in a schoolboy international match against Scotland at Roker Park. However, two in particular, I would mention. Herbie Addo, a delightful Ghanaian, and Nigel Bennett. Of the former, I wrote: 'Immensely gifted in the context of school football, he scored some sixty goals in four seasons and was always master of the ball.' His knowledge of the game was considerable, his distribution unselfish and mature. He looked a lazy player, with a suspect work-rate, which his critics invariably held against him. But he could turn it on and score with consummate ease when all around him were floundering. He played with a happy disposition and a rhythmic grace. He now coaches the international youth side of Ghana, and manages their top team, Ashanti Goldfield.

Nigel Bennett was the most accomplished player I had during my twenty-two years coaching soccer at Lancing and had already attracted the attention of Wolves when playing for Oxford University. Tall and powerful, with skill on the ground and in the air, I could see no real weakness. In the ninety-seventh Oxford and Cambridge match which Oxford won 2-0, he scored both goals. The second was considered at the time to be the best goal seen in a varsity match at Wembley. The move began from the dark Blue penalty area with a headed clearance from a corner during a period of concerted light Blue pressure. The ball was headed out to the Oxford winger, Sadler, who broke clear from wide on the right, deep inside his own half. Eluding two successive challenges he sped down the touchline into the Cambridge half, to deliver a great low curving cross which Nigel — who had

Above: A good side:
Arthur Dunn Cup 1984
Lanccing Old Boys 2 Old Carthusians 0
Arthurian League Champions 1983/84

Back row: A. J. Hodgkinson, N. J. Bell (sub), M. O. Wyatt, C. A. Sutherland,
R. C. C. H. Broadhurst, G. J. Sheridan, J. H. Todd.
Front row; P. M. Stallibrass, A. M. F. Todd, N. B. Pitcher, N. I. G. Bennett, N. G. W. Triggs

sprinted the length of the Wembley pitch in a support run — met with his left foot, on the edge of the penalty area, cleanly side-footing it low into the right-hand corner of the Cambridge goal, leaving the keeper stranded, solitary and transfixed. It was a fine goal in any context, created by two passes, a fast break and a splendid finish. I wish I had been there to see it.

Nigel went on to play a few games for the Wolves reserves and, on one occasion, was on the bench as a substitute at Anfield watching his side play against Liverpool. In the end, probably wisely, he decided against pursuing a professional career as a footballer. Had he done so, I have not the slightest doubt he would have made his mark.

The fact that he was now playing regularly for the Old Boys was a great bonus. With his help and that of Nigel Pitcher, the captain, who led the side by his sharp and determined play, the prospects looked good. By the end of that first year we reached the final of the Arthur Dunn Cup, losing in extra time on a hard, uneven ground at the Crystal Palace National Athletics Stadium.

Two years later, the jigsaw complete, the pieces in place, the Lancing Old Boys completed the double for three consecutive years, winning the Arthurian League and the Arthur Dunn Cup. Since then they have won the cup and the league several more times. The dinner to which the Lancing Old Boys invited me and the gift of cut-glass and a generous cheque, well into four figures, meant more to me than the Sheikh of Kuwait's ten thousand pounds could ever have done.

It would be incomplete, indeed odd, if I made no mention of the actual business of teaching. Over the years, as a thoroughly undistinguished historian, I taught the Tudor and Stuart period, preparing classes for the now extinct 'O' level examinations at the end of summer terms. I found teaching history enjoyable, never tedious and, supported by Edwards' Notes — they were more than handy — together with plenty of encouragement and humour, as well as a good bark or two at the indolent, most got through their examinations, a number surprisingly well. Above all, I like to think I never discouraged a boy from pursuing the subject at a higher level.

Successive heads of Lancing's history department, Roger Lockyer, Robin Reeve, Ted Maidment, Mark Buck, all Cambridge historians with first-class degrees and publications under their belts, generously left me to my own devices, for which I was grateful.

Much to my astonishment, when I finished teaching, Dr Buck, my last head of department, a former fellow of Caius, Cambridge and author of a study entitled *Politics, Finance and the Church in the Reign of Edward II,* created an award, the Ken Shearwood Prize for Tudor and Stuart History. I felt most honoured and, to be frank, a bit of a fraud.

To mark the occasion, Dr Roger Lockyer, a Reader in History at Royal Holloway and Bedford New College, London, who had written a biography of George Villiers, Duke of Buckingham, and a specialist work on the early Stuarts, as well as a standard text-book on Tudor and Stuart Britain, came down and delivered a beautifully crafted lecture. Beginning and ending with James I's Declaration of Sports, re-issued by his son in 1633, Roger demonstrated how hostility to Charles I was, to a large degree, the fruit of the Puritanism of the godly gentry which was engendered by the catholicity (with a small 'c') of Charles I's social and religious policies. Charles I identified with the 'old' England, the England of organic communities, of church ales and parish feasts, of maypoles and morris dances, thereby alienating those who took a newer and narrower view, believing that sports were an incitement to wantonness, and that life, Christian life, was far too serious a business to be dissipated in thoughtless merriment. So, the question of sport was an important issue in determining allegiances and preparing the ground for the Great Rebellion.

Now I sit on a panel of examiners each year and, having read the scripts, watch and listen as the young candidates are gently but rigorously interviewed. It is all done with academic courtesy and distinction, reminiscent of an Oxford viva and I enjoy being present though, on one occasion, I became distinctly alarmed.

John Wilks, historian, housemaster and friend — he had played no less than five times for Cambridge in the varsity soccer matches at Wembley — said to one of the candidates about to be interviewed, who was in his house, "Ask Mr Shearwood a question," and suggested one that he knew would be well beyond my capability. Fortunately Mark saved my bacon, dexterously fending off and handling the question on my behalf, much to the amusement of two of the panel, Christopher Kemp — a Harrovian and Oxford first-class historian — and Father Simon Heans.

But what I enjoyed most of all was teaching English literature, in particular introducing classes to poetry. I taught youngsters at the start of their Lancing careers and those at the lower sixth stage. One book I read unfailingly, year after year, with the new intake, was Siegfried Sassoon's *Memoirs of a Fox-Hunting Man*. I read it with them, not because I was remotely interested in hunting or horses, far from it, but because his memoirs are written with such clarity and evocation, concerning a boy's youth, set in the Kentish Weald at the turn of the century. Perhaps because it was so different from my early upbringing at 24 Normanton Road, Derby, perhaps it was the memory of the Pytchley hunt meeting outside Maidwell Hall, the headmaster, in pink coat astride his horse, surrounded by baying hounds on a winter's morning — whatever it was, I never tired of the book.

My window was wide open when I went to bed, and I had left the curtains half-drawn. I woke out of my deep and dreamless sleep to a gradual recognition that I was at home and not in the cubicled dormitory at Ballboro'. Drowsily grateful for this, I lay and listened. A cock was crowing from a neighbouring farm; his shrill challenge was faintly echoed by another cock a long way off.

I loved the early morning; it was luxurious to lie there, half-awake, and half-aware that there was a pleasantly eventful day in front of me ... Presently I would get up and lean on the window-ledge to see what was happening in the world outside ... There was a starling's nest under the window where the jasmine grew thickest and, all of a sudden I heard one of the birds dart away with a soft flurry of wings. Hearing it go, I imagined how it would fly boldly across the garden. Soon I was up and staring at the tree-tops which loomed motionless against a flushed and brightening sky. Slipping into some clothes I opened my door very quietly and tiptoed along the passage and down the stairs. There was no sound except the first chirping of the sparrows in the ivy. I felt as if I had changed since the Easter holidays. The drawing-room door creaked as I went softly in and crept across the beeswaxed parquet floor. Last night's half-consumed candles and the cat's half-empty bowl of milk under the gate-legged table seemed to belong neither here nor there, and my own silent face looked queerly at me out of the mirror. And there was the familiar photograph of 'Love and Death', by Watts, with its secret meaning which I could never quite formulate in a thought, though it often touched me with a vague emotion of pathos. When I unlocked the door into the garden the early morning air met me with its cold purity; on the stone step were the bowls of roses and delphiniums and sweet peas which Aunt Evelyn had carried out there before she went to bed; the scarlet disc of the sun had climbed an inch above the hills. Thrushes and blackbirds hopped and pecked busily on the dew-soaked lawn, and a pigeon was cooing monotonously from the belt of woodland which sloped from the garden toward the Weald. Down there in the belt of river-mist a goods train whistled as it puffed steadily away from the station with a distinctly heard clanking of buffers. How little I knew of the enormous world beyond that valley and those low green hills.

And how about this splendid passage, by John Masefield, describing a clipper, sighted to windward one morning watch, just as the sun was beginning to climb from the ocean and the stars to fade.

When I saw her first there was a smoke of mist about her as high as her foreyard. Her topsails and flying kites had a faint glow upon them where the dawn caught them. Then the mist rolled away from her, so that we could see her hull and the glimmer of the red sidelight as it was hoisted inboard. She was rolling slightly, tracing an arc against the heaven, and as I watched her the glow upon her deepened, till every sail she wore burned rosily like an opal turned to the sun, like a fiery jewel. She was radiant, she was of an immortal beauty, that swaying, delicate clipper. Coming as she came, out of the mist into the dawn, she was like a spirit, like an intellectual presence. Her hull glowed, her rails glowed; there was colour upon the boats and tackling. She was a lofty ship with skysails and royal staysails, and it was wonderful to watch her, blushing in the sun, swaying and curveting. She was alive with a more than mortal life. One thought that she would speak in some strange language or break out into a music which would express the sea and that great flower in the sky. She came trembling down to us, rising up high and plunging; showing the red lead below her waterline; then diving down till the smother bubbled over her hawseholes. She bowed and curveted; the light caught the skylights on the poop; she gleamed and sparkled; she shook the sea from her as she rose. There was no man aboard of us but was filled with the beauty of that ship.

The choice of poetry is personal, and a poem enjoyed can be turned to repeatedly, as can a painting or a piece of music. Dylan Thomas advised: "Read the poems you like reading. Don't bother whether they are important or if they'll live. All that matters about poetry is the enjoyment of it, however tragic it may be."

Over the years I have shared poetry with numerous English sets at Lancing. And who knows? Perhaps one or two minds may have pursued the subject further and discovered what Wordsworth meant, when he spoke of 'the still sad music of humanity'.

And, when the night is long and sleep elusive, I try recalling opening lines to some of the poems we used to read. The following selection of verses, mostly from works of familiar poets, were chosen with difficulty, for there are many others I would have liked to include. I am aware, however, that it is impossible to win approval for inclusions or exclusions, and that readers may feel it is wrong not to quote the complete poem. I accept this, but I never intended to write an anthology, merely to present a glimpse of poems I once read with boys at Lancing.

from In Memoriam
The flowers left thick at nightfall in the wood
This Eastertide call into mind the men,
Now far from home, who, with their sweethearts, should
Have gathered them and will do never again.

Edward Thomas

from Anthem for Doomed Youth
What passing bells for these who die as cattle?
Only the monstrous anger of the guns.
Only the stuttering rifles' rapid rattle
Can patter out their hasty orisons.

Wilfred Owen

from Death Bed
He drowsed and was aware of silence heaped
Round him, unshaken as the steadfast walls;
Aqueous like floating rays of amber light,
Soaring and quivering in the wings of sleep.
Silence and safety; and his mortal shore
Lipped by the inward, moonless waves of death.

Siegfried Sassoon

If any question why we died
Tell them because our fathers lied.

Rudyard Kipling

from **Naming of Parts**

Today we have naming of parts. Yesterday
We had daily cleaning. And tomorrow morning
We shall have what to do after firing. But today,
Today we have naming of parts. Japonica
Glistens like coral in all of the neighbouring gardens,
And today we have naming of parts.

Henry Reed

from **Adlestrop**

Yes. I remember Adlestrop —
The name, because one afternoon
Of heat the express-train drew up there
Unwontedly. It was late June.

Edward Thomas

from **Six Young Men**

The celluloid of a photograph holds them well, —
Six young men, familiar to their friends.
Four decades that have faded and ochre-tinged
This photograph have not wrinkled the faces or the hands.
Though their cocked hats are not now fashionable,
Their shoes shine. One imparts an intimate smile,
One chews a grass, one lowers his eyes, bashful,
One is ridiculous with cocky pride —
Six months after this picture they were all dead.

Ted Hughes

from **Song of the Dying Gunner AA1**

Farewell, Aggie Weston, the Barracks at Guz
Hang my tiddley suit on the door
I'm sewn up neat in a canvas sheet
And I shan't be home no more.

Charles Causley

from **O What is that Sound**

O what is that sound so thrills the ear
Down in the valley drumming, drumming?
Only the scarlet soldiers, dear,
The soldiers coming.

W. H. Auden

from **For Johnny**
Do not despair
For Johnny-head-in-air
He sleeps as sound
As Johnny underground.

John Pudney

from **High Flight**
Oh I have slipped the surly bonds of earth,
And danced the skies on laughter-silvered wings;
Sunward I've climbed and joined the tumbling mirth
Of sun-split clouds — and done a hundred things
You have not dreamed of — wheeled and soared and swung
High in the sunlit silence.

John Magee

from **Sea Fever**
I must go down to the seas again, to the lonely sea and the sky,
And all I ask is a tall ship and a star to steer her by,
And the wheel's kick and the wind's song and the white sails shaking
And a grey mist on the sea's face and a grey dawn breaking.

John Masefield

from **The Old Ship**
It was so old a ship — who knows, who knows?
And yet so beautiful, I watched in vain
To see the mast burst open with a rose
And the whole deck put on its leaves again.

James Elroy Flecker

from **Meeting at Night**
The grey sea and the long black land;
And the yellow half-moon large and low;
And the startled little waves that leap
In fiery ringlets from their sleep
As I gain the cove with pushing prow
And quench its speed i' the slushy sand.

Robert Browning

428

from Crossing the Bar

Sunset and evening star,
And one clear call for me!
And may there be no moaning of the bar
When I put out to sea.

Alfred, Lord Tennyson

from A Prayer for my Daughter

Once more the storm is howling, and half hid
Under this cradle-hood and coverlid
My child sleeps on. There is no obstacle
But Gregory's wood and one bare hill
Whereby the haystack- and roof-levelling wind,
Bred on the Atlantic, can be stayed;
And for an hour I have walked and prayed
Because of the great gloom that is in my mind.

W. B. Yeats

from He Wishes for the Cloths of Heaven

Had I the heavens' embroidered cloths
Enwrought with golden and silver light,
The blue and the dim and the dark cloths
Of night and light and the half-light,
I would spread the cloths under your feet:
But I, being poor, have only my dreams;
I have spread my dreams under your feet;
Tread softly because you tread on my dreams.

W. B. Yeats

from Afterwards

When the Present has latched its postern behind my tremulous stay
And the May month flaps its glad green leaves like wings,
Delicate-filmed as new-spun silk, will the neighbours say,
'He was a man who used to notice such things'?

Thomas Hardy

from Beeny Cliff

O the opal and the sapphire of that wandering western sea,
And the woman riding high above with bright hair flapping free —
The woman whom I loved so, and who loyalty loved me.

Thomas Hardy

from **Preludes**
The winter evening settles down
With smells of steaks in passageways.
Six o'clock.
The burnt-out ends of smoky days.
And now a gusty shower wraps
The grimy scraps
Of withered leaves about your feet
And newspapers from vacant lots;
The showers beat
On broken blinds and chimney-pots,
And at the corner of the street
A lonely cab-horse steams and stamps.
And then the lighting of the lamps.

T. S. Eliot

from **Piano**
Softly in the dusk, a woman is singing to me;
Taking me back down the vista of years, till I see
A child sitting under the piano, in the boom of the tingling strings
And pressing the small, poised feet of a mother who smiles
as she sings.

D. H. Lawrence

from **Bredon Hill**
In summertime on Bredon
The bells they sound so clear;
Round both the shires they ring them
In steeples far and near,
A happy noise to hear.

A. E. Housman

from **The Solitary Reaper**
Behold her, single in the field,
Yon solitary Highland Lass!
Reaping and singing by herself;
Stop here, or gently pass!
Alone she cuts and binds the grain,
And sings a melancholy strain;
O listen! for the vale profound
Is overflowing with the sound.

William Wordsworth

from **Dover Beach**
The sea is calm to-night.
The tide is full, the moon lies fair
Upon the straits; — on the French coast the light
Gleams and is gone; the cliffs of England stand,
Glimmering and vast, out in the tranquil bay.
Come to the window, sweet is the night-air!
Only, from the long line of spray
Where the sea meets the moon-blanched land,
Listen! you hear the grating roar
Of pebbles which the waves draw back, and fling,
At their return, up the high strand,
Begin, and cease, and then again begin,
With tremulous cadence slow, and bring
The eternal note of sadness in.

Matthew Arnold

from **Sonnet 18**
Shall I compare thee to a summer's day?
Thou art more lovely and more temperate:'
Rough winds do shake the darling buds of May
And summer's lease hath all too short a date.

William Shakespeare

from **The World is too much with Us**
It moves us not. — Great God! I'd rather be
A Pagan suckled in a creed outworn;
So might I, standing on this pleasant lea,
Have glimpses that would make me less forlorn;
Have sight of Proteus rising from the sea;
Or hear old Triton blow his wreathed horn.

William Wordsworth

from **To Daffodils**
Fair daffodils, we weep to see
You haste away so soon;
As yet the early-rising sun
Has not attained his noon.

Robert Herrick

from **I Am**
I long for scenes where man has never trod,
A place where woman never smiled or wept;
There to abide with my Creator, God,
And sleep as I in childhood sweetly slept:
Untroubling and untroubled where I lie,
The grass below — above the vaulted sky.

John Clare

from **The Clod and the Pebble**
'Love seeketh not itself to please,
Nor for itself hath any care,
But for another gives its ease,
And builds a Heaven in Hell's despair.'

William Blake

from **To Autumn**
Season of mists and mellow fruitfulness!
Close bosom-friend of the maturing sun;
Conspiring with him how to load and bless
With fruit the vines that round the thatch-eaves run;

John Keats

from **Ode to the West Wind**
O Wild West Wind, thou breath of Autumn's being,
Thou from whose unseen presence the leaves dead
Are driven like ghosts from an enchanter fleeing,
Yellow, and black, and pale, and hectic red,
Pestilence-stricken multitudes!

Percy Bysshe Shelley

from **A Red, Red Rose**
My love is like a red, red rose
That's newly sprung in June:
My love is like the melody
That's sweetly played in tune.

Robert Burns

from **London Snow**

When men were all asleep the snow came flying,
In large white flakes falling on the city brown,
Stealthily and perpetually settling and loosely lying,
Hushing the latest traffic of the drowsy town;
Deadening, muffling, stifling its murmurs failing;
Lazily and incessantly floating down and down:

Robert Bridges

from **Pied Beauty**

Glory be to God for dappled things —
For skies of couple-colour as a brinded cow;
For rose-moles all in stipple upon trout that swim;

Gerard Manley Hopkins

from **The Burning of the Leaves**

Now is the time for the burning of the leaves.
They go to the fire; the nostril pricks with smoke
Wandering slowly into a weeping mist.
Brittle and blotched, ragged and rotten sheaves!
A flame seizes the smouldering ruin and bites
On stubborn stalks that crackle as they resist.

Laurence Binyon

from **Les Sylphides**

Life in a day: he took his girl to the ballet;
Being shortsighted himself could hardly see it -
The white skirts in the grey Glade and the swell of the music
Lifting the white sails.

Louis MacNeice

from **Elegy for Margaret**

Poor girl, inhabitant of a strange land
Where death stares through your gaze,
As though a distant moon
Shone through midsummer days
With the skull-like glitter of night.

Stephen Spender

from **She Walks in Beauty**
She walks in beauty, like the night
Of cloudless climes and starry skies;
And all that's best of dark and bright
Meet in her aspect and her eyes:
Thus mellow'd to that tender light
Which heaven to gaudy day denies.

George Gordon, Lord Byron

from **Fern Hill**
Now as I was young and easy under the apple boughs
About the lilting house and happy as the grass was green,
The night above the dingle starry,
Time let me hail and climb
Golden in the heydays of his eyes,
And honoured among wagons
I was prince of the apple towns
And once below a time I lordly had the trees and leaves
Trail with daisies and barley
Down the rivers of the windfall light.

Dylan Thomas

from **The Pike**
And nigh this toppling reed, still as the dead
The great pike lies, the murderous patriarch
Watching the waterpit shelving and dark,
Where through the plash his lithe bright vassals thread.

Stephen Spender

from **Death of a Peasant**
You remember Davies? He died, you know,
With his face to the wall, as the manner is
Of the poor peasant in his stone croft
On the Welsh hills. I recall the room
Under the slates, and the smirched snow
Of the wide bed in which he lay,
Lonely as an ewe that is sick to lamb
In the hard weather of mid-March.

R. S. Thomas

from **Lament for a Sailor**
Here, where the night is clear as sea-water
And stones are white and the sticks are spars,
Swims on a windless, mackerel tide
The dolphin moon in a shoal of stars.

Paul Dehn

from **anyone lived in a pretty how town**
anyone lived in a pretty how town
(with up so floating many bells down)
spring summer autumn winter
he sang his didn't he danced his did.

e. e. cummings

from **Hospital for Defectives**
By your unnumbered charities
A miracle disclose
Lord of the images, whose love
The eyelid and the rose
Take for a language, and today
Tell to me what is said
By these men in a turnip field
And their unleavened bread

Thomas Blackburn

from **The Listeners**
"Is there anybody there?" said the Traveller
Knocking on the moonlit door;
And his horse in the silence champed the grasses
Of the forest's ferny floor.

Walter De La Mare

from **Death the Leveller**
The glories of our blood and state
Are shadows, not substantial things
There is no armour against Fate
Death lays his icy hand on kings

James Shirley

from **Leisure**
What is this life if, full of care,
We have no time to stand and stare?

W. H. Davies

from **Church Going**
Once I am sure there's nothing going on
I step inside, letting the door thud shut.
Another church: matting, seats, and stone,
And little books; sprawlings of flowers, cut
For Sunday, brownish now; some brass and stuff
Up at the holy end; the small neat organ;
And a tense, musty, unignorable silence,
Brewed God knows how long.

Philip Larkin

from **Timothy Winters**
Timothy Winters comes to school
With eyes as wide as a football-pool,
Ears like bombs and teeth like splinters:
A blitz of a boy is Timothy Winters.

Charles Causley

from **Indoor Games Near Newbury**
In among the silver birches winding ways of tarmac wander
And the signs to Bussock Bottom, Tussock Wood and Windy Brake,
Gabled lodges, tile-hung churches, catch the lights of our Lagonda
As we drive to Wendy's party, lemon curd and Christmas cake.

John Betjeman

from **To my Mother**
Most near, most dear, most loved and most far,
Under the window where I often found her
Sitting as huge as Asia, seismic with laughter,
Gin and chicken helpless in her Irish hand,
Irresistible as Rabelais, but most tender for
The lame dogs and hurt birds that surround her,
She is a procession no one can follow after
But be like a little dog following a brass band.

George Barker

from **Death of a Son**
Something has ceased to come along with me.
Something like a person: something very like one.
And there was no nobility in it Or anything like that.

Jon Silkin

from **Auguries of Innocence 1**
It is right it should be so;
Man was made for Joy and Woe;
And when this we rightly know,
Thro' the world we safely go,
Joy and Woe are woven fine,
A clothing for the soul divine.
Under every grief and pine
Runs a joy with silken twine.

William Blake

Winter Morning
Did you see the moon?
still, huge wraith
In the everlasting blue
of a winter morn.
Opaque bubble, widening
Till the edge break softly, softly break
over His land,
Given unseen, unseeing,
God's Holy Wafer
'light on all.

Biddie Shearwood

Ian Beer left Lancing for Harrow and we were, once more, under 'new management'. Jim Woodhouse, son of a suffragan bishop, was educated at St Edwards, Oxford. He read English at Cambridge and, on going down, taught at Westminster, where he became Master of the Queen's Scholars. He was married to Sarah, a woman of considerable determination and courage. Their marriage had all the ingredients of a future headship. The headmaster of Rugby, Walter Hamilton, who had been head of Westminster, and had appointed Jim Woodhouse to his first teaching post, was soon to be leaving, and it all dovetailed together. Jim became the new headmaster of Rugby and was there for twelve years, before his appointment to Lancing in 1981.

A tall man, well over six feet, he was a natural games player and, like all good games players, did not like losing nor, come to that, did he enjoy being on the wrong side of an argument. In conversation he often gave the impression of being detached and had a habit of gazing over one's shoulder into the far distance. Warm and welcoming, at the same time slightly withdrawn and not prepared to give much away when he felt so inclined, from his considerable height he presented a scholarly, if slightly aloof figure. Was it perhaps how he thought a headmaster should be? I found when we were both separately interviewing prospective parents he would, at times, make a hasty judgement as to whether he liked, or disliked, a father or mother or both. I shall always be grateful to Jim Woodhouse for allowing me to continue teaching until I was sixty-five, and then inviting me to become the first Registrar at Lancing, a post I held for a further ten years, giving me an opportunity to save enough, though only just, in order to retire without being constantly in the red, which, for the most of my career as a schoolmaster, has been the case.

An early intention of our new headmaster was that every department should face an inspection and I immediately recalled John Dancy's week of inspections back in the 50s. Alan Black, head of the English department, a Glasgow MA, scholar of Balliol, a shrewd Scot and a close friend, broke the news that we were to be inspected first. "So, you'd better be prepared," he advised us over a cup of coffee up in his flat at the top of Second's House, with its distant view across the Downs on the north side of the school.

Now I cannot pretend it is a particularly enjoyable experience having somebody sitting at the back of a class, listening, judging, making the odd note, solely to report on how one was performing. For many this can be a taxing experience. But this time I rather looked forward to the occasion, for I knew exactly what I intended to do, compare the following extract from *Sons And Lovers* with Lawrence's poem, 'Child In Discord'.

> ...Then they went to bed. Their mother sat sewing below. Having such a great space in front of the house gave the children a feeling of night, of vastness, and of terror. This terror came in from the shrieking of the tree and the anguish of the home discord. Often Paul would wake up, after he had been asleep a long time, aware of thuds downstairs. Instantly he was wide awake. Then he heard the booming shouts of his father, come home nearly drunk, then the sharp replies of his mother, then the bang, bang of his father's fist on the table, and the nasty snarling shout as the man's voice got higher and higher. And then the whole was drowned in a piercing medley of shrieks and cries from the great, windswept ash-tree. The children lay silent in suspense, waiting for a lull in the wind to hear what their father was doing. He might hit their mother again. There was a feeling of horror, a kind of bristling in the darkness, and a sense of blood. They lay with their hearts in the grip of an intense anguish.

The poem, intense and devastating, reflects the passage.

> Outside the house an ash-tree hung its terrible whips,
> And at night when the wind rose, the lash of the tree
> Shrieked and slashed the wind, as a ship's
> Weird rigging in a storm shrieks hideously.

Within the house two voices arose, a slender lash
Whistling she-delirious rage, and the dreadful sound
Of a male thong booming and bruising, until it had
drowned The other voice in a silence of blood, 'neath the noise of the ash.

I was about to begin taking a lower sixth set when the inspector arrived and, without preamble, quietly found a seat at the back of the form. I enjoyed the lesson, forgot about the inspector, there was plenty of discussion, and we finished the period reading Lawrence's poem, 'Piano', its gentle cadence in stark contrast to 'Discord in Childhood'.

Softly, in the dusk, a woman is singing to me;
Taking me back down the vista of years, till I see
A child sitting under the piano, in the boom of the tingling strings
And pressing the small, poised feet of a mother who smiles as she sings.

In spite of myself, the insidious mastery of song
Betrays me back, till the heart of me weeps to belong
To the old Sunday evenings at home, with winter outside
And hymns in the cosy parlour, the tinkling piano our guide.

So now it is vain for the singer to burst into clamour
With the great black piano *appassionato.* The glamour
Of childish days is upon me, my manhood is cast
Down in the flood of remembrance, I weep like a child for the past.

The following day I needed to phone the headmaster about the common room contracts.

"Your ears should be burning," he said, "the inspector has just suggested we should all come and listen to you teaching."

"Good God," I said, really taken aback, "I sincerely hope not."

Nevertheless, I felt pleased, very pleased indeed, for I have no illusions but that I am indeed 'hardly a scholar'.

Biddie, at 3 Valentine Close, Shoreham-by-Sea

Chapter 42

Registrar

FOR TEN YEARS I was Registrar of Lancing, the first to be appointed as such. The days seemed to pass more quickly than ever. My study was a pleasant one, spacious and light, bang in the centre of things, with four low windows, so that I could talk and wave to passers by, just as I had done when teaching. "Give them a wave," I'd tell the class as a master or passer-by crossed the Tower Quad, and wave they would, and usually got a warm response. "For, after all," I'd remind them, "we are the wave-and-smile school." Across one corner of the room I placed the same big desk I had used when housemaster of Sanderson's and President of the Common Room. With some nineteenth century etchings of the college on the walls, a relief print by my daughter Vanessa, two very large photographs of the Wembley Cup Finals, several comfortable chairs and a large half-moon-shaped sofa, I felt I could not go wrong.

My objective was to sell the school and ensure that, when prospective parents came to see me, they would leave convinced that Lancing was the right place for their offspring. I found the job a good deal easier and enjoyable than my brief experience trying to open accounts with the London clothing stores. I met and interviewed over two thousand parents and never once ceased to anticipate each occasion with enjoyment.

I saw prospective parents first, and was grateful to Jim Woodhouse for allowing me to do so, for first impressions are often vital. Jim would see them next, followed by a housemaster and finally, probably most important of all, a boy would talk to them, and show them any parts of the school they had not seen. It was comprehensive and effective.

I met a wide and varied selection of parents from all walks of life and our discussions ranged from school matters — often not too much of these — to the war, fishing, sailing, Cornwall, writing, bullying, varicose veins, Wembley, and our family. The half-hour I had with them was never long enough. At times when the headmaster was unavailable a housemaster would call and take them off.

"How do we meet and choose a housemaster?" some of them would ask occasionally, and I'd explain that there were parents who know the house they want their sons to enter, while others, who have no connection with or knowledge of the school, simply take pot luck as to whom they see. In that case they could always arrange a further visit and meet another housemaster.

"And whom are we going to meet now?"

"Well," I'd say, "you're going to meet a married housemaster with a delightful wife, son and daughter. He is small, possesses a quick precise manner of speech, has a very good mind, and looks not unlike a member of the Gestapo. But if you can get your boy into his house, you'll do well, because he's a nice person, and an excellent housemaster, always in demand."

Shortly there'd be a knock on the door, in he would come and I'd introduce them. Out would shoot his hand and, with a brusque "hello", off they'd go, but not before I had said goodbye to the parents and caught a glint of amused acknowledgement in their eyes.

I visited over fifty preparatory schools, many of them more than once, often taking a housemaster with me. The schools would give us lunch and we'd meet boys who were coming our way and others who had not made up their minds. One or two of the schools were difficult to find, often tucked away down a drive in a fold of the countryside. David Lutwyche, who succeeded Ted Maidment as housemaster of Sanderson's, and had previously run the football at Lancing, was an expert navigator — but Jim Sheppe, a brilliant, somewhat eccentric, American linguist was not.

"It's down here, Ken," he said on one occasion, when we were hopelessly lost, deep in the heart of the Kent countryside, on a bitter morning in February. Following his instruction I turned down a steep lane with snow banked on either side. "Yes, this must be it," said Jim, pointing to a narrow drive up which I proceeded with considerable misgivings to end up outside a substantial Victorian residence.

"Doesn't look much like a school to me, Jim," I remarked, before getting out to climb some steep steps and ring the bell at the side of a heavy oak door. I rang it twice before it was eventually opened by a young nurse.

"We're looking for Northbourne Park preparatory school. This isn't it, by any chance?" I asked.

"No," she replied, "this is a nursing home for the elderly."

"Ah," I said, "I'm sorry to have troubled you. Can you tell me where it is?" She had no idea and went off to find someone who might help.

As I waited a little old lady approached me across the hall.

"Come in, dear," she said, her voice and manner gentle and charming, "do come in out of the cold, dear," and, reaching out with a frail hand, which I could not ignore, I stepped inside with her, just as a man in a white coat appeared and led the little old lady away, still looking over her shoulder at me, still asking that I be let in out of the cold. We did not find our way to Northbourne Park preparatory school on that occasion.

At the start of my last summer term at Lancing the headmasters and their wives of all the preparatory schools that had connections with us were invited to a dinner, an occasion at which I spoke and mentioned the incident of the 'little old lady'. To my astonishment I was given a standing ovation and presented with a cheque for six hundred pounds.

So my years at Lancing slipped away, but not before a new headmaster had been appointed in 1993, my sixth and certainly my last. I knew who I hoped it would be, and did my best to see that it came about. When eventually Christopher Saunders was appointed, I was delighted. Once my head of house in Sanderson's, he had completed twelve successful years as headmaster of Eastbourne, having previously been a housemaster at Bradfield. By no stretch of the imagination an academic, he was a fluent and witty speaker, known to have an excellent relationship with preparatory schools and parents. Unlike his predecessor, he preferred to interview prospective parents first.

"You are now going to meet someone who has been running longer than *The Mousetrap*," he would announce when he brought parents in to see me. I had a happy last three years working with Chris, and many a chat and laugh over a glass of sherry at the end of a day.

But his reign was to prove short and, a year after I retired, he dropped in one evening to inform me that he had resigned. "I wanted to tell you personally," he began and went on to explain how disillusioned he had become.

In fact I had already guessed that something was amiss, on greeting him one Sunday morning, attending a ten o'clock chapel service at the start of a new term. Clad in gown and hood, he was standing at the west end watching the school enter, occasionally stepping forward to demand that a tie be straightened, a shirt buttoned up.

"Had a good holiday, Chris?" I asked him. "No longer enjoyable," came his prompt reply. "It's a different ball game, Ken. There's no fun in it any more," and he gave me a quick wry smile.

I was aware that during the previous term he had been confronted with an unpleasant bullying incident and an understandably irate mother, who was determined that the press and each member of the governing body should be informed of what had happened. To make matters worse a drug problem came to light and eight boys were expelled. The troubles had pursued him throughout the holidays and there were internal problems and pressures building up. Finally, poor academic results, falling numbers, and the knowledge that the school faced a full HMC inspection, convinced him that it was in Lancing's interest, and his own, that he should call it a day. At the annual dinner, held at the end of the summer term of 1998, I was asked by the President of the Common Room to propose the health of Christopher and Cynthia Saunders. I was privileged and glad to do so.

3 Valentine Close faces west, looking across the River Adur and beyond to where the school is situated high on the Downs. Through our windows we have often watched the chapel and its cluster of grey, gothic buildings, sharply outlined against a glorious sunset, fade into the night. Later, before drawing our curtains and preparing for bed, we would catch a further glimpse of the great building, this time lit up and standing on its own, shining in solitary splendour for all to see, a jewel in the night.

To conjure up a vision of Lancing that excludes the chapel is inconceivable, for Lancing is the Chapel, the Chapel is Lancing. What part, however, it has played in the lives of its congregations is another matter and one we shall never know about. At a guess, it is probably no more than the chapel services at Maidwell Hall and Shrewsbury did for me, where for ten years I was instilled with the tenets of

Christianity as historical fact, going along with it all, keeping an open mind, becoming more confused as to the existence or non-existence of the Almighty as the years passed, aware there are other gods and many millions who believe in them. The Greeks and Romans, Egyptians and Scandinavians all believed in the existence of Gods, but no one today sees them as anything other than myth. Yet the concept of God persists. Is it the fear of the unknown, a void within that drives us to seek God? Over the years I have attended many school services in this beautiful chapel — I still do — sometimes bored, sometimes amused, sometimes deeply moved, still awaiting a convincing explanation of why a loving God allows so much suffering and inequality in a world He has created. In the end I have come to the conclusion that there is only one God and He is in the minds of us all. I look upon this Unseen Presence as a personal friend, with whom I can always talk, share my joys and sorrows, my hopes and fears, ask forgiveness and count my blessings. Perhaps I am merely being superstitious, playing safe, touching wood, hedging my bets, better to believe and be safe, than disbelieve and find I am on the wrong side of the Pearly Gates. Whatever it is, it is my way forward into the unknown.

The words of Minnie Louise Harkins, used by George VI in his 1939 Christmas broadcast, for me, do more than just ring a bell.

I said to the man who stood at the Gate of the Year: 'Give me a light that I may tread safely into the unknown.'

And he replied: 'Go out into the darkness, and put your hand into the Hand of God. That shall be to you better than light and safer than a known way.'

So I went forth, and finding the Hand of God, trod gladly into the night.

And He led me towards the hills, and the breaking of the day in the lone East.

"Do you believe in God, sir," I have been asked occasionally by a class.

"I do not disbelieve," I would reply. "In the end you will all have to form your own idea of God. But one thing I am certain of, you must keep an open mind, and always remember, there is a still, small voice that speaks at unexpected times and in unexpected places." I did not add that someone very close and dear to me has heard that still, small voice more than once.

Above: KAS, Registrar

Chapter 43

Epilogue

THE CHRISTMAS Carol Service was almost over. Within the great chapel a congregation of eight hundred, consisting of boys, staff, girls and parents had just sung 'Hark the Herald Angels Sing', a fitting end to another Michaelmas term at Lancing.

The Blessing had been given. The choir, which had moved from their stalls to sing the final carol massed before the High Altar, had descended in a long column towards the steps that lead up from the nave. Before the headmaster's stall, the tall leading figure of the verger paused, to ensure that all was in order behind him, the two chaplains ready to follow the choir down the aisle.

For several long seconds, Charles Welling, late of the Welsh Guards, stood motionless, dignified, staring impassively ahead, upon his chest two rows of medals, one decorated with the insignia of an oak leaf. In his long black cassock, his polished oak stick held firmly before him, he made an impressive figure upon whom all eyes were now fixed.

Just as he took that first measured step down the long nave, and the white column followed faithfully forward in his wake, a solitary blue balloon appeared, sixty feet overhead, to hover momentarily, as though heralding what was to come. Sure enough, above the astonished upturned young faces, bright beneath the glittering chandeliers, there erupted along the north triforium, a cascade of coloured balloons that sallied gently hither and thither, slowly drifting down upon a delighted and expectant congregation. Softly a balloon touched and floated off the grey head of the verger who, nothing daunted, as one would expect of a guardsman, continued sedately to lead the hilarious choir out through the west end, without a flicker of emotion on his face.

Not unnaturally, as the balloons came within reach, the school began to bat them around, until the inevitable first sharp explosion was followed by a series of intermittent bursts, which continued while the headmaster and his staff filed out, the organ played on, and the amused, but slightly puzzled parents watched a spectacle that now had all the atmosphere of a New Year's Ball.

Outside the west end, beneath the magnificent rose window, the crowd were assembling, as parents and their offspring met up, and a slow procession of cars began to move off in the gathering gloom of a cold December afternoon. Watching the scene, occasionally smiling and addressing a few words to shivering parents, the headmaster, a tall figure in a billowing MA gown and Cambridge hood, looked pensive. It did not help particularly when one of his staff, a talented young mathematician, not noted for tact, remarked in passing that he didn't normally attend chapel — a fact of which the headmaster was aware.

"Never knew you had balloons on these occasions," said the young master waggishly, "I shall come again."

"And what did the headmaster say?" I enquired.

"Nothing. But I could have told him that something was afoot."

"Then I should keep very quiet about that, if I were you," I suggested.

"Well," commented a senior member of the common room a little later over a cup of tea, "at least they had the good grace to wait to the end of the service. It would have been disastrous had they let them go in the middle."

"It may teach the head not to place too much faith in his school prefects," said a bearded Lawrentian figure, whose independence of mind was not always appreciated by the headmaster. "Never pays, they're only children."

By now it was strongly rumoured that the head boy was behind the prank.

"I must say I thought it rather amusing," remarked another, "and it really didn't do any harm. There was no malice in it; I'm sure the good Lord would have had a quiet smile."

"Not sure all the parents would agree with that," announced a housemaster cryptically.

A brief silence followed, and then the elder statesman, once a pupil at Lancing, a pillar of the Chapel, an honorary member of the common room, born at the turn of the century, a first in Greats, who would preface his statements with a noisy intake of breath and a quick touch of his goat-like beard, suddenly pronounced that it didn't really worry him at all. "You know, I don't think we should make too much of a 'hullaballoon' about the whole thing," he concluded with a dry chuckle.

It was the spectacle of those balloons that urged me to write something about Lancing, not how to be a schoolmaster — God forbid — but simply to recall a few memories of the place set against the background of my own schooldays, the war, some inshore fishing off Cornwall, and a stint at Oxford. So, back to the beginning and 24 Normanton Road, Derby.

Lancing, looking towards Shoreham-by-Sea

Index